PAYROLL ACCOUNTING

1994 EDITION

BERNARD J. BIEG, C.P.A.
Professor, Business Studies
Bucks County Community College
Newtown, Pennsylvania

B. LEWIS KEELING
Professor Emeritus
Bucks County Community College
Newtown, Pennsylvania

COLLEGE DIVISION South-Western Publishing Co.

Cincinnati Ohio

Sponsoring Editor: David L. Shaut
Editor: Judy Toland
Software Editor: Mary H. Draper
Production Editor: Peggy A. Williams
Production Editor—Software: Tim Butz
Associate Editor—Software: Sally Neiman
Cover and Internal Design: Craig LaGesse Ramsdell
Photo Editor: Jennifer Mayhall
Marketing Manager: Michael O'Brien

ISBN: 0-538-81658-9

1 2 DH 4 3

Printed in the United States of America

I(T)P
International Thomson Publishing
South-Western Publishing Co. is an ITP company. The ITP
trademark is used under license.

INTRODUCTION

Tax Freedom Day

In 1993, May 3 was the date on which the average American worker's income, since the beginning of the year, equaled his or her tax obligation to federal, state and local governments. In 1992, "Tax Freedom Day" was May 5. On a day-to-day basis, 2 hours and 41 minutes (1 hour and 43 minutes for federal taxes) of each 8-hour workday are used to pay for the deduction of government taxes of all varieties. These tax deductions and employee-authorized deductions have significantly increased the volume of clerical work and the complexity of accounting entries necessary in connection with payroll operations. Payroll accounting has emerged as one of the most important components of the organization's total accounting system.

Payroll Taxes Surge Upward

Total employer-employee taxes for old-age, survivors, and disability insurance have reached 12.4% of the first $60,600 in wages paid each covered employee. The hospital insurance part of the social security taxes amounts to an additional employer-employee tax of 2.9% on all covered wages. In addition to these social security taxes are federal and state unemployment taxes, and state and local income taxes in many states. The total federal and state payroll taxes for which an employer is liable may now exceed 10% of the wages paid to most employees. Payroll taxes, obviously, have come to represent a considerable portion of the operating costs of doing business.

Keeping Abreast of Legislative Changes

At the federal, state, and local levels, frequent changes are being made in the laws that affect a company's payroll tax structure. This year, the Omnibus Budget Reconciliation Act of 1993 will have a significant impact on every worker's take-home pay. Thus, payroll accounting is an active field of endeavor that requires a constant updating on the part of the persons charged with planning and organizing the payroll system.

The Need for Internal Control

The steady increase in the portion of a company's operating expenses that payroll, payroll taxes, and fringe benefits occupy dictates that each business exercise adequate control over every detail of its payroll system in order to improve the accuracy, reliability, and timeliness of the payroll information being processed. This includes not only the calculation of the payroll and the payroll taxes but also the preparation of those records and reports that form the foundation of an efficient payroll system.

Goals of This Course

The major objectives of this course may be summarized as follows:

1. To develop an appreciation and an understanding of the personnel and payroll records that provide the information required under the numerous laws affecting the operations of a payroll system.
2. To familiarize students with the payroll-record life of employees from their initial applications for employment to their applications for the first social security benefits checks.
3. To introduce students to the various aspects of the Fair Labor Standards Act and the other laws that affect payroll operations and employment practices.

4. To describe the basic payroll accounting systems and procedures used in computing wages and salaries and the timekeeping methods used to record time worked.

5. To acquaint students with the various phases of the Social Security Act, the federal income tax withholding law, and other laws relating to the payment of wages and salaries. Anyone involved in clerical or accounting work relating to payroll systems must have an understanding of the various federal, state, and local laws as they affect payroll accounting.

6. To provide practice in all payroll operations, the preparation of payroll registers, the recording of accounting entries involving payroll, and the preparation of payroll tax returns that are required of businesses.

7. To offer instructors and students an opportunity to complete a payroll project through the use of microcomputers. Students can use the optional diskette package to update employee files, to complete payroll reports, and to display quarterly reports and W-2 forms.

Features of 1994 *Payroll Accounting*

- The most current tax laws for both federal and state and newest required filled-in forms with line-by-line instructions are included.

- As We Go To Press section summarizes the latest developments three weeks before text delivery.

- Unique, three-month simulated payroll project uses actual forms to prepare students for the business world.

- **NEW!** "Professional Tips" give students realistic advice for success as payroll accountants.

- **NEW!** "News Alerts" add realism with focus on real-world payroll issues.

- **NEW!** *Computerized Payroll Accounting by Klooster & Allen* models the *Integrated Accounting* software and prepares future business professionals for today's computer payroll environment. The software includes pull-down menus that provide quick access to lists, reports, and help information. Well-documented instructions, found in Appendix B of this text, guide students through an automated, comprehensive payroll problem.

- Each of the seven units of the textbook opens with Goals of This Unit, which gives the reader a preview of what is to be accomplished in that unit.

- Each of the first six units ends with a Glossary of important terms that are introduced and defined in that unit.

- Tests for each of the first six units are available in quantity, free of charge, from the publisher.

- Additional test questions, including ones for *Computerized Payroll Accounting,* are included in the solutions manual.

We express our appreciation to the many instructors and students who have contributed suggestions to make this course more understandable and more practical to those who pursue the study of payroll accounting. As a result of these very helpful recommendations, each new edition has better satisfied the learning needs of students and the teaching needs of instructors.

Bernard J. Bieg
B. Lewis Keeling

As We Go To Press . . .

Unit 1—President Clinton's Health-Care Plan

At the time of this writing, President Clinton had presented his health-care plan, with the aim of providing health-care benefits for all Americans by 1997. A few provisions of the plan, which will have a significant effect upon the human resources and payroll accounting systems of business organizations, are:

1. All citizens, including those abroad, will be covered.
2. The estimated annual health-care premiums are: individuals, $1,800; families, $4,200. The maximum copayment above the premium amount would be $1,500 for individuals and $3,000 for families.
3. Business firms would pay 80% of the premium; employees would pay 20%. Thus, for the individual's $1,800-a-year policy, the employer would pay $1,440; the worker would pay $360. For the family's $4,200-a-year policy, the employer would pay $3,360; the worker would pay $840. Part-time workers would be covered on a pro rata basis, and small businesses would get discounts. Self-employeds would receive a 100% tax deductibility for the purchase of health insurance.
4. States would create alliances to secure health-care coverage at the best price from insurers. All companies with fewer than 5,000 workers would be required to join the alliances. Organizations with more than 5,000 employees could create their own alliances.
5. The benefits package would be comprehensive, including mental health and prescription drugs. Incentives will be provided to enroll in managed care programs, such as health maintenance organizations (HMOs).

Months of debate lie ahead, and most of the provisions outlined above will be modified by the health-care plan that finally emerges.

Unit 3—OASDI Taxable Wage Base

Throughout this edition, we have used the OASDI taxable wage base of $59,700, the amount estimated earlier by the Social Security Board of Trustees. In mid-October, the Social Security Administration announced that the actual taxable wage base would be $60,600. As we indicate throughout the text, there is no HI taxable wage base; the tax applies to the employee's *total earnings* for the year.

Units 3, 4, and 5—Retroactive Extension of Educational Assistance Income Exclusion

The Omnibus Budget Reconciliation Act of 1993 (OBRA) retroactively extended the income and payroll tax exclusion for educational assistance contained in Section 127 of the Internal Revenue Code from July 1, 1992, through December 31, 1994. Under Section 127, employees can exclude from income up to $5,250 in benefits provided under an employer's qualified educational assistance plan (EAP). (Before OBRA '93, the most recent extension of the income exclusion had expired on June 30, 1992.)

Employers and employees who treated EAP benefits as taxable income after June 30, 1992, are entitled to refunds of overwithheld and overpaid taxes. Employers and employees who continued to treat such benefits as nontaxable did not overwithhold or overpay taxes and are not entitled to refunds. Further, they are not subject to penalties for failing to treat the EAP benefits as taxable before OBRA '93 was enacted on August 10, 1993.

Employee Income Tax Refunds. Employees who are entitled to a refund of income taxes paid for 1992 because their employer withheld federal income tax from EAP benefits they received during the second half of 1992 can claim a refund. To do so, they must file a 1992 Form 1040X, *Amended U.S. Individual Income Tax Return*.

Most employees need only include their name, address, social security number, and "1992 tax year" on the 1992 Form 1040X, and sign the form. They must attach a Form W-2c, *Statement of Corrected Income and Tax Amounts*, provided by their employer. Form W-2c will show the corrected amount of income for 1992.

The processing of Form 1040X will be expedited if the employee writes "IRC 127" in the top margin of the form.

1992 Earned Income Credit. Employees who receive Form W-2c from their employer showing corrected wages of $22,370 or less for 1992 may qualify for the earned income credit for that year. To claim the credit, the employee must complete a 1992 Schedule EIC. If the qualifications set forth in Part I are met, the employee should attach Schedule EIC to Form 1040X being submitted.

Employees who received earned income credit in 1992 and already filed Schedule EIC should not file another one. When the IRS processes Form 1040X, it will automatically recalculate the 1992 earned income credit and adjust the refund owed accordingly.

Employee Recovery of Income Taxes Withheld in 1993.
Employees who had federal income taxes withheld from EAP benefits provided to them in 1993 can ask their employers for a refund of the amount withheld. Or, employees can have the amount credited against future withholdings during the remainder of the year. They can also wait and claim a refund on any overwithheld taxes on their personal 1993 tax return.

Employee OASDI and HI Tax Refunds for 1992 and 1993.
Employees should request their employers to reimburse them for withheld OASDI and HI taxes for both 1992 and 1993.

For 1992, they are entitled to a refund if their corrected wages for the year are below the OASDI and HI wage bases for that year—$55,500 and $130,200, respectively.

For 1993, employees are entitled to be reimbursed for any amount withheld so far from qualified EAP benefits for OASDI and HI taxes, either through direct repayment or a credit against taxes owed on wages paid later in the year.

If employees are unable to get a refund of 1992 or 1993 OASDI and HI taxes from their employer, they can obtain a refund by filing Form 843, *Claim for Refund and Request for Abatement*, with the IRS. To expedite the processing of their claims, employees should write "IRC 127" in the top margin of Form 843.

Employer Responsibilities Regarding Income Tax Refunds and Repayment.
Employers must provide Form W-2c for 1992 to employees who received EAP benefits, which were included in their wages on their 1992 Form W-2. Form W-2c should show the wage and tax information originally shown on Form W-2, along with the corrected information and the difference. NOTE: Corrections to 1992 wage and tax amounts CANNOT be made on 1993 Forms W-2; Form W-2c must be used to make the corrections.

Employers must provide employees with Copies B, C, and 2 of Form W-2c. The employer must send Copy A of all Forms W-2c to the Social Security Administration, along with Form W-3c, *Transmittal of Corrected Income and Tax Statements*.

For income taxes withheld from EAP benefits provided in 1993 and later deposited, employers may repay their employees the withheld amount at any time during the year. Or they may reimburse the employees by withholding less income tax during the year. If employers repay the withheld tax, they must keep in their records a written receipt from employees showing the date and amount paid. NOTE: Employers must repay or reimburse employees for amounts withheld from qualified EAP benefits during 1993 by December 31, 1993.

Employer Responsibilities Regarding Employee and Employer OASDI and HI Tax Refunds.
Employers may refund the employee's share of OASDI and HI taxes withheld from EAP benefits after June 30, 1992. The employer may also reimburse the employee with respect to 1993 overwithholdings by applying the previously withheld amounts against future amounts owed by the employee on wages paid in 1993.

If the employer does not wish to pay the employee the previously withheld amounts, the employer can obtain the employee's written consent to the employer's filing a refund claim on the employee's behalf on Form 843.

Before repaying or reimbursing, the employer must recalculate the employee's 1992 OASDI and HI wages to determine if the employee is entitled to a refund. If the employee's corrected wages exceed the wage bases for 1992, no refund may be provided.

All refunds and reimbursements should be made to eligible employees no later than December 31, 1993.

Employer Refunds of Overpaid FUTA Tax.
Employers who paid FUTA taxes on employees' EAP benefits for the second half of 1992 may seek a refund of the amount overpaid. However, the EAP benefits must be subtracted from each employee's wages to make sure that the corrected wages are under the FUTA wage base of $7,000. Employers can claim the refund by filing Form 843.

Tax Treatment of Employer's Refunds.
Any refunds received by the employer of OASDI, HI, and FUTA taxes paid and deducted in 1992 must be reflected as income tax refunds on the employer's 1993 income tax return.

For special IRS telephone assistance, call 800-829-1040. For forms, call 800-829-3676.

Unit 4—Combined Electronic Filing of State and Federal Tax Returns

In 1994, 24 states will be trying the combined electronic filing of state and federal tax returns. Under this system, all filings go to the Internal Revenue Service, which then relays state returns to the states. In 1993, most of the 600,000 returns handled by the system were from South Carolina, North Carolina, and Kansas. Eight states that tested the system and which plan to accept all filers in 1994 are Indiana, Louisiana, Mississippi, New Mexico, New York, Utah, West Virginia, and Wisconsin. Limited testing will get underway in 1994 in Arkansas, Colorado, Connecticut, Delaware, Idaho, Iowa, Missouri, Nebraska, and Oregon. The other states that are testing combined filing are Kentucky, Maine, Michigan, and Oklahoma.

Unit 4—Personal Allowances and Standard Deductions

For the calendar year 1994, a personal allowance of $2,450 is permitted in computing an employee's taxable income, provided the employee is not claimed as a dependent on another person's tax return.

For 1994, the following standard deductions apply (whether or not an individual is age 65 or older or is blind):

Joint return filers and surviving spouses . . $6,350
Married filing separately 3,175
Head of household filers 5,600
Single filers 3,800

Unit 5—Expiration of Unemployment Insurance "Emergency" Benefits

At the time of this writing, the federal unemployment insurance "emergency" benefits had expired on October 2, 1993. It was doubtful that unemployed workers would receive the standard 26 weeks of benefits after using up state benefits. However, in mid-October, the House passed a bill that would offer up to 13 weeks of additional benefits. Labor Secretary Reich announced that eventually the outlays of federal money should be linked to job counseling and training.

CONTENTS

UNIT 1   THE NEED FOR PAYROLL AND PERSONNEL RECORDS/1

The Payroll Profession 1
Fair Labor Standards Act 2
State Minimum Wage and Maximum Hours Laws 4
Fair Employment Laws 4
Federal Insurance Contributions Act (FICA) 6
Income Tax Withholding Laws 6
Unemployment Tax Acts 6
Other Federal Laws Affecting the Need for Payroll and Personnel
    Records 7
Other State Laws Affecting the Need for Payroll and Personnel
    Records 9
Human Resources and Payroll Accounting Systems 10
Human Resources System 11
Payroll Accounting System 17
Glossary 20
Questions for Review 21
Questions for Discussion 22
Case Problems 22

UNIT 2   COMPUTING AND PAYING WAGES AND SALARIES/25

Fair Labor Standards Act 25
Determining the Employee's Working Time 34
Keeping a Record of Time Worked 36
Methods of Computing Wages and Salaries 42
Methods of Paying Wages and Salaries 46
Unclaimed Wages 48
Glossary 49
Questions for Review 49
Questions for Discussion 50
Practical Problems 53
Continuing Payroll Problem 67
Case Problems 68

UNIT 3   SOCIAL SECURITY TAXES/69

Coverage Under FICA   69
Self-Employed Persons—Their Income and Taxes   78
Application for Employer Identification Number (Form SS-4)   79
Employee's Application for a Social Security Card (Form SS-5)   79
Request for Earnings and Benefit Estimate Statement
    (Form SSA-7004-SM)   82
Returns Required Under FICA   82
Employer's Quarterly Federal Tax Return (Form 941)   88
Penalties   92
Glossary   95
Questions for Review   95
Questions for Discussion   96
Practical Problems   97
Continuing Payroll Problem   113
Case Problems   113

UNIT 4   WITHHOLDING FOR INCOME TAXES/117

Coverage Under Federal Income Tax Withholding Law   118
Withholding Allowances and Withholding Certificates   122
The Main Methods of Withholding   126
Other Methods of Withholding   128
Withholding Tax on Supplemental Wage Payments   130
Withholding Tax on Tips   132
Advance Payment of Earned Income Credit (EIC)   132
Individual Retirement Accounts (IRA)   134
Wage and Tax Statements   135
Major Returns Completed by Employers   140
Information Returns   143
Employer's Records for Income Taxes Withheld   145
Withholding State Income Taxes   145
Withholding Local Income Taxes   147
Glossary   148
Questions for Review   149
Questions for Discussion   150
Practical Problems   153
Continuing Payroll Problem   171
Case Problems   171

UNIT 5   UNEMPLOYMENT COMPENSATION TAXES/173

Coverage Under FUTA and SUTA   174
Unemployment Compensation Taxes and Credits   179
Unemployment Compensation Reports Required of the Employer   186
Unemployment Compensation Benefits   193
Glossary   196
Questions for Review   197
Questions for Discussion   198
Practical Problems   199
Continuing Payroll Problem   213
Case Problems   213

UNIT 6   ANALYZING AND JOURNALIZING PAYROLL TRANSACTIONS/217

The Payroll Register 217
The Employee's Earnings Record 219
Recording the Gross Payroll and Withholdings 220
Recording Payroll Taxes 222
Recording Workers' Compensation Insurance Expense 225
Recording the Deposit or Payment of Payroll Taxes 226
Recording End-of-Period Adjustments 227
Recording Transactions Pertaining to Other Payroll Deductions 227
Summary of Accounts Used in Recording Payroll Transactions 229
Illustrative Case 230
Glossary 236
Questions for Review 237
Questions for Discussion 237
Practical Problems 239
Continuing Payroll Problem 261
Case Problems 261

UNIT 7   PAYROLL PROJECT/263

Books of Account and Payroll Records 264
General Information 264
Narrative of Payroll Transactions 266
Questions on the Payroll Project 277

APPENDIX A   SOCIAL SECURITY BENEFITS/327

Old-Age, Survivors, and Disability Benefits 327
Kinds of Social Security Benefits 329
Medical Care for Aged and Needy 332
Applying for Social Security Benefits 332
Glossary 334

APPENDIX B   *COMPUTERIZED PAYROLL ACCOUNTING* BY KLOOSTER & ALLEN/335

Introduction 335
Software Program Overview 336
Windows 338
Start-Up Procedures 344
Operating Procedures 345
Tutorial Problem 355
Tutorial Problem Audit Test 361
Student Project 363
Student Project Audit Tests 369
Mastery Project 377
Mastery Project Audit Test 379

TAX TABLE A   TABLES FOR PERCENTAGE METHOD OF WITHHOLDING/381

TAX TABLE B   WAGE-BRACKET WITHHOLDING TABLES/385

INDEX/397

THE NEED FOR PAYROLL AND PERSONNEL RECORDS

GOALS OF THIS UNIT

After completing your study of this unit, you should be able to:

1. Identify the various laws that affect employers in their payroll operations.
2. Know the record-keeping requirements of these laws.
3 Realize the importance of a thorough record-keeping system.
4. Describe the procedures generally followed in a Human Resources Department.
5. Recognize the various personnel records used by businesses and know the type of information shown on each form.
6. Understand the procedures employed in a typical payroll accounting system.
7. Identify the *payroll register* and the *employee's earnings record*.

With the increased capabilities of today's computer technology, the demands on payroll professionals have been magnified. Their skills as administrators and technicians are being challenged with every new payroll processing. Their work is being monitored by all who are affected by the payroll—the employees, the employer, and the government.

Payroll professionals are responsible for over four billion paychecks issued each year to over a hundred million people in the workforce of the United States. In their processing of payrolls, there is no margin for error.

A payroll accounting system is the only operation in a business that is almost completely governed by various federal, state, and local laws and regulations. Rules establish who is an employee, when to pay an employee, when overtime is to be paid, what deductions are made, and when taxes are paid. Lack of compliance with these laws and regulations can result in both fines and back-pay awards.

The preparation and processing of payroll data have become more difficult as changes in legislation have been enacted. With each new year, rates and taxable amounts vary so that payroll administrators must keep abreast of the changes that affect their firms' payroll record keeping.

Only by understanding the requirements of the various laws affecting payroll operations can you know which payroll and personnel records and procedures are necessary. This unit examines briefly the various laws that affect employers in their payroll operations. You will be shown the payroll and personnel records that employers use to meet the requirements of the laws. First, however, let's take a brief look at payroll accounting as a profession.

THE PAYROLL PROFESSION

With the increased responsibilities of payroll specialists, the profession has seen a significant increase in salary compensation. In a survey done by the job placement agency, Robert Half International, the 1993 salary range for payroll clerks was $19,000 to $23,000.[1]

---

[1]*INC.* (April 1993): 45.

Typically, an entry-level payroll clerk collects, reviews, approves, and records time records. Also, the clerk is in charge of updating attendance records, including vacation, sick, and personal days. Once a payroll is processed, the clerk reviews the information to insure the accuracy of each employee's paycheck.

As the clerk progresses in the Payroll Department, job responsibilities will include entering the following information into the payroll system:

1. Time-worked data.
2. Pay rate changes.
3. Tax rate changes.
4. Employee authorized payroll deductions.
5. New employee information.
6. Marital and employee allowance changes.

Providing information to the Finance Department concerning the amounts to be paid for taxes, health insurance premiums, retirement plans, etc., may also be part of the evolving duties of the advancing payroll professional. One of the final stages in the payroll progression involves the completion of payroll tax returns, employee information returns, federal and state census returns, and fringe benefit and welfare plan returns.

In many cases, becoming the supervisor of the Payroll Department is not the end of the line for the payroll professional. This path can also lead to high-level positions in both the finance and human resources areas.

As with other highly trained specialists, payroll professionals have moved closer to the top echelon of the organizational chart. It is, therefore, important that payroll professionals keep abreast of the changes in their field so that they can remain technically proficient. This need has spurred the development of an association of payroll practitioners—The American Payroll Association (APA).

Membership in the association is open to anyone interested in or engaged in the support of payroll accounting. The APA offers professional training seminars and various publications to its members. In addition, each year the APA administers an examination for the payroll accountant, and those who pass the exam are awarded a certificate (Certified Payroll Professional). This testing and certification process has helped the payroll profession to gain its needed recognition in the business community.

The APA has also established guidelines for the conduct of the payroll professional. This "Code of Ethics," shown in Illustration 1-1, sets the direction for the profession.[2]

CODE OF ETHICS

1. To be mindful of the personal aspect of the payroll relationship between employer and employee, and to ensure that harmony is maintained through constant concern for the Payroll Professional's fellow employees.
2. To strive for perfect accuracy and timeliness of all payroll activities.
3. To keep abreast of the state of the payroll art with regard to developments in payroll technologies.
4. To be current with legislative developments, actions on the part of regulatory bodies, and the like, in so far as they affect payroll.
5. To maintain the absolute confidentiality of the payroll, within the procedures of the employer.
6. To refrain from using Association activities for one's personal self-interest or financial gain.
7. To take as one's commitment the enhancement of one's professional abilities through the resources of the American Payroll Association.
8. To support one's fellow Payroll Professionals, both within and outside one's organization.

Illustration 1-1. APA Code of Ethics

FAIR LABOR STANDARDS ACT

In the processing of payrolls, the first step is to determine gross pay. The act that affects this calculation is the Fair Labor Standards Act (FLSA) of 1938. Commonly referred to as the Federal Wage and Hour Law, this law sets up minimum wage and overtime pay requirements. Recent changes have brought the minimum wage rate to $4.25 an hour.

Other provisions of this law concern equal pay for equal work regardless of sex, restrictions upon the employment of child labor, public service contracts, and wage garnishment. These basic provisions apply to employers engaged in interstate commerce or in the production of goods and services for interstate commerce and to employees in certain enterprises which are so engaged, unless specifically exempted.

The FLSA also imposes record-keeping requirements on employers. However, no specific form of record is prescribed. The basic requirements imposed on the employer concerning payroll and personnel records are shown in Illustration 1-2. In addition to satisfying those demands, employers of white-collar workers who are *exempt* from federal minimum wage and overtime pay standards must keep records that permit the calculation of such employees' total remuneration for each pay period. *Total remuneration*

---

[2]For more information on the organization, write to: American Payroll Association, New York Educational Division, 30 E. 33rd Street, New York, NY 10016.

	Item	Fair Labor Standards Act	Social Security	Income Tax Withholding	Unemployment Tax
EMPLOYEE DATA	Name	Yes	Yes	Yes	Yes
	Address	Yes	Yes	Yes	Yes
	Sex	Yes	. . . .	. . . .	. . . .
	Date of birth	Yes	. . . .	. . . .	. . . .
	Social security number	Yes	Yes	Yes	Yes
	Withholding allowances claimed	. . . .	. . . .	Yes	. . . .
	Occupation	Yes	Yes	Yes	Yes
	Period employed	. . . .	Yes	Yes	Yes
	State where services rendered	. . . .	Yes	. . . .	Yes
EMPLOYMENT DATA	Day and time of day when workweek begins	Yes	. . . .	. . . .	. . . .
	Regular hourly rate of pay	Yes	. . . .	. . . .	. . . .
	Basis of wage payments; e.g. $5 per hour; $40 per day	Yes	. . . .	. . . .	. . . .
	Hours worked each day	Yes	. . . .	. . . .	. . . .
	Hours worked each week	Yes	. . . .	. . . .	. . . .
	Daily or weekly straight-time pay, exclusive of overtime pay	Yes	. . . .	. . . .	. . . .
	Amount and nature of exempt pay	Yes	. . . .	. . . .	. . . .
	Weekly overtime pay	Yes	. . . .	. . . .	. . . .
	Total additions to or deductions from wages	Yes	. . . .	. . . .	. . . .
	Total remuneration for payroll period	Yes	Yes	Yes	. . . .
	Total remuneration for calendar year	. . . .	Yes	. . . .	Yes
	Date of payment	Yes	Yes	Yes	Yes
	Payroll period	Yes	Yes	Yes	Yes
TAX DATA	Employees' wages subject to tax for payroll period	. . . .	Yes	Yes	. . . .
	Employee's wages subject to tax for calendar year	. . . .	Yes	. . . .	Yes
	Taxable remuneration — if different from total remuneration, reason for difference	. . . .	Yes	Yes	Yes
	Tax deductions from employees' wages	. . . .	Yes	Yes	Yes
	Date tax collected if other than date of payment	. . . .	Yes	Yes	. . . .
	Tax paid by employer but not deducted from employee's wages	. . . .	Yes	Yes	Yes
GEN'L	Specific form of records	No	No	No	No
	No. of years records must be kept	2–3	4	4	4

Illustration 1-2. Summary of Information Required by Major Federal Payroll Laws

includes not only the payment for services rendered but also employee benefits and perquisites of employment such as board, lodging, or other facilities provided the worker.

All employers are required to keep records explaining the basis of wage differentials paid to employees of opposite sex for equal work performed in the same establishment. Included in such records are those relating to job evaluations, job descriptions, merit systems, seniority systems, and union contracts.

The employer is also required to display a poster, available from the regional office of the Wage and Hour Division, that informs employees of their minimum wage, equal pay, overtime pay, and wage-collection rights, as well as of child-labor restrictions.

A detailed discussion of this act and the standards established will be presented in Unit 2.

STATE MINIMUM WAGE AND MAXIMUM HOURS LAWS

Most states have established minimum wage rates for covered employees either by legislation or by administrative order of the legislature whereby minimum wage rates are fixed for specific industries. As noted earlier, there are also minimum wage and maximum hour provisions applicable to employers under the Fair Labor Standards Act, a federal law. Where both federal and state regulations cover the same employee, the higher of the two rates prevails. For example, the federal minimum wage is $4.25 an hour. However, the minimum hourly wage in Oregon is $4.75, or 50¢ greater than the federal minimum wage. All workers covered by that state's legislation would receive the higher state rate.

As payroll managers, you must be familiar with the administrative orders of your particular states since the wage orders not only set minimum wages but also contain provisions affecting pay periods, pay for call-in time and waiting time, rest and meal periods, absences, meals and lodging, tips, uniforms, and other matters dealing with wages and hours. The state wage orders usually provide that the employer must keep records showing the wages paid, the hours worked, and such other information that will aid enforcement by state officials.

FAIR EMPLOYMENT LAWS

Federal and state legislation has been enacted to enforce fair employment practices. Many of these laws deal with discrimination on the basis of age, race, color, religion, sex, or national origin as a condition of employment.

Civil Rights Act of 1964

Several fair employment practices are provided for in Title VII of the Civil Rights Act of 1964, entitled "Equal Employment Opportunity." The act, as amended, forbids employers to discriminate in hiring, firing, promoting, or in any other condition of employment on the basis of race, color, religion, sex, or national origin. Guidelines, established by the Equal Employment Opportunity Commission (EEOC), also include physical characteristics in the definition of national origin discrimination. For example, unnecessary height or weight requirements could exclude some individuals on the basis of their national origin. The EEOC has also declared that sexual harassment is a violation of the Civil Rights Act. Unwelcome sexual advances, requests for sexual favors, and other verbal or physical conduct of a sexual nature can constitute sexual harassment.

Employment agencies may not refer or refuse to refer applicants for employment on the basis of race, color, religion, sex, or national origin. Unions are prohibited from including or segregating their members on these bases, and unions may not cause employers to discriminate on these bases.

This act covers all employers who engage in an industry "affecting commerce" and who employ 15 or more workers for each working day in each of 20 or more weeks in the current or preceding calendar year. Employers specifically excluded from coverage of the fair employment practices legislation include: the United States government (state and local governments are covered), a corporation that is wholly owned by the United States, Indian tribes, private membership clubs (other than labor unions) that are exempt from federal income tax, and religious societies in the employment of members of a particular religion to work on the societies' religious activities. Although the United States government is classed as an exempt employer, the act states that it is the policy of the United States government to provide equal employment opportunities without discrimination, and that the President should use his existing authority to implement this policy.

To accomplish the purpose of eliminating discrimination, the Equal Employment Opportunity Commission tries to obtain voluntary compliance with the law before a court action for an injunction is filed. Where a state or local law forbids discriminatory practices, relief must first be sought under the state or local law before a complaint is filed with the Commission. The EEOC is authorized to institute court proceedings for an injunction if there is reason to believe that any person or group of persons is not complying with the law.

In addition to federal fair employment legislation, more than half the states and some cities have laws that prohibit employers from discriminating on the basis of race, creed, color, or national origin. In most of the states the laws are administered by a special commission or the state Department of Labor, which may authorize cease and desist orders that are enforceable in the courts.

Executive Orders

Employers not subject to Title VII coverage discussed above may come within the scope of the Civil Rights Act by reason of a contract or subcontract involving federal funds. In a series of *executive orders*, the federal government has banned, in employment on government contracts, discrimination that is based on race, color, religion, sex, or national origin. More significantly, the orders have been held to require that some contractors take affirmative action to ensure equal opportunity.

Affirmative Action. Affirmative action is designed to eliminate employment barriers to minorities, women, persons of various religious and ethnic groups, handicapped persons, and veterans. The concept of affirmative action was developed to clarify what firms seeking to conduct business with the federal government must do to be truly equal opportunity employers.

An *affirmative action plan* prescribes a specific program to eliminate, limit, or prevent discriminatory treatment on the basis of race, ethnic group, and sex. Some plans are required by law, while others are developed voluntarily. Usually the plan involves an analysis of the work force utilization; the establishment of attainable results-oriented goals and timetables for recruiting, hiring, training, and promoting any underrepresented classes; an explanation of the methods to be used to eliminate discrimination; and the establishment of responsibility for implementing the program. Only companies with more than 250 employees and a federal contract exceeding $1 million have to write a formal affirmative action plan.

Executive Order 11246. This is the major antidiscrimination regulation for government contractors and subcontractors who perform work under a federal construction contract exceeding $10,000, and for the United States government itself. Examples of discrimination forbidden by Executive Order 11246 include a contractor's refusal to hire women for certain jobs because of overtime requirements or weightlifting requirements.

In their affirmative action plans, covered contractors are required to scrutinize tests and other screening procedures and to make all changes necessary to assure that they are nondiscriminatory. Contractors must post notices announcing their nondiscrimination responsibilities in places conspicuous to employees, applicants, and representatives of each labor union with which the contractors deal. In all advertisements for employment, contractors must state that there will be no discrimination in hiring for any position.

Age Discrimination in Employment Act (ADEA)

Under the Age Discrimination in Employment Act of 1967 (ADEA), employers, employment agencies, and labor unions are prohibited from discriminating on the basis of age in their employment practices. Only employers (those who employ 20 or more workers), employment agencies, and labor unions engaged in an industry affecting interstate commerce are covered. The act also covers federal, state, and local government employees, other than elected officials and certain aides not covered by civil service.

Under the ADEA, protection is provided for virtually all workers over 40. There is no longer an upper age cap. A key exception involves executives who are 65 or over and who hold high policymaking positions. If such an employee is entitled to an annual retirement benefit from the employer of at least $44,000, the employee can be forcibly retired.

In order to prove compliance with the various fair employment laws, employers must keep accurate personnel and payroll records. All employment applications, along with notations as to their disposition and the reasons for the disposition, should be retained. A complete file of job descriptions and copies of employment tests should be kept. All records pertaining to promotions, discharges, seniority plans, merit programs, incentive payment plans, etc., should also be retained.

Americans with Disabilities Act (ADA)

The Americans with Disabilities Act of 1990 prohibits employers (with 25 or more employees), employment agencies, labor organizations, or joint labor-management committees from discriminating against qualified persons with disabilities because of their disability. The prohibition of disability-based discrimination applies to job application procedures, hiring, advancement, termination, compensation, job training, and other conditions of employment. In addition, reasonable accommodations, such as wheelchair accessible restrooms and ramps, for qualified disabled job applicants and workers must be provided.

FEDERAL INSURANCE CONTRIBUTIONS ACT (FICA)

The Federal Insurance Contributions Act (FICA) is part of the social security program planned by the federal government to provide economic security for workers and their families. Under the act, a tax is levied on employers and employees in certain industries to be paid to the federal government and credited to the Federal Old-Age and Survivors' Trust Fund and the Federal Disability Insurance Trust Fund. The old-age, survivors, and disability insurance (OASDI) tax levied on employees is a set percent of their gross wages, and it must be withheld from their pay. From these funds payments are made to persons who are entitled to benefits under the Social Security Act.

FICA also provides a two-part health insurance program, commonly known as Medicare, for the aged and the disabled. The Hospital Insurance (HI) plan is financed by a separate tax on both employers and employees. The Supplementary Medical Insurance plan is voluntary and is financed by those who desire coverage, with a matching payment by the federal government.

Social security benefits are also available to the self-employed person under the provisions of the Self-Employment Contributions Act (SECA). This act imposes a tax on the net earnings from self-employment derived by an individual from any trade or business carried on by that person.

Detailed information about FICA and exemptions from its coverage is given in Unit 3, and the benefits available are briefly discussed in Appendix A.

Although no specific form of records is recommended for employers under FICA, the act requires that employers keep records providing certain specific information. The information needed and the period of time for which it is to be retained are shown in Illustration 1-2 on page 3.

INCOME TAX WITHHOLDING LAWS

With the passage of the 16th Amendment in 1913, taxation of income became constitutional. Today, an *income tax* is levied on the earnings of most employees and is deducted from their gross pay. In some cases, this may involve three separate deductions from the employee's gross pay—a federal income tax, a state income tax, and a local (city) income or wage tax. All of the acts that levy these various income taxes provide for the collection of taxes at the source of the wages paid (payroll withholding).

Federal Income Tax Withholding Law

The collection of federal income taxes at the source of wages paid came into being with the enactment of the Current Tax Payment Act of 1943. This act is commonly referred to as a withholding tax law. A percentage formula is used in an attempt to collect the approximate tax on wages or salaries by requiring the employer to withhold a specified amount from each wage or salary payment. These withholdings are then turned over to the federal government for the employee's tax account. Over the years many changes have been made in the tax rates, exemptions, and allowable deductions. The present requirements are discussed in detail in Unit 4.

Employers are required to keep records showing the information referred to in Illustration 1-2 on page 3. However, the law does not prescribe any specific forms to be used for such record keeping.

State and Local Income Tax Withholding Laws

State income taxes are imposed on individuals in most states. The laws vary from state to state as to the amount to be withheld, exemptions from withholding, and the time for withholding reports to be filed. Employers may also be required by *local* income tax laws to deduct and withhold local income taxes on salaries or wages paid. The withholding of state and local income taxes is further discussed in Unit 4.

UNEMPLOYMENT TAX ACTS

The purpose of *unemployment insurance taxes* is to provide funds at the state level for compensating unemployed workers. The employer is affected by taxes levied both by the federal government (Federal Unemployment Tax Act) and by the state government (State Unemployment Tax Acts).

Federal Unemployment Tax Act (FUTA)

Like the Federal Insurance Contributions Act, the Federal Unemployment Tax Act is incorporated in the

Internal Revenue Code. If an employer employs one or more individuals in each of 20 or more weeks in occupations covered by FUTA or pays wages of $1,500 or more during any calendar quarter in the current or preceding calendar year, a federal unemployment insurance tax must be paid. The tax paid to the federal government is used for paying state and federal administrative expenses of the unemployment program. Employers subject to FUTA receive credit against most of the federal tax when they contribute to their state unemployment compensation funds. Detailed information as to employers and employees who are subject to the requirements of the act is given in Unit 5.

Employers subject to FUTA must keep permanent records that provide the information listed in Illustration 1-2 on page 3. No particular form is prescribed for these records. However, each employer must use forms and accounting systems that will enable the District Director of the Internal Revenue Service to ascertain whether the tax is correctly computed and paid.

State Unemployment Tax Acts (SUTA)

All the states and the District of Columbia have enacted unemployment insurance laws. Each employer receives a credit against the FUTA tax because of the contribution (tax) to a state's unemployment compensation program. The taxes paid to the individual states by employers are used primarily for the payment of unemployment benefits.

The Social Security Act specifies certain standards that each state had to meet in passing an unemployment compensation law. These standards have resulted in a fairly high degree of uniformity in the requirements of state unemployment laws and in the records that must be kept by businesses. State laws do differ, however, making it necessary for employers to be familiar with the laws of the states in which they operate.

The state unemployment compensation laws require employers to keep payroll records similar to those required under the federal law. Penalties may be imposed for failure to keep the required records or for failure or delinquency in making the required returns or for default or delinquency in paying the contributions. The required period for retaining records varies in different states, but in no case should the records be kept for a period of less than four years because of the federal requirement.

State unemployment compensation and tax acts are discussed in Unit 5.

OTHER FEDERAL LAWS AFFECTING THE NEED FOR PAYROLL AND PERSONNEL RECORDS

Generally the payroll and personnel records and reports that a business prepares and retains to meet the requirements of the laws already discussed provide sufficient information needed under the laws which are outlined in Illustration 1-3, on page 8, and discussed below.

Employee Retirement Income Security Act of 1974 (ERISA)

This act covers employee pension and welfare plans that are established or maintained (1) by any employer engaged in commerce or in any industry or activity affecting commerce and (2) by any employee organization representing employees engaged in commerce or in any industry or activity affecting commerce. The legislation insures that workers will earn pension rights, and safeguards those pension funds by regulating how the funds are to be raised, how they are to be disbursed, who controls them, and what is to be done when funds are insufficient to pay promised benefits. However, the law *does not* require any employer to establish a pension plan.

ERISA was primarily designed to insure that workers who are covered by private pension plans receive benefits from those plans in accordance with their credited years of service with their employers. *Vesting* is the process of conveying to employees the right to share in a retirement fund in the event they are terminated before the normal retirement age. The vesting process is linked to the number of years needed for workers to earn an equity in their retirement plans and to become entitled to full or partial benefits at some future date if they leave the company before retirement. Once vested, a worker has the right to receive a pension at retirement age, based on years of covered service, even though the worker may not be working for the firm at that time. Most retirement plans provide for vesting after the worker has been covered under the plan for a specified number of years. Currently, the law provides for full vesting in five years or gradually over seven years (20% after three years and 20% a year for the next four). To protect against potential benefit losses because of a plan's termination, ERISA set up a government insurance program (The Pension Benefit Guaranty Corporation) to pay any benefits that could not be met with funds from the plan.

Individual Retirement Account (IRA).

An *individual retirement account (IRA)* is a pension plan established and funded by an individual employee. The employee's contributions to an IRA may be made through the employer or a union or placed in an individual retirement savings account specified in the law. *Under certain conditions*, employees may put aside each year the lesser of $2,000 or 100% of their compensation without paying federal income taxes on their contributions.

A more detailed discussion of IRA accounts is presented in Unit 4.

Simplified Employee Pension (SEP) Plan.

By means of a *simplified employee pension (SEP) plan*, employers may make contributions to individual retirement accounts on behalf of their employees. Employers may make annual contributions of up to 25% of each employee's compensation, but in no case may the contribution exceed $30,000. The contributions are placed in an individual retirement account for the employee. The employee can also contribute to the plan.

Employers must contribute for all employees who are 21 years of age or older and who have worked for the employer at least three of the past five years. The

Law	Coverage	Contract Dollar Minimum	Major Provisions
Davis-Bacon Act (1931)	Laborers for contractors or subcontractors on federal government contracts for construction, alteration, or repair of public buildings or works.	$2,000	Minimum wage set by Secretary of Labor (weight is given to union wage scale prevailing in the project area).
Walsh-Healey Public Contracts Act (1936)	Laborers for contractors who furnish materials, supplies, articles, and equipment to any agency of the United States.	$10,000	Single minimum wage determined by Secretary of Labor for all covered employees in a given industry.
McNamara-O'Hara Service Contract Act (1965)	Service employees on contracts with the United States or the District of Columbia for the furnishing of services.	$2,500	Minimum wage set by Secretary of Labor based on minimum wage found to be prevailing in that locality.
Occupational Safety and Health Act (OSHA) (1970)	Any business involved in interstate commerce.	-0-	Sets specific occupational and health standards for employers; requires that records be kept of work-related deaths, illnesses, and injuries.
Vocational Rehabilitation Act (1973)	Companies with federal agency contracts.	$2,500	Must include in the contract an affirmative action clause requiring that the handicapped applicant or employee will be given appropriate consideration.
Vietnam Era Veterans' Readjustment Act (1974)	Government contractors with federal contracts or subcontracts.	$10,000	Requires contractors to take affirmative action to employ and advance in employment qualified veterans of the Vietnam era and disabled veterans.

Illustration 1-3. Federal Laws Affecting the Need for Payroll and Personnel Records

NEWS ALERT NEWS ALERT NEWS ALERT

During the aftermath of serious natural disasters, such as Hurricanes Andrew and Iniki, the federal government suspends the Davis-Bacon Act for those regions of the country that are hardest hit by the catastrophes. Once the regions have recovered sufficiently, the Act is restored by Presidential Proclamation.

contributions made by the employer are fully and immediately vested.

Disclosure Requirements. The reporting and disclosure requirements set forth by ERISA have tremendous implications for the record-keeping requirements of employers. Informational reports must be filed with the U.S. Department of Labor, the IRS, and the government insurance program.

In general, the reports are composed of descriptions of the plans and the annual financial data. The plan descriptions include the eligibility requirements for participation and for benefits; provisions for non-forfeitable pension benefits; circumstances which may result in disqualification, loss, or denial of benefits; and procedures for presenting claims. The annual reports include financial statements and schedules showing the current value of plan assets and liabilities, receipts and disbursements, and employer contributions; the assets held for investment purposes; insurance data; and an opinion of an independent qualified public accountant.

Upon written request from the participants, the administrator must also furnish a statement, not more than once in a 12-month period, of the total benefits accrued, accrued benefits that are vested, if any, or the earliest date on which accrued benefits will become vested.

Immigration Reform and Control Act of 1986 (IRCA)

This act bars employers from hiring aliens unauthorized to work in the United States. It also requires all employers to verify employment eligibility for all individuals hired after November 6, 1986. To do this, the employer must examine the employee's verification documents and have the employee complete Form I-9, Employment Eligibility Verification (not illustrated). The document or documents that the employee must furnish to the employer are listed on Form I-9. These documents are used for two purposes: to identify the employee, and, if an alien, to verify authorization to work in the United States.

Form I-9 must be completed within three business days of the date the employee starts to work. The form must be retained for three years after the date of hiring or for one year after the date the employment is terminated, whichever is longer.

The Immigration and Naturalization Service (INS) can levy fines if an audit uncovers record-keeping violations. Civil penalties range from $100 to $1,000 for each violation.

Family and Medical Leave Act of 1993 (FMLA)

This law requires employers that have 50 or more employees within a 75-mile radius to grant workers unpaid leave for a family or medical emergency. In cases of childbirth or adoption, and serious illness of the employee or the employee's child, spouse, or parent, the employer is required to offer the worker as many as 12 weeks of unpaid leave.

Employers can exempt the following:

1. The highest-paid 10% of their workforce.
2. Those who have not worked at least one year and at least 1,250 hours in the previous 12 months for the company.

In addition, the employer can substitute an employee's earned paid leave for any part of the 12-week family leave.

OTHER STATE LAWS AFFECTING THE NEED FOR PAYROLL AND PERSONNEL RECORDS

States have enacted other laws which have a direct bearing on the payroll and personnel records that an employer must maintain and on the rights that must be extended to employees.

Workers' Compensation Laws

By means of *workers' compensation insurance*, employees and their dependents are protected against losses due to injury or death incurred during employment. Most states have passed laws that require employers to provide workers' compensation insurance by one of the following plans:

1. Contribution to a state compensation insurance fund administered by an insurance department of the state.
2. Purchase of workers' compensation insurance from a private insurance company authorized by the state to issue this type of policy.

3. Establishment of a self-insurance plan, approved by the state, under which the company bears all risk itself.

The cost of the workers' compensation insurance premiums is borne by the employer, except in New Mexico, Oregon, and Washington, where both the employer and the employee contribute to the workers' compensation fund. Benefits are paid to the injured worker, or to the survivors in the event of death, by the state, by the insurance company, or by the risk-assuming employer according to the adopted plan.

The insurance premiums are often based upon the total gross payroll of the business and may be stated in terms of an amount for each $100 of weekly wages paid to employees. The premium rates vary among types of jobs and vary in amount with the pay rate involved.

EXAMPLE:

The rate for the office workers of the Volpe Parts Company is $0.60 per $100 of payroll, while the rate for machine-shop workers is $6 per $100 of payroll.

Because the premium rates vary according to the different degrees of danger in various classes of jobs, it is necessary that payroll records be planned and carefully maintained to indicate job classifications for rate purposes. If the employer's accident experience is low, the rates may be reduced to a certain minimum. Every business should determine whether it comes under a workers' compensation insurance law and should keep any records required in connection with the law.

State Disability Benefit Laws

California, Hawaii, New Jersey, New York, Rhode Island, and Puerto Rico have passed laws to provide *disability benefits* to employees who are absent from their jobs because of illness, accident, or disease *not arising out of their employment*. State disability benefit laws are further discussed in Unit 5.

State Time-Off-To-Vote Laws

In many states employees are allowed to take time off from work to vote, and the United States Supreme Court has upheld the validity of time-off-to-vote laws. Although the laws of the states vary, generally the legislation provides that if employees who are entitled to vote in an election are absent from work for a specified period, they will not be penalized nor will there be a deduction from their wages. In most states the employee is required to have applied for the time off prior to the date of the election. Usually penalties are provided if the employer refuses an employee the right-to-vote privileges that have been conferred by state law.

Legal Holidays

Payroll administration requires that we know what holidays are legally recognized by our state. For example, the due dates for returns and tax payments are extended by the federal government and many states when the scheduled due date falls on a Saturday, a Sunday, or a legal holiday.

The federal government has declared New Year's Day (January 1), Independence Day (July 4), Veterans Day (November 11), Thanksgiving Day (fourth Thursday in November), and Christmas Day (December 25) to be legal public holidays. In addition, the following "Monday Holidays" are legal public holidays:

- Martin Luther King, Jr.'s Birthday, the third Monday in January.
- Presidents' Day, the third Monday in February.
- Memorial Day, the last Monday in May.
- Labor Day, the first Monday in September.
- Columbus Day, the second Monday in October.

Although almost all states have enacted legislation declaring most of the "Monday Holidays," we must be familiar with the legislation of our own state and those states wherein other employees of our firm may be working.

Professional Tip
The "Monday Holidays" affect only agencies under federal or state jurisdiction. Private firms are not required to observe these holidays.

HUMAN RESOURCES AND PAYROLL ACCOUNTING SYSTEMS

Up to this point in the unit, we have seen that a business must keep *human resources* (or *personnel*) and *payroll* records to meet the requirements of the various laws under which it is operating. In addition, these records form an integral part of an effective business system.

In developing its human resources system and payroll accounting system, a business should design basic forms and records that satisfy the requirements of all the laws applicable to that organization. Properly designed forms and records, as described in the closing pages of this unit, not only supply the information required by the various laws but also provide management with information needed in its decision-making process. Thus, properly designed human resources and payroll accounting forms and records result in savings in both time and work because the necessary information is recorded, stored, retrieved, and distributed economically, efficiently, and quickly.

Before studying the employment process, it is important to examine the close relationship between the Payroll Department and the Human Resources Department. Some businesses consider payroll to be strictly an accounting function and, as such, place it under the direct control of the director of finance. However, because of the need for quick interchange of information between the Payroll and the Human Resources Departments, the recent trend has been to place payroll under the control of the Director of Human Resources.

This movement toward centralization eliminates the duplication of many tasks, such as information reviews on both federal and state tax and census returns. With the required information in one department, the process of completing these forms is shortened and done more accurately. Further, questions from employees concerning sick pay, vacation pay, and other benefits can be answered from one source.

Individual computer programs have been developed for the combined needs of payroll and human resources. Information concerning such diverse activities as attendance, retirement benefits, health insurance coverages, and bonus pays is now available to designated employees in the Human Resources Department through a computer terminal.

In the remainder of this unit, we will assume that the two departments are operating separately.

HUMAN RESOURCES SYSTEM

In many medium-size and large companies, the *human resources system* embodies all those procedures and methods related to recruiting, selecting, orienting, training, and terminating personnel. Extensive record-keeping procedures are required in order to:

1. Provide data for considering promotions and changes in the status and earnings of workers.
2. Provide the information required by various federal, state, and local laws.
3. Justify company actions if investigated by national or state labor relations boards.

4. Justify company actions in discussions with local unions or plant committees.

Before the Payroll Department can pay newly hired employees, the Human Resources Department must process those employees. The procedure that the Human Resources Department follows in this hiring process is charted in Illustration 1-4.

A number of companies that manufacture business forms have available standard personnel forms

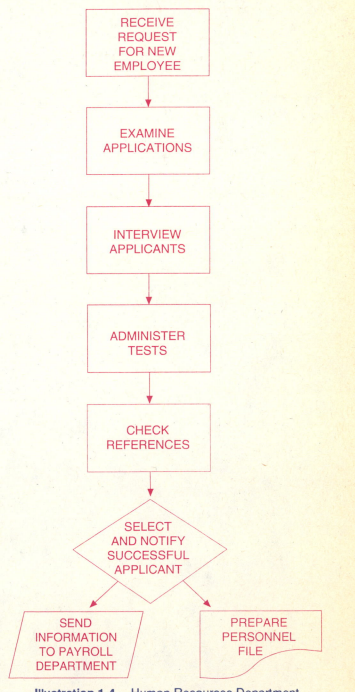

Illustration 1-4. Human Resources Department Procedure in the Hiring Process

and records that may be successfully used if a business does not care to design its own special forms.

In small companies it may not be necessary to keep such extensive personnel records. Frequently an application form or an employee history record may be the only document needed.

Throughout the remainder of this unit, the discussion of the various human resources and payroll records is augmented by the use of several illustrations. In the examples of these records, we shall follow Mary Louise Mosworth from her initial application for employment with the United Chemicals Company to her entry onto the company's payroll records.

Requisition for Personnel

The *requisition for personnel* form is used to notify the Human Resources Department of the need for additional or replacement employees. The requisition for new employees can be initiated in a number of ways. In some companies a memo is sent to the Human Resources Department, stating the title of the position to be filled, a brief description of the duties of the job, and the salary range. Other companies may use preprinted forms. If a preprinted form is utilized, it should indicate the type and number of persons needed, the position to be filled, the rate of pay for the job, the salary range, the date the employee is needed, a summary of any special qualifications, and whether the position is permanent or temporary.

Illustration 1-5 shows a typical personnel requisition that is very suitable in businesses requiring a record of this kind. Usually, two copies of the form are prepared by the department head or other person making the request. The original copy is sent to the Human Resources Department, and the duplicate is retained by the person making the request.

Application for Employment

Every business, regardless of size, should have an application form to be filled out by a person seeking employment. The *application form* gives the applicant an opportunity to provide complete information as to personal qualifications, training, and experience. The form serves as a permanent record for the business and provides a means of obtaining information needed for various purposes. When the people who interview the applicant have the information before them, as requested on the application blank, they are reminded of questions that should be asked of the applicant, and of facts that should be given the applicant.

United Chemicals

PERSONNEL REQUISITION

Department Accounting Position Payroll Clerk Date Wanted July 1, 19--

Name of person being replaced Martin W. Scruggs
(If addition, attach explanation)

Job Title Payroll Clerk Job Grade 4

*Name of person terminating ---

*Job Title --- *Job Grade ---

Date of Termination June 25, 19--

If temporary, for how long? ---

If part-time, what hours or days? ---

*Complete only if person being requested will not be performing the same job duties as the person terminating.

EDUCATION

HIGH SCHOOL ___ BUSINESS SCHOOL X

COLLEGE 1 (2) 3 4 YEARS

OTHER ___

LIST ANY SPECIAL QUALIFICATIONS NOT COVERED BY JOB DESCRIPTION:

Approval E. J. Dunn Date June 15, 19-- Signed Margaret T. Johnson
Supervisor—Department Head

(FOR HUMAN RESOURCES DEPARTMENT USE)

POSITION FILLED BY	CODE NO.	STARTING DATE	STARTING SALARY	PAYROLL NOTIFIED BY
Mary Louise Mosworth	33-4	7/1/--	$1,500 mo.	Vernon T. Hansen

Illustration 1-5. Personnel Requisition

Other purposes of the application form are to provide information for the checking of references, to serve as a guide to effective interviewing, and to provide information for correlation with data obtained from employment tests. The basic information that should be provided by the application for employment form is the following:

1. Personal information including the name, address, telephone number, and social security account number of the applicant.
2. Educational background including a summary of the schools attended, whether the applicant graduated, and degrees conferred.
3. Employment and experience record.
4. Type of employment desired.
5. References.

Employers who are subject to fair employment laws must make certain that all aspects of the prehire inquiries are free of discrimination on the basis of race, color, religion, sex, national origin, or age. *Prehire inquiries* include questions asked in the employment interview and on application forms, resumes of experience or education required of an applicant, and any kind of written testing. None of the federal civil rights laws specifically outlaw questions concerning the race, color, religion, sex, national origin, or age of an applicant. However, if the employer can offer no logical explanation for asking such questions, the Equal Employment Opportunity Commission and the Wage and Hour Administrator view such questions as discriminatory. Of course, prehire questions pertaining to religion, sex, national origin, or age are allowed when these factors are bona fide occupational qualifications for a job.

Asking an applicant's age or date of birth may tend to deter the older worker. Thus, if such information is asked for on an application form, a statement should appear on that form notifying the applicant that discrimination on the basis of age with respect to individuals who are at least 40 is prohibited by the Age Discrimination in Employment Act. Some businesses have removed the "date of birth" and "year of graduation" questions from their application forms.

Generally an employer may not require information of a minority, a female, or an older applicant that would not be required of another applicant. It has also been held by the EEOC that asking a job applicant to list arrests on the job application violates the Civil Rights Act. An employer may seek or use information concerning criminal convictions of applicants or employees and may refuse to hire a convicted criminal only if there is a valid business need for doing so. The employer is also prohibited from making inquiries about an applicant's honorable discharge from the military service unless it can be proved that there is a proper business interest that justifies the asking of such information.

As shown in Illustration 1-6 on pages 14 and 15, an application blank may provide space for an interview record. This section of the form is completed by the interviewer either while the interview is in process or after it has been completed. The comments appearing on the application blank in Illustration 1-6 were those of Vernon T. Hansen, the Director of Human Resources. Often the applicant is interviewed by the potential supervisor as well as by a member of the Human Resources Department.

In case an applicant is rejected, a notation on the application form enumerating the reasons for rejection will prove helpful in the future. This would simplify the restudy of the applicant's qualifications if the individual should later reapply. In addition, a record of the reasons for rejecting an applicant will be needed in the event the company is accused of unfair labor practices.

Reference Inquiry

Before an applicant is employed, a company may check some of the references given on the application blank. Many businesses use a standard *reference inquiry form*, which is usually mailed to the person or company given as a reference. In some cases, businesses do not use a specially designed form for inquiring about references but instead write special letters. Other companies prefer a telephone reference check because they feel that a more frank opinion of the candidate is received over the telephone than in a letter. Some companies prefer not to check on personal references given by the job applicant since these tend to be less objective than business references. Today, any type of reference checking has taken on new meaning—expensive litigation. Because of this, many human resources departments give references only a cursory glance.

Professional Tip

Job applicants can now find out what previous employers are saying about them. A company, Documented Reference Check of Alto Loma, California, will for a fee check job references just as a prospective employer would, except that the reference check company reports back to the applicant.[3]

---

[3]Joseph Busler, "Employers Have to Be Careful When Employees Come and Go," *Camden Courier Post*, 28 March 1993, D-1.

United Chemicals

PERSONAL

Name *Mary Louise Mosworth*	Date *June 18, 19--*
7 North Street	Phone Number *555-5136*
City *Huntington* State *WV* Zip *25703-2234*	Social Security Number *293-77-1388*

In case of emergency, who would we notify? Phone Number
Name *Robert Mosworth* Address *7 North Street, Huntington* *555-5136*

STATEMENT OF HEALTH

Is There Any Reason Why You Would Be Unable to Perform Any of the Duties of the Position for Which You Are Applying?
No

If Yes, Explain:

EMPLOYMENT INFORMATION

Type Work Preferred *Accounting – clerical*	When Available for Work *at once*
Are You Now Employed? *No*	Reasons for Desiring Change

Have You Ever Supervised People *No*	How Many	Where

List Special Skill and Office Equipment You Operate Efficiently *typewriter, office copier,*
video display terminal

Present Typing Speed	No. Years in School?	In Experience?	Present Shorthand Speed	No. Years in School	In Experience?
65	3	1	—	—	—

PREVIOUS EMPLOYMENT

SHOW LAST POSITION FIRST. ANSWER ALL QUESTIONS

1 Name and Address of Company
White Transfer Co., P.O. Box 801, Huntington, WV 25701-2231

Date Employed *Feb 1, 19--*	Date Terminated *Dec. 31, 19--*	Final Salary *$5.80/hr.*	Name of Supervisor *Jean Sanning*

Reason for Termination
To enter Business College

Duties and Positions Held
Clerk-typist – Verify extensions and prepare waybills

2 Name and Address of Company
Palmer Drugs, Broad & Center, Huntington, WV 25701-2232

Date Employed *Aug. 10, 19--*	Date Terminated *Jan. 31, 19--*	Final Salary *$4.25/hr.*	Name of Supervisor *William Palmer*

Reason for Termination
To accept full-time job at higher hourly rate

Duties and Positions Held
Cash register operator at check-out counter

Illustration 1-6. Application Blank (page 1)

EDUCATION		Name and Address of School	Years Attended	Average Grade	Major Course	Minor Course	Graduate?
	High School	Valley High School Huntington, WV	19__ To 19__	B	Business	English	Yes
	College		19__ To 19__				
			19__ To 19__				
	Business School	Huntington College of Business—Huntington, WV	19__ To 19__	A	Accounting	Office Procedures	Yes
	Other		19__ To 19__				

Your Most Interesting Subjects in Last School Attended.	Your Most Difficult Subjects in Last School Attended.
Accounting and Law	Economics

Honors and Extracurricular Activities in Last School Attended

Vice-President, Young Business Executives Club

PROFESSIONAL CERTIFICATES

Type	Issuing State	Date	No.
None			
Type	Issuing State	Date	No.
Type	Issuing State	Date	No.

REFERENCES

List below three references not previously mentioned in application. and not related to you. who have known you at least three years.

Name	Address	Occupation or Profession
Rev. Stephen M. Keel	51 Parker Rd. Huntington, WV 25710-2237	Minister, Central Presbyterian Church
George P. Russell	163 21st Street Nitro, WV 25143-2139	Chemical Engineer
Mrs. Ethel Carson	416 Eighth Street Huntington, WV 25701-2236	Instructor

The above statements are true to the best of my knowledge and belief. I am willing to undergo a medical examination as a basis for further consideration of my application.

Signature _____ Mary L. Mosworth _____

DO NOT WRITE IN SPACE BELOW

Employed?	Hold Application in Pending File
☒ Yes ☐ No	☐ Yes ☒ No

Date to Report to Work	Department
July 1, 19—	Accounting

Position	Job Grade	Salary
Payroll Clerk	4	$1,500/mo.

Remarks:

Very pleasing personality, well poised. Excellent scholastic background. Anxious to advance in accounting-related position.

Interviewed By	Interviewed By	Interviewed By
		Vernon T. Hansen

Illustration 1-6. Application Blank (page 2)

Under the Fair Credit Reporting Act of 1968, employers are subject to certain disclosure obligations when they seek an *investigative consumer report* from a consumer reporting agency on a job applicant or in certain instances on present employees. An investigative consumer report usually contains information about the individual's character, general reputation, and mode of living. Generally, the employer must notify the applicant or the employee in writing that such a report is being sought. Also, the employer must notify the applicant or employee that he or she may request information from the employer about the nature and scope of the information sought. In the event employment is denied because of the consumer report information, the employer is required to inform the individual that this was the reason or part of the reason for denying employment. Also, the employer must furnish the applicant with the name and address of the consumer reporting agency that made the report.

Hiring Notice

After the successful applicant is notified of employment and is informed as to the starting date, time, and to whom to report, a *hiring notice* is sent to the Payroll Department so that the new employee can be added properly to the payroll. A hiring notice such as that shown in Illustration 1-7 usually gives the name, address, and telephone number of the new employee, the department in which employed, the starting date,

the rate of pay, the number of withholding allowances claimed, and any other information pertaining to deductions that are to be made from the employee's wages. Usually two copies of this form are prepared, with the original going to the Payroll Department and the duplicate being kept by the Human Resources Department.

Employee History Record

Although many businesses keep no personnel records other than the application blank, there is need for a more detailed record such as the *employee history record*, which provides a continuous record of the relationship between the employer and the employee. The employee history record, in addition to providing personal and other information usually found on an application blank, provides space to record the employee's progress, attendance, promotions, performance appraisals, and salary increases.

Change in Payroll Rate

The *change in payroll rate form* is used to notify the proper departments of a change in the employee's rate of remuneration. The change in rate may originate in the Human Resources Department or with the head of the department in which the employee works. In either event, the Payroll Department must be informed of the change for the employee so that the rate change is put into effect at the proper time and so that

---

HIRING NOTICE

NO. 220

SOCIAL SECURITY NO. 293-77-1388

DATE _____ June 28, 19--

NAME Mary Louise Mosworth

CLOCK NO. 418

ADDRESS 7 North St., Huntington, WV   ZIP 25703-2234   PHONE NO. 555-5136

OCCUPATION Payroll Clerk   DEPT. Accounting   GROUP NO. --

STARTING DATE July 1, 19--   TIME 8:00   A.M. P.M.   RATE $1,500 mo.

MARRIED   SINGLE   x   BIRTH DATE   8/1/--

LAST EMPLOYMENT   White Transfer Co.   LOCATION Huntington, WV

DATE LEFT 12/31/--   REASON Enrolled in college

NO. OF WITHHOLDING ALLOWANCES   1

IN EMERGENCY NOTIFY   Robert Mosworth   PHONE NO.   555-5136

EMPLOYEE'S SIGNATURE IN FULL   *Mary Louise Mosworth*

SUPERVISOR'S SIGNATURE   *Margaret T. Johnson*

EMPLOYMENT DEPARTMENT

ORIGINAL TO PAYROLL DEPT.
DUPLICATE RETAINED BY HUMAN RESOURCES DEPT.

Illustration 1-7. Hiring Notice

the records reflect the new rate. Illustration 1-8 shows a form that may be used for this purpose. Ordinarily one copy is sent to the Payroll Department, one to the Human Resources Department, and one to the employee's department.

PAYROLL ACCOUNTING SYSTEM

A *payroll accounting system* embodies all those procedures and methods related to the disbursement of pay to employees. A typical payroll accounting system includes the procedures shown in Illustration 1-9, page 18.

The nature of the payroll records depends to a great extent on the size of the work force and the degree to which the record keeping is automated. Throughout this course, manual payroll accounting systems are described and illustrated. Computerized payroll accounting systems are described in Appendix B, along with operating instructions for using the software available with this text.

In most payroll systems—manual or automated—there are two basic records: the payroll register and the employee's earnings record.

Payroll Register

The *payroll register* is a multicolumn form used to assemble and summarize the data needed at the end of each payroll period. It is a detailed listing of a company's complete payroll for that particular pay period. Thus, the payroll register lists all the employees who earned remuneration, the amount of remuneration, the deductions, and the net amount paid. The information provided in the payroll register is used primarily to meet the requirements of the Fair Labor Standards Act. However, the register is also used to provide information for recording the payroll entries in the journal and to prepare reports required by other federal, state, and local laws.

One form of payroll register is shown in Illustration 1-10 on page 19. Another form, used in the Continuing Payroll Problem at the end of Units 2 through 6, is shown in the fold-out at the back of this book. Further discussion of the payroll register is presented in Unit 6.

Employee's Earnings Record

In addition to the information contained in the payroll register, businesses are required to provide more complete information about the accumulated earnings of each employee. For that reason, it is necessary to keep a separate payroll record on each employee—the *employee's earnings record*. Each payday, after the information has been recorded in the payroll register, the information for each employee is transferred, or posted, to the employee's earnings record.

CHANGE OF STATUS

Please enter the following change(s) as of   January 1, 19--

Name   Mary L. Mosworth   Clock or Payroll No.   418   Soc. Sec. Number   293-77-1388

FROM

Job	Dept.	Shift	Rate
Payroll Clerk	Acct.	--	$1,500

TO

Job	Dept.	Shift	Rate
Accounting Clerk (A)	Acct.	--	$1,750

REASON FOR CHANGE:

- ☐ Hired
- ☐ Re-hired
- ☒ Promotion
- ☐ Demotion
- ☐ Transfer
- ☐ Merit Increase
- ☐ Leave of Absence to _____
- ☐ Length of Serv. Increase
- ☐ Re-eval. of Existing Job
- ☐ Resignation
- ☐ Retirement
- ☐ Layoff
- ☐ Discharge

Date

Other reason or explanation: _____

_____

_____

AUTHORIZED BY *Margaret T. Johnson*   APPROVED BY *E. J. Dunn*

Prepare in triplicate: (1) Human Resources (2) Payroll (3) Employee's Department

Illustration 1-8. Change of Status Form

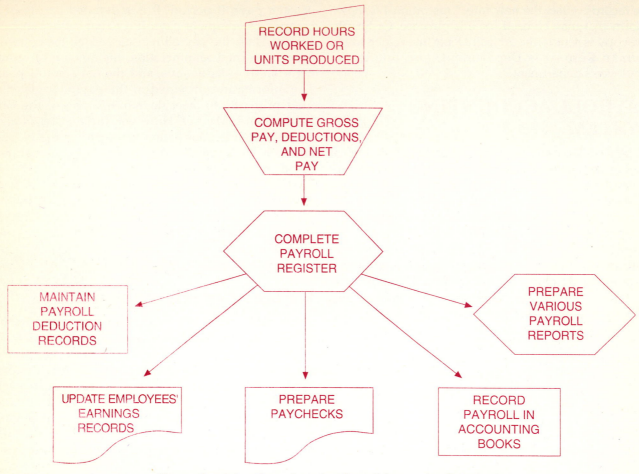

Illustration 1-9. Procedures in a Payroll Accounting System

The employee's earnings record provides the information needed to prepare periodic reports required by the withholding tax laws, the FICA tax law, and state unemployment or disability laws. Employers also use the employee's earnings record in preparing *Form W-2, Wage and Tax Statement.* This form is used by the employer to report the amount of wages paid each worker in the course of the trade or business of the employer. An example of the employee's earnings record is shown in Illustration 1-11 on page 19. A more detailed discussion of the preparation and use of the earnings record is presented in Unit 6.

Paycheck

When employees are paid by check, a check is written for each worker, using as the amount of net pay that figure appearing in the Net Paid column of the payroll register. Most paychecks, such as that depicted in Illustration 1-12 on page 20, carry a stub, or voucher, that shows the earnings and deductions. Paying workers in cash, by check, or by means of an electronic transfer of payroll funds is explained in the following unit.

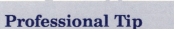

Professional Tip
The retention requirements imposed on employers by various government agencies set a limit of seven years on payroll registers and eight years on employees' earnings records.

PAYROLL REGISTER

FOR WEEK ENDING   January 19   19 --

	No.	Name	Total Hours Worked	Regular Earnings			Overtime Earnings			Total Earnings	Deductions				Net Paid	
				Hrs.	Rate	Amount	Hrs.	Rate	Amount		OASDI Tax	HI Tax	Fed. Income Tax	State Income Tax	Check No.	Amount
1	403	Springs, Carl A.	40	40	5.15	206.00				206.00	12.77	2.99	17.00	3.92	504	169.32
2	409	Wiegand, Sue T.	42	40	4.80	192.00	2	7.20	14.40	206.40	12.80	2.99	13.00	3.92	505	173.69
3	412	O'Neill, John B.	38	38	4.50	171.00				171.00	10.60	2.48	19.00	5.10	506	133.82
4	413	Bass, Marie S.	44	40	5.00	200.00	4	7.50	30.00	230.00	14.26	3.34	14.00	4.67	507	193.73
5	418	Mosworth, M. L.	41	40	S	403.85	1	15.15	15.15	419.00	25.98	6.08	48.00	13.15	508	325.79
47		Totals				3,895.75			317.20	4,212.95	261.20	61.09	808.00	124.24		2,958.42

Illustration 1-10.   Payroll Register

EMPLOYEE'S EARNINGS RECORD

Week	Week Ending	Total Hours Worked	Regular Earnings			Overtime Earnings			Total Earnings	Deductions				Net Paid		Cumulative Earnings
			Hrs.	Rate	Amount	Hrs.	Rate	Amount		OASDI Tax	HI Tax	Fed. Income Tax	State Income Tax	Check No.	Amount	
1	1/5	40	40	S	403.85				403.85	25.04	5.86	47.00	12.75	419	313.20	403.85
2	1/12	42	40	S	403.85	2	15.15	30.30	434.15	26.92	6.30	51.00	13.94	463	335.99	838.00
3	1/19	41	40	S	403.85	1	15.15	15.15	419.00	25.98	6.08	48.00	13.15	508	325.79	1,257.00

Sex		Department	Occupation	State Employed	S.S. Account No.	Name—Last First Middle	No. W/H Allow.
F	M	Accounting	Accounting Clerk (A)	West Virginia	293-77-1388	Mosworth, Mary Louise	1
√							Marital Status S

Illustration 1-11.   Employee's Earnings Record

REGULAR HOURS	O.T.B. HOURS	REGULAR EARNINGS	O.T.B. EARNINGS	GROSS EARNINGS	OASDI	HI	FIT	SIT	CODE	DEDUCTIONS
40	1	403.85	15.15	419.00	25.98	6.08	48.00	13.15		

			DEDUCTIONS							
		1. MISC.		5. SPECIAL INSURANCE		9. TOOLS				
		2. BONDS		6. WELFARE FUND		10. RELIEF ASSOC.				
		3. CREDIT UNION		7. ADVANCES		11. SHOES				
		4. GROUP INSURANCE		8. UNIFORMS		12.				

CLOCK NO.	RATE	PERIOD ENDING	GROSS EARNINGS	OASDI	HI	FIT	SIT	
418	S	1:19:	1,257.00	77.94	18.24	146.00	39.84	
				YEAR TO DATE				325.79

RETAIN THIS STUB
IT IS A STATEMENT OF YOUR
EARNINGS AND DEDUCTIONS

NET PAY ↑

United Chemicals

CLOCK NO.
418

United Chemicals
Huntington, WV

DATE   January 19, 19—

69–21
513

No. 508

PAYROLL ACCOUNT

PAY TO THE ORDER OF   Mary L. Mosworth   325.79

DOLLARS | CENTS
325 | 79

the 1st national bank
Huntington, WV

BY   *S. Hollis Stevenson*

⑆051300212⑆ 6139 ⑈

Illustration 1-12.   Paycheck with Stub Showing Current and Year-to-Date Earnings and Deductions

GLOSSARY

Affirmative action plan—a formal plan that pre-scribes a specific program to eliminate, limit, or prevent discriminatory treatment on the basis of race, ethnic group, and sex.

Application for employment form—personnel re-cord which gives the applicant an opportunity to provide complete information as to personal qualifications, train-ing, and experience.

Change in payroll rate form—document used to notify the proper departments of a change in the employee's rate of remuneration.

Disability benefits—payments to employees who are absent from their jobs because of illness, accident, or disease not arising out of their employment.

Employee history record—continuous record of the relationship between the employer and the employee.

Employee's earnings record—payroll record for each employee that is used to provide complete infor-mation about the accumulated earnings of each employee.

Executive order—regulation issued by the federal government that bans, in employment on government contracts, discrimination based on race, color, religion, sex, or national origin.

Fair employment legislation—laws that deal with discrimination on the basis of age, race, color, religion, sex, or national origin as a condition of employment.

Form W-2, Wage and Tax Statement—form used by the employer to report the amount of wages paid each worker in the course of the trade or business of the employer.

Gross pay—the total regular earnings plus the total overtime earnings.

Hiring notice—form that is sent to the Payroll Department so that new employees are properly added to the payroll.

Human resources system—those procedures and methods related to recruiting, selecting, orienting, training, and terminating personnel.

Income tax—levy on the earnings of most employees that is deducted from their gross pay.

Individual retirement account (IRA)—employee's pension plan which is established and funded by the individual employee.

Investigative consumer report—study done by a consumer reporting agency on a job applicant or current employee concerning the individual's character, general reputation, and mode of living.

Net pay—the total earnings of the employee less the deductions from the earnings.

Payroll accounting system—those procedures and methods related to the disbursement of pay to employees.

Payroll register—multicolumn form used to assemble and summarize the data needed at the end of each payroll period. It lists all employees who earned remuneration, the amount of remuneration, the deductions, and the net amount paid.

Prehire inquiries—questions asked in the employment interview and on application forms, resumes of experience or education required of an applicant, and any kind of written testing.

Reference inquiry form—document used by the employer to investigate the references given on the application blank by the job applicant.

Remuneration—payment for services rendered, including employee benefits and perquisites of employment such as board, lodging, or other facilities provided the worker.

Requisition for personnel—document submitted by a department head to the Human Resources Department asking for additional or replacement employees.

Simplified employee pension (SEP) plan—formal plan by means of which employers may make contributions to individual retirement accounts on behalf of their employees.

Unemployment insurance taxes—the source of funds at the state level which are used to provide benefits for unemployed workers.

Vesting—the process of conveying to employees the right to share in a retirement fund in the event they are terminated before the normal retirement age.

Workers' compensation insurance—protection provided employees and their dependents against losses due to injury or death incurred during employment.

QUESTIONS FOR REVIEW

1. Under the FLSA, what information concerning employees' wages earned must be maintained by the employer?
2. Which act sets the minimum wage and what is the current wage rate?
3. What records must the employer who is subject to FLSA keep for white-collar workers who are exempt from federal minimum wage and overtime standards?
4. Under FLSA, what is included in the definition of employees' total remuneration?
5. What types of unfair employment practices are prohibited by the Civil Rights Act of 1964 as amended?
6. What is the purpose of the Age Discrimination in Employment Act (ADEA)?
7. Who pays the social security taxes that are levied by the Federal Insurance Contributions Act?
8. What are the two parts of the health insurance (HI) program provided by FICA?
9. What are the tax data requirements that an employer must meet in keeping payroll records that conform to the Federal Income Tax Withholding Law?
10. How are the funds used which are provided by FUTA and SUTA?
11. Who is covered by the Walsh-Healey Public Contracts Act?
12. Explain the concept of vesting.
13. What is the maximum amount of tax-free contributions that an eligible employee can place in his or her IRA account each year?
14. Under the Family and Medical Leave Act, what is the maximum number of weeks of unpaid leave that a covered employer is required to offer an employee whose spouse is seriously ill?
15. What is the purpose of workers' compensation insurance?
16. List the reasons why extensive record-keeping procedures are needed in a human resources system.
17. Summarize the procedure that may be followed by the Human Resources Department in hiring new employees.

18. What kinds of information are commonly provided by the jobseeker on the application for employment form?
19. What is the significance of the Civil Rights Act of 1964 and the Age Discrimination in Employment Act in the employer's use of prehire inquiries?
20. What reasons can be advanced for including in the personnel file the records of applicants who were not hired?

21. What obligations are imposed upon the employer by the Fair Credit Reporting Act of 1968?
22. a. What is the purpose of a hiring notice?
    b. What information is usually included in this form?
23. What procedures are usually included in a typical payroll accounting system?
24. What is the purpose of the payroll register?
25. What use is made of the information contained in the employee's earnings record?

QUESTIONS FOR DISCUSSION

1. What personnel records would you suggest for a small retailer with three employees?
2. What kind of problem can be encountered when requesting references from previous employers of job applicants?
3. In staffing their offices, some firms encourage in-house referrals (recommendations of their present employees). What are some possible objections to this practice as a means of obtaining job applicants? What advantages may be realized by the firm that uses in-house referrals?
4. Some companies have every applicant for a job fill out an application blank, even though some are obviously not fitted for the position. Why is this done?
5. The main office of a large bank has an annual turnover of 500 office workers. As an employment officer of this bank, discuss the sources you would use in obtaining replacement employees.
6. Among the questions asked on the application for employment form of Horner Company are the following:
   a. Have you ever worked for Horner Company under another name?
   b. Give the name of your church and list the religious holidays you observe.
   c. Indicate the name of your birthplace.
   d. Are you a citizen of the United States?
   e. Indicate the foreign languages you can read, write, or speak fluently.
   In view of federal and state civil rights laws, do you believe that Horner Company is acting legally or illegally in asking each of the questions listed above?

CASE PROBLEMS

Case 1-1   Streamlining Payroll Records

After working in the accounting department of the Brooher Steel Company for the past year, Claire Gieber has been promoted to head payroll clerk. In a recent meeting, the controller of the company, Matthew Watson, tells Gieber that he is very concerned over the time that is being spent in processing the weekly payroll. Top on his list of priorities for her is a review of the entire payroll accounting system and the implementation of any changes that can save the company time and money.

The company's payroll is presently being prepared manually. Earlier this year the company evaluated the use of computers for the processing of its payroll. In this evaluation the purchase and the leasing of a computer, as well as the use of an outside data processing company, were analyzed. In each of these proposals, the cost was considered too high.

Gieber's first step in her investigation is to study the payroll records that are currently used by the company. In reviewing the information presented on the company's three main records (the payroll register, the employee's earnings record, and the paycheck), Gieber finds, that in addition to the usual payroll data, space is provided for recording the following deductions from each weekly gross pay:

FICA tax (OASDI and HI)
Federal income tax
State income tax
Union Dues
Blue Cross/Blue Shield
U.S. savings bonds
Group life insurance

Further, Gieber discovers that the data recorded on each form are, for the most part, exactly the same. Since each of the forms is written individually, most of the data are being separately recorded three times.

In order to alleviate this duplication, Gieber feels that by using carbonless paper (paper that reproduces on the following sheet of paper without the use of carbon paper) for the three records, the data could be entered on all of them at the same time with only one manual writing. However, in order to convert to records made of carbonless paper, the three forms will have to be redesigned so that data recorded on the top record will be correctly lined up on all forms lying below.

Prepare a new format for each of the three payroll records (the payroll register, the employee's earnings record, and the paycheck) that will permit use of a "one-write" manual recording on the carbonless paper. Particular attention should be devoted to the category headings that are listed at the top of each of these payroll records, so that they will be lined up on each sheet. In addition, prepare an instruction sheet on the steps that are to be followed in preparing the weekly payroll. In these instructions, the mechanics of placing the forms in proper sequence and entering the information on the top form should be explained.

Case 1-2   Paycheck Pickup

Jack works the night shift for Lemon Auto and sleeps during the day. Jack's wife customarily drops by on payday to pick up his check and take it to the bank. Lemon thought nothing of the practice since it had been going on for five years. One day Jack came bursting into the payroll department demanding to know where his paycheck was. It appears that he and his wife had separated the week before. Jack's wife cashed the check and took the money without his knowledge or permission. How do you think Lemon Auto settled this dispute?[4]

---

[4]Reprinted with permission from *Payroll Guide Newsletter*. Volume 52, No. 5, Copyright © 1993 by Warren Gorham Lamont, Inc., 210 South St., Boston, MA 02111. 1-800-950-1211. All rights reserved.

COMPUTING AND PAYING WAGES AND SALARIES

GOALS OF THIS UNIT

After completing your study of this unit, you should be able to:

1. Understand the major provisions of the Fair Labor Standards Act that affect: (a) minimum wages, (b) equal pay for equal work regardless of sex, (c) overtime pay, (d) record keeping, and (e) child labor.

2. Distinguish between the employees' *principal* activities and their *preliminary* and *postliminary* activities.

3. Describe the main types of time records—time sheets and time cards—and indicate the kind of payroll data collected on each.

4. Perform the following arithmetic operations:
    a. Convert weekly wage rates to hourly rates.
    b. Convert monthly and annual salary rates to hourly rates.
    c. Calculate regular earnings and overtime earnings to arrive at total gross earnings.
    d. Apply two different methods in calculating overtime payment for pieceworkers.
    e. Calculate earnings under incentive and commission plans.

5. Describe how wages and salaries are paid (a) in cash, (b) by check, and (c) by electronic transfer of funds.

In this unit, we shall investigate the major provisions of the Fair Labor Standards Act and show how to determine the hours worked by employees. In addition, we shall examine in detail the records that are commonly used to record time worked, the major methods of computing salaries and wages, and the methods of paying employees.

Even though we find that the 40-hour, 5-day workweek is the most common work schedule, the schedules of American workers have been changing and becoming increasingly diverse. To improve declining productivity, to decrease job dissatisfaction, and to reduce absenteeism, many firms have adopted alternative work schedules such as those briefly described in Illustration 2-1 on pages 26 and 27.

FAIR LABOR STANDARDS ACT

The Fair Labor Standards Act (FLSA), commonly known as the Federal Wage and Hour Law, contains provisions and standards concerning minimum wages, equal pay for equal work regardless of sex, overtime pay, record keeping, and child labor. The act is administered by the Wage and Hour Division of the U.S. Department of Labor. Since its enactment in 1938, the FLSA has been amended several times to broaden the definition of employees and enterprises that are covered by the law.

Coverage

The FLSA provides for two bases of coverage—enterprise coverage and individual employee coverage.

Enterprise Coverage. Under *enterprise coverage*, all employees of an enterprise are covered if:

1. At least two employees are engaged in interstate commerce or in producing goods for interstate commerce. *Interstate commerce* refers to the trade, transportation, or communication among several states or between a state and any place outside that state. Employees are also covered if they handle, sell, or otherwise work on goods or materials that have been moved in or produced for interstate commerce, and

2. The business has annual gross sales of at least $500,000.

Coverage has also been extended, *without regard to annual sales volume*, to those who operate:

1. A hospital.
2. A nursing home.
3. An institution for the mentally ill.
4. A school for mentally or physically handicapped or gifted children.
5. A preschool, elementary, or secondary school.
6. An institution of higher education. (Coverage applies to hospitals, institutions, and schools whether or not they are operated for profit.)
7. A public agency.

Family establishments, often referred to as "mom and pop stores," are not considered part of the enterprise coverage under the FLSA. Thus, if the only regular employees of an establishment are the owner and his or her parent, spouse, child, or other immediate family member, the establishment is exempt from FLSA coverage.

Type of Work Schedule	Description	Example(s)	Advantages	Disadvantages
Compressed Workweek	The usual number of full-time hours are worked in fewer than 5 days (the regular workweek).	4/40 workweek (4 workdays during the week, with each day 10 hours in duration).	1) Improves employee morale by providing more flexible leisure time, thus enabling workers to schedule commitments such as dental appointments outside work time. 2) Boosts productivity. 3) Reduces absenteeism.	1) Employees not available full workweek or at critical times. 2) Nonlabor costs (heating and cooling) increase as the result of longer hours of operation. 3) Employees become more fatigued. 4) Increases stress on supervisors.
Staggered Work Schedule	Fixed work schedule under which groups of employees arrive at their workplaces at different times and work a predetermined number of hours each workday.	Group A works 7:30 a.m. to 3:30 p.m., overlapping with Group B, which works 10:00 a.m. to 6:00 p.m.	1) Alleviates commuter tie-ups. 2) Reduces waiting time for elevators and lessens lobby congestion.	1) Increased scheduling problems. 2) Nonlabor costs increase as the result of longer hours of operation.
Flexible Work Schedule	Workday is divided into *core time* (those hours during which all employees must be present for work) and *flexible time* (those hours from which employees choose their arrival and departure times); also known as *flextime*.	In a workday with a span of 12 hours, employees working a regular 8-hour shift must be on the job during the peak workload hours 9:00 a.m. to 3:00 p.m. (core time). During the hours 6:00 a.m. to 9:00 a.m. and 3:00 p.m. to 6:00 p.m. (flexible time), employees select their arrival and departure times.	1) Improves customer service. 2) Increases employee performance by strengthening motivation and improving employee morale and attitudes toward jobs. 3) Eases rush-hour traffic peaks. 4) Decreases tardiness. 5) Attracts and retains employees having outside commitments, such as child care and elder care.	1) Added need for managers and supervisors to schedule and plan the work flow and ensure the coverage of critical functions. 2) Possible lack of supervision during all hours of work. 3) Increased nonlabor costs associated with more hours of operation.

Illustration 2-1. Types of Work Schedules (Continued)

Type of Work Schedule	Description	Example(s)	Advantages	Disadvantages
Job Sharing	One full-time job is shared by two people who generally split their working hours, job responsibilities, and employee benefits.	Employee A works from 8:00 a.m. to 12:00 p.m. Employee B works on the same job from 12:00 p.m. to 4:00 p.m.	1) Strengthens employee motivation by allowing larger blocks of leisure time, thus accommodating persons having outside commitments. 2) Improves employee attitudes toward their jobs and the organization, thus boosting employee morale. 3) Reduces turnover and increases job performance.	1) Increased costs of employee benefits such as group health insurance, social security taxes, and on-site child care. 2) Increases training costs. 3) Supervisory difficulties in relating to two different persons in one job, with possibility of communication breakdowns. 4) Possible conflicts of responsibility between two workers holding same job.
Telecom-muting	Employees work off site, such as in their homes, rather than in offices.	Data-entry personnel, secretaries, typists, programmers, researchers, forms processors.	1) Working during off hours improves turnaround time and increases around-the-clock use of computer facilities. 2) Reduces workers' costs and problems associated with day care and baby-sitting services. 3) Offers productive outlet to persons who have had their mobility restricted by illness or accident but who are otherwise able and willing to work.	1) Difficulties in effectively managing and supervising telecommuters. 2) Loss of information because of unreliable communication units linking off-site units to firm's central computer. 3) Off-site workers feel socially isolated and thus unable to build rapport with peer office workers.
Permanent Part-Time Employment	Regular employment (not temporary or casual) is carried out during working hours that are shorter than normal.	Telemarketers who sell by phone several hours each day, and employees staffing departments where workload is not sufficient to warrant full-time staffs.	1) Appeals to workers attending school and those having family responsibilities and physical handicaps. 2) Part-timers may obtain job security and employee rights that full-time employees have.	Increased administrative problems related to managing and supervising a predominantly part-time staff.
Work Sharing	Employees work a shorter than normal week, have their salaries reduced accordingly, and receive partial state unemployment compensation benefits for lost days' pay.	In the dozen or so states having unemployment insurance programs that legally allow workers to receive partial temporary unemployment benefits in the event workers suffer moderate reductions in their work hours.	1) Enables employer to reduce employee hours rather than lay off workers. 2) Employer realizes savings on severance pay and other labor turnover costs.	1) Possible lack of job dedication by employees. 2) Employers may be faced with increased unemployment insurance benefit charges.

Illustration 2-1.   Types of Work Schedules (Concluded)

Individual Employee Coverage. Under *individual employee coverage*, a worker is covered by the FLSA if the employee is either engaged in interstate commerce or in producing goods for such commerce. Employment in a fringe occupation closely related and directly essential to the production of goods for interstate commerce is sufficient to constitute engagement in the production of goods for interstate commerce.

Coverage depends on the activities of the individual employee and not on the work of fellow employees, nor the nature of the employer's business, nor the character of the industry as a whole. Thus, we find that even though a business does not meet the enterprise coverage test, it must pay FLSA wages to those workers eligible for individual coverage.

EXAMPLE:

James Rineheart works for a small manufacturing firm that has an annual sales volume of $370,000. Thus, the firm does not meet the $500,000 volume-of-sales requirement for enterprise coverage. However, Rineheart is individually covered since he operates machinery used to produce goods for interstate commerce.

Domestic service consists of services of a household nature performed in or about a private home of the person by whom the domestic is employed. Some typical domestics include cooks, waiters, butlers, valets, maids, housekeepers, nurses, janitors, caretakers, handymen, gardeners, and chauffeurs of automobiles used by the family. The term also includes a babysitter employed on *other than a casual basis*, such as a person who sits for a child five days a week. Domestics must be paid the minimum wage if:

1. They are employed in one or more homes for a total of more than 8 hours in any workweek, *or if*
2. They earn wages of at least $50 in any calendar quarter.

If the domestics do *not* live in the household, they must be paid overtime compensation as well as the minimum wage. However, live-in domestics do not have to be paid overtime. A *casual* babysitter (one employed on an irregular or intermittent basis) or a companion for the aged or infirm is completely exempt.

Wages

Under the FLSA, *wages* includes the remuneration or compensation paid employees—salaries, commissions, vacation pay, overtime pay, severance or dis-

missal pay, earned bonuses, and any other amounts agreed upon by the employer and the employee. Wages also includes the reasonable cost or fair value to the employer of board, lodging, or other facilities ordinarily furnished the employee.

You will find that the terms wages and salaries are commonly used interchangeably. However, the term *wage* refers to remuneration paid on an hourly, weekly, or piecework basis. The remuneration paid on a monthly, *biweekly* (every two weeks), *semimonthly* (twice a month), or yearly basis is ordinarily called *salary*. In either event, the employer agrees to pay the employees a certain amount for their time, whether it is by the hour, the week, the month, or the year, or based on output under a piece-rate system.

Minimum Wages

The FLSA of 1938 established a minimum wage of 25¢ an hour for a straight-time workweek of 44 hours. Following the first year of operation, the law provided for graduated rises in the minimum-wage figure and graduated decreases in the maximum weekly straight-time hours. Two years later when the standard workweek had decreased to 40 hours, the minimum wage had risen to 30¢. Several years later the minimum hourly wage rose to 40¢. With the objective of improving the purchasing power of covered workers, succeeding amendments to the FLSA increased the minimum hourly rate. In 1989, the FLSA was amended to increase the minimum hourly wage to $4.25 as of April 1, 1991.

Paying Workers Less Than the Minimum Wage

Under certain conditions, we may find that wages lower than the minimum wage are paid some employees.[1]

EXAMPLES:

1. Retail or service establishments and farms may employ full-time students at 85% of the minimum wage.
2. Institutions of higher education may employ their own full-time students at 85% of the minimum wage.
3. Student-learners may be employed at 75% of the minimum wage if they are participating in a bona fide vocational training program conducted by an accredited school.
4. Persons whose earning capacity is impaired by age, physical or mental deficiency, or injury may be employed at special minimum wage rates. However, a certificate authorizing employment at such rates

---

[1] Under the Minimum Wage Law of 1989, employers paid eligible trainees a subminimum training wage of $3.6125 per hour. However, this training wage provision expired April 1, 1993.

must first be obtained. The handicapped workers are entitled to the full benefits of the law, which requires premium pay for overtime hours and equal pay for equal work regardless of sex.

NEWS ALERT NEWS ALERT NEWS ALERT

In August, 1993, the Labor Secretary announced plans to boost the minimum wage by at least 25 cents from its $4.25-an-hour level. Thereafter, the minimum wage would be automatically indexed each year.

Tips

A *tip* (to *i*nsure *p*romptness) is a gift or gratuity given by a customer in recognition of some service performed for him or her. A *tipped employee* is one who is engaged in an occupation in which tips of more than $30 a month are customarily and regularly received.

An employer may consider, within prescribed limits, the tips received by a tipped employee as part of the employee's wages. An employer can credit up to 50% of a tipped employee's minimum wage as coming from tips actually received.

EXAMPLE:

In July, 1994, Barbara Rivera, a hair stylist, is paid $120 plus tips for a 40-hour workweek. The weekly wage paid Rivera is $50 less than the minimum wage for a 40-hour workweek ($4.25 x 40 = $170). Rivera regularly receives at least $250 in tips each week. Thus, each week her employer claims a credit of $50 from her tips in order to meet the weekly minimum wage requirement of $170. The maximum weekly credit that could have been available to the employer is $85 ($170 x 50%). Therefore, her employer could have paid Rivera as little as $85 a week and not have violated the provisions of the FLSA.

If the tips received by a worker are less than 50% of the minimum wage rate, the amount received is the maximum permissible tip credit. In such a case, the employer must pay the balance so that a combination of the tips received and of the wages paid in cash (or in the form of board, lodging, or other facilities) equals the minimum wage.

EXAMPLE:

In November, 1994, Bill Hunt, a waiter, is paid a weekly wage of $85 plus tips for a 40-hour workweek. The weekly wage paid Hunt is $85 less than the minimum wage

requirement for a 40-hour workweek ($170 – $85). Over the past few months, Hunt has received tips totaling $80 each week. Each week his employer claims a credit for the tips that Hunt receives. However, the amount of tips received, $80, is less than the 50% tip credit taken ($170 x 50% = $85). Thus, the maximum credit that the employer may take is $80, the tips received by Hunt. The employer must pay the balance, $5, along with the weekly wage of $85 so that the combined wages paid and the tip credit taken equal $170.

The rules for the reporting of tips by employees and employers are discussed in Unit 3.

Workweek

The FLSA defines a *workweek* as a fixed and regularly recurring period of 168 hours—7 consecutive 24-hour periods. The individual employee's workweek is the statutory or contract number of hours to be worked regularly during that period. The workweek may begin on any day of the week and need not coincide with the calendar week. An employer may establish the same workweek for the business operations as a whole or assign different workweeks to individual workers or groups of workers.

An employer may change the day a workweek begins if the change is intended to be permanent and not to evade the overtime pay requirements of the FLSA. If, however, the workweek is fixed by union contract, the employer's right to change the workweek depends upon the wording in the contract. Each workweek is considered to stand alone, and the overtime hours worked in one week may not be shifted to another workweek. Thus, each workweek is a separate unit for the purpose of computing overtime pay.

Overtime Hours and Overtime Pay

The FLSA states that overtime pay is required for all hours worked in excess of 40 in a workweek. Under the law the overtime pay required is time and one half the employee's regular hourly rate of pay. The regular hourly rate of pay at which the worker is employed may in no event be less than the statutory minimum. If the employee's regular rate of pay is higher than the statutory minimum, overtime compensation must be computed at a rate not less than one and one-half times such higher rate.

EXAMPLE:

Marcia Averre's regular rate of pay is $4.40 an hour. Her overtime rate must be at least $4.40 x 1.5, or $6.60, an hour.

Over the years, as the result of union contracts, hours beyond a certain number each day have become known as overtime. Work on Saturdays, Sundays, or on the sixth and seventh days of the workweek, holidays, and days of rest is thought of as overtime because this work often commands overtime pay. The FLSA, however, generally requires no overtime pay for daily hours worked in excess of any given number or for work on Saturdays, Sundays, holidays, or other special days.

Exceptions to Overtime Hours and Overtime Pay Provisions.

An exception to the preceding statement regarding overtime hours and overtime pay is available for *hospital employees*. Hospitals are authorized to enter into an agreement with their employees under which a 14-day period, rather than a workweek, becomes the basis for computing overtime pay. Employees with whom such an agreement exists must receive overtime pay at not less than one and one-half times their regular hourly rate for hours worked in excess of 8 hours in any workday or in excess of 80 hours in a 14-day period, whichever is the greater number of overtime hours. Although employers have the option of using the normal workweek or the 14-day period, they cannot change from one method to the other arbitrarily.

EXAMPLE:

Pam Valenti, a lab technician at Metro Hospital, agreed that a 14-day period would be used to figure her overtime pay. She works 12 hours in one day during the period and 8 hours in each of the 9 other days during the period, a total of 84 hours. Valenti is entitled to 80 hours of straight-time pay and 4 hours of overtime pay for the 14-day period.

Let's say that Valenti worked only 7 hours in each of the 9 other days during the period, or a total of 75 hours. In this case, she would be entitled to 71 hours of straight-time pay and 4 hours of overtime pay for the 14-day period.

The minimum wage legislation provides an exception for *employees who are receiving remedial education*. Under this law, employees who are receiving remedial education offered by their employers would be permitted to work up to 10 hours overtime each week without receiving overtime compensation. To qualify as *remedial* education, it must be provided to employees who lack a high school diploma or educational attainment at the eighth-grade level. The remedial training, which does not include training for a specific job, must be designed to provide reading and other basic skills at an eighth-grade level or below.

Compensatory Time Off.

The employees of a state, a political subdivision of a state, or an interstate governmental agency are allowed use of compensatory time off in lieu of overtime compensation. Thus, we find that employees whose work includes public safety, emergency response, or seasonal activities are allowed to accumulate compensatory time off up to 480 hours. (The 480-hour limit represents 320 hours of overtime actually worked at the one and one-half overtime rate.) These employees may "bank" their hours and use them later as time off at time and one-half during the course of their employment.

Employees whose work does not include the preceding activities are allowed to bank 240 hours for compensatory time off. (The 240-hour limit represents 160 hours of overtime actually worked at the one and one-half overtime rate.) Upon reaching the 480- or 240-hour limit, an employee must receive either cash for additional hours of overtime worked or use some compensatory time before receiving further overtime compensation in the form of compensatory time off. Note that not all 480 or 240 hours have to be accrued before compensatory time off may be used.

State and local government employers must continue to pay their employees not less than the statutory minimum wage. (Note that employees of private employers or of the federal government are not affected by the amendments.) Volunteers of state and local governments are exempted from both the wage and hour provisions of the FLSA.

Equal Pay Law

The Equal Pay Act, effective in 1964, amended the FLSA to require that men and women performing equal work must receive equal pay. Any employer having workers subject to the minimum pay provisions of the Wage and Hour Law is subject to the Equal Pay Law. The law applies to *any establishment* wherein such workers are employed. The equal-pay requirements also apply to white-collar workers, including outside salespersons, even though they are exempt from the minimum wage standards.

The Equal Pay Law states that an employer must not discriminate by paying wages to employees of one sex at a lower rate than is paid the opposite sex for equal work on jobs that require equal skill, effort, and responsibility, and that are performed under similar working conditions. However, wage differentials between sexes are allowable if the differences are based on a seniority system, a merit system, a payment plan that measures earnings by quantity or quality of production, or any factor other than sex. If there is an unlawful pay differential between men and women, the employer is required to raise the lower rate to equal the higher rate.

Exemptions from FLSA Requirements

Exempt employees are those workers who are exempt from some, or all, of the FLSA requirements such as minimum wages, equal pay, and overtime pay. As you see in Illustration 2-2, many workers are exempt from one or more of these requirements.

Executive, Administrative, and Professional Employees. Some workers, such as executive, administrative, and professional employees, are exempt from the minimum wage and overtime pay provisions of the FLSA if certain tests regarding their duties and salaries are satisfied. In order for an employee to be granted this exemption as an *executive*, all of the following requirements must be met:

1. The primary duty must be that of managing an enterprise or department or subdivision thereof.
2. The employee must customarily and regularly direct the work of two or more full-time employees.
3. The employee can hire and fire and suggest changes in the status of other employees.

Employee Job Description	Minimum Wage Exemption	Equal Pay Exemption	Full Overtime Exemption
Agricultural employees.			X
Agricultural workers who are members of the employer's immediate family.	X	X	X
Air carrier employees if the carrier is subject to Title II of the Railway Labor Act.			X
Amusement or recreational establishment employees, provided the business has seasonal peaks.	X	X	X
Announcers, news editors, and chief engineers of radio or television stations in small communities.			X
Babysitters (casual) and companions to ill or aged persons unable to care for themselves.	X	X	X
Drivers and drivers' helpers who make local deliveries and are paid on a trip-rate or similar basis following a plan approved by the government.			X
Executive, administrative, and professional employees including teachers and academic administrative personnel in schools.	X		X
Fruit and vegetable employees who are engaged in the local transportation of these items or of workers employed or to be employed in the harvesting of fruits or vegetables.			X
Household domestic service employees who reside in the household.			X
Motion picture theater employees.			X
Motor carrier employees if the carrier is subject to regulation by the Secretary of Transportation.			X
Newspaper employees if the newspaper is published on a weekly, semiweekly, or daily basis and if the circulation is less than 4,000 copies, with the major circulation in the county of publication or contiguous counties.	X	X	X
Outside sales personnel.	X		X
Railroad, express company, and water carrier employees if the companies are subject to Part I of the Interstate Commerce Act.			X
Salespersons for automobile, truck, or farm implement dealers; parts stock clerks or mechanics; salespersons for boat, trailer, or aircraft dealers.			X
Taxicab drivers.			X

Illustration 2-2. Exemption Status of Workers under FLSA

4. The employee must customarily and regularly exercise discretionary powers.
5. The nonexempt work must be no more than 20% of the executive's weekly hours worked, or 40% in the case of executives of retail or service establishments.
6. The executive's salary must be at least $155 a week, exclusive of board, lodging, or other facilities. In Puerto Rico, the Virgin Islands, and American Samoa, the test is $130 a week; for the motion picture producing industry, a base rate of $250 a week applies.[2]

Short Test of Exemption.
A shorter test of exemption status may be applied to higher salaried employees who earn $250 or more each week. In this test, most highly paid employees need meet only the first two requirements listed above so long as their weekly salary (exclusive of board, lodging, or other facilities) is $250 or more.

Employees *who are paid by the hour* are not exempt from the minimum wage and overtime pay requirements and thus do not qualify for the salary test even if their total weekly compensation exceeds the limits specified.

Highly Skilled Computer Professionals.
Employees who are highly skilled in computer systems analysis, programming, or related work in software functions may be exempt from the minimum wage and overtime requirements. Some of the job titles included in this exemption are: computer programmer, systems analyst, computer programmer analyst, applications programmer, applications systems analyst, software engineer, software specialist, and systems engineer. The exemption does *not* apply to workers who operate computers or manufacture, repair, or maintain computer hardware and related equipment.

To be exempt from the overtime requirements, the computer professional must be paid:

1. On an *hourly* basis.
2. At a rate greater than 6½ times the minimum wage, or more than $27.63 an hour ($4.25 × 6.5).

As pointed out on page 31, a *salaried* computer professional may qualify for exemption as a *professional* and thus also be exempt from the overtime requirements, provided the employee:

1. Earns at least $170 a week.

The Labor Department warns employers that they may deduct pay from *salaried* employees for full-day absences but not for partial-day absences. Salaried workers who are docked for partial-day absences are "hourly" employees and should receive overtime pay for hours worked over 40 in a week.

2. Meets the other requirements of a professional (work is primarily intellectual and nonstandard in character, uses discretion and independent judgment, and spends no more than 20% of the workweek on nonexempt work).

Child-Labor Restrictions

A business is prohibited from the interstate shipment of its goods or services if it employs child labor unlawfully. Under the FLSA, the Secretary of Labor issues regulations that restrict the employment of individuals under the age of 18. The restrictions on child employment are divided into nonfarm occupations and agricultural occupations.

Nonfarm Occupations.
The basic minimum age for most jobs is 16 years. This is the minimum age for work in manufacturing and processing jobs or in any other occupations except those that are declared by the Secretary of Labor as hazardous for minors under 18. Some of the jobs classified as hazardous include motor-vehicle drivers and helpers; occupations in plants manufacturing or storing explosives, in coal mines, and in slaughtering and meat-packing establishments; operating power-driven woodworking machines; doing excavation work; and wrecking and demolishing buildings. In some of the hazardous occupations, you may employ a child under 18 as an apprentice, student learner, or trainee under narrowly restricted conditions. For a list of these hazardous occupations, contact the Wage and Hour Division of the U.S. Department of Labor to obtain a copy of the child-labor laws.

Children under 16 years of age may *not* be employed in manufacturing, mining, or processing of goods; operating or tending power-driven machinery other than office machines; public messenger service; and jobs (other than office or sales work) connected with the transportation of persons or property by rail,

---

[2]The salary or fee for an *administrative* employee must also be at least $155 a week. The salary tests in Puerto Rico, the Virgin Islands, and American Samoa, and for the motion picture producing industry are the same as for executives. However, for a *professional* employee, the salary or fee must be at least $170 a week, exclusive of board, lodging, or other facilities. In Puerto Rico, the Virgin Islands, and American Samoa, the amount is $150 a week; for the motion picture industry, the base rate is $250 a week.

highway, air, water, pipeline, or other means; warehousing and storage; communications and public utilities; construction, including demolition and repair.

Within certain limits 14- and 15-year-olds may be employed in retail, food service, and gasoline service establishments. For example, this age group may be employed in office and clerical work, including the operation of office machines; cashiering; selling; price marking and tagging by hand or by machine; errand and delivery work; kitchen work and other work involved in preparing and serving food and beverages; dispensing gasoline and oil; and car cleaning. The employment of minors between the ages of 14 and 16 is permitted only to the extent that it will not interfere with their schooling, health, and well-being. In addition, the following conditions must be met:

1. All work must be performed outside school hours.
2. There is a maximum 3-hour day and 18-hour week when school is in session (8 hours and 40 hours when not in session).
3. All work must be performed between 7 a.m. and 7 p.m. (9 p.m. during the summer).

Agricultural Occupations.
The employment of children under age 12 is generally prohibited in agricultural occupations (1) during hours when school is in session, (2) outside school hours on farms, including conglomerates, that used more than 500 man-days of labor in any quarter of the preceding calendar year, and (3) outside school hours on noncovered farms without parental consent. However, children may work on farms owned or operated by their parents or guardians. Children 10 and 11 years old may be employed as hand harvest laborers outside school hours for up to eight weeks between June 1 and October 15, provided a number of strict conditions are met by the employer.

Children aged 12 and 13 are permitted to be employed only during hours when school is not in session provided there is parental consent or the employment is on a farm where the parents are employed.

Children aged 14 and 15 may be employed, but only during hours when school is not in session. No child under the age of 16 may be employed in a farm occupation that is declared hazardous, such as operating large tractors, corn pickers, cotton pickers, grain combines, and feed grinders.

Certificate of Age.
Employers cannot be charged with having violated the child-labor restrictions of the law if they have on file an officially executed *certificate of age* which shows that the minor has reached the stipulated minimum age. In most states a state employment or age certificate, issued by the Federal Wage and Hour Division or by a state agency, is accepted as proof of age.

In some states a state or federal certificate of age, a state employment certificate, or a work permit may not be available. In such cases, the employer may rely on any one of the following documents as evidence of age for minor employees:

1. Birth certificate (or attested transcript thereof) or a signed statement of the recorded date and place of birth issued by a registrar of vital statistics or other officer charged with the duty of recording births.
2. Record of baptism (or attested transcript thereof) showing the date of birth of the minor.
3. Statement on the census records of the Bureau of Indian Affairs and signed by an administrative representative thereof showing the name and date and place of the minor's birth.

The employer should maintain a copy of the document or indicate in the payroll records which document was checked to verify the minor's age.

Penalties

The U.S. Government may bring civil or criminal actions against employers who violate the FLSA. Employers who willfully violate the wage and hour provisions of the law or the wage orders fixed by the Administrator of the Wage and Hour Division of the Department of Labor will be prosecuted and will be subject to a fine of not more than $10,000, or imprisonment for up to six months, or both. However, no person may be imprisoned for a first offense violation. If an imposed fine goes unpaid, however, the courts have the power to order imprisonment as an incident to the nonpayment. Violators of the child-labor provisions of the Act are subject to fines of $10,000 for each violation.

Payroll managers should read the Fair Labor Standards Act and its amendments very carefully. If there is any question whether their companies are governed by the provisions of the law, managers should consult a representative of the Wage and Hour Division.

Areas Not Covered by the FLSA

As we saw earlier, the FLSA does not require employers to pay extra wages for work on Saturday, Sunday, or holidays. It does not require vacation, holiday, or severance pay; nor does it limit the number of hours of work for persons 16 years of age or over, as long as the overtime pay provisions are met.

In addition, the law does not require the employer to give employees the day off on holidays, nor to give them vacations. If the employee does work on a holiday, the employer is not required to pay the employee time and one-half. Thus, holidays, like Sundays, are treated the same as any other day. Whether time off is granted or overtime rates are paid depends on the employment agreement.

DETERMINING THE EMPLOYEE'S WORKING TIME

To avoid paying for time not actually spent on the job and to eliminate payment for unnecessary overtime work, we must know what types of employee activities should and should not be counted as working time under the law. Generally the hours that must be counted as working time include all the time that employees are actually at work or are required to be on duty.

A distinction must be made between an employee's principal activities and the preliminary and postliminary activities.

Principal Activities

The *principal activities* of employees are those tasks they are required to perform and include any work of consequence performed for the employer. Principal activities include those that are indispensable to the performance of productive work and those that are an integral part of a principal activity.

Professional Tip

Be sure that your workers use their time spent on call for their own pursuits. The Supreme Court tests for compensability by determining if the on-call employee's waiting time is spent predominantly for the benefit of the employer or the employee.

EXAMPLE:

Ted Jambro is a lathe operator who oils and cleans his machines at the beginning of each workday and installs new cutting tools. These activities performed by Jambro are part of his principal activity.

The test of compensability, with respect to principal activities, requires that there be physical or mental exertion, controlled or required by the employer and performed for the employer's benefit.

Clothes-Changing Time and Wash-Up.

Because of the nature of their work, some employees are required to change clothes or to wash on the employer's premises. Statutes or ordinances may also require clothes changing or washing. When employees spend time in changing clothes or washing on the employer's premises, this time is regarded as part of their principal activities. However, even where the clothes changing or wash-up is required by the nature of the job or by law, it may be excluded from time worked either expressly or by custom and practice under a collective bargaining contract.

Travel Time.

The time spent by employees in traveling to and from work need be counted as time worked only if contract, custom, or practice so requires. In some situations, however, travel time between home and work is counted as time worked.

EXAMPLE:

Lisa Rubini receives an emergency call outside her regular working hours and is required to travel a substantial distance to perform a job away from her usual work site for one of her employer's customers. The travel time is counted as time worked.

Also, if an employee who regularly works at a fixed location is given a special one-day work assignment in another city, the travel time is counted as time worked.

When travel is performed during the workday as part of an employee's principal activities, the travel time is treated as time worked.

EXAMPLE:

Reba Ferguson travels throughout the city from job site to job site during her working hours, 9 a.m. to 5 p.m., Mondays through Fridays. Such travel time is counted as part of her time worked.

Occasionally Ferguson is required to travel between workdays from one city to another. Her travel time is counted as working time when the hours involved correspond to her regular working hours, even though the hours may occur on days that are not normally her working days. The time spent in travel outside these regular working hours is not counted as time worked, however.

Let's say that Ferguson is sent on a trip that requires traveling on Saturday and Sunday in order to be at a job site the first thing Monday morning. Her travel time on Saturday and Sunday between the hours of 9 a.m. and 5 p.m. is counted as time worked, but travel time before 9 a.m. and after 5 p.m. is not counted.

Rest Periods and Coffee Breaks.
The FLSA does not require that an employer give employees a rest period or a coffee break. However, the employer may grant such rest periods voluntarily; or the union contract or municipal or state legislation may require them. In these cases, if the time spent on a rest period is 20 minutes or less, the time must be counted as part of the hours worked. If the rest period is longer than 20 minutes, the compensability for the time depends upon the employee's freedom during that time or upon the provisions of the union contract.

Meal Periods.
Bona fide meal periods (not including coffee breaks or snack times) during which the employee is completely relieved from duty are not considered working time. Lunch periods during which the employee is required to perform some duties while eating are not bona fide meal periods.

EXAMPLE:

Virginia Sherr, an office worker, is required to eat at the desk in order to operate the switchboard at lunch time. Sherr must be paid for the lunch period.

Training Sessions.
Generally the time spent by employees in attending lectures and meetings for training purposes must be counted as working time.

EXAMPLE:

The working time spent by postal clerks in learning mail-distribution practices and the operation of letter-sorting machines counts as compensable time under the FLSA. The study and training time put in by the employees constitutes compensable work because it is (a) controlled and required by the employer, (b) for the primary benefit of the employer, and (c) an integral and indispensable part of the employees' principal work activities.

However, time spent in training sessions need not be counted as working time if *all* the following conditions are met:

1. Attendance by the employee is voluntary.
2. The employee does not produce any goods or perform any other productive work during the meeting or lecture.
3. The meeting or lecture takes place outside regular working hours.
4. The meeting or lecture is not directly related to the employee's work.

Preliminary and Postliminary Activities

Activities regarded as *preliminary* and *postliminary* need not be counted as time worked unless required by contract or custom. Some examples of activities regarded as preliminary and postliminary are: walking, riding, or traveling to or from the actual place where employees engage in their principal activities; checking in and out at the plant or office and waiting in line to do so; changing clothes for the convenience of the employee; washing up and showering unless directly related to the specific type of work the employee is hired to perform; and waiting in line to receive paychecks.

Absences

The FLSA does not require an employer to pay an employee for hours not worked because of illness. In the case of employees on an hourly wage basis, the time card shows the exact hours worked; and the time off is *not* counted toward the 40 hours for overtime pay purposes even if the employee is paid for the absences.

Employees on a salary basis are frequently paid for a certain number of days of excused absences after they have been employed by their company for a certain length of time. When the employee is absent from work, the department head usually is required to approve the time card for payment of salaries for hours not worked.

Tardiness

We find that employers handle tardiness in many ways. Frequently when an employee is late or leaves early, causing the time clock to print in red, the supervisor must O.K. the time card. Some companies require the employee to sign a special slip indicating the reason for being late or leaving early.

In some cases, time is kept according to the decimal system whereby each hour is divided into units of tens (6 minutes times 10 periods in each hour). An employee who is late 1 through 6 minutes is penalized or "docked" one tenth of an hour. One who is 7 through 12 minutes late is "docked" one fifth of an hour, etc. Many businesses following this procedure claim that when employees are "docked" each one-tenth hour, there is a tendency to reduce tardiness.

Working During Daylight-Saving Time

Under the Uniform Time Act, daylight-saving time is observed in most of the United States and its territories.[3] Daylight-saving time is in effect from the first Sunday in April until the last Sunday in October.

Shift workers on duty when daylight-saving time goes into effect will work an hour less. Giving such workers a full 8 hours' pay causes some questions under the FLSA. The additional hour's pay given to an employee who works a 7-hour shift need not be included in figuring the worker's regular rate of pay for the purpose of any overtime due that week. On the other hand, the extra hour's pay may not be credited toward any overtime compensation due.

EXAMPLE:

John Yetter is a nighttime clerk for a national hotel chain. His schedule requires him to work the first Saturday night in April from 11:00 p.m. to 7:00 a.m. Because daylight-saving time went into effect early Sunday morning, Yetter had to work only 7 hours. He will be paid for 8 hours of work, however. Further, Yetter's employer may not deduct the extra hour's pay from any overtime compensation due.

In the fall, when daylight-saving time ends, an employee who works a 9-hour shift must be paid for all 9 hours. This time must be counted in determining the hours worked in that week.

KEEPING A RECORD OF TIME WORKED

As you saw in Illustration 1-2, page 3, the FLSA requires that certain time and pay records be kept by employers subject to the law. For example, employers must keep records that indicate the hours each employee worked each workday and each workweek. Most of the information required by the FLSA is the kind that a company would usually keep in following ordinary business practices.

The methods of keeping time records are left to the discretion of the employer. Selection of the type of record depends on the size of the company, and whether employees are paid on an hourly, weekly, biweekly, semimonthly, or monthly basis. Employees on a salary basis usually work a given number of hours each day, generally on a definite schedule. Employees on an hourly wage basis may work a varying number of hours with some "down time" and layoffs and some overtime work. All of this time must be recorded in some way. As you will learn in the following sections, time sheets or time cards may be used to keep this record.

Time Sheets

Many small businesses that must keep a record of time worked by each employee require each person to sign a *time sheet*, indicating the time of arrival for work and the time of departure. The time sheet can be found in many different forms. There may be a sheet used for each working day with employees signing their names on arrival in the morning and indicating the time they started and quit work. Some businesses have someone in each department serving in the capacity of a timekeeper, who uses a similar form to record the hours worked by each person in the department. Some businesses require a record of the exact time an employee arrives and leaves, while others require only the total hours worked each day. In any event, the time sheets provide the information required by law and the data used in computing the payroll. Illustration 2-3 shows a time sheet that contains the weekly work time information for an employee.

Time Cards

Under this timekeeping system, each employee is furnished a *time card* on which the time worked is recorded manually by the employee or automatically by a time clock. The time card is designed to fit various lengths of pay periods.

Illustration 2-4 on page 38 shows one type of time card frequently used for a weekly pay period. The card provides space to record the hours worked, the rate of pay, deductions, and net pay. The handwritten figures are inserted by the payroll department to be used in computing total earnings, deductions, and net pay for the payroll period.

On some time clocks the *continental system* of recording time on the time card is used. Under this system, each day consists of one 24-hour period,

---

[3]Areas that do not observe daylight-saving time include Arizona, Hawaii, Puerto Rico, the Virgin Islands, American Samoa, and that portion of Indiana within the Eastern Time Zone.

WEEKLY TIME REPORT

EMPLOYEE NAME _Alma Chapman_

DEPARTMENT _Packing_

REPORT FOR WEEK ENDING SATURDAY _June 12, 19--_

DAY	TIME IN	LUNCH PERIOD	TIME OUT	HOURS WORKED	EXCEPTIONS
Sunday	—	XXXXXXXXX	—	—	
Monday	8:00	– 45 minutes	10:05	2	S-6
Tuesday	7:50	– 45 minutes	4:40	8	
Wednesday	7:45	– 45 minutes	4:30	8	
Thursday	7:30	– 45 minutes	5:15	9	
Friday	8:00	– 45 minutes	4:45	8	
Saturday	—	XXXXXXXXX	—	—	
			WEEKLY TOTAL	35	6

Exception Code
S - Sickness   H - Holiday
V - Vacation   E - Other

EMPLOYEE'S SIGNATURE: _Alma Chapman_

APPROVED BY: _James S. Malek_

Illustration 2-3. Time Sheet

instead of two 12-hour periods. The time runs from 12 midnight to 12 midnight. Eight o'clock in the morning is recorded as 800; 8 o'clock in the evening, as 2000; 5 o'clock in the evening, as 1700. Illustration 2-5 on page 38 shows a time card that uses the continental system of recording time.

For many office workers the time card most commonly used is that which registers from 1 to 12 a.m. or p.m. with full minutes. However, for many mass-production jobs and in job shops, managers need additional information such as how and where each employee's time is spent. Accurate accounting of time spent enables managers and first-line supervisors to determine why certain materials were not available when needed in the production process, to learn what caused machine set-up or break-down time, and to investigate other factors relating to efficient operations. In mass-production operations, information is needed about how time was spent by an employee on a particular operation as the product passed along the line. In a job shop such as an auto or appliance repair shop, information is needed on how employees allocate their time to a single job. Where incentive plans are used, standards must be compared with actual time for the purposes of determining pay as well as for cost analysis of the individual parts produced.

For job costing, the continental time system, with minutes indicated in fractional equivalents, may be effectively used. As shown in Illustration 2-6 on page 39, the labor time or charge is made against a specific job. The *job cost card*, prepared in advance by the scheduling or production control department, identifies the job and may accompany the job throughout the shop. Each employee who works on the job signs his or her name or clock number on the card in the space provided, together with the time registration on and off the job. Such a time record gives a complete summation of time spent on the job as soon as the job is completed and allows a study of the total time spent on a particular job.

Mechanical Time-Clock System

The following summary indicates how a mechanical time-clock works. A mechanical time-clock is shown in Illustration 2-7 on page 39.

1. The number of time-clock stations used by an employer depends on the number of hourly employees, the number of employee entrances, etc. Usually each station has a centrally located time clock with an *In* rack on one side and an *Out* rack on the other. Before employees report for work on Monday morning, a card for each employee is placed in the rack. Each slot in the rack is identified by a clock number and the cards are arranged chronologically by clock number. The cards are kept in the *Out* rack when employees are not at work, and in the *In* rack when employees are at work.

2. Each employee's card shows the clock number, name of employee, and a record of the hours worked.

3. When employees arrive on Monday morning, they remove their time cards from the *Out* rack and place them in the slot provided in the time clock. The insertion of the card actuates a device that prints in the *Morning In* column of the card the day of the week and the exact starting time. The employees then place their cards in the proper place in the *In* rack. At noon when the employees go to lunch, they remove their cards from the *In* rack, register the time in the *Morning Out* column, and place the cards in the *Out* rack. When they return to work after lunch, they take the cards

No. **312**   Pay Ending _October 17, 19--_

NAME   GARY A. SCHNEIDER   262-09-7471

	Hours	Rate	Amount			
Reg.	40	10.75	430 00	OASDI	32	66
O/T	6	16.13	96 78	HI	7	64
				FIT	81	00
				SIT	10	54
				Group Life Ins.	1	60
				Hospital Ins.	3	15
Total Earnings			526 78	U.S. Sav. Bonds	5	00
Less Deductions			141 59	Other		
NET PAY			385 19	Total	141	59

(DEDUCTIONS)

Days	MORNING IN	MORNING OUT	AFTERNOON IN	AFTERNOON OUT	OVERTIME IN	OVERTIME OUT	Daily Totals
1	M 7⁵⁹	M 12⁰³	M 1⁰⁰	M 5⁰⁵			8
2	TU 7⁵⁰	TU 12⁰⁴	TU 12⁵⁹	TU 5⁰⁷			8
3	W 7⁵¹	W 12⁰¹	W 12⁵⁰	W 5⁰⁴	W 5²⁹	W 7³⁵	10
4	TH 8⁰⁰	TH 12⁰²	TH 12⁵⁸	TH 5⁰³			8
5	FR 8⁰⁰	FR 12⁰⁵	FR 1⁰¹	FR 5⁰⁶			8
6	SA 7⁵⁵	SA 12⁰⁴					4
7							

Signature   *Gary A. Schneider*

Illustration 2-4.   Time Card

DEPT. **34** — NUMBER **943**

SPECIAL INSTRUCTIONS

Deduct ¼ hr.

Unexcused absence

TOTAL HOURS WORKED   **39¾**

NAME   DOROTHY Y. MANNINO   943

| M 17⁰⁵ | TU 17⁰⁷ | W 17⁰⁴ | TH 17⁰³ | FR 17⁰⁶ | | |

| M 13⁰⁰ | TU 12⁵⁹ | W 12⁵⁰ | TH 12⁵⁸ | FR 12⁵⁵ | | |
| M 12⁰³ | TU 12⁰⁰ | W 12⁰¹ | TH 12⁰² | FR 12⁰⁵ | | |

| | | | TH 8¹⁰ | | | |
| M 7⁵⁹ | TU 7⁵⁰ | W 7⁵¹ | | FR 8⁰⁰ | | |

MON.	TUE.	WED.	THUR.	FRI.	SAT.	SUN.
8	8	8	7¾	8		

TOTAL HOURS SHOWN IS CORRECT.   *Dorothy Y. Mannino*   SIGNATURE

PP   3 17   PAY PERIOD   STORE 2   DEPT 34   SOCIAL SECURITY NUMBER 320-10-4410

Illustration 2-5.   Continental System Time Card

from the *Out* rack, register the *Afternoon In* time, and place the cards in the *In* rack. At closing time in the afternoon, they take the cards from the *In* rack, register the *Afternoon Out* time, and place the cards in the *Out* rack. Overtime is recorded in a similar manner. On each succeeding day during the week, a similar procedure is followed. Each day there is an automatic adjustment in the time clock which makes it print on the next lower line. Although the time clock described here prints the time automatically when a time card is properly inserted in the machine, some time clocks require pressing a lever to record the time after the card has been inserted.

4. The time clock is equipped with a two-color ribbon. The clock can be set so that all regular time is printed in black, and irregular time in red. For example, if regular working hours were from 8:00 a.m. to 5:00 p.m., with an hour from noon to 1:00 p.m. for lunch, the regular working day would be eight hours. The clock would record as follows:

a. Black when the person rings in before 8:00 a.m. or 1:00 p.m.; also when the person rings out after 12:00 p.m. and 5:00 p.m.

b. Red when the person rings in after 8:00 a.m. or 1:00 p.m.; also when the person rings out before 12:00 p.m. and 5:00 p.m. In other words, when the clock prints red, the person arrived late or left early.

c. Red for both in and out for overtime work, so that special attention is called to the extra hours worked. (In Illustrations 2-4 and 2-5, red is indicated by the shaded areas.)

5. Blank spaces on the card indicate that the employee was absent or had neglected to "punch in" that day. For example, if the *Morning In* and *Out* columns were blank but time was recorded in the afternoon columns, it might indicate that the employee was absent in the morning.

6. At the end of the week, a clerk in the payroll department collects the time cards. The total hours worked, including regular and overtime, during the week are computed. This information is needed in calculating payroll and in preparing the information for the payroll register.

PART NO. *A-14583*		JOB NO. *1771*
JOB COST CARD		
DESCRIPTION *SWITCH BRACKET*		
CARD NO. *1*	EST. TIME *11*	HRS.

Employee		Time	Clock Time Record
	OFF		
	ON		
	OFF		
	ON		
	OFF		
	ON		
	OFF		
	ON		
	OFF		
	ON		
	OFF		
	ON		
	OFF		17 SEP 10 75
311 Max First	ON	.19	17 SEP 10 56
	OFF		17 SEP 10 56
247 J. Sharpe	ON	.54	17 SEP 10 02
	OFF		17 SEP 10 02
125 John Smith	ON	1.96	17 SEP 8 06
	OFF		17 SEP 8 06
109 H. Hinkle	ON	1.06	17 SEP 7 00
	OFF		16 SEP 15 30
109 H. Hinkle	ON	.76	16 SEP 14 54
	OFF		16 SEP 14 54
166 B. Brinkman	ON	2.54	16 SEP 12 00
	OFF		16 SEP 11 50
166 B. Brinkman	ON	1.52	16 SEP 9 98
	OFF		16 SEP 9 98
131 G. Davis	ON	2.98	16 SEP 7 00
TOTAL TIME *11.55*			

Cincinnati Time

Illustration 2-6. Job Cost Card with Time Recorded in Hundredths of an Hour

Illustration 2-7. Mechanical Time-Clock

Computerized Time and Attendance Recording Systems

The main kinds of computerized time and attendance recording systems include:

1. *Card-generated systems* in which employees use time cards similar to the traditional time cards illustrated earlier. Daily and weekly totals are calculated and printed on the time cards for data entry into the firm's computer system.
2. *Badge systems* in which employees are issued plastic laminated badges containing punched holes or having magnetic strips or bar codes. The badges are used with electronic time clocks that collect and store data, which later become input to the computer system.
3. *Cardless and badgeless systems* in which employees enter only their personal identification numbers (PIN) on a numerical or alphanumerical key pad. This system, like the badge system, uses time clocks to collect and store data for transmission to and processing by the firm's computer system.

For illustrative purposes, one kind of computerized time-clock system—a card-generated system—is explained below.

The Timekeeper is a self-contained, wall-mounted time clock that contains a computer system.[4] This time clock is capable of accepting time and attendance data from time cards and computing complex payroll and on-the-job information. By means of time-clock systems, such as the Timekeeper, most manual payroll processing operations are eliminated.

Employees are provided with their own time cards that show their daily attendance record, thus complying with federal, state, and union regulations. The Timekeeper also totals employee hours and rounds out employee time to fractions of an hour in accordance with the payroll practice of the firm.

The Timekeeper card, shown in Illustration 2-8 is similar to the time cards illustrated previously. However, in addition to recording time in and time out, the card prints total hours worked each day and total hours worked from the beginning of the pay period indicated on the time card. The mark sense field at the bottom of the card identifies each employee or supervisor and authorizes access to and use of the Timekeeper. Prior to the use of the card, the mark sense field is marked with the employee's identification number, the shift, and the department. This marking may be done by the Timekeeper or with a pencil. The supervisors' time cards are used to activate the keyboard of the Timekeeper to enter data or to print summary reports on blank time cards. Some of the typical summary reports prepared by the Timekeeper are:

1. List of employee's daily and/or cumulative hours worked by shift and/or department.
2. Absentee list.
3. Tardy list.
4. List of employees on premises.
5. List of employees off premises.

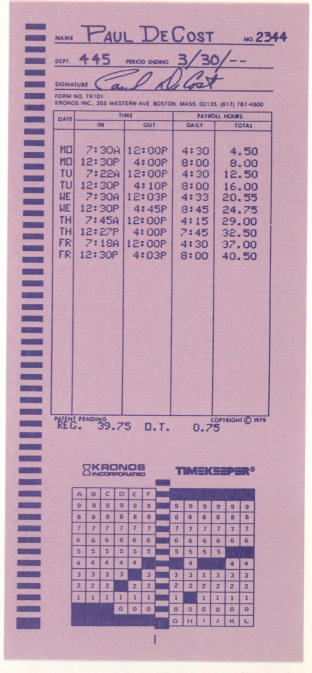

Kronos, Inc.

Illustration 2-8. Mark-Sense Time Card Used in the Timekeeper Computerized Time-Clock System

---

[4]Information supplied the authors by Kronos, Incorporated.

When an employee places the card in the time clock, the computer scans the card. The employee's number is optically verified in the computer memory, and the last print line on the card is located. The time of entry is then printed on the next line. Simultaneously, the computer stores the punch-in time in the system's memory. When an employee punches out, the Timekeeper again verifies the employee's identification number and calculates and rounds off the daily and cumulative payroll hours. Next, the actual punch-out time and the calculated cumulative hours are printed on the card and stored within the Timekeeper for transmission to a computer for payroll processing.

A computerized time and attendance recording system is charted in Illustration 2-9.

Fractional Parts of an Hour

The FLSA requires that employees be paid for *all* time worked, including fractional parts of an hour. An employer cannot use an arbitrary formula or an estimate as a substitute for determining precisely the compensable working time which is part of an employee's fixed or regular hours. However, there is an exception to this rule. Employers may adopt the practice of recording an employee's starting and stopping time to the nearest five minutes, or the nearest tenth of an hour, or the nearest quarter of an hour. Nevertheless, the employer must be able to show that over a period of time the averages so recorded result in the employees being paid for all the time they actually worked.

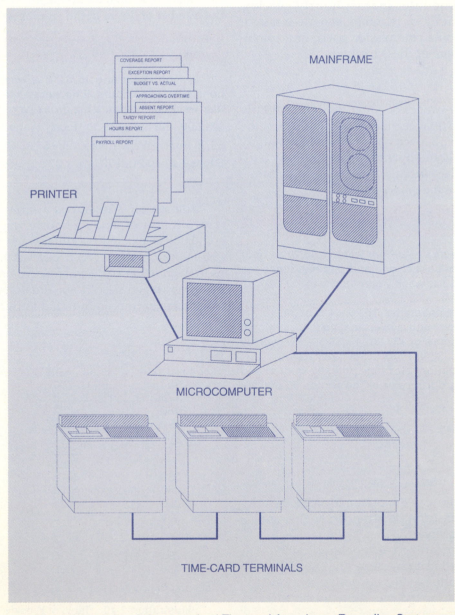

Illustration 2-9. A Computerized Time and Attendance Recording System

Uncertain and indefinite working periods beyond the scheduled working hours cannot be practically determined. Therefore, a few seconds or minutes may be disregarded since the law does not concern itself with trifles. Some courts have allowed from 10 to 20 minutes to be ignored, while other courts have refused to apply the law to periods as small as 10 minutes. Generally a few minutes of time spent by employees on the company premises for their own convenience before or after their workday are not included in the hours worked.

METHODS OF COMPUTING WAGES AND SALARIES

As you saw earlier, remuneration for time worked is usually at a time rate, that is, hourly, weekly, biweekly, semimonthly, or monthly; at a piece rate; at an incentive rate; on a commission basis; or a combination of one or more of these methods.

Time Rate

To calculate the wages of employees on an hourly basis, multiply the total regular hours worked by the regular hourly rate. If overtime is involved, multiply the total overtime hours by the overtime rate. By adding the total regular earnings and the total overtime earnings, we obtain the *gross earnings*.

EXAMPLE:

Nick Sotakos works a 40-hour week at $6.20 an hour with overtime hours paid at one and one-half times the regular rate. His regular weekly earnings are: 40 x $6.20, or $248.

Sotakos's overtime rate is: $6.20 x 1.5, or $9.30.

If Sotakos works 4 hours overtime, he has additional earnings for the 4 hours of $37.20 (4 x $9.30). His weekly gross earnings are: $248 + $37.20, or $285.20.

If Sotakos is paid only for time actually worked and works only 36 hours during a week, he earns: 36 x $6.20, or $223.20.

Professional Tip

Don't allow your nonexempt employees to be at their workstations until it is time to begin regular work duties. Even if the early arrivals say they do not want to be paid for their catch-up work done prior to starting time, the employer is legally obligated to pay for the duties performed even though the work was done without the employer's permission.

In many factories, we find that the actual time spent on a certain job is charged to that job.

EXAMPLE:

Sonja Butta spent 100 minutes on a certain job. Her wages chargeable to that job at the regular hourly rate of $5.58 would be computed as follows:

$$\$5.58 \times \frac{100}{60} = \$9.30$$

Converting Weekly Wage Rates to Hourly Rates.

When an employee is paid on a weekly basis, sometimes we must convert the weekly wage rate to an hourly rate, especially to figure overtime earnings. To do this, we divide the weekly wage rate by the number of hours in the regular workweek.

EXAMPLE:

Joseph Gallo is paid $212 a week for a workweek consisting of 40 hours. If he worked 43 hours in a particular week, we compute his gross pay as follows:

$212.00 ÷ 40 hrs. = $5.30 Hourly Wage Rate

$5.30 Hourly Wage Rate x 1.5 = $7.95 Overtime Wage Rate

Gross Pay = $212 + (3 hrs. x $7.95) = $235.85

Illustration 2-10 shows a table of weekly wage rates with corresponding hourly wage rates based on a 40-hour week, and overtime wage rates at time and one-half for hours worked beyond 40. Practice varies as to the number of decimal places used in calculating overtime wage rates. In our illustration, the overtime wage rates have been rounded to two decimal places.

Weekly Wage Rate	Hourly Wage Rate (40-hr. week)	Overtime Wage Rate* (over 40 hrs.)
$160	$4.00	$ 6.00
170	4.25	6.38
180	4.50	6.75
190	4.75	7.13
200	5.00	7.50
210	5.25	7.88
220	5.50	8.25
230	5.75	8.63
240	6.00	9.00
250	6.25	9.38
260	6.50	9.75
270	6.75	10.13
280	7.00	10.50
290	7.25	10.88
300	7.50	11.25

*Rounded to two decimal places.

Illustration 2-10 Table of Weekly Wage Rates Converted to Hourly Rates

Converting Monthly Salary Rates to Hourly Rates.

Many workers paid on a monthly basis earn overtime pay for work beyond a 40-hour week. In such cases, we must convert the monthly salary rate to an hourly rate in order to obtain the hourly overtime rate.

EXAMPLE:

Elaine Manera is paid a monthly salary of $900, and she receives overtime for hours worked beyond 40 in each workweek. During one weekly pay period she worked 6 hours overtime. We convert her monthly salary rate to its equivalent weekly salary by multiplying the monthly salary by 12 (the number of months) and dividing by 52 (the number of weeks), as follows:

$900 Monthly Rate x 12 Months = $10,800 Yearly Rate

$10,800 Yearly Rate ÷ 52 Weeks = $207.69 Weekly Rate

Next, we divide the weekly rate by the standard number of hours in the workweek to determine the equivalent hourly rate:

$207.69 Weekly Rate ÷ 40 Hours = $5.19 Hourly Rate

Then, we determine her hourly overtime rate:

$5.19 Hourly Rate x 1.5 = $7.79 Overtime Rate

Finally, we calculate Manera's weekly gross pay as follows:

6 Hrs. x $7.79 Overtime Rate = $46.74 (Overtime Earnings)

$207.69 (Regular Weekly Rate) + $46.74 (Overtime Earnings) = $254.43

Illustration 2-11 shows a table of monthly salary rates with corresponding yearly rates, weekly rates, hourly rates based on a 40-hour week, and overtime rates at time and one half for hours worked beyond 40.

When employees are paid semimonthly, we follow the same plan in converting to an hourly basis except we must multiply the semimonthly earnings by 24 instead of by 12 to arrive at the yearly earnings.

Monthly Salary Rate	Yearly Salary Rate	Weekly Salary Rate	Hourly Salary Rate* (40-hr. week)	Overtime Salary Rate* (over 40 hrs.)
$ 725	$ 8,700	$167.31	$4.18	$6.27
750	9,000	173.08	4.33	6.50
775	9,300	178.85	4.47	6.71
800	9,600	184.62	4.62	6.93
825	9,900	190.38	4.76	7.14
850	10,200	196.15	4.90	7.35
875	10,500	201.92	5.05	7.58
900	10,800	207.69	5.19	7.79
925	11,100	213.46	5.34	8.01
950	11,400	219.23	5.48	8.22
975	11,700	225.00	5.63	8.45
1,000	12,000	230.77	5.77	8.66
1,025	12,300	236.54	5.91	8.87
1,050	12,600	242.31	6.06	9.09
1,075	12,900	248.08	6.20	9.30
1,100	13,200	253.85	6.35	9.53
1,125	13,500	259.62	6.49	9.74

*Rounded to two decimal places.

Illustration 2-11   Table of Monthly Salary Rates Converted to Yearly, Weekly, and Hourly Rates

Similarly, if employees are paid biweekly, we multiply the biweekly earnings by 26 to arrive at the yearly earnings.

There are numerous tables of decimal equivalents, such as the one shown in Illustration 2-12, and other devices on the market to help in computing wages at the hourly rate. Stationery and office supply firms usually sell such timesaving devices.

Fractional Cents.

In computing the hourly and overtime rates shown in Illustrations 2-10 and 2-11 we ignored a fraction amounting to less than a half cent. We treated a fraction amounting to a half cent or more as a whole cent. Practice in the treatment of fractions varies with different employers. In the case of union and other employment contracts, the method of computing

	To convert into:		
	Weekly Salary Rate	Hourly Salary Rate*	Hourly Overtime Salary Rate*
Multiply the:			
Weekly salary rate by	. . .	.025	.0375
Semimonthly salary rate by	.4615	.01154	.0173
Monthly salary rate by	.2308	.00577	.00866
Yearly salary rate by	.01923	.00048	.000721

*Based on a 40-hour workweek.

Illustration 2-12.   Table of Decimal Equivalents Used for Conversion into Weekly, Hourly, and Hourly Overtime Salary Rates

regular and overtime hourly rates may be prescribed in the contracts. Use of tables of decimal equivalents may yield weekly, hourly, and hourly overtime equivalents that differ by a cent or more from the amounts shown in Illustrations 2-10 and 2-11. Such differences are due to the process of rounding at various stages in the calculations.

Piece Rate

Under the *piece-rate system*, we pay workers according to their output or so much for each unit or piece produced. Thus, the wages increase as production increases.

EXAMPLE:

Jay White receives 14½¢ for every unit produced. He produces 450 units in an 8-hour workday. His daily wages are: 450 x .145, or $65.25.

The Fair Labor Standards Act specifies that under a piece-rate system, we compute the regular hourly rate of pay by adding together the total weekly earnings from piece rates and all other sources, such as production bonuses. Then, we divide this sum by the number of hours worked in the week for which such compensation was paid to arrive at the pieceworker's "regular hourly rate" for that week. This rate must *at least equal* the statutory minimum wage rate.

EXAMPLE:

Peggy Zagst earns daily wages of $47.20 during a 5-day, 40-hour workweek. Her weekly earnings, $236, divided by 40 hours, gives an average hourly earnings of $5.90. Zagst's average hourly earnings for nonovertime work in each workweek must at least equal the minimum wage.

Overtime Earnings for Pieceworkers—Method A.
For overtime work, the pieceworker is entitled to be paid, in addition to piecework earnings for the entire period, a sum equal to one-half the regular hourly rate of pay multiplied by the number of hours worked in excess of 40 in the week.

EXAMPLE:

Marge Adkins produced 3,073 pieces in a 44-hour workweek and is paid 14¾¢ for every unit produced. We calculate Adkins's total piecework and overtime earnings as follows:

3,073 Pieces x .1475 = $453.27 Piecework Earnings

$453.27 ÷ 44 Hours = $10.30 Regular Hourly Rate of Pay

.5 x $10.30 (Regular Hourly Rate of Pay) = $5.15 Overtime Rate Of Pay

4 Hours x $5.15 = $20.60 Overtime Earnings

$453.27 + $20.60 = $473.87 Piecework and Overtime Earnings

Overtime Earnings for Pieceworkers—Method B.
There is another method of computing overtime payment for pieceworkers that complies with the requirements of the FLSA. Under this method, employees who are paid on the basis of a piece rate may agree with their employer in advance of the performance of the work that they shall be paid at a rate not less than one and one-half times the piece rate for each piece produced during the overtime hours. No additional overtime pay will be due the employees.

EXAMPLE:

Assume that in the preceding example, we paid Adkins overtime at a piece rate of one and one-half times the regular rate for all pieces produced during overtime hours. Of the total 3,073 pieces produced, 272 were produced in the 4 overtime hours. We calculate Adkins's total piecework and overtime earnings as follows:

2,801 pieces x .1475 = $413.15 Piecework Earnings

272 pieces x .2213 = $60.19 Overtime Earnings

$413.15 + $60.19 = $473.34 Piecework and Overtime Earnings

In some instances we may pay a worker an hourly rate for some hours and a piece rate for other hours during the week. In such cases the hourly rate must be at least the minimum rate and the piece-rate earnings for the piece-rate hours must average at least the minimum.

When the piece-rate system is used, production records are kept for each employee so that these records will be available in the payroll department when the time comes to compute the wages earned by each employee.

Special Incentive Plans

Most wage systems involving special incentives are modifications of the piece-rate system described previously.

EXAMPLE:

Le Tourneau pays its production workers according to the following incentive schedule:

Output	Rate
1st 100 units	$ 9.90 per C (hundred)
2d 100 units	10.05 per C
3d 100 units	10.25 per C
all units over 300	10.50 per C

On Monday, Adele Roche produced 410 pieces. We calculate her daily earnings as follows:

1st 100 units	$ 9.90
2d 100 units	10.05
3d 100 units	10.25
110 units over 300	11.55
Total daily earnings ..	$41.75

Under many incentive plans, the company determines a standard for the quantity that an average worker can produce in a certain period of time. Workers failing to reach the standard are paid at a lower piece rate, while those who produce more than the standard receive a higher rate for the quantity produced. When incentive plans are used, the computation of payroll is usually more complicated than under the time-rate or piece-rate systems. Records of time worked as well as the production of each employee must be available in computing wages under most incentive plans.

EXAMPLE:

Chu Wang, Inc., pays its blade polishers according to the following piece-rate incentive plan:

No. of Blades Polished Per 8-Hour Workday	Earnings Per Blade Polished
less than 1,850	$.0150
1,850 to 1,999	.0165
2,000 (Daily Standard)	.0180
2,001 to 2,100	.0198
2,101 to 2,250	.0217
over 2,250	.0240

For one regular 5-day workweek, we determine the gross pay of Lee Kum Choy from the company's production records as follows:

	No. of Blades Polished Daily	Earnings Per Blade Polished	Daily Earnings
M	2,097	.0198	$ 41.52
T	2,012	.0198	39.84
W	1,990	.0165	32.84
Th	2,253	.0240	54.07
F	1,992	.0165	32.87
Total weekly earnings			$201.14

Commissions

The entire remuneration, or at least part of the remuneration, of certain employees may be on a commission basis. A *commission* is a stated percentage of revenue paid an employee who transacts a piece of business or performs a service. Thus, a salesperson working in a certain territory may receive a fixed salary each year plus a bonus for sales in excess of a certain amount.

EXAMPLE:

Maria Fontana receives an annual $22,500 base salary for working a certain territory. A quota of $800,000 in sales has been set for that territory for the current year. It is agreed that Fontana will receive 6% commission on all sales in excess of $800,000. For the current year the sales in the territory are $830,000. The bonus paid Fontana would be 6% of $30,000, or $1,800. Her total earnings for the year would be $22,500 + $1,800, or $24,300.

There are numerous variations of the commission method of remuneration. Some businesses offer special premiums or bonuses for selling certain merchandise. For example, to help move merchandise in a ready-to-wear department, a department store will frequently pay a premium or a bonus to the salesperson who sells specific items of merchandise.

Commissions are considered to be payments for hours worked and must be included in determining the "regular" hourly rate. This is so regardless of whether the commission is the sole source of the employee's compensation or is paid in addition to a salary or hourly rate. It does not matter whether the commission earnings are computed daily, weekly, monthly, or at some other interval. However, in the case of outside salespeople who are exempt from the FLSA, commissions paid to them would not have to meet the minimum wage criteria. This also applies to all employees who are exempt because they are employed in establishments that meet the requirements for exemption.

Profit-Sharing Plans

Many businesses have developed *profit-sharing plans* whereby the employer shares with the employees a portion of the profits of the business. Generally, profit-sharing plans are of three types:

1. Cash payments are based upon the earnings of a specified period.
2. Profits are placed in a special fund or account to be drawn upon by employees at some future time. This plan may be in the form of a savings account, a pension fund, or an annuity.

3. Profits may be distributed to employees in the form of capital stock.

The payments made pursuant to a bona fide profit-sharing plan that meets the standards fixed by the Secretary of Labor's regulations are not deemed wages in determining the employee's regular rate of pay for overtime purposes.

METHODS OF PAYING WAGES AND SALARIES

The three main methods used in paying wages and salaries are (1) by cash, (2) by check, and (3) by electronic transfer. A small business may pay wages and salaries in cash, but most medium-size and large firms pay wages and salaries by check. As we look ahead to a "checkless society" in which the workers' pay is transferred electronically to bank accounts of their choice, the first two methods of paying wages and salaries may become obsolete for many business firms.

Paying Wages and Salaries in Cash

When a company pays wages and salaries in cash, a common procedure is:

1. Compute the total wages earned, the deductions, and the net amount to be paid and record this information in the payroll register, as shown in Illustration 1-10 on page 19. Later, we shall transfer this information to the employees' earnings records, such as that presented in Illustration 1-11 on page 19.

2. Prepare a supplementary payroll sheet that shows the various denominations of bills and coins needed to pay the salary of each employee. The form in Illustration 2-13 provides columns to list the names of the employees, the net amount to be paid, the denominations needed to pay each employee, the total amount needed to pay all employees, and the total number of each denomination needed to pay all employees.

In determining the denominations needed to pay each employee in Illustration 2-13, we have followed the practice of giving employees the least possible number of denominations needed for their net pays. However, no employees will be given $100 bills.

3. Prepare a payroll slip by using the total amount of each denomination needed for the payroll. Illustration 2-14 shows a payroll slip similar to one that many banks furnish to list the amount of each denomination needed for the payroll. The illustration shows the money needed to pay the payroll listed in Illustration 2-13.

4. Write a check for the total amount of the payroll and present it to the bank with the payroll slip so that we may obtain the proper denominations.

5. Place the amount due each employee in an envelope with a receipt showing the total earnings, the deductions, and the net amount paid. Next, we distribute the prepared envelopes to the employees.

		Bills					Coins				
Name of Employee	Net Amount to Be Paid	$50	$20	$10	$5	$1	50¢	25¢	10¢	5¢	1¢
Brandon, Paul C.	$ 268.62	5		1	1	3	1		1		2
Connor, Rose T.	271.40	5	1			1		1	1	1	
Day, Joseph R.	297.28	5	2		1	2		1			3
Gee, Margaret F.	204.92	4			4		1	1	1	1	2
Hawke, Sidney O.	271.64	5	1			1	1		1		4
Kirk, Evelyn A.	288.24	5	1	1	1	3			2		4
Lerro, Doris B.	268.12	5		1		3			1		2
Pesiri, Armand G.	378.80	7	1		1	3	1	1		1	
Topkis, Christine W.	284.65	5	1	1		4	1		1	1	
Vogel, John C.	224.10	4	1			4			1		
Total	$2,757.77	50	8	4	5	28	5	4	9	4	17

HENDRIX, INC. SUPPLEMENTARY PAYROLL SHEET — June 30, 19--

Illustration 2-13. Supplementary Payroll Sheet

Paying Wages and Salaries by Check

When we pay wages and salaries by check, we prepare and sign the checks in the usual way. The one preparing the checks should be sure that the names of the payees and the amounts are correct. The checks are made out for the net amounts to be paid employees.

Employers are required under the Social Security Act to give employees a periodic statement showing the deductions that have been made from their wages for social security tax purposes. We may distribute these statements each payday when the wages are

paid, or we may give them out monthly, quarterly, or annually. Also, we give a statement to an employee at the time the person leaves the employ of the company. Most employers who pay wages and salaries by check indicate on each check issued or on the check stub or earnings statement the various deductions made. (See Illustration 2-15 on page 48.)

Many businesses maintain a payroll account at their bank in addition to their regular checking account. In such a case, we issue all checks to pay wages and salaries against the payroll account rather than against the regular checking account. When the company maintains a separate payroll account, a common procedure is:

1. Set up a payroll account with a certain balance to be maintained at all times. We do this by issuing a check against the regular checking account and depositing the check in the payroll account. A small balance is desirable in the payroll account because it may be necessary to issue payroll checks before the regular payday. For example, if employees are leaving for vacation, we may give them their next payroll checks before the regular payday. Therefore, some balance will be needed in the payroll account to cover the payment of these checks.

2. After the payroll for each period has been computed, issue a check payable to *Payroll*, which will be drawn on the regular checking account and deposited in the special payroll account at the bank.

3. Prepare individual checks, which will be drawn against the special payroll account, and record the numbers of the payroll checks in the payroll register. Many companies having a large number of employees may use automatic means of signing the checks.

By maintaining a separate payroll account at the bank, we simplify the reconciliation of the regular bank statement. The canceled payroll checks, accompanied by a statement of the payroll account balance, are returned separately from the canceled checks drawn upon the regular checking account. The payroll account balance as shown on the bank statement should always be equal to the sum of the total of the outstanding payroll checks and any maintained balance, less any service charge.

Paying Wages and Salaries by Electronic Transfer

The use of checks has expanded to the point where today about 40 billion checks are processed each year. To overcome their paperwork problems and

Bank of Middleton
PAYROLL WITHDRAWAL FROM THE ACCOUNT OF
HENDRIX, INC.

Date _June 30_ 19_--_

Per _J. Stephens_

		DOLLARS	CENTS
BILLS:	100s		
	50s	2 500	00
	20s	160	00
	10s	40	00
	5s	25	00
	1s	28	00
HALF DOLLARS		2	50
QUARTERS		1	00
DIMES			90
NICKELS			20
PENNIES			17
TOTAL		2 757	77

Illustration 2-14.   Payroll Slip

EMPLOYEE'S NAME	ARTHUR T. COCO					PENLAND EQUIPMENT COMPANY, SAN MATEO, FL 32088-2279				
PAY PERIOD ENDING	HOURS	RATE	GROSS EARNINGS	OASDI TAX	HI TAX	FED. WITH. TAX	STATE WITH. TAX	UNION DUES		NET EARNINGS PAID
5/16/--	REG. T. 40 O.T. 12	5.50 8.25	319.00	19.78	4.63	20.00		3.00		271.59

EMPLOYEE: THIS IS A STATEMENT OF YOUR EARNINGS AND DEDUCTIONS FOR PERIOD INDICATED. KEEP THIS FOR YOUR PERMANENT RECORD.

Illustration 2-15   Earnings Statement (Check Stub) Showing Payroll Deductions

mounting information processing costs, many banks, business firms, and government agencies are trying to eliminate payroll and other kinds of checks. Automatic payroll depositing is not new to the banking system or to employers. For many years employers have been able to send one check to each of the banks used by participating employees, along with a list of the amounts to be credited to the employees' specific accounts. Under such a plan the number of checks passing through the banking system is reduced, but the employees' banks are required to prepare numerous deposit slips or a computer tape to process the payroll, either of which is time consuming and costly.

Under an *electronic funds transfer system (EFTS)*, we do not issue a paycheck to each worker, although the worker is given a stub showing the amounts deducted. Instead, we create a computer tape that indicates for each employee: the employee's bank; account number at the bank; and net amount to be paid. A day or two before payday we send the tape to the company's bank where the amounts due any employees who also keep their accounts at that bank are removed from the tape and deposited to the appropriate accounts. That bank sends the remaining names to an automated clearinghouse which sorts out the other bank names and prepares a computer tape for each bank that is to receive funds electronically. For banks that are unable to receive entries in electronic form, the clearinghouse creates a printed statement showing the customers' names and the amounts for which their accounts are to be credited. The actual crediting of accounts and the settlement occur on payday.

Under a "paperless" deposit and bill-paying system, we may deposit wages in bank accounts designated by the employees if the deposits are voluntarily authorized by the employees. Thus, no paper paychecks ever pass hands. Millions of written checks may be eliminated each month, partly by electronically transferring some payroll dollars directly from the accounts of the employers to those of employees. After we have electronically transferred each employee's net pay directly into the worker's account, the employee is able to authorize the bank to automatically transfer funds from that account to the accounts of creditors such as the utility company and the department store.

UNCLAIMED WAGES

Occasionally a worker may terminate employment or be terminated and not claim the final wage payment. The payroll manager is then faced with the question of what to do with the worker's unclaimed wages.

Even though there is a uniform law on the subject of unclaimed or abandoned property, varying practices are found in those states that provide for the disposition of unclaimed property, such as unclaimed wages. The uniform law, which is followed by most states, provides that the holder of any unclaimed property must file a report after a specified statutory period and then surrender the property to the state. The length of the statutory period varies widely from state to state. In other states the holder of unclaimed property files a report with the state and the state then files suit for possession of the property.

Because of the different practices among states, payroll managers must be well acquainted with the laws of their own states in the event they are faced with the difficult problem of disposing of unclaimed wages.

GLOSSARY

Biweekly—every two weeks.

Commission—stated percentage of revenue paid an employee who transacts a piece of business or performs a service.

Continental system—method of recording time on time cards in which the day is divided into one 24-hour period, with time running from 12 midnight to 12 midnight.

Domestic service—those services of a household nature performed in or about a private home of the person by whom the domestic is employed.

Electronic funds transfer system (EFTS)—system whereby the employer transfers employees' net pays to employees' bank accounts with electronic equipment rather than issuing paychecks.

Enterprise coverage—test applied to determine if employees of an enterprise are covered under the provisions of the Fair Labor Standards Act. The test criteria are: at least two employees engaged in interstate commerce, and an annual gross sales volume of at least $500,000.

Exempt employee—worker who is exempt from some, or all, of the FLSA requirements such as minimum wages, equal pay, and overtime pay.

Gross earnings—summation of total regular earnings and total overtime earnings; also known as *gross pay*.

Individual employee coverage—test applied to determine if an employee is covered under the provisions of the Fair Labor Standards Act. The test is that the employee is either engaged in interstate commerce or in producing goods for such commerce.

Job cost card—time card prepared for each job in process, showing the time spent by each employee on that particular job.

Piece-rate system—compensation plan under which workers are paid according to their output (units or pieces produced).

Principal activities—those tasks employees are required by the employer to perform.

Profit-sharing plan—compensation plan in which employer shares with employees a portion of the profits of the business.

Salary—remuneration paid on a monthly, biweekly, semimonthly, or yearly basis.

Semimonthly—twice a month.

Time card—form on which employee's time worked is recorded manually by the worker or automatically by a time clock.

Time sheet—form that indicates an employee's time of arrival and time of departure.

Tip—gift or gratuity given by a customer in recognition of service performed for him or her.

Tipped employee—one engaged in an occupation in which tips of more than $30 a month are customarily and regularly received.

Wage—remuneration paid on an hourly, weekly, or piecework basis.

Wages—remuneration or compensation paid employees plus the reasonable cost or fair value of any facilities furnished the employees by the employer.

Workweek—fixed and regularly recurring period of 168 hours—7 consecutive 24-hour periods.

QUESTIONS FOR REVIEW

1. What factors may cause business organizations to adopt alternative work schedules?
2. Explain the two bases of coverage provided by the FLSA.
3. Distinguish between the terms wage and salary.
4. What kinds of establishments may employ full-time students at 85% of the minimum wage?
5. What is the FLSA definition of *tipped employee*?
6. To what extent are tips considered wages under the FLSA?
7. Explain the requirement set forth by the FLSA for overtime pay.
8. Explain how a state employee working in the area of public safety may use compensatory time off in lieu of overtime compensation.
9. What is the basic provision of the Equal Pay Law?
10. What requirements must be met by employees in order to be classified as an executive under the FLSA?
11. The following employees are exempt from various requirements of the FLSA. Indicate from which requirement or requirements each of the following employees is exempt:
   a. Amusement park employee
   b. Taxicab driver
   c. Casual babysitter
   d. Elementary school teacher
   e. Outside salesperson
12. Under what conditions may children under the age of 18 be employed in nonfarm occupations?

13. Why should an employer require a minor to furnish a state employment or age certificate at time of employment?

14. In determining the working time of employees, how are the principal activities of employees defined?

15. Under what conditions is travel time counted as time worked?

16. A company grants its employees a 15-minute rest period twice each workday. Must the employees be paid for each rest period?

17. When is time spent by employees in attending lectures and meetings for training purposes not counted as working time?

18. A production worker is employed on the third shift (usually 8 hours) when daylight-saving time goes into effect. Explain how the additional hour's pay given the worker is considered in determining the worker's regular pay rate and overtime compensation.

19. How may an employee's absence be indicated on a time card?

20. Explain how to calculate the overtime hourly rate for employees who are paid biweekly.

21. How are wages calculated under the piece-rate system?

22. Explain the two methods that may be used to calculate overtime wages for a pieceworker.

23. Outline the steps usually followed in paying wages and salaries (a) by cash and (b) by check.

24. How is the issuance of paychecks eliminated under an electronic funds transfer system?

25. What is the uniform law on the subject of unclaimed or abandoned property?

QUESTIONS FOR DISCUSSION

1. At Struthers, Inc., factory employees work Monday through Friday at their regular hourly rates. On occasion they work on Saturdays, when they receive time and a half provided they worked 40 hours Monday through Friday.

   One week Sam Rico was absent Wednesday in order to attend a relative's funeral. Under the company's death-in-family policy, Rico's absence was paid for. Therefore, during the workweek Rico worked 32 hours and was paid for 40. That same week Struthers scheduled overtime for Saturday, and Rico worked 8 hours. He expected to be paid for 12 hours. However, the payroll manager informed him that he was entitled to only 8 hours' pay on Saturday because he had worked only 40 hours during the entire week. Do you agree that Rico is entitled to overtime pay for Saturday's hours? Explain.

2. Peter Massey, a machinist for Star Motors, worked 4 hours overtime in the first week of a 2-week pay period. During the second week of the pay period, the company laid Massey off for 6 hours to offset the amount of overtime he worked during the first week. As a result, Massey's total earnings for the 2-week period were the same as they would have been had he worked no overtime hours. Did Star Motors violate any provision of the FLSA in this instance? Explain.

3. Along with many other companies, Gomez Printers observes the Friday after Thanksgiving as a paid holiday. The company requires each employee to make up Friday's lost hours in the following workweek by working extra hours without pay. Is Gomez Printers proceeding legally by requiring its employees to work extra hours without compensation to make up for the hours lost on the Friday holiday? Explain.

4. The cashiers at a drugstore like to make a preliminary count of the $50 "cash bank" in their registers before the store is opened for business. Is the time required to count the "cash bank" compensable under the overtime provisions of the FLSA?

5. In the payroll department of DuMont, there is a policy of waiting one full week before correcting any paycheck errors of $30 or less. However, any pay shortages that exceed $30 are made up the same day. Also, any amounts less than $30 are made up the same day when the particular circumstances of the employees indicate that it would place an undue hardship on them to wait until the next pay one week later.

   Denise Harris, an order checker in DuMont's shipping department, discovered an error of $28.34 in her weekly check. Upon reporting the error, Harris was informed by a payroll clerk that she would have to wait until the next week's paycheck to recover the amount since the underpayment was less than $30.

   What is your reaction to DuMont's policy of providing for paycheck corrections? Assume that Harris protests the delay and in court argues that her earned wages should be paid on the date due. As the judge hearing the case, how would you decide?

6. It is 9:30 p.m. and while Hank Rodgers is watching the ballgame on TV, the doorbell rings. When he opens the door, he finds Bobby, a neighbor, who is delivering the pizza he had ordered. The following conversation takes place:

   Hank: Hi, Bobby. You made it within the 30-minute time limit! I didn't know you were working at the pizza shop. Hey, are you old enough to be driving that jazzy delivery truck?

Bobby: Yeah, no sweat! I'll be 16 in two months, just as soon as school is out.

Is Bobby's employer violating any federal child-labor law? Explain.

7. In some companies employees are permitted to pick up the payroll check of another employee as a favor. What is your reaction to this practice?

8. Many banks in the United States participate in various types of *check truncation* or *check safekeeping* programs. Under such a program, instead of returning to a firm its canceled checks along with the monthly statement, the bank microfilms the checks and stores the truncated checks. For its customers participating in the program, the bank sends a periodic statement listing the numbers, dates, and amounts of checks posted to the customer's account during the previous month. If a customer should ask for a copy of a specific check, the bank sends a photograph or a computer image of the check reproduced from its microimage files.

Assume that you are a payroll manager in a company participating in a check truncation program for the payroll checks written as well as for those written on your firm's commercial checking account. What advantages does the check truncation program offer your company? Do you see any disadvantages?

9. Consult the minimum wage and overtime law of your state, or of another state as directed by your instructor, and prepare a short report in which you discuss each of the following topics:
   a. Coverage and exceptions from coverage.
   b. Minimum wage.
   c. Overtime requirements.
   d. Subminimum wage rates.
   e. Gratuities and tips—how counted toward meeting the minimum wage.
   f. Requirements for publicly displaying certain items by the employer.
   g. Recordkeeping requirements.
   h. Penalties for violation of the law and its regulations.
   i. Remedies available to employees to recover unpaid wages.
   j. Existence of a statute of limitations, which imposes a time restriction on the starting of any action to recover a liability imposed by the law.

10. Consult your state law (or those of several states as directed by your instructor) to find out when termination payments must be made to workers who are discharged, who quit, or who are on strike.

Date _____   Name _____

PRACTICAL PROBLEMS

Special forms required to solve the Practical Problems are provided along with the problems in each unit.

NOTE: In this unit and in all succeeding work throughout the course, *unless instructed otherwise*, calculate hourly rates and overtime rates as follows:

1. Carry the hourly rate and the overtime rate to 3 decimal places and then round off to 2 decimal places.
2. If the third decimal place is 5 or more, round to the next higher cent.
3. If the third decimal place is less than 5, simply drop the third decimal place.

Examples: $4.765 should be rounded to $4.77.
$4.764 should be rounded to $4.76.

Also, use the minimum hourly wage of $4.25 in solving these problems and all that follow.

2-1. The hours worked and the hourly wage rates for five employees of the Cooley Company for the week ended September 10 follow.

a. For each employee, calculate the gross earnings.
b. Determine the total gross earnings for all employees.

Employee	Hours Worked	Regular Hourly Wage Rate	(a) Gross Earnings
Dempski, R.	38	$8.40	$ _____
Floyd, B.	40	5.25	_____
Iskin, J.	37	6.30	_____
Macintyre, H.	40	6.95	_____
Serock, P.	32½	4.25	_____
		(b) Total gross earnings	$ _____

2-2. The wages and hours information for five employees of Serbu Enterprises for the week ended July 5 is given below. Employees work a standard 40-hour workweek and are paid time and one-half for all hours over 40 in each workweek.

a. For each employee, calculate the regular earnings, overtime rate, overtime earnings, and total gross earnings.
b. Determine the total gross earnings for all employees.

(a)

Employee	Hours Worked	Regular Hourly Wage Rate	Regular Earnings	Overtime Rate	Overtime Earnings	Total Gross Earnings
Clay, T.	48	$6.45	$_____	$_____	$_____	$_____
DeMusis, G.	44	6.25	_____	_____	_____	_____
Kliny, A. ...	42	5.70	_____	_____	_____	_____
Ostrow, B. .	49	4.85	_____	_____	_____	_____
Wax, W. ...	45½	7.40	_____	_____	_____	_____
		(b) Total gross earnings				$_____

2-3. Bruce Cabot is a waiter at the Towne House, where he receives a weekly wage of $80 plus tips for a 40-hour workweek. Cabot's weekly tips usually range from $180 to $200.

    a. Under the Fair Labor Standards Act, the minimum amount of wages that Cabot must receive for a 40-hour workweek is .... $_____

    b. The maximum amount of tip credit that may be claimed that week by the Towne House is .... $_____

    c. In addition to the $80 weekly wage, the amount the Towne House must pay Cabot each week is .... $_____

2-4. Tony Franco is a full-time student at Southern Junior College. After school hours he is employed by the college as a clerk at $3.50 per hour. One week he worked 18½ hours.

    a. Franco's earnings for the week are .... $_____

    b. Is the hourly rate in violation of the FLSA? Explain.

    c. If the hourly rate is in violation of the FLSA, the amount the college should pay Franco is .... $_____

2-5. May Kim, a full-time student at Central University, is employed by Gifford's Dress Shop as a salesperson. Her hourly rate is $3.25. One week Kim worked 32¾ hours.

    a. Kim's earnings for the week are .... $_____

    b. Is the hourly rate in violation of the FLSA? Explain.

    c. If the hourly rate is in violation of the FLSA, the amount the dress shop should pay Kim is .... $_____

2-6. Joe Vacca receives an hourly wage of $6.90 for a 40-hour week of 5 days, 8 hours daily. For Saturday work, he is paid one and one-half times the regular rate; for Sunday work, he is paid double the regular rate. During a certain week, he works the full 5-day week, plus 8 hours on Saturday and 4 hours on Sunday.

For this workweek, compute:

    a. The regular earnings .... $_____

    b. The overtime earnings .... _____

    c. The total earnings .... $_____

2-7. Annette Henri is paid an hourly wage of $5.30 for a 32-hour workweek of 4 days, 8 hours daily. For any work on the fifth day and on Saturdays, she is paid one and one-half times her regular hourly rate. During a certain week, in addition to her regular 32 hours, Henri worked 6 hours on the fifth day and 5 hours on Saturday.

For this workweek, compute:

    a. The regular earnings .... $_____

    b. The overtime earnings .... _____

    c. The total earnings .... $_____

2-8. Peter Romez receives $215 for a regular 40-hour week and time and one-half for overtime. For a workweek of 46 hours, compute:

    a.   The regular earnings .... $_____

    b.   The overtime earnings .... _____

    c.   The total earnings .... $_____

2-9. Chris Donato earns $1,450 each month and works 40 hours each week. Compute:

    a.   The hourly rate .... $_____

    b.   The overtime rate at time and one-half .... $_____

2-10. Richard Gentile is paid an annual salary of $18,900 by the Lett Company. Based on a 52-week year during which Gentile works 37½ hours each week, his hourly pay rate is .... $_____

2-11. Kathleen Otto, a medical secretary, is paid $1,075 monthly for a 35-hour week. For overtime work she receives extra pay at the regular hourly rate up to 40 hours, and time and one-half beyond 40 hours in any week. During one semimonthly pay period, Otto worked 10 hours overtime. Only 2 hours of this overtime were beyond 40 hours in any one week. Compute:

    a.   The regular semimonthly earnings .... $_____

    b.   The overtime earnings .... _____

    c.   The total earnings .... $_____

2-12. Cynthia Porrini receives $4.90 per hour for a workweek of 5 days, 7½ hours daily. She is paid time and one-half for overtime, but the overtime rate is not effective until she works 40 hours during the week. Porrini is not paid for time off. During a certain week, she is absent 2 hours on Monday and works 8 hours on Saturday. Compute:

    a.   The regular earnings .... $_____

    b.   The overtime earnings .... _____

    c.   The total earnings .... $_____

2-13. Refer to Problem 2-12. Assume that Porrini was paid for her absence on Monday and received time and one-half for all of her Saturday work. Compute:

    a.   The regular earnings .... $_____

    b.   The overtime earnings .... _____

    c.   The total earnings .... $_____

2-14. The time card below shows the time worked one week by Peter Van Horn. The employer disregards any time before 8:00 a.m. or 1:00 p.m. and after 5:00 p.m. Employees do not begin work until 8:00 a.m. or 1:00 p.m., and do not work beyond 5:00 p.m., unless they are asked to work overtime. Hours worked beyond the regular 8-hour day and on Saturday are paid at one and one-half times the regular rate. Hours worked on Sunday are paid double the regular rate.

No. 72						
Name Peter Van Horn					(a)	
Day	Morning		Afternoon		Overtime		Hours Worked
	In	Out	In	Out	In	Out	
M	7:50	12:00	12:50	5:01			
T	7:56	12:01	12:49	5:02	5:30	7:31	
W	7:59	12:02	12:58	5:03			
T	7:45	12:00	12:55	5:00	5:29	8:02	
F	8:01	12:01	1:00	5:01	6:00	7:30	
S	7:48	12:02					
S			2:00	6:03			
(b)	Total Hours Worked						
Remarks							

Van Horn's regular wage rate is $4.78 per hour, and the regular workweek is 40 hours with five 8-hour days. Compute:

a. The hours worked each day. (Ignore the one-minute tardiness on Friday.)

b. The total hours worked.

c. The regular earnings . . . . $_____

d. The overtime earnings . . . . _____

e. The total earnings . . . . $_____

2-15. Under the decimal system of calculating time worked at the Silverman Company, production workers who are tardy are "docked" according to the schedule shown below.

(a)

Minutes Late in Ringing In	Fractional Hour Deducted
1 through 6	1/10
7 through 12	2/10
13 through 18	3/10
19 through 24	4/10
etc.	

DAY	AM		PM		HRS WORKED
	In	Out	In	Out	
M	7:28	11:31	12:29	4:31	
T	7:35	11:30	12:30	4:30	
W	7:50	11:33	12:27	4:32	
Th	7:27	11:31	12:50	4:33	
F	7:28	11:32	12:40	4:30	

The regular hours of work, Monday through Friday, are from 7:30 to 11:30 a.m. and from 12:30 to 4:30 p.m. During one week Henry Vanderhoff, who earns $6.15 an hour, reports in and checks out as shown above. Employees are not paid for ringing in a few minutes before 7:30 and 12:30 nor for ringing out a few minutes after 11:30 and 4:30. Compute:

a. The hours worked each day.

b. The total hours worked . . . . _____

c. The gross earnings for the week . . . . $_____

2-16. Refer to Problem 2-15. Assume that Vanderhoff worked 5 hours overtime on Monday and that he is paid time and one-half for any hours over 8 each workday. Compute:

a.   The regular earnings . . . . $_____

b.   The overtime earnings . . . .   _____

c.   The gross earnings for the week . . . . $_____

2-17. The Toland Gear Company pays its employees according to the incentive schedule shown below.

Output	Rate per C (hundred)
1st 2,000 units	$1.95
next 100 units (2,001 to 2,100)	$2.00
all units over 2,100	$2.05

Using the following production data, compute:

a.   The daily earnings for each employee.
b.   The total daily earnings for all employees.

Employee	Units Produced		(a) Daily Earnings
Rocco D'Orazio	2,975	_____	
		_____	
		_____	$_____
John Ervin	2,480	_____	
		_____	
		_____	$_____
Kenneth Hicks	2,870	_____	
		_____	
		_____	$_____
Joseph Mylotte	2,710	_____	
		_____	
		_____	$_____
Thomas Wade	2,902	_____	
		_____	
		_____	$_____
(b) Total daily earnings			$_____

2-18. Zeller Parts, Inc., pays its employees according to the incentive schedule shown below.

Output	Rate per C (hundred)
1st 500 units	$6.15
next 100 units (501 to 600)	$6.25
all units over 600 . .	$6.45

Using the following production data, compute:

a. The daily earnings for each employee.
b. The total daily earnings for all employees.

Employee	Units Produced		(a) Daily Earnings
Pauline Bonovitz	560		
			$_____
Jose DeLaRosa	570		
			$_____
Harlan Girard	730		
			$_____
Anna Mayne	800		
			$_____
Betty Shore	835		
			$_____
(b) Total daily earnings			$_____

2-19. During the first week in November, Esther Coulter worked 45½ hours and produced 1,215 units under a piece-rate system. The regular piece rate is 18¢ a unit. Coulter is paid overtime according to the FLSA ruling for overtime work under a piece-rate system. Calculate:

a. The piecework earnings . . . . $_____

b. The regular hourly rate . . . . $_____
   The overtime hourly rate . . . . $_____

NOTE: In your calculations, carry the regular hourly rate and the overtime rate each to 4 decimal places and then round off each rate to 3 decimal places.

c. The overtime earnings . . . .   _____

d. The total earnings . . . . $_____

2-20. Refer to Problem 2-19. Assume that Coulter had agreed with her employer prior to the performance of the work that she shall be paid one and one-half times the regular piece rate for all pieces produced during the overtime hours. Assume that her production totals for the week were: 1,075 pieces during regular hours and 140 pieces during overtime hours. Calculate:

a. The piecework earnings . . . . $_____

b. The overtime earnings . . . . _____

c. The total earnings . . . . $_____

2-21. The hours worked and units produced by five production workers at the Charles Steel Company for the period ending December 12 are given below. The regular piece rate for each worker is 24¢ a unit. All workers are paid according to the FLSA ruling for overtime work under a piece-rate system. Calculate:

a. The piecework earnings for each employee.
b. The regular hourly rate.
c. The overtime rate.

NOTE: In your calculations, carry the regular hourly rate and the overtime rate each to 4 decimal places and then round off each rate to 3 decimal places.

d. The overtime earnings for each employee.
e. The total earnings for each employee.

Employee	Hrs. Worked	Units Produced	(a) Piecework Earnings	(b) Reg. Hrly. Rate	(c) Overtime Rate	(d) Overtime Earnings	(e) Total Earnings
M. Bell	44	1,322	$_____	$_____	$_____	$_____	$_____
E. Carter	40	1,175	_____	_____	_____	_____	_____
D. Erk	45	1,408	_____	_____	_____	_____	_____
F. Kitei	48½	1,555	_____	_____	_____	_____	_____
D. Soong	49¾	1,580	_____	_____	_____	_____	_____

2-22. The production record for Chu Wang, Inc., for the week ending April 16 is given on page 60. This record shows the weekly output for six of the firm's blade polishers. The company's piece-rate incentive plan is described on page 45.

For overtime work a premium is paid the employees. The premium rate for each piece produced during the overtime hours is one and one-half times the piece rate the employee earned that day for the total pieces produced. The production record shows that of the six blade polishers, only Correro worked overtime during the week. Of the total 2,757 blades polished by Correro on Wednesday, 584 were produced in two overtime hours.

On the production record, calculate:

a. The earnings per blade polished for each employee.
b. The daily earnings for each employee.
c. The weekly earnings for each employee.

CHU WANG, INC.

Production Record for Week Ending April 16, 19—

Employee	Day	No. of Blades Polished	(a) Earnings Per Blade Polished	(b) Daily Earnings
Luis Agosto	M	2,000	$_____	$_____
	T	2,170	_____	_____
	W	Absent	_____	_____
	T	2,116	_____	_____
	F	2,009	_____	_____
			(c) Total	$_____
Ana Correro	M	2,240	$_____	$_____
	T	2,298	_____	_____
	W	2,173 (Regular)	_____	_____
		584 (Overtime)	_____	_____
	T	2,284	_____	_____
	F	2,069	_____	_____
			(c) Total	$_____
Pearl Gaines	M	1,900	$_____	$_____
	T	1,950	_____	_____
	W	2,005	_____	_____
	T	2,107	_____	_____
	F	2,003	_____	_____
			(c) Total	$_____
Thomas Kelman	M	1,980	$_____	$_____
	T	2,050	_____	_____
	W	2,010	_____	_____
	T	2,000	_____	_____
	F	2,007	_____	_____
			(c) Total	$_____
Eloise Miller	M	2,217	$_____	$_____
	T	2,130	_____	_____
	W	2,020	_____	_____
	T	960	_____	_____
	F	2,010	_____	_____
			(c) Total	$_____
David Rotberg	M	2,200	$_____	$_____
	T	2,195	_____	_____
	W	1,998	_____	_____
	T	2,090	_____	_____
	F	2,000	_____	_____
			(c) Total	$_____

Date _____   Name _____

2-23. Refer to Problem 2-22. On the form given below, determine:

a. The average earnings per blade polished by each of the six workers during the week.
b. The average earnings per blade polished for all six workers during the week.
c. How the average earnings per blade polished for all six workers during the week compare with the daily standard earnings of $.0180 per blade.

Employee	Weekly Earnings	÷	No. Blades Polished	=	(a) Average Earnings Per Blade
Luis Agosto	$_____		_____		$_____
Ana Correro	_____		_____		_____
Pearl Gaines	_____		_____		_____
Thomas Kelman	_____		_____		_____
Eloise Miller	_____		_____		_____
David Rotberg	_____		_____		_____
Total	$_____		_____		

(b) $_____ ÷ _____ = $_____
       (Total weekly earnings)   (Total blades polished)   (Average earnings per blade
                                                                       polished by all six workers)

(c) Average earnings per blade polished by all six workers: .... $_____

Daily standard earnings per blade polished: .... ____.0180____

The actual average for the week is (less than or greater than) the daily
standard earnings by .... $_____

2-24. Joan Sullivan, a sales representative, earns an annual salary of $17,750. She is also paid a commission on that portion of her annual sales that exceeds $60,000. The commission is 7% on all sales up to $45,000 above the quota. Beyond that amount, she receives a commission of 9½%. Her total sales for the past year were $128,000. Calculate:

a. The regular annual salary .... $_____
b. The commission .... _____
c. The total annual earnings .... $_____

2-25. Ferry Furriers pays its sales personnel a base salary plus commissions on sales that exceed a stated annual sales quota. From the information given below, calculate each salesperson's (a) commission and (b) total annual earnings.

Salesperson	Annual Sales	Annual Base Salary	Annual Sales Quota	Commission Percentage for Sales Above Quota	(a) Commission	(b) Total Annual Earnings
J. Fosco	$105,750	$25,700	$ 95,000	13½%	$_____	$_____
T. Glenn	150,540	27,500	135,000	10½%	_____	_____
A. Kehoe	97,220	20,000	90,000	8¾%	_____	_____
P. Luss	189,600	30,500	180,000	7%	_____	_____
J. Osti	87,290	24,375	70,000	12½%	_____	_____

61

2-26. Joyce Sand is employed as a salesperson in the men's department of Lukens Fashions. In addition to her weekly base salary of $240, Sand is paid a commission of 1% on her total net sales for the week (total gross sales less any customer returns). During the past week, to promote the sale of its fine cashmere sweaters, Lukens agreed to pay Sand an additional PM (push money) of 2% of the total net sales of cashmere sweaters. Sand's weekly sales tally is given below.

Item	Gross Sales	Customer Returns
Regular sweaters	$350	$48
Cashmere sweaters	995	75
Ties	180	-0-
Dress shirts	445	20
Sports shirts	185	15

Calculate Sand's total weekly earnings, showing her (a) weekly base salary, (b) commission, (c) PM, and (d) total weekly earnings.

(a) Weekly base salary . . . . $ 240.00

    Weekly gross sales . . . . $_____

       Less customer returns . . . . _____

    Weekly net sales . . . . $_____

(b) Commission: $_____ x 1% . . . . _____

    Weekly gross sales of cashmere sweaters . . . . $_____

       Less customer returns . . . . _____

    Weekly net sales of cashmere sweaters . . . . $_____

(c) PM: $_____ x 2% . . . . _____

(d) Total weekly earnings . . . . $_____

2-27. Potts, Inc., recently converted from a 5-day, 40-hour workweek to a 4-day, 40-hour workweek, with overtime continuing to be paid at one and one-half times the regular hourly rate for all hours worked beyond 40 in the week. In this company, time is recorded under the continental system, as shown on the time card at the right.

Sue Ellen Boggs is part of the Group B employees whose regular workweek is Tuesday through Friday. The working hours each day are 800 to 1200; 1230 to 1630; and 1800 to 2000. The company disregards any time before 800, 1230, and 1800, and permits employees to ring in up to 10 minutes late before any deduction is made for tardiness. Deductions are made to the nearest ¼ of an hour for workers who are more than 10 minutes late in ringing in.

Refer to the time card and compute:

a. The daily total hours.

b. The total hours for the week.

c. The regular weekly earnings . . . . $_____

d. The overtime earnings . . . .

e. The total weekly earnings . . . . $_____

No. 160					Hr. Rate $4.45	
Name Sue Ellen Boggs					O.T. Rate $6.675	

Time		Mon	Tues	Wed	Thurs	Fri	Sat
Evening	Out		2002	2001	2005	2000	
	In		1801	1809	1802	1800	
Afternoon	Out		1630	1631	1630	1635	
	In		1230	1231	1230	1238	
Morning	Out		1200	1202	1200	1203	1201
	In		755	750	813	759	800	Total for Week
Daily Totals	(a)						(b)

Remarks *13 minutes late Thursday – deduct ¼ hr.*

62

2-28. The job cost card used by Gamma Manufacturing Company to record the time spent in assembling its micro relays is illustrated below.

JOB COST CARD

Part No. *B-640*   Job No. *12*

Description *MICRO RELAY 640*

Card No. *1*   Estimated Time *6* Hrs.

No.	Employee	Time		Time Clock Record
		OFF		
		ON		
		OFF		
		ON		
		OFF		
		ON		
		OFF		
		ON		
		OFF		
		ON		
64	Bill Fleming	OFF		4 JUN 15^{12}
		ON		4 JUN 15^{00}
31	Laura Packard	OFF		4 JUN 14^{74}
		ON		4 JUN 13^{00}
44	HARRY O'NEILL	OFF		4 JUN 11^{82}
		ON		4 JUN 10^{00}
27	Ella Poole	OFF		4 JUN 09^{75}
		ON		4 JUN 08^{50}
47	Martha Ayers	OFF		4 JUN 08^{48}
		ON		4 JUN 08^{25}
19	Peter Wilson	OFF		4 JUN 08^{20}
		ON		4 JUN 07^{30}

TOTAL TIME _____

On the form given below:

a. Determine the time spent on the job by each employee and the total time spent by all employees. *Note that the time is recorded in hundredths of an hour.*

b. Use the hourly wage rates given to calculate the total labor cost for producing the one relay. In your calculations, carry out the labor cost for each employee and the total labor cost to 4 decimal places.

No.	Employee	(a) Time	Hourly Wage Rate	(b) Labor Cost
64	Bill Fleming	_____	$5.75	$ _____
31	Laura Packard	_____	6.10	_____
44	Harry O'Neill	_____	6.30	_____
27	Ella Poole	_____	5.25	_____
47	Martha Ayers	_____	6.75	_____
19	Peter Wilson	_____	6.50	_____
	Totals	_____		$ _____

c. The company's time study engineer has determined that the standard labor cost for producing one micro relay is $36.5025. Calculate by what percentage (plus or minus) the actual labor cost on June 4 varied from the predetermined standard. . . . .   _____

2-29. Hendrix, Inc., pays its employees' weekly wages in cash. A supplementary payroll sheet that lists the employees' names and their earnings for a certain week is shown below. Complete the payroll sheet by calculating the total amount of payroll and indicating the least possible number of denominations that can be used in paying each employee. However, no employees are to be given bills in denominations greater than $20.

HENDRIX, INC.

Supplementary Payroll Sheet

For Period Ending August 15, 19—	Net Amount Paid	Bills				Coins				
Name of Employee		$20	$10	$5	$1	50¢	25¢	10¢	5¢	1¢
Chad T. Biskis	$251.75									
Nicole A. Cibik	256.52									
Domingo M. Diaz	184.94									
Laura B. Elias	202.59									
Ari M. Fleischer	253.64									
Diane Y. Germano	296.50									
Arnold B. Herst	194.26									
Edward C. Kenner	199.89									
Kathleen J. Marfia	234.01									
Kimberly A. Picket	195.80									
Total										

64

2-30. Refer to Problem 2-29. After you have completed the supplementary payroll sheet, prepare the payroll slip and check below. Sign your name on the "Per" line of the payroll slip. The check should be made payable to *Payroll* and signed with your signature below the company name.

⑈042205022⑈

Bank of Middleton

PAYROLL WITHDRAWAL FROM THE ACCOUNT OF
HENDRIX, INC.

Date _____ 19 _____

Per _____

		DOLLARS	CENTS
BILLS:	100s		
	50s		
	20s		
	10s		
	5s		
	1s		
HALF DOLLARS			
QUARTERS			
DIMES			
NICKELS			
PENNIES			
	TOTAL		

No. **1915**

56—456
422

19 _____

$ _____

_____ DOLLARS

HENDRIX, INC.

HENDRIX, INC.
PAYROLL ACCOUNT

PAY TO
THE ORDER OF _____

Bank of Middleton

⑈042204563⑈ 121 ⑈63229⑈

✳ CONTINUING PAYROLL PROBLEM

In the Continuing Payroll Problem, which is presented at the end of succeeding units, you will gain experience in computing wages and salaries and preparing a payroll register for the Steimer Company, Inc., a newly formed corporation. At the end of subsequent units, information will be presented so that the payroll register can be completed step by step as you proceed through the discussion material relating to that particular section of the payroll register.

The Steimer Company is a small manufacturing firm located in Philadelphia, PA. The company has a work force of both hourly and salaried employees. Each employee is paid for hours actually worked during each week, with the time worked being recorded in quarter-hour increments. The standard workweek consists of 40 hours, with all employees being paid time and one-half for any hours worked beyond the 40 regular hours.

Wages are paid every Friday, with one week's pay being held back by the company. Thus, the first payday for the Steimer Company is January 14 for the workweek ending January 7.

The information at the top of the next column will be used in preparing the payroll for the pay period ending January 7.

Ms. Nancy B. Costello prepares the time clerk's report for each pay period. Her report for the first week of operations is given below.

Using the payroll register for the Steimer Company, which is reproduced on a fold-out at the back of the book, proceed as follows:

Time Card No.	Employee Name	Hourly Wage or Salary
11	Mary L. Lopenski	$4.50 per hour
12	Anthony P. Wren	$4.25 per hour
13	Leroy A. Young	$5.10 per hour
21	Lester D. Hayes	$4.90 per hour
22	Meredith O. McGarry	$5.75 per hour
31	Nancy B. Costello	$215 per week
32	Gloria D. Hopstein	$1,700 per month
33	Vernon U. Porth	$1,350 per month
51	Marsha T. Stone	$1,510 per month
99	Harold Y. Steimer	$52,000 per year

1. Enter each employee's time card number and name in the appropriate columns.
2. Record the regular hours and the overtime hours worked for each employee, using the time clerk's report as your reference.
3. Complete the Regular Earnings columns (Rate Per Hour and Amount) and the Overtime Earnings columns (Rate Per Hour and Amount) for each employee.
4. Record the Total Earnings for each employee by adding the Regular Earnings and the Overtime Earnings.

Note: Retain your partially completed payroll register for use at the end of Unit 3.

TIME CLERK'S REPORT NO. 1

For Period Ending January 7, 19--

Time Card No.	Employee	Time Record						Time Worked	Time Lost
		M	T	W	T	F	S		
11	Mary L. Lopenski	8	8	8	8	8	—	40	
12	Anthony P. Wren	8	8	8	8	8	8	48	
13	Leroy A. Young	8	5½	8	8	8	—	37½	2½ hrs. tardy
21	Lester D. Hayes	10	10	8	8	10	—	46	
22	Meredith O. McGarry	8	8	8	8	8	—	40	
31	Nancy B. Costello	9	8	8	8	8	1¼	41¼	
32	Gloria D. Hopstein	8	8	8	8	8	—	40	
33	Vernon U. Porth	8	8	8	8	8	—	40	
51	Marsha T. Stone	8	8	8	8	8	4	44	
99	Harold Y. Steimer	8	8	8	8	8	—	40	

CASE PROBLEMS

Case 2-1   Reducing the Cost of Compensated Leave Time

For the past several weeks, Adele Delgado, payroll manager for the Petrillo Packing Company, has been studying the mounting costs of accrued vacations and sick leave. Most of her firm's employees are entitled to two weeks' vacation each year and the privilege of accruing their vacation time for future use. Also, the workers have a generous sick-leave plan that reimburses them while they are ill at home or in the hospital.

Scanning the employees' accrued vacation times on the computer printout, Delgado notes the line entry for John Mannick. Mannick recently retired and cashed in 14 weeks of accrued vacation—all paid at his current wage, which was much more than when he originally earned the vacations. And, of course, the firm's payroll taxes for the accrued vacation payout were significantly increased.

Delgado also knows that some workers feel short-changed if they do not use their sick leave each year. They realize that if the leave is not used, they lose it for that year. Probably, she thinks, this accounts for those who regularly become ill on Mondays or Fridays.

What solutions can you offer to limit the cost of and more effectively manage the firm's policies for compensated leave time?

Case 2-2   Selecting A Computerized Time and Attendance Recording System

Assume you are the payroll clerk for Yours Truly, Inc., which employs 23 full-time workers. At the present time all of the company's employees record their time and attendance on one electromechanical time clock, which is adequate for the number of workers in your firm. As part of a feasibility study, you have been given the responsibility to investigate which kind of automated equipment will enable your company to process its payroll more efficiently and economically.

During your study you accumulate the following information:

1. Cost of the electromechanical time clock now in use, $1,000.
2. Cost of one calculating time clock that prints in and out times and automatically figures daily and weekly totals, $1,500.
3. Cost of one calculating time clock that will interface with your company's computer, $2,500. This system feeds all payroll data directly to the computer, thus eliminating the step of data entry from hard-copy time cards.
4. Cost of a badge-based system, for firms employing 50 or more employees, $5,000; for businesses with 1,000 employees or more, $50,000.

   This system, depending on the use of an employee's coded identification badge, eliminates time cards. The data are collected at a terminal, where the time is automatically recorded and sent to a central computer.
5. Estimated time required for you to process manually one time card, 7 minutes.
6. Your present hourly wage, $8.50.
7. Cost of an outside part-time bookkeeper to do the payroll work, $10 an hour.

Based upon the information you have obtained, prepare a report in which you recommend the type of equipment that should be installed to automate the payroll accounting operations, along with the estimated savings your company will realize during the first year.

SOCIAL SECURITY TAXES

GOALS OF THIS UNIT

After completing your study of this unit, you should be able to:

1. Identify, for social security purposes, those persons covered under the law, those services that constitute employment, and the kinds of compensation that are defined as wages.

2. Apply the current tax rates for purposes of the Federal Insurance Contributions Act and the Self-Employment Contributions Act.

3. Understand the importance of obtaining and correctly using the Employer's Identification Number and the Employee's Social Security Number.

4. Complete Form 941, Employer's Quarterly Federal Tax Return, and Form 8109, Federal Tax Deposit Coupon.

5. Understand the different requirements and procedures for depositing FICA taxes and income taxes withheld from employees' wages.

6. Recognize that, as collection agents for the government, employers may be subject to civil and criminal penalties if they fail to carry out their duties.

In this unit we center our discussion on the *old-age, survivors, disability and health insurance program (OASDHI)*. This program provides monthly benefits to workers who qualify under the provisions of the Social Security Act. To cover the cost of this program, the act imposes taxes on employers and their employees. The statutes that provide the taxes are:

1. The *Federal Insurance Contributions Act (FICA)*, which imposes *two* taxes on employers and *two* taxes on employees. One of the taxes is used to finance the *federal old-age, survivors, and disability insurance program (OASDI)*; the other is used to finance the *hospital insurance (HI)*, or *Medicare*, program.
2. The *Self-Employment Contributions Act (SECA)*, which levies a tax upon the net earnings of the self-employed.

COVERAGE UNDER FICA

Today most workers in the United States are covered by the retirement and disability aspects of the social security program. Before individuals are considered to be "covered" for social security purposes, we must determine (a) if they are "employees," (b) whether the services they render are "employment," and (c) whether the compensation they receive is "wages" within the meaning of the law. The determination of a "covered" employee and "covered" employment is related to who pays the tax and who is entitled to benefits.

Employee

Every individual is an *employee* if that person performs services in a covered employment. As long as the common-law relationship of employer and employee exists and the employment is not exempt from the provisions of the law, both are covered and must observe its provisions.

The Common-Law Test.

A *common-law relationship* of employer and employee exists when the employer has the *right to control* both what work will be done and how it will be done. To determine if a worker may be classified as an employee and if the employer has the right to control, the Internal Revenue Service uses the 20-factor *common-law test* shown in Illustration 3-1. (If workers do not meet these tests, generally they are classified as *independent contractors*, as discussed in a later section.)

THE COMMON-LAW TEST

Workers are *generally* classified as employees if they:

1. Must comply with the employer's instructions about when, where, and how to work.
2. Receive training from or at the direction of the employer. This may include working along with an experienced employee or attending meetings.
3. Provide services that are integrated into the business. That is, the success or continuation of the employer's business depends significantly on the performance of certain services provided by the worker.
4. Perform the work personally.
5. Hire, supervise, and pay assistants *for the employer*.
6. Have a continuing relationship with the employer. This may exist where the work is performed at frequently recurring, although irregular, intervals.
7. Must follow set hours of work.
8. Work full-time for the employer.
9. Do their work on the employer's premises.
10. Must do their work in a sequence set by the employer.
11. Must submit regular oral or written reports to the employer.
12. Receive payments of regular amounts at set intervals.
13. Receive payments for business and/or traveling expenses.
14. Rely on the employer to furnish tools and materials.
15. Lack a significant investment in facilities used to perform the service.
16. Cannot make a profit or suffer a loss from their services.
17. Work for one employer at a time.
18. Do not offer their services to the general public.
19. Can be fired by the employer.
20. May quit their job at any time without liability.

Illustration 3-1. The Common-Law Test

Employees of a Corporation.

In a corporation, there is no distinction between classes or grades of employees. Thus, managers, superintendents, supervisors, department heads, and other executives are employees. All the officers, such as the president, vice-presidents, the secretary, and the treasurer, are employees of the corporation. Their salaries are taxable the same as the wages paid to other employees. If, however, the corporation officers perform no services as such and receive no remuneration in any form, they are not considered employees of the corporation. Also, the definition of employee excludes a director of a corporation who performs no services other than attending and participating in meetings of the board of directors.

Partnerships.

Partners generally are not employees of the partnership or of the other partners with regard to the business of the partnership. In some cases, however, a partnership may operate as an association that may be classified as a corporation. In such situations, any partner who renders services similar to those of corporate officers would be an employee.

Occupations Specifically Covered by FICA.

The law also provides FICA coverage for the following four occupations:

1. Agent-drivers and commission-drivers who distribute food and beverage products, or handle laundry or dry cleaning.
2. Full-time life insurance salespersons.
3. Full-time traveling or city salespersons.
4. Homeworkers who receive at least $100 in cash by one employer in a calendar year. *Homeworkers* are persons who perform services for another, generally on a contract or piecework basis, and usually in their homes or in the home of another.

However, such persons are not covered by FICA if they have a substantial interest in the facilities used in connection with their jobs, or if the services consist of a single transaction.

Independent Contractors.

Independent contractors are persons who follow an independent trade, business, or profession in which they offer their services to the public. Examples of independent contractors are physicians, lawyers, public accountants, consultants, advertising agencies, and data service centers. According the Small Business Administration, there are nearly 5 million workers classified as independent contractors who are hired each year by 31% of all employers.[1]

Workers are generally classified as independent contractors if they meet the test listed in Illustration 3-2. Persons properly identified as independent contractors

---

[1]Virginia M. Gibson, "Unraveling the Mystery of Independent Contractors," *HR Focus* (May 1992): 23.

are *not* considered employees and thus not subject to the employer's payroll taxes. If the IRS determines that an employer has misclassified a worker as an independent contractor, the employer faces substantial fines and penalties.

NEWS ALERT NEWS ALERT NEWS ALERT

The IRS has decided that a temporary employment agency hiring out legal secretaries was the employer of those workers for FICA, FUTA, and federal income tax withholding purposes. The workers were not, as the agency claimed, independent contractors. [PLR 9311001]

Government Employees

For many years, employees of the federal, state, and local governments were excluded from FICA coverage. However, as noted below, most government employees are now covered by FICA.

Federal Government.
All federal government employees hired on or after April 1, 1986, are covered under FICA. Before that date, coverage was extended only to specific groups of federal workers, as we briefly indicate below.

In 1983, all federal employees became subject to the *hospital insurance (HI)* portion of the FICA tax, with the exception of medical interns, student nurses, inmates of U.S. penal institutions, and those serving temporarily in case of fire, storm, earthquake, flood, and similar emergency.

Certain federal employees became subject to both OASDI and HI taxes on or after January 1, 1984. As of

---

TEST FOR INDEPENDENT CONTRACTOR STATUS

Workers *may* be classified as independent contractors if they:

1. Hire, supervise, and pay assistants.
2. Determine the sequence of their work.
3. Set their own hours of work.
4. Work for as many employers as they wish.
5. Are paid by the job.
6. Make their services available to the public.
7. Have an opportunity for profit or loss.
8. Furnish their own tools.
9. Have a substantial investment in their trade.
10. May be dismissed only under the terms of a contract.

Illustration 3-2. The Test for Independent Contractor Status

---

that date, these groups included (1) all newly hired employees; (2) employees of the legislative branch and those not covered by the civil service retirement system; (3) members of Congress, the President, and the Vice President; and (4) sitting federal judges and political appointees at the executive level and in senior executive service. Still remaining exempt from both OASDI and HI taxes are those workers listed above as exempt from the HI portion of the FICA tax.

State and Local Governments.
The wages of state and local government employees hired after March 31, 1986, became subject *only* to the HI portion of the FICA tax. However, beginning July 1, 1991, full OASDHI coverage was extended to all state and local government employees who were not currently covered by a public employee retirement program.

Government Payments and Employer Payments.
Members of the uniformed services on active duty are covered by OASDHI, with their contributions and benefits computed on their *basic* pay. However, amounts paid in excess of their basic pay (such as for sea or foreign duty, hazardous duty, etc.) are *not* subject to FICA.

Some employers pay their workers the difference between the workers' salaries and the amounts they receive from the federal or state government while on duty with the armed forces or the state National Guard. If the worker is *temporarily* serving with the state National Guard, the payments are treated as wages and thus are subject to FICA. If, however, the employment relationship is terminated, as when the employee enlists or is drafted into the U.S. Armed Forces or is called to active duty in the state National Guard, the payments are *not* considered wages for employment.

Exempt Employees

Employees of not-for-profit organizations became subject to FICA taxes on January 1, 1984. However, some services, such as those performed by duly ordained ministers of churches, remain exempt from FICA taxes. Ministers, certain members of religious orders, and Christian Science practitioners who had previously elected to be exempt from social security coverage may now be covered by filing a waiver form with the IRS. Once an election to be covered by social security is made, it is irrevocable.

Employer

Every person is an *employer* if the person employs one or more individuals for the performance of services in the United States, unless such services or employment are specifically excepted by the law. The term *person* as defined in the law means an individual, a trust or estate, a partnership, or a corporation.

Employment

The term *employment* means any service performed by employees for their employer, regardless of the citizenship or residence of either. Most types of employment are covered under FICA, but we do find specific exclusions. Some types of employment are wholly exempt from coverage; others are exempt only if the cash wages received are less than a stipulated dollar amount. Among the kinds of employment *excluded* are:

1. *Agricultural services* when the remuneration paid *all* farm workers is less than $2,500 in any calendar year. Employers who do not meet the $2,500 annual payroll test may exclude remuneration for agricultural services when it amounts to less than $150 paid *each* worker in a calendar year. Payment for farm work with remuneration other than cash is not taxed.
2. *Domestic service* performed in a local college club, or local chapter of a college fraternity or sorority, or service performed in the employ of a school, college, or university by a *student* who is *enrolled* and *regularly attending classes* at the school, college, or university.
3. *Domestic service* in a private home (cooks, waiters, butlers, maids, babysitters, gardeners, etc.) if performed for *cash* remuneration of less than $50 a calendar quarter.
4. *Service performed by children under the age of 18* in the employ of their father or mother. This "under 18" exclusion applies to children employed by a father or a mother whose business is a sole proprietorship or by parents whose husband-wife business is organized as a partnership. However, the exclusion does *not* apply to children under age 18 who are employed by a family-owned corporation.
5. *Services performed by civilians for the United States government* or any of its instrumentalities (agencies) if such agencies are *specifically* exempt from the employer portion of the FICA tax, or if such services are covered by a retirement system established by law.
6. *Service performed by railroad workers* for employers covered by the Railroad Retirement Tax Act.
7. *Services performed in the employment of foreign governments,* such as ambassadors, ministers, and other diplomatic officers and employees.

8. *Services performed by student nurses* in the employ of a hospital or a nurses' training school if the nurses are *enrolled* and *regularly attending classes* in that school, which must be chartered or approved under state law. Note that the pay received by student nurses is *not* exempt from FICA taxes *unless* the pay is nominal and the nurses' work is part-time and an integral part of the curriculum.
9. *Service performed by an individual under the age of 18* in the delivery or distribution of newspapers or shopping news, not including delivery or distribution to any point for subsequent delivery or distribution.

If an employee's services performed during one-half or more of any period constitute covered employment, then all the employee's services for that pay period must be counted as covered employment. On the other hand, if the employee's services during more than one-half of a pay period do not constitute covered employment, then none of the services for that pay period are counted as covered employment. A pay period cannot exceed 31 consecutive days.

Voluntary Coverage

Coverage under FICA can be extended to certain classes of services that otherwise would be excluded. For example, prior to March 31, 1986, service in the employ of a state or local government had been exempt from the OASDI as well as the HI portion of the FICA tax. However, these state and local government employees are now subject to the HI portion of the tax. Coverage for the OASDI portion can also be extended to state and local government employees by means of a voluntary agreement entered into by the state and the Secretary of Health and Human Services. When a state elects voluntary coverage, it becomes responsible for the collection and payment of the FICA tax as if it were a covered employer.

Taxable Wages

OASDHI taxes are measured by the amount of wages paid by employers to their employees during the calendar year. In most instances the term *wages* includes not only the actual money received by employees but also the cash value of remuneration paid in other forms, such as meals and lodging provided *for the convenience of the employees.* The term *wages* is not the governing factor, since salaries, bonuses, fees, and commissions are all classified as wages if they are paid by an employer with respect to employment covered under the social security laws. Further, it does not matter upon what basis the payment is made. Wages may be paid hourly, daily, weekly, biweekly, semimonthly, monthly, annually, or on the basis of piecework or as a percentage of profits.

Other common types of payments made to workers that are considered wages under FICA are listed below:

1. *Advance payments* for work to be done in the future if the individual who receives the advance does the work or part of it and if the employer considers the work as satisfaction for the advance.
2. *Cash and noncash prizes and awards* made for doing outstanding work, for exceeding sales quotas, or for contributing suggestions that increase productivity or efficiency.
3. *Back pay awards* (pay received in one period for employment in an earlier period) unless the back pay is a settlement for a failure to employ the workers.
4. *Bonuses* if they are remuneration for services rendered by employees for an employer.
5. *Christmas gifts* unless the gifts are of nominal value such as a turkey or a ham.
6. *Commissions on sales or on insurance premiums* if paid as compensation for services performed.
7. *Death benefits*, or wage payments to an employee's dependents after the employee's death. However, if the payments are in the nature of a gratuity rather than compensation for services, the payments do not constitute wages. Payments made by an employer to an employee's estate or an employee's survivors after the calendar year in which the employee died are excluded from the definition of "wages" and are not taxed. Some employers provide a death-benefit plan for all employees generally or for certain classes of employees under which payments are made to the employee, or on behalf of an employee, or any of the employee's dependents at the time of the employee's death. Such death benefits are excluded from the term "wages" for FICA purposes.
8. *Dismissal pay*—payments made by an employer because of the involuntary separation of an employee from the employer's service.
9. *Guaranteed annual wage payments*, such as contained in union contract agreements whereby an employer guarantees that certain employees will either work during or be paid for each normal workweek in a calendar year.
10. *Idle time or standby payments*—amounts paid workers who are at the beck and call of an employer but who are performing no work.
11. *Jury duty pay*, where the difference between the employee's regular wages and the amount received for jury duty is paid by the employer.
12. *Moving expense reimbursements* unless at time of payment it is reasonable to believe that the employee will be entitled to deduct these moving expenses in determining taxable income for federal income tax purposes. Present tax rules allow individuals, when they are transferred or move closer to work, to deduct (subject to limitations) all direct moving expenses and some indirect costs. (Indirect costs include the cost of house hunting before the move, temporary living expenses at the new location, and the cost of selling an old residence and buying a new one.) These same rules apply to the self-employed person who moves to be nearer a new work site. When employer reimbursements exceed the deduction limitations, the employee may have taxable income to report.
13. *Retroactive wage increases.*
14. *Stock payments* made by the employer, who transfers its stock to employees as remuneration for services. The transfers are taxed at the fair market value of the stock at the time of payment.
15. *Vacation pay.*
16. *Employees' federal income and social security taxes paid for by the employer.* However, payment of the employee portion of the FICA tax by the employer for domestics working in the employer's home and for agricultural laborers is an exception to this rule.
17. *The first six months of sick pay* paid employees on account of sickness or accident disability. Payments made under a state temporary disability law are also subject to FICA taxes.
18. *Noncash fringe benefits*, such as personal use of company car, use of employer-provided vehicles for commuting (vanpooling), flights on employer-provided airplanes, and free or discounted flights on commercial airlines.
19. *Employer-paid premiums for an employee's group term life insurance coverage* that exceeds $50,000. For retired workers, the cost of their group term life insurance that exceeds $50,000

is also subject to FICA taxes. If the employer elects not to pay the retirees' share of FICA taxes nor to collect the taxes from the retirees, the retired workers must pay the taxes at the time of filing their personal income tax returns on Form 1040.

Tips. Under FICA, cash tips of $20 or more in a calendar month are looked upon as taxable wages. Employees must report their tips in writing to their employers by the 10th of the month following the month in which the tips were received. *Form 4070, Employee's Report of Tips to Employer*, shown in Illustration 3-3, may be used for this purpose. Form 4070 also contains an employee's daily record of tips (not illustrated) which provides workers a form for recording their daily tips conveniently and for retention in their personal files.

If employees receive tips of $20 or more in any month and do not report them to their employer, the employees must complete *Form 4137, Social Security and Medicare Tax on Unreported Tip Income* (not illustrated). On this form, the employees compute the amount of FICA tax due on their unreported tip income. Later, the employees report the amount of FICA tax due when they file their personal income tax returns. Failure to report tips to their employers may subject employees to a penalty of 50% of the FICA tax due on the tips. Therefore, employees should attach a statement to their income tax returns explaining why they did not initially report the tips to their employers. Further, the Tax Court may rule that the nonreporting of tip income constitutes a fraud.

Employers must collect the employee's FICA tax on the tips that each employee reports. The employer deducts the employee's FICA tax from the wages due the employee or from other funds the employee makes available. The employer collects the employee's FICA tax throughout the year until the employee's combined wages and tips total the taxable wage base for that year. Employers are also liable for their share of the FICA tax on any tips that are subject to the employee's FICA tax.

Large food and beverage establishments (those with 11 or more employees and where tipping is customary) are required to allocate to their tipped employees the excess of 8% of the establishments' gross receipts over the tips reported by their employees. However, employers withhold FICA taxes *only* from the tips reported by employees, not from the tips that are merely allocated. The amount of allocated tip income appears as a separate entry on the employee's *Wage and Tax Statement (Form W-2)*, as explained in Unit 4.

Professional Tip

Employers and employees of large food or beverage establishments where the tips average less than 8% of the gross receipts may petition the IRS to reduce the tip allocation. The tip allocation may be set as low as 2%. The IRS Revenue Procedure that provides the guidelines for petitioning states that more than one-half of the directly tipped employees must consent to the petition.

Every large food or beverage establishment must report annually to the IRS the amount of its receipts from food or beverage operations and the amount of tips reported by its employees. In some cases, as noted before, the establishment is required to allocate amounts as tips to its employees. *Form 8027, Employer's Annual Information Return of Tip Income and Allocated Tips*, (not illustrated) is used. Detailed instructions for calculating the amount of allocated tips accompany this form.

Form **4070**	**Employee's Report of Tips to Employer**	
Department of the Treasury Internal Revenue Service	▶ For Paperwork Reduction Act Notice, see back of this form.	OMB No. 1545-0065

Employee's name and address	Social security number
Morton O. Tanenbaum 1704 Elm St., San Diego, CA 92121-8837	269 : 21 : 7220

Employer's name and address (include establishment name, if different.)
Holland House Inn 9 Fairway, San Diego, CA 92123-1369

Month or shorter period in which tips were received	Tips
from July 1, 19--, to July 31, 19--	$389.10
Signature *Morton O. Tanenbaum*	Date August 10, 19--

Illustration 3-3. Form 4070, Employee's Report of Tips to Employer

Tax Savings for the Employer and the Employee. The payroll manager must be careful to apply the FICA tax only to those kinds of compensation that are regarded as taxable wages for social security purposes. Otherwise, both the company and the employee suffer when the tax is applied to exempt payments. Several examples of compensation that are *excluded* from the definition of wages for FICA tax purposes are described below.

Meals and Lodging.

The value of meals or lodging furnished employees *for the convenience of the employer* is not wages for FICA purposes. If the meals and lodging do not meet the convenience-of-employer test, their value will be wages subject to FICA taxes.

The IRS has placed no specific value on meals or lodging furnished by employers to employees. Instead, the IRS relies on state valuations. Where a state has no law or regulation on the subject, fair value is defined as the reasonable prevailing value of the meals or lodging. In determining this value, some of the factors used are: (a) the value employers charge in their accounting records for meals or lodging, (b) any agreement between employer and employees as to the value, and (c) the specific type of meal or lodging provided.

Sick Pay.

Sick pay is defined as any payment made to individuals, because of their personal injury or sickness, that does not constitute wages. The sick pay payments must be part of a plan to which the employer is a party. Further, sick pay must be paid for a period during which employees are *temporarily* absent from work because of injury or sickness. Sick pay does not include amounts paid under a plan if paid to individuals who are *permanently* disabled. As indicated earlier, the first six months of sick pay that employees receive are considered wages and thus are subject to withholding for FICA tax purposes. The period off the job must be continuous for six months. A relapse after a return to work starts a new six-month period. Payments made after the expiration of six calendar months following the last month in which the employee worked for the employer are not taxed.

Sick-pay payments may be made by a third party rather than by the employer. Typically, the third party is an insurance company. However, third parties also include trusts that provide incidental sick and accident benefits, and employers' associations funded to pay sickness and accident benefits. When sickness and accident benefits are paid by a third party, the third party is treated as a separate employer and is required to withhold and deposit the FICA taxes. However, the third party may be relieved of the liability for the employer's share of the FICA taxes. Thus, the employer may be charged with the liability for paying the employer portion of the FICA taxes if the third party fulfills each of these requirements:

1. Withholds the employee portion of the FICA tax.
2. Deposits the employee portion of the FICA tax.
3. Notifies the employer of the amount of wages or compensation involved.

For administrative convenience, an employer may contract with the third party to have it deposit the employer portion of the tax as well as the employee portion.

Generally payments made to employees or their dependents for medical or hospital expenses in connection with sickness or accident disability are not considered wages. However, these payments must be part of a system or a plan established by the employer for all employees or for a particular class of employees.

Simplified Employee Pension (SEP) Plans.

Employers are permitted to contribute to individual retirement accounts and annuities that have been set up by or on behalf of employees. As indicated in Unit 1, such contribution arrangements are called *simplified employee pension (SEP) plans*. Employer contributions to SEP plans are *exempt* from FICA taxes if there is reason to believe that employees will be entitled to deduct the employer contributions for federal income tax purposes.

Payments for Educational Assistance.

Educational assistance refers to the expenses that an employer pays for an employee's education, such as tuition, fees, and payments for books, supplies, and equipment. Also, educational assistance includes the cost of employer-provided courses of instruction (books, supplies, and equipment). Educational assistance *does not* include payment for tools or supplies that are kept by employees after they complete a course of instruction. Also, not included is any payment for courses or other education involving sports, games, or hobbies. The benefits received by employees under their employer's educational assistance plan are not includible in an employee's gross income. Further, these benefits are specifically excluded from "wages," as defined by FICA.

The Internal Revenue Code specifies that an employer's *nondiscriminatory educational assistance plan* must be in writing and designed for the exclusive purpose of providing employees with educational assistance. Further, the plan must not discriminate in favor of company officers, shareholders, owners, or highly compensated employees. The exclusion for employer-paid educational assistance does not apply to courses on sports, gardening, photography, etc.

Often employees take educational courses to improve their job skills or to meet the requirements for retaining their current jobs. If the employer pays the tuition costs to, or on behalf of, employees for such courses, the reimbursements are ordinary business expenses of the employer and thus are *not* subject to FICA taxes.

Up to July 1, 1992, the maximum amount of educational assistance benefits an employee could receive, free of FICA taxes during the year, was limited to $5,250. Any benefits in excess of this amount were subject to FICA taxes.

NEWS ALERT NEWS ALERT NEWS ALERT

The exclusion of benefits paid under an employer's nondiscriminatory educational assistance plan expired June 30, 1992. However, the tax bill of 1993 provided that the exclusion would be extended through 1994.

In their annual income tax reporting, employers may deduct the educational assistance payments as business expenses, and employees may exclude the amounts from their gross income. If, however, the plan does not meet the requirements of the Code, the educational assistance payments must ordinarily be treated as wages subject to withholding for FICA tax purposes.

Taxable Wage Bases

The *taxable wage base* is the maximum amount of wages during a calendar year that is subject to the OASDI and the HI taxes. At the time of this writing, it was estimated by the Social Security Board of Trustees that the taxable OASDI wage base for 1994 would be $59,700. The tax bill of 1993 repealed the taxable wage base provisions on the HI portion of the FICA tax. Thus, commencing in 1994, with no lid on the HI taxable wage base, the HI tax applies to the *total wages and salaries paid during the year*.

The actual OASDI taxable wage base is not released until October or November each year. For future years, the Social Security Board's estimates of the OASDI taxable wage base are given in Illustration 3-4.

Once the OASDI taxable wage base has been reached, all payments made to the employee during the remainder of the year, even though they are clearly wages, cease to be *taxable* wages. Thus, the collection of the OASDI taxes from that employee is no longer required. The wage base applies to amounts *paid* employees in a calendar year and not to the time when the services were performed by the employees.

Year	OASDI
1995	$61,800
1996	64,500
1997	67,500
1998	70,200

Illustration 3-4. Estimated Taxable Wage Bases for OASDI

EXAMPLE:

Renee Riley is paid on January 6, 1995, for work done during the last week of December, 1994. The wages would be taxed as income in the calendar year 1995, using 1995 tax rates.

The OASDI taxable wage base is subject to *escalator* increases whereby it is automatically adjusted whenever a *cost-of-living adjustment (COLA)* in social security benefits becomes available. The amount of the social security COLA each year is based on the growth from year to year in average annual wages in *all* employment.

Tax Rates

Under the Social Security Act as amended, a separate tax is imposed on employers and employees for old-age, survivors, and disability insurance (OASDI) benefits, and for hospital insurance (HI) benefits. The 1994 OASDI tax rate is 6.2% for both the employer and the employee portions of the tax. The HI tax rate is 1.45% for both the employer and the employee portions. No further tax rate increases are scheduled for OASDI or HI.

Employees' FICA (OASDHI) Taxes and Withholdings

Under FICA, employers are required to collect the OASDHI taxes from their employees and pay the taxes to the IRS at the same time they pay their own tax. The employee's portion of each tax is collected by deducting it from the wages at the time of payment. The amount of each tax to be withheld is computed by applying to the employee's taxable wages the tax rate in effect at the time that the wages are received.

Employees are liable for the tax only until the employer has collected it from them. In other words, the liability for the tax extends to both the employee and the employer; but after the employer has collected the tax, the employee's liability ceases.

The following examples illustrate the computation of the FICA taxes to be withheld.

EXAMPLES:

1. **Virgil Hooper, who is employed by the Gobel Company, earned $460 during the week ended February 4, 1994. He is paid for these earnings on February 11. Prior to this pay his cumulative gross earnings for the year were $2,765.70. The computation of the FICA taxes to be withheld is:**

OASDI

Taxable Wages	$ 460
Tax Rate	x 6.2%
OASDI Tax to be Withheld	$28.52

HI

Taxable Wages	$ 460
Tax Rate	x 1.45%
HI Tax to be Withheld	$ 6.67

2. **Anne Fergo is a salaried employee of the Lafayette Advertising Agency, and she is paid $1,410 every Friday. Prior to the pay of October 28, 1994 (the 43d pay of the year), she had earned $59,220. The FICA taxes to be withheld from Fergo's pay on October 28 are calculated as follows:**

OASDI

Taxable Wage Limit	$59,700
Wages Paid to Date	59,220
Taxable Wages This Pay	$ 480
Tax Rate	x 6.2%
OASDI Tax to be Withheld	$ 29.76

HI

Taxable Wage Limit	NONE
Wages Paid to Date	$59,220
Taxable Wages This Pay	1,410
Tax Rate	x 1.45%
HI Tax to be Withheld	$ 20.45

3. **Marc Todd, president of Uni-Sight, Inc., is paid $5,885 semimonthly. Prior to his last pay on December 30, 1994, Todd had earned $135,355. The FICA taxes to be withheld from Todd's pay on December 30 are calculated as follows:**

OASDI

Taxable Wage Limit	$ 59,700
Wages Paid to Date	135,355
Taxable Wages This Pay	-0-
OASDI Tax to be Withheld	-0-

HI

Taxable Wage Limit	NONE
Wages Paid to Date	$135,355
Taxable Wages This Pay	5,885
Tax Rate	x 1.45%
HI Tax to be Withheld	$ 85.33

In calculating the taxes, you may disregard any fractional part of a cent that results from applying the tax rate to the employee's taxable wages if it is less than half a cent. If the fractional part amounts to one-half cent or more, increase the amount of FICA tax withheld to the next whole cent.

Sometimes we find that an employee has paid FICA taxes on wages in excess of the taxable base because of having worked for more than one employer. If so, the employee is entitled to a refund for the overpayment. The amount of the overpayment is credited against the employee's federal income taxes for that year. Instructions are given on the *Individual Income Tax Return (Form 1040)* that explain how the overpayment should be treated.

Through error an employer may withhold too much FICA tax from employees' earnings and turn the money over to the IRS. In such a case the employer should repay the amount to the employees and make an adjustment on the quarterly tax return, as explained later in this unit.

Employer's FICA (OASDHI) Taxes

In addition to withholding the correct amount of FICA tax from the employees' taxable earnings, the employer must make contributions to the program. The employer's portion of the tax is based on the wages paid to the employees. The OASDI tax is 6.2% of each employee's wages paid; the HI tax is 1.45% of each employee's wages paid. However, as with employee withholdings, once the OASDI taxable wage base is reached, the employer no longer contributes for that particular employee. The employer's taxes, however, are not computed on the wages paid each employee, but on the total wages paid all employees.

EXAMPLE:

The LeFevre Company has 100 employees, each earning $375.25 a week.

OASDI

The amount of OASDI tax withheld from each employee's paycheck each week is $23.27 (6.2% x $375.25). The total tax withheld from the 100 employees' wages is $2,327.00. The tax on the employer is 6.2% of the total payroll for the week, or $2,326.55 (6.2% x $37,525).

HI

The amount of HI tax withheld from each employee's paycheck each week is $5.44 (1.45% x $375.25). The total tax withheld from the 100 employees' wages is $544. The tax on the employer is 1.45% of the total payroll for the week, or $544.11 (1.45% x $37,525).

SELF-EMPLOYED PERSONS—THEIR INCOME AND TAXES

Coverage under the social security system was extended to the self-employed in 1951 under the *Self-Employment Contributions Act (SECA)*. Over the years we find that most self-employed persons have become covered by the law.

Self-Employment Income

An individual's self-employment income is the basis for levying taxes under SECA, and for determining the amount of income that may be credited toward old-age, survivors, and disability insurance benefits or hospital insurance coverage. *Self-employment income* generally consists of the net earnings derived by individuals from a business or profession carried on by them as sole proprietors or by a partnership of which they are members.

We determine net earnings from self-employment by finding the sum of the following:

1. The gross income derived by an individual from any business or profession carried on, less allowable deductions attributable to such business or profession, and
2. The individual's distributive share (whether or not distributed) of the ordinary net income or loss from any business or profession carried on by a partnership of which the individual is a member.

Ordinarily the net business income of individuals as shown in their income tax returns constitutes their net earnings from self-employment for the purpose of the Social Security Act. Earnings of less than $400 from self-employment are ignored. For calculating the OASDI taxes, the maximum self-employment taxable income of any individual for 1994 is $59,700. For calculating the HI taxes, however, there is no lid on the self-employment taxable income. If any wages are received, we reduce the maximum amount of taxable self-employment income by the amount of such wages.

EXAMPLE:

Elizabeth Brown receives a salary of $60,000 in 1994. In calculating her OASDI taxes, any earnings derived from self-employment do not constitute taxable self-employment income. However, in calculating her HI taxes, all of her earnings from self-employment are taxed.

If the wages received in 1994 amount to less than $59,700, any self-employment earnings amounting to $400 or more must be counted as self-employment income up to an aggregate amount of $59,700 for OASDI taxes.

EXAMPLE:

Paul Bixby receives wages in 1994 amounting to $46,300. His net earnings from self-employment amount to $14,600. Therefore, Bixby must count $13,400 ($13,400 + $46,300 = $59,700) of his earnings in determining taxable self-employment income for OASDI taxes. All of his earnings represent taxable self-employment income for HI taxes.

Taxable Year

In computing the taxes on self-employment income, the taxable year is the same as that used for income tax purposes. In the case of a partnership, the taxable year of the partners may not correspond with that of the partnership. In such instances the partners are required to include in computing net earnings from self-employment their distributive share of the income or loss of the partnership for any taxable year ending with or within their taxable year.

Reporting Self-Employment Income

Individuals report their self-employment income by transferring certain data from the *Profit or Loss From Business* schedule of their income tax return, *Schedule C*, Form 1040, to the *Self-Employment Tax* schedule, *Schedule SE*, on the same return.

Self-employed persons are required to include SECA taxes in their quarterly payment of estimated income taxes. The taxpayer's estimated income tax is the sum of the estimated income taxes and SECA taxes less any credits against the tax. Thus, each quarter the self-employed person is currently paying SECA taxes into the social security and Medicare funds.

Self-Employment OASDHI Taxes

The 1994 social security tax rates for self-employed persons are: OASDI—12.4% and HI—2.9%. However, self-employed persons are able to reduce their taxable self-employment income in order to lessen the impact of the higher tax rates. This deduction is calculated according to the instructions that accompany Form 1040 and Schedule SE.

APPLICATION FOR EMPLOYER IDENTIFICATION NUMBER (FORM SS-4)

Every employer of one or more persons is required to file an application for an identification number (Form SS-4). A filled-in copy of Form SS-4 is shown in Illustration 3-5 on page 80. The application form is available from any IRS or social security office.

An employer should file Form SS-4 early enough to allow for its processing, preferably four weeks before the number will be needed. The application must be filed with the IRS center where the federal tax returns are filed. (See page 91.) If the employer has no legal residence, or principal place of business, or principal office in any IRS district, the application should be filed with the IRS Service Center, Philadelphia, PA 19255.

An employer may not have received an identification number prior to the time the required returns are to be filed. In such a case, the employer should write "Applied for" and the date of the application in the space shown on the return for the identification number. Each employer receives but one identification number regardless of how many different establishments, offices, stores, factories, warehouses, or branches may be maintained or operated. If a business is sold or otherwise transferred and the new owner does not have an identification number, the number assigned to the former owner cannot be used. The new owner must file an application for a new identification number.

The employer must enter the identification number on all returns, forms, and correspondence relating to the taxes imposed under FICA that are sent to the District Director of Internal Revenue. The identification number should be used in any correspondence with the Social Security Administration (SSA) and should be entered on forms that are issued by the SSA. The penalty for failure to supply identification numbers is discussed later in this unit.

EMPLOYEE'S APPLICATION FOR A SOCIAL SECURITY CARD (FORM SS-5)

Under the Social Security Act every employee and every self-employed person must have an account number. The application for an account number is available at any social security or IRS office. The *Application for a Social Security Card (Form SS-5)* can be filed with any field office of the SSA. A filled-in copy of Form SS-5 is shown in Illustration 3-6 on page 81.

The application for an employee's social security card should be made far enough in advance of its first required use to allow for the processing of the application. The Social Security Act requires applicants for an account number card to furnish evidence of their age, identity, and U.S. citizenship or lawful alien status. Applicants may apply either by mailing the required documents and forms to their nearest Social Security office or by bringing them in person. However, individuals must apply *in person* at their Social Security office if they are age 18 or older and have never had a Social Security number card, or if they are aliens whose immigration documents should not be sent through the mail.

After filing Form SS-5, the employee will receive from the SSA a card showing the social security account number that has been assigned. See Illustration 3-7 on page 82.

Upon receipt of their account numbers, employees should advise their employers of the number assigned them. Care should be taken to see that employers are advised of the correct number. Should employees change positions, they must notify the new employer of their account number as soon as they commence employment. Should an employee change his or her name by court order or by marriage, the individual should request a new social security card by completing Form SS-5. Employees may have their account number changed at any time by applying to the SSA and showing good reasons for a change. Otherwise, only one account number is assigned to an employee and the employee will continue to use that number regardless of the number of changes in positions or the number of employers for whom service is rendered.

The Secretary of Health and Human Services is authorized to assure that social security numbers are issued to or on behalf of children who are below school age at the request of their parents or guardians and to children of school age when they first enroll in school. Further, Social Security account numbers must be obtained for children age one or over who are claimed as dependents on federal income tax returns. To thwart cheaters who claim dogs, cats, and nonexistent people as dependents, taxpayers are required to

Form **SS-4**	**Application for Employer Identification Number**	EIN
Department of the Treasury Internal Revenue Service	(For use by employers and others. Please read the attached instructions before completing this form.)	OMB No. 1545-0003

Please type or print clearly.

1 Name of applicant (True legal name) (See instructions.)
Montana Mining, Inc.

2 Trade name of business, if different from name in line 1

3 Executor, trustee, "care of" name
Care of Carla P. Ortiz

4a Mailing address (street address) (room, apt., or suite no.)
P.O. Box 447

5a Address of business (See instructions.)
1200 High Gap

4b City, state, and ZIP code
Butte, MT 59701-0210

5b City, state, and ZIP code
Butte, MT 59701-1200

6 County and state where principal business is located
Silver Bow, MT

7 Name of principal officer, grantor, or general partner (See instructions.) ▶ Grant X. Bilton, President

8a Type of entity (Check only one box.) (See instructions.)
☐ Individual SSN _____
☐ REMIC   ☐ Personal service corp.
☐ State/local government   ☐ National guard
☐ Other nonprofit organization (specify) _____
☐ Other (specify) ▶ _____
☐ Estate
☐ Plan administrator SSN _____
☒ Other corporation (specify) Extraction
☐ Federal government/military   ☐ Church or church controlled organization
If nonprofit organization enter GEN (if applicable) _____
☐ Trust
☐ Partnership
☐ Farmers' cooperative

8b If a corporation, give name of foreign country (if applicable) or state in the U.S. where incorporated ▶
Foreign country
State
Montana

9 Reason for applying (Check only one box.)
☒ Started new business
☐ Hired employees
☐ Created a pension plan (specify type) ▶ _____
☐ Banking purpose (specify) ▶ _____
☐ Changed type of organization (specify) ▶ _____
☐ Purchased going business
☐ Created a trust (specify) ▶ _____
☐ Other (specify) ▶ _____

10 Date business started or acquired (Mo., day, year) (See instructions.)
July 3, 19--

11 Enter closing month of accounting year. (See instructions.)
June

12 First date wages or annuities were paid or will be paid (Mo., day, year). Note: If applicant is a withholding agent, enter date income will first be paid to nonresident alien. (Mo., day, year) · · · · · · · · · · · · ▶ July 12, 19--

13 Enter highest number of employees expected in the next 12 months. Note: If the applicant does not expect to have any employees during the period, enter "0." · · · · · · · ▶

Nonagricultural	Agricultural	Household
450		

14 Principal activity (See instructions.) ▶ Copper Extraction

15 Is the principal business activity manufacturing? · · · · · · · · · · · · · · · · · · · ☐ Yes ☒ No
If "Yes," principal product and raw material used ▶

16 To whom are most of the products or services sold? Please check the appropriate box.
☐ Public (retail)   ☐ Other (specify) ▶   ☒ Business (wholesale)   ☐ N/A

17a Has the applicant ever applied for an identification number for this or any other business? · · · · · · · · · ☐ Yes ☒ No
Note: If "Yes," please complete lines 17b and 17c.

17b If you checked the "Yes" box in line 17a, give applicant's true name and trade name, if different than name shown on prior application.

True name ▶   Trade name ▶

17c Enter approximate date, city, and state where the application was filed and the previous employer identification number if known.

Approximate date when filed (Mo., day, year)	City and state where filed	Previous EIN

Under penalties of perjury, I declare that I have examined this application, and to the best of my knowledge and belief, it is true, correct, and complete.

Telephone number (include area code)

Name and title (Please type or print clearly.) ▶ Carla P. Ortiz, V.P., Finance

406-555-2400

Signature ▶ *Carla P. Ortiz*   Date ▶ 7/3/--

Note: Do not write below this line.   For official use only.

Please leave blank ▶	Geo.	Ind.	Class	Size	Reason for applying

Form **SS-4**

Illustration 3-5. Form SS-4, Application for Employer Identification Number

SOCIAL SECURITY ADMINISTRATION
Application for a Social Security Card

Form Approved
OMB No. 0960-0066

INSTRUCTIONS

- Please read "How To Complete This Form" on page 2.
- Print or type using black or blue ink. DO NOT USE PENCIL.
- After you complete this form, take or mail it along with the required documents to your nearest Social Security office.
- If you are completing this form for someone else, answer the questions as they apply to that person. Then, sign your name in question 16.

1 NAME
To Be Shown On Card
▶ Bertha   Mary   Davis
FIRST   FULL MIDDLE NAME   LAST

FULL NAME AT BIRTH IF OTHER THAN ABOVE
FIRST   FULL MIDDLE NAME   LAST

OTHER NAMES USED

2 MAILING ADDRESS
Do Not Abbreviate
▶ 18 Dundee Avenue
STREET ADDRESS, APT. NO., PO BOX, RURAL ROUTE NO.
Akron   Ohio   44320-2968
CITY   STATE   ZIP CODE

3 CITIZENSHIP
(Check One)
[X] U.S. Citizen   [ ] Legal Alien Allowed To Work   [ ] Legal Alien Not Allowed To Work   [ ] Foreign Student Allowed Restricted Employment   [ ] Conditionally Legalized Alien Allowed To Work   [ ] Other (See Instructions On Page 2)

4 SEX
[ ] Male   [X] Female

5 RACE/ETHNIC DESCRIPTION
(Check One Only—Voluntary)
[ ] Asian, Asian-American Or Pacific Islander   [ ] Hispanic   [X] Black (Not Hispanic)   [ ] North American Indian Or Alaskan Native   [ ] White (Not Hispanic)

6 DATE OF BIRTH   8   1   76
MONTH DAY YEAR

7 PLACE OF BIRTH
(Do Not Abbreviate)   Lima   Ohio
CITY   STATE OR FOREIGN COUNTRY   FCI

Office Use Only

8 MOTHER'S MAIDEN NAME
Ruth   Ann   Archer
FIRST   FULL MIDDLE NAME   LAST NAME AT HER BIRTH

9 FATHER'S NAME
Roger   Paul   Davis
FIRST   FULL MIDDLE NAME   LAST

10 Has the person in item 1 ever applied for or received a Social Security number before?
[ ] Yes (If "yes", answer questions 11-13.)   [X] No (If "no", go on to question 14.)   [ ] Don't Know (If "don't know", go on to question 14.)

11 Enter the Social Security number previously assigned to the person listed in item 1.
□□□ – □□ – □□□□

12 Enter the name shown on the most recent Social Security card issued for the person listed in item 1.
FIRST   MIDDLE   LAST

13 Enter any different date of birth if used on an earlier application for a card.
MONTH   DAY   YEAR

14 TODAY'S DATE ▶ 1   12   --
MONTH DAY YEAR

15 DAYTIME PHONE NUMBER ▶ (419) 555-4321
AREA CODE

DELIBERATELY FURNISHING (OR CAUSING TO BE FURNISHED) FALSE INFORMATION ON THIS APPLICATION IS A CRIME PUNISHABLE BY FINE OR IMPRISONMENT, OR BOTH.

16 YOUR SIGNATURE
▶ *Bertha M. Davis*

17 YOUR RELATIONSHIP TO THE PERSON IN ITEM 1 IS:
[X] Self   [ ] Natural Or Adoptive Parent   [ ] Legal Guardian   [ ] Other (Specify)

DO NOT WRITE BELOW THIS LINE (FOR SSA USE ONLY)

NPN		DOC	NTI	CAN		ITV
PBC	EVI	EVA	EVC	NWR	DNR	UNIT

EVIDENCE SUBMITTED

SIGNATURE AND TITLE OF EMPLOYEE(S) REVIEWING EVIDENCE AND/OR CONDUCTING INTERVIEW

DATE

DCL   DATE

Form SS-5

Illustration 3-6. Form SS-5, Application for a Social Security Card

Illustration 3-7. Social Security Card

list the taxpayer identification numbers of any claimed dependents age one or over. The Secretary also insures that social security numbers are assigned to aliens when they are admitted to the United States under conditions that permit them to work.

Criminal penalties are provided (a) if one knowingly and willfully uses a social security number that was obtained with false information; (b) if one uses someone else's social security number; (c) if a person knowingly alters a social security card; buys or sells a card that is, or purports to be, a card issued by the Secretary; counterfeits a social security card; or possesses a social security card or counterfeit social security card with the intent to sell or alter it. The penalty involves a fine of up to $5,000 or imprisonment of up to 5 years, or both.

NEWS ALERT NEWS ALERT NEWS ALERT

Employers may verify employees' social security numbers through the SSA's Enumeration Verification System (EVS). To use the system, you must use round tapes, 3480 cartridges, or paper; and there is a limit of 300 employees per paper submission. For further information, call the EVS service at 410-965-7140.

REQUEST FOR EARNINGS AND BENEFIT ESTIMATE STATEMENT (FORM SSA-7004-SM)

Each employee who has received taxable wages under the Social Security Act has an account with the SSA. This account shows the amount of wages cred-

ited to the employee's account. When employees or members of their family claim benefits, the wage credits in the employees' social security account are used to calculate the amount of benefits payable, as discussed in Appendix A.

The SSA makes it possible for employees to check the accuracy of the wage credits in their accounts. Form SSA-7004-SM (not illustrated) is the official form to use in requesting a statement of wages credited to an individual's account. Copies of this form are available by contacting the district office of the SSA or by calling the toll-free number, 1-800-772-1213.

After filing Form SSA-7004-SM, the worker will receive a statement showing the yearly earnings, the social security taxes paid each year, and a projection of the benefits the worker or the survivors will receive if the worker retires, dies, or is disabled.

Because of errors that employers make in reporting wage information to the SSA and the IRS, from time to time workers should compare their wage records with those of the SSA. As a result of errors, many workers lose credits for the social security taxes they have paid. If workers find any discrepancies between their records and the accounts kept by the SSA, claims can be made for adjustment. Errors will be corrected if they are reported within 3 years, 3 months, and 15 days following the close of any taxable year.

RETURNS REQUIRED UNDER FICA

Employers covered under FICA are liable for their own FICA taxes and for their employees' FICA and income taxes that are withheld from the employees' wages. The withholding of income taxes is discussed in Unit 4. Every employer, except those employing agricultural workers, who is required to withhold income taxes from wages or who is liable for social security taxes must file:

1. A *quarterly* tax and information return. This return shows the total taxable FICA wages paid and the total FICA taxes (employer and employee contributions) and federal income taxes withheld.
2. An *annual* return of withheld federal income taxes. This return covers *nonpayroll* items such as backup withholding and withholding on gambling winnings, pensions, and annuities.
3. An *annual* record of federal tax liability. Certain depositors, discussed later, are required to report on a *daily* basis their liability for backup withholding and income taxes withheld on gambling winnings, pensions, and annuities.

Generally an employer must deposit the income taxes and social security taxes withheld and the employer's FICA taxes in an authorized depositary or a Federal Reserve bank that serves the employer's geographic area. In other instances, as explained later in this section, the employer is not required to deposit the taxes but, instead, may remit them with the quarterly return.

Any employer who fails to pay the withheld income taxes and FICA taxes, or fails to make deposits and payments, or does not file the tax returns as required by law may be required to deposit such taxes in a special trust account for the U.S. government and file monthly tax returns.

The major forms used in preparing FICA tax returns and deposits are listed and briefly described in Illustration 3-8.

Deposit Requirements for Employers of Nonagricultural Workers

The requirements for depositing FICA taxes and income taxes withheld from employees' wages vary according to the amount of such taxes accumulated with respect to wages paid during the deposit period. Depending on the aggregate amount of taxes involved (federal income tax and FICA tax withheld from employees' earnings plus the employer's portion of the FICA tax), employers may have to deposit their taxes several times a month or monthly. Some employers may not have to make any deposits, but, instead, may pay their taxes at the time of filing their quarterly return, Form 941, which is discussed on

Form 941, Employer's Quarterly Federal Tax Return	Required of all covered employers, except employers of household employees and agricultural employees, who withhold income tax and social security taxes. (See Illustration 3-12, page 89.)
Form 941c, Supporting Statement to Correct Information	Used to correct income and social security tax information previously reported on Forms 941, 941E, 941-M, 941SS, or 943.
Form 941-V, Form 941 Payment Voucher	Filled in by employers with a total tax liability of less than $500 for the quarter who are making payment with Form 941.
Form 941-M, Employer's Monthly Federal Tax Return	Required of employers who have not complied with the requirements for filing returns or paying or depositing all taxes reported on quarterly returns. Notification to file Form 941-M is received from the District Director, and preaddressed forms are mailed the employer monthly.
Form 941PR, Employer's Quarterly Federal Tax Return	Required of employers to report social security taxes for workers in Puerto Rico.
Form 941SS, Employer's Quarterly Federal Tax Return	Required of employers to report social security taxes for workers in American Samoa, Guam, the Northern Mariana Islands, and the Virgin Islands.
Form 942, Employer's Quarterly Tax Return for Household Employees	Used by employers of household workers for reporting FICA and income taxes on wages paid.
Form 943, Employer's Annual Tax Return for Agricultural Employees	Used by employers of agricultural workers for reporting FICA and income taxes on wages paid.
Form 8109, Federal Tax Deposit Coupon	Completed at the time of depositing various types of taxes such as withheld income and FICA (Form 941), agricultural withheld income and FICA (Form 943), and federal unemployment (Form 940, as discussed in Unit 5).

Illustration 3-8. Major Forms for Preparing FICA Tax Returns and Deposits

pages 88-92. Most employers, however, are either *monthly* or *semiweekly* depositors.

The amount of employment taxes that the employer reports on the quarterly returns for the four quarters in the lookback period determines if the employer is a monthly or a semiweekly depositor. A *lookback period* consists of four quarters beginning July 1 of the second preceding year and ending June 30 of the prior year. These four quarters are the employer's lookback period even if no taxes were reported for any of the quarters. Illustration 3-9 shows the lookback period for 1994.

Monthly Depositors.
A *monthly depositor* is one who reported employment taxes of *$50,000 or less* for the four quarters in the lookback period. (An employer ceases to be a monthly depositor any day on which the employer becomes subject to the $100,000 one-day rule discussed later. At that time, the employer becomes a semiweekly depositor for at least the remainder of the calendar year and for the following calendar year.)

EXAMPLE:

At the beginning of 1994, Huan Company determined its deposit status using the lookback period shown in Illustration 3-9. During the two quarters of 1992, Huan reported employment taxes of $16,000. For *each* of the two quarters in 1993, the firm reported taxes of $10,000.

Since the taxes reported by Huan during the lookback period do not exceed $50,000, the firm is classed as a monthly depositor. Thus, Huan is subject to the monthly rule for the current year, 1994.

Monthly depositors are required to deposit their taxes in a Federal Reserve bank or an authorized financial institution by the 15th day of the following month. If a deposit is required to be made on a day that is not a banking day, the deposit is considered timely if it is made by the close of the next banking day.

LOOKBACK PERIOD FOR CALENDAR YEAR 1994

Calendar Year 1994

Jan. – Mar.	Apr. – June	July – Sept.	Oct. – Dec.

———— Lookback Period ————

1992		1993	
July – Sept.	Oct. – Dec.	Jan. – Mar.	Apr. – June

Illustration 3-9. Lookback Period for Calendar Year 1994

EXAMPLE:

Valencia, Inc., is a monthly depositor. During April, 1994, Valencia accumulated taxes totaling $11,000. Under the monthly rule, Valencia is required to deposit the $11,000 on or before May 15, 1994. Since May 15 is Sunday, a nonbanking day, Valencia must deposit the taxes by the close of the next banking day, Monday, May 16.

Semiweekly Depositors.
A *semiweekly depositor* is one who reported employment taxes of *more than $50,000* for the four quarters in the lookback period. Depending upon what day of the week the employer makes payments, deposits must be made as follows:

Payment Days	Deposit by
Wednesday, Thursday, and/or Friday	Following Wednesday
Saturday, Sunday, Monday, and/or Tuesday	Following Friday

EXAMPLES:

1. At the beginning of 1994, Meyer Company determined its deposit status by using the lookback period shown in Illustration 3-9. In the two quarters of 1992, Meyer reported taxes of $35,000. The taxes reported in the two quarters of 1993 totaled $30,000. Since the total taxes reported during the four quarters of the lookback period exceeded $50,000, Meyer is subject to the semiweekly rule for the current year, 1994.

2. The employees of DeVeau, a semiweekly depositor, are paid every Monday. On Monday, October 3, 1994, DeVeau accumulated taxes totaling $24,000. DeVeau is required to deposit the $24,000 on or before the following Friday, October 7.

$100,000 One-Day Rule.
If on any day during a deposit period, an employer has accumulated $100,000 or more in employment taxes, the taxes must be deposited by the close of the next banking day. When determining whether the $100,000 threshold is met, a monthly depositor takes into account only those taxes accumulated in the calendar month in which the day occurs. A semiweekly depositor takes into account only those taxes accumulated in the Wednesday-Friday or Saturday-Tuesday semiweekly periods in which the day occurs.

1. On Tuesday, January 18, 1994, Parker Company accumulated $105,000 in employment taxes for wages paid on that day. Regardless of Parker's deposit status, the firm is required to deposit the $105,000 by the next banking day, Wednesday, January 19.

   Note that if Parker was not subject to the semiweekly rule on January 18, 1994, the company would become subject to that rule as of January 19, 1994.

2. The Quincy Company is subject to the semiweekly rule. On Monday, February 7, 1994, Quincy accumulated $120,000 in employment taxes. The firm is required to deposit the $120,000 by the next banking day, Tuesday, February 8. On Tuesday, February 8, Quincy accumulates $30,000 more in employment taxes. Even though Quincy had a previous $120,000 deposit obligation that occurred earlier in the semiweekly period, Quincy now has an additional and separate deposit obligation that must be met by the following Friday, February 11.

Accumulated Employment Taxes Less Than $500 at the End of a Calendar Quarter.

If during a calendar quarter the accumulated employment taxes are less than $500, no deposits are required. The taxes may be paid to the IRS at the time of filing the quarterly return, Form 941, discussed on pages 88–92. However, if the employer wishes, the taxes may be fully deposited by the end of the next month.

The Safe Harbor Rule.

The amount deposited by an employer may be affected by the *safe harbor rule*. Under this rule, an employer is considered to have satisfied the deposit obligations provided:

1. The amount of any shortfall does not exceed the greater of $100 or 2% of the amount of employment taxes required to be deposited.
2. The employer deposits the shortfall on or before the shortfall make-up date.

A *shortfall* is the excess of the amount of employment taxes required to be deposited over the amount deposited on or before the last date prescribed for the deposit. The shortfall make-up rules are as follows:

1. *Monthly depositors:* The shortfall must be deposited or remitted by the due date for the quarterly return, in accordance with the applicable form and instructions.
2. *Semiweekly depositors and those subject to the $100,000 one-day rule:* The shortfall must be deposited on or before the first Wednesday or Friday, whichever is earlier, falling on or after the 15th day of the month following the month in which the deposit was required to be made.

1. On Friday, June 3, 1994, Rogers, Ltd., a semiweekly depositor, pays wages and accumulates employment taxes. Rogers makes a deposit on Wednesday, June 8, in the amount of $4,000. Later, it was determined that Rogers was actually required to deposit $4,080 by Wednesday. Rogers has a shortfall of $80. The shortfall is less than the greater of $100 or 2% of the amount required to be deposited. Therefore, Rogers satisfies the safe harbor rule so long as the $80 shortfall is deposited by July 15.

2. On Friday, November 4, 1994, Stacy Company, a semiweekly depositor, pays wages and accumulates employment taxes. Stacy makes a deposit of $30,000 but later finds that the amount of the deposit should have been $32,000. The $2,000 shortfall ($32,000 – $30,000) exceeds the greater of $100 or 2% of the amount required to be deposited (2% x $32,000 = $640). Thus, the safe harbor rule was not met. As a result, Stacy is subject to a failure-to-deposit penalty, as described later in this unit.

Summary of Deposit Rules.

The deposit rules for nonagricultural employers are summarized in Illustration 3-10.

Accumulated Unpaid Liability	Deposit Requirement
1. $50,000 or less in the lookback period—	1. Monthly taxes must be deposited on or before the 15th of the following month.
2. More than $50,000 in the lookback period—	2. (a) Payday on Wednesday, Thursday, and/or Friday—must be deposited on or before following Wednesday. (b) Payday on Saturday, Sunday, Monday, and/or Tuesday—must be deposited on or before following Friday.
3. $100,000 or more on any day—	3. Must be deposited by the close of the next business day.
4. Less than $500 at end of calendar quarter—	4. Must be paid by end of following month, either as a deposit or with the quarterly tax return (Form 941).

Illustration 3-10. Summary of Deposit Rules for Nonagricultural Employers

Deposit Requirements for Employers of Agricultural Workers

The deposit-making rules that apply to employers of agricultural laborers (farm workers) are similar to those for employers of nonagricultural workers. However, there are exceptions, which are explained in the instructions accompanying *Form 943, Employer's Annual Tax Return for Agricultural Employees.* Employers of agricultural workers, as well as those who employ nonagricultural workers, must use the *Federal Tax Deposit Coupon (Form 8109)*. The procedures to be followed in making deposits and completing Form 8109 are discussed in a later section.

Deposit Requirements for Employers of Household Employees

Household or domestic employees are usually not subject to federal income tax withholding, but they may voluntarily request that federal income taxes be withheld from their wages. Even though federal income taxes are not withheld from household employees' wages, their wages are subject to FICA taxes if each worker has been paid cash wages of $50 or more in a calendar quarter. The value of food, lodging, clothing, car tokens, and other noncash items given to household employees is not subject to FICA taxes. However, cash given in place of these items is considered wages.

Employers who withhold and pay FICA taxes or federal income taxes based on the wages paid domestic workers should follow the instructions that accompany *Form 942, Employer's Quarterly Tax Return for Household Employees.*

Deposit Requirements for State and Local Government Employers

As you saw earlier, provision is made for the coverage of employees of state and local governments by means of voluntary agreement entered into between the state and the Secretary of Health and Human Services. Each state and local government employer covered under a voluntary agreement must file its return on Form 941 with the IRS and deposit its FICA taxes through the federal deposit system, as explained below. State and local government employers are required to make their tax deposits according to the same deposit schedule used by private employers.

Procedures for Making Deposits

Deposits of FICA taxes and employees' federal income taxes withheld are made by using one of the preprinted *Federal Tax Deposit Coupons, Form 8109.* This coupon is used for depositing various types of taxes in a Federal Reserve bank or in an authorized commercial depositary. Employers indicate on the coupon the type of tax being deposited and include a coupon with each deposit. A sample coupon and part of the instructions for its completion are reproduced in Illustration 3-11.[2]

Under a program called *Autogen*—the automatic generation of federal tax deposit (FTD) coupon books—the IRS automatically supplies employers with new coupon books when needed. If the resupply of FTD coupons has not been received, the employer should contact the local IRS office. The FTD coupon books can be sent to a branch office, tax preparer, or service bureau that is making the employer's deposits by showing the appropriate address on the address change form provided in the coupon book.

Employers who make their deposits at a Federal Reserve bank must make them at the Federal Reserve bank that serves their geographic area. Also, they must make payment with an "immediate credit item." An *immediate credit item* is a check or other instrument of payment for which immediate credit is given by the receiving bank in accordance with its check-collection schedule. If a deposit is not made with an immediate credit item, the bank stamps the coupon to reflect the name of the bank and the date on which the proceeds of the accompanying payment instrument are collected by the Federal Reserve bank. This date is used to determine the timeliness of the payment.

Authorized depositaries are required to accept cash, postal money orders drawn to the order of the depositary, or checks and drafts drawn on and to the order of the depositary. Employers may make a tax deposit by means of a check drawn on another financial institution only if the depositary is willing to accept that payment as a deposit of federal taxes.

The timeliness of deposits is determined by the date they are received by the commercial bank depositary or the Federal Reserve bank. However, a deposit received after the due date will be considered timely if the employer establishes that it was mailed at least 2 days before the due date. A tax deposit of $20,000 or more must be at the depositary or the Federal Reserve

---

[2]Form 8109-B, Federal Tax Deposit Coupon, is used by employers *only* if: (1) preprinted deposit coupons, Forms 8109, have been reordered but have not yet been received; or (2) the employer is a new entity and an employer identification number has been assigned but the initial supply of preprinted deposit coupons has not been received.

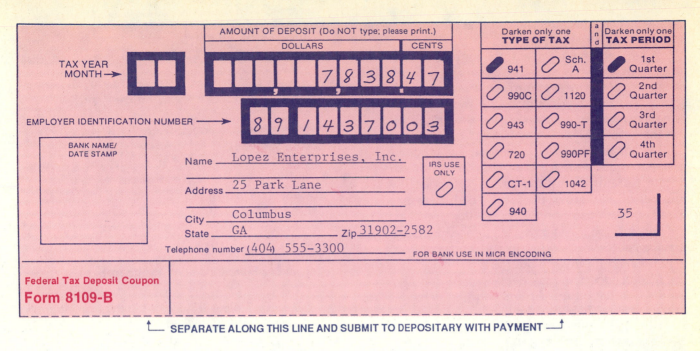

Federal Tax Deposit Coupon
Form 8109-B

↑—— SEPARATE ALONG THIS LINE AND SUBMIT TO DEPOSITARY WITH PAYMENT ——↑

IMPORTANT

Read instructions carefully before completing Form 8109-B, Federal Tax Deposit Coupon.

Note: *Except for the name, address, and telephone number, entries are processed by optical scanning equipment and must be made in pencil. Please use a soft lead (for example, a #2 pencil) so that the entries can be read more accurately by the optical scanning equipment. The name, address, and telephone number may be completed other than by hand. You CANNOT use photocopies of the coupons to make your deposits. DO NOT staple, tape or fold the coupons.*

Paperwork Reduction Act Notice.—We ask for the information on this form to carry out the Internal Revenue laws of the United States. You are required to give us the information. We need it to ensure that you are complying with these laws and to allow us to figure and collect the right amount of tax.

The time needed to complete and file this form will vary depending on individual circumstances. The estimated average time is 3 min. If you have comments concerning the accuracy of this time estimate or suggestions for making this form more simple, we would be happy to hear from you. You can write to both the **Internal Revenue Service,** Washington, DC 20224, Attention: IRS Reports Clearance Officer T:FP; and the **Office of Management and Budget,** Paperwork Reduction Project (1545-0257), Washington, DC 20503. **DO NOT** send this form to either of these offices. Instead, see the instructions on the back of this page for information on how to make deposits.

Purpose of Form.—Use Form 8109-B deposit coupons to make tax deposits **only** in the following two situations:

(1) You have not yet received your resupply of preprinted deposit coupons (Form 8109); or

(2) You are a new entity and have already been assigned an employer identification number (EIN), but have not yet received your initial supply of preprinted deposit coupons (Form 8109).

Note: *If you do not receive your resupply of the deposit coupons and a deposit is due or you do not receive your initial supply within 5-6 weeks of receipt of your EIN, please contact your local IRS office.*

If you have applied for an EIN, have not received it, and a deposit must be made, send your payment to your internal Revenue Service Center. Make your check or money order payable to the Internal Revenue Service and show on it your name (as shown on **Form SS-4,** Application for Employer Identification Number), address, kind of tax, period covered, and date you applied for an EIN. Also attach an explanation to the deposit. Do **NOT** use Form 8109-B in this situation. Do **NOT** use Form 8109-B to deposit delinquent taxes for which you have been assessed by the IRS. Pay those taxes directly to the IRS.

How To Complete the Form.—Enter your name exactly as shown on your return or other IRS correspondence, address, and EIN in the spaces provided on the coupon. If you are required to file a Form 1120, Form 990-C, Form 990-PF (with net investment income), Form 990-T, or Form 2438, enter the month in which your tax year ends in the **TAX YEAR MONTH** boxes. For example, if your tax year ends in January, enter 01; if it ends in June, enter 06; if it ends in December, enter 12. Please make your entries for EIN and tax year month (if applicable) in the manner specified in *Amount of Deposit* below. Darken one box each in the *Type of Tax* and *Tax Period* columns as explained below.

Amount of Deposit.—Enter the amount of the deposit in the space provided. Enter the amount legibly, forming the characters as shown below:

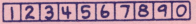

Hand-print money amounts without using dollar signs, commas, a decimal point, or leading zeros. The commas and the decimal point are already shown in the entry area. For example, a deposit of $7,635.22 would be entered like this:

If the deposit is for whole dollars only, enter "00" in the CENTS boxes.

Illustration 3-11. Form 8109-B, Federal Tax Deposit Coupon, and a Portion of the Accompanying Instructions

bank on the due date. The 2-day mail rule does not apply in this situation.

When making a deposit, the employer enters the amount of the payment in the accounting records. The check or money order number is also recorded and serves as a source document for the entry. The employer may make a photocopy of the form if desired, but the canceled check may be used as a receipt. Form 8109 is not returned by the bank to the employer but is used as the basis for crediting the employer's tax account identified by the employer's identification number on the face of the form. The bank stamps the date and bank name on the form where indicated. The tax deposits are then forwarded by the bank to the IRS service center for posting to the taxpayer's account. When each employer's quarterly return is received, the IRS reconciles the tax deposits with the payments claimed on the return. At this point, settlement of the employer's tax liability is made.

NEWS ALERT NEWS ALERT NEWS ALERT

In 1992, the IRS began testing TAXLINK, a new system that would replace tax deposits made via the 8109 deposit coupon with a process that allows employers to make their payments electronically. Depositors in Florida, Georgia, and South Carolina may now participate in a prototype test system in which payments are made via telephone, PC dial-up, or bank-directed initiation. Employers in these states may obtain further information by calling 1-800-829-5469.

EMPLOYER'S QUARTERLY FEDERAL TAX RETURN (FORM 941)

Generally the employer must make a quarterly return of FICA taxes and withheld income taxes for the three months of each calendar quarter, using *Form 941, Employer's Quarterly Federal Tax Return.* A filled-in copy of Form 941 is shown in Illustration 3-12. Once Form 941 has been filed, the employer receives preaddressed forms every three months. If the form is not received, the employer should request one from an IRS office in time to file the return when due.

NOTE: At the time this edition was being prepared, the 1994 Form 941 was not available. Therefore, we are illustrating an advance proof of this form throughout the remainder of the textbook.

NEWS ALERT NEWS ALERT NEWS ALERT

Beginning with the first quarter of 1994, all non-payroll items (backup withholding and withholding from pensions, annuities, and gambling winnings) were removed from Form 941. A new form, *Form 945, Annual Return of Withheld Federal Income Tax,* will be used to report these nonpayroll items for 1994. The nonpayroll items are discussed and Form 945 is illustrated in Unit 4.

Completing the Return

Fill in the State Code box in the upper left corner as follows:

1. Use the Postal Service two-letter state abbreviation as the State Code.
2. If you made your deposits in a state other than that shown in the address on the form, enter the state code for that state.
3. Enter the Code "MU" in the box if you deposit in more than one state.
4. If you deposit in the same state as shown in your address, do not make an entry in this box.

To complete Lines 1 through 17 of Form 941, we may obtain the information from various sources, such as those listed in Illustration 3-13 on page 90.

Signing Form 941

Form 941 must be signed by the employer or other person who is required to withhold and pay the tax. If the employer is:

1. An *individual,* the return should be signed by that person.
2. A *corporation,* the return should be signed by its president, vice president, or other principal officer given authority to sign the return.

   Corporate officers or duly authorized agents may use facsimile signatures under certain conditions. Each group of returns must be accompanied by a letter signed by the person authorized to sign the returns declaring (a) that the facsimile signature appearing on the returns is the signature adopted by him or her, and (b) that the signature was affixed to the returns by the officer or agent or at his or her direction.
3. A *partnership* or *other unincorporated organization,* a responsible and duly authorized partner or officer having knowledge of the firm's affairs should sign the return.

Form **941**

4141

Employer's Quarterly Federal Tax Return

▶ See separate instructions for information on completing this return.

Please type or print.

Department of the Treasury
Internal Revenue Service

OMB No. 1545-0029

Enter state code for state in which deposits made . ▶ ☐

(see page 2 of instructions).

Name (as distinguished from trade name)

Date quarter ended
MAR 31, 1994

Trade name, if any
LOPEZ ENTERPRISES, INC.

Employer identification number
89-1437003

Address (number and street)
25 PARK LANE   COLUMBUS, GA 31902-2582

City, state, and ZIP code

T	
FF	
FD	
FP	
I	
T	

If address is different from prior return, check here ▶ ☐

IRS Use

1 1 1 1 1 1 1 1 1 1   2   3 3 3 3 3 3   4 4 4

5 5 5   6   7   8 8 8 8 8   9 9 9   10 10 10 10 10 10 10 10 10 10

If you do not have to file returns in the future, check here ▶ ☐ and enter date final wages paid ▶

If you are a seasonal employer, see **Seasonal employers** on page 2 and check here (see instructions) ▶ ☐

1 Number of employees (except household) employed in the pay period that includes March 12th ▶		24
2 Total wages and tips subject to withholding, plus other compensation	**2**	74,895 92
3 Total income tax withheld from wages, tips, and sick pay	**3**	12,372 13
4 Adjustment of withheld income tax for preceding quarters of calendar year	**4**	-0-
5 Adjusted total of income tax withheld (line 3 as adjusted by line 4—see instructions)	**5**	12,372 13
6a Taxable social security wages . . . . $ 74,895 92 × 12.4% (.124) =	**6a**	9,287 09
b Taxable social security tips . . . . $ -0- × 12.4% (.124) =	**6b**	-0-
7 Taxable Medicare wages and tips . . . $ 74,895 92 × 2.9% (.029) =	**7**	2,171 98
8 Total social security and Medicare taxes (add lines 6a, 6b, and 7). Check here if wages are not subject to social security and/or Medicare tax . . . . ▶ ☐	**8**	11,459 07
9 Adjustment of social security and Medicare taxes (see instructions for required explanation) Sick Pay $ _____ ± Fractions of Cents $ _____ ± Other $ _____ =	**9**	41 Fractions only
10 Adjusted total of social security and Medicare taxes (line 8 as adjusted by line 9—see instructions)	**10**	11,459 48
11 **Total taxes** (add lines 5 and 10)	**11**	23,831 61
12 Advance earned income credit (EIC) payments made to employees, if any	**12**	-0-
13 Net taxes (subtract line 12 from line 11). This should equal line 17, column (d) below (or line D of Schedule B (Form 941))	**13**	23,831 61
14 Total deposits for quarter, including overpayment applied from a prior quarter	**14**	23,831 61
15 Balance due (subtract line 14 from line 13). Pay to Internal Revenue Service	**15**	-0-
16 Overpayment, if line 14 is more than line 13, enter excess here ▶ $ _____ and check if to be: ☐ Applied to next return OR ☐ Refunded.		

17 **Monthly Summary of Federal Tax Liability.**

• **Monthly depositors:** Complete line 17, columns (a) through (d) and check here . . . . ▶ ☒

• **Semiweekly depositors:** Complete Schedule B and check here . . . . ▶ ☐

• **All filers:** If line 13 is less than $500, you need not complete line 17 or Schedule B.

(a) First month liability	(b) Second month liability	(c) Third month liability	(d) Total liability for quarter
7,838.47	7,940.78	8,052.36	23,831.61

Sign Here

Under penalties of perjury, I declare that I have examined this return, including accompanying schedules and statements, and to the best of my knowledge and belief, it is true, correct, and complete.

Signature ▶ *David S. Lopez*

Print Your Name and Title ▶ David S. Lopez, President

Date ▶ 5/2/94

Form **941**

Illustration 3-12. Form 941, Employer's Quarterly Federal Tax Return

SOURCES OF INFORMATION FOR COMPLETING FORM 941

Line No.	Source of Information
1	Payroll register
2	General ledger account(s) for wages and salaries; Forms 4070, or employees' written statements to report cash tips
3	General ledger account(s)
4	Forms 941 previously filed and general ledger accounts—to determine amount of errors made in income tax withheld from wages paid in earlier quarters of the calendar year.
5	Add lines 4 and 3 if additional income tax withheld is being reported; subtract line 4 from line 3 if the amount of income tax withheld is being reduced.
6a	Payroll register; include any social security taxes (OASDI) paid for employees, sick pay, and taxable fringe benefits subject to OASDI. Do not include any tips. Do not report any employees' wages that exceed $59,700, the taxable wage base for 1994.
6b	Forms 4070, or employees' written statements to report cash tips. Enter all tips reported until tips and wages for each employee reach $59,700. Report this information even if you are unable to withhold the employee OASDI tax. Do not include allocated tips, which should be reported on Form 8027.
7	Payroll register; Forms 4070, or employees' written statements to report cash tips. Report amounts paid to certain federal, state, and local government employees who are subject only to the HI (Medicare) portion of the FICA tax.
8	Add lines 6a, 6b, and 7.
9	Forms 941 previously filed. Correct errors in social security taxes reported on earlier return or correct errors in credits for overpayments of penalty or interest paid on tax for an earlier quarter. If you report both an underpayment and an overpayment, show only the difference.
	Use Form 941c to explain any amount on line 9, other than adjustments for fractions of cents or third-party sick pay. Or, you may attach a statement that shows the nature of error(s) being corrected.
	Use Form W-2c, Statement of Corrected Income and Tax Amounts, to adjust an employee's social security wages, tips, or tax withheld for a prior year. Also, complete Form W-3c, Transmittal of Corrected Income and Tax Statements.
	To adjust for the tax on tips: Include the total uncollected employee social security tax for lines 6b and 7.
	To adjust for the tax on third-party sick pay: Deduct the social security tax on third-party sick pay for which you are not responsible. Write "Sick pay" in the margin.
	To adjust for fractions of cents: If there is a difference between the total tax on line 8 and the total deducted from your employees' wages or tips plus the employer's tax on those wages or tips (general ledger accounts) because of fractions of cents added or dropped in collecting the tax, report the difference. If this difference is the only entry, write "Fractions only" in the margin.
10	Add line 9 to line 8 if you are reporting additional taxes for an earlier quarter. Subtract line 9 from line 8 if you are reducing the amount of taxes reported for an earlier quarter or claiming credit for overpayments of penalty or interest paid on tax for an earlier quarter.
11	Record total taxes by adding lines 5 and 10.
12	If applicable, show the amount of any *advance earned income credit (EIC)* payments made to low-income workers (payroll register). As discussed in the next unit, the credit may be paid out periodically as part of the workers' paychecks. The amount of the advance EIC payments does not change the amount you must deduct and withhold from employees' pay for income tax and employee FICA taxes. Advance EIC payments that you make are treated as made from the amounts withheld as income tax and employee FICA taxes, and your FICA tax contributions.
13	Determine net taxes by subtracting line 12 from line 11.
14	General ledger account(s), previous Form 941; record the total deposits for the quarter, including any overpayment applied from previous quarter.
15	Calculate balance due by subtracting line 14 from line 13. Pay balance due to IRS.
16	Calculate overpayment by subtracting line 13 from line 14 and indicate if amount is to be applied to the next return or refunded.
17	General ledger account(s).

Illustration 3-13. Sources of Information for Completing Form 941

4. A *trust* or *estate*, the return should be signed by the fiduciary of that trust or estate.
5. A *political body*, such as a state or territory, the return should be signed by the officer or employee who has control of the wage payments or an officer properly designated for that purpose.

Filing Form 941

The return is due on or before the last day of the month following the close of the calendar quarter for which the return is made. If, however, we have made timely deposits of the taxes for a quarter, we may file the quarterly return on or before the 10th day of the second month following the close of the calendar quarter for which the return is made. If no deposits have been made during the quarter, we may still obtain the 10-day extension by making a deposit of any taxes due on or before the last day of the first calendar month following the close of the quarter.

If the last day for filing a quarterly return falls on Saturday, Sunday, or a legal holiday, we may file the return on the next business day. If the return is filed by mailing, we should mail the return in sufficient time for it to reach the IRS Center no later than the next business day under ordinary handling of the mail.

Individual employers file their quarterly returns with the IRS Center of the region in which the employer's principal place of business or office or agency is located. The locations of the IRS Centers are given in Illustration 3-14. Even though the IRS requires that a particular return be filed at a regional service center, the return may still be filed at the local office of the district director of the IRS if the return is hand delivered by the taxpayer.

Paying the FICA Taxes

We may pay our FICA taxes directly to the IRS by check or money order, which should be made payable to the "Internal Revenue Service." Cash payments made in person are permissible, but we should not send cash through the mail. However, we may mail checks, drafts, and money orders.

Privately Printed Forms

Under certain conditions, Form 941 may be privately printed. The forms must be exact facsimile reproductions of the officially printed Form 941 and meet other requirements contained in the Revenue Procedures, which are available from the IRS. In addition to providing specifications for substitute forms, the IRS provides reproduction proofs of its own forms at a prescribed per-page charge.

If the Legal Residence, Principal Place of Business, Office, or Agency Is in	File with the Internal Revenue Service Center at
Florida, Georgia, South Carolina	Atlanta, GA 39901
New Jersey, New York (New York City and counties of Nassau, Rockland, Suffolk, and Westchester)	Holtsville, NY 00501
New York (all other counties), Connecticut, Maine, Massachusetts, New Hampshire, Rhode Island, Vermont	Andover, MA 05501
Illinois, Iowa, Minnesota, Missouri, Wisconsin	Dept. 6884 Chicago, IL 60680-6884
Delaware, District of Columbia, Maryland, Pennsylvania, Virginia	Philadelphia, PA 19255
Indiana, Kentucky, Michigan, Ohio, West Virginia	Cincinnati, OH 45999
Kansas, New Mexico, Oklahoma, Texas	Austin, TX 73301
Alaska, Arizona, California (counties of Alpine, Amador, Butte, Calaveras, Colusa, Contra Costa, Del Norte, El Dorado, Glenn, Humboldt, Lake, Lassen, Marin, Mendocino, Modoc, Napa, Nevada, Placer, Plumas, Sacramento, San Joaquin, Shasta, Sierra, Siskiyou, Solano, Sonoma, Sutter, Tehama, Trinity, Yolo, and Yuba), Colorado, Idaho, Montana, Nebraska, Nevada, North Dakota, Oregon, South Dakota, Utah, Washington, Wyoming	Return only (without a payment): Ogden, UT 84201-0049 Return with a payment: P.O. Box 7922 San Francisco, CA 94120-7922
California (all other counties), Hawaii	Fresno, CA 93888
Alabama, Arkansas, Louisiana, Mississippi, North Carolina, Tennessee	Memphis, TN 37501
If there is no legal residence or principal place of business in any state	Philadelphia, PA 19255

Illustration 3-14.   Where to File Form 941

Reporting FICA Information on Magnetic Media

The IRS permits reporting agents for groups of employers to furnish the information required for Form 941 on magnetic tape instead of paper documents. Agents who wish to file their returns on magnetic tape must first file a letter of application or submit *Form 8655, Reporting Agent Authorization.* Also, at the option of the employer, the IRS may permit the use of a composite employment tax return in lieu of Form 941. A single form, together with magnetic tapes or other approved media, is used for the returns of more than one employer.

Professional Tip

The IRS provides free software to employers in Delaware, Maryland, Pennsylvania, Virginia, and Washington, D.C., for preparing Forms 941, 941E, and 940. This prototype program gives users the choice of filing the forms via diskette or modem. For more information, contact the Philadelphia Service Center at 11601 Roosevelt Boulevard, DP: 115, Philadelphia, PA 19154.

Some states that require employers to file detailed quarterly wage reports authorize the combined reporting on magnetic tape of social security and state unemployment compensation reporting data. Using such combined reporting on tape enables employers to prepare and submit more easily the social security and state wage data. By means of the combined tape format, employers forward one tape or diskette to the SSA and a copy to the appropriate participating state unemployment insurance agency.

The magnetic media filing of Form 8027 (Employer's Annual Information Return of Tip Income and Allocated Tips) as well as other information returns is discussed in Unit 4.

Professional Tip

The SSA provides an electronic bulletin board that allows employers to access wage reporting information, such a magnetic media specifications, via a computer and modem. The bulletin board may be accessed 24 hours a day, seven days a week through a modem at 410-965-1133. Users may also communicate directly with their regional SSA Magnetic Media Coordinators.

PENALTIES

In this unit we have discussed only one of the employment taxes—FICA taxes on employees and employers. In the following unit, we shall examine the withholding of a second tax—employees' income taxes. Then, in Unit 5, we present another employment tax—unemployment compensation. *The following discussion of penalties applies to each of the employment taxes discussed in Units 3, 4, and 5.*

Employers act as collection agents for the government by collecting employment taxes and paying them to the appropriate governmental agency. If employers fail to carry out their duties as collection agents, they are subject to civil and criminal penalties. The penalties may take the form of additions to the tax, interest, and fines and imprisonment.

As you see in Illustration 3-15 on pages 93 and 94, penalties are imposed upon employers who fail to: (1) file employment tax returns, (2) pay over employment taxes when due, (3) make timely deposits, (4) furnish wage and tax statements, (5) file or furnish information returns, and (6) supply identification numbers. The severity of the penalty varies depending on the degree of willfulness present in the employer's conduct. The penalties may be assessed not only against the employer but may also be imposed on any person who has the duty or responsibility for collecting, accounting for, and paying over any tax. As we shall see, penalties are also imposed for passing bad checks.

FAILURE TO FILE EMPLOYMENT TAX RETURNS

The civil and criminal penalties facing employers who *fail to file employment tax returns* are discussed below.

Additions to Tax

If an employer *fails to file an employment tax return on the date prescribed for its filing*, a certain percentage of the amount of tax required to have been reported will be added to the tax. Such an addition to the tax is not applicable, however, when employers show to the satisfaction of the IRS that the failure to file was due to reasonable cause and not to willful neglect.

The amount to be added to the tax is 5% of the *net* amount of tax required to have been reported if the failure to report is for not more than one month. An additional 5% is levied for each additional month or fraction of a month during which the failure continues, not to exceed 25% in the aggregate. Thus, if a failure to file continued for four months, an employer would be liable for an addition to the tax equal to 20% of the net tax that should have been reported.

If the failure to file a return is *fraudulent*, the penalty is increased to 15% per month, not to exceed 75% in the aggregate.

Criminal Penalties

If employers *willfully* attempt to evade the payment of employment taxes by failing to file a return or by filing a false return, upon conviction, they may be fined up to $10,000 or imprisoned for not more than 5 years, or both.

Employment tax returns are signed under a statement declaring that the return is made under penalties of perjury. Thus, an employer who willfully signs a return knowing that it is not true and correct as to every material statement will, upon conviction, be subject to a fine of not more than $5,000, or imprisonment for not more than 3 years, or both.

FAILURE TO PAY OVER EMPLOYMENT TAXES

Employers who *fail to pay over the required amount of employment taxes when due* are faced with the following civil and criminal penalties.

Additions to Tax

Employers who fail to pay over the required amount of tax when due face a penalty of an additional tax amounting to ½% of the *net* amount due if the failure to pay lasts no longer than a month. For each month during which the failure to pay continues, an additional ½% penalty is levied, not to exceed 25% in the aggregate. Thus, if an employer's delinquency continues for six months, the addition will be equal to 3% of the net tax shown on the return or that should have been shown on the return. Along with any penalties that may be imposed, taxes due and unpaid will bear interest at the rate of 7% per year. The interest rate on a *large corporate underpayment* (an underpayment of $100,000 for any tax period) is 9%.[3]

If any part of a deficiency in the amount of taxes paid is due to *negligence or an intentional disregard* of the payment rules (but without intent to defraud), a penalty of 20% of any underpayment will be imposed. *Negligence* includes any failure to make a reasonable attempt to comply with the provisions of the law. *Disregard* includes any careless, reckless, or intentional disregard of the law. However, the negligence penalty will not be imposed if it is shown that there was reasonable cause for the underpayment and that the taxpayer acted in good faith.

If any part of an underpayment is due to *fraud with an intent to evade* the tax, a penalty of 75% of the underpayment will be added to the tax due. In such a case, the fraud penalty will be imposed in place of the negligence penalty; the fraud penalty will also be imposed in place of the additions to the tax provided for failure to pay the tax.

The 100% Penalty

Employers who *willfully* fail to collect, account for or pay over employment taxes, or willfully attempt in any manner to evade or defeat the taxes, may be liable for a penalty equal to the total amount of the tax evaded, or not collected, or not accounted for and paid over. This *100% penalty* (or *responsible person penalty*) may be assessed on the person(s) responsible for collecting, accounting for, and paying over the tax. Generally excluded from the penalty are non-owner employees, volunteers, and employees who perform merely administrative duties such as signing checks. If the 100% penalty is imposed, the 75% fraud penalty noted above may not be imposed for the same offense.

Tax Levies

If, within 10 days after notice and demand for payment, an employer fails to pay any tax for which he or she is liable, the IRS is authorized to levy on and seize any property and property rights held by the employer at the time of the levy. If the IRS concludes that the collection of any tax is in jeopardy, it may immediately demand payment of the tax and, upon the employer's failure or refusal to pay, may levy and seize the employer's property without regard to the 10-day period.

Criminal Penalties

The *willful* failure to pay any tax constitutes a felony. Upon conviction of such a felony, the employer will be subject to a fine of not more than $10,000, or imprisonment for not more than 5 years, or both. These penalties are in addition to the 75% fraud penalty.

Illustration 3-15. Penalties That Apply to Employment Taxes (Continued)

---

[3]Each calendar quarter the Internal Revenue Service sets the interest rate to be charged for tax underpayments (and on refunds for tax overpayments). The rate is based on the short-term Treasury bill rate for the first month in each calendar quarter, plus 3 percentage points, and applies for the following calendar quarter.

FAILURE TO MAKE TIMELY DEPOSITS

Penalties are imposed for the *failure to make timely deposits of employment taxes*. These penalties are based on applicable percentages of the amount of the underpayment of a deposit as determined by the number of days the deposit is late. An *underpayment* is the excess of the amount of tax required to be deposited over the tax that was actually deposited.

If the failure to make a timely deposit is:

1. *Not more than 5 days late*, the penalty is 2% of the undeposited taxes.

2. *More than 5 days late but less than 15 days late*, the penalty is 5% of the undeposited taxes.

3. *More than 15 days late*, the penalty is 10%.

Also, a penalty of 15% of the underpayment may be imposed if the undeposited taxes are not paid on or before the earlier of:

1. 10 days after the first delinquency notice, or
2. The day on which notice and demand for immediate payment is given.

Any person who makes an overstated deposit claim is subject to a penalty of 25% of such claim. (This penalty is in addition to any other penalty imposed.) An *overstated deposit claim* refers to a claim of tax deposits in excess of the amount actually deposited. An overstated deposit claim also refers to claims for deposits not actually made. However, the penalty for overstated deposit claims does not apply if the overstated claims were due to reasonable cause and not due to willful neglect.

FAILURE TO FURNISH WAGE AND TAX STATEMENTS

If employers *willfully* fail to furnish their employees with properly executed wage and tax statements, or *willfully* furnish false or fraudulent statements, the civil penalty is $50 for each such statement. This fine is in addition to any criminal penalties that may be imposed. There is a maximum penalty of $100,000 in any calendar year. If such failures are due to *intentional disregard*, the penalty for each failure is $100 per statement or, if greater, 10% of the amount required to be shown on the statement. In this case there is no limit on the maximum penalty each calendar year.

The criminal penalty for the offenses noted, upon conviction, is a fine of not more than $1,000, or imprisonment for not more than 1 year, or both, for each offense.

FAILURE TO FILE OR FURNISH INFORMATION RETURNS

Employers who fail to timely file their information returns are subject to a penalty of $50 for each failure, with a maximum penalty of $250,000 in any calendar year. However, if a failure is *corrected within 30 days* after the required filing date, the penalty for each failure is $15 and the maximum penalty is $75,000. If a failure is corrected *after the 30th day but before August 1* of the calendar year in which the required filing date occurs, the penalty for each failure is $30 and the maximum penalty is $150,000.

If the failure to timely file information returns or to include all the information required to be shown on the returns, or the inclusion of incorrect information, is due to *intentional disregard*, the penalty is $100 per statement or, if greater, 10% of the amount required to be shown on the statement. In such cases, there is no limit on the maximum penalty for the calendar year.

FAILURE TO SUPPLY IDENTIFICATION NUMBER

Employers and employees are often required to include their identification number on tax returns, statements, and other documents. If any person fails to comply with such a requirement, a penalty of $5 is levied for each failure to include the identifying number.

Employers and employees may also be required to (a) furnish their identifying number to another person or (b) in-clude another person's identifying number in the tax return, statement, or document made for that person. The penalty for failing to meet either requirement in (a) or (b) is $50 for each such failure. The total amount of penalty for all failures will not exceed $100,000.

BAD CHECKS

A specific penalty is imposed for giving the IRS a bad check or money order in payment of any employment taxes. The penalty is an amount equal to 2% of the amount of the check or money order. If the check is for less than $750, the penalty is $15 or the amount of the check, whichever is less. The penalty does not apply, however, if the check or money order was tendered in good faith and with reasonable cause to believe that it would be paid upon presentment.

Illustration 3-15. Penalties That Apply to Employment Taxes (Concluded)

GLOSSARY

Common-law relationship—the state existing when the person for whom services are rendered has the right to control and direct the individual who performs the services, not only as to the result to be accomplished by the work but also as to the details and means by which that result is to be accomplished.

Educational assistance—the expenses that an employer pays for an employee's education, such as tuition, fees, and payments for books, supplies, and equipment.

Employee—any individual who performs services in covered employment.

Employer—any person who employs one or more individuals for the performance of services, unless such services or employment are specifically excepted by law.

Employment—any service performed by employees for their employer, regardless of the citizenship or residence of either.

Immediate credit item—a check or other instrument of payment for which immediate credit is given the payee by the receiving bank in accordance with its check-collection schedule.

Independent contractor—a person who follows an independent trade, business, or profession in which services are offered to the public.

Lookback period—the block of time, consisting of four quarters beginning July 1 of the second preceding year and ending June 30 of the prior year, used to determine if an employer is a monthly or a semiweekly depositor.

Monthly depositor—one who reported employment taxes of $50,000 or less for the four quarters in the lookback period.

Person—an entity defined by law as an individual, a trust or estate, a partnership, or a corporation.

Safe harbor rule—rule that determines if an employer has satisfied the deposit obligations by (a) having no shortfall that exceeds the greater of $100 or 2% of the amount of employment taxes required to be deposited and (b) having deposited the shortfall on or before the shortfall make-up date.

Self-employment income—the net earnings derived by individuals from a business or profession carried on by them as sole proprietors or by a partnership of which they are members.

Semiweekly depositor—one who reported employment taxes of more than $50,000 for the four quarters in the lookback period.

Shortfall—the excess of the amount of employment taxes required to be deposited over the amount deposited on or before the last date prescribed for the deposit.

Sick pay—any payment made to individuals, because of their personal injury or sickness, that does not constitute wages.

Taxable wage base—the maximum amount of wages during a calendar year that is subject to a particular tax, such as FICA.

QUESTIONS FOR REVIEW

1. Under FICA what are the two taxes that are imposed on both employers and employees?
2. For social security purposes, what conditions must an individual meet to be classed as a "covered" employee?
3. Under what conditions does a common-law relationship exist between an employee and an employer?
4. Summarize the test conditions under which a worker is classed as an independent contractor.
5. For social security purposes, what conditions must an individual meet to be classed as a "covered" employer?
6. Jill Kravitz, 17 years of age, works in a grocery store for her father, who owns the store. Are the wages paid Jill subject to FICA taxes? Why?
7. Explain what is meant by the term *voluntary coverage*.
8. For the purpose of determining the amount of wages subject to FICA taxes, how are wages defined?
9. Under what conditions are the following types of remuneration considered wages under FICA?
   a. Advances
   b. Christmas gifts
   c. Death benefits
   d. Sick pay
10. What are an employer's responsibilities for FICA taxes:
    a. On tips reported by tipped employees?
    b. On wages paid tipped employees?
11. The value of meals and lodging furnished employees may or may not represent wages for FICA tax purposes. Explain.
12. Under what condition is sick pay excluded from the definition of wages for FICA tax purposes?

13. What is the OASDI tax rate and the estimated taxable wage base for 1994?
14. What is the HI tax rate for 1994?
15. How are the employee's FICA taxes collected and paid to the IRS?
16. a. John Luis receives taxable wages from three employers during 1994. Is he entitled to a refund on the OASDI taxes paid on wages in excess of $59,700?
    b. If Luis is entitled to a refund on the excess OASDI taxes he paid, how should he proceed in claiming such a refund?
17. Explain the procedure for calculating the employer's OASDI and HI taxes.
18. From what sources may self-employment income be obtained?
19. What are the SECA tax rates on self-employed persons for 1994?
20. What procedure should an employer follow in filing an application for an employer identification number?
21. Explain how individuals may check the accuracy of the wage credits in their social security insurance accounts.

22. Indicate the deposit requirement for each of the following nonagricultural employers:
    a. On payday, Thursday, April 18, the employer, a semiweekly depositor, has accumulated employment taxes that total $3,490.
    b. At the end of the second calendar quarter, the employee and employer FICA taxes and income taxes withheld total $455.
    c. On payday, Friday, November 15, the employee and employer FICA taxes and income taxes withheld total $101,230.
23. For what purpose does an employer complete Form 8109?
24. Explain how the timeliness of a deposit of employment taxes is determined.
25. a. How often must an employer file Form 941?
    b. By what date must an employer file Form 941?
    c. For employers who have their legal residences in your city, with which IRS Center should they file Form 941?
26. What penalty is imposed on an employer who:
    a. Does not file Form 941 by the due date?
    b. Is 7 days late in making the monthly deposit of employment taxes?
    c. Gives the IRS a bad check for $1,250?

QUESTIONS FOR DISCUSSION

1. Strapped for cash to pay his suppliers and meet his weekly payrolls, Amos Nash decided several months ago to postpone depositing all employment taxes. As Nash told his sales manager, "I'll pay up before the IRS catches up with me." What risks does Nash face by diverting his payroll-tax money to business uses?
2. On Wednesday, August 15, 19—, LaPoint Company, a semiweekly depositor, had employment taxes of $25,000 that were required to be deposited on or before Wednesday, August 22, 19—. The deposit was mailed and postmarked on Wednesday, August 22, 19—, and was delivered on Thursday, August 23, 19—. Was the tax deposit timely made by LaPoint Company? Explain.
3. When employees of the County Bank are summoned to serve on jury duty, the firm pays its workers the difference between their regular wages and the amount received for jury duty, even though the workers are absent from work.

    Amy Kane, a correspondence secretary with the bank, has been receiving a weekly salary of $365. Kane has just completed her first 5-day week of jury duty, for which she was paid $65 ($9 per day plus 20 cents per mile from her home to the court house, a 20-mile round trip).

    How much of Kane's earnings for this week is considered to be wages subject to FICA tax withholding?
4. During their first month of employment at Perez Company, all new workers are looked upon as probationary employees. During this period of time the new workers do not qualify for many employee benefits, such as the company-sponsored hospitalization-medical insurance program. Are the earnings received by the new workers during the probationary period properly defined as taxable wages for purposes of FICA?
5. During a recent strike at the Hulett Shoe Company, the union members were paid strike benefits by their union. One of the company workers, Tim Dopson, is employed by the union to serve as a union representative. In this capacity Dopson sits down at the bargaining table and represents the union in negotiating contracts with the company.
    a. Are the strike benefits paid by the union to its members subject to FICA tax withholding?
    b. Are the payments Dopson receives from the union for his services as union representative subject to FICA tax withholding?
6. Ivan McCullers, owner of a large retail store, has been making his deposits of FICA taxes and income taxes by mailing these amounts to his IRS service center. McCullers reasons that by making his deposits at the service center, he can have use of his money for several extra days during the delay required by the center to turn over his deposit to the Treasury Department. Is McCullers proceeding correctly in gaining more days' usage of his funds in his checking account? Explain.

Date _____   Name _____

PRACTICAL PROBLEMS

NOTE: In these and succeeding Practical Problems, the OASDI tax rate is 6.2% on employers and employees on the first $59,700 of taxable wages. The HI tax rate is 1.45% on employers and employees on the total wages paid.

3-1. The biweekly taxable wages for the employees of Barkan Graphics are given below. On the appropriate lines, record:

   a. The FICA taxes (OASDI and HI) that should be withheld from each employee's biweekly pay.

   b. The total OASDI and HI taxes to be withheld.

   c. The employer's FICA taxes for the biweekly pay period.

BARKAN GRAPHICS

Employee No.	Employee Name	Biweekly Taxable Wages	(a) FICA Taxes OASDI	HI
711	Bechette, Mel M.	$479.68	$ _____	$ _____
512	Calderon, Karen T.	485.00	_____	_____
624	Fletcher, Rickey P.	394.55	_____	_____
325	Honeycuff, Eric X.	397.70	_____	_____
422	Lansford, William R.	778.00	_____	_____
210	Plunk, Floyd A.	775.50	_____	_____
111	Tolleson, Audrey S.	495.73	_____	_____
	(b) Totals		$ _____	$ _____

(c) Employer's OASDI Tax = $ _____ x _____ = $ _____
                                 Total Taxable   OASDI Tax Rate   Employer's OASDI
                                   Wages   Tax

    Employer's HI Tax = $ _____ x _____ = $ _____
                                   Total Taxable   HI Tax Rate   Employer's HI Tax
                                   Wages

3-2. During 1994, Melido Canseco, president of the Oak Company, was paid a semimonthly salary of $6,030. Calculate the amount of FICA taxes that should be withheld from his:

	OASDI	HI
a. 9th pay	$ _____	$ _____
b. 10th pay	$ _____	$ _____
c. 24th pay	$ _____	$ _____

3-3. The annual salary paid each of the officers of Sabo, Inc., is given below. The officers are paid semimonthly on the 15th and the last day of the month. Determine the FICA taxes to be withheld from each officer's semimonthly pay on (a) July 31 and (b) December 31.

SABO, INC.

Name and Title	Annual Salary	(a) July 31				(b) December 31			
		OASDI Taxable Earnings	OASDI Tax	HI Taxable Earnings	HI Tax	OASDI Taxable Earnings	OASDI Tax	HI Taxable Earnings	HI Tax
Larkin, Andrew T. President	$144,000								
Oliver, Carla O. V-P, Finance	108,000								
Benzinger, Ryne J. V-P, Sales	106,000								
Armstrong, Sidney T. V-P, Manufacturing ..	105,500								
Winningham, Arlene C. V-P, Personnel	90,600								
Decker, Jessie R. V-P, Secretary	98,950								

98

3-4. Audrey Rucker and Jill Rodgers are partners engaged in operating the R&R Gift Shop, which employs the persons listed below. Paychecks are distributed every Friday to all employees. Based upon the information given, compute:

a. The amount of FICA taxes to be withheld from the paychecks of March 18, 1994.
b. The amount of the employer's FICA taxes for the March 18 payroll.

R&R GIFT SHOP

Name and Position	Salary	(a) OASDI Taxable Earnings	OASDI Tax	HI Taxable Earnings	HI Tax
Jessica Palmer, general office worker	$335 per week	$	$	$	$
Brenda Whalen, salesperson	$1,980 per month				
Rob Stoll, part-time deliveryperson	$285 per week				
Audrey Rucker, partner	$650 per week				
Jill Rodgers, partner	$650 per week				
Totals		$	$	$	$

(b) Employer's OASDI Tax = $ _____ × _____ = $ _____
                              OASDI Taxable   OASDI Tax Rate   OASDI Tax
                              Earnings

Employer's HI Tax = $ _____ × _____ = $ _____
                       HI Taxable   HI Tax Rate   HI Tax
                       Earnings

99

3-5. Vicki DeVault began working as a part-time waitress on June 1, 1994, at Leonardo's Restaurant. The cash tips of $140 that she received during June were reported on Form 4070, which she submitted to her employer on July 1. During July, she was paid wages of $495 by the restaurant. Determine:

a. The amount of FICA taxes that the employer should withhold from
   DeVault's wages during July . . . . OASDI $_____

   HI $_____

b. The amount of the employer's FICA taxes on DeVault's wages and
   tips during July . . . . OASDI $_____

   HI $_____

3-6. Sue Ellen Stein was paid a salary of $35,800 during 1994 by the Farrell Company. In addition, during the year Stein started her own business as a public accountant and reported a net business income of $26,500 on her income tax return for 1994. Determine:

a. The amount of FICA taxes that was withheld from her earnings during
   1994 by the Farrell Company . . . . OASDI $_____

   HI $_____

b. Stein's self-employment taxes (OASDI and HI) on the income derived from her
   public accounting business for 1994 . . . . $_____

3-7. The Bond Printing Company pays its salaried employees monthly on the last day of each month. The annual salary payroll for 1994 is given below. Compute:

a. The FICA taxes withheld from each employee's wages for December.
b. The total taxable wages (OASDI and HI) and the total OASDI and HI taxes withheld from all employees' wages for December.
c. The employer's FICA taxes (OASDI and HI) on the taxable wages for December.

BOND PRINTING COMPANY

Employee	Annual Salary	OASDI Taxable Wages	(a) OASDI Tax on Employees	HI Taxable Wages	(a) HI Tax on Employees
DAVIS, Sara	$20,160				
DAWSON, Martha	19,800				
FRANCO, Betty	20,400				
GLADDEN, Arthur	60,000				
HEATH, Maria	19,400				
KELLY, Laura	19,820				
KITTLE, Madge	17,990				
QUINTANA, Emilio	58,800				
RIPKEN, Elisa	19,980				
WASHINGTON, Teri	51,600				
(b) Totals	. . .				

(c) Employer's OASDI Tax . . . $_____   Employer's HI Tax . . . . $_____

3-8. The weekly and hourly wage schedule for the employees of Abrams, Inc., is given below. All employees work a full 40-hour week. Compute:

a. The OASDI and HI taxable wages earned by each employee for a full week in February, 1994.
b. The FICA taxes (OASDI and HI) withheld from each employee's wages.
c. The net wages paid each employee.
d. The total taxable wages (OASDI and HI), FICA taxes (OASDI and HI), and net wages.
e. The employer's FICA taxes.

ABRAMS, INC.

Employee	Weekly (W) or Hourly (H) Wage	(a) OASDI Taxable Wages	HI Taxable Wages	(b) OASDI Tax	HI Tax	(c) Net Wages
Arlene Benedetti	$270 W	$	$	$	$	$
Gary Combs	285 W					
Bruce Earle	415 W					
Joan Gill	450 W					
Dwight Kaiser	$5.60 H					
Joel Perkowski	5.85 H					
Phillip Stieber	6.40 H					
Chi Yee	6.80 H					
(d) Totals		$	$	$	$	$

(e) Employer's FICA taxes: $ _____ OASDI Tax $ _____ HI Tax

102

3-9. The monthly salaries and part-time hourly wage rates of the office employees of Thornton Payroll Service during 1994 are given below. Assume that the monthly salaries were in effect during the entire year. In December, the part-time employees worked the number of hours and at the hourly rates as shown. None of the part-time employees earned as much as $59,700 during the year. Compute:

a. The total wages of each part-time employee for December, 1994.
b. The OASDI and HI taxable wages earned by each employee.
c. The FICA taxes (OASDI and HI) withheld from each employee's wages for December.
d. The total monthly payroll, the OASDI and HI taxable wages, and the OASDI and HI taxes withheld.
e. The employer's FICA taxes for the month.

THORNTON PAYROLL SERVICE

Employees	(a) Total Monthly Salary Payroll	(b) OASDI Taxable Wages	HI Taxable Wages	(c) OASDI Tax	HI Tax
FULL-TIME OFFICE:					
Asad, Gordon	$1,300	$	$	$	$
Cella, Paul	1,300				
Essex, Joanna	1,875				
Gorzo, Marvin	1,875				
Lentini, Larry	1,800				
Price, Billie	5,230				
Ryan, Donna	2,400				
Sams, Richard	3,925				
Tona, Jeannette	4,825				
Wagner, Grace	1,500				

Employees	Hrs. Worked	Hourly Rate	Total Part-Time Wages	OASDI Taxable Wages	HI Taxable Wages	OASDI Tax	HI Tax
PART-TIME OFFICE:							
Kaplan, Judy	170	$4.95	$				
Law, Sherri	170	4.95					
Miller, Sandy	140	6.00					
Quinn, Debra	145	5.00					
Stabinsky, Kim	162	5.50					
(d) Totals			$	$	$	$	$

(e) Employer's FICA taxes: $_____ OASDI Tax $_____ HI Tax

3-10. Wayne P. Roney opened Wayne's Service Station on January 3, 1994. The business, whose fiscal year is the same as the calendar year, is subject to FICA taxes. At the end of the first quarter of 1994, Roney is required to file an Employer's Quarterly Federal Tax Return. Using Form 941, reproduced on page 105, prepare the return on the basis of the following information obtained from the payroll records of the company.

Employer's address: 114 Center Street, Sycamore, South Carolina 29846-3477
Employer's identification number: 61-0230450

The employees' names, occupations, social security numbers, and semimonthly wages are given below. Assume that the same amounts of wages were paid semimonthly during the quarter on the 15th and the last day of each month.

Employee's Name and Occupation	Soc. Sec. Account No.	Semimonthly Wage
Alan T. Frank, attendant	384-10-7233	$ 580.00
Patty R. Collett, attendant	345-90-8451	565.00
Patrick O. Hume, mechanic	528-09-3667	1,290.00
Denise B. Dow, cashier	766-43-6527	650.00
Total taxable wages		$3,085.00

None of the four employees reported tips during the quarter. No advance earned income credit (EIC) payments were made to the workers.

The federal income taxes withheld from the employees' wages each semimonthly pay period totaled $412. All deposits of federal income taxes withheld and the employer-employee FICA taxes were timely made.

Note that on Lines 6a and 7, the total taxable OASDI and HI wages are multiplied by a combined tax rate for both employer and employee. Often there is a small difference between (a) this total and (b) the total taxes withheld from employees each pay period and the amount of the employer's taxes calculated each pay period. This difference is attributable to the rounding of fractional parts of cents because the FICA taxes calculated on Lines 6a and 7 are based on the total taxable wages for the calendar quarter. When such a difference in amounts occurs, the difference is reported on Line 9 as a deduction or addition, as the case may be. The words "Fractions only" should be inserted in the margin of Form 941 to indicate the type of adjustment made.

Practical Problem 3-10

Form 941	4141	**Employer's Quarterly Federal Tax Return**

Department of the Treasury
Internal Revenue Service

► See separate instructions for information on completing this return.
Please type or print.

Enter state code for state in which deposits made ► ☐☐ (see page 2 of instructions).

Name (as distinguished from trade name)

Trade name, if any

Address (number and street)

Date quarter ended

Employer identification number

City, state, and ZIP code

OMB No. 1545-0029

| T |
| FF |
| FD |
| FP |
| I |
| T |

If address is different from prior return, check here ► ☐

IRS Use

1 1 1 1 1 1 1 1 1 1   2   3 3 3 3 3 3   4 4 4

5 5 5   6   7   8 8 8 8 8   9 9 9   10 10 10 10 10 10 10 10 10 10

If you do not have to file returns in the future, check here ► ☐ and enter date final wages paid ►

If you are a seasonal employer, see **Seasonal employers** on page 2 and check here (see instructions) ► ☐

1	Number of employees (except household) employed in the pay period that includes March 12th ►	
2	Total wages and tips subject to withholding, plus other compensation	2
3	Total income tax withheld from wages, tips, and sick pay	3
4	Adjustment of withheld income tax for preceding quarters of calendar year	4
5	Adjusted total of income tax withheld (line 3 as adjusted by line 4—see instructions) .	5
6a	Taxable social security wages . . . . $_____ × 12.4% (.124) =	6a
b	Taxable social security tips . . . . $_____ × 12.4% (.124) =	6b
7	Taxable Medicare wages and tips . . . . . $_____ × 2.9% (.029) =	7
8	Total social security and Medicare taxes (add lines 6a, 6b, and 7). Check here if wages are not subject to social security and/or Medicare tax . . . . ► ☐	8
9	Adjustment of social security and Medicare taxes (see instructions for required explanation) Sick Pay $_____ ± Fractions of Cents $_____ ± Other $_____ =	9
10	Adjusted total of social security and Medicare taxes (line 8 as adjusted by line 9—see instructions)	10
11	**Total taxes** (add lines 5 and 10)	11
12	Advance earned income credit (EIC) payments made to employees, if any	12
13	Net taxes (subtract line 12 from line 11). **This should equal line 17, column (d) below** (or line D of Schedule B (Form 941))	13
14	Total deposits for quarter, including overpayment applied from a prior quarter	14
15	**Balance due** (subtract line 14 from line 13). Pay to Internal Revenue Service	15
16	**Overpayment,** if line 14 is more than line 13, enter excess here ► $_____ and check if to be: ☐ Applied to next return OR ☐ Refunded.	

17   **Monthly Summary of Federal Tax Liability.**
- **Monthly depositors:** Complete line 17, columns (a) through (d) and check here . . . . ► ☐
- **Semiweekly depositors:** Complete Schedule B and check here . . . . ► ☐
- **All filers:** If line 13 is less than $500, you need not complete line 17 or Schedule B.

(a) First month liability	(b) Second month liability	(c) Third month liability	(d) Total liability for quarter

Sign Here

Under penalties of perjury, I declare that I have examined this return, including accompanying schedules and statements, and to the best of my knowledge and belief, it is true, correct, and complete.

Signature ►

Print Your Name and Title ►

Date ►

Form 941

3-11. During the fourth calendar quarter of 1994, the Riverside Inn employed the persons listed below. Also given are the employees' salaries or wages and the amount of tips reported to the owner, Diane R. Peters, during the quarter.

Employee	Salary or Wage	Tips Reported
Grant P. Frazier, manager	$25,000/year	. . .
Joseph R. LaVanga, ass't. manager . . .	18,000/year	. . .
Susanne T. Ayers, waitress	$250/week	$2,240.90
Howard P. Cohen, waiter	225/week	2,493.10
Lee W. Soong, waitress	250/week	2,640.30
Mary E. Yee, waitress	250/week	2,704.00
Helen O. Woods, hostess/cashier	325/week	. . .
Koo C. Shin, ass't. chef	325/week	. . .
Aaron Y. Abalis, chef	400/week	. . .
David T. Harad, dishwasher	170/week	. . .

Employees are paid weekly on Friday. During this calendar quarter, there were 4 weekly paydays in October, 4 in November, and 5 in December. Tips were reported by the four tipped employees by the 10th of each month. The federal income taxes and FICA taxes to be withheld from the tips were estimated by Peters and withheld equally over the 13 weekly pay periods. For the employer's weekly FICA taxes on the tips reported, Peters used the same estimate as the amount of employees' FICA taxes withheld.

The total federal income taxes withheld during the quarter were $5,720. The total FICA taxes on *tips* reported during the quarter were $118.61 each week. All deposits of federal income taxes withheld and the employer-employee FICA taxes were timely made.

No advance earned income credit (EIC) payments were made to the workers.

Based upon the information given above, complete Form 941, reproduced on page 107.

Practical Problem 3-11

Form 941

4141

Employer's Quarterly Federal Tax Return

Department of the Treasury
Internal Revenue Service

▶ See separate instructions for information on completing this return.

Please type or print.

Enter state code for state in which deposits made . ▶ [:]
(see page 2 of instructions).

Name (as distinguished from trade name)

Trade name, if any
RIVERSIDE INN

Address (number and street)
404 UNION AVE.

Date quarter ended
DEC 31, 1994

Employer identification number
65-4263607

City, state, and ZIP code
MEMPHIS, TN 38112-1404

OMB No. 1545-0029

T	
FF	
FD	
FP	
I	
T	

If address is different from prior return, check here ▶ [ ]

IRS Use

1	1	1	1	1	1	1	1	1	1		2		3	3	3	3	3	3		4	4	4			
5	5	5		6		7		8	8	8	8	8		9	9	9		10	10	10	10	10	10	10	10

If you do not have to file returns in the future, check here ▶ [ ]   and enter date final wages paid ▶

If you are a seasonal employer, see **Seasonal employers** on page 2 and check here (see instructions) ▶ [ ]

1	Number of employees (except household) employed in the pay period that includes March 12th ▶		
2	Total wages and tips subject to withholding, plus other compensation	2	
3	Total income tax withheld from wages, tips, and sick pay	3	
4	Adjustment of withheld income tax for preceding quarters of calendar year . . .	4	
5	Adjusted total of income tax withheld (line 3 as adjusted by line 4—see instructions)	5	
6a	Taxable social security wages . . . . $	× 12.4% (.124) =	6a	
b	Taxable social security tips . . . . $	× 12.4% (.124) =	6b	
7	Taxable Medicare wages and tips . . . . . $	× 2.9% (.029) =	7	
8	Total social security and Medicare taxes (add lines 6a, 6b, and 7). Check here if wages are not subject to social security and/or Medicare tax . . . . ▶ [ ]	8	
9	Adjustment of social security and Medicare taxes (see instructions for required explanation) Sick Pay $ _____ ± Fractions of Cents $ _____ ± Other $ _____ =	9	
10	Adjusted total of social security and Medicare taxes (line 8 as adjusted by line 9—see instructions)	10	
11	**Total taxes** (add lines 5 and 10)	11	
12	Advance earned income credit (EIC) payments made to employees, if any	12	
13	Net taxes (subtract line 12 from line 11). This should equal line 17, column (d) below (or line D of Schedule B (Form 941))	13	
14	Total deposits for quarter, including overpayment applied from a prior quarter	14	
15	**Balance due** (subtract line 14 from line 13). Pay to Internal Revenue Service	15	
16	Overpayment, if line 14 is more than line 13, enter excess here ▶ $ _____ and check if to be: [ ] Applied to next return OR [ ] Refunded.		

17	Monthly Summary of Federal Tax Liability.
	● Monthly depositors: Complete line 17, columns (a) through (d) and check here . . . . . . ▶ [ ]
	● Semiweekly depositors: Complete Schedule B and check here . . . . . . ▶ [ ]
	● All filers: If line 13 is less than $500, you need not complete line 17 or Schedule B.

(a) First month liability	(b) Second month liability	(c) Third month liability	(d) Total liability for quarter

Sign Here

Under penalties of perjury, I declare that I have examined this return, including accompanying schedules and statements, and to the best of my knowledge and belief, it is true, correct, and complete.

Signature ▶

Print Your Name and Title ▶

Date ▶

Form **941**

3-12. The Trainer Company is a monthly depositor whose tax liability (amount withheld from employees' wages for federal income tax and FICA tax plus the company's portion of the FICA tax) for March, 1994, was $205. The Trainer Company's employer identification number is 73-1456654.

Based on the information above and the instructions given in Illustration 3-11, page 87, complete the Federal Tax Deposit Coupon, Form 8109, shown below. In the space provided below the form, show the date by which the deposit must be made.

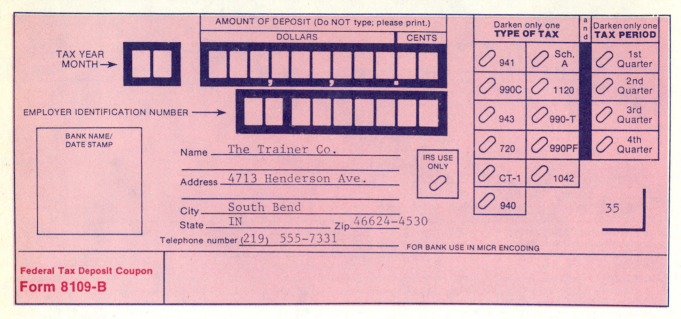

Date to be filed: _____

3-13. Assume that in Problem 3-12 no deposit was made by The Trainer Company until May 20. Determine the:

a. Penalty for failure to make timely deposit . . . . $_____

b. Penalty for failure to pay tax when due . . . . _____

c. Interest on taxes due and unpaid . . . . _____

d. Total penalty imposed . . . . $_____

3-14. At the Payne Die Company, office workers are employed for a 40-hour workweek on either an annual or a monthly salary basis. In the plant, most workers are paid according to a units-of-production (piece-rate) plan under which the overtime rate is equal to ½ the regular hourly pay rate.

Given on the form on pages 110 and 111 are the current annual and monthly salary rates for five office workers and the number of units produced by six plant workers for the week ended November 4, 1994.

All workers are entitled to overtime pay for all hours worked beyond 40 each workweek at 1½ times the regular hourly rates.

    a.   For each worker calculate:

        NOTE: In calculating all hourly rates, overtime rates, etc., carry out the cents to 3 decimal places and round back to 2 places.

        (1) The regular earnings for the weekly payroll period ended November 4, 1994. In 1994, there are 52 weekly Friday payrolls.
        (2) The overtime earnings, if any.
        (3) The total regular and overtime earnings.
        (4) The FICA taxable wages (OASDI and HI) for this pay period.
        (5) The amount of FICA taxes (OASDI and HI) to be withheld by the employer this pay period.
        (6) The net pay for this pay period.

    b.   Determine the employer's FICA taxes (OASDI and HI) for the week ended November 4, 1994.

Practical Problem 3-14

a.

PAYNE DIE COMPANY

Employee	Salary or Unit Rate	Hrs. Worked and Units Produced	(1) Regular Earnings	(2) Overtime Earnings	(3) Total Reg. and O/T Earnings
OFFICE:					
LENTZ, R.	$16,900 per yr.	40			
STEYER, C.	$28,080 per yr.	40			
LONG, S.	$5,760 per mo.	40			
RICHEY, S.	$1,400 per mo.	48			
TAVEAU, G.	$900 per mo.	40			
PLANT:					
MANELLA, V.	$8.50/M (thousand)	30 hrs. 18M units			
PLATT, R.	$12.50/M	46 hrs. 19M units			
FLORA, L.	$11.80/M	48 hrs. 17M units			
VALADEZ, M.	$12.50/M	40 hrs. 16M units			
YAU, C.	$12.50/M	48 hrs. 19.5M units			
KATZ, B.	$8.50/M	33 hrs. 16.5M units			
Totals					

b.   Employer's FICA taxes for week ended November 4, 1994: $ _____ $ _____
                                                                                          OASDI   HI

110

Date _____   Name _____

| Cum. FICA Taxable Wages as of Last Pay Period (10/28/94) | | (4) FICA Taxable Wages This Pay Period | | (5) FICA Taxes to be Withheld | | (6) Net Pay |
OASDI	HI	OASDI	HI	OASDI	HI	
$14,950.00	$14,950.00					
25,380.00	25,380.00					
59,256.89	59,256.89					
17,600.02	17,600.02					
9,553.74	9,553.74					
8,380.00	8,380.00					
17,570.10	17,570.10					
10,418.13	10,418.13					
11,603.90	11,603.90					
16,145.67	16,145.67					
6,513.50	6,513.50					
. . . . .	. . . . .					

✳ CONTINUING PAYROLL PROBLEM

Refer to the partially completed payroll register which you started at the end of Unit 2. You will now determine the amount of FICA taxes to be withheld from each employee's pay for the pay period ending January 7 by proceeding as follows:

1. In the Taxable Earnings columns—OASDI and HI, record the amount of each employee's weekly earnings that is subject to the two taxes.

2. Using the amounts you recorded in step (1), determine the taxes for each employee by multiplying the taxable earnings by the current OASDI and HI tax rates. Record these amounts in the appropriate Deductions columns for each employee.

NOTE: Retain your partially completed payroll register for use at the end of Unit 4.

CASE PROBLEMS

Case 3-1   Auditing Form 941

Ron Harte, payroll clerk for the Coastal Company, has just completed a rough draft of Form 941, the Employer's Quarterly Federal Tax Return, for the quarter ending March 31, 1994. The rough draft is shown on page 115. As Harte's supervisor and the person authorized to sign Form 941, you are auditing the form before it is mailed to make sure that the information on the form is accurate.

The information available to you in four of the company's general ledger accounts is shown below and on page 114. Employees are paid on the 15th and the last day of each month. When these days fall on Saturday or Sunday, employees are paid the previous Friday. Indicate what changes, if any, should be made on Form 941 before the final copy is prepared, signed, and mailed.

FICA TAXES PAYABLE—OASDI   Account No. 214

Date		Debit	Credit	Balance Debit	Balance Credit
1994					
Jan. 14			773.96		773.96
14			773.94		1,547.90
19		1,547.90			--------
31			843.78		843.78
31			843.78		1,687.56
Feb. 4		1,687.56			--------
15			833.74		833.74
15			833.72		1,667.46
18		1,667.46			--------
28			803.79		803.79
28			803.79		1,607.58
Mar. 4		1,607.58			--------
15			786.72		786.72
15			786.73		1,573.45
18		1,573.45			--------
31			787.88		787.88
31			787.87		1,575.75
Apr. 6		1,575.75			--------

FICA TAXES PAYABLE—HI
Account No. 215

Date		Debit	Credit	Balance Debit	Balance Credit
1994					
Jan. 14			181.01		181.01
14			181.01		362.02
19		362.02			--------
31			197.34		197.34
31			197.32		394.66
Feb. 4		394.66			--------
15			194.98		194.98
15			194.98		389.96
18		389.96			--------
28			187.98		187.98
28			187.98		375.96
Mar. 4		375.96			--------
15			184.01		184.01
15			183.99		368.00
18		368.00			--------
31			184.26		184.26
31			184.24		368.50
Apr. 6		368.50			--------

EMPLOYEES FEDERAL INCOME TAXES PAYABLE
Account No. 216

Date		Debit	Credit	Balance Debit	Balance Credit
1994					
Jan. 14			1,980.00		1,980.00
19		1,980.00			--------
31			2,217.00		2,217.00
Feb. 4		2,217.00			--------
15			2,016.00		2,016.00
18		2,016.00			--------
28			2,007.00		2,007.00
Mar. 4		2,007.00			--------
15			1,970.00		1,970.00
18		1,970.00			--------
31			1,887.00		1,887.00
Apr. 6		1,887.00			--------

WAGES AND SALARIES
Account No. 511

Date		Debit	Credit	Balance Debit	Balance Credit
1994					
Jan. 14		12,483.16		12,483.16	
31		13,609.40		26,092.56	
Feb. 15		13,447.13		39,539.69	
28		12,964.43		52,504.12	
Mar. 15		12,689.02		65,193.14	
31		12,707.69		77,900.83	

Form **941**
4141
Department of the Treasury
Internal Revenue Service

Employer's Quarterly Federal Tax Return
▶ See separate instructions for information on completing this return.
Please type or print.

Enter state code for state in which deposits made . ▶ [:]
(see page 2 of instructions).

		OMB No. 1545-0029
Name (as distinguished from trade name)	Date quarter ended	T
	MAR 31, 1994	FF
Trade name, if any	Employer identification number	FD
COASTAL COMPANY	77-2267142	FP
Address (number and street)	City, state, and ZIP code	I
77 CASTRO SAN FRANCISCO, CA 94117-6903		T

If address is different from prior return, check here ▶ [ ]

IRS Use

```
1 1 1 1 1 1 1 1 1 1 1    2    3 3 3 3 3 3    4 4 4
5 5 5   6   7   8 8 8 8 8   9 9 9   10 10 10 10 10 10 10 10 10 10
```

If you do not have to file returns in the future, check here ▶ [ ]   and enter date final wages paid ▶

If you are a seasonal employer, see **Seasonal employers** on page 2 and check here (see instructions) ▶ [ ]

1	Number of employees (except household) employed in the pay period that includes March 12th ▶		19
2	Total wages and tips subject to withholding, plus other compensation	2	77,900 38
3	Total income tax withheld from wages, tips, and sick pay	3	12,077 00
4	Adjustment of withheld income tax for preceding quarters of calendar year	4	—0—
5	Adjusted total of income tax withheld (line 3 as adjusted by line 4—see instructions) . .	5	12,077 00
6a	Taxable social security wages . . . . $ 77,900 38 × 12.4% (.124) =	6a	9,659 65
b	Taxable social security tips . . . . $ —0— × 12.4% (.124) =	6b	—0—
7	Taxable Medicare wages and tips . . . . . $ 77,900 38 × 2.9% (.029) =	7	2,259 11
8	Total social security and Medicare taxes (add lines 6a, 6b, and 7). Check here if wages are not subject to social security and/or Medicare tax . . . . ▶ [ ]	8	11,918 76
9	Adjustment of social security and Medicare taxes (see instructions for required explanation) Sick Pay $ _____ ± Fractions of Cents $ _____ ± Other $ _____ =	9	04
10	Adjusted total of social security and Medicare taxes (line 8 as adjusted by line 9—see instructions)	10	11,918 80
11	**Total taxes** (add lines 5 and 10)	11	23,995 80
12	Advance earned income credit (EIC) payments made to employees, if any	12	—0—
13	Net taxes (subtract line 12 from line 11). **This should equal line 17, column (d) below** (or line D of Schedule B (Form 941))	13	23,995 80
14	Total deposits for quarter, including overpayment applied from a prior quarter	14	23,977 80
15	Balance due (subtract line 14 from line 13). Pay to Internal Revenue Service	15	18 00
16	Overpayment, if line 14 is more than line 13, enter excess here ▶ $ _____ and check if to be: [ ] Applied to next return OR [ ] Refunded.		

17 Monthly Summary of Federal Tax Liability.
- **Monthly depositors:** Complete line 17, columns (a) through (d) and check here . . . . ▶ [ ]
- **Semiweekly depositors:** Complete Schedule B and check here . . . . ▶ [ ]
- **All filers:** If line 13 is less than $500, you need not complete line 17 or Schedule B.

(a) First month liability	(b) Second month liability	(c) Third month liability	(d) Total liability for quarter
8,189.14	8,063.96	7,742.70	23,995.80

Sign Here

Under penalties of perjury, I declare that I have examined this return, including accompanying schedules and statements, and to the best of my knowledge and belief, it is true, correct, and complete.

Signature ▶   Print Your Name and Title ▶   Date ▶

Form **941**

Case 3-2   Hiring a Former Employee for the Summer

To provide coverage for a programmer who will be vacationing during July and August, Ann Langford, payroll supervisor for New Ventures, Inc., has decided to contact Marc Cruz, who retired from the company six months ago. The closing part of Langford's interview with Cruz went something like this:

Langford: It will be good, Marc, having you back with us tomorrow. In fact, you can use your old office. Your former assistant, Ted, is still with us and will be able to lend a helping hand and get all the supplies you need. We are in a rush to get the bugs out of this new program, and I know you are just the one to help us out.

Cruz: Sounds fine with me. It will be good to see all the old familiar faces again. You know, for the past two months I have been doing some part-time consulting work for Rox-Moor and that debugging is now finished. It's going to be a challenge working on your new payroll deductions program. By the way, will I be able to use one of your new notebook computers?

Langford: I've already requisitioned one for you and it will be on your desk tomorrow morning. Oh, I almost forgot. We are now "flexing" in our department. So, you should plan to be here between 9:00 and 9:30. That way, you can feel free to leave any time after 4:00. Okay?

Cruz: Good. By the way, is the company still paying every other week?

Langford: Yes. But, we shall carry you as an independent contractor, doing seasonal consulting work for us. This means that we shall be paying you a weekly flat fee—with no deducts.

Is Langford proceeding correctly by classifying Cruz as an independent contractor? Explain.

WITHHOLDING FOR INCOME TAXES

GOALS OF THIS UNIT

After completing your study of this unit, you should be able to:

1. Determine coverage under the federal income tax withholding law by examining (a) the employer-employee relationship, (b) the kinds of payments defined as wages, and (c) those kinds of employment that are excluded under the law.

2. Complete Form W-2 and be familiar with other wage and tax statements.

3. Calculate the amount of federal income taxes to be withheld under the percentage method and the wage-bracket method.

4. Describe alternative methods of withholding federal income taxes such as quarterly averaging of wages, annualizing of wages, and cumulative withholding.

5. Calculate the withholding of federal income taxes on supplementary wage payments such as vacation pay, bonuses, commissions, dismissal pay, and tips.

6. Reinforce your knowledge of completing employers' returns such as Forms 941 and 8109, which we discussed in Unit 3.

7. Describe briefly the major kinds of information returns.

8. Understand how the task of payroll accounting is further complicated by the imposition of state and local income taxes.

The federal government has taxed our income since March 1, 1913, and over the years many tax statutes have been enacted. With the passage of the Current Tax Payment Act of 1943, employers were required to withhold federal income taxes from our wages and salaries on a "pay-as-you-go" basis. The amount of taxes withheld is not our exact tax liability because the amount withheld is based upon a system of graduated withholding rates that approximates the actual tax liability. If the actual tax is more or less than the amount withheld, when we file our annual income tax returns, we may have to pay more than the amount withheld or we may be entitled to a refund.[1]

In this unit we describe the obligations of employers to withhold from each payment of wages and salaries the amount required by law and to turn this amount over to the federal government for the employee's income tax account. After employers have remitted this amount, their responsibility for the collection of income taxes from their employees ends.

---

[1]Those persons interested in tax planning and completing tax returns for individuals, partnerships, and corporations are directed to the many publications of the Internal Revenue Service. These publications and tax forms are available from the IRS Forms Distribution Center of the taxpayer's state and are in many public libraries that maintain reference sets of IRS publications.

Payroll accounting is further complicated as a result of the number of states, cities, and counties that require the withholding of income taxes on wages and salaries. Thus, in order to avoid costly penalties, today's payroll managers, especially those in organizations having employees in many states, must have at their fingertips up-to-date information on laws and regulations such as those we describe in this unit.

COVERAGE UNDER FEDERAL INCOME TAX WITHHOLDING LAW

Before you may withhold any tax under the tax law, the following conditions must exist:

1. There must be, or must have been, an employer-employee relationship.
2. The payments received by the employee must be properly defined as wages.
3. The employment must not be exempted by the law.

We shall discuss each of these qualifying conditions in the following paragraphs. You will see that, under both the federal income tax withholding law and the social security law (discussed in Unit 3), the definitions of *employer*, *employee*, and *wages* are very similar.

Employers

An *employer* is any person or organization for whom an individual performs any service as an employee. Sole proprietors are employers regardless of whether they have one or more employees. Partners are also employers regardless of the number of employees and regardless of whether or not the partners draw compensation for services rendered. Corporations are employers, and the officers of a corporation including the president, vice-president, secretary, and treasurer are employees. Not-for-profit corporations, which are themselves exempt from income tax, are also employers and are subject to the withholding requirements. Such corporations include religious and charitable organizations, educational institutions, clubs, and social organizations. Employers also include the federal government, state governments, the governments of Puerto Rico and the District of Columbia, as well as any of their respective agencies, instrumentalities, or political subdivisions.

Employees

Every individual is an *employee* if there is a *common-law relationship* between the employee and the person for whom the services are performed. At this point, you may wish to review the 20-factor *Common-Law Test* presented in Illustration 3-1, page 70.

In some cases it is rather difficult to determine whether the relationship of employer and employee exists. If such a relationship does exist, the designation of the relationship by the parties as anything other than that of employer and employee is immaterial. Thus, if such relationship exists, it does not matter whether the employee is designated as a partner, an agent, or an independent contractor. Generally physicians, lawyers, dentists, veterinarians, public accountants, auctioneers, and others who follow an independent trade, business, or profession in which they offer their services to the public are *independent contractors* and not employees. See the *Test for Independent Contractor Status* in Illustration 3-2, page 71.

In defining the term employee, no distinction is made between classes or grades of employees. Thus, superintendents, managers, and other administrative and executive personnel are employees. As we stated above, the officers of a corporation are employees of that corporation. However, the directors of a corporation are not employees unless they perform services other than attending and participating in meetings of the board of directors. Partners are not considered employees even though they may draw compensation for services rendered the partnership. In the case of federal, state, or local governmental agencies, the term employee includes both officers and elected officials.

Wages

The term *wages* includes the total compensation paid for services whether in the form of wages, salaries, commissions, or bonuses, including the cash value of remuneration paid in a medium other than cash. When employers pay wages in the form of noncash property, they are not relieved of their duty to withhold. Rather, they must withhold on the fair value of the property.

Vacation allowances, dismissal payments, and other supplementary payments representing compensation for services rendered constitute wages. Any deductions from the wages paid employees are considered to be part of the employees' remuneration at the time the deductions are made. This means that the amount of federal income taxes to be withheld is determined from the *gross amount* of wages without regard to deductions made from gross wages for local, state, or federal taxes; insurance premiums; savings bond purchases; employee contributions to profit-sharing plans; and union dues.

Meals and Lodging.
Generally the cash value of meals and lodging furnished employees is included in taxable wages. Under federal income tax withholding, however, the tax does *not* apply if employers furnish the meals and lodging on their premises and for their convenience, and require that employees accept the lodging.

EXAMPLE:

Jersey Hospital requires certain employees to live and to eat on the hospital's premises in order to be available for emergency calls. The hospital does *not* need to withhold federal income taxes on the cash value of the meals and lodging since the value of these items does not represent taxable income to employees.

If employees receive a cash allowance for their meals or lodging, the exclusion does not apply because only meals and lodging furnished *in kind* are free from withholding. An exception exists when employees receive supper money in cash for voluntarily working overtime. Generally the payment is regarded as for the employer's convenience and thus is not subject to federal income tax withholding.

Noncash Fringe Benefits.
Examples of *noncash fringe benefits* that employers provide their employees include the personal use of company cars, use of vehicles for commuting (vanpooling), flights on employer-provided airplanes, and free or discounted flights on commercial airlines. Such fringe benefits are considered to be taxable income to employees and thus are subject to the withholding of federal income taxes.

Employers have much flexibility in deciding when to withhold federal income taxes on noncash fringe benefits so long as the withholding occurs in the calendar year in which the benefits are provided. For example, the withholding may be in the final paycheck in December, or the amount to be withheld may be spread over several pay periods. The timing of the withholding need not be the same for all employees nor for all benefits. However, if personal property such as securities or real estate is provided as a noncash fringe benefit, the withholding of federal income taxes must occur at the time of transferring the personal property.

Tips.
Cash tips of $20 or more received in a calendar month, in the course of employment with a single employer, are treated as remuneration subject to income tax withholding. *Noncash* tips, such a those in the form of passes, tickets, or other goods, are not considered wages and thus are not subject to federal income tax withholding.

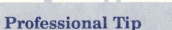

Professional Tip
Do not confuse this treatment of cash tips with the definition of a tipped employee given in the Fair Labor Standards Act. As noted in Unit 2, the FLSA defines a *tipped employee* as a person engaged in an occupation in which tips of more than $30 a month are customarily received.

An employee must furnish the employer a statement of the cash tips received if they amount to at least $20 in a month. The employee must report the amount of the cash tips in writing to the employer by the tenth day of the following month. Failure on the part of the employee to make a timely report will subject the employee to a penalty. The Internal Revenue Service (IRS) issues a special pamphlet, consisting of Forms 4070 and 4070-A, that may be used by the employee in recording tips and reporting them to the employer. (See Illustration 3-3 on page 74.) The employer is not required to audit or verify the accuracy of the tip income reported for purposes of federal income tax withholding.

There are special reporting rules for large food and beverage establishments. A *large food or beverage establishment* is one that provides food or beverages for consumption on the premises, where tipping is customary, and where the employer normally employs more than 10 workers on a typical business day in all food or beverage operations.

If employees report tips that total 8% or more of the gross receipts (less carryout sales and sales with a 10% or more service charge added), no tip allocation is needed. However, if the tips reported do not equal 8% of the gross receipts, the employer must allocate to the tipped employees an amount equal to the difference between 8% of the gross receipts and the total tips reported. The allocation may be made according to an agreement between the employer and the employees or in accordance with the method contained in the regulations issued by the IRS.

EXAMPLE:

The tips reported during October by the employees of La Cruz Restaurant total $4,840. The gross receipts for that month are $78,500. The restaurant is required to allocate additional income of

($78,500 x .08) – $4,840, or $1,440,

among all of the tipped employees.

As we indicated earlier, federal income taxes are to be withheld *only* on the tips reported to the employer; no taxes are withheld on the tips that are merely allocated.

Employers who allocate tips are required to file annually with the IRS *Form 8027, Employer's Annual Information Return of Tip Income and Allocated Tips,* which contains information such as:

1. Total charged tips.
2. Total charged receipts (other than nonallocable receipts) showing charged tips.
3. Total amount of service charges less than 10% paid as wages to employees.
4. Total tips reported by indirectly tipped and directly tipped employees.
5. Gross receipts from food or beverage operations (other than nonallocable receipts).
6. Amount that must be allocated as tips and recorded on the employee's Wage and Tax Statement, Form W-2. (Form W-2 is described and illustrated later in this unit.)

Regardless of whether employees receive an allocation, at the time of filing their personal income tax returns, employees are required to report as income all tips received. If employees fail to report the full amount of allocation as gross income, they must be able to furnish adequate records to substantiate the lesser amount reported.

Payments Exempt from Withholding

The law excludes from the definition of "wages" certain payments such as those described below. Thus, persons making such payments are *not* required to withhold federal income taxes.

Advances. Amounts paid in advance or reimbursements made to employees for traveling or other business expenses incurred or reasonably expected to be incurred are not subject to withholding. Any reasonable segregation of wages paid will be acceptable. Thus, you may issue one check indicating the amount that represents wages and the amount that represents reimbursed expenses, or you may issue a separate check covering the expenses.

Educational Assistance. Many employers reimburse their employees for the cost of tuition, fees, books, and supplies that is incurred when the employees are attending school. Such amounts are excluded from the definition of wages and thus are not subject to federal income tax withholding. In 1994, the maximum amount of educational assistance that can be excluded is $5,250. However, withholding *is* required from employer-paid tuition payments for hobby-type courses such as photography and gardening.

The employer's educational assistance plan must be in writing and limited to providing employees with educational assistance. The plan must not discriminate in favor of employees who are officers, shareholders, self-employed individuals, or highly compensated employees or their dependents.

Note that employer-paid tuition for *job-related* courses is tax free and thus not subject to withholding. These tuition payments are one of several fringe benefits that employees may receive. To be considered job-related, a course must maintain or improve the employee's skills required for the job, or be required by the employer as a condition of continuing employment in the employee's current job. Courses that are needed by the employee to meet the minimum education requirements for a job or that prepare an employee for a new trade or business do *not* qualify as job-related.

Other Payments Exempt from Withholding. Some other types of employment and payments excluded for income tax *withholding* purposes are:

1. Agricultural workers, *all* of whom are paid cash remuneration *less* than $2,500 in any calendar year. Employers who do not meet the $2,500 annual payroll test may exclude remuneration for agricultural services when it

amounts to less than $150 paid *each* worker in a calendar year. Payment for farm work with remuneration other than cash is not taxed.

2. Domestic service in a private home, local college club, or local chapter of a college fraternity or sorority.

3. Persons not employed in the course of the employer's trade or business (casual laborers) provided the cash remuneration paid for service performed in the calendar quarter is less than $50 and employees work on fewer than 24 days in that or the preceding quarter.

4. Citizens or residents of the United States employed by a foreign government or an international organization such as the United Nations.

5. U.S. citizens residing abroad if (a) they have been bona fide residents of a foreign country or countries for an uninterrupted period that includes an entire taxable year, or (b) they show that they have been present in a foreign country or countries for at least 330 full days during a period of 12 consecutive months.

6. Ministers of churches and members of religious orders performing duties as such.

7. Public officials (fees only, not salaries).

8. Individuals under age 18 for delivery or distribution of newspapers or shopping news and vendors of newspapers and magazines whose remuneration consists of difference between purchase and sales price.

9. Deceased person's wages paid to the employee's beneficiary or estate.

10. Sickness or injury payments made under workers' compensation law or contract of insurance. (However, as we explain later, employees receiving sick pay may voluntarily authorize insurers and other third parties to withhold federal income taxes on the payments.)

11. Tips if less than $20 a month.

12. Moving expenses reimbursed by the employer if at time of payment it is reasonable to believe that the employee will be entitled to a deduction for these expenses on the individual's federal income tax return. When moving expenses are reimbursed (whether to the employee, to a third party for the employee, or by providing services in kind to the employee), the employee should be given a completed *Form 4782, Employee Moving Expense Information* (not illustrated).

13. Employer's cost of *group-term* life insurance on the life of an employee. However, the cost of group-term life insurance in excess of $50,000 is includible in the employee's gross

Professional Tip

Retired employees are subject to the same tax rules that apply to active employees for the cost of coverage above $50,000 of group-term life insurance purchased by employers.

income and must be reported by the employer as part of the employee's "wages, tips, and other compensation" on the worker's Wage and Tax Statement (Form W-2).

14. Strike benefits and lockout benefits paid by a union to its members.

15. Amounts received by service personnel on active service in an area declared by the President to be a combat zone. For example, when the Persian Gulf area was designated a combat zone, the military pay received by service personnel serving in the combat zone (or while hospitalized from injuries or disease incurred in the combat zone) was exempted from income tax.

16. Supper money paid occasionally to employees who work overtime, if the amounts can be classified as a *de minimis* fringe benefit. (*De minimis* fringe benefits are those of so little value as to make accounting for the benefits unreasonable or administratively impracticable.)

17. Employer contributions to cash or deferred arrangements, such as salary-reduction agreements (Code Sec. 401[k] plans). In such plans, an employee elects to have the employer contribute an amount to the plan on the employee's behalf or to receive the amount directly from the employer in cash. The amounts contributed to the plan following the employee's election are treated as employer contributions to the plan and are not subject to federal income tax withholding. In 1993, the amount an employee could defer under these arrangements was limited to $8,994.

18. Employer contributions to employer-sponsored individual retirement accounts (IRA) and simplified employee pension plans (SEP). Employees must include in their gross income the employer's contributions, but income tax withholding is not required if the employer reasonably expects that the employees will be able to deduct such contributions on their income tax returns. In 1993, employees could

elect to defer up to $8,994 of employer contributions into a qualified SEP plan. In a qualified plan, employers must have 25 or fewer employees at the beginning of the year, and at least 50% of the employees must elect to contribute to the SEP plan.

Under certain conditions federal income tax withholding is permitted from some wage payments that are ordinarily exempt from withholding. For example, domestic workers and members of the clergy may request their employers to withhold federal income taxes from their wage payments during the year. Such a procedure benefits these workers who are thus able to decrease their year-end tax liability.

WITHHOLDING ALLOWANCES AND WITHHOLDING CERTIFICATES

For purposes of computing the withholding tax, employees are entitled to personal allowances and allowances for dependents provided the employees properly furnish their employers with a claim for the allowances. In addition to the personal allowances and allowances for dependents, employees may claim other allowances such as a special withholding allowance and allowances for itemized deductions and tax credits.

Personal Allowances

A *personal allowance* (sometimes called a *personal exemption*) is a deduction allowed in computing taxable income. For the calendar year 1993, a personal allowance of $2,350 was permitted in computing an employee's taxable income, provided the employee was not claimed as a dependent on another person's tax return. The value of the personal allowance was reduced for employees with an adjusted gross income over $108,450 ($162,700 if married and filing jointly, $135,600 if a head of household, or $81,350 if married and filing separately). This exemption amount is annually adjusted, or indexed, for inflation.

If an employee is *married* and the spouse is not claimed as a dependent on another person's tax return, the employee may also claim one personal allowance for the spouse.

If employees hold more than one job, they may not claim the *same* withholding allowances with more than one employer at the same time. They may claim all of their allowances on one job, or they may divide their allowances among jobs.

An employee who is divorced or legally separated by a decree of separate maintenance is not to be treated as married. Also, if an employee is a nonresident alien (other than a resident of Canada, Mexico, or Puerto Rico), he or she may claim only *one* withholding allowance.

Allowances for Dependents

Employees may claim one allowance for each dependent (other than a spouse) who can be claimed on their federal income tax returns. To qualify as a dependent, the person must meet specific requirements that are listed in the instructions accompanying the individual's federal income tax return.

Special Withholding Allowance

To insure that wages below the level to which income taxes apply will not be subject to withholding, a worker may claim an additional allowance. This *special withholding allowance* may be claimed by workers whether or not they plan to itemize deductions on their tax returns. Note that the special withholding allowance is used *only* to figure the employee's income tax withholding; the allowance is *not* claimed when the employee files his or her tax return.

A special withholding allowance can be claimed by a person under any *one* of the following situations:

1. The person is single and has only one job.
2. The person is married, has only one job, and the spouse is not working.
3. The person's wages from a second job or the spouse's wages (or the total of both) are $1,000 or less.

The special withholding allowance may be claimed by workers when they complete the Employee's Withholding Allowance Certificate, which we shall discuss and illustrate in a later section.

Other Withholding Allowances

Withholding allowances are designed to reduce the overwithholding of income taxes of employees. In addition to personal allowances and allowances for dependents, employees may be entitled to withholding allowances based on estimated tax credits (such as child and dependent care credit) and estimated itemized deductions (such as medical expenses and charitable contributions).

Employees may take these credits and deductions when filing their federal income tax returns. The number of withholding allowances is determined on the worksheets that accompany the withholding allowance certificate and then reported on the certificate itself, as shown in Illustration 4-1.

Form W-4—Employee's Withholding Allowance Certificate

Employees are required to furnish their employers with a signed *Employee's Withholding Allowance Certificate, Form W-4.* This form sets forth the number of withholding allowances that an employee claims, which shall in no event exceed the number to which the employee is entitled.

Form W-4 contains the withholding allowance certificate and detailed instructions and worksheets for employees to use in completing the certificate. Illustration 4-1 shows a filled-in withholding allowance certificate, Form W-4, which the employee detaches and gives to the employer.

You must retain the withholding certificates as a supporting record of the withholding allowances used in deducting income taxes from the employees' salaries and wages. Once filed, the withholding allowance certificate remains in effect until an amended certificate takes effect. You must retain the withholding certificates for as long as the certificates are in effect and for four years thereafter.

If there is a change in the status of employees with respect to the number of withholding allowances to which they are entitled, they should file an amended Form W-4 with you. In case there is a *decrease* in the number of withholding allowances, the employee must furnish you with a new certificate within 10 days. If, however, the reduction in allowances results from the death of a dependent or a spouse, the amended certificate need not be filed until December 1 since the personal allowance is not lost by death of the dependent during the current taxable year. Should there be an *increase* in the number of withholding allowances to which an employee is entitled, he or she should file a new certificate. However, an employee is not required to do so, as the claiming of additional allowances is optional with the employee.

When an employee files an amended certificate as a result of a change in status, you may put the certificate into effect at any time. However, you must put the certificate into effect no later than the start of the first payroll period ending (or the first payment of wages) on or after the 30th day you receive the certificate.

If an employee furnishes you with an amended Form W-4, you may not repay or reimburse the employee for income taxes overwithheld before the effective date of the new certificate. However, you may repay or reimburse the employee for income taxes overwithheld on or after the effective date of the amended form if you failed to take the new certificate into account.

It is important that employees file Form W-4 to avoid having amounts withheld that are not close to the amount of tax due at the time they file their tax returns. If an employee does not file a withholding allowance certificate, you must withhold federal income tax as if the employee had claimed no allowances.

If married employees do not claim their marital status on Form W-4, you must withhold according to

---

1 Type or print your first name and middle initial: Alberta V.   Last name: Barrera   **2** Your social security number: 173-68-3201

Home address (number and street or rural route): 550 South State Street

3 [X] Single ☐ Married ☐ Married, but withhold at higher Single rate.
Note: *If married, but legally separated, or spouse is a nonresident alien, check the Single box*

City or town, state, and ZIP code: Troy, ME 04987-0550

4 If your last name differs from that on your social security card, check here and call 1-800-772-1213 for more information · · · · ▶ ☐

5 Total number of allowances you are claiming (from line G above or from the worksheets on page 2 if they apply) .   **5**   5

6 Additional amount, if any, you want withheld from each paycheck . . . .   **6** $ 0

7 I claim exemption from withholding for 1993 and I certify that I meet **ALL** of the following conditions for exemption:
- Last year I had a right to a refund of **ALL** Federal income tax withheld because I had **NO** tax liability; **AND**
- This year I expect a refund of **ALL** Federal income tax withheld because I expect to have **NO** tax liability; **AND**
- This year if my income exceeds $600 and includes nonwage income, another person cannot claim me as a dependent.

If you meet all of the above conditions, enter "EXEMPT" here . . . . ▶   **7**

Under penalties of perjury, I certify that I am entitled to the number of withholding allowances claimed on this certificate or entitled to claim exempt status.

Employee's signature ▶ *Alberta V. Barrera*   Date ▶ January 2 , 19 93

8 Employer's name and address (Employer: Complete 8 and 10 only if sending to the IRS)   **9** Office code (optional)   **10** Employer identification number

Illustration 4-1. Form W-4, Employee's Withholding Allowance Certificate

the withholding tables for single employees. Thus, to take advantage of the lower withholding provided for married employees, married workers must indicate their marital status in Box 3 of Form W-4. In this box, the marital status entitled "Married, but withhold at higher Single rate" appears. Married couples with both spouses employed or a married person with more than one employer may use this status to increase the amount of income taxes withheld.

No-Tax-Liability Exemption

Employees who had no income tax liability in 1993 and do not expect to have any in 1994 qualify for exemption from withholding of federal income tax from their wages. Such employees include students working during the summer, retired persons, and other part-time workers. Single persons who made less than $6,050 in 1993 owed no federal income tax. During 1993 a married couple entitled to file a joint return could earn combined wages up to $10,900 without incurring any federal income tax liability. However, if someone else claimed the employee as a dependent on his or her tax return, the employee probably would have to pay some income tax. For example, in 1993, employees were *not* exempt from withholding if they had any nonwage income, such as interest on savings or dividends, and if their total income (wages and nonwage income) was more than $600.

Part-time and summer employees who are exempt from the withholding of federal income taxes should complete and submit to you their Form W-4 showing the no-tax-liability status. In such cases, you *must not* withhold federal income tax from their wages. (This exemption does not affect your liability for collecting the employee's FICA taxes.) Employees claiming the exemption from withholding must file Form W-4 with you each year.

Additional and Voluntary Withholding Agreements

In some instances, employees wish to have additional federal income tax withheld from their wages. For example, a person with two or more jobs or a married couple, both of whom are working, may need to have additional income tax withheld. The simplest way to increase the amount of tax withheld is to reduce the number of withholding allowances claimed. However, this approach may not be satisfactory for employees who claim only one or even zero allowances. Therefore, employees may request on Form W-4 that their employer withhold an additional amount from their wages.

In other cases, employees may have no income tax withheld from their wages because the payments received do not represent wages; or the relationship between the one making the payment and the payee is not that of employer and employee. For example, the person receiving remuneration for services may be a clergyman or a domestic worker in a private home. As we indicated earlier in this unit, these types of payments do not constitute wages for income tax withholding purposes. However, such persons may voluntarily request that you withhold federal income taxes from their payments. Employees who wish to enter into an additional or a voluntary withholding agreement with their employer need only furnish you with Form W-4. The filing of this form constitutes a request for withholding.

Other persons may need to have additional taxes withheld if they receive income other than wages, such as interest and dividends. Procedures are available for these persons to enter into voluntary withholding agreements under which federal income taxes will be withheld from payments not ordinarily subject to withholding.

Requests for additional and voluntary withholding become effective when you accept them and commence to withhold the tax. The agreements remain in effect until the stipulated termination date or until the termination is mutually agreed upon by you and the employee. Either you or the employee may terminate an agreement before its stipulated or mutually agreed-upon termination date by furnishing to the other party a signed, written notice of termination.

Withholding Less Than the Required Amount

The full amount of the income tax for which employees are liable must be withheld. You may not withhold a lesser amount than required under the law. In determining the amount of tax required to be withheld, you consider the number of withholding allowances that an employee claims on Form W-4. In no event may the number of allowances claimed be greater than the number to which the employee is entitled.

A civil fine of $500 may be charged for filing a Form W-4 that decreases the tax withheld with no reasonable basis at the time of the decrease. Also, criminal penalties apply for willfully supplying false or fraudulent information or failing to supply information in an attempt to evade the tax.

Invalid Withholding Certificates

The number of allowances that a worker claims is used in computing the amount of federal income taxes to be withheld. However, you are under no obligation to determine whether the number of allowances claimed is greater than the number to which the employee is entitled.

A withholding certificate is deemed to be invalid and void if:

1. The withholding certificate has been altered by the employee.
2. Extraneous unauthorized material has been added to the form.
3. The employee has otherwise indicated that the data on the form are false.

In such cases, the employee should be told that the form is invalid and that another one should be completed. If the employee does not complete a valid form, you must withhold federal income taxes at the rate for a single person claiming no exemptions. However, if there is a prior valid certificate in effect with respect to the employee, you must continue to withhold in accordance with the prior certificate.

Submitting Forms W-4 to IRS

To curb the practice of filing false Forms W-4 by claiming unreasonable numbers of allowances or total exemption from withholding, the IRS requires employers to submit a copy of each form on which:

1. An employee claims 11 or more withholding allowances, or
2. An employee, usually earning more than $200 a week at the time the certificate was filed, claims to be exempt from withholding.

Employers should submit such copies of Form W-4 at the time and place of filing Form 941, Employer's Quarterly Federal Tax Return, for the reporting period. You may submit the W-4 information on magnetic tape instead of filing paper returns if you first receive permission from the IRS. Employers may submit their Forms W-4 to the IRS more often if they wish. If so, employers should include a cover letter giving their name, address, employer identification number, and the number of forms included.

Employees who claim allowances inconsistent with the IRS regulations may submit new Forms W-4 with supporting statements either directly to the IRS or to the employer, who must then forward the forms to the IRS. Until receipt of notice from the IRS, you are required to withhold on the basis of the statements made in the certificates submitted. The IRS may find that the copies of the Forms W-4 submitted contain materially incorrect statements. If the IRS verifies that the forms are defective, it will furnish you the reasons for such a determination. The IRS will advise you that

employees who submitted defective Forms W-4 cannot claim an exempt status nor can they claim the number of allowances that is in excess of the number specified by the IRS in the written notice.

You must give the employees a copy of the notice and ask them to furnish new Forms W-4. Until new forms are received, you must withhold on the basis of the maximum number of allowances set by the IRS in the written notice. If the employees' new forms claim more allowances than the number set by the IRS, you should disregard the amended forms and continue withholding on the basis of the number of allowances set by the IRS.

Other Withholdings

Federal income taxes are also withheld from other kinds of payments made to current and former employees. We briefly describe several of the different kinds of payments below. You will find additional information about the withholdings in the instructions accompanying each withholding allowance form.

Form W-4P—Withholding Certificate for Pension or Annuity Payments. Generally the withholding of federal income taxes applies to payments made from pension, profit-sharing, stock bonus, annuity, and certain deferred compensation plans and individual retirement arrangements. You treat the payments from any of these sources as wages for the purpose of withholding. Unless the recipients of pension or annuity payments elect *not* to have federal income taxes withheld from such payments, the taxes will be withheld. Payers must withhold on monthly pension and annuity payments exceeding $1,104 ($13,250 a year) unless the payees elect otherwise. If the recipients do not instruct the payers to the contrary, the payers are required to withhold income taxes as if the recipients were married and claiming three withholding allowances.

By completing Form W-4P or a substitute form furnished by the payer, an employee can elect to have no income tax withheld from the payments received. The form may also be used to change the amount of tax that would ordinarily be withheld by the payers. Once completed, Form W-4P remains in effect until the recipient changes or revokes the certificate. The payer must notify the recipients each year of their right to elect to have no taxes withheld or to revoke their election.

Form W-4S—Request for Federal Income Tax Withholding From Sick Pay. Form W-4S must be filed with the *payer of sick pay* if the employee wants federal income taxes withheld from the payments. The form should *not* be filed with

the worker's employer who makes such payments since employers are already required to withhold income taxes from sick pay. *Thus, Form W-4S is filed only if the payer is a third party, such as an insurance company.*

Withholding for Child Support.

To enforce the collection of child-support funds, legislation was passed to require the withholding of these amounts. Under the law, procedures are developed by state agencies for the automatic withholding of child-support payments from employees' wages. The Family Support Act of 1988 requires the *immediate* withholding for child-support payments for all cases supported by a court order. The amount withheld is equal to the amount of the delinquency, subject to the limits prescribed in the federal garnishment law, which we shall discuss in Unit 6. Also, employers are entitled to withhold a fee, set by each state, for the administrative costs they incur in relation to the withholding.

Withholding to Collect Delinquent Taxes.

The collection of delinquent federal taxes by means of payroll deductions has been authorized by the IRS. Under this procedure, employees use the *Payroll Deduction Agreement, Form 2159*. On this form, employees authorize their employer to deduct specified amounts from their salaries or wages each payday. The employer remits the amounts withheld to the IRS at regular, agreed-upon intervals.

THE MAIN METHODS OF WITHHOLDING

After the number of withholding allowances has been determined, your next step is to select the method of computing the amount of federal income tax to be withheld. Usually one of two main methods of withholding—the *percentage method* or the *wage-bracket method*—is used. Under both methods, unmarried persons (either single or head of household) are distinguished from married persons. Both methods provide for giving employees the full benefit of the allowances they claim. As you will see below, both methods use withholding tables to determine the amount to be withheld.

In making a choice between the two methods, you are primarily concerned with the number of employees and the type of payroll accounting system used. You may change from one method to another at will and may use one method for one group of employees and the other method for other groups.

The two withholding methods take into account the standard deduction amounts. A *standard deduction* is an amount of money that is used to reduce a person's adjusted gross income in arriving at the taxable income. The standard deduction varies according to the taxpayer's filing status. For 1993, the following standard deductions apply (whether or not an individual is age 65 or older or is blind):

Joint return filers and surviving spouses	$6,200
Married filing separately	3,100
Head of household filers	5,450
Single filers	3,700

These amounts are increased for single and married individuals or surviving spouses age 65 or older or blind.

Each year the standard deductions are adjusted for inflation. The adjustment also applies to the additional standard deductions available to elderly or blind persons.

Percentage Method

To determine the tax under the percentage method, take the following steps:

Step 1: Determine the amount of gross wages earned. If the employee's wage ends in a fractional dollar amount, round the gross pay to the nearest dollar; if the gross pay ends in 50¢, the rounding off must be to the next higher dollar. Or, you may round the last digit of the gross pay to 0.

Step 2: Multiply the number of allowances claimed by the amount of one allowance for the applicable payroll period, as determined in the Table of Allowance Values shown in Illustration 4-2.

TABLE OF ALLOWANCE VALUES FOR 1993

PAYROLL PERIOD	AMOUNT OF ONE WITHHOLDING ALLOWANCE
Weekly	$ 45.19
Biweekly	90.38
Semimonthly	97.92
Monthly	195.83
Quarterly	587.50
Semiannual	1,175.00
Annual	2,350.00
Daily or miscellaneous (per day of such period)	9.04

Illustration 4-2. Table of Allowance Values for Percentage Method

Step 3: Subtract the amount for the number of allowances claimed from the employee's gross pay to find the excess of wages over allowances claimed.

Step 4: Determine the withholding tax on the excess of wages over allowances claimed by referring to the appropriate Percentage Method Withholding Table. These tables, in effect January 1, 1993, are shown in Tax Table A at the end of the textbook.

The percentage method of computation is further explained in the following illustrative examples.

EXAMPLES:

A. Sean Yan is single and claims one allowance. His income for the taxable year is $19,320, payable at the rate of $805 semimonthly.

Computation of Amount to be Withheld

Step 1:	Semimonthly wages	$805.00
Step 2:	Amount of one withholding allowance (from Allowance Table) . . .	97.92
Step 3:	Excess of wages over allowance	$707.08
Step 4:	Amount to be withheld from Table 3(a) in Tax Table A: 15% of ($707.08 less $105.00)	$ 90.31

B. Jose Fernandez, married with one dependent child, claims three allowances. Neither the wife nor the child has any separate income. Fernandez receives a salary of $48,000, payable at the rate of $923.08 each week.

Computation of Amount to be Withheld

Step 1:	Weekly wages (rounded to nearest dollar)		$923.00
Step 2:	Amount of one withholding allowance (from Allowance Table)	$45.19	
	Number of allowances claimed	x 3	135.57
Step 3:	Excess of wages over allowances . . .		$787.43
Step 4:	Amount to be withheld from Table 1(b) in Tax Table A: $99.75 + .96 [28% of ($787.43 less $784.00)]		$100.71

As we indicated before, to determine the amount of tax to be withheld under the percentage method, you may round the last digit of the wage amount to zero. Or, you may round the wage amount to the nearest dollar, as done in Example B. Thus, if an employee receives a weekly wage of $395.37, you may eliminate the last digit and determine the amount of the tax to be withheld on $395.30. Or, you may compute the amount to be withheld on $395. In other words, in such a case, you have the option of computing the amount of tax to be withheld on (a) $395.37, (b) $395.30, or (c) $395. If you decide to round wage payments ending in an even half dollar, you must compute the amount to be withheld on the higher dollar. Thus, if the wage payment amounted to $395.50, you must compute the amount to be withheld on $396. Where the amount to be withheld is determined on the basis of a miscellaneous payroll period, you may round only the aggregate wages for the period (not the average daily wage) to the nearest dollar.

To calculate more easily an employee's excess of wages over allowances claimed, you may use the table shown in Illustration 4-3 on page 128. To use this table:

Step 1: Locate in the left-hand column the total number of withholding allowances claimed by the employee.

Step 2: Determine the total dollar amount of the employee's withholding allowances in the corresponding line in the payroll period column.

Step 3: Subtract the amount obtained in Step 2 from the total wages earned by the employee for the payroll period to arrive at the excess of wages.

Step 4: Determine the withholding tax on the excess of wages over allowances claimed by referring to the appropriate Percentage Method Withholding Table in Tax Table A.

The IRS makes available formula tables and wage-bracket tables for percentage method withholding. These tables are especially useful in automated payroll systems.

Wage-Bracket Method

Under the wage-bracket method, the IRS provides statutory wage-bracket tables for weekly, biweekly, semimonthly, monthly, and daily or miscellaneous pay periods. You may obtain copies of the tables from the District Director of Internal Revenue. Tables for 10-day and 28-day payroll periods also are available at the office of the District Director and will be supplied upon request. The weekly, biweekly, semimonthly, monthly, and daily tables for married and single persons, in effect January 1, 1993, are reproduced in Tax Table B at the end of the textbook.

If the payroll period is quarterly, semiannual, or annual, you must use the percentage method of withholding since there are no wage-bracket withholding tables available for these payroll periods. You may also use the percentage method for payroll periods for which statutory tables are provided.

If the number of allowances is	And wages are paid—							
	Weekly	Bi-weekly	Semi-monthly	Monthly	Quarterly	Semi-annually	Annually	Daily or Misc.
	The total amount of withholding allowances for that payroll period is—							
0	$ 0	$ 0	$ 0	$ 0	$ 0	$ 0	$ 0	$ 0
1	45.19	90.38	97.92	195.83	587.50	1,175.00	2,350.00	9.04
2	90.38	180.76	195.84	391.66	1,175.00	2,350.00	4,700.00	18.08
3	135.57	271.14	293.76	587.49	1,762.50	3,525.00	7,050.00	27.12
4	180.76	361.52	391.68	783.32	2,350.00	4,700.00	9,400.00	36.16
5	225.95	451.90	489.60	979.15	2,937.50	5,875.00	11,750.00	45.20
6	271.14	542.28	587.52	1,174.98	3,525.00	7,050.00	14,100.00	54.24
7	316.33	632.66	685.44	1,370.81	4,112.50	8,225.00	16,450.00	63.28
8	361.52	723.04	783.36	1,566.64	4,700.00	9,400.00	18,800.00	72.32
9	406.71	813.42	881.28	1,762.47	5,287.50	10,575.00	21,150.00	81.36
10	451.90	903.80	979.20	1,958.30	5,875.00	11,750.00	23,500.00	90.40
11 or more	Multiply the amount of one withholding allowance for the specific payroll period by the number of allowances claimed							

Illustration 4-3. Easy-Reference Table for Computing Employee's Excess of Wages over Allowances Claimed

To use the wage-bracket method to determine the amounts to be withheld from the wages earned by employees, you should take the following steps:

Step 1: Select the withholding table that applies to the employee's marital status and the payroll period. (You can save time during this step by first separating all employees into groups of "Not Married" and "Married" according to the payroll period. Then determine the amount of federal income tax for all employees in the one group before selecting the appropriate withholding table to be used for the second group.)

Step 2: Locate the wage bracket (the first two columns of the table) in which the employee's gross wages fall.

Step 3: Follow the line for such wage bracket across to the right to the column headed by the figure that represents the number of withholding allowances claimed by the employee. This amount is the tax to be withheld.

NOTE: If the amount of an employee's wages exceeds the amount shown in the last bracket of the table, use the percentage method of withholding. Before using the percentage method tables, however, be sure to reduce the employee's wages by the value of the total withholding allowances claimed.

If, instead of using the percentage method to compute the amount to be withheld from the semimonthly wages of Yan (Example A, page 127), you had elected to use the wage-bracket method, you would have withheld $91 each payday instead of $90.31. (Refer to semimonthly, not married table in Tax Table B.)

If, instead of using the percentage method to compute the amount to be withheld from the weekly wages of Fernandez (Example B, page 127), you had elected to use the wage-bracket method, you would have withheld $101 each payday instead of $100.71. (Refer to weekly, married table in Tax Table B.)

OTHER METHODS OF WITHHOLDING

In addition to the two principal methods of withholding we have described above, you may use other methods such as quarterly averaging of wages, annualizing wages, cumulative withholding, and withholding for part-year employment. Of these four alternative procedures, two methods—cumulative withholding and withholding for part-year employment—may be initiated only upon an employee's request. If you should find the alternative methods unsatisfactory for your particular payroll operations, you may devise your own withholding procedure, as we discuss later in the section, "Substantially Similar" Methods.

We discuss the features of the four alternative methods in this section. You may round to the nearest dollar the tax withheld under any of the alternative methods, following the rounding rules given on page 127.

Quarterly Averaging of Wages

Under this method of withholding, proceed as follows:

Step 1: Estimate the wages that will be paid the employee in the calendar quarter.

Step 2: Calculate an appropriate average payment.

Step 3: Withhold an amount based on the average payment instead of on the actual payment.

During the quarter you should make any needed adjustment to bring the amount of tax withheld on the basis of average payments into line with the amount required to be withheld without any averaging.

EXAMPLE:

Ortiz, Inc., estimates that Helene Ligonnier will be paid $6,000 during the second quarter of the year. Ligonnier's W-4 shows that she is married and claims seven withholding allowances. Divide the estimated quarterly wages by six—the number of semimonthly pay periods in the quarter—to determine the average payment of $1,000. From Tax Table B, you will find that the amount of federal income taxes to withhold from each semimonthly pay is $10.

The quarterly averaging of wages method works best where there is steady employment and little fluctuation in wages between pay periods. Thus, you can estimate a reasonably accurate average wage. If the only wage payments involved are tips, you cannot use the quarterly averaging method.

Annualizing Wages

For withholding purposes, you may annualize the wage payments and prorate the income tax applicable to those wage payments. Under the annualizing method, proceed as follows:

Step 1: Multiply the wages for one payroll period by the number of payroll periods in the year.

Step 2: Determine the annual amount of withholding required on the total wages.

Step 3: Divide the annual withholding amount by the number of payroll periods to arrive at the amount of withholding for one payroll period.

EXAMPLE:

Marc Field, a married employee with three allowances, is paid $1,050 semimonthly. Under the annualizing method, multiply the $1,050 semimonthly wage by 24 to arrive at an annual wage of $25,200. Next, subtract the withholding allowances of $7,050 (3 x $2,350) from the

$25,200 annual wage to arrive at $18,150, the amount of wages subject to tax.

Table 7(b) in Tax Table A indicates that the tax to be withheld on $18,150 is 15% of the excess over $6,200. The excess, computed to be $11,950 ($18,150 − $6,200) and multiplied by .15, equals $1,792.50, the total amount to be withheld on an annual basis. Prorate this amount over the 24 semimonthly payrolls to arrive at $74.69, the amount to withhold from each semimonthly paycheck.

The annualizing method is especially advantageous if you wish to conserve computer memory, since only the rates, brackets, and allowance values for an annual payroll period need be stored in the computer.

Cumulative Withholding

Upon an employee's written request, you may withhold income taxes on the basis of the employee's cumulative wages. This method of withholding is primarily used when the amount of the employee's wage payments is very irregular and when the percentage method or the wage-bracket method would cause overwithholding. The cumulative withholding method may be used, however, only when the employee's wages since the beginning of the current calendar year have been paid in payroll periods that are all of the same length. Employees who may benefit from use of this method include commission salespeople and those working on a piece-rate basis.

Under the cumulative withholding method, proceed as follows:

Step 1: Add the wages for the payroll period to the total wages already paid during the calendar year.

Step 2: Divide the aggregate amount of wages by the number of payroll periods to which it pertains.

Step 3: Compute the total taxes on the average amount of wages just as if that amount had been paid to the employee in each of the payroll periods to which the total amount relates.

Step 4: Subtract from this amount of tax any amount already withheld during the preceding payroll periods.

Step 5: Deduct any excess tax from the current payment of wages.

EXAMPLE:

Roger Samuel, a salesperson for Drury Motors, is single and claims one withholding allowance. Samuel has been paid $28,000 in commissions during the first three quarters of this year (19 biweekly pay periods). Because he surpassed his quota of new cars to be sold, Samuel's next commission check at the beginning of the fourth quarter amounts to $3,700. Calculate the amount of federal income taxes to be withheld under the cumulative withholding method as follows:

1. $28,000 (commissions paid in 19 biweekly pay periods of the past three quarters) + $3,700 (commissions for first biweekly pay in fourth quarter) = $31,700.
2. $31,700 ÷ 20 (biweekly pay periods) = $1,585 (average biweekly wages).
3. Using the percentage method, from Table 2(a), the income taxes on $1,585 are $286.68.
   $286.68 x 20 pay periods = $5,733.60 (total income taxes).
4. $5,733.60 less $5,105.56 (actual taxes withheld during the first three quarters) = $628.04.
5. From his commissions of $3,700 during the 20th biweekly pay period, deduct $628.04 for federal income taxes.

Note: Had Samuel's employer used the percentage method instead of cumulative withholding, the federal income taxes to withhold on commissions of $3,700 would be $930.65.

Part-Year Employment

Upon the request of an employee who works only part of a year, you may withhold according to a complicated averaging method that reduces the amount to be withheld. To be eligible for this alternative method, the employee must reasonably expect that he or she will be employed for a total of no more than 245 calendar days in all terms of continuous employment during the calendar year. The employee must also use a calendar-year accounting method.

"Substantially Similar" Methods

If your firm has a computerized payroll accounting system, possibly none of the withholding methods described above may be entirely satisfactory. In such cases you may devise any withholding method that will meet the needs of your organization. However, that method must yield deductions substantially similar to those withheld under the percentage method for the payroll period involved. A "substantially similar" method is defined as one that provides for amounts withheld that are within $10 either way of the amounts required to be withheld annually under the percentage method.

You need not submit your alternative method to the IRS for approval before putting it to use. However, you should make sure that the alternative method is tested against the full range of wage and allowance situations to make sure that the method meets the tolerances prescribed by the IRS.

WITHHOLDING TAX ON SUPPLEMENTAL WAGE PAYMENTS

Those responsible for payroll preparation are often faced with the problem of properly handling additional compensation known as supplemental wage payments. *Supplemental wage payments* include items such as vacation pay, bonuses, commissions, and dismissal pay. The problem arises since supplemental wages often are paid at a different time than the regular wage payments. Then, too, supplemental wages may be based on a different wage rate or for a wage period that differs from the regular wage period. Further, supplemental wages may be related to no particular payroll period.

When a supplemental wage payment is involved in payroll preparation, you should decide whether the payment must be lumped together with a regular wage payment or whether the supplemental wages may be treated separately. If the supplemental wages must be lumped together with a regular payment, the amount of tax withheld may be disproportionately high when compared with the effect of the payment on the employee's actual tax liability. This problem is created by the nature of the graduated withholding system.

To aid in solving problems such as those described above, the IRS has issued tax computation rules that indicate when supplemental wage payments must be lumped together with regular wage payments and when they may be treated separately. Generally the tax computation rules apply to any kind of supplemental wages. However, in the case of vacation pay, as we discuss below, different rules apply depending upon whether or not the vacation pay is paid at the same time as an employee's regular wages.

Supplemental Wages Paid Along with Regular Wages

When you pay supplemental wages at the same time as regular wages, the method of calculating the withholding tax depends on whether the payment is vacation pay or some other kind of supplemental wage.

Vacation Pay. When employees receive vacation pay along with their regular pay for a payroll period, the vacation pay is subject to withholding as though it were a regular payment made for the payroll period or periods occurring during the vacation.

EXAMPLE:

Josh Gayle, who is married, claims two allowances and is paid $620 biweekly. According to the wage-bracket table in Tax Table B, his usual withholding amount is $32. Gayle schedules his three weeks' vacation from Saturday, August 19, through Friday, September 8. For this period, his vacation pay is $930 ($310 each week for three weeks) and is paid him *with his regular pay* on the second biweekly payroll period on Friday, August 18. For withholding purposes, the first two weeks' vacation pay are deemed to be paid on Friday, September 1, and the third week is considered to be paid on Friday, September 15. Given below are the details of Gayle's paychecks for the second payroll period in August and the two payroll periods in September:

Payday	Pay	Withholding
August 18	$1,550	$80
September 1	-0-	-0-
September 15	310	16

The $80 withheld on August 18 consists of $32 on Gayle's regular biweekly wages, $32 on two weeks' vacation pay (deemed paid on September 1), and $16 (one half of $32) on one week's vacation pay. The $16 withheld from the September 15 check relates to Gayle's regular pay for the week of September 11-15, his first week back from vacation.

If you had lumped the vacation pay with the regular wages and treated the entire amount as a single payment, the tax withheld, according to the wage-bracket table in Tax Table B, would have been $170, or $90 greater than the amount properly withheld under the procedure described above.

Other Supplemental Wages. You may pay a supplemental wage other than vacation pay at the same time as a regular wage payment. In such cases, you must combine the supplemental wages with the wage payment. Then, you determine the amount to be withheld from the aggregate payment as if the combined payment were a single payment for the payroll period involved.

EXAMPLE:

Jenny Wright, a married sales representative with three withholding allowances, is employed at a monthly salary of $1,800. She also receives an annual bonus of 10% of her total annual sales in excess of $50,000. Her sales for the current year amount to $96,000, on which the bonus is $4,600. The total of her bonus for the year and her salary for December amounts to $6,400. According to Table 4(b) in Tax Table A, the amount to withhold from her December paycheck is $1,108.47.

When you combine the regular wages and supplemental wages in a single payment, you may wish to indicate specifically the amount of each payment. In such cases, you may withhold federal income taxes at a flat 28% rate on the supplemental wages, if the tax is withheld on the employee's regular wages at the appropriate rate.

EXAMPLE:

Referring to the preceding example, you may indicate separately on Wright's paycheck stub the amount of each payment. In this case, calculate the amount of federal income taxes withheld as follows:

		Federal Income Taxes Withheld
Regular monthly earnings	$1,800	$ 104.33*
Annual bonus	4,600	1,288.00
Totals	$6,400	$1,392.33

*Using the percentage method.

Under this approach, the amount of federal income taxes withheld from Wright's last monthly pay is $283.86 more than under the preceding example.

Supplemental Wages Paid Separately from Regular Wages

In those situations where supplemental wages are not paid at the same time as regular wage payments, you need to determine whether or not federal income tax was withheld from the employee's prior wage payment. The computation rules we describe below pertain to all types of supplemental wage payments—vacation pay as well as other supplemental wage payments.

Federal Income Tax Not Withheld from Prior Wage Payment.
In some instances federal income taxes are not withheld from employees' regular wages because their allowances exceed their wages. In these cases you must combine the supplemental wages with the wages paid for the last preceding payroll period or with the wages to be paid for the current payroll period. Then, determine the amount of tax to be withheld as if the aggregate of the supplemental wages and the regular wages were a single wage payment for the payroll period involved.

EXAMPLE:

Heng May, married with eight allowances, received his last weekly paycheck for the year on December 29.

Since his total regular wages were $475, according to the wage-bracket table in Tax Table B, no federal income taxes were withheld. Two days later, May is paid a year-end bonus amounting to $600. Add the amount of this supplemental wage ($600) to the wages paid for the last preceding payroll period ($475), and withhold federal income taxes of $89 on the aggregate, $1,075.

Federal Income Tax Already Withheld from Regular Wages.

When the federal income tax has already been withheld from the employee's regular wages, you may select one of two alternative methods for withholding the tax on the supplemental wages.

Method A. Under this method combine the supplemental wage with the wages for the last preceding or the current payroll period. Then, determine the amount to be withheld as if the supplemental wages and the regular wages were a single payment. However, since the federal income tax has already been withheld from the regular wages, subtract that amount from the tax due on the aggregate. Deduct only the excess federal income tax from the payment of the supplemental wages.

EXAMPLE:

Brent Einstein, married with two allowances, is paid $985 semimonthly. The tax to be withheld under the wage-bracket method on each semimonthly pay is $80. Einstein is paid his regular wage on June 15. On June 18 he receives a bonus of $500. The tax on the bonus is calculated as follows:

Regular wage payment	$ 985
Bonus	500
Total	$1,485
Tax on total from wage-bracket table in Tax	
Table B	$155
Less tax already withheld on $985	80
Tax to be withheld from $500 bonus	$ 75

Method B. Under this alternative method for withholding federal income taxes, withhold a flat 28% of the supplemental wages. As indicated above, this method may be used only if you have already withheld federal income taxes from the employee's regular wages. Further, if you elect to withhold at the 28% rate, this must be done without considering any withholding allowances claimed by the employee. Thus, referring to the example given above, under this method you would withhold 28% of the $500 bonus payment, or $140, from the June 18 bonus paid Einstein.

WITHHOLDING TAX ON TIPS

As we noted earlier in this unit, tips amounting to $20 or more in a calendar month must be reported by employees to their employers. When reported, the tips are subject to federal income tax withholding. When employees report tips in connection with employment in which they also receive regular wages, calculate the amount of tax to be withheld on the tips as if the tips were a supplemental wage payment. Generally the rules for withholding federal income tax on tips are the same as those given in the preceding section for withholding taxes on supplemental wage payments.

You must withhold the employee's income tax and FICA taxes on the reported tip income, but this withholding is made from the wages (other than tips) that are under the employer's control. The amount of tax due on the employee's tip income may exceed the amount of wages under the employer's control and available for making a deduction (or the amount of additional funds supplied by the employee). In such a case, the employee must pay the uncollected portion of the taxes directly to the IRS when the annual income tax return is filed.

ADVANCE PAYMENT OF EARNED INCOME CREDIT (EIC)

The *earned income credit (EIC)* is a reduction in the computation of the federal income taxes mostly for workers who have dependent children and maintain a household. In 1994, for taxpayers with one qualifying child, the maximum credit is $2,038 (26.3% of the first $7,750 in earned income). For taxpayers with two or more qualifying children, the maximum credit is $2,527 (30% of the first $8,425 in earned income). The credit has also been extended to low-income taxpayers age 26 to 64 years of age who have no qualifying children. For them, the maximum credit is $306 (7.65% of the first $4,000 in earned income). The maximum amount of each credit is adjusted annually for inflation.

Eligible employees may elect to receive payment of their earned income credit in advance of filing their annual personal income tax returns. To be eligible for the EIC payments, employees must meet the criteria given in the instructions accompanying Form W-5, which is discussed below.

Form W-5

Eligible employees who want to receive advance EIC payments must file *Form W-5, Earned Income Credit Advance Payment Certificate*, with their employer. A filled-in Form W-5 is shown in Illustration 4-4. If employees choose not to get the advance payments, they will still obtain the full benefit of the EIC when filing their annual personal income tax returns.

Employees who have had no income taxes withheld must be informed about refundable earned income credits, unless the employees have filed Form W-4 claiming full exemption from withholding. To meet this requirement, employers have four options: (a) give employees IRS Notice 797, "You May Be Eligible for a Refund on Your Federal Income Tax Return Because of the Earned Income Credit"; (b) supply employees with a written notice containing an exact reproduction of the wording in Notice 797; (c) furnish employees with Forms W-2 that have the required statement on the back of Copy C; or (d) provide employees with a substitute Form W-2 that contains the exact wording found on the back of Copy C.

When completing Form W-5, employees must show if they are married and if their spouse has a Form W-5 in effect that year with an employer. The form remains in effect until the end of the calendar year. Thereafter, eligible employees must file a new certificate annually. The signed form should be made effective with the first payroll period ending on or after the date the certificate is given to the employer.

After an employee has given you a signed Form W-5, circumstances may change that make the employee ineligible for the credit. Or the employee's spouse may file a Form W-5. In such cases, the employee must, within 10 days after such a change, either revoke the previously filed form or file a new Form W-5 showing that the spouse has a Form W-5 in effect with an employer.

An employee may have filed a Form W-5 certifying that his or her spouse has a Form W-5 in effect, and the spouse later ceases to have a form in effect. In such an instance, the employee should file a new Form W-5 with you to certify that the spouse no longer has a Form W-5 in effect.

Computing the Advance Payment of the EIC

Employers must include the advance EIC payment with wages paid their eligible employees who have filed Form W-5. For purposes of the advance payment, wages are defined as amounts subject to income tax withholding. For employers of domestic and agricultural workers, wages mean amounts subject to FICA taxes.

In determining the amount of the advance payment, the following factors are taken into account:

1. Wages paid—including tips reported.
2. Whether a married employee's spouse has a Form W-5 in effect with an employer.

The amount of the payment to include in eligible employees' wage payments is determined from either the percentage method or wage-bracket tables provided by the IRS (not reproduced in this textbook). Separate tables are available for married employees whose spouses have a certificate in effect.

Paying the Advance EIC to Employees

The advance EIC payments do not affect the amount of income taxes or FICA taxes that is withheld from employees' wages and paid over to the IRS. Since the advance EIC payments are not compensation for services rendered, they are not subject to payroll taxes.

Generally employers will pay the amount of the advance EIC payments from withheld income taxes and FICA taxes. As indicated in Unit 3, these taxes are

Form **W-5**	**Earned Income Credit** **Advance Payment Certificate**		OMB No. 1545-1342	
Department of the Treasury Internal Revenue Service	▶ This certificate expires on December 31, 1993.		19**93**	
Type or print your full name Jean Claude LaFitte			Your social security number 277 : 09 : 2413	
Note: *If you get advance payments of the earned income credit for 1993, you **must** file a 1993 Form 1040A or Form 1040. To get advance payments, your filing status must be any status **except** married filing a separate return.*			Yes	No
1 I expect to be able to claim the earned income credit for 1993, I do not have another Form W-5 in effect with any other current employer, and I choose to get advance payment of the earned income credit			X	
2 Are you married?				X
3 If you are married, does your spouse have a Form W-5 in effect for 1993 with any employer?				
Under penalties of perjury, I declare that the information I have furnished above is, to the best of my knowledge, true, correct, and complete.				
Signature ▶ *Jean Claude LaFitte*		Date ▶ March 2, 1993		

Illustration 4-4. Form W-5, Earned Income Credit Advance Payment Certificate

usually paid over to the IRS either through federal tax deposits or along with the employer's tax returns.

It is possible that for a payroll period the advance EIC payments may be more than the withheld income taxes and the FICA taxes. In such a case, you have the option of:

1. Reducing each advance EIC payment proportionately, or
2. Electing to make full payment of the advance EIC amount and treating such full amounts as an advance payment of your company's tax liability.

Employer's Returns and Records

As you saw above, the amount of the advance EIC payments does not change the amount that employers must deduct and withhold from their employees' pay for income taxes and FICA taxes. Advance EIC payments made by the employer are treated as having been made from amounts withheld as income tax and employee FICA taxes, and from the employer's FICA taxes. The amount of advance EIC payments is treated as if the employer had paid over the amount of the payments to the IRS on the day the wages are paid employees.

Employers take into account the amount of their advance EIC payments when completing their quarterly employment tax returns, Form 941. The amount of the advance EIC payments is subtracted from the total amount of income taxes and FICA taxes in order to determine the net taxes for the quarter.

All records of advance EIC payments should be retained four years and be available for review by the IRS. These records include: (a) copies of employees' Forms W-5, (b) amounts and dates of all wage payments and advance EIC payments, (c) dates of each employee's employment, (d) dates and amounts of tax deposits made, and (e) copies of returns filed.

INDIVIDUAL RETIREMENT ACCOUNTS (IRA)

As we pointed out in Unit 1, an individual retirement account (IRA) is a pension plan that is established and funded by an individual employee. Depending upon the existence of a company-funded retirement plan, employees may authorize that either one of two types of contributions—deductible or nondeductible—be withheld by their employer or union. Or employees may place their contributions in individual retirement savings accounts as specified in the law.

Deductible Contributions

Under certain conditions, employees may put aside each year the lesser of $2,000 or 100% of their compensation *without paying federal income taxes on their contributions*. To be eligible for such *deductible* (tax-free) contributions, either of the following two conditions must be met:

1. The individual does not belong to a company-funded retirement plan. (In the case of a married person filing a joint return, neither the person nor the person's spouse belongs to the employer's maintained retirement plan.)
2. The individual has adjusted gross income that is less than $25,000. (A married couple filing a joint return must have adjusted gross income of less than $40,000.)

For a married individual entitled to take a tax-free IRA deduction, an additional benefit is allowed where the spouse has no earned income or only income less than $250. Thus, another $250 may be added to the couple's individual retirement accounts to permit a total contribution as great as $2,250.

> **EXAMPLE:**
>
> Frank and Connie Rivera file a joint tax return in 1994. In 1993, Frank earned $20,000 and Connie earned $220. In 1993, the couple contributed $2,250 to their IRA accounts and took the deductions on their joint return. Since Connie had earned less than $250 compensation in 1993, she will be treated as having no compensation for the year. Thus, Frank and Connie may take advantage of the spousal deduction.

The only restriction on the division between the employee's IRA and the spouse's IRA is that at least $250 must be placed in the spouse's account. The tax advantage of these IRAs is lost if the worker withdraws the money prematurely.

If the employee does belong to a company-funded retirement plan, *partial* tax-free deductions are allowed if:

1. The employee has adjusted gross income less than $35,000.
2. A married couple files a joint return with adjusted gross income less than $50,000.
3. A married couple files separately with one spouse having adjusted gross income less than $10,000.

Nondeductible Contributions

A person who is ineligible to make a deductible IRA contribution is permitted to make *nondeductible* contributions to a separate IRA account. The earnings on the nondeductible contributions are not subject to federal income tax until they are withdrawn. The limit on such nondeductible contributions for a taxable year is the lesser of $2,000 or 100% of the employee's compensation.

WAGE AND TAX STATEMENTS

You are required to furnish *wage and tax statements* to your firm's employees informing them of the wages paid during the calendar year and the amount of taxes withheld from those wages. You are also required to send copies of these statements to the federal government and in most cases to state, city, and local governments.

Form W-2

Form W-2, Wage and Tax Statement, shown in Illustration 4-5, is prepared if *any* of the following items applied to an employee during the calendar year:

1. Income tax or social security (FICA) taxes were withheld.

2. Income tax would have been withheld if the employee had not claimed more than one withholding allowance or had not claimed exemption from withholding on Form W-4.

3. *Any* amount was paid for services, if the employer is in a trade or business. The cash value of any noncash payments made should be included.

4. Any advance EIC (earned income credit) payments were made.

In Illustration 4-6 on pages 136 and 137, we have summarized the instructions for completing each of the boxes on Form W-2. If an entry does not apply to your firm or the employee, leave the box blank.

You must give employees Form W-2 on or before January 31 following the close of the calendar year. When employees leave the service of your employer, you may give them Form W-2 any time after employment ends. If employees ask for Form W-2, you should give it to them within 30 days of their request or the final wage payment, whichever is later. In some instances the services of workers will be terminated

a Control number	22222	Void ☐	For Official Use Only ▶			
b Employer's identification number 13-5407221				1 Wages, tips, other compensation 29360.18		2 Federal income tax withheld 4610.00
c Employer's name, address, and ZIP code				3 Social security wages 29360.18		4 Social security tax withheld 1820.33
Stone Metal Products 600 Third Avenue Philadelphia, PA 19103-5600				5 Medicare wages and tips 29360.18		6 Medicare tax withheld 425.72
				7 Social security tips		8 Allocated tips
d Employee's social security number 382-13-7478				9 Advance EIC payment		10 Dependent care benefits
e Employee's name (first, middle initial, last) Henry T. Tate 483 Monroe Street Philadelphia, PA 19119-4821				11 Nonqualified plans		12 Benefits included in Box 1
				13 See Instrs. for Box 13 C 78.00		14 Other BC/BS Premium w/h 296.00

			15 Statutory employee ☐	Deceased ☒	Pension plan ☒	Legal rep. ☐	942 emp. ☐	Subtotal ☐	Deferred compensation ☐
f Employee's address and ZIP code									

16 State	Employer's state I.D. No.	17 State wages, tips, etc.	18 State income tax	19 Locality name	20 Local wages, tips, etc.	21 Local income tax
PA	46-8-0013	29360.18	822.09	Phila.	29360.18	1456.26

Department of the Treasury—Internal Revenue Service

Form **W-2** Wage and Tax Statement **1993**

For Paperwork Reduction Act Notice, see separate instructions.

Copy A For Social Security Administration

Illustration 4-5. Form W-2, Wage and Tax Statement

HOW TO COMPLETE FORM W-2

NOTE: Type the entries, using black ink if possible. Do not make any erasures, whiteouts, or strikeovers. Also, do not use script type. Make all dollar entries without the dollar sign and comma but with the decimal point (000.00). Show the cents portion of the money amounts. File Forms W-2 either alphabetically by employees' last names or numerically by employees' SSNs.

Box a—Control number: The control number is for the employer to identify the individual Forms W-2. Up to 7 digits may be assigned the control number, which the employer uses when writing the Social Security Administration about the form. You do not have to use this box. The form identifying number 22222 is used by optical scanning equipment in the SSA to tell which information document (Form W-2) is being "read."

Void: Put an X in this box when an error has been made. Amounts shown on void forms should *not* be included in your subtotal Form W-2.

Box b—Employer's identification number (EIN): Enter the number assigned to you by the IRS (00-0000000). Do not use a prior owner's EIN. If you do not have an EIN when filing Forms W-2, enter "Applied For" in Box b. You can get an EIN by filing Form SS-4, *Application for Employer Identification Number.* (See Unit 3.)

Box c—Employer's name, address, and ZIP code: Record the employer's name, address, and ZIP code. This entry should be the same as shown on your Form 941, 942, or 943.

Box d—Employee's social security number: Enter the number shown on the employee's social security card. If the employee does not have a card, he or she should apply for one by completing Form SS-5, *Application for a Social Security Card.* (See Unit 3.)

Box e—Employee's name: Enter the name as shown on the employee's social security card (first, middle initial, last). If the name has been changed, have the employee get a corrected card from any SSA office. Use the name on the original card until you see the corrected one.

Box f—Employee's address and ZIP code: This box is combined with Box e (Employee's name) on all copies except Copy A to allow you to mail employees' copies in a window envelope or as a self-mailer.

Box 1—Wages, tips, other compensation: Record, before any payroll deductions, the total of (1) wages, prizes, and awards paid; (2) noncash payments (including certain fringe benefits); (3) tips reported by employee to employer (not allocated tips); (4) certain employee business expense reimbursements; (5) cost of accident and health insurance premiums paid on behalf of 2% or more shareholder-employees by an S corporation; (6) taxable benefits made from a Section 125 (cafeteria plan); and (7) all other compensation including scholarships and fellowship grants and payments for moving expenses. Other compensation is an amount you pay your employee from which federal income tax is not withheld. If you prefer, you may show other compensation on a separate Form W-2.

Box 2—Federal income tax withheld: Record the amount of federal income tax withheld from the employee's wages for the year.

Box 3—Social security wages: Enter the total wages paid (before payroll deductions) subject to employee social security (OASDI) tax. Do *not* include social security tips and allocated tips. Generally noncash payments are considered wages. Include employee business expenses reported in Box 1. Include employer contributions to qualified cash or deferred compensation plans and to retirement arrangements described in Box 13 (Codes D, E, F, and G), even though the contributions are not includible in Box 1 as wages, tips, and other compensation. Include any employee OASDI and HI taxes and employee state unemployment compensation taxes you paid for your employee rather than deducting it from wages. Report in this box the cost of group-term life insurance coverage over $50,000 that is taxable to former employees. Report the cost of accident and health insurance premiums paid on behalf of 2% or more shareholder-employees by an S corporation only if the exclusion under Section 312(a)(2)(B) is not satisfied. Do not enter more than the maximum OASDI taxable wage base for the year.

Box 4—Employee social security tax withheld: Record the total social security (OASDI) tax (not your share) withheld or paid by you for the employee. Include only taxes withheld for the year's wages.

Box 5—Medicare wages and tips: Enter the Medicare (HI) wages and tips, but do not enter more than the maximum HI wage base for the year. Be sure to enter tips the employee reported even if you did not have enough employee funds to collect the HI tax for those tips. Report in this box the cost of group-term life insurance coverage over $50,000 that is taxable to former employees.

Box 6—Medicare tax withheld: Enter the total employee Medicare (HI) tax (not your share) withheld or paid by you for your employee. Include only taxes withheld for the year's wages.

Box 7—Social security tips: Record the amount the employee reported even if you did not have enough employee funds to collect the social security (OASDI) tax for the tips. The total of Boxes 3 and 7 should not be more than the maximum OASDI wage base for the year. But report all tips in Box 1 along with wages and other compensation.

Box 8—Allocated tips: If you are a large food or beverage establishment, record the amount of tips allocated to the employee. Do *not* include this amount in Boxes 1, 5, or 7.

Box 9—Advance EIC payment: Record the total amount paid to the employee as advance earned income credit payments.

Box 10—Dependent care benefits: Record the total amount of dependent care benefits paid or incurred by you for your employee. This total should include any amount in excess of the exclusion.

Box 11—Nonqualified plans: Enter the amount from a nonqualified deferred compensation plan or a Section 457 plan that was distributed or became taxable because the substantial risk of forfeiture lapsed. Include this amount in Box 11 only if it is also includible in Boxes 1, 3, and 5. Report distributions to beneficiaries of deceased employees on Form 1099-R.

Illustration 4-6. Instructions for Completing Form W-2 (Continued)

HOW TO COMPLETE FORM W-2 (Continued)

Box 12—Benefits included in Box 1: Record the total value of the taxable fringe benefits included in Box 1 as other compensation. Do not include amounts reported in Boxes 10 and/or 13. You may use a separate statement, Box 14, or multiple Forms W-2, if necessary, to report all Box 12 entries. If you use multiple Forms W-2, do not report the same federal wage and tax data to SSA on more than one Copy A.

Box 13: Complete and code this box for all applicable items listed below in the *Reference Guide*. Additional information about any coded item may be found in the IRS's *Instructions for Form W-2*. Do not report in Box 13 any items not listed as Codes A-N. Do *not* enter more than three codes in this box. If you are reporting more than three items, use a separate Form W-2 or a substitute Form W-2 to report the additional items.

Use a capital letter when entering each code. Leave one space blank after the code and enter the dollar amount on the same line. Use decimal points but not dollar signs or commas, such as J 358.00.

Box 14—Other: Use this box for any other information you want to give your employee. Label each item. Examples are union dues, health insurance premiums deducted, moving expenses paid, nontaxable income, or educational assistance payments.

Box 15: Mark the boxes that apply.

Statutory employee: Mark this box for statutory employees whose earnings are subject to social security (OASDI) and Medicare (HI) taxes but *not* subject to federal income tax withholding.

Deceased: Mark this box if the employee is now deceased. If an employee is deceased, you must report wages or other compensation for services performed and paid in the year of death to the estate or beneficiary. Report wages paid after the date of death that are not subject to federal income tax withholding on Form 1099-MISC, Miscellaneous Income.

Pension plan: Mark this box if the employee was an active participant (for any part of the year) in a retirement plan such as 401(k) and SEP.

Legal representative: Mark this box when the employee's name is the only name shown but is shown as a trust account (for example, John Doe Trust), or another name is shown in addition to the employee's name and the other person or business is acting on behalf of the employee.

942 employee: For household employers only. Mark this box if you are a household employer filing a single Form W-2. See Form 942 instructions.

Subtotal: Do not subtotal if you are submitting 41 or fewer Forms W-2. If you are submitting *42 or more Forms W-2,* give subtotal figures for every 41 individual forms and the last group of forms. Mark the "Subtotal" box on the form that shows the subtotal dollar amounts for the preceding 41 forms and for the last group of forms, even if less than 41 forms. Show subtotal amounts for Boxes 1 through 11, and 13.

Deferred compensation: Mark this box if the employee has made an elective deferral to a section 401(k), 403(b), 408(k)(6), or 501(c)(18)(D) retirement plan. Also, mark this box if an elective or nonelective deferral was made to a section 457(b) plan.

Box 16—Employer's state I.D. number: You do not have to complete this box, but you may want to if you use copies of this form for your state return. The number is assigned by each individual state. This box is separated by a dotted line so you may report two state I.D. numbers. If you are reporting for only one state, enter the number above the dotted line.

Boxes 17 through 21—State or local income tax information: The state and local information boxes can be used to report wages and taxes on two states and two localities. Keep each state's and locality's information separated by the dotted line.

Reference Guide for Box 13 Codes

A—Uncollected social security (OASDI) tax on tips
B—Uncollected Medicare (HI) tax on tips
C—Group-term life insurance over $50,000
D—Elective deferrals to a Section 401(k) cash or deferred arrangement
E—Elective deferrals to a Section 403(b) salary reduction agreement
F—Elective deferrals to a section 408(k)(6) salary reduction SEP
G—Elective and nonelective deferrals to a Section 457(b) deferred compensation plan (state and local government and tax-exempt employers)
H—Elective deferrals to a Section 501(c)(18)(D) tax-exempt organization plan
J—Nontaxable sick pay
K—20% excise tax on excess golden parachute payments
L—Substantiated Employee Business Expense (federal rate)
M—Uncollected social security (OASDI) tax on group-term life insurance coverage
N—Uncollected Medicare (HI) tax on group-term life insurance coverage

---

Illustration 4-6. Instructions for Completing Form W-2 (Concluded)

but there is a reasonable expectation that they may be rehired at some time before the year ends. In such a situation you need not give Form W-2 to the employees. Instead, you may delay furnishing the form until January 31 following the close of the calendar year.

Copies of the six-part Form W-2 are distributed as follows:

1. *Copy A* → to the Social Security Administration by the end of February following the year for which Form W-2 is applicable.
2. *Copy 1* → to the state, city, or local tax department.
3. *Copy B* } to employees for filing with their federal income tax returns.
4. *Copy C* → to employees for retention in their personal records.
5. *Copy 2*) to employees for filing with their state, city, or local income tax returns.
6. *Copy D* → retained by employer.

If Form W-2 has been lost or destroyed, you are authorized to furnish substitute copies to the employee. The substitute form should be clearly marked REISSUED STATEMENT. Do *not* send Copy A of the reissued statement to the Social Security Administration.

Occasionally you will prepare Forms W-2 which, after reasonable effort, you are unable to deliver to employees. Do *not* send the forms to the Social Security Administration, but instead retain them for a four-year period. You are deemed to have made a "reasonable effort" to deliver the Forms W-2 if you mailed them to the last known address of the employee.

Form W-2c

Form W-2c, Statement of Corrected Income and Tax Amounts, is used to correct errors in previously filed Forms W-2. File Copy A of Form W-2c with the Social Security Administration and distribute the remaining copies of the form as noted on the bottom of each form. A separate form, Form W-3c (discussed later in this unit), is used to transmit the corrected wage and tax statements. However, if the correction is for only one employee or is to correct an employee's name and/or social security number only, you need not prepare a transmittal form.

Illustration 4-7.   Form W-2c, Statement of Corrected Income and Tax Amounts

Professional Tip

The SSA estimates that it costs about 38 cents to process an accurate W-2; but the cost to process an inaccurate W-2 is around $307. Besides all the extra work for you, the cost factor is an important reason to properly file your W-2s.[2]

Illustration 4-7 shows how Form W-2c has been used to correct an error made in Tate's Form W-2 (Illustration 4-5, page 135).

Form W-3

Form W-3, Transmittal of Wage and Tax Statements, must be filed with the Social Security Administration by employers and other payers as a transmittal for Forms W-2. On Form W-3 you indicate the number of documents being transmitted. Form W-3 and the accompanying copies of the documents enable the Social Security Administration (and at a later date, the IRS) to compare the taxes withheld as reported on Forms W-2 with the amount of taxes withheld as reported on the employers' Forms 941. A filled-in Form W-3 is shown in Illustration 4-8.

Since Forms W-3 are read by optical scanning machines, type all entries if possible. Also, record all dollar entries without the dollar sign and comma but with the decimal point (0000.00). You should not staple or tape Forms W-3 to the related Forms W-2 since staple holes or tears cause the optical scanning equipment to jam.

File all Forms W-2 with one W-3. When a large number of forms are to be transmitted, you may forward the forms in separate packages of convenient size, each of which is clearly identified with the

a	Control number	For Official Use Only ▶ OMB No. 1545-0008	1 Wages, tips, other compensation 2620736.40	2 Federal income tax withheld 330317.19
b	**Kind of Payer** ▶ 941/941E ☒ Military ☐ 943 ☐ CT-1 ☐ 942 ☐ Medicare govt. emp. ☐		3 Social security wages 2066400.00	4 Social security tax withheld 128116.80
c Total number of statements 132	d Establishment number		5 Medicare wages and tips 2527620.95	6 Medicare tax withheld 36650.50
	e Employer's identification number 88-1936281		7 Social security tips	8 Allocated tips
f Employer's name Grove Electronics 33 Vista Road Vallejo, CA 94590-0033			9 Advance EIC payments 778.00	10 Dependent care benefits
			11 Nonqualified plans	12 Deferred compensation 319530.00
			13 Adjusted total social security wages and tips 2066400.00	
			14 Adjusted total Medicare wages and tips 2527620.95	
g Employer's address and ZIP code				
h Other EIN used this year			15 Income tax withheld by third-party payer	
i Employer's state I.D. No.				

Under penalties of perjury, I declare that I have examined this return and accompanying documents, and, to the best of my knowledge and belief, they are true, correct, and complete.

Signature ▶ *Carl W. Tolan*   Title ▶ President   Date ▶ 2/28/94

Telephone number (415) 555-3200

Form **W-3 Transmittal of Wage and Tax Statements 1993**   Department of the Treasury Internal Revenue Service

Illustration 4-8.   Form W-3, Transmittal of Wage and Tax Statements

---

[2] *Payroll Manager's Letter (May 7, 1993): 3.*

payer's name and identifying number. Postal regulations require that all forms and packages sent by mail be sent by first-class mail.

You should file Form W-3 and the related documents with the Social Security Administration by the end of February each year at the locations shown in Illustration 4-9.

Form W-3 is mailed to you during the fourth quarter as part of Publication 393, Federal Employment Tax Forms.

Form W-3c

The *Transmittal of Corrected Income and Tax Statements, Form W-3c* (not illustrated in this textbook), is used to accompany copies of Form W-2c, Statement of Corrected Income and Tax Amounts, sent to the Social Security Administration. You may also use Form W-3c

If employer's residence, principal place of business, office, or agency is located in	File Form W-3 at this address
Alaska, Arizona, California, Colorado, Hawaii, Idaho, Iowa, Minnesota, Missouri, Montana, Nebraska, Nevada, North Dakota, Oregon, South Dakota, Utah, Washington, Wisconsin, Wyoming	Social Security Administration Data Operations Center Salinas, CA 93911
Alabama, Arkansas, Florida, Georgia, Illinois, Kansas, Louisiana, Mississippi, New Mexico, Oklahoma, South Carolina, Tennessee, Texas	Social Security Administration Data Operations Center Albuquerque, NM 87180
Connecticut, Delaware, District of Columbia, Indiana, Kentucky, Maine, Maryland, Massachusetts, Michigan, New Hampshire, New Jersey, New York, North Carolina, Ohio, Pennsylvania, Rhode Island, Vermont, Virginia, West Virginia	Social Security Administration Data Operations Center Wilkes-Barre, PA 18769
If no legal residence or principal place of business in any state	Use address given above.

Illustration 4-9. Where to File Form W-3

to correct an employer identification number or establishment number.

Privately Printed Forms

Some employers prefer to use their own privately printed forms, such as Forms W-2, rather than the ones provided by the IRS. To make sure that the same information is included on the substitute forms as that required by those provided by the IRS, specifications have been established for the private printing of forms. You may obtain specifications for the private printing of Forms W-2 from any IRS center or district office. To the extent that the privately printed forms meet the specifications set forth, you may generally use them without prior approval of the IRS.

MAJOR RETURNS COMPLETED BY EMPLOYERS

Beginning with the first quarter in which taxable wages are paid, you are required at prescribed times to file returns reporting the amount of wages paid and the amount of taxes withheld. Such reporting continues until you prepare a final return showing that your organization has gone out of business or otherwise has ceased to pay taxable wages.

Your accounting tasks and payroll procedures are further complicated as a result of rules that require different returns for different types of employees, differing deposit requirements, and different time periods for which the returns must be filed. The major returns completed by employers are briefly summarized in Illustration 4-10. The most recent information with regard to the withholding, deposit, payment and reporting of federal income taxes, FICA taxes, and FUTA taxes is available in Circular E, "Employer's Tax Guide." Circular E is available at the district offices of the IRS.

Form 945

In the past, *Form 941, Employer's Quarterly Federal Tax Return,* was used to report (a) *payroll items,* such as social security and Medicare wages and taxes and income taxes withheld on wages, and (b) *nonpayroll items,* such as income tax withheld on pensions, annuities, and gambling winnings, and backup withholding (discussed later in this section).

To simplify the completion of Form 941, beginning with the first quarter in 1994, the IRS has restricted Form 941 to the reporting of payroll items only. A new form, *Form 945, Annual Return of Withheld Federal Income Tax,* will be used for 1994 to report income tax withholdings on nonpayroll items—pensions, annuities, gambling winnings, and backup

Form 941, Employer's Quarterly Federal Tax Return	For reporting federal income taxes withheld during the calendar quarter and the employer and employee portions of the FICA taxes. See Form 941 on page 89. Detailed information about the use of depositaries and the payment of taxes is given on pages 83–85.
Form 941-M, Employer's Monthly Federal Tax Return	For reporting federal income taxes withheld and FICA taxes on a *monthly* basis. IRS may require monthly returns and payments of taxes from employers who have not complied with the requirements for filing returns or the paying or depositing of taxes reported on quarterly returns. You are not required to file monthly returns unless you receive written notification from the IRS.
Form 942, Employer's Quarterly Tax Return for Household Employees	For reporting federal income taxes withheld as a result of voluntary withholding agreements between employers and their domestic employees. Form 942 is also completed by employers who are liable for FICA taxes on wages paid domestic workers.
Form 943, Employer's Annual Tax Return for Agricultural Employees	For reporting the withholding of federal income taxes and FICA taxes on wages paid agricultural workers. Form 943 is used for agricultural employees even though the employer may employ nonagricultural workers.
Form 945, Annual Return of Withheld Federal Income Tax	Used to report tax liability for *nonpayroll* items such as backup withholding and withholding on gambling winnings, pensions, and annuities, and deposits made for the year.
Form 945-A, Annual Record of Federal Tax Liability	Completed by all semiweekly depositors and monthly depositors who accumulate $100,000 or more on any day to report on a *daily* basis their backup withholding and income taxes withheld from gambling winnings, pensions, and annuities.

Illustration 4-10. Summary of Major Returns Filed by Employers

withholding. As shown in Illustration 4-11 on page 142, Form 945 provides lines to report the nonpayroll amounts and a reconciliation of the total taxes with the total deposits. If the total taxes (Line 3) is less than $500, you do not need to complete the monthly summary of federal tax liability at the bottom of the form. However, monthly depositors must use the schedule to summarize their monthly tax liabilities.

Form 945-A

Semiweekly depositors and those who have accumulated $100,000 or more on any day do not complete the schedule at the bottom of Form 945. Instead, they must attach *Form 945-A, Annual Record of Federal Tax Liability* (not illustrated in this textbook), upon which the tax liability is reported on a daily basis.

With the availability of new Forms 945 and 945-A, you no longer need complete *Form 941, Schedule A, Record of Federal Backup Withholding Tax Liability.* Also, *Form 941E, Quarterly Return of Withheld Federal Income Tax and Medicare Tax,* is eliminated since employers will be using Forms 941 and/or 945.

Backup Withholding

Certain recipients of taxable interest, dividends, and other payments are required to provide the payers with correct *Taxpayer Identification Numbers (TINs)*. The IRS uses the TINs for identification purposes to make sure that taxpayers are reporting accurately all sources of income received. Payers must be given the TINs whether or not the recipients are required to file tax returns.

Payers must generally withhold 31% of taxable interest, dividends, and certain other payments if the payees fail to furnish their correct TINs. This type of withholding is called *backup withholding.* Generally payments are subject to backup withholding if:

1. The payees fail to furnish TINs to the payers.
2. The IRS notifies the payers that the payees furnished incorrect TINs.
3. The payers are notified by the IRS that the payees are subject to backup withholding.
4. The payees fail to certify to the payers that they are not subject to backup withholding or fail to certify their TINs.

Form **945**	**Annual Return of Withheld Federal Income Tax**	OMB No. 1545-0029

Department of the Treasury
Internal Revenue Service

▶ See Circular E for more information concerning income tax withholding.
Please type or print.

1994

IRS USE ONLY

Enter state code for state in which deposits made. ▶ ☐ (See page 2 of instructions).

Name (as distinguished from trade name)

Taxpayer identification number
31-7207411

| T |
| FF |
| FD |
| FP |
| I |
| T |

Trade name, if any
LICITRA'S

Address (number and street)
1410 MAIN STREET

City, state, and ZIP code
WIMAUMA, FL 33598-0527

If address is different from prior return, check here ▶ ☐

IRS Use

| 1 | 1 | 1 | 1 | 1 | 1 | 1 | 1 | 1 | 1 | 2 | 3 | 3 | 3 | 3 | 3 | 4 | 4 | 4 | | | | | | | | |
| 5 | 5 | 5 | 6 | 7 | 8 | 8 | 8 | 8 | 8 | 9 | 9 | 10 | 10 | 10 | 10 | 10 | 10 | 10 | 10 | 10 | 10 |

If you do not have to file returns in the future, check here ▶ ☐   Date final payments paid ▶ _____

1	Federal income tax withheld from pensions, annuities, gambling, etc.	1	470	00
2	Backup withholding (see instructions)	2		
3	Total taxes (add lines 1 and 2)	3	470	00
4	Total deposits for 1994 from your records	4	470	00
5	Balance due (subtract line 4 from line 3). Pay to the Internal Revenue Service	5	-0-	

6 If line 3 is less than line 4, enter overpayment here ▶ $ _____ and check if to be:

☐ Applied to next return   **OR** ☐ Refunded

7 **Monthly Summary of Federal Tax Liability.**—If line 3 is less than $500, you need not complete this section (line 7). If you are a monthly depositor, summarize your monthly tax liability below. If you are a semiweekly depositor or have accumulated $100,000 or more on any day, do not complete the lines A-M below. Instead, attach Form 945-A and check here (see instructions) . . . . ☐

The total tax liability for the year (line M) should equal total taxes (line 3) above.

	Tax liability for month			Tax liability for month			Tax liability for month
A January		F June		K November	
B February . . .		G July		L December	
C March		H August . . .		M Total liability for year (add lines A through L) . . .	
D April		I September . .			
E May		J October . . .			

Sign Here

Under penalties of perjury, I declare that I have examined this return, including accompanying schedules and statements, and to the best of my knowledge and belief, it is true, correct, and complete.

Signature ▶ *Pauline V. Licitra*

Print Your Name and Title ▶ Pauline V. Licitra
Owner/Manager

Date ▶ 1/31/95

Form **945**

Illustration 4-11. Form 945, Annual Return of Withheld Federal Income Tax

Further information about those payments subject to backup withholding and the period of time for which the 31% should be withheld may be found in the instructions that accompany Form 1099.

INFORMATION RETURNS

You may be required to file an *information return* upon which you report the compensation paid to individuals who are not employees. Thus, you may need to file information returns in addition to preparing

statements that reflect the amount of wages and other compensation paid to employees. The IRS requires that information returns be filed as an aid in determining whether the true income of a taxpayer has been reported; for, like Form W-2, copies of the information returns are filed with the IRS as well as being sent to the payee of the amount involved. We have briefly described several of the major information returns in Illustration 4-12. As an example of one type of information return, Form 1099-MISC is shown in Illustration 4-13, page 144.

Form 1099-MISC, Miscellaneous Income	For reporting miscellaneous types of income, such as rents, royalties, commissions, fees, prizes, and awards, of at least $600 paid to nonemployees, and any backup withholding. Gross royalty payments of $10 or more must also be reported on this form. (Life insurance companies may use either Form W-2 or 1099-MISC for reporting payments of commissions to full-time life insurance sales agents.) See Illustration 4-13.
Form 1099-INT, Interest Income	For reporting payments of (a) interest of $10 or more paid or credited on earnings from savings and loan associations, credit unions, bank deposits, corporate bonds, etc.; (b) interest of $600 or more from other sources; (c) forfeited interest due on premature withdrawals of time deposits; (d) foreign tax eligible for the recipient's foreign tax credit withheld and paid on interest; and (e) payments of any interest on bearer certificates of deposit.
Form 1099-DIV, Dividends and Distributions	For reporting payments of dividends totaling $10 or more to any person; foreign tax withheld and paid on dividends and other distributions on stock for a person; and distributions made by corporations and regulated investment companies (including money market funds) as part of a liquidation.
Form 1099-PATR, Taxable Distributions Received from Cooperatives	For cooperatives to report patronage dividends paid and other distributions made that total $10 or more during the year.
Form 1099-R, Distributions From Pensions, Annuities, Retirement or Profit-Sharing Plans, IRAs, Insurance Contracts, etc.	For reporting all distributions from pensions, annuities, profit-sharing and retirement plans, and individual retirement arrangements made by employees' trusts or funds; federal, state, or local government retirement systems; and life insurance companies.
Form 1099-G, Certain Government Payments	For reporting unemployment compensation payments and state and local income tax refunds of $10 or more, taxable grants, income tax refunds, and agricultural subsidy payments.
Form 5498, Individual Retirement Arrangement Information	For reporting contributions received from each person to an individual retirement account (IRA) or a simplified employee pension plan (SEP) and qualified deductible voluntary employee contributions to a plan maintained by the employer.
Form 8027, Employer's Annual Information Return of Tip Income and Allocated Tips	For large food or beverage establishments to report the amount of receipts from food or beverage operations, the amount of tips reported by employees, and the amounts allocated as tips to employees.

Illustration 4-12. Major Information Returns

```
           9595        ☐ VOID     ☐ CORRECTED

 PAYER'S name, street address, city, state, and ZIP code   | 1 Rents            | OMB No. 1545-0115  |
                                                           | $                  |                    | Miscellaneous
  Worldwide Publishing Co.                                 | 2 Royalties        |    1993            | Income
  40 Fifth Avenue                                          | $34,970.65         |                    |
  New York, NY 10011-4000                                  | 3 Prizes, awards, etc. |                |
                                                           | $                  |                    |
 PAYER'S Federal identification number | RECIPIENT'S identification number | 4 Federal income tax withheld | 5 Fishing boat proceeds | Copy A
   75-4013736                          |   461-91-4821                     | $                             | $                       | For
 RECIPIENT'S name                                          | 6 Medical and health care payments | 7 Nonemployee compensation | Internal Revenue
                                                           | $                  | $                  | Service Center
  Laurie T. Musberger                                      | 8 Substitute payments in lieu of | 9 Payer made direct sales of | File with Form 1096.
 Street address (including apt. no.)                       |   dividends or interest          |   $5,000 or more of consumer | For Paperwork
  1043 Maple Drive                                         | $                  |   products to a buyer          | Reduction Act
 City, state, and ZIP code                                 | 10 Crop insurance proceeds | 11 State income tax withheld | Notice and
  Chicago, IL 60615-3443                                   | $                  | $                  | instructions for
 Account number (optional)              | 2nd TIN Not. | 12 State/Payer's state number |                   | completing this form,
                                        |    ☐         |   85-33378                    |                   | see Instructions for
                                                                                                            Forms 1099, 1098,
 Form 1099-MISC                                            Department of the Treasury - Internal Revenue Service   5498, and W-2G.
```

Illustration 4-13. Form 1099-MISC, Miscellaneous Income

Generally you must file an information return whenever payments totaling $600 or more are made in the form of (1) salaries, wages, commissions, fees, and other forms of compensation for services, or (2) interest, dividends, rents, royalties, annuities, pensions, and other gains, profits, and income paid by a person engaged in a trade or business in the course of that trade or business. When you pay employees any of the items listed in (1) above, your obligation to file an information return is satisfied by filing Form W-2.

Professional Tip

Do you have questions about the proper filing of Form W-2 or about the Form 1099 series? If so, contact the Martinsburg, WV Computing Center, which has installed an information reporting customer service call site. The site can be reached by dialing 304-263-8700 (not toll free) from 8:00 a.m. to 6:00 p.m. EST.

Use *Form 1096, Annual Summary and Transmittal of U.S. Information Returns*, to transmit to the IRS the information contained on Forms 1099. You must use a Form 1096 to transmit each separate type of information return. Thus, you must use a 1096 to transmit all Forms 1099-INT, and another 1096 to transmit all Forms 1099-MISC issued for the year. You must file Form 1096 and the accompanying information returns on or before the last day of February of the year following the payment.

Magnetic Media/ Electronic Reporting

The Secretary of the Treasury issues regulations that provide standards for determining which information returns must be filed on magnetic media or in other machine-readable form. The magnetic reporting requirements are contained in Revenue Procedures, which may be obtained from the District Director's office, and in the publications of the Social Security Administration.

By means of a dial-up modem, employers can electronically submit their *original* Forms 5498 (Individual Retirement Arrangement Information) and all *corrected* returns for the Forms 1099 series. Those interested in obtaining information about electronic filing should contact the IRS Martinsburg Computing Center, at (304) 263-8700.

Form W-2 and Other Information Returns. If you file 250 or more Forms W-2 or other information returns, you must use magnetic media instead of paper forms. To obtain approval of a magnetic medium for filing Forms W-2, you must file your application with the Social Security Administration, P.O. Box 2317, Baltimore, MD 21203, Attn: Magnetic Media Group. For other information returns, you must complete *Form 4419, Application for Filing Information Returns Magnetically/Electronically* and file the form with the IRS.

If you can prove that the filing of Forms W-2 or other information returns on magnetic media would be costlier than filing on paper returns, you may request a hardship waiver. To do so, complete and submit *Form 8508, Request for Waiver From Filing Information Returns on Magnetic Media,* to the IRS. Or, you may send a letter containing all necessary information to Magnetic Media Reporting, IRS National Computer Center, P.O. Box 1359, Martinsburg, WV 25401-3159. Written requests for a waiver are required at least 90 days before the return due date.

Form W-4. As you saw earlier, you must submit copies of Forms W-4 on which 11 or more withholding allowances are claimed. If you are filing on magnetic media, you should include a signed *Form 6466, Transmittal of Magnetic Media of Form W-4, Employee's Withholding Allowance Certificate.*

EMPLOYER'S RECORDS FOR INCOME TAXES WITHHELD

If you withhold federal income taxes from your employees' wages, you must keep the records required by the Director of Internal Revenue. The information required by the income tax withholding laws is summarized in Illustration 1-2, page 3.

There is no prescribed form in which you must keep the records. However, they must be maintained in a manner that will enable the IRS to determine whether any tax liability has been incurred and, if so, the extent of that liability. Although you may microfilm your general books of account, such as cash books, journals, and ledgers, the microfilm reproduction must be in accordance with procedures and standards set forth by the IRS. The IRS will grant permission to microfilm the general books of account only after it has examined your micrographic system.

To facilitate preparing the returns and reports for the federal, state, and local governments, you must keep certain payroll and earnings records, as indicated in the preceding units of this textbook. In most payroll accounting systems, a column is provided in both the payroll register and the employee's earnings record to show the amount of each kind of tax withheld from each employee's wages on each payday.

Your payroll records must be made available for inspection at all times by officers of the IRS. The records must be kept for a period of at least four years after the date the tax to which they relate becomes due, or the date the tax is paid, whichever is later.

WITHHOLDING STATE INCOME TAXES

In 41 states, the District of Columbia, and Puerto Rico, employers must withhold income taxes on wage payments.[3] Thus, the payroll manager may be faced with the complex task of keeping informed of the latest tax developments at the state level. The problem becomes more acute if a firm has employees in several states. In this instance the payroll manager must know if there is an income tax in each of the states, if withholding from wages is required, how much must be withheld, what kinds of employees and payments are exempt from the state law, and how the tax is to be paid. Further, information may be needed about each state's regulations as to: (a) the required frequency with which you must make wage payments, (b) acceptable media of payment, (c) the maximum permissible interval between the end of a pay period and the payday for that pay period, (d) the time within which you must make a final wage payment to an employee who is discharged or laid off or who quits or goes on strike, (e) the frequency with which you must tell employees of the deductions made from their wage payments, and (f) the maximum amount of unpaid wages that you may pay to the surviving spouse or family of a deceased worker.

Employers in most states use wage-bracket tables and percentage method formulas to determine the amount of state income taxes to withhold from their employees' wages. However, when the size of wage payments and the frequency of such payments are irregular, overwithholding may result. Thus, employees become dissatisfied with the amount of their take-home pay. Although the federal income tax law and regulations provide for the use of alternative withholding methods (see pages 128 to 130) in such situations, the methods are not automatically adopted by the states. Therefore, payroll managers must decide for their individually affected states which, if any, of the federal alternative withholding methods may be used to determine the amount of state income taxes to be withheld.

Withholding from Nonresidents or Residents or Both

In those states imposing personal income taxes, the laws vary as to the withholding of taxes from wages paid. For example, Arizona does not require the withholding of state income tax from *nonresidents* engaged in motion picture production in that state. In Hawaii, *nonresidents* who perform temporary services are not subject to withholding of the state income tax. In the District of Columbia, employers are required to withhold the tax from wages paid to *residents* only. In Oklahoma, *nonresidents* are exempt from state income tax withholding on the first $300 or less each calendar

---

[3] Those states that do not have a personal income tax law requiring withholding from wage payments are: Alaska, Florida, Nevada, New Hampshire, South Dakota, Tennessee, Texas, Washington, and Wyoming.

quarter. However, in most states having income tax laws, you are required to withhold the tax from *both nonresidents and residents*, unless, as described below, there is a reciprocal agreement with one or more states to the contrary. In most states a "covered employee" is any person from whose pay you are required to withhold federal income taxes under the Internal Revenue Code.

Other variations in state income tax laws result from *reciprocal agreements* among the states. For example, in Kentucky, reciprocal agreements have been entered into with Illinois, Indiana, Michigan, Ohio, West Virginia, and Wisconsin. Thus, if a resident of one of these states works in Kentucky, the employee will not be subject to withholding of Kentucky income tax if the other state grants an exemption from the withholding of its income tax to Kentucky residents who earn income in that state. Also, Kentucky has an agreement with Virginia whereby residents of Virginia who commute daily to work in Kentucky are not subject to Kentucky withholding, and vice versa.

Types of State Income Tax Returns or Reports

In connection with state income tax laws, there are four main types of returns or reports the payroll manager should be familiar with:

1. *Periodic withholding returns* on which you report the wages paid and the state tax withheld during the reporting period. Illustration 4-14 shows the *Employer Deposit Statement of Income Tax Withheld* used by employers in Pennsylvania. Depending on the amount of state income taxes withheld for each quarterly period, employers may be required to pay over the taxes semimonthly, monthly, or quarterly.

Some states require employers to deposit their withheld income taxes through electronic funds transfer (EFT), which was discussed in Unit 2, pages 47-48. The requirements for using EFT vary among the states, depending upon the amounts withheld. Thus, payroll managers should contact their state to obtain information on EFT and their bank to determine its EFT capabilities.

2. *Reconciliation returns* that compare the total amount of state tax paid as shown on the periodic returns with the amounts of state tax declared to have been withheld from employees' wages. The *Employer Quarterly Reconciliation Return of Income Tax Withheld* for use by employers in Pennsylvania is shown in Illustration 4-15. Employers who have computer systems may submit their information on magnetic tapes.

3. *Annual statements to employees* showing the amount of wages paid during the year and the state tax withheld from those wages. Form W-2, Wage and Tax Statement, was shown in Illustration 4-5.

4. *Information returns* used to report payments to individuals that are not subject to withholding and/or are not reported on the annual employee wage and tax statements. See Illustration 4-12 for a listing of the major information returns.

PA-501R PA DEPARTMENT OF REVENUE					19 --		EMPLOYER DEPOSIT STATEMENT OF INCOME TAX WITHHELD Use Only When Employers Do Not Have Preprinted Coupons ALL EMPLOYERS MUST FILE A PA-W3 RETURN FOR EACH QUARTER	
EIN	QUARTER	QUARTER ENDING	DUE DATE	TYPE FILER		EXPECTED 3-MONTH WITHHOLDING WILL BE:		
71-3456798	9-04	12/31/--	1/4/--	MONTHLY ☐ SEMI-MONTHLY ☒		$300 OR MORE BUT LESS THAN $1,000 TAX $1,000 OR MORE TAX		

DATE WAGES WERE FIRST PAID
6/15/--

BUSINESS NAME AND ADDRESS

Weiner, Inc.
820 Allen Drive
Ambler, PA 19002-0882

1.	GROSS COMPENSATION	11,614	29
2.	PA INCOME TAX WITHHELD	325	20
3.	LESS CREDITS	-0-	
4.	PLUS INTEREST	-0-	
5.	PAYMENT	325	20

DATE 1/4/--	TELEPHONE NUMBER (215) 555-6700	SIGNATURE *Robert T. Rojas*	TITLE Controller

Illustration 4-14. Form PA-501R, Pennsylvania Employer Deposit Statement of Income Tax Withheld

Since the requirements for transmitting returns and reports vary from state to state, you should be familiar with the tax regulations of the state in which your business firm is located and of the state or states in which your employees reside.

As a result of federal regulations that require the filing of information returns on magnetic media, many states permit you to submit your wage information on magnetic tape, disk, and diskette. Also, many states take part in the Combined Federal/State Filing Program. This program enables you to file information returns with the federal government and to authorize the release of the information to the applicable state rather than file a separate state return. To participate in this program, you must first obtain permission from the IRS.

NEWS ALERT NEWS ALERT NEWS ALERT

Studies are underway to simplify the costly and complex reporting of wage and tax data by combining and standardizing the reporting to the IRS, SSA, Labor Department, and state agencies. Some states have joined in a test where the SSA sends state data from the Forms W-2 to the IRS, which in turn, routes the data to the states for their analysis of taxpayer compliance.

WITHHOLDING LOCAL INCOME TAXES

In addition to state income tax laws, cities and counties in Alabama, California, Colorado, Delaware, Georgia, Indiana, Kentucky, Maryland, Michigan, Missouri, New Jersey, New York, Ohio, Oregon, and Pennsylvania have passed local income tax legislation requiring employers to deduct and withhold income taxes or license fees on salaries or wages paid.

As a few examples, in Alabama, several cities have license fee ordinances that require the withholding of the fees from employees' wages. Certain employees in Denver, Colorado, are subject to the withholding of the Denver Occupational Privilege Tax from their compensation. In Wilmington, Delaware, the Earned Income Tax is withheld from the taxable wages paid employees. In Kentucky, a license fee (payroll tax) is imposed by a number of cities and counties.

Illustration 4-16 on page 148 shows the return that must be completed by employers in Philadelphia, all of whom are required to withhold wage taxes from compensation paid their employees. Depending upon the amount of wage taxes withheld, employers may be required to make deposits weekly, semimonthly, monthly, or quarterly. For any late payment of the withheld tax, the city imposes a penalty on the underpayment. Employers are required to file annual summary returns with respect to the wage taxes deducted during the preceding calendar year. The annual reconciliation of wage tax return is due January 31.

Illustration 4-15. Form PA-W3R, Pennsylvania Employer Quarterly Reconciliation Return of Income Tax Withheld

THE CITY OF PHILADELPHIA EMPLOYER'S DEPOSITORY RETURN OF TAX WITHHELD (W7)				

THE CITY OF PHILADELPHIA
EMPLOYER'S DEPOSITORY RETURN
OF TAX WITHHELD (W7)

WEINER, INC.
820 ALLEN DRIVE
AMBLER, PA 19002-0882

FILE RETURN AND PAY TAX FOR

Week No.	52
FROM	12/22/--
TO	12/28/--

W - 7

PERIOD	TYPE	S.I.C.	ACCOUNT NO.
4	1	501	3256301

T.D.		TOT. P.
T.P.		T.B.
I.&P.		I.&P. BAL.

1. TOTAL COMPENSATION (INCLUDE VALUE OF PERSONAL USE OF EMPLOYER OWNED VEHICLE)	5,543.18
2. DEDUCT COMPENSATION PAID NON-RESIDENTS FOR SERVICES OUTSIDE PHILADELPHIA	-0-.
3. TAXABLE COMPENSATION (LINE 1 MINUS LINE 2)	5,543.18
4A NUMBER OF RESIDENTS 12 — PORTION OF LINE 3 PAID TO RESIDENTS	5,543.18
4B NUMBER OF NON-RESIDENTS 0 — PORTION OF LINE 3 PAID TO NON-RESIDENTS NOTE: (4A + 4B MUST EQUAL LINE 3)	-0-.

5. LINE 4A-TAX Withheld at 4.96%	6. LINE 4B-TAX Withheld at 4.3125%	7. TOTAL Block 5 Plus Block 6	8. Penalty + Interest (See Reverse)	9. TOTAL - Block 7 plus Block 8
274.94	-0-	274.94	-0-	274.94

PLEASE ANSWER FULLY
Have you ceased being an employer? ...... No
Have you discontinued or sold business? ...... No
If yes, give date ....
If sold, give name of new owner(s) ....

Illustration 4-16. Form W-7, City of Philadelphia Employer's Depository Return of Tax Withheld

GLOSSARY

Annualizing wages—plan of determining amount of income taxes to be withheld by multiplying the wages for one payroll period by the number of periods in the year, determining the annual amount of withholding required on the total wages, and dividing the annual withholding by the number of payroll periods.

Backup withholding—amount of income tax withheld by payers of taxable interest, dividends, and certain other payments made to payees who have failed to furnish the payers with correct identification numbers.

Cumulative withholding—plan of determining amount of income taxes to be withheld by adding wages for a particular payroll period to total wages already paid during the year, dividing the aggregate by the number of payroll periods to which it pertains, computing the tax on the average amount of wages, subtracting the amount of tax already withheld during preceding payroll periods, and deducting any excess tax from current payment of wages.

Earned income credit (EIC)—reduction in the computation of the federal income taxes mostly for workers who have dependent children and maintain a household.

Employee—any individual performing services for an employer in the legal relationship of employer and employee.

Employer—any person or organization for whom an individual performs any service as an employee.

Information return—form upon which an employer reports compensation paid to individuals who are not employees.

Percentage method—plan of determining amount of income taxes to be withheld through use of Table of Allowance Values and Percentage Method Withholding Table.

Personal allowance—a deduction allowed in computing taxable income; also known as a *personal exemption.*

Quarterly averaging of wages—plan of determining amount of income taxes to be withheld by estimating the employee's average wages for the calendar quarter, calculating an average payment, and withholding an amount based on the average payment.

Reciprocal agreement—arrangement entered into by two or more states whereby the resident of one state working in another state will not be subject to the withholding of income taxes by the state in which the person is employed if that state has entered into a similar agreement with the employee's resident state.

Special withholding allowance—allowance claimed by employees so that wages which are below the level subject to the income tax will not be subject to withholding.

Standard deduction—amount of money used to reduce a person's adjusted gross income in arriving at the taxable income.

Supplemental wage payments—additional compensation such as vacation pay, bonuses, and commissions paid to employees.

Wage and tax statement—statement furnished by employers to their employees informing them of the wages paid during the calendar year and the amount of taxes withheld from those wages.

Wage-bracket method—plan of determining amount of income taxes to be withheld by reading amount from tables provided by the IRS, which take into consideration length of payroll period, gross earnings, marital status, and number of withholding allowances claimed.

Wages—total compensation paid for services whether in the form of wages, salaries, commissions, or bonuses, including the cash value of remuneration paid in a medium other than cash.

QUESTIONS FOR REVIEW

NOTE: *Tax Tables A and B at the back of this textbook and the tax regulations presented in this unit are to be used in answering all questions and solving all problems.*

1. What three conditions must exist before any tax may be withheld under the federal income tax withholding law?
2. Define *wages* under the federal income tax law.
3. To what extent are cash tips treated as remuneration subject to federal income tax withholding?
4. Under what conditions must a large food establishment allocate tips to its tipped employees?
5. For each of the following kinds of wage payments, indicate whether or not the wages are exempt from the withholding of federal income taxes:
   a. Three weeks' vacation pay.
   b. Weekly advance to a sales representative for traveling expenses to be incurred.
   c. Weekly wages paid the housekeeper in a college fraternity.
   d. Monthly salary received by Rev. Cole Carpenter.
   e. Benefits paid by a union to its members who are on strike.
6. a. What is a personal allowance?
   b. What was the amount of a personal allowance in 1993?
7. Brock Armstrong is married and his only dependent is his wife, Norma. Norma is claimed as a dependent on her father's federal income tax return. Is Brock entitled to claim a personal allowance for Norma? Explain.
8. Are all employees entitled to claim one special withholding allowance? Explain.
9. For what purpose does an employer ask that a completed Form W-4 be on file for each employee?
10. On July 15, William Mitchell amended his Form W-4 to increase the number of withholding allowances from four to seven. Mitchell asked for a refund of the amount of overwithheld income taxes from January 1 to July 15 when the number of allowances was only four. Should Mitchell be reimbursed for the income taxes overwithheld before the effective date of the amended Form W-4?

11. a. Under what conditions may employees be exempt from the withholding of federal income taxes during 1994?
    b. How do such employees indicate their no-tax-liability status?
12. a. May an employee agree with the employer to withhold income tax *in excess of* that required under the law?
    b. May an employee agree with the employer to withhold income tax *less than* that required under the law?
13. Under what conditions are employers required to submit copies of Form W-4 to the IRS?
14. Commencing in June, Slade Exon is eligible to receive monthly payments from a pension fund. What procedure should Exon follow if he does not wish to have federal income taxes withheld from his periodic pension payments?
15. What is a standard deduction?
16. a. Rhonda Gramm is single and her wages are paid weekly. What is the amount of her withholding allowance?
    b. Howard Heinz, married, claims two withholding allowances and his wages are paid semimonthly. What is the total amount of his withholding allowance?
17. Max Lieberman, a married employee, fails to furnish his employer with a withholding allowance certificate. His weekly wages amount to $445. Under the percentage method, will any portion of his wages be subject to withholding? If so, indicate what portion.
18. Compare the percentage method and the wage-bracket method of withholding federal income taxes.
19. What steps should be taken by an employer to calculate the amount of income tax to be withheld by the annualizing of wages method?
20. Nancy Wallop is to receive her two weeks' vacation pay along with her regular semimonthly pay this Friday. Wallop's employer has decided to combine her two weeks' vacation pay with her

regular semimonthly pay and withhold federal income taxes on the aggregate payment. Is the employer properly following the computation rules issued by the IRS? Explain.

21. The Baucus Company has just completed the processing of its year-end payroll and distributed all the weekly paychecks. The payroll department is now calculating the amount of the annual bonus to be given each worker. What methods may be used by the company in determining the amount of federal income taxes to be withheld from the annual bonus payments?

22. Gerry Jeffords is eligible to receive advance earned income credit (EIC) payments. How should she proceed to obtain her payments?

23. From what source do employers obtain the funds needed to make advance EIC payments to their eligible employees?

24. Orrin D'Amato, single, participates in his firm's pension retirement plan. This year his adjusted gross income will be about $42,000. How much of his compensation may D'Amato contribute to an IRA this year without paying federal income taxes on the contribution?

25. a. For what purpose are employers required to prepare Form W-2?
   b. When are employers required to furnish their employees with copies of Form W-2?

26. Ross, Inc., a semiweekly depositor, withholds $2,500 in federal income taxes from employees' wages each Friday. When and to whom should the amount withheld be paid?

27. For what purpose is Form W-3 completed by the employer?

28. What is backup withholding?

29. Why are certain organizations and persons required to file information returns?

30. Why are some employers required to file Form 1096?

31. For how long a period of time should employers retain their payroll records?

32. Identify the main types of returns or reports that an organization may be required to file under a state income tax law.

QUESTIONS FOR DISCUSSION

1. Virginia Skelton, a former office layout consultant and now a full-time homemaker, was recently elected to the board of directors of Lantos, Inc. In addition to attending monthly board meetings, Skelton has assumed a short-term responsibility, along with the office manager, for developing a new word processing center. For her consulting services, Skelton is to be paid $950. The company will furnish an office, clerical help, and all materials and supplies to be used by Skelton. Will her earnings of $950 be subject to federal income tax withholding? Explain.

2. Alex Oberstar, a cook in the Lagomarsino company cafeteria, is furnished two meals each day during his eight-hour shift. Oberstar's duties require him to have his meals on the company's premises. Should the cash value of Oberstar's meals be included as part of his taxable wages? Explain.

3. The Solomon Company ordinarily pays its employees on a weekly basis. Recently one of the employees, Bernard Nagle, was sent from the home office on a three-week trip. Nagle has now returned to the office and you are preparing a single check covering his three-weeks' services. Should you withhold federal income taxes on the total gross earnings for the three-week period or should you calculate the federal income taxes as if Nagle were receiving three separate weekly wage payments?

4. Investigate your state's income tax withholding law (or that of some other state assigned by your instructor) and find the answers to the following questions:
   a. Who must withhold the tax?
   b. How are covered employers and covered employees defined?
   c. Are there any reciprocal agreements the state has entered into? If so, describe them.
   d. How is the withholding rate determined?
   e. What payments are subject to withholding?
   f. What payments are not subject to withholding?
   g. Are there any employee withholding exemptions?
   h. What methods of withholding are permitted?
   i. Describe each of the returns required by the state.
   j. What kinds of information must be retained by employers in their withholding tax records?
   k. What penalties are imposed for failure to comply with the withholding law?
   l. Are any employers required to deposit their withheld income taxes through electronic funds transfer (EFT)? If so, what requirements are imposed by the state?

5. Janice Sikorski, one of your firm's workers, has just come into the Payroll Department and says to you: "I am thinking of amending my Form W-4 so that an additional $10 is withheld each week. That way I will get a fat refund next year. What do you think of my idea?" How would you reply to Sikorski?

6. Anita Leland, a waitress in the Atlantis Casino, reported tips of $467 to her employer last year. Two months after she filed her federal income tax return, Leland received a letter from the IRS informing her that she had earned $5,260 in tips rather than the $467 reported. She was notified that she owed the government $1,872.94 in back taxes.

    a. How is the IRS able to determine the amount of tips received by a waitress in a casino?

    b. If the IRS is correct in its determination of the tips received, is Atlantis subject to a penalty for not having withheld payroll taxes on all the tips Leland received during the year?

7. Research the regulations your state may have issued regarding the filing of information returns to learn: (a) whether your state *permits* or *requires* the use of magnetic media, (b) which forms may be filed on magnetic media, and (c) whether your state participates in the Combined Federal/State Filing Program.

PRACTICAL PROBLEMS

4-1. Use the percentage method to determine the federal income taxes to withhold from the wages or salaries of each employee listed below.

Employee's Name	Marital Status	No. of W/H Allow.	Gross Wage or Salary	Amount to be Withheld
1. Amoroso, A.	Married	4	$610 weekly	$_____
2. Dorbuck, J.	Single	0	$825 biweekly	_____
3. Gleason, R.	Single	5	$9,630 quarterly	_____
4. Quinto, K.	Married	8	$925 semimonthly	_____
5. Sweeney, R.	Married	3	$1,975 monthly	_____

4-2. Use the (a) percentage method and (b) wage-bracket method to determine the federal income taxes to withhold from the wages or salaries of each employee listed below.

Employee's Name	Marital Status	No. of W/H Allow.	Gross Wage or Salary	Amount to be Withheld (a) Percentage Method	(b) Wage-Bracket Method
1. Anastasi, B. . .	Single	2	$475 weekly	$_____	$_____
2. Caplan, J.	Single	1	$960 weekly	_____	_____
3. Jones, H.	Married	6	$1,775 biweekly	_____	_____
4. Schiff, W.	Married	4	$1,480 semimonthly	_____	_____
5. Yarrow, K.	Married	9	$5,380 monthly	_____	_____

4-3. Donato Bakery uses the wage-bracket method in determining the amount of federal income taxes to withhold from the wages of its employees. Calculate the amount to withhold from the wages paid each employee listed below.

DONATO BAKERY

Employee	Marital Status	No. of W/H Allow.	Payroll Period W=Weekly S=Semimonthly M=Monthly D=Daily	Wage	Amount to be Withheld
William Bowen . .	M	1	W	$1,550	$_____
Elizabeth Carden	S	1	W	490	_____
Mel Jergensen . .	S	3	W	575	_____
Jessie Kelley	M	6	M	4,095	_____
Rose Lechner . . .	M	2	M	2,830	_____
Catherine Marcus	M	8	S	850	_____
Sarah Schartz . . .	S	1	D	96	_____
Jeffrey Singer . . .	S	4	S	2,090	_____
Manuel Torres . . .	M	10	M	3,225	_____

4-4. The names of the employees of the Lambright Music Shop are listed on the payroll register illustrated below. The payroll register also shows the marital status, number of withholding allowances claimed, and the total weekly earnings for each employee. Complete the payroll register for the payroll period ending October 7, showing the following:

a. Amount to withhold from each employee's earnings under FICA. This pay period ending October 7 is the 40th weekly pay period of the year. Assume that during the year the employees received the same weekly pay.

b. Amount to withhold from each employee's earnings for federal income taxes (FIT). Use the wage-bracket method to compute the amount to withhold.

c. Amount to withhold from each employee's earnings for the state income tax (SIT). In this state the entire amount of earnings is subject to a 2% tax.

d. Amount to withhold from each employee's earnings for the city income tax (CIT). In this city the entire amount of earnings is subject to a 1½% tax.

e. Net pay for each employee.

LAMBRIGHT MUSIC SHOP
PAYROLL REGISTER

FOR PERIOD ENDING _____ 19__

EMPLOYEE'S NAME	MARITAL STATUS	NO. OF W/H ALLOW.	TOTAL EARNINGS	(a) FICA OASDI	HI	(b) FIT	(c) SIT	(d) CIT	(e) NET PAY
Blue, Marion E.	M	4	1500 00						
Good, Ralph C.	S	1	275 00						
Irwin, Robert A.	M	0	195 00						
Larue, Stella V.	S	3	302 50						
Mayers, Charles D.	S	1	365 70						
Nash, Donald L.	S	2	464 80						
Syler, John T.	S	1	470 10						
Yost, Robert J.	M	5	360 00						
Totals									

Calculate the employer's FICA taxes for the pay period ending October 7.

OASDI taxes:

OASDI taxable earnings . . . . $ _____

OASDI taxes . . . . $ _____

HI taxes:

HI taxable earnings . . . . $ _____

HI taxes . . . . $ _____

(Practical Problems continued on page 156.)

Date _____   Name _____

4-5. The names of the employees of Cox Security Systems and their regular salaries are shown in the payroll register below. Note that Hill and Van Dyne are paid monthly on the last day, while all others are paid weekly.

In addition to the regular salaries, the company pays an annual bonus based on the amount of earnings for the year. For the current year, the bonus amounts to 8% of the annual salary paid each employee. The bonus is to be paid along with the regular salaries on December 31, but the amount of the bonus and the amount of the regular salary will be shown separately on each employee's earnings statement. Assume that all employees received their regular salary during the entire year.

Prepare the payroll for the pay period ending December 31, showing the following for each employee:

a. Supplementary earnings.
b. Total earnings.
c. FICA taxes to withhold.
d. Federal income taxes (FIT) to withhold. Use the wage-bracket method to compute the amount to withhold from the regular salary. Withhold a flat 28% of the annual bonus.
e. State income taxes (SIT) to withhold. In this state the entire amount of earnings is subject to a 2% tax.
f. City income taxes (CIT) to withhold. In this city the entire amount of earnings is subject to a 1% tax.
g. Net pay.

COX SECURITY SYSTEMS
PAYROLL REGISTER

19

FOR PERIOD ENDING

EMPLOYEE'S NAME	MARITAL STATUS	NO. OF W/H ALLOW.	EARNINGS REGULAR	(a) SUPP'L.	(b) TOTAL	(c) FICA OASDI	HI	(d) FIT	(e) SIT	(f) CIT	(g) NET PAY
Hill, J. Harvey	M	5	4 7 0 0 00								
Van Dyne, Joyce S.	M	2	2 6 5 0 00								
Abbott, Leslie N.	S	1	4 7 0 00								
Bunger, Russell L.	M	4	3 6 5 00								
Noblet, Thomas D.	M	2	2 8 0 00								
Short, Frank C.	S	1	3 5 0 00								
Toban, Harriette O.	M	2	3 7 5 00								
Wyeth, Amy R.	S	0	4 0 5 00								
Totals											

Calculate the employer's FICA taxes for the pay period ending December 31:

OASDI taxes:

OASDI taxable earnings .... $ _____

OASDI taxes .... $ _____

HI taxes:

HI taxable earnings .... $ _____

HI taxes .... $ _____

156

4-6. During the quarter ending December 31 of the current year, Cox Security Systems had 13 weekly paydays and three monthly paydays. Using the data given in Problem 4-5, complete the form below to show the:

a. Total earnings paid during the quarter, including both the regular and the supplementary earnings.
b. Total amount of FICA taxes withheld during the quarter.
c. Total amount of federal income taxes (FIT) withheld during the quarter.
d. Total amount of state income taxes (SIT) withheld during the quarter.
e. Total amount of city income taxes (CIT) withheld during the quarter.
f. Total net amount paid each employee during the quarter.

COX SECURITY SYSTEMS

19___

EMPLOYEE'S NAME	(a) TOTAL EARNINGS	(b) FICA OASDI	(b) FICA HI	(c) FIT	(d) SIT	(e) CIT	(f) NET PAY
Hill, J. Harvey							
Van Dyne, Joyce S.							
Abbott, Leslie N.							
Bunger, Russell L.							
Noblet, Thomas D.							
Short, Frank C.							
Toban, Harriette O.							
Wyeth, Amy R.							
Totals							

157

4-7. The employees of Talbott Hosiery, Inc., are paid biweekly. The names of five employees of the company are given on the payroll register illustrated below. The payroll register also shows the marital status, number of withholding allowances claimed, and the total biweekly earnings for each worker. Assume that each employee is paid the same biweekly wage on each payday in 1994. Also shown below is the Wage-Bracket Table for Advance Earned Income Credit (EIC) Payments for a Biweekly Payroll Period. Each of the employees listed on the payroll register has completed a Form W-5 indicating that the worker is not married.

Complete the payroll register for the biweekly payroll period ending December 2, 1994, showing the following:

a. Amounts to withhold from each employee's earnings under FICA.
b. Amount to withhold from each employee's earnings for federal income taxes (FIT). Use the wage-bracket method to compute the amount to be withheld.
c. Amount to withhold from each employee's earnings for the state income tax (SIT). In this state the entire amount of earnings is subject to a 1½% tax.
d. Amount of advance EIC payments to be paid each employee. Use the wage-bracket table below.
e. Net pay for each employee.

TALBOTT HOSIERY, INC.

PAYROLL REGISTER

FOR PERIOD ENDING _____ 19 ____

EMPLOYEE'S NAME	MARITAL STATUS	NO. OF W/H ALLOW.	TOTAL EARNINGS	(a) FICA OASDI	(a) FICA HI	(b) FIT	(c) SIT	(d) ADVANCE EIC PAYMENT	(e) NET PAY
Allen, N.	S	4	393 00						
Diehl, M.	S	1	347 00						
McDowell, J.	S	2	473 50						
Ronsini, J.	S	3	522 00						
Wheeler, D.	S	5	454 00						
Totals									

Wage-Bracket Table for Advance EIC Payments

BIWEEKLY Payroll Period

SINGLE or MARRIED Without Spouse Filing Certificate

Wages— At least	But less than	Payment to be made	Wages— At least	But less than	Payment to be made	Wages— At least	But less than	Payment to be made	Wages— At least	But less than	Payment to be made
$0	$6	$0	$152	$157	$28	$470	$477	$54	$682	$689	$26
6	11	1	157	163	29	477	485	53	689	697	25
11	17	2	163	168	30	485	493	52	697	704	24
17	22	3	168	173	31	493	500	51	704	712	23
22	28	4	173	179	32	500	508	50	712	720	22
28	33	5	179	184	33	508	515	49	720	727	21
33	38	6	184	190	34	515	523	48	727	735	20
38	44	7	190	195	35	523	530	47	735	742	19
44	49	8	195	200	36	530	538	46	742	750	18
49	55	9	200	206	37	538	545	45	750	757	17
55	60	10	206	211	38	545	553	44	757	765	16
60	65	11	211	217	39	553	561	43	765	773	15
65	71	12	217	222	40	561	568	42	773	780	14
71	76	13	222	228	41	568	576	41	780	788	13
76	82	14	228	233	42	576	583	40	788	795	12
82	87	15	233	238	43	583	591	39	795	803	11
87	92	16	238	244	44	591	598	38	803	810	10
92	98	17	244	249	45	598	606	37	810	818	9
98	103	18	249	255	46	606	614	36	818	826	8
103	109	19	255	260	47	614	621	35	826	833	7
109	114	20	260	265	48	621	629	34	833	841	6
114	119	21	265	271	49	629	636	33	841	848	5
119	125	22	271	276	50	636	644	32	848	856	4
125	130	23	276	282	51	644	651	31	856	863	3
130	136	24	282	287	52	651	659	30	863	871	2
136	141	25	287	292	53	659	667	29	871	879	1
141	146	26	292	297	54	667	674	28	879	- - -	0
146	152	27	297	470	55	674	682	27			

Date _____   Name _____

4-8. During the fourth quarter of 1994 there were seven biweekly paydays on Friday (October 7, 21; November 4, 18; and December 2, 16, and 30) for Talbott Hosiery, Inc. Assume that each of the seven biweekly payments was the same as that calculated in Problem 4-7.

Using the forms supplied below and on pages 161-163, complete the following for the fourth quarter, 1994:

a. Federal Tax Deposit Coupons, Forms 8109. Below each coupon, indicate the due date of the deposit. The employer's telephone number is: (501) 555-7331.

b. Employer's Quarterly Federal Tax Return, Form 941. The form is to be signed by the company's president, Wilbur B. Kroft.

Each pay period the amount of the advance EIC payments is subtracted from the employer's liability for the federal income taxes withheld, the employees' FICA taxes, and the employer's FICA taxes. Thus, on each payday, the tax liability is calculated as follows:

Federal income taxes withheld	$ 78.00
Employees' OASDI taxes	135.75
Employees' HI taxes	31.75
Employer's OASDI taxes	135.75
Employer's HI taxes	31.75
Total	$413.00
Less advance EIC payments	267.00
Tax liability	$146.00

c. Employer's Quarterly Report of State Income Taxes Withheld. The report, due on or before January 31, 1995, is to be signed by Kroft.

EMPLOYER'S REPORT OF STATE INCOME TAX WITHHELD

(DO NOT WRITE IN THIS SPACE)

IMPORTANT: PLEASE REFER TO THIS NUMBER IN ANY CORRESPONDENCE →

IF YOU ARE A SEASONAL EMPLOYER AND THIS IS YOUR FINAL REPORT FOR THIS SEASON, CHECK HERE ☐ AND SHOW THE NEXT MONTH IN WHICH YOU WILL PAY WAGES.

WITHHOLDING IDENTIFICATION NUMBER: 42-7-3301   MONTH OF OR QUARTER ENDING: DEC. 94

TALBOTT HOSIERY, INC.
10 SUMMIT SQUARE
CITY, STATE 00000-0000

IF NAME OR ADDRESS IS INCORRECT, PLEASE MAKE CORRECTIONS.
THIS REPORT MUST BE RETURNED EVEN IF NO AMOUNT HAS BEEN WITHHELD

Under penalties prescribed by law, I hereby affirm that to the best of my knowledge and belief this return, including any accompanying schedules and statements, is true and complete. If prepared by a person other than taxpayer, his affirmation is based on all information of which he has any knowledge.

SIGNATURE: TITLE: DATE:

1. GROSS PAYROLL THIS PERIOD $
2. STATE INCOME TAX WITHHELD $
3. ADJUSTMENT FOR PREVIOUS PERIOD(S) (ATTACH STATEMENT) $
4. TOTAL ADJUSTED TAX (LINE 2 PLUS OR MINUS LINE 3) $
5. PENALTY (25% OF LINE 4)
6. INTEREST
7. TOTAL AMOUNT DUE AND PAYABLE $

MAIL THIS REPORT WITH CHECK OR MONEY ORDER PAYABLE TO THE DEPT. OF REVENUE ON OR BEFORE DUE DATE TO AVOID PENALTY.

Practical Problem 4-8

	AMOUNT OF DEPOSIT (Do NOT type; please print.)				Darken only one **TYPE OF TAX**	a n d	Darken only one **TAX PERIOD**

Mark the "X" in this box only if there is a change to Employer Identification Number (EIN) or Name.

See Instructions on page 1.

DOLLARS   CENTS

EIN [70-2204701]

BANK NAME/
DATE STAMP

TALBOTT HOSIERY, INC.
10 SUMMIT SQUARE
CITY, STATE 00000-0000

IRS USE ONLY

TYPE OF TAX		TAX PERIOD
941	Sch. A	1st Quarter
990C	1120	2nd Quarter
943	990T	3rd Quarter
720	990PF	4th Quarter
CT-1	1042	
940		6 2

Telephone number ( )

FOR BANK USE IN MICR ENCODING

Federal Tax Deposit Coupon
Form 8109

To be deposited on or before _____

Mark the "X" in this box only if there is a change to Employer Identification Number (EIN) or Name.

See Instructions on page 1.

AMOUNT OF DEPOSIT (Do NOT type; please print.)

DOLLARS   CENTS

EIN [70-2204701]

BANK NAME/
DATE STAMP

TALBOTT HOSIERY, INC.
10 SUMMIT SQUARE
CITY, STATE 00000-0000

IRS USE ONLY

TYPE OF TAX		TAX PERIOD
941	Sch. A	1st Quarter
990C	1120	2nd Quarter
943	990T	3rd Quarter
720	990PF	4th Quarter
CT-1	1042	
940		6 2

Telephone number ( )

FOR BANK USE IN MICR ENCODING

Federal Tax Deposit Coupon
Form 8109

To be deposited on or before _____

Practical Problem 4-8

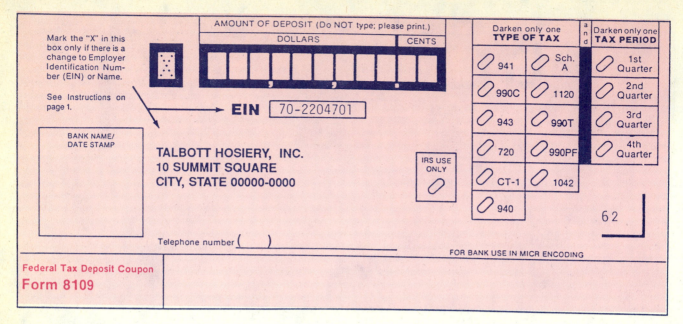

To be deposited on or before _____

Practical Problem 4-8

Form **941**	4141	**Employer's Quarterly Federal Tax Return**		
		▶ See separate instructions for information on completing this return.		
Department of the Treasury Internal Revenue Service		Please type or print.		

Enter state code for state in which deposits made ▶ [:] (see page 2 of instructions).

Name (as distinguished from trade name)	Date quarter ended DEC. 31, 1994	OMB No. 1545-0029
		T
Trade name, if any	Employer Identification number	FF
TALBOTT HOSIERY, INC.	70-2204701	FD
Address (number and street)	City, state, and ZIP code	FP
10 SUMMIT SQUARE	CITY, STATE 00000-0000	I
		T

If address is different from prior return, check here ▶ [ ]

IRS Use

1	1	1	1	1	1	1	1	1	2		3	3	3	3	3	3		4	4	4		
5	5	5	6	7	8	8	8	8	8		9	9	9	10	10	10	10	10	10	10	10	10

If you do not have to file returns in the future, check here ▶ [ ] and enter date final wages paid ▶

If you are a seasonal employer, see **Seasonal employers** on page 2 and check here (see instructions) ▶ [ ]

1	Number of employees (except household) employed in the pay period that includes March 12th ▶		
2	Total wages and tips subject to withholding, plus other compensation	**2**	
3	Total income tax withheld from wages, tips, and sick pay	**3**	
4	Adjustment of withheld income tax for preceding quarters of calendar year	**4**	
5	Adjusted total of income tax withheld (line 3 as adjusted by line 4—see instructions)	**5**	
6a	Taxable social security wages	$ _____ × 12.4% (.124) =	**6a**	
b	Taxable social security tips	$ _____ × 12.4% (.124) =	**6b**	
7	Taxable Medicare wages and tips	$ _____ × 2.9% (.029) =	**7**	
8	Total social security and Medicare taxes (add lines 6a, 6b, and 7). Check here if wages are not subject to social security and/or Medicare tax . . . . ▶ [ ]	**8**	
9	Adjustment of social security and Medicare taxes (see instructions for required explanation) Sick Pay $ _____ ± Fractions of Cents $ _____ ± Other $ _____ =	**9**	
10	Adjusted total of social security and Medicare taxes (line 8 as adjusted by line 9—see instructions)	**10**	
11	**Total taxes** (add lines 5 and 10)	**11**	
12	Advance earned income credit (EIC) payments made to employees, if any	**12**	
13	Net taxes (subtract line 12 from line 11). This should equal line 17, column (d) below (or line D of Schedule B (Form 941))	**13**	
14	Total deposits for quarter, including overpayment applied from a prior quarter	**14**	
15	**Balance due** (subtract line 14 from line 13). Pay to Internal Revenue Service	**15**	
16	Overpayment, if line 14 is more than line 13, enter excess here ▶ $ _____ and check if to be: [ ] Applied to next return OR [ ] Refunded.		

17 **Monthly Summary of Federal Tax Liability.**
- **Monthly depositors:** Complete line 17, columns (a) through (d) and check here . . . ▶ [ ]
- **Semiweekly depositors:** Complete Schedule B and check here . . . ▶ [ ]
- **All filers:** If line 13 is less than $500, you need not complete line 17 or Schedule B.

(a) First month liability	(b) Second month liability	(c) Third month liability	(d) Total liability for quarter

Sign Here — Under penalties of perjury, I declare that I have examined this return, including accompanying schedules and statements, and to the best of my knowledge and belief, it is true, correct, and complete.

Signature ▶ _____ Print Your Name and Title ▶ _____ Date ▶ _____

Form **941**

4-9. During the first week of 1995 the payroll department of the Figley Corporation is preparing the Forms W-2 for distribution to its workers along with their paychecks on January 6. In this problem you will complete six of the forms in order to gain some experience in recording the different kinds of information required.

Assume that each worker earned the same weekly salary for each of the 52 paydays in 1994.

Using the following information obtained from the personnel and payroll records of the firm, complete Copy A of the six Forms W-2 reproduced on pages 165 to 169.

Company Information:

Address: 4800 River Road
                 Philadelphia, PA 19113-5548
Federal identification number: 13-7490972
State identification number: 46-3-1066

Income Tax Information:

1. The wage-bracket method is used to determine the amount of federal income taxes to withhold each week.
2. The Pennsylvania tax rate is 2.8% of the worker's weekly gross earnings.
3. The city tax rate for residents of Philadelphia is 4.96% of the worker's weekly gross earnings.

Personnel and Payroll Information:

a. Patricia A. Grimes   Single 1 allowance
    54 Gradison Place $415/week
    Philadelphia, PA 19113-4054   SS#: 376-72-4310
    Union dues withheld, $102

b. Roberta P. Kurtz   Married 1 allowance
    56 Andrews Court, Apt. 7 $485/week
    Philadelphia, PA 19103-3356   SS#: 272-33-8804
    Dependent care payments, $950

c. David P. Markle   Single 0 allowance
    770 Camac Street $365/week
    Philadelphia, PA 19101-3770   SS#: 178-92-3316
    Union dues withheld, $102

d. Harold W. Rasul   Married 7 allowances
    338 North Side Avenue $1,200/week
    Philadelphia, PA 19130-6638   SS#: 269-01-6839
    Cost of Rasul's group-term life
    insurance exceeding $50,000:
    $262.75

e. Christine A. Shoemaker   Married 2 allowances
    4900 Gladwynne Terrace $320/week
    Philadelphia, PA 19127-0049   SS#: 368-14-5771
    Advance EIC payments made to
    Shoemaker: $16 each week
    Union dues withheld, $102

f. Angelo Zickar   Single 1 allowance
    480-A Hopkinson Tower $390/week
    Philadelphia, PA 19101-3301   SS#: 337-99-8703
    Educational assistance
    payments, $675

Practical Problem 4-9

a Control number	22222	Void ☐	For Official Use Only ▶		
b Employer's identification number			1 Wages, tips, other compensation	2 Federal income tax withheld	
c Employer's name, address, and ZIP code			3 Social security wages	4 Social security tax withheld	
			5 Medicare wages and tips	6 Medicare tax withheld	
			7 Social security tips	8 Allocated tips	
d Employee's social security number			9 Advance EIC payment	10 Dependent care benefits	
e Employee's name (first, middle initial, last)			11 Nonqualified plans	12 Benefits included in Box 1	
			13 See Instrs. for Box 13	14 Other	

	15 Statutory employee ☐	Deceased ☐	Pension plan ☐	Legal rep. ☐	942 emp. ☐	Subtotal ☐	Deferred compensation ☐
f Employee's address and ZIP code							

16 State	Employer's state I.D. No.	17 State wages, tips. etc.	18 State income tax	19 Locality name	20 Local wages, tips, etc.	21 Local income tax

Department of the Treasury—Internal Revenue Service

Form **W-2** **Wage and Tax Statement** **1994**

Copy A For Social Security Administration

For Paperwork Reduction Act Notice, see separate instructions.

---

a Control number	22222	Void ☐	For Official Use Only ▶		
b Employer's identification number			1 Wages, tips, other compensation	2 Federal income tax withheld	
c Employer's name, address, and ZIP code			3 Social security wages	4 Social security tax withheld	
			5 Medicare wages and tips	6 Medicare tax withheld	
			7 Social security tips	8 Allocated tips	
d Employee's social security number			9 Advance EIC payment	10 Dependent care benefits	
e Employee's name (first, middle initial, last)			11 Nonqualified plans	12 Benefits included in Box 1	
			13 See Instrs. for Box 13	14 Other	

	15 Statutory employee ☐	Deceased ☐	Pension plan ☐	Legal rep. ☐	942 emp. ☐	Subtotal ☐	Deferred compensation ☐
f Employee's address and ZIP code							

16 State	Employer's state I.D. No.	17 State wages, tips. etc.	18 State income tax	19 Locality name	20 Local wages, tips, etc.	21 Local income tax

Department of the Treasury—Internal Revenue Service

Form **W-2** **Wage and Tax Statement** **1994**

Copy A For Social Security Administration

For Paperwork Reduction Act Notice, see separate instructions.

Practical Problem 4-9

a Control number 22222 Void ☐ For Official Use Only ▶		
b Employer's identification number	**1** Wages, tips, other compensation	**2** Federal income tax withheld
c Employer's name, address, and ZIP code	**3** Social security wages	**4** Social security tax withheld
	5 Medicare wages and tips	**6** Medicare tax withheld
	7 Social security tips	**8** Allocated tips
d Employee's social security number	**9** Advance EIC payment	**10** Dependent care benefits
e Employee's name (first, middle initial, last)	**11** Nonqualified plans	**12** Benefits included in Box 1
	13 See Instrs. for Box 13	**14** Other
	15 Statutory employee ☐ Deceased ☐ Pension plan ☐ Legal rep. ☐ 942 emp. ☐ Subtotal ☐ Deferred compensation ☐	
f Employee's address and ZIP code		

16 State Employer's state I.D. No.	17 State wages, tips, etc.	18 State income tax	19 Locality name	20 Local wages, tips, etc.	21 Local income tax

Department of the Treasury—Internal Revenue Service

Form W-2 Wage and Tax Statement **1994**

Copy A For Social Security Administration

For Paperwork Reduction Act Notice, see separate instructions.

a Control number 22222 Void ☐ For Official Use Only ▶		
b Employer's identification number	**1** Wages, tips, other compensation	**2** Federal income tax withheld
c Employer's name, address, and ZIP code	**3** Social security wages	**4** Social security tax withheld
	5 Medicare wages and tips	**6** Medicare tax withheld
	7 Social security tips	**8** Allocated tips
d Employee's social security number	**9** Advance EIC payment	**10** Dependent care benefits
e Employee's name (first, middle initial, last)	**11** Nonqualified plans	**12** Benefits included in Box 1
	13 See Instrs. for Box 13	**14** Other
	15 Statutory employee ☐ Deceased ☐ Pension plan ☐ Legal rep. ☐ 942 emp. ☐ Subtotal ☐ Deferred compensation ☐	
f Employee's address and ZIP code		

16 State Employer's state I.D. No.	17 State wages, tips, etc.	18 State income tax	19 Locality name	20 Local wages, tips, etc.	21 Local income tax

Department of the Treasury—Internal Revenue Service

Form W-2 Wage and Tax Statement **1994**

Copy A For Social Security Administration

For Paperwork Reduction Act Notice, see separate instructions.

Practical Problem 4-9

a Control number	22222	Void ☐	For Official Use Only ▶		
b Employer's identification number				**1** Wages, tips, other compensation	**2** Federal income tax withheld
c Employer's name, address, and ZIP code				**3** Social security wages	**4** Social security tax withheld
				5 Medicare wages and tips	**6** Medicare tax withheld
				7 Social security tips	**8** Allocated tips
d Employee's social security number				**9** Advance EIC payment	**10** Dependent care benefits
e Employee's name (first, middle initial, last)				**11** Nonqualified plans	**12** Benefits included in Box 1
				13 See Instrs. for Box 13	**14** Other

15 Statutory employee ☐	Deceased ☐	Pension plan ☐	Legal rep. ☐	942 emp. ☐	Subtotal ☐	Deferred compensation ☐

f Employee's address and ZIP code

16 State	Employer's state I.D. No.	17 State wages, tips, etc.	18 State income tax	19 Locality name	20 Local wages, tips, etc.	21 Local income tax

Department of the Treasury—Internal Revenue Service

Form **W-2** **Wage and Tax Statement** **1994**

Copy A For Social Security Administration

For Paperwork Reduction Act Notice, see separate instructions.

---

a Control number	22222	Void ☐	For Official Use Only ▶		
b Employer's identification number				**1** Wages, tips, other compensation	**2** Federal income tax withheld
c Employer's name, address, and ZIP code				**3** Social security wages	**4** Social security tax withheld
				5 Medicare wages and tips	**6** Medicare tax withheld
				7 Social security tips	**8** Allocated tips
d Employee's social security number				**9** Advance EIC payment	**10** Dependent care benefits
e Employee's name (first, middle initial, last)				**11** Nonqualified plans	**12** Benefits included in Box 1
				13 See Instrs. for Box 13	**14** Other

15 Statutory employee ☐	Deceased ☐	Pension plan ☐	Legal rep. ☐	942 emp. ☐	Subtotal ☐	Deferred compensation ☐

f Employee's address and ZIP code

16 State	Employer's state I.D. No.	17 State wages, tips, etc.	18 State income tax	19 Locality name	20 Local wages, tips, etc.	21 Local income tax

Department of the Treasury—Internal Revenue Service

Form **W-2** **Wage and Tax Statement** **1994**

Copy A For Social Security Administration

For Paperwork Reduction Act Notice, see separate instructions.

✳ CONTINUING PAYROLL PROBLEM

Refer to the partially completed payroll register upon which you were working at the end of Unit 3. You will now determine the amount of income taxes to withhold for each employee, proceeding as follows:

(1) In the appropriate columns of your payroll register, record the marital status and number of withholding allowances claimed for each employee, using the information given at the right.
(2) Record the amount of:
   a. Federal income taxes (FIT) to withhold, using the wage-bracket method.
   b. State income taxes (SIT). The Pennsylvania tax rate is 2.8% of the worker's weekly gross earnings.
   c. City income taxes (CIT). In Philadelphia, the city tax rate on residents is 4.96% of the worker's weekly gross earnings. All employees reside in Philadelphia.

Time Card No.	Marital Status	No. of Allowances
11	S	1
12	S	0
13	M	2
21	M	4
22	S	2
31	M	3
32	M	6
33	S	1
51	M	5
99	M	7

NOTE: Retain your partially completed payroll register for use at the end of Unit 5.

CASE PROBLEMS

Case 4-1   Processing the Pay for a Deceased Worker

On June 1 Bill Melville called his supervisor and indicated that he was not feeling well. Later that day Melville was admitted to a hospital, where two weeks later he died. Melville's last monthly payday was on May 31. Under his company's policy Melville was entitled to full pay during the period of his absence; and upon his death, any unpaid salary was to be paid his beneficiary or estate. At the time of Melville's death, his beneficiary was given $950 representing Melville's salary for the month of June in which his death occurred, plus $750 representing the vacation allowance earned by Melville prior to his death.

a. Should federal income taxes be withheld on (1) the $950 monthly salary and (2) the $750 vacation allowance?
b. Assume that the paycheck for the month ending May 31 (from which federal income taxes had been withheld) was not cashed by Melville prior to his death. Should the employer prepare a new paycheck? If so, should the new paycheck reflect any deduction for federal income taxes?

Case 4-2   Answering Employees' Questions About Wage Reporting

During the past week, one of your newly employed payroll associates dropped into your office to ask several questions regarding wage reporting for federal income and social security tax purposes. If you were the payroll supervisor, how would you answer each of the following questions raised by your associate?

1. I just noticed that the social security number is wrong on three of the workers' W-2 forms. How do I go about correcting the forms? Will the workers be penalized for filing incorrect forms?

2. Eileen Huang informed me today that I had withheld too much Medicare tax from her pay last year. She is right! What forms do I use to make the correction?

3. You asked me last week to locate one of our former employees, Warren Bucks. I can't seem to track him down. What should I do with his Form W-2?

4. Is it okay to use titles like "M.D." and "Esq." when I keyboard data in the W-2 forms?

UNEMPLOYMENT COMPENSATION TAXES

GOALS OF THIS UNIT

After completing your study of this unit, you should be able to:

1. Describe the basic requirements for an individual to be classified as an employer or an employee under the Federal Unemployment Tax Act.
2. Understand the factors considered in determining the coverage of interstate employees.
3. Identify generally what is defined as taxable wages by the Federal Unemployment Tax Act.
4. Calculate the federal unemployment tax and the credit against this tax.
5. Describe how an experience rating system is used in determining employers' contributions to state unemployment compensation funds.
6. Complete the reports required by the Federal Unemployment Tax Act.
7. Describe the types of information reports under the various state unemployment compensation laws.
8. Understand the factors that determine eligibility for unemployment compensation benefits.

Under the Social Security Act of 1935, every state was mandated to set up an unemployment compensation program in order to provide payments to workers during periods of temporary unemployment. This unemployment insurance program is a coordinated federal-state program that is funded by payroll taxes at both federal and state levels.

Under the Federal Unemployment Tax Act (FUTA), a tax is imposed on employers and is based on wages paid for covered employment. It is *not* collected or deducted from employees' wages. The funds collected by the federal government as a result of this tax are used primarily to pay the cost of administering both the federal and the state unemployment insurance programs. The FUTA tax is *not* used for the payment of weekly benefits to unemployed workers. Such benefits are paid by the states in accordance with each state's unemployment tax law (SUTA). These unemployment benefits are paid out of each state's trust fund, which is financed by unemployment taxes lev-ied on employers. Because all states conform to standards specified in FUTA, there is considerable uniformity in the provisions of the state unemployment compensation laws. However, there are many variations in eligibility requirements, rates of contributions, benefits paid, and duration of benefits. All the states, Puerto Rico, the Virgin Islands, and the District of Columbia have enacted unemployment compensation laws that have been approved by the Social Security Administration.

You can realize the extent of the federal-state unemployment insurance program in terms of the people involved by the fact that in September, 1993, the number of unemployed persons was 8.5 million out of a civilian labor force of about 128.0 million. At that time the jobless rate was 6.7%. *Unemployed persons* include young people seeking positions for the first time, seasonal workers unemployed a part of each year, and workers who lost their jobs through various causes and cannot find other suitable employment.

COVERAGE UNDER FUTA AND SUTA

Other than a few significant exceptions as explained in this section, the coverage under FUTA is similar to that under FICA, as described in Unit 3.

Employers—FUTA

The federal law levies a payroll tax on employers for the purpose of providing more uniform administration of the various state unemployment compensation laws. A person or a business is considered an employer if *either* of the following two tests is met:

1. Pays wages of $1,500 or more during any calendar quarter in the current or preceding calendar year, or
2. Employs one or more persons, on at least some portion of one day, in each of 20 or more calendar weeks during the current or preceding taxable year.

A number of points serve to clarify the meaning of the two alternative tests: (a) a calendar week is defined as seven successive days beginning with Sunday; (b) it is not necessary that the 20 weeks be consecutive; (c) the employees need not be the same employees; (d) regular, part-time, and temporary workers are considered to be employees; (e) individuals on vacation or sick leave are counted as employees in determining the employer's status; and (f) members of a partnership are not considered to be employees.

As soon as an employer meets either test, the employer becomes liable for the FUTA tax for the entire calendar year.

EXAMPLE:

In the Vemor Company, the 20th week of having one or more employees does not occur until November of 1994. The company is liable for FUTA tax on all taxable wages paid beginning with January 1, 1994.

Once the employer status is attained, it continues for two calendar years. Thus, an employer may be covered in the second calendar year even though the coverage requirements are not met for that year. Once the second calendar year has ended, the employer's FUTA liability terminates until the coverage requirements are once again met.

Generally the nature of the business organization has no relevance in determining who is an employer. Thus, the employer may be an individual, corporation, partnership, company, association, trust, or estate. There may be instances where it is difficult to determine which of two entities is the employer for purposes of FUTA. As under FICA, the question is answered by determining which entity has the ultimate right to direct and control the employees' activities. It is not necessary that the employer actually direct or control the manner in which the services are performed; it is sufficient if the employer has the right to do so. The right to discharge is also an important factor indicating that the person possessing that right is an employer. Another factor characteristic of an employer is the furnishing of tools and a place to work for the individual who performs services.

Employers—SUTA

In general, employers specifically excluded under the federal law are also excluded under the state laws. However, as a result of variations found in state unemployment compensation laws, not all employers covered by the unemployment compensation laws of one or more states are covered by FUTA. For example, the services performed by some charitable organizations may be covered by a state's unemployment compensation act, but these same services may be exempt from FUTA coverage.

In order to have their state unemployment insurance laws approved by the federal government, the states must provide coverage for most state and local government workers, including employees in nonprofit elementary and secondary schools. In addition, coverage is extended to employers of domestic workers who pay $1,000 or more for such services in any calendar quarter of the current or preceding year.

> ### Professional Tip
> Domestic service is not to be considered when determining employer status under FUTA for the wage test or the "1-in-20" test.

Also covered are employers of farm workers (a) who employ 10 or more farm workers during any 20 different weeks, or (b) who pay $20,000 or more in quarterly wages for farm services during the current or preceding calendar year.

Employees—FUTA

Every individual is considered an employee if the relationship between the worker and the person for whom the services are performed is the legal common-law relationship of employer and employee. This individual would then be counted in determining whether the employer is subject to FUTA. The nature of this common-law relationship is discussed in Unit 3, page 70.

No distinction is made between classes or grades of employees. Thus, superintendents, managers, and other supervisory personnel are employees. An officer of a corporation is an employee of the corporation, but a director, as such, is not.

For the purpose of the FUTA tax, the term "employee" also means any of the following who perform service for remuneration:

1. An agent-driver or a commission-driver who distributes food or beverages (other than milk) or laundry or dry-cleaning services for the principal.
2. A traveling or a city salesperson engaged in full-time soliciting and transmitting to the principal orders for merchandise for resale or supplies for use in business operations.

If a person in one of these categories has a substantial investment in facilities used to perform the services (not including transportation facilities), the individual is an independent contractor and not a covered employee. Also, individuals are not covered if their services are a single transaction that is not part of a continuing relationship with the persons for whom they are performed.

The work performed by the employee for the employer includes any services of whatever nature performed within the United States, regardless of the citizenship or residence of either. FUTA coverage also includes service of any nature performed outside the United States by a citizen of the United States for an American employer. The major exception is that service performed in Canada or in any other adjoining country with which the United States has an agreement relating to unemployment does not constitute covered employment.

An employee may perform both included and excluded employment for the same employer during a pay period. In such a case, the services which predominate in the pay period determine the employee's status with that employer for the period.

Under FUTA some services are wholly exempt from coverage. In other cases the services are exempt from coverage until the cash wages paid for the services reach a certain level. Once this level is exceeded, the services become covered employment.

Among those *excluded* from coverage in 1994 are the following:

1. Independent contractors, such as physicians, lawyers, dentists, veterinarians, contractors, subcontractors, public stenographers, auctioneers, and others who follow an independent trade, business, or profession in which they offer their services to the public.
2. Directors of corporations, unless they perform services for the corporation other than those required by attending and participating in meetings of the board of directors.
3. Members of partnerships.
4. Insurance agents or solicitors paid solely on a commission basis.
5. Agricultural laborers; however, if the employer employs 10 or more during any 20 different weeks in a year or pays $20,000 or more in a quarter during the current or preceding year, the exemption is lost.
6. Casual laborers, unless cash remuneration paid for such service is $50 or more in a calendar quarter, and the person to whom it is paid is regularly employed by the one for whom the services were performed during that period.
7. Domestic workers, students or nonstudents, rendering service in a private home, local college club, or local chapter of a college fraternity or sorority. If the work is performed for an employer who paid $1,000 or more for such services in any calendar quarter of the current or preceding year, the exemption is lost.
8. Foreign students and exchange visitors who are carrying out the purposes for which they are admitted into the United States, such as in studying, teaching, or conducting research. If employed for other purposes, they would not be excluded.
9. Students enrolled full-time in a work-study or internship program, for work that is an integral part of the student's academic program.
10. Service performed by an individual for a son, daughter, or spouse, or by a child under the age of 21 for a parent.

Professional Tip
If a person works for an employer on some part of at least 24 days during the calendar quarter, he or she is considered to be regularly employed.

11. Services performed by individuals in fishing and related activities if the vessel is less than ten net tons.
12. Service performed in the employ of foreign, federal, state, or local governments and certain of their instrumentalities. However, taxes imposed by FUTA apply to these federal instrumentalities: federal reserve banks, federal loan banks, and federal credit unions.
13. Government employees of international organizations, such as the United Nations.
14. Individuals under 18 years of age who deliver or distribute newspapers or shopping news (other than delivery or distribution to any point for subsequent delivery and distribution) and retail vendors of any age who sell and distribute newspapers and magazines to the ultimate consumer.
15. Services performed by employees or employee representatives for employers covered by either the Railroad Retirement Tax Act or the Railroad Unemployment Insurance Act.
16. Services performed by a student who is enrolled and regularly attending classes at a school, college, or university, if service is performed for school, college, or university.
17. Student nurses and hospital interns.
18. Services performed in the employ of a religious, educational, or charitable organization that is exempt from federal income tax. This exemption includes service in church-sponsored elementary and secondary schools.

Employees—SUTA

The definition of "employee" as established by FUTA applies to a majority of the states, although minor variations exist in the state laws. One variation involves firms that employ persons who work in more than one state. In these cases, we must determine which state covers the workers for unemployment compensation purposes.

Coverage of Interstate Employees.
An *interstate employee* is an individual who works in more than one state. To prevent duplicate contributions on the services of interstate employees, all states have adopted a uniform definition of employment in terms of where the work is localized. Under this definition, the entire services of an interstate worker are covered in one state only—that state in which the worker will most likely look for a job if he or she becomes unemployed.

The several factors that must be considered in determining coverage of interstate employees, in their order of application, are:

1. Place where the work is localized.
2. Location of base of operations.
3. Location of place from which operations are directed or controlled.
4. Location of employee's residence.

Place Where the Work is Localized. Under this main criterion of coverage adopted by the states, if all the work is performed within one state, it is clearly "localized" in that state and constitutes "employment" under the law of that state. In some cases, however, part of the person's work may be performed outside the state. In such instances the entire work may be treated as localized within the state if the services performed in other states are temporary or transitory in nature.

EXAMPLE:

Carson Thomson is a sales representative whose regular sales territory lies within Arizona. Thomson is covered by the laws of Arizona, with respect to his total employment, even though he makes frequent trips to the firm's showrooms in Los Angeles to attend sales meetings and to look over new lines of goods.

Location of Base of Operations. Often a worker may perform services continually in two or more states. In such situations it cannot be said that the employment in one state is incidental to the employment in the other state. Thus, the test of localization is not applicable since the services cannot be considered as localized within one state. Therefore, the base of operations test must be considered.

Under this test, the employee's services may be covered by the laws of a single state even though the services are not localized within that state. The base of operation is the place of a more or less permanent nature from which the employee starts work and to which he or she customarily returns. It could be a particular place where his or her (a) instructions are received, (b) business records are maintained, (c) supplies are sent, or (d) office is maintained (may be in the employee's home).

EXAMPLE:

Mitch Goldman travels through four southern states for the Irwin Company, which is headquartered in Georgia. His work is equally divided among the four states. When working in Georgia, he reports to the main office for instructions. The location of his base of operations is clearly Georgia, and his services are subject to the Georgia laws.

Location of Place from Which Operations Are Directed or Controlled.

Often it may be impossible to say that an employee's services are localized in any state. Or it may be impossible to determine any base of operations of such services. If it is possible to fix the place of control in a particular state in which some service is performed, that will be the state in which the individual is covered.

EXAMPLE:

Joyce Mendes is a sales representative whose sales territory is so widespread that she does not retain any fixed business address or office. All of her orders or instructions are received by mail or wire wherever she may happen to be. Clearly the work is not localized in any state, and there is no fixed base of operations. However, the services performed by Mendes may still come under the provisions of a single state law—the law of that state in which is located the place of direction or control, provided that some of Mendes's work is also performed in that state.

Location of Employee's Residence.

If an employee's coverage cannot be determined by any of the three tests described above, a final test, that of the employee's residence, is used. Thus, the worker's service is covered in its entirety in the state in which the employee lives, provided some of the service is performed in that state.

EXAMPLE:

Robert Donald is employed by the Prang Company of Indiana. He lives in Iowa, and his work territory includes Iowa, Minnesota, and Wisconsin. Since neither the base of operations nor the place from which his work is directed is in a state in which he works, he is covered in his state of residence (Iowa).

Reciprocal Arrangements and Transfers of Employment.

The states have entered into several types of interstate agreements to provide unemployment insurance coverage and payment of benefits to interstate workers. These agreements are known as *reciprocal arrangements*. The most widely accepted type of interstate coverage arrangement is the Interstate Reciprocal Coverage Arrangement. Under this arrangement, an employer is permitted to elect to cover all of the services of a worker in any one state in which (a) any work is performed by the employee, or (b) the employee has his or her residence, or (c) the employer maintains the place of business.

EXAMPLE:

Morris Davidson is a salesperson for the Tannenbaum Company. His sales territory includes parts of Connecticut and Massachusetts, and his services can be considered localized in both states. Under the Interstate Reciprocal Coverage Arrangement, the company elects to cover Davidson under the law of Massachusetts.

Once the employer chooses the state in which all the services of the interstate workers are to be covered, this state approves the election of coverage. Then, the appropriate agencies of the other states in which services are performed are notified so that they can agree to the coverage in the state of election.

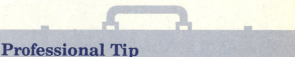

Professional Tip
The only states that do not participate in reciprocal arrangements are Alaska, Kentucky, Mississippi, New Jersey, and New York, plus Puerto Rico.

Another aspect of reciprocal arrangements concerns the transfer of an employee from one state to another during the same calendar year. In all the states, an employer can include, for purposes of determining the taxable wage base in the second state, wages paid an employee with respect to employment covered by the unemployment compensation law of the previous state.

EXAMPLE:

The Karlson Company has paid wages of $4,000 to an employee in State A. During the year the employee is transferred to State B, which has a $7,000 taxable salary limitation for its state unemployment tax. The company has a credit of $4,000 against this $7,000 limit. Thus, the company has to pay State B's unemployment tax on only the next $3,000 of wages earned by that worker in State B during the remainder of the calendar year.

Coverage of Americans Working Overseas.

As mentioned before, coverage is extended to U.S. citizens working abroad for American employers. The state where the employer's principal place of business is located would provide the coverage. If the principal place of business cannot be determined, the state of incorporation or the state of residence of the individual owners would be the state of coverage.

Wages—FUTA

Generally *wages* means all remuneration for employment, including the cash value of all remuneration paid in any medium other than cash, with certain exceptions.

EXAMPLE:

An exemption from FUTA exists for commissions paid to insurance agents and solicitors who are paid solely by commission.

During 1994, only the first $7,000 of remuneration paid by an employer to an employee with respect to employment during any calendar year is included in computing taxable wages. The basis upon which the remuneration is paid is immaterial. It may be paid on a piece-work basis or it may be a percentage of profits; it may be paid hourly, daily, weekly, biweekly, semi-monthly, monthly, or annually.

Some of the more common types of payments made to employees and the taxability status of these payments are:

Taxable Wages for Unemployment Purposes

1. Advance payment for work to be done in the future.
2. Cash and noncash prizes and awards for doing outstanding work, for exceeding sales quotas, or for contributing suggestions that increase productivity or efficiency.
3. Bonuses as remuneration for services.
4. Christmas gifts, excluding noncash gifts of nominal value.
5. Commissions as compensation for covered employment.
6. Payments representing compensation for services by an employee which are paid to the dependents of an employee after his or her death. If the payments are in the nature of a gratuity rather than compensation for services, the payments are nontaxable. Any payments made by an employer to an employee's estate or to the employee's survivors after the calendar year in which the employee died are excluded from the definition of wages and thus may not be taxed.
7. Dismissal payments.
8. Idle time and standby payments.
9. Retroactive wage increases.

10. Transfer of stock by an employer to the employees as remuneration for services. (The fair market value of the stock at the time of payment is the taxable base.)
11. Payments under a guaranteed annual wage plan.
12. Contributions by an employer to a supplemental unemployment individual-account plan, to which the employee has a fully vested and nonforfeitable right.
13. All tips, including charged tips, reported by the employee to the employer.
14. Vacation pay.
15. Payment by the employer of the employee's FICA tax or the employee's share of any state unemployment compensation tax without deduction from the employee's wages.
16. Payments to employees or their dependents on account of sickness or accident disability. These payments are *not* taxable after the expiration of six months following the last calendar month in which the employee worked. Payments for work missed due to pregnancy are not classified as taxable wages during the first six months of absence.
17. Employer contributions to cash or deferred arrangements to the extent that the contributions are not included in the employees' gross income.

Nontaxable Wages for Unemployment Purposes

1. Advances or reimbursement of ordinary and necessary business expenses incurred in the business of the employer.
2. Bonuses under a supplemental compensation plan paid upon retirement, death, or disability of an employee.
3. Caddy fees.
4. Commissions paid to insurance agents and solicitors who are paid solely by commission. Such persons are classified as independent contractors, not employees.
5. Courtesy discounts to employees and their families.
6. Payments made by an employer under a plan established by the employer for health, accident, or life insurance, or retirement benefits on behalf of the employees or their dependents.
7. Reimbursement of an employee's moving expenses if at the time of payment, it is reasonable to believe that the employee will be entitled to a deduction for those expenses at the time of filing his or her federal income tax return.

8. Allowances made to an individual by a prospective employer for expenses incurred in connection with interviews for possible employment.
9. Retirement pay.
10. Strike benefits paid by a union to its members.
11. Workers' compensation payments.
12. Educational assistance payments to workers. The maximum excludable amount for 1994 is $5,250.
13. Value of meals and lodging furnished employees for the convenience of the employer.

Wages—SUTA

The definition of taxable wages is fairly uniform under the various state unemployment compensation laws. However, there are some variations among the states as to the status of particular kinds of payments. For example, about one sixth of the states have ruled that Christmas bonuses or gifts are "wages" where they are substantial, contractual, or where they are based on a percentage of the employee's wages or length of service. New Hampshire, however, provides that gifts or gratuities of $25 or less are not wages, unless paid under a contract related to past or future employment.

A further variation in defining taxable wages among the states arises in the treatment of *dismissal payments*, sometimes called payments in lieu of notice, separation pay, or terminal leave pay. Generally such payments are considered wages whether or not the employer is legally obligated to make the payments. However, in some states dismissal payments do not constitute wages unless the employer is legally required to make them. In Puerto Rico, no type of dismissal payment is considered to be wages.

UNEMPLOYMENT COMPENSATION TAXES AND CREDITS

The base of the unemployment compensation tax is wages *paid* rather than *wages payable*. Thus, an employer is liable for the unemployment compensation tax in the year in which wages are paid employees, not necessarily in the year in which the services are rendered. Thus, if an employee performs services in 1994 but is not paid for them until 1995, the employer is liable for the tax in 1995 and the 1995 tax rates apply.

Wages are considered paid when they are actually paid or when they are *constructively paid*. Wages are considered constructively paid when credited to the account of, or set apart for, an employee so that they

may be drawn upon at any time, even though they are not actually possessed by the employee.

Tax Rate—FUTA

Under FUTA, all employers, as defined earlier, are subject to a tax with respect to having individuals in their employ. For 1994, the employer's tax rate is 6.2% of the first $7,000 wages paid each employee during the calendar year. Thus, an employer is liable for the FUTA tax on wages paid each employee until the employee's wages reach the $7,000 level. If an employee has more than one employer during the current year, the taxable wage base applies separately to each of those employers, unless one employer has transferred the business to the second.

EXAMPLE:

Assume that in 1994 an employer had charged the wages account for $63,910. Of this amount, $720 will not be paid until the first payday in 1995. Further, the wages actually paid to employees in 1994 in excess of $7,000 each amounted to $19,840. The gross FUTA tax imposed on the employer is computed as follows:

Total amount charged to wages during 1994		$63,910.00
Less:		
Wages not to be paid until 1995	$ 720	
Wages paid in excess of $7,000 limit	19,840	20,560.00
Total taxable wages		$43,350.00
Rate of tax		6.2%
Amount of gross FUTA tax		$ 2,687.70

Credits Against FUTA Tax. Employers are entitled to a credit against their FUTA tax liability for contributions made under approved state unemployment compensation laws. The maximum credit permitted is 5.4%. Thus, in the preceding example where the *gross* FUTA tax rate is 6.2%, the *net* FUTA rate would be .8% if the full 5.4% credit applied. The net FUTA tax may be calculated in two ways:

EXAMPLES:

1. Total taxable earnings (above example) .		$43,350.00
Net rate of tax (6.2% – 5.4%)		.8%
Amount of net FUTA tax		$ 346.80
2. Amount of gross FUTA tax		$ 2,687.70
Total taxable wages	$43,350	
Credit against tax	5.4%	
Total credit		2,340.90
Amount of net FUTA tax		$ 346.80

To obtain the maximum credit of 5.4% against the federal tax, the employer must make the state contributions on or before the due date for filing the annual return under FUTA (see page 186). If the employer is tardy in paying the state contributions, the maximum credit that the employer may claim against the federal tax is 95% of 5.4%, or 5.13%.

EXAMPLE:

The Sutcliffe Company had taxable wages totaling $87,500 in 1994. During the year the company was late in paying its state contributions. The penalty for tardiness is shown in the following calculation of the firm's net FUTA tax for 1994:

Amount of gross FUTA tax ($87,500 x 6.2%)		$5,425.00
Total taxable wages	$87,500	
Credit against tax	5.13%	
Total credit		4,488.75
Amount of net FUTA tax ($87,500 x 1.07%)		$ 936.25

If the company had made timely payments of its state contributions, the amount of its net FUTA tax would have been reduced to $700, for a savings of $236.25, as shown below.

Amount of gross FUTA tax ($87,500 x 6.2%)		$5,425.00
Total taxable wages	$87,500	
Credit against tax	5.4%	
Total credit		4,725.00
Amount of net FUTA tax ($87,500 x .8%)		$ 700.00

$936.25 – $700.00 = $236.25, savings

Experience Rating.

In some cases, employers are permitted to pay contributions into their state unemployment fund at a rate lower than 5.4%. The method by which the employer contributions may be adjusted because of a favorable employment record is referred to as *experience rating* or *merit rating*. Thus, an employer's favorable experience rate (employment record) qualifies the employer for a SUTA rate lower than 5.4%. In such a case, FUTA provides for a credit equal to the employer's SUTA rate plus an additional credit so that the full 5.4% credit still applies. In this way, employers who have steady employment histories and, therefore, lower SUTA tax rates, are not penalized when the FUTA tax is paid.

EXAMPLE:

The Jaro Company pays taxable wages of $88,000 during 1994. The state's unemployment compensation law sets a range of unemployment tax rates from 2.7% to 6.8% under its experience rating system. Because of its past employment record, the Jaro Company is taxed at the rate of 4.4% by the state for 1994. The computation of the net FUTA and SUTA taxes is:

SUTA tax: 4.4% of $88,000 = $3,872		
Gross federal tax: 6.2% of $88,000		$5,456
Less credits against tax:		
Contributions actually paid to state	$3,872	
Additional credit*	880	4,752
Remainder of tax (net FUTA) ($88,000 x .8%)		$ 704

*The additional credit is computed as follows:		
SUTA tax, had the rate been 5.4%	$4,752	
Contributions at experience rate (4.4%)	3,872	
Additional credit allowed	$ 880	

The Jaro Company is entitled to the maximum credit of 5.4%, even though the contributions paid to the state amounted to only 4.4%. Since the Jaro Company paid only $3,872 to the state fund and $704 to the federal fund, the total unemployment tax amounted to $4,576, or 5.2% of taxable wages. Thus, due to the experience rating of the employer, there was a savings of 1.0% (6.2% – 5.2%) in the combined tax.

Where contributions are paid into more than one state unemployment compensation fund, the credit against the federal tax is based on the contributions paid to each state. In some states the contribution rate might be less than 5.4%; however, the employer would receive the 5.4% credit against the gross FUTA tax. In those states where the employer's SUTA contribution is more than 5.4%, the credit against the gross FUTA tax is limited to 5.4%.

EXAMPLE:

The contribution rate of Domski Supply in Kansas is 5.5% and in Missouri, 2%. The credit against the gross FUTA tax on the wages paid is 5.4% in each state.

Under the unemployment compensation laws of certain states, the taxable wage base is set at a figure higher than the first $7,000 paid to each employee. For example, in Arkansas, the wage base for 1994 was the first $8,500. In such states, the total contributions that the employer is required to pay into the state fund may exceed 5.4% of the taxable wages as established by FUTA (first $7,000 of each employee's earnings). However, the maximum credit that can be claimed against the gross FUTA tax for the state contributions is 5.4% of the first $7,000 of each individual employee's earnings.

Title XII Advances.

States, who due to financial difficulties cannot pay their unemployment compensation benefits, may borrow funds from the federal government under Title XII of the Social

Security Act. These funds, called *Title XII advances*, are used by the states to pay their regular unemployment benefits.

Under the repayment provisions established by the federal government, if a state defaults in its payments, the credit against the gross FUTA tax is reduced by 0.3% beginning the *second taxable year after the advance*. This penalty is increased by an additional 0.3% for each succeeding year in which there is a balance due the federal government. Thus, employers in those states have their gross FUTA tax rate increased by 0.3% the second year after the advance, then by 0.6%, 0.9%, etc. The credit reductions for the affected states will appear in the Annual FUTA Tax Return, Form 940 (see pages 187 and 188), which is filed by each employer.

However, a cap—a limitation on the amount the federal credit may be reduced—has been established for states that meet certain solvency requirements as determined by the Secretary of Labor. The determination of the credit reduction is made on or before November 10 of each year. The credit reduction (cap) applicable to employers in the affected states is limited to 0.6%. Other states that do not qualify for the total cap can have their annual credit reduction decreased by 0.1% or 0.2% if they meet some of the solvency requirements.

For 1992, only employers in the state of Michigan were subject to FUTA credit reduction. Because the state had not repaid the borrowings from the federal unemployment fund, employers in Michigan were subject to a 1.9% net FUTA tax. The tax rate for 1993 was not determined until the end of 1993, so that repayments made during the year could be used in the calculation of the credit reduction.

NEWS ALERT NEWS ALERT NEWS ALERT

The grace period for payment of loans has been extended by one year if the state amended its unemployment law in 1993 to increase estimated revenues by at least 25% in the first year after enactment of the state legislation.

Tax Rates—SUTA

A summary of each state's 1993 unemployment compensation laws, including the tax rates and the wage limitations, is presented in Illustration 5-1 on pages 182 and 183.

The tax rate applied to each employer within a particular state yields the funds used by that state in paying benefits to its unemployed workers. Currently, all states have enacted *pooled-fund laws* as a basis for their unemployment insurance systems. By means of pooled funds, the cost of unemployment benefits is spread among all the employers in a particular state.

Employer Contributions. Every state has its own unemployment compensation law with varying tax rates and taxable wage bases. To minimize the impact of unemployment insurance taxes on newly covered employers, each state sets an initial contributions rate for new employers that will apply for a specific period of time. During this period of time the new employer's employment record can be developed and an experience rating later established. A state may assign a contributions rate of not less than 1% to newly covered employers on some "reasonable basis" other than employment experience. Once the new employer has accumulated the experience required under the provisions of the state law, a new rate will be assigned. For example, in North Carolina, the rate applied to new employers is 2.25%.

Employee Contributions. Some states, as shown in Illustration 5-1, impose a contributions requirement on employees in addition to the contributions made by the employer.

EXAMPLES:

1. **Fay Nannen earns $320 during the first week of February while working for Dango, Inc. Since the company is located in New Jersey, Nannen would have $3.60 deducted from her pay (1.125% of $320). This 1.125% tax would be deducted on the first $16,100 paid to her during the year. (In New Jersey, .5% of the employees' contributions is for the disability benefit plan and .625% for the unemployment insurance fund.)**

2. **John Garrison works in Puerto Rico, and earns $450 each week. He would contribute $1.35 (.3% of $450) of each pay to a disability fund. This .3% deduction would continue until his cumulative pay for the year reached $9,000.**

Experience Rating. As indicated earlier, the concept of experience rating is based upon the payment of state unemployment taxes according to the employer's stability of employment. As an employer experiences a lower employee turnover, generally the state unemployment tax rate is lower. Similarly, a high employee turnover generally leads to a higher tax rate. By qualifying for reduced state unemployment contributions, an employer can realize substantial tax savings.

SUMMARY OF STATE UNEMPLOYMENT COMPENSATION LAWS (1993)

Warning: The provisions of the state laws are subject to change at any time.

State	Size of Firm (1 employee in specified time and/or size of payroll[1])	Contributions (On first $7,000 unless otherwise indicated)		Benefits (Excluding dependency allowances)			
		Employer Min.-Max.	Employee	Waiting Period (weeks)	Max. per Week	Min. per Week	Max. Duration (weeks)
ALABAMA	20 weeks	0.59%-6.19% on first $8,000		none	$165	$22	26
ALASKA	any time	1.0%-5.4% on first $23,200	.5% on first $23,200	1	212	44	26
ARIZONA	20 weeks	0.1%-5.4%		1	185	40	26
ARKANSAS	10 days	1.2%-7.1% on first $8,500		1	240	43	26
CALIFORNIA	over $100 in any calendar quarter	1.1%-5.4%	1.30% on first $31,767 (disability ins.)	1	446	30	26
COLORADO	any time	0.0%-5.4% on first $10,000		1	250	25	26
CONNECTICUT	20 weeks	1.5%-6.4% on first $7,100		none	306	15	26
DELAWARE	20 weeks	1.0%-9.5% on first $8,500		none	245	20	26
DISTRICT OF COLUMBIA	any time	2.0%-7.5% on first $9,000		1	335	13	26
FLORIDA	20 weeks	0.2%-5.4%		1	250	10	26
GEORGIA	20 weeks	0.06%-8.64% on first $8,500		1	185	37	26
HAWAII	any time	0.0%-5.4% on first $23,900	.5% of maximum weekly wages of $555.81, not to exceed $2.78 per week (disability ins.)	1	322	5	26
IDAHO	20 weeks or $300 in any calendar quarter	0.5%-5.4% on first $19,200		1	223	44	26
ILLINOIS	20 weeks	0.6%-7.7% on first $9,000		1	227	51	26
INDIANA	20 weeks	0.2%-5.5%		1	140	50	26
IOWA	20 weeks	0.06%-7.46% on first $13,100		1	200	30	26
KANSAS	20 weeks	0.05%-6.4% on first $8,000		1	239	59	26
KENTUCKY	20 weeks	0.3%-9.0% on first $8,000		none	217	22	26
LOUISIANA	20 weeks	0.29%-5.77% on first $8,500		1	181	10	26
MAINE	20 weeks	2.4%-7.5%		1	192	35	26
MARYLAND	any time	2.3%-8.1% on first $8,500		none	233	25	26
MASSACHUSETTS	13 weeks or more than $200 per quarter	2.2%-8.1% on first $10,800		1	312	21	30
MICHIGAN	20 weeks or $1,000 in calendar year	1.0%-10.0% on first $9,500		none	293	42	26
MINNESOTA	20 weeks	0.6%-9.1% on first $14,300		1	279	38	26
MISSISSIPPI	20 weeks	1.2%-5.4%		1	165	30	26
MISSOURI	20 weeks	0.0%-7.8% on first $7,500		1	175	45	26
MONTANA	over $1,000 in current or preceding year	0.3%-6.4% on first $14,500		1	209	50	26
NEBRASKA	20 weeks	0.1%-5.4%		1	154	20	26

[1] $1,500 in any calendar quarter in current or preceding calendar year unless otherwise specified.

Illustration 5-1. Summary of State Unemployment Compensation Laws (1993)

SUMMARY OF STATE UNEMPLOYMENT COMPENSATION LAWS (1993)

Warning: The provisions of the state laws are subject to change at any time.

State	Size of Firm (1 employee in specified time and/or size of payroll[1])	Contributions (On first $7,000 unless otherwise indicated)		Benefits (Excluding dependency allowances)			
		Employer Min.-Max.	Employee	Waiting Period (weeks)	Max. per Week	Min. per Week	Max. Duration (weeks)
NEVADA	$225 in any quarter	0.25%-5.4% on first $14,800		none	$217	$16	26
NEW HAMPSHIRE	20 weeks	0.05%-6.5%		none	188	32	26
NEW JERSEY	$1,000 in any year	0.4%-5.4% on first $16,100	1.125% (.5% for disability ins.; .625% for unempl. comp.)	1	325	61	26
NEW MEXICO	20 weeks or $450 in any quarter	0.6%-5.4% on first $12,600		1	191	38	26
NEW YORK	$300 in any quarter	2.5%-7.0%	.5% of weekly wages, not to exceed 60¢ per week (disability ins.)	1	300	40	26
NORTH CAROLINA	20 weeks	0.01%-5.7% on first $12,500		1	267	22	26
NORTH DAKOTA	20 weeks	0.4%-5.4% on first $12,600		1	212	43	26
OHIO	20 weeks	0.725%-8.425% on first $8,500		1	228	10	26
OKLAHOMA	20 weeks	0.1%-5.5% on first $10,400		1	229	16	26
OREGON	18 weeks or $225 in any quarter	1.6%-5.4% on first $18,000		1	271	63	26
PENNSYLVANIA	any time	2.1395%-10.5556% on first $8,000	.05% on first $8,000	1	317	35	26
PUERTO RICO	any time	1.0%-5.4%	.3% on first $9,000 (disability ins.)	1	133	7	26
RHODE ISLAND	any time	2.3%-8.4% on first $15,600	1.3% on first $38,000 (disability ins.)	1	374	42	26
SOUTH CAROLINA	20 weeks	1.3%-5.4%		1	186	20	26
SOUTH DAKOTA	20 weeks	0.0%-7.7%		1	166	28	26
TENNESSEE	20 weeks	0.10%-10.0%		1	185	30	26
TEXAS	20 weeks	0.35%-6.35% on first $9,000		1	245	40	26
UTAH	$140 in calendar quarter in current or preceding calendar year	0.3%-8.0% on first $15,700		1	240	16	26
VERMONT	20 weeks	0.6%-5.9% on first $8,000		1	199	29	26
VIRGIN ISLANDS	any time	0.1%-8.5% on first $22,000		1	211	15	26
VIRGINIA	20 weeks	0.17%-6.27% on first $8,000		none	208	65	26
WASHINGTON	any time	0.5%-5.42% on first $18,500		1	273	68	30
WEST VIRGINIA	20 weeks	1.5%-8.5% on first $8,000		1	270	24	28
WISCONSIN	20 weeks	0.02%-9.75 on first $10,500		none	243	46	26
WYOMING	$500 in current or preceding calendar year	0.99%-9.49% on first $11,100		1	250	40	26

[1]$1,500 in any calendar quarter in current or preceding calendar year unless otherwise specified.

Illustration 5-1. (Concluded)   Summary of State Unemployment Compensation Laws (1993)

In all states, some type of experience-rating plan provides for a reduction in the employer's tax contributions based on the employer's experience with the risk of unemployment. Of the several formulas used to determine the contribution rates, the most commonly used is the *reserve-ratio formula*:

$$\text{Reserve Ratio} = \frac{\text{Contributions less Benefits Paid}}{\text{Average Payroll}}$$

The amount of the unemployment compensation contributions (taxes paid), the benefits paid by the state, and the employer's payroll are entered by the state on each employer's record. The benefits paid are subtracted from the contributions, and the balance of the employer's account is divided by the average payroll for a stated period of time to determine the reserve ratio.

Under this plan, the balance carried forward each year is the difference between the employer's total contributions and the total benefits paid to former employees by the state. Employers must accumulate and maintain a specified reserve before their contribution rate can be reduced. The contribution rates are established according to a schedule under which the higher the reserve ratio, the lower the tax rate. The formula is designed to make sure that no employers are granted a rate reduction unless during the year they contribute more to the fund than has been withdrawn.

Employers who have built up a balance in their reserve account (contributions paid in less benefits charged) are sometimes referred to as *positive-balance employers*. The larger the positive balance in a company's reserve account, the lower will be its tax rate. Employers whose reserve accounts have been charged for more benefits paid out than contributions paid in are referred to as *negative-balance employers*, and their high tax rates reflect this fact.

Calculating the Contribution Rate.

In an experience-rating system, the rate of contributions for employers is based on the employment experience of the employer. The rate is determined by computing the total of the reserve built up by employer contributions over a certain period of time and by determining the ratio of the amount in the reserve account to the employer's average annual payroll as determined under the state's formula.

EXAMPLE:

The Parson Company is an employer located in a state with an unemployment compensation law containing merit-rating provisions for employers who meet certain requirements. Below is a summary of the total wages for the years 1990 to 1993, inclusive. For the purpose of the illustration, assume that the total wages and taxable wages are the same amount.

Quarter	1990	1991	1992	1993
1st	$11,000	$10,000	$ 8,500	$10,500
2d	10,000	9,000	9,500	11,000
3d	10,000	9,500	10,000	11,000
4th	10,500	9,750	9,500	9,500
Total	$41,500	$38,250	$37,500	$42,000

A separate account is maintained by the State Unemployment Compensation Commission for each employer. The account is credited with contributions paid into the unemployment compensation fund by the employer and is charged with unemployment benefits that are paid from the fund.

For 1994, the state law set up the following contribution rate schedule for employers:

Reserve Ratio	Rate
Negative reserve balance	6.7%
0.0% to less than 8%	5.9%
8% to less than 10%	5.0%
10% to less than 12%	4.1%
12% to less than 15%	3.2%
15% and over	2.5%

The state law under discussion defines "annual payroll" as the wages paid during a 12-month period ending with the last day of the third quarter of any calendar year. The average annual payroll is the average of the last three annual payrolls.

The following computations show the state contributions made by the Parson Company for the calendar years 1990 to 1993, inclusive, the federal tax imposed under FUTA, and the method of arriving at the contribution rate for the calendar year 1994:

1990

Taxable wages	$41,500	
Rate (SUTA)	x 2.7%	
State contributions:		$1,120.50
Federal tax: .8% of $41,500		332.00
Total unemployment tax		$1,452.50

1991

Taxable wages	$38,250	
Rate (SUTA)	x 2.7%	
State contributions:		$1,032.75
Federal tax: .8% of $38,250		306.00
Total unemployment tax		$1,338.75

1992

Taxable wages	$37,500	
Rate (SUTA)	x 3.4%	
State contributions:		$1,275.00
Federal tax: .8% of $37,500		300.00
Total unemployment tax		$1,575.00

1993

Taxable wages	$42,000	
Rate (SUTA)	x 3.7%	
State contributions:		$1,554.00
Federal tax: .8% of $42,000		336.00
Total unemployment tax		$1,890.00

In computing the average annual payroll and the ratio of the balance in the reserve account to the average annual payroll, you must remember that the average annual payroll is the average of the last three annual payrolls, with each annual payroll period running from October 1 to September 30.

Assume that the Parson Company paid state contributions of $960 in 1988 and $1,010 in 1989 and that $1,850 was charged to the employer's account for unemployment compensation benefits during 1992 and 1993. The contribution rate for 1994 is computed as follows:

Computation of rate for 1994:

Annual payroll period ending 9/30/91	$ 39,000
Annual payroll period ending 9/30/92	37,750
Annual payroll period ending 9/30/93	42,000
Total of last 3 annual payroll periods	$118,750

Average annual payroll:

$118,750 divided by 3 = $39,583

Contributions for 1988	$ 960.00
Contributions for 1989	1,010.00
Contributions for 1990	1,120.50
Contributions for 1991	1,032.75
Contributions for 1992	1,275.00
Contributions for 1993 (first nine months)	1,202.50
Total contributions	$6,600.75
Less amount of benefits paid	1,850.00
Balance in reserve account 9/30/93	$4,750.75

$4,750.75, divided by average annual payroll, $39,583 = 12%

Since the reserve is 12% of the average annual payroll, the tax rate for 1994 is 3.2% (the ratio is between 12% and 15%).

Voluntary Contributions.

In some states, employers may obtain reduced unemployment compensation rates by making *voluntary contributions* to the state fund. These contributions are deliberately made by employers in addition to their regularly required payments of state unemployment taxes. The purpose of voluntary contributions is to increase the balance in the employer's reserve account so that a lower contributions rate may be assigned for the following year. Thus, the new lower tax rate will save the employer more in future state unemployment tax payments than the amount of the voluntary contribution itself.

EXAMPLE:

To illustrate the tax saving that may be realized as a result of making voluntary contributions, consider the following case of the Werner Company, which is subject to the unemployment compensation law of a state that uses the reserve-ratio formula to determine experience

ratings. The following contribution rate schedule will be in effect for 1995:

Reserve Ratio	Rate
0.0% to less than 1%	6.2%
1.0% to less than 1.4%	5.6%
1.4% to less than 1.8%	5.0%
1.8% to less than 2.2%	4.4%
2.2% to less than 2.6%	3.8%
2.6% to less than 3.0%	3.2%
3.0% and over	2.6%

For the three 12-month periods ending on June 30, 1994, the company had an average annual taxable payroll of $330,000. This is the base that the state uses as the average payroll. As of June 30, 1994, the credits to the employer's account exceeded the benefits paid by $6,800. Thus, the 1995 reserve ratio is 2.06% ($6,800 ÷ $330,000), which would result in the assignment of a 4.4% tax rate, as shown in the preceding table. If the employer's 1995 total taxable payroll were $390,000, the SUTA contribution would amount to $17,160.

If the Werner Company makes a voluntary contribution into the state fund within the time period specified by the state law, the tax for 1995 will be less. For example, if a $460 contribution is made, the reserve ratio will be 2.2% ($7,260 ÷ $330,000). As a result, the tax rate will be reduced to 3.8%, with the following savings realized in 1995:

Tax Payment with No Voluntary Contribution (4.4% x $390,000) = ...		$17,160
Tax Payment with Voluntary Contribution	$ 460	
(3.8% x $390,000) =	14,820	15,280
Tax Savings		$ 1,880

An employer who desires to make a voluntary contribution usually must determine without the aid of the state administrative agency the amount of the contribution needed in order to obtain a lower contribution rate. In some states, the agencies provide worksheets that aid employers in determining the amount of voluntary contributions required. If the amount of voluntary contribution is not sufficient to bring about a reduction in the employer's contribution rate, the contribution ordinarily will not be refunded. Instead, the state may give the employer credit against any future SUTA taxes due.

As with the regular contributions, the state must receive the voluntary contributions by a certain date before they can be credited to the employer's account and be used in computing a new tax rate. In some states, the employer may have a certain number of days following the mailing of the tax rate notice to make the voluntary contributions. For instance, in Arizona and New York, the voluntary contributions must be paid by January 31. In West Virginia, the contribution must be sent in within 30 days of the mailing of the rate notice.

UNEMPLOYMENT COMPENSATION REPORTS REQUIRED OF THE EMPLOYER

Employers liable for both the FUTA and the SUTA tax must file periodic reports with both the federal and the state governments. For FUTA tax reporting, there is an annual return (either Form 940 or 940-EZ) and a tax deposit form (Form 8109). Employers covered by state unemployment compensation laws are also generally required to submit two major kinds of reports. One is a tax return, on which the employer reports the tax due the state. The other is a wage report, which reflects the amount of taxable wages paid to each of the employer's covered employees.

Annual FUTA Return—Form 940

Form 940, Employer's Annual Federal Unemployment (FUTA) Tax Return, is the prescribed form for making the return required of employers in reporting the tax imposed under FUTA. A filled-in copy of this form is reproduced in Illustration 5-2 on pages 187 and 188.

Completing the Return. All employers complete Questions A, B, C, and D. If all of these questions are answered "YES," the employer can file the simplified annual tax return, Form 940-EZ, which is shown in Illustration 5-4 on page 190. If the employer answers "NO" to any of the questions, Form 940 must be completed.

The specific information needed to complete Form 940 may be obtained from the sources listed in Illustration 5-3 on page 189.

Payment of Balance Due. After calculating the final net FUTA tax (Part II, Line 7), the employer compares the net tax with the total deposits for the year in order to determine the balance due. Depending on the amount of the liability, the employer either deposits the balance due or remits it directly to the IRS with Form 940.

Signing Form 940. Form 940 must be signed by:

1. The individual, if the employer is an individual.
2. The president, vice-president, or other principal officer, if the employer is a corporation.
3. A responsible and duly authorized member, if the employer is a partnership or other unincorporated organization.
4. A fiduciary, if the employer is a trust or estate.

Filing the Return. The employer must file the annual return not later than January 31 next following the close of the calendar year. If, however, the employer has made timely deposits that pay the FUTA tax liability in full, as discussed below, we may delay the filing of Form 940 until February 10. We must file the return on a calendar-year basis even though our company operates on a fiscal-year basis different from the calendar year. If January 31 falls on Saturday, Sunday, or a legal holiday, we may file the return on the following business day.

A mailed return bearing a postmark indicating it was mailed on or before the due date will be considered to have been timely filed even though it is received after the due date. If we send the return by registered mail, the date of registration is treated as the postmark date. If we send the return by certified mail, the postmark date on the employer's receipt is treated as the postmark date.

Upon application of the employer, the district director or the director of a service center may grant a reasonable extension of time in which to file the return, but not for payment of the tax. However, no extension will be granted for a period longer than 90 days. Generally, we must file the application for an extension in writing on or before the due date for filing the return.

We must file the return with the IRS center for the district in which our employer's principal place of business or office or agency is located. The locations of the IRS centers are given in Illustration 3-14, page 91.

If Form 940 is not available, the employer may make a statement disclosing the amount of wages paid and the amount of tax due. This statement will be accepted as a tentative return until the return is made on the proper form. A privately designed and printed or a computer-prepared substitute Form 940 is permitted if certain IRS specifications are met. For specific approval, a sample of the new form must be sent to the IRS.

Revenue Procedures have been issued for magnetic media filing of Form 940 by reporting agents. A letter of application must first be filed with the appropriate Internal Revenue Service Center if the agents desire to use this method of filing.

Illustration 5-2. Form 940, Employer's Annual Federal Unemployment (FUTA) Tax Return (page 1)

Once an employer has filed Form 940, the IRS will send the employer a preaddressed Form 940 near the close of each subsequent calendar year. In addition, a Federal Tax Deposit Coupon Book, Form 8109, will be mailed to the employer.

NEWS ALERT NEWS ALERT NEWS ALERT

Employers in Delaware, the District of Columbia, Maryland, Pennsylvania, and Virginia can file Form 940 electronically. To participate in the program, filers must get advance approval from the IRS. Write IRS, Magnetic Media Project Office, D.P. 115, Box 21028, Philadelphia, PA 19114, or phone 215-969-7533.

Annual FUTA Return— Form 940-EZ

A streamlined Form 940 is available for employers who have uncomplicated tax situations. In order to use *Form 940-EZ, Employer's Annual Federal Unemployment (FUTA) Tax Return*, an employer must satisfy four simple tests:

1. Must have paid state unemployment taxes to only one state.
2. Must have made the state unemployment tax payments by the due date of Form 940-EZ.
3. All wages that were taxable for FUTA purposes were also taxable for state unemployment tax purposes.
4. Must not be located in a state that is subject to a FUTA credit reduction due to nonpayment of Title XII advances.

Form 940   Page 2

Part II   Tax Due or Refund

| 1 | Gross FUTA tax. Multiply the wages in Part I, line 5, by .062 . . . . | 1 | 3,745 | 59 |
| 2 | Maximum credit. Multiply the wages in Part I, line 5, by .054 . . . | 2 | 3,262 | 29 | | | |

3   Computation of tentative credit:

(a) Name of state	(b) State reporting number(s) as shown on employer's state contribution returns	(c) Taxable payroll (as defined in state act)	(d) State experience rate		(e) State experience rate	(f) Contributions if rate had been 5.4% (col. (c) x .054)	(g) Contributions payable at experience rate (col. (c) x col. (e))	(h) Additional credit (col. (f) minus col. (g) if 0 or less, enter 0	(i) Contributions actually paid to state
			From	To					
PA	20747	40,000.00	1/1	12/31	2.4	2,160.00	960.00	1,200.00	960.00
IN	83-48032	7,040.58	1/1	12/31	2.2	380.19	154.89	225.30	154.89
KY	7321	13,372.22	1/1	12/31	2.0	722.10	267.44	454.66	267.44
3a	Totals . . . ▶	60,412.80						1,879.96	1,382.33

3b	Total tentative credit (add line 3a, columns (h) and (i) only—see instructions for limitations on late payments) ▶		3,262	29
4	Credit: Enter the smaller of the amount in Part II, line 2, or line 3b.	4	3,262	29			
5	Enter the amount from Part I, line 6	5	-0-	
6	Credit allowable (subtract line 5 from line 4). (If zero or less, enter 0.)	6	3,262	29
7	Total FUTA tax (subtract line 6 from line 1)	7	483	30
8	Total FUTA tax deposited for the year, including any overpayment applied from a prior year . .	8	483	30
9	Balance due (subtract line 8 from line 7). This should be $100 or less. Pay to the Internal Revenue Service . . . . ▶	9	-0-	
10	Overpayment (subtract line 7 from line 8). Check if it is to be: ☐ Applied to next return, or ☐ Refunded . . . . ▶	10		

Part III   Record of Quarterly Federal Tax Liability for Unemployment Tax *(Do not include state liability)*

Quarter	First	Second	Third	Fourth	Total for year
Liability for quarter	203.42	159.95	98.83	21.10	483.30

Under penalties of perjury, I declare that I have examined this return, including accompanying schedules and statements, and to the best of my knowledge and belief, it is true, correct, and complete, and that no part of any payment made to a state unemployment fund claimed as a credit was or is to be deducted from the payments to employees

Signature ▶ *J. D. Shannon*   Title (Owner, etc.) ▶ Owner   Date ▶ 1/31/95

Illustration 5-2.   Form 940, Employer's Annual Federal Unemployment (FUTA) Tax Return (page 2)

As you can see from Illustration 5-4 on page 190, Form 940-EZ, many payroll managers will have an easier time completing this year-end tax report than Form 940. This time-saving feature is apparent when you compare the IRS's estimates of the average time spent in completing the two forms:

	940	**940-EZ**
Recordkeeping	12 hours, 55 minutes	5 hours, 55 minutes
Learning about the law or the form	18 minutes	7 minutes
Preparing and sending the form to the IRS	31 minutes	28 minutes

Quarterly Deposit Form—FUTA

We compute the net FUTA tax on a quarterly basis during the month following the end of each calendar quarter. We determine the tax by multiplying .8% by that part of the first $7,000 of each of the employee's annual wages that the employer paid during the quarter. If the employer's tax liability is more than $100, we must deposit it with a Federal Reserve bank or an authorized commercial bank on or before the last day of the month following the end of the quarter. The deposit is considered timely if the bank receives it by the due date or if the employer can establish that it was mailed two days before the due date. We make a similar computation and deposit for each of the first three quarters of the year. Each quarterly deposit is to be accompanied by a preinscribed *Federal Tax Deposit*

SOURCES OF INFORMATION FOR COMPLETING FORM 940

Line No.	Source of Information
A	State unemployment tax forms
B	General ledger account for SUTA Taxes Payable
C	State unemployment tax forms
D	State unemployment tax forms

Part I—Computation of Taxable Wages

1	General ledger account(s) for wages and salaries
2	Personnel records, time sheets, and employee earnings records
3	Employee earnings records
4	Follow directions for addition.
5	Follow directions for subtraction.
6	Follow directions for multiplication, if applicable.

Part II—Tax Due or Refund

1 and 2	Follow directions for multiplication.
3	From the appropriate states' unemployment tax returns
4	Determine the smaller of Part II, line 2, or line 3b.
5	Take the amount from Part 1, line 6.
6 and 7	Follow the directions for subtraction.
8	General ledger account for FUTA Taxes Payable
9 and 10	Compare the net tax with the total deposits for the year.

Part III—Record of Quarterly Federal Tax Liability for Unemployment Tax

1	From the quarterly balances in the FUTA Taxes Payable account in the general ledger

Illustration 5-3. Sources of Information for Completing Form 940

Coupon (Form 8109). A filled-in copy of this deposit form is reproduced in Illustration 5-5 on page 191.

If the tax liability for the first quarter is $100 or less, a deposit is not required; however, we must add the amount of the liability to the amount subject to deposit for the next quarter, in order to compare the total tax due with the $100 minimum for that quarter.

EXAMPLE:

As shown in Illustration 5-2, page 188, the tax liability of the Shannon Heating Company for the 1st quarter of 1994 was $203.42; since the liability exceeded $100, a deposit was made on May 2, 1994. The tax liability for the 2d quarter was $159.95, and a deposit was made on August 1, 1994. The tax liability for the 3d quarter was $98.83, but since this amount was less than the $100 limit, no deposit was required. The tax liability for the 4th quarter was $21.10. Since the accumulated liability of $119.93 exceeded the $100 limit, a deposit of $119.93 was made on January 31, 1995, as shown on Form 8109 in Illustration 5-5 on page 191.

At the time of filing the annual return on Form 940, the employer pays the balance of tax owed for the prior year and not yet deposited. If the amount of tax reportable on Form 940 exceeds by more than $100 the sum of amounts deposited each quarter, the employer must deposit the total amount owed and undeposited (Form 8109) on or before January 31 following the year for which Form 940 is filed. If the amount owed is $100 or less, the employer may remit it with the annual form.

In the case of an employer in a state subject to the FUTA credit reduction because of Title XII advances, we calculate the deposits by multiplying the taxable wages by .8% during each of the first three quarters of the year. Since the penalty rate cannot be known with certainty until November of the current year, the procedure for the first three quarters is the same as that used by an employer in any state. However, since the amount of the penalty imposed for the year will be known during the fourth quarter, the deposit for the last quarter of the year will include the penalty for the entire year. This deposit is due by January 31 of the next year.

Penalties—FUTA

As indicated in Unit 3, under the Internal Revenue Code, employers are subject to civil and criminal penalties for failing to file returns, pay the employment taxes when due, and make timely deposits. These penalties apply, generally, without regard to the type of tax or return involved. All of the penalties are discussed in Illustration 3-15, pages 93 and 94.

Information Reports—SUTA

There is wide variation in the official forms that the states provide for filing the reports required under the unemployment compensation laws. It is, therefore, necessary for us to become familiar with the law and regulations of each state in which liability might be incurred.

The reports that are required of the employers by the individual states are used to determine: (1) the employer's liability for the contributions, (2) the amount of the contribution due on a quarterly basis, and (3) the amount of benefits to which employees

Form 940-EZ

Department of the Treasury
Internal Revenue Service

Employer's Annual Federal Unemployment (FUTA) Tax Return

1994

OMB No. 1545-1110

T	
FF	
FD	
FP	
I	
T	

If incorrect, make any necessary changes. ▶

Name (as distinguished from trade name)

Calendar year
1994

Trade name, if any
YANGO SUPPLY COMPANY

Address and ZIP code
13 M STREET   SALEM, OR 97311-9595

Employer identification number
15 - 8590113

Follow the chart under **Who May Use Form 940-EZ** on page 2. If you cannot use Form 940-EZ, you must use Form 940 instead.

A Enter the amount of contributions paid to your state unemployment fund. (See instructions for line A on page 4.) ▶ $ 12,410 00

B (1) Enter the name of the state where you have to pay contributions . . . . ▶ Oregon

(2) Enter your state reporting number as shown on state unemployment tax return. ▶ 163-97557

If you will not have to file returns in the future, check here (see *Who Must File*, on page 2) complete, and sign the return . . . . . . ▶ ☐

If this is an Amended Return check here . . . . ▶ ☐

Part I   Taxable Wages and FUTA Tax

1	Total payments (including payments shown on lines 2 and 3) during the calendar year for services of employees	1	478,231 19

		Amount paid	
2	Exempt payments. (Explain all exempt payments, attaching additional sheets if necessary.) ▶	2	
3	Payments for services of more than $7,000. Enter only amounts over the first $7,000 paid to each employee. Do not include any exempt payments from line 2. Do not use state wage limitation. The $7,000 amount is the Federal wage base. Your state wage base may be different . . .	3 303,231 19	

4	Total exempt payments (add lines 2 and 3)	4	303,231 19
5	**Total taxable wages** (subtract line 4 from line 1) . . . . ▶	5	175,000 00
6	FUTA tax. Multiply the wages on line 5 by .008 and enter here. (If the result is over $100, also complete Part II.) . .	6	1,400 00
7	Total FUTA tax deposited for the year, including any overpayment applied from a prior year (from your records)	7	1,400 00
8	**Amount you owe** (subtract line 7 from line 6). This should be $100 or less. Pay to "Internal Revenue Service". ▶	8	-0-
9	**Overpayment** (subtract line 6 from line 7). Check if it is to be: ☐ Applied to next return, or ☐ Refunded ▶	9	

Part II   Record of Quarterly Federal Unemployment Tax Liability (Do not include state liability.) Complete only if line 6 is over $100.

Quarter	First (Jan. 1 – Mar. 31)	Second (Apr. 1 – June 30)	Third (July 1 – Sept. 30)	Fourth (Oct. 1 – Dec. 31)	Total for year
Liability for quarter	719.90	360.18	319.92	-0-	1,400.00

Under penalties of perjury, I declare that I have examined this return, including accompanying schedules and statements, and, to the best of my knowledge and belief, it is true, correct, and complete, and that no part of any payment made to a state unemployment fund claimed as a credit was, or is to be, deducted from the payments to employees.

Signature ▶ *William H. Yango*   Title (Owner, etc.) ▶ President   Date ▶ 1/31/95

Form **940-EZ**

Illustration 5-4.   Form 940-EZ, Employer's Annual Federal Unemployment (FUTA) Tax Return

will be entitled if they become unemployed. The most important of the required reports are the following:

1. Status reports
2. Contribution reports
3. Wage information reports
4. Separation reports
5. Partial unemployment notices

Status Reports. Under the unemployment compensation laws of most states, new employers are required to register or file an initial statement or *status report*. The principal purpose of this report is to determine the employer's liability to make contributions into the state unemployment compensation fund. A status report may be required of employers regardless of whether they are liable for contributions under the state law.

Contribution Reports. All employers liable for contributions under the unemployment compensation law of any state are required to submit a quarterly *contribution report* or tax return. The purpose of this report is to provide a summary of the wages paid during the period and to show the computation of the tax or contribution. Usually, we must file this report on or before the last day of the month following the close of the calendar quarter, and the tax or contribution must be paid at the same time.

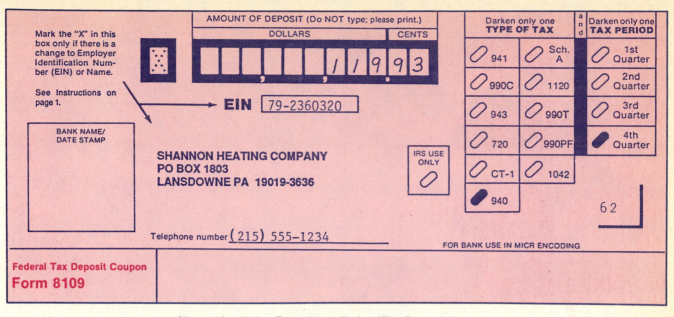

Illustration 5-5. Form 8109, Federal Tax Deposit Coupon

Wage Information Reports.

In most states we are required to make *wage information reports* concerning individual employees. Usually we file these reports with the quarterly contribution reports. An example of a quarterly wage information report is shown in Illustration 5-6, page 192.

On the report we may list all employee names, social security account numbers, taxable wages, taxable tips, state in which worker was employed during the reported quarter, and employer's federal account number. We may also be required to list for each employee the number of credit weeks earned during the quarter. (A *credit week* is defined by the state's unemployment compensation law; for example, in Pennsylvania, a credit week is defined as any calendar week in the quarter during which the person earned remuneration of not less than $50). Commercially printed forms may also be used provided the form includes all the necessary information required by the state.

About three fourths of the states permit the use of the same magnetic tape for reporting state wage information that is used for federal social security reporting purposes. By using the same magnetic tape and reporting specifications to satisfy both state and federal requirements, we eliminate the need to transcribe information from the tape prepared for the federal government for submission to the state. The payroll manager should contact the state agency to determine whether federal-state combined magnetic tape reporting is acceptable.

Separation Reports.

Whenever a worker becomes separated from employment, we may be required to furnish a *separation report* providing a wage and employment record of the separated employee and the reason for leaving. Usually we must give a copy of the report to the worker in order that the individual may be informed of any entitlement to unemployment insurance benefits.

Partial Unemployment Notices.

Most states require employers to give partial unemployment notices to those workers who become "partially unemployed" so that they are informed of their potential eligibility for partial unemployment benefits. *Partial unemployment* refers to employment by the individual's regular employer but on a reduced scale because of lack of work. In most states the notice must be given to the worker immediately after a week of partial employment has been completed. After that, the employer ordinarily furnishes the worker with some kind of low-earnings report during each week of partial employment so that the worker will be assured of the receipt of supplemental or partial benefits.

Penalties—SUTA

In all states there is some form of penalty for failure to pay, or for the late payment of, contributions, and also for failure to file reports. Some states impose a 10% penalty if the failure to pay the tax is due to negligence, and in a few states, a 50% penalty is imposed if the failure to pay is due to fraud. Many states also deny experience rates to employers who are delinquent in filing reports or paying contributions. In some states employers who have been delinquent in paying their contributions may be required to pay the contributions monthly rather than quarterly.

EMPLOYER'S REPORT FOR UNEMPLOYMENT COMPENSATION	PA FORM	QTR.	YEAR
READ INSTRUCTIONS ON REVERSE SIDE OF EMPLOYER'S COPY	UC-2	1ST	19--
ANSWER EACH ITEM. TYPE OR PRINT IN INK			

UC-2A'S

EMPL. ALPHA INDEX   CASHIER'S TRANSMITTAL NUMBER

INV. OR R.D. CLEARANCE

1. TOTAL NUMBER OF COVERED EMPLOYES IN PAY PERIOD INCL. 12TH OF MONTH. INCLUDE EMPLOYES WHOSE WAGES EXCEED TAXABLE LIMIT. IF NONE ENTER "0"

| | FIRST MONTH | SECOND MONTH | THIRD MONTH |
| | 6 | 6 | 7 |

I CERTIFY THAT THE INFORMATION ON FORMS UC-2/2A/2B IS TRUE AND CORRECT TO THE BEST OF MY KNOWLEDGE AND BELIEF. NO PART OF THE AMOUNT OF EMPLOYER CONTRIBUTIONS REPORTED ON TAXABLE WAGES WAS DEDUCTED OR IS TO BE DEDUCTED FROM THE EMPLOYE'S WAGES.

SIGN HERE DO NOT PRINT   *Jack B. Kiel*
SIGNATURE OF OWNER, PARTNER, RESPONSIBLE OFFICER OR AUTHORIZED AGENT

TITLE President   DATE 5-2-94

EMPLOYER'S CONTRIBUTION RATE ▶ .041   EMPLOYER'S ACCT. NO.
79-16093-0

FOR DEPT. USE

2	GROSS WAGES	31,790	00
2A	EMPLOYE CONTRIBUTIONS WITHHELD WITHHOLDING RATE IS .0015	47	69
3	TAXABLE WAGES FOR EMPLOYER CONTRIBUTIONS	29,290	00
4	EMPLOYER CONTRIBUTIONS DUE (RATE X ITEM 3)	1,200	89
4A	TOTAL CONTRIBUTIONS DUE (ITEM 2A +4)	1,248	58
5	INTEREST DUE SEE INSTRUCTIONS	-0-	
6	PENALTY DUE SEE INSTRUCTIONS	-0-	
7	TOTAL REMITTANCE (ITEM 4A +5 +6)	1,248	58

DO NOT WRITE IN THIS SPACE

KIELSO COMPANY
8101 ARCHER LANE
NORRISTOWN, PA 19401-1936

MAKE CHECKS PAYABLE TO: PA UC FUND   SUBJECTIVITY DATE

DATE PAYMENT RECEIVED
REPORT TIMELY
REPORT DELINQUENT DATE

POST CASH CREDIT
WE $
C $
I $
P $
EXAMINED BY

IF ADDRESS HAS CHANGED, PLEASE CORRECT UC-2B PORTION OF THIS FORM

EMPLOYER'S QUARTERLY REPORT OF WAGES PAID TO EACH EMPLOYE

	PA FORM UC-2A
	QTR.	YEAR
	1ST	19--

7A. TEL. NO. OF PREPARER 215-555-8210

FOR DEPT. USE

8. TOTAL NUMBER OF PAGES IN THIS REPORT	1
9. GROSS WAGES (MUST AGREE WITH ITEM 2 ABOVE AND TOTALS OF ITEM 14)	31,790 00
10. TOTAL NUMBER OF EMPLOYES LISTED IN ITEM 13 ON ALL PAGES	7
11. PLANT NUMBER	N/A

12. EMPLOYE'S SOC. SEC. ACCT. NO.	13. NAME OF EMPLOYE (TYPE OR PRINT IN INK)			14. GR. WAGES PD. THIS QTR.	15. CREDIT WEEKS
	FIRST NAME	INITIAL	LAST NAME		
111 09 8271	Janet	L	Carroll	6,300 00	13
095 19 1918	Carson	H	Long	1,900 00	5
212 16 3790	Heidi	M	Dorsey	2,990 00	13
091 78 6510	Mary	F	Ernst	2,100 00	13
109 05 0093	Jack	B	Kiel	10,500 00	13
170 91 9008	Alan	W	Pinkett	4,100 00	13
089 87 1792	Lawrence	B	Golic	3,900 00	13

LIST ANY ADDITIONAL EMPLOYES ON FORM UC-2A SUPPLEMENT OR ON CONTINUATION SHEETS APPROVED BY THE DEPARTMENT.

TOTAL FOR THIS PAGE _____   31,790 00

Illustration 5-6. Pennsylvania Form UC-2, Employer's Report for Unemployment Compensation

An employer's failure to file reports or pay contributions when due may, in addition to subjecting the employer to penalties and interest, result in paying contributions at a higher rate than would have been required otherwise. Where contributions are one of the factors used in the experience-rating formula, only payments made by a certain date may be used in figuring the new tax rates.

UNEMPLOYMENT COMPENSATION BENEFITS

Unemployment compensation benefits, which are payments made to workers who are temporarily unemployed, are provided primarily under the unemployment compensation law of each state. Each state specifies the qualifications to be met by the unemployed worker in order to be eligible for benefits, the amount of the benefits to be paid each individual, and the duration of the period for which benefits will be paid.

As discussed in Unit 4, payers of unemployment compensation benefits must send copies of Form 1099-G to the Internal Revenue Service and to the person receiving the benefits. This form is used only when the total benefits paid are $10 or more. These benefits are includable in the recipient's gross income for federal income tax purposes if the unemployment benefits plus the individual's adjusted gross income exceed certain dollar limits.

Employee Benefits—SUTA

There is no uniform rate of unemployment benefits payable by all states. The amount of the benefits that an unemployed worker is entitled to receive usually is about 50% of the regular weekly wages subject to minimum and maximum amounts specified by law. Maximum weekly benefits vary widely among states, from 50% to 70% of average weekly wages. Illustration 5-1 on pages 182 and 183 shows the minimum and maximum amounts of benefits (excluding dependency allowances) provided under the laws of each state.

Under the laws of all the states there is a limit to the total amount of benefits an unemployed worker may receive in any year. Usually the limit is expressed in the terms of amounts rather than weeks. Thus, the maximum amount of benefits allowed under the various state laws ranges from 26 to 30 times the individual's weekly benefit amount. Therefore, if a certain employee should qualify for weekly benefits of $150 and the maximum benefits payable during the year are $4,500, the employee would be entitled to receive benefits during a period of 30 weeks.

Dependency Allowances. The state unemployment compensation laws often provide for payment of a *dependency allowance*, which is an additional weekly benefit to unemployed workers with dependents. For example, the law in Connecticut provides for a weekly dependency allowance of $10 each for the claimant's nonworking spouse and each child and stepchild (but for no more than five dependents). However, the total dependency allowance cannot exceed 50% of the benefit otherwise payable to the claimant. In those states that provide dependency allowances, the allowances are sometimes made only to workers with dependent children of a stipulated age.

Eligibility for Benefits. The unemployment compensation laws of all the states require that a claimant meet certain conditions before becoming eligible to receive benefits. An analysis of the required qualifications in most states reveals that the claimant must:

1. File a claim for benefits.
2. Be able to work.
3. Be available for work.
4. Be actively seeking work or make a reasonable effort to obtain work.
5. Have earned a certain amount of wages or worked a certain number of weeks in covered employment.
6. Have registered at the local state employment office.
7. Have served the required waiting period.
8. Not be disqualified under any of the other provisions of the law.

Disqualification of Benefits. Certain disqualifications are set up in the state laws to conserve the funds and to insure the intended purpose of unemployment insurance, which is to compensate for involuntary unemployment. While there is wide variation in the state laws, the following are some of the more common reasons for disqualification:

1. Discharge for misconduct.
2. Voluntarily leaving work without good cause.
3. Unemployment due to a labor dispute.[1]
4. Leaving work to attend school.
5. Commitment to penal institution.
6. False or fraudulent representation to obtain benefits.
7. Refusal of suitable employment.
8. Receipt of certain kinds of remuneration.

---

[1]Most states provide benefits to strikers who have been replaced by nonstriking employees, and many states allow strikers to collect benefits in cases where their employers continue to operate.

Professional Tip
In Maine, applicants for benefits who quit to follow their spouses to a new area are not disqualified.

Most state laws provide that an unemployed individual shall not be entitled to unemployment compensation benefits during any week in which the person receives remuneration from other sources such as workers' compensation for temporary partial disability, old-age benefits under the Social Security Act, vacation allowances, dismissal wages, earnings from self-employment, or unemployment compensation benefits from another state. In some cases, however, it is provided that if such remuneration is less than the benefits due the individual, the person shall receive the amount of the benefits less such remuneration.

An individual otherwise qualified may receive unemployment compensation benefits regardless of age. Thus, minors and persons over the age of 65 may qualify for unemployment compensation benefits.

Benefits for the Unemployed as a Result of Major Disaster.
Under the *Disaster Relief Act*, unemployment benefits are provided to persons who become unemployed as a result of a major disaster. The benefits will be available so long as the individual's unemployment caused by a major disaster continues or until the individual is reemployed in a suitable position. In no event, however, will the benefits be paid for longer than one year after the disaster has been declared.

Benefits for Federal Employees.
Under the *Federal Employee Unemployment Compensation* program of the Social Security Act, unemployment insurance is provided for federal civilian employees. If a federal civilian worker becomes unemployed, eligibility for benefits is determined under the unemployment law of the state in which the person last worked in federal civilian employment. If eligible, the person is entitled to unemployment benefits in the amounts and under the conditions provided by the state unemployment insurance law. Upon request by the state, the federal employing agencies make available their findings pertaining to federal civilian employment, wages, and reasons for job separation.

Benefits for Ex-Service Personnel.
Unemployment compensation benefits for ex-service personnel are provided by the *Federal Unemployment Compensation for Ex-Servicemen* program of the Social Security Act. The benefits are determined by the unemployment insurance law of the state in which the person first files a claim that establishes a benefit year as the most recent separation from active military service.

Disability Benefits.
Five states—California, Hawaii, New Jersey, New York, and Rhode Island—and Puerto Rico provide for the payment of *disability benefits* to workers who suffer wage losses through unemployment due to nonoccupational disease or injury. The programs in these states have developed in response to the need for protecting workers who are not eligible for either workers' compensation or unemployment insurance. The programs are not health insurance as such, for benefits are paid only to offset the wage loss of an employee who becomes sick or suffers an accident not connected with work.

Payment of disability benefits under the state laws are, for the most part, financed by employee contributions. In Hawaii, New Jersey, New York, and Puerto Rico, however, employers are required to contribute. In California, New Jersey, and Puerto Rico, the benefits are provided under a state-administered plan; but employers may substitute their own plans if they so wish. However, such "private" or "voluntary" plans must provide benefits at least as favorable as those payable under the state plan. Rhode Island does not provide for the use of private plans, and all employees covered by the law are insured under the state fund. In Hawaii, the employer may provide for the benefits by means of private insurance, by deposit of securities or bonds with the State Director of Finance, by furnishing proof of ability to pay, or by private plans.

Supplemental Unemployment Benefits (SUB).
Many union contracts provide for the private supplementation of state unemployment compensation benefits to provide payments to employees during periods of layoff. In nearly all of the states that have investigated the *Supplemental Unemployment Benefits (SUB)* plan benefits in relation to state unemployment compensation benefits, it has been ruled that workers who receive SUB may also simultaneously be paid unemployment compensation benefits. A SUB plan is usually one of two types: (a) the pooled-fund plan or (b) the individual-account plan.

Pooled-Fund Plan.
This plan, which is also known as the "auto" or "Ford-type" plan, is the most common type of SUB plan. Under this plan employers contribute to a general fund a certain number of cents

for each hour worked by employees currently on the job. Employees usually have a right to benefits from the fund only upon layoff and only after meeting stipulated eligibility requirements.

Individual-Account Plan. Under this plan, found mainly in the plate glass industry, contributions are paid to separate trusts for each employee and the employee has a vested and nonforfeitable right to the amount in the fund. Workers are entitled to the fund upon layoff and have a right to the fund when their employment is terminated. In the event the worker dies, the designated beneficiary is paid the content of the trust.

FUTA Funds

As indicated earlier, the net FUTA tax the employer pays to the federal government is used primarily to pay the state and federal administrative expenses of the total unemployment insurance program. However, there is a program of *federal emergency benefits* for employees who exhaust their regular state unemployment insurance benefits. Generally, under this program, unemployment benefits are provided for an extra 20 or 26 weeks to jobless workers. However, these emergency benefits are payable only if the nation's seasonally adjusted unemployment rate is 7% or higher. Each individual state's adjusted insured

unemployment rate determines whether the extension is for 20 or 26 weeks.

Current legislation also provides for a drop in duration of benefits to 10 or 15 weeks if the nation's unemployment rate falls below 7% for two consecutive months, and to 7 or 13 weeks if it falls below 6.8% for two consecutive months.

As indicated earlier, the FUTA provides that when a state's unemployment compensation fund is insufficient to meet its benefit obligations, the state may obtain an advance from its federal account in the unemployment trust fund. Such advances constitute loans that must be repaid. If the loans (Title XII advances) are not repaid within the specified period, the net FUTA tax on employers in the *affected state* is increased until the loan has been recaptured through the increased taxes (see pages 180-181).

Summary of Sources and Duration of Benefits

The chart below shows how the federal-state unemployment insurance system operates in a state in which the basic duration of benefits is 26 weeks. In addition to the kinds of benefits listed in the chart, legislation may be enacted that extends the federal-state benefits program.

Weeks of Unemployment	Source of Benefits	Starting Point	Life of Program
1st to 26th	Regular state program (funded entirely from state unemployment accounts)	Operates continuously	Permanent
27th up to 52nd	Emergency Unemployment Compensation Act (funded entirely with federal funds)	Nation's seasonally adjusted unemployment rate 7% or higher. State's adjusted insured unemployment rate determines whether extension is for 20 or 26 weeks	Expires January 15, 1994

GLOSSARY

Constructively paid wages—remunerations that are credited to the account of, or set apart for, an employee so that they may be drawn upon at any time, even though they are not actually possessed by the employee.

Contribution report—quarterly tax return filed with the state by the employer to provide a summary of the wages paid during the period and to show the computation of the tax or contribution.

Dependency allowance—an additional weekly benefit paid to unemployed workers with dependents.

Disability benefits—payments to workers who suffer wage losses through unemployment due to nonoccupational disease or injury.

Dismissal payments—amounts paid by employers to workers who have been separated from employment; also known as *payments in lieu of notice, separation pay,* or *terminal leave pay.*

Experience rating—method by which employer contribution payments may be adjusted because of a favorable employment record; also known as *merit rating.*

Federal emergency benefits program—a plan for the payment of extended benefits to employees who exhaust their regular state unemployment insurance benefits.

Individual-account plan—supplemental unemployment benefits plan in which the employer's contributions are paid into a separate trust for each employee.

Interstate employee—an individual who works in more than one state.

Merit rating—*see* experience rating.

Negative-balance employers—those whose reserve accounts have been charged for more benefits paid out than contributions paid into the fund.

Partial unemployment—employment by the individual's regular employer on a reduced scale because of lack of work.

Partial unemployment notice—form completed by employer and given to partially unemployed workers so that supplemental unemployment benefits may be obtained.

Pooled-fund laws—unemployment insurance system wherein the cost of unemployment benefits is spread among all employers in a particular state.

Pooled-fund plan—supplemental unemployment benefits plan financed by employers' contributions into a general fund; also known as the *auto* or *Ford-type plan.*

Positive-balance employers—those who have built up a balance in their reserve accounts (contributions paid in less benefits charged).

Reciprocal arrangements—agreements between states to provide unemployment insurance coverage and payment of benefits to interstate workers.

Reserve-ratio formula—experience-rating plan used in most states, based on: Contributions less Benefits Paid ÷ Average Payroll.

Separation report—report that provides a wage and employment record of the separated employee and the reason for leaving.

Status report—initial statement filed by new employers with their state unemployment office, which determines their liability to make contributions into the state unemployment compensation fund.

Supplemental unemployment benefits—private supplementation of state unemployment compensation benefits to employees during periods of layoff.

Title XII advances—funds borrowed from the federal government by states who, due to financial difficulties, cannot pay their unemployment compensation benefits.

Unemployment compensation benefits—payments made to workers who are temporarily unemployed.

Unemployment insurance—a federal-state program that provides economic security for workers during periods of temporary unemployment.

Voluntary contributions—payments deliberately made by employers to their state funds in order to qualify for a lower unemployment compensation tax rate.

Wage information report—statement filed by the employer, usually with the quarterly contribution report, which lists employee names, social security account numbers, taxable wages, taxable tips, state in which worker was employed during the reported quarter, and employer's federal account number.

QUESTIONS FOR REVIEW

1. How are the employer's contributions to FUTA used by the federal government?
2. What are the two alternative tests that are applied to a business in order to judge whether it is an "employer" and, therefore, subject to the FUTA tax?
3. Explain how one of two entities is determined to be the employer for purposes of FUTA.
4. Under what conditions are agricultural laborers included in the coverage of FUTA?
5. To what extent does FUTA coverage extend to services that a citizen of the United States performs for an American employer outside the United States?
6. Explain how an employee who works in more than one state may be covered under the state unemployment compensation law of one state.
7. As far as SUTA is concerned in most states, how does an employer account for the wages that are paid to an employee who is transferred to another plant location in a different state during the same calendar year?
8. Which of the following types of payments are taxable under FUTA:
   a. Commissions as compensation for covered employment.
   b. Christmas gifts of nominal value.
   c. Courtesy discounts to employees.
   d. Reimbursement of ordinary and necessary business expenses.
   e. Dismissal payments.
9. a. What is the basis upon which the FUTA tax is calculated?
   b. What portion of each employee's annual wages is subject to the FUTA tax?
   c. What is the current gross FUTA tax rate?
   d. What is the maximum credit an employer may claim for state contributions in computing the net FUTA tax?
10. Explain how experience rating allows an employer to pay an overall unemployment tax (FUTA and SUTA) of less than 6.2%.
11. An employer, because of a favorable experience rating, is permitted to pay a state contribution at a reduced rate of 1.5%. What percentage of taxable wages must be paid in the aggregate to the federal and state governments?
12. What are two situations in which an employer could be liable for a net FUTA tax greater than .8%?
13. What is the purpose of Title XII advances?
14. How is the SUTA tax rate determined for a new employer?
15. In 1993:
   a. Which state(s) had the widest range of SUTA tax rates for employers?
   b. Which state(s) paid the highest weekly maximum benefit (excluding dependency allowances) to qualified unemployed workers?
   c. Which state(s) had the highest taxable wage base for the SUTA tax?
16. Describe briefly the formula most commonly used to calculate the experience-rating contributions of an employer.
17. How might an employer's payroll taxes be reduced by means of voluntary contributions to the state's unemployment compensation plan?
18. Which employers can file Form 940-EZ?
19. a. For an employer who is subject to FUTA, what are the basic forms that must be filed with the federal government?
   b. When must these forms be filed?
   c. How are taxable wages computed on the annual return?
20. For 1994, the Baxter Company paid a 2.2% state unemployment tax to Rhode Island. What percentage of taxable wages would be paid in the aggregate to the federal and state governments for unemployment?
21. How may an employer obtain an extension of time in filing Form 940?
22. What is a separation report?
23. Why do some states require employers to furnish partial unemployment notices to workers?
24. Why might an unemployed worker be disqualified from receiving unemployment compensation benefits?
25. a. What is the purpose of the federal emergency benefits program?
   b. How many additional weeks of benefits are added?
   c. How is this program financed?

QUESTIONS FOR DISCUSSION

1. Can the owner of a small business receive unemployment compensation? Explain.
2. What arguments could be made for raising the upper limits of the SUTA tax rates?
3. Check the unemployment compensation law of your state and determine the answers to the following questions:
   a. How do nonprofit organizations, subject to coverage, make payments to the unemployment compensation fund?
   b. Can part-time teachers collect unemployment compensation between school terms?
   c. Can professional athletes receive unemployment compensation?
   d. Are aliens covered by the unemployment compensation law?
   e. How do employers protest or appeal benefit determinations and charges against their accounts?
   f. Briefly describe how a person's weekly benefit rate and maximum benefit amount are determined.
   g. Can an unemployed worker collect additional benefits if he or she has dependents? If so, how much is paid for each dependent?
   h. Does the state provide payment of partial benefits?
   i. Are benefits payable to a female during pregnancy?
   j. Can employers make voluntary contributions to their state unemployment reserve accounts?
   k. For what reasons may an unemployed worker be disqualified from receiving unemployment benefits?
   l. What steps are taken by the state unemployment agency to prevent the improper payment of claims?
4. As a way of curbing the unemployment rate, California has instituted a "shared-work compensation" program. Under this program, a company faced with a layoff of its workers may place its entire work force on a four-day workweek during the period of hardship. During this period of reduced workweeks, the employees collect partial unemployment benefits. When business rebounds, the firm returns to its normal five-day workweek, and the unemployment compensation benefits cease. Participation in the program must be approved by both the employer and the unions. If, however, the firm is not unionized, management has the discretion of putting the plan into effect.
   a. What are the benefits of such a shared-work compensation program to (1) the employer and (2) the employees?
   b. What disadvantages do you see in the operation of a shared-work compensation program, especially from the viewpoint of organized labor?

PRACTICAL PROBLEMS

5-1. During the year, the Hernandez Company is required to pay FUTA and SUTA taxes. The state's tax rate for the company is 3.8%. The taxable payroll for the year for FUTA and SUTA is $45,000. Compute:

a. The net FUTA tax . . . . $_____

b. The net SUTA tax . . . .   _____

c. The total unemployment taxes . . . . $_____

5-2. During the year, the Nanchez Company has a SUTA tax rate of 5.9%. The taxable payroll for the year for FUTA and SUTA is $67,000. Compute:

a. The net FUTA tax . . . . $_____

b. The net SUTA tax . . . .   _____

c. The total unemployment taxes . . . . $_____

5-3. The Parrett Company's payroll for the year is $737,910. Of this amount, $472,120 is for wages paid in excess of $7,000 to each individual employee. The SUTA rate in the state in which the Parrett Company is located is 2.9% on the first $7,000 of each employee's earnings. The FUTA tax also applies to the company. Determine:

a. The net FUTA tax . . . . $_____

b. The net SUTA tax . . . .   _____

c. The total unemployment taxes . . . . $_____

5-4. The Garrison Shops had a SUTA tax rate of 3.7%, and their state's taxable limit was $8,000 of each employee's earnings. For the year, the Garrison Shops had FUTA taxable wages of $67,900 and SUTA taxable wages of $83,900. Determine:

a. The net FUTA tax . . . . $_____

b. The net SUTA tax . . . . $_____

5-5. Due to its experience rating, Ianelli, Inc., is required to pay unemployment taxes on its payroll as follows:

1. Under SUTA for Illinois on taxable wages of $18,000, the contribution rate is 4%.
2. Under SUTA for Indiana on taxable wages of $24,000, the contribution rate is 2.65%.
3. Under SUTA for Ohio on taxable wages of $79,000, the contribution rate is 2.9%.
4. Under FUTA, the taxable wages are $103,500.

Determine:

a. SUTA taxes paid to Illinois .... $_____

b. SUTA taxes paid to Indiana .... $_____

c. SUTA taxes paid to Ohio .... $_____

d. FUTA taxes paid .... $_____

5-6. The Brooks Company began its operations in August of the current year. During August and September, the company paid wages of $6,950. For the last quarter of the year, the taxable wages paid amounted to $12,910. None of the employees were paid more than $7,000 this year.

a. Is the Brooks Company liable for FUTA tax this year? Explain.

b. If so, what is the amount of the *gross* FUTA tax before any credit is granted for the SUTA tax? .... $_____

5-7. In September, 1994, the Haley Paint Corporation began operations in a state that requires new employers of one or more individuals to pay a state unemployment tax of 3.5% of the first $7,000 of wages paid each employee.

An analysis of the company's payroll for the year shows total wages paid of $177,610. The salaries of the president and the vice-president of the company were $20,000 and $15,000, respectively, for the four-month period; but there were no other employees who received wages in excess of $7,000 for the four months. Included in the total wages were $900 paid to a director who only attended director meetings during the year, and $6,300 paid to the factory superintendent.

Besides the total wages of $177,610, there was a payment of $2,430 made to the O'Hara Accounting Company for an audit they performed on the company's books in December, 1994. Determine:

a. The net FUTA tax .... $_____

b. The SUTA tax .... $_____

5-8. In April of the current year, the Korn Steel Company transferred Harry Marsh from its factory in Tennessee to its plant in South Carolina. The company's SUTA tax rates based on its experience ratings are 3.2% in Tennessee and 3.8% in South Carolina. Both states base the tax on the first $7,000 of each employee's earnings. This year the Korn Steel Company paid Harry Marsh wages of $9,900; $2,800 were paid in Tennessee and the remainder in South Carolina. Compute:

a. The amount of SUTA tax the company must pay to Tennessee on Marsh's wages .... $_____

b. The amount of SUTA tax the company must pay to South Carolina on Marsh's wages .... $_____

c. The amount of the net FUTA tax on Marsh's wages .... $_____

200

5-9. The partnership of Edward and Farnam paid the following wages during this year:

M. Edward (partner)	$21,000
S. Farnam (partner)	19,000
N. Pearson (supervisor)	12,500
T. Grunhart (factory worker)	9,700
R. Rice (factory worker)	9,200
D. Brown (factory worker)	7,900
S. Koenig (bookkeeper)	10,900
C. Chang (maintenance)	4,500

In addition, the partnership owed $200 to Chang for work he performed during December. However, payment for this work will not be made until January of the following year.

a.   The *gross* FUTA tax for the partnership for this year is .... $_____

b.   The *net* FUTA tax for this year is .... $_____

5-10. This year Katherine Thomason was paid wages of $9,340 by the Wexter Company. Due to its experience rating, the company's SUTA tax rate is 2.5%. The state's tax rate applies to the first $8,000 paid each employee. Determine:

a.   The amount that the Wexter Company must pay for net FUTA and SUTA taxes
     in connection with Thomason's salary this year .... $_____

b.   The net FUTA and SUTA taxes on Thomason's salary if the Wexter Company's
     tax rate was a less favorable 3.6% on the first $8,000 of each employee's earn-
     ings .... $_____

5-11. The Demigold Company paid wages of $170,900 this year. Of this amount, $114,000 was taxable for net FUTA and SUTA purposes. The state's contribution tax rate is 3.1% for the Demigold Company. Due to cash flow problems, the company was late in making its SUTA payments throughout the year. Compute:

a.   The amount of credit the company would receive against the FUTA tax for its
     SUTA contributions .... $_____

b.   The amount that the Demigold Company would pay to the federal government
     for their FUTA tax .... $_____

c.   The amount that the company lost because of their late payments .... $_____

5-12. During 1994, the Jordan Company was subject to the Alaska state unemployment tax of 4.2%. The company's taxable earnings for FUTA were $86,700 and for SUTA, $171,000. Determine:

a.   The SUTA tax that the Jordan Company would pay to the State of Alaska ..... $_____

b.   The net FUTA tax for 1994 .... $_____

c.   The amount of the employees' disability insurance tax for 1994 (use the
     employee's tax rate that is shown in Illustration 5-1 on page 182) .... $_____

5-13. The following unemployment tax-rate schedule is in effect during the calendar year 1994 in State A, which uses the reserve-ratio formula in determining employer contributions:

Reserve Ratio	Contributions Rate
0.0% or more, but less than 1%	6.7%
1.0% or more, but less than 1.2%	6.4%
1.2% or more, but less than 1.4%	6.1%
1.4% or more, but less than 1.6%	5.8%
1.6% or more, but less than 1.8%	5.5%
1.8% or more, but less than 2.0%	5.2%
2.0% or more, but less than 2.2%	4.9%
2.2% or more, but less than 2.4%	4.6%
2.4% or more, but less than 2.6%	4.3%
2.6% or more, but less than 2.8%	4.0%
2.8% or more, but less than 3.0%	3.7%
3.0% or more, but less than 3.2%	3.4%
3.2% or more	3.1%

The Grant Company, which is located in State A, had an average annual payroll of $850,000 for the three 12-month periods ending on June 30, 1993 (the computation date for the tax year 1994). As of June 30, 1993, the total contributions that had been made to the Grant Company's reserve account, in excess of the benefits charged, amounted to $17,440. Compute:

a. The Grant Company's reserve ratio for 1994 .... _____ %

b. The 1994 contributions rate for the company .... _____ %

c. The smallest contribution that the company can make in order to reduce its tax rate if State A permits voluntary contributions .... $ _____

d. The tax savings realized by the company taking into consideration the voluntary contribution made in "c" if the taxable payroll in 1994 is $980,000 .... $ _____

5-14. As of June 30, 1993 (the computation date for the 1994 tax rate), the Zimfer Company had a negative balance of $867 in its unemployment reserve account in State A. The company's average payroll over the last three 12-month periods amounted to $360,000. The unemployment compensation law of State A provides that the tax rate of an employer who has a negative balance on the computation date shall be 7.2% during the following calendar year. Using the tax-rate schedule presented in Problem 5-13, determine:

a. The smallest voluntary contribution that the Zimfer Company should make in order to effect a change in its tax rate .... $ _____

b. The amount of the tax savings as a result of the voluntary contribution if the Zimfer Company's taxable payroll for 1994 is $420,000 .... $ _____

5-15. Marlene Grady and Pauline Monroe are partners engaged in operating the MGM Doll Shop, a partnership, which has employed the following persons since the beginning of the year:

V. Hoffman (general office worker) .... $1,700 per month
A. Drugan (saleswoman) .... $15,000 per year
G. Beiter (stock clerk) .... $180 per week
S. Egan (deliveryman) .... $220 per week
B. Lin (cleaning and maintenance, part-time) .... $160 per week

Grady and Monroe are each paid a weekly salary allowance of $450.

The doll shop is located in a state that requires unemployment compensation contributions of employers of one or more individuals. The company is subject to state contributions at a rate of 3.1% for wages not in excess of $8,100. Determine each of the following amounts based upon the 41st weekly payroll period for the week ending October 14, 1994:

a. The amount of FICA taxes (OASDI and HI) to be withheld from the earnings of each person.

	OASDI	**HI**
M. Grady	$_____	$_____
P. Monroe	_____	_____
V. Hoffman	_____	_____
A. Drugan	_____	_____
G. Beiter	_____	_____
S. Egan	_____	_____
B. Lin	_____	_____

b. The amount of the employer's FICA taxes for the weekly payroll ....   _____   _____

c. The amount of state unemployment contributions for the weekly payroll .... $_____

d. The amount of the net FUTA tax on the payroll .... $_____

e. The total amount of the employer's payroll taxes for the weekly payroll .... $_____

5-16. The Glavine Steel Company is located in State H, which enables employers to reduce their contribution rates under the experience-rating system. During 1980 to 1989, inclusive, the company's total contributions to state unemployment compensation amounted to $14,695. For the calendar years 1990 to 1993, inclusive, the contribution rate for employers was 2.7%.

The contributions of each employer are credited to an account maintained by the State Unemployment Compensation Commission. This account is credited with contributions paid into the account by the employer and is charged with unemployment benefits that are paid from the account.

Starting January 1, 1994, the contributions rate for all employers in State H will be based on the following tax-rate schedule:

Reserve Ratio	Contributions Rate
Contributions falling below benefits paid	7.0%
0.0% to 7.9%	5.5%
8.0% to 9.9%	4.5%
10.0% to 11.9%	3.5%
12.0% to 14.9%	2.5%
15.0% or more	1.5%

The annual payroll is the total wages payable during a 12-month period ending with the last day of the third quarter of any calendar year. The average annual payroll is the average of the last three annual payrolls. The SUTA tax rate for the year is computed using the information available as of September 30 of the preceding year.

The schedule below shows the total payroll and the taxable payroll for the calendar years 1990 to 1993.

GLAVINE STEEL COMPANY

CALENDAR YEAR	1990		1991		1992		1993	
	Total Payroll	Taxable Payroll	Total Payroll	Taxable Payroll	Total Payroll	Taxable Payroll	Total Payroll	Taxable Payroll
First Quarter	$12,000	$12,000	$11,000	$11,000	$13,000	$13,000	$10,000	$10,000
Second Quarter	11,750	11,750	11,500	11,400	12,750	12,700	9,300	9,300
Third Quarter	12,500	12,250	12,750	12,400	12,200	12,000	9,350	9,350
Fourth Quarter	13,000	12,500	12,500	12,200	14,000	13,750	—	—

Unemployment benefits became payable to the company's qualified unemployed workers on January 1, 1981. Between that time and September 30, 1993, total benefits amounting to $15,100.90 were charged against the employer's account. Compute:

a. The contribution rate for 1994 ....   _____ %

b. The rate for 1994 if $2,000 additional benefits had been charged by mistake to the account of the Glavine Steel Company by the State Unemployment Compensation Commission ....   _____ %

5-17. As the accountant for the Monroe Trucking Company, you are preparing the company's annual return, Form 940. Use the following information to complete Form 940 on pages 205 and 206.

The net FUTA tax liability for each quarter of 1994 was as follows: 1st, $97; 2d, $87; 3d, $69.70; and 4th, $59.50. Since the net FUTA tax liability did not exceed $100 until the end of the 2d quarter, the company was not required to make its first deposit of FUTA taxes until August 1, 1994. The second deposit was not required until January 31, 1995. Assume that the federal tax deposit coupons (Form 8109) were completed and the deposits made on these dates.

a. State F's reporting number: 73902.
b. The Monroe Trucking Company has one employee who performs all of his duties in another state—State P. The employer's identification number for this state is 7-115180.
c. Total payments made to employees during calendar year 1994:

State F	$53,450
State P	9,100
Total	$62,550

d. Payments made to employees in excess of $7,000: $23,400.
e. Amount contributed to unemployment compensation fund of State F under merit rating, 1.8% of $32,150, or $578.70, for calendar year 1994. For State P, the contribution was 3.6% of $7,000 (the taxable salary limit), or $252.
f. Form is to be signed by Elmer P. Lear, Vice-President.

Practical Problem 5-17

Form **940**	**Employer's Annual Federal Unemployment (FUTA) Tax Return**	OMB No. 1545-0028
Department of the Treasury Internal Revenue Service	▶ For Paperwork Reduction Act Notice, see separate Instructions.	**19 94**

	T	
	FF	
	FD	
	FP	
	I	
	T	

If incorrect, make any necessary change. ▶

Name (as distinguished from trade name)   Calendar year
1994

Trade name, if any
MONROE TRUCKING COMPANY

Address and ZIP code   Employer identification number
423 BRISTOL PIKE   54-0663793
NEWTOWN, STATE F 18940-4523

A Are you required to pay unemployment contributions to only one state? . . . . ☐ Yes ☐ No

B Did you pay all state unemployment contributions by January 31, 1995? (If a 0% experience rate is granted check "Yes.") . . . . ☐ Yes ☐ No

C Were all wages that were taxable for FUTA tax also taxable for your state's unemployment tax? . . . . . ☐ Yes ☐ No

D Did you pay all wages in a state other than Michigan? . . . . ☐ Yes ☐ No

If you answered "No" to any of these questions, you must file Form 940. If you answered "Yes" to all the questions, you may file Form 940-EZ which is a simplified version of Form 940. You can get Form 940-EZ by calling 1-800-TAX-FORM (1-800-829-3676).

If you will not have to file returns in the future, check here, complete, and sign the return . . . . ▶ ☐
If this is an Amended Return, check here . . . . ▶ ☐

Part I Computation of Taxable Wages

		Amount paid			
1	Total payments (including exempt payments) during the calendar year for services of employees .			**1**	
2	Exempt payments. (Explain each exemption shown, attach additional sheets if necessary.) ▶	**2**			
3	Payments of more than $7,000 for services. Enter only amounts over the first $7,000 paid to each employee. Do not include payments from line 2. The $7,000 amount is the Federal wage base. Your state wage base may be different. **Do not use the state wage limitation**	**3**			
4	Total exempt payments (add lines 2 and 3)			**4**	
5	**Total taxable wages** (subtract line 4 from line 1) . . . . ▶			**5**	
6	Additional tax resulting from credit reduction for unpaid advances to the State of Michigan. Enter the wages included on line 5 for Michigan and multiply by .011. (See the separate Instructions for Form 940.) Enter the credit reduction amount here and in Part II, line 5: Michigan wages _____ × .011 = ... ▶			**6**	

Form **940**

Practical Problem 5-17

Form 940   Page **2**

Part II   Tax Due or Refund

1	Gross FUTA tax. Multiply the wages in Part I, line 5, by .062	1
2	Maximum credit. Multiply the wages in Part I, line 5, by .054 . . .	2	
3	Computation of tentative credit:	

(a) Name of state	(b) State reporting number(s) as shown on employer's state contribution returns	(c) Taxable payroll (as defined in state act)	(d) State experience rate		(e) State experience rate	(f) Contributions if rate had been 5.4% (col. (c) x .054)	(g) Contributions payable at experience rate (col. (c) x col. (e))	(h) Additional credit (col. (f) minus col. (g)) If 0 or less, enter 0	(i) Contributions actually paid to state
			From	To					

3a	Totals . . . ▶	
3b	Total tentative credit (add line 3a, columns (h) and (i) only—see instructions for limitations on late payments) ▶	
4	Credit: Enter the smaller of the amount in Part II, line 2, or line 3b. 4	
5	Enter the amount from Part I, line 6	5
6	Credit allowable (subtract line 5 from line 4). (If zero or less, enter 0.)	6
7	Total FUTA tax (subtract line 6 from line 1)	7
8	Total FUTA tax deposited for the year, including any overpayment applied from a prior year . .	8
9	Balance due (subtract line 8 from line 7). This should be $100 or less. Pay to the Internal Revenue Service . . . . ▶	9
10	Overpayment (subtract line 7 from line 8). Check if it is to be: ☐ **Applied to next return,** or ☐ **Refunded** . . . . ▶	10

Part III   Record of Quarterly Federal Tax Liability for Unemployment Tax *(Do not include state liability)*

Quarter	First	Second	Third	Fourth	Total for year
Liability for quarter					

Under penalties of perjury, I declare that I have examined this return, including accompanying schedules and statements, and to the best of my knowledge and belief, it is true, correct, and complete, and that no part of any payment made to a state unemployment fund claimed as a credit was or is to be deducted from the payments to employees

Signature ▶   Title (Owner, etc.) ▶   Date ▶

5-18. The information listed below refers to the employees of the Dumas Company for the year ended December 31, 1994. The wages are separated into the quarters in which they were paid to the individual employees.

DUMAS COMPANY

Name	Social Security #	1st Qtr.	2d Qtr.	3d Qtr.	4th Qtr.	Total
Robert G. Cramer	173-68-0001	$ 1,800	$ 2,000	$ 2,000	$ 2,200	$ 8,000
Daniel M. English (Foreman)	168-95-0003	3,000	3,400	3,400	3,400	13,200
Ruth A. Small	199-99-1998	2,000	2,300	2,300	2,400	9,000
Harry B. Klaus	168-75-7413	1,600	1,700	1,700	1,700	6,700
Kenneth N. George (Mgr.)	179-18-6523	3,600	4,000	4,500	5,000	17,100
Mavis R. Jones	123-45-6789	1,600	1,700	1,700	-0-	5,000
Marshall T. McCoy	131-35-3334	1,400	1,400	-0-	-0-	2,800
Bertram A. Gompers (President) ..	153-00-1014	4,500	5,000	5,500	6,300	21,300
Arthur S. Rooks ....:	171-71-7277	-0-	700	1,700	1,700	4,100
Mary R. Bastian	186-83-8111	3,000	3,200	3,200	3,200	12,600
Klaus C. Werner	143-21-2623	2,300	2,500	2,500	2,500	9,800
Kathy T. Tyler	137-36-3534	-0-	-0-	1,300	1,700	3,000
Totals		$24,800	$27,900	$29,800	$30,100	$112,600

For 1994, State D's contributions rate for the Dumas Company, based on the experience rating system of the state, was 2.8% of the first $7,000 of each employee's earnings. The state tax returns are due one month after the end of each calendar quarter. During 1994, the company paid $1,976.80 of contributions to State D's unemployment fund.

Employer's phone number: (613) 555-0029. Employer's State D reporting number: 80596.

Using the forms supplied on pages 209-212, complete the following for 1994:

a. Federal Tax Deposit Coupons—Form 8109
b. Employer's Report for Unemployment Compensation, State D—4th Quarter only
c. Employer's Annual Federal Unemployment (FUTA) Tax Return—Form 940-EZ

Indicate on each form the date that the form should be submitted and the amount of money that must be paid.

The president of the company signs all tax forms.

Practical Problem 5-18

Mark the "X" in this box only if there is a change to Employer Identification Number (EIN) or Name.

See Instructions on page 1.

AMOUNT OF DEPOSIT (Do NOT type; please print.)

DOLLARS	CENTS

EIN [53-0006421]

BANK NAME/ DATE STAMP

DUMAS COMPANY
123 SWAMP ROAD
PIKESVILLE, D STATE 10777-2017

Telephone number ( )

IRS USE ONLY

Darken only one **TYPE OF TAX**		a n d	Darken only one **TAX PERIOD**
⬭ 941	⬭ Sch. A		⬭ 1st Quarter
⬭ 990C	⬭ 1120		⬭ 2nd Quarter
⬭ 943	⬭ 990T		⬭ 3rd Quarter
⬭ 720	⬭ 990PF		⬭ 4th Quarter
⬭ CT-1	⬭ 1042		
⬭ 940			6 2

FOR BANK USE IN MICR ENCODING

Federal Tax Deposit Coupon
Form 8109

Mark the "X" in this box only if there is a change to Employer Identification Number (EIN) or Name.

See Instructions on page 1.

AMOUNT OF DEPOSIT (Do NOT type; please print.)

DOLLARS	CENTS

EIN [53-0006421]

BANK NAME/ DATE STAMP

DUMAS COMPANY
123 SWAMP ROAD
PIKESVILLE, D STATE 10777-2017

Telephone number ( )

IRS USE ONLY

Darken only one **TYPE OF TAX**		a n d	Darken only one **TAX PERIOD**
⬭ 941	⬭ Sch. A		⬭ 1st Quarter
⬭ 990C	⬭ 1120		⬭ 2nd Quarter
⬭ 943	⬭ 990T		⬭ 3rd Quarter
⬭ 720	⬭ 990PF		⬭ 4th Quarter
⬭ CT-1	⬭ 1042		
⬭ 940			6 2

FOR BANK USE IN MICR ENCODING

Federal Tax Deposit Coupon
Form 8109

Mark the "X" in this box only if there is a change to Employer Identification Number (EIN) or Name.

See Instructions on page 1.

BANK NAME/
DATE STAMP

AMOUNT OF DEPOSIT (Do NOT type; please print.)

DOLLARS | CENTS

EIN 53-0006421

DUMAS COMPANY
123 SWAMP ROAD
PIKESVILLE, D STATE 10777-2017

IRS USE ONLY

Telephone number (   )

FOR BANK USE IN MICR ENCODING

Darken only one TYPE OF TAX		a n d	Darken only one TAX PERIOD
941	Sch. A		1st Quarter
990C	1120		2nd Quarter
943	990T		3rd Quarter
720	990PF		4th Quarter
CT-1	1042		
940			62

Federal Tax Deposit Coupon
Form 8109

Mark the "X" in this box only if there is a change to Employer Identification Number (EIN) or Name.

See Instructions on page 1.

BANK NAME/
DATE STAMP

AMOUNT OF DEPOSIT (Do NOT type; please print.)

DOLLARS | CENTS

EIN 53-0006421

DUMAS COMPANY
123 SWAMP ROAD
PIKESVILLE, D STATE 10777-2017

IRS USE ONLY

Telephone number (   )

FOR BANK USE IN MICR ENCODING

Darken only one TYPE OF TAX		a n d	Darken only one TAX PERIOD
941	Sch. A		1st Quarter
990C	1120		2nd Quarter
943	990T		3rd Quarter
720	990PF		4th Quarter
CT-1	1042		
940			62

Federal Tax Deposit Coupon
Form 8109

Practical Problem 5-18

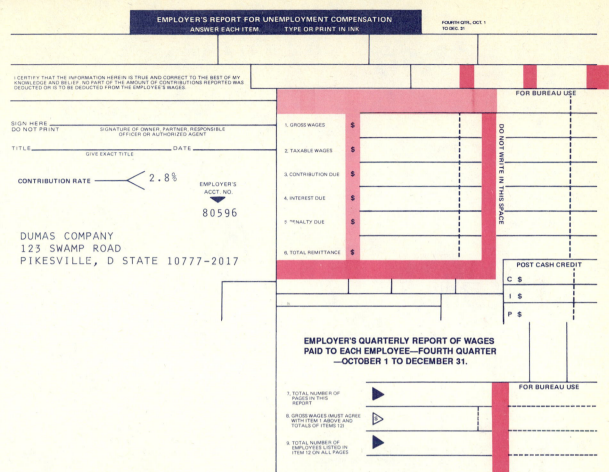

| **EMPLOYER'S REPORT FOR UNEMPLOYMENT COMPENSATION** | FOURTH QTR., OCT. 1 TO DEC. 31 |
| ANSWER EACH ITEM.   TYPE OR PRINT IN INK | |

I CERTIFY THAT THE INFORMATION HEREIN IS TRUE AND CORRECT TO THE BEST OF MY KNOWLEDGE AND BELIEF. NO PART OF THE AMOUNT OF CONTRIBUTIONS REPORTED WAS DEDUCTED OR IS TO BE DEDUCTED FROM THE EMPLOYEE'S WAGES.

FOR BUREAU USE

SIGN HERE _____
DO NOT PRINT   SIGNATURE OF OWNER, PARTNER, RESPONSIBLE OFFICER OR AUTHORIZED AGENT

TITLE _____ DATE _____
GIVE EXACT TITLE

CONTRIBUTION RATE — 2.8%

EMPLOYER'S ACCT. NO.
80596

DUMAS COMPANY
123 SWAMP ROAD
PIKESVILLE, D STATE 10777-2017

1. GROSS WAGES $
2. TAXABLE WAGES $
3. CONTRIBUTION DUE $
4. INTEREST DUE $
5. PENALTY DUE $
6. TOTAL REMITTANCE $

DO NOT WRITE IN THIS SPACE

POST CASH CREDIT
C $
I $
P $

**EMPLOYER'S QUARTERLY REPORT OF WAGES
PAID TO EACH EMPLOYEE—FOURTH QUARTER
—OCTOBER 1 TO DECEMBER 31.**

7. TOTAL NUMBER OF PAGES IN THIS REPORT ▶
8. GROSS WAGES (MUST AGREE WITH ITEM 1 ABOVE AND TOTALS OF ITEMS 12) ▷ $
9. TOTAL NUMBER OF EMPLOYEES LISTED IN ITEM 12 ON ALL PAGES ▶

FOR BUREAU USE

10. EMPLOYEE'S SOC. SEC. ACCT. NO.	11. NAME OF EMPLOYEE (TYPE OR PRINT IN INK)			12. GR. WAGES PD. THIS QTR.
	FIRST NAME	INITIAL	LAST NAME	
	TOTAL FOR THIS PAGE-------------------			

Practical Problem 5-18

Form 940-EZ

Department of the Treasury
Internal Revenue Service

Employer's Annual Federal Unemployment (FUTA) Tax Return

OMB No. 1545-1110

1994

T	
FF	
FD	
FP	
I	
T	

If incorrect, make any necessary changes. ▶

Name (as distinguished from trade name)

Trade name, if any
DUMAS COMPANY

Address and ZIP code
123 SWAMP ROAD PIKESVILLE,
D STATE 10777-2017

Calendar year
1994

Employer identification number
53-0006421

Follow the chart under **Who May Use Form 940-EZ** *on page 2. If you cannot use Form 940-EZ, you must use Form 940 instead.*

A   Enter the amount of contributions paid to your state unemployment fund. (See instructions for line A on page 4.)▶ $ ....

B   (1) Enter the name of the state where you have to pay contributions . . . . ▶ ....

   (2) Enter your state reporting number as shown on state unemployment tax return. ▶ ....

If you will not have to file returns in the future, check here (see *Who Must File*, on page 2) **complete, and sign the return** . . . . . . ▶ ☐

If this is an Amended Return check here . . . . ▶ ☐

Part I   Taxable Wages and FUTA Tax

1	Total payments (including payments shown on lines 2 and 3) during the calendar year for services of employees	1	
2	Exempt payments. (Explain all exempt payments, attaching additional sheets if necessary.) ▶		
3	Payments for services of more than $7,000. Enter only amounts over the first $7,000 paid to each employee. Do not include any exempt payments from line 2. Do not use state wage limitation. The $7,000 amount is the Federal wage base. Your state wage base may be different		
4	Total exempt payments (add lines 2 and 3)	4	
5	**Total taxable wages** (subtract line 4 from line 1) . . . . ▶	5	
6	FUTA tax. Multiply the wages on line 5 by .008 and enter here. (If the result is over $100, also complete Part II.)	6	
7	Total FUTA tax deposited for the year, including any overpayment applied from a prior year (from your records)	7	
8	**Amount you owe** (subtract line 7 from line 6). This should be $100 or less. Pay to "Internal Revenue Service" . ▶	8	
9	Overpayment (subtract line 6 from line 7). Check if it is to be: ☐ Applied to next return, or ☐ Refunded ▶	9	

Amount paid

Part II   Record of Quarterly Federal Unemployment Tax Liability (Do not include state liability.) Complete only if line 6 is over $100.

Quarter	First (Jan. 1 – Mar. 31)	Second (Apr. 1 – June 30)	Third (July 1 – Sept. 30)	Fourth (Oct. 1 – Dec. 31)	Total for year
Liability for quarter					

Under penalties of perjury, I declare that I have examined this return, including accompanying schedules and statements, and, to the best of my knowledge and belief, it is true, correct, and complete, and that no part of any payment made to a state unemployment fund claimed as a credit was, or is to be, deducted from the payments to employees.

Signature ▶   Title (Owner, etc.) ▶   Date ▶

Form **940-EZ**

✳ CONTINUING PAYROLL PROBLEM

Refer to the partially completed payroll register that you worked on at the end of Unit 4. You will now calculate the employees' SUTA contributions and the employer's liability for unemployment taxes (FUTA and SUTA) for the pay of January 14. These computations will be used at the end of Unit 6 in recording the payroll tax entries.

The employee's SUTA tax rate is 0.15% on all wages paid during the year. Record each employee's SUTA contribution in the SUTA Deductions column.

To determine the employer's liability for unemployment taxes, proceed as follows:

1. Enter each employee's gross earnings in the Taxable Earnings—FUTA and SUTA columns.
2. Total the Taxable Earnings—FUTA and SUTA columns.

3. At the bottom of your payroll register, calculate the following for the total payroll:
   a. Net FUTA tax. Since this is the first pay period of the year, none of the employees are near the $7,000 ceiling; therefore, each employee's gross earnings is subject to the FUTA tax.
   b. Since the Steimer Company is a new employer, Pennsylvania has assigned the company a contribution rate of 3.5% on the first $8,000 of each employee's earnings.

NOTE: Retain your partially completed payroll register for use at the end of Unit 6.

CASE PROBLEMS

Case 5-1   Reducing a High Unemployment Tax Rate

Over the past two years, Kermit Stone, the controller of the Hilton Company, has been concerned that the company has been paying a large amount of money for state unemployment taxes. On reviewing the "unemployment file" with the head accountant, Deborah Murtha, he learns that the company's tax rate is near the top of the range of the state's experience-rating system.

After calling the local unemployment office, Stone realizes that the turnover of employees at the Hilton Company has had an adverse effect on the company's tax rates. In addition, after consulting with Murtha, he discovers that the eligibility reports that come from the state unemployment office are just signed and sent back to the state without any review.

The eligibility reports are notices that an ex-employee has filed a claim for unemployment benefits. By signing these reports "blindly," the company, in effect, tells the state that the employee is eligible for the benefits. Any benefits paid are charged by the state against the Hilton Company's account.

Stone is convinced that the rates the company is paying are too high, and he feels that part of the reason is the "blind" signing of the eligibility reports. Besides this, he wonders what other steps the company can take to lower its contribution rate and taxes.

Submit recommendations that might help Stone reduce the "unfair" burden that the unemployment compensation taxes are leveling on the Hilton Company.

Case 5-2   Auditing Form 940-EZ

Harvey Jones, owner of the Jones Company, Inc., has completed Form 940-EZ for the year just ended, and he asks you to help him find and correct the errors that exist on the form. The tax form indicates a FUTA tax for the year of $273.92 (line 6), but the Record of Quarterly Federal Unemployment Tax Liability (Part II) shows a total of $257.92.

The information that Jones presents to you (on page 214) includes the general ledger accounts for

the FUTA and SUTA taxes payable, and the quarterly wages of his employees. He also informs you that each employee received a $500 Christmas bonus, which is included in the employees' fourth quarter totals.

Indicate the changes that should be made on Form 940-EZ, page 215, and explain to Jones the procedure that should be used to make the final FUTA tax payment.

PAYROLL INFORMATION

	First Quarter	Second Quarter	Third Quarter	Fourth Quarter		Total
Mary Foster	$ 5,200	$ 5,200	$ 5,200	-----		$15,600
Stanley Morris	-----	3,100	3,100	$ 3,600		9,800
Harvey Jones	8,600	8,600	8,600	9,100		34,900
Carson Heldt	-----	-----	2,520	3,220		5,740
Renee Butcher	-----	-----	-----	6,500		6,500
	$13,800	$16,900	$19,420	$22,420		$72,540
FUTA Taxable Wages	$12,200	$4,900	$5,620	$9,520		
FUTA Tax Rate	x .008	x .008	x .008	x .008		
FUTA Tax	$ 97.60	$39.20	$44.96	$76.16	=	$257.92

FUTA TAXES PAYABLE — Account No. 210

Date		Debit	Credit	Balance Debit	Balance Credit
19--					
Mar. 31			97.60		97.60
June 30			39.20		136.80
July 31		136.80			--------
Sept. 30			44.96		44.96
Dec. 31			76.16		121.12

SUTA TAXES PAYABLE — Account No. 220

Date		Debit	Credit	Balance Debit	Balance Credit
19--					
Mar. 31			414.80		414.80
Apr. 30		414.80			--------
June 30			166.60		166.60
July 31		166.60			--------
Sept. 30			191.08		191.08
Oct. 31		191.08			--------
Dec. 31			323.68		323.68

Form **940-EZ**

Department of the Treasury
Internal Revenue Service

**Employer's Annual Federal
Unemployment (FUTA) Tax Return**

OMB No. 1545-1110

19--

T	
FF	
FD	
FP	
I	
T	

If incorrect,
make any
necessary
changes. ▶

Name (as distinguished from trade name)

Calendar year
19--

Trade name, if any
JONES COMPANY, INC.

Address and ZIP code
121 HENDERSON DRIVE MAINVILLE,
P STATE 97133-0191

Employer identification number
53-0006429

Follow the chart under **Who May Use Form 940-EZ** on page 2. If you cannot use Form 940-EZ, you must use Form 940 instead.

A   Enter the amount of contributions paid to your state unemployment fund. (See instructions for line A on page 4.) ▶ $ 1,096 16

B   (1) Enter the name of the state where you have to pay contributions . . . . ▶ P STATE

       (2) Enter your state reporting number as shown on state unemployment tax return. ▶ 765012

If you will not have to file returns in the future, check here (see *Who Must File*, on page 2) **complete, and sign the return.** . . . . . ▶ ☐

If this is an Amended Return check here . . . . ▶ ☐

Part I   Taxable Wages and FUTA Tax

1	Total payments (including payments shown on lines 2 and 3) during the calendar year for services of employees	**1**		72,540	00
		Amount paid			
2	Exempt payments. (Explain all exempt payments, attaching additional sheets if necessary.) ▶ *CHRISTMAS BONUS PAYMENTS TO HELDT AND BUTCHER*	**2**	1,000 00		
3	Payments for services of more than $7,000. Enter only amounts over the first $7,000 paid to each employee. Do not include any exempt payments from line 2. Do not use state wage limitation. The $7,000 amount is the Federal wage base. Your state wage base may be different	**3**	37,300 00		
4	Total exempt payments (add lines 2 and 3)	**4**		38,300	00
5	**Total taxable wages** (subtract line 4 from line 1) ▶	**5**		34,240	00
6	FUTA tax. Multiply the wages on line 5 by .008 and enter here. (If the result is over $100, also complete Part II.)	**6**		273	92
7	Total FUTA tax deposited for the year, including any overpayment applied from a prior year (from your records)	**7**		136	80
8	Amount you owe (subtract line 7 from line 6). This should be $100 or less. Pay to "Internal Revenue Service" ▶	**8**		137	12
9	Overpayment (subtract line 6 from line 7). Check if it is to be: ☐ **Applied to next return, or** ☐ Refunded ▶	**9**			

Part II   Record of Quarterly Federal Unemployment Tax Liability (Do not include state liability.) Complete only if line 6 is over $100.

Quarter	First (Jan. 1 – Mar. 31)	Second (Apr. 1 – June 30)	Third (July 1 – Sept. 30)	Fourth (Oct. 1 – Dec. 31)	Total for year
Liability for quarter		136.80		121.12	257.92

Under penalties of perjury, I declare that I have examined this return, including accompanying schedules and statements, and, to the best of my knowledge and belief, it is true, correct, and complete, and that no part of any payment made to a state unemployment fund claimed as a credit was, or is to be, deducted from the payments to employees.

Signature ▶   Title (Owner, etc.) ▶   Date ▶

Form **940-EZ**

ANALYZING AND JOURNALIZING PAYROLL TRANSACTIONS

GOALS OF THIS UNIT

After completing your study of this unit, you should be able to:

1. Record payrolls in payroll registers and post to employees' earnings records.
2. Journalize the entries to record the payroll, payroll taxes, and payment of payroll-related liabilities.
3. Post to the various general ledger accounts that are used to accumulate information from the payroll entries.
4. Understand the payment and the recording of the payroll tax deposits.
5. Use the information in the payroll registers and earnings records to prepare the various reports required by government agencies.

In this unit, we shall discuss with you the procedures for recording the payroll in a payroll register and for transferring information from the payroll register to the employees' earnings records. Also, we shall analyze typical transactions pertaining to a company's payroll, record these transactions in the company's book of original entry, and post them to the proper ledger accounts.

THE PAYROLL REGISTER

As you have seen in Illustration 1-10 on page 19 and in completing the Continuing Payroll Problem, the payroll register gives detailed information about the payroll for each pay period. To summarize, the payroll register may provide the following types of information:

1. The title of the form.
2. The period covered by the payroll and the date on which the pay period ends.
3. Department or branch. Some large businesses with many departments or branches prepare a

separate sheet in the payroll register for each department or branch on each payday. Other firms provide "distribution" columns such as "Sales Salaries," "Office Salaries," and "Plant Wages" for classifying the gross wages and salaries according to the nature of the wage and salary expense. The total of each distribution column shows the total amount for that particular operating expense.
4. A column to record the name of each employee. Many businesses provide a column to record an identifying number such as the time clock number for each employee.
5. Marital status and number of withholding allowances. This information is used in determining the income tax deductions.
6. A record of time worked. Many companies show detailed information in the payroll register as to hours worked each day by each employee.
7. Some companies provide separate columns to show a total of regular hours worked and a total of overtime hours worked during the

pay period. This information may be of help in a business that schedules much overtime work.

8. The payroll register should show the regular rate of pay and the amount earned at the regular rate.

9. A space should be provided to record the overtime rate and the total earnings at the overtime rate.

10. A column should be provided to record the total earnings.

11. A section of the payroll register should provide information about deductions from total earnings. A separate column may be provided for each type of deduction. The various deductions will be discussed later in this unit.

12. A column to show the net amount paid, which is the total earnings less deductions. When wages or salaries are paid by check, a company usually provides a column for inserting the number of the check used in paying the employee.

13. Some firms provide special columns in the payroll register to indicate that portion of the employee's wages that is taxable under the Federal Insurance Contributions Act (OASDI and HI) and other laws that require payment of taxes only on wages up to the taxable limits.

The partial payroll register shown in Illustration 6-1 contains most of the information outlined above. This register is used to calculate the pay for hourly workers for a weekly pay period. The layout of the section devoted to time or hours worked will vary, depending on the payroll period and the work schedules of each individual business.

A payroll register may be a bound book with ruled sheets, or it may be a loose-leaf book with sheets to be inserted. Many companies that manufacture business forms design and produce payroll registers that are sold through stationery stores and office supply houses. Very often these forms can be adapted to meet the needs of a business without making any major change in the layout of the forms. Although some small businesses still prepare the payroll by hand, most businesses use calculating machines and computers of various sizes to process their payrolls.

Proving the Totals of the Payroll Register

As shown later in this unit, the payroll register provides the information needed in preparing the *journal entries* to record (1) the wages earned, deductions from wages, and net amount paid each payday and (2) the employer's payroll taxes. Prior to making the journal entry to record the payroll, you must check the accuracy of the amounts entered in the payroll register by proving the totals of the money columns. The partial payroll register shown in Illustration 6-1 is proved as follows:

Proof:

Regular earnings ...	$2,497.20	
Overtime earnings ..	265.50	
Total earnings		$2,762.70

PAYROLL REGISTER

FOR WEEK ENDING *January 17*   19 --

	NO.	NAME	MARITAL STATUS	NO. W/H ALLOW.	M	T	W	T	F	S	HOURS	RATE PER HOUR		AMOUNT		HOURS	RATE PER HOUR		AMOUNT	
							TIME RECORD					REGULAR EARNINGS					OVERTIME EARNINGS			
1	10	Amand, Jorge L.	M	2	8	8	8	8	8	4	40	5 20	2 0 8	00	4	7 80	3 1	20
2	12	Basile, Carole O.	M	4	8	8	8	8	10		40	7 10	2 8 4	00	2	10 65	2 1	30
3	13	Darnell, Robert T.	S	1	8	8	8	8	8		40	6 30	2 5 2	00				
4	23	Gorbus, Glen A.	M	2	8	8	8	8	8	8	40	5 90	2 3 6	00	8	8 85	7 0	80
5	24	Granger, Mary I.	S	1	8	8	8	0	8		32	5 10	1 6 3	20				
36		Totals											2 4 9 7	20			2 6 5	50

Illustration 6-1. Payroll Register (left side)

FICA tax withheld— OASDI	$ 171.29
FICA tax withheld— HI	40.06
Federal income taxes withheld	215.00
State income taxes withheld	55.25
Group insurance withheld	54.70
Total deductions	$ 536.30
Total net pay	2,226.40
Total earnings	$2,762.70

In preparing the journal entry to record a payroll, you do not need to make a separate journal entry to record the wages of each employee; instead, you make an entry each payday to record the aggregate amount of wages earned, deductions made, and net payments to all employees, as determined from the Totals line of the payroll register. Depending upon the nature of the accounting system in use, a business may record the journal entry in a two-column general journal, a cashbook, a cash payments journal, or a combined cash journal. After the journal entry has been made, you must transfer, or post, the information from the journal to the appropriate accounts in the general ledger.

Some companies use a formal *payroll journal* instead of a payroll register to record each payroll. When you record the payroll originally in a payroll journal, you post from the payroll journal to the general ledger accounts.

In most companies having computer-driven payroll systems, the payroll programs are interfaced with the general ledger programs. In these systems, the payroll entries are generated by computers into a printed journal-entry format. Then the postings to the various general ledger accounts are completed automatically from these entries.

Using the Information in the Payroll Register

In addition to serving as the source of authority for preparing journal entries to record the payroll and the employer's payroll taxes, the payroll register provides information that meets the record-keeping requirements of the Fair Labor Standards Act. Also, the payroll register provides data that are used in preparing periodic reports required by various laws.

Besides the information contained in the payroll register, businesses are required to provide information about the accumulated earnings of each employee. Therefore, it is necessary to keep a separate payroll record on each employee—the employee's earnings record. This record, which we introduced in Illustration 1-11 on page 19, is discussed in the following section.

THE EMPLOYEE'S EARNINGS RECORD

The employee's earnings record is a supplementary record that provides information for:

1. *Preparing the payroll register.* For example, the earnings record contains information such as the hourly rate, marital status, and number of withholding allowances claimed, which is

DEPT. ACCOUNTING—10

TOTAL EARNINGS	DEDUCTIONS					NET PAID		TAXABLE EARNINGS			
	FICA		FED. INCOME TAX	STATE INCOME TAX	GROUP INS.	CHECK NO.	AMOUNT	FICA		FUTA & SUTA	
	OASDI	HI						OASDI	HI		
2 3 9 20	1 4 83	3 47	4 00	4 78	9 00	898	2 0 3 12	2 3 9 20	2 3 9 20	2 3 9 20	1
3 0 5 30	1 8 93	4 43	1 00	6 11	9 00	899	2 6 5 83	3 0 5 30	3 0 5 30	3 0 5 30	2
2 5 2 00	1 5 62	3 65	2 4 00	5 04	3 90	900	1 9 9 79	2 5 2 00	2 5 2 00	2 5 2 00	3
3 0 6 80	1 9 02	4 45	1 4 00	6 14	9 00	901	2 5 4 19	3 0 6 80	3 0 6 80	3 0 6 80	4
1 6 3 20	1 0 12	2 37	1 0 00	3 26	3 90	902	1 3 3 55	1 6 3 20	1 6 3 20	1 6 3 20	5
27 6 2 70	17 1 29	4 0 06	21 5 00	5 5 25	5 4 70		22 2 6 40	27 6 2 70	27 6 2 70	27 6 2 70	36

Illustration 6-1.   Payroll Register (right side)

needed to calculate gross earnings and to determine the amount to withhold for income tax purposes.

2. *Preparing reports* required by state unemployment compensation or disability laws.

3. *Determining when the accumulated wages of an employee reach the cutoff level* for purposes of FICA (OASDI), FUTA, or SUTA. As shown in Illustration 6-2, a special "Cumulative Earnings" column is provided so that the total amount of accumulated wages can be recorded each pay period. Thus, when the FICA (OASDI), FUTA, or SUTA cutoff has been reached, the record shows that the employee or the employer no longer has a liability for that particular tax during the rest of the calendar year. (In Illustration 6-1, the FUTA and SUTA taxable wage cutoffs are the same [$7,000]. However, if there were a different cutoff for the SUTA tax, another separate column would be needed in the payroll register.)

4. *Preparing payroll analyses* for governmental agencies and for internal management control. Information such as the department in which the employee works and the job title may be used as the basis for such analyses.

5. *Settling employee grievances* regarding regular pay and overtime pay calculations and the withholding of amounts for income taxes and other purposes.

6. *Completing Forms W-2*, which show for each employee the annual gross earnings, income taxes withheld, wages subject to FICA taxes, and FICA taxes withheld.

An employee's earnings record is kept for each employee whose wages are recorded in the payroll register. Each payday, after the information has been recorded in the payroll register, the information for each employee is posted to the employee's earnings record. The columns are arranged so that the information can be transferred easily. The earnings record shown in Illustration 6-2 is arranged for weekly pay periods. You will note that totals are provided for each quarter so that you can enter information easily on the quarterly tax returns. At the bottom of page 1 of the earnings record, there is a line for semiannual totals. At the bottom of page 2 of the form, which is not illustrated, there is a line for annual totals that you will need in preparing Form 940 or Form 940-EZ and other year-end reports.

If a business pays wages once a month, the employee's earnings record would need only one line for each month, or three lines for a quarter. Similarly, if a business paid wages semimonthly, the form would have six lines for each quarter.

RECORDING THE GROSS PAYROLL AND WITHHOLDINGS

After you have recorded the payroll in the payroll register and posted to the employees' earnings records, you must enter the information in the employer's accounting system. An entry for the totals of each payroll period should be made in the general journal and posted to the general ledger. You can obtain the amounts needed for this entry from the Totals line at the bottom of the last payroll register sheet.

The following journal entry to record the payroll includes a debit to the appropriate expense account(s) for the gross payroll and credits to the various liability accounts for the withholdings from the pay and for the net amount to be paid employees:

	Debit	Credit
Salary Expense	XXX	
Liabilities (Withholdings)		XXX
Cash or Salaries Payable		
(Net Pay)		XXX
To record the payment of		
salaries and the liabilities		
for the employees' taxes		
withheld.		

Gross Payroll

You should record the total gross payroll (regular earnings and overtime earnings) as the debit portion of the payroll entry. The account to be used has a title such as *Wages Expense* or *Salaries Expense*. In the case of a company with many departments or cost centers, the accounts would have titles such as *Wages Expense—Department A*, *Wages Expense—Maintenance*, and *Wages Expense—Residential Services*. These accounts show the total gross earnings that the employer incurs as an *expense* each payday.

FICA Taxes—Employee

The employer is required by law to withhold FICA taxes of 6.2% for OASDI and 1.45% for HI of the taxable wages of each employee. Since the employer has withheld these taxes from the pay of the employees and now owes this amount to the IRS, the taxes withheld represent a *liability* of the employer. When recording the payroll, you should credit accounts entitled *FICA Taxes Payable—OASDI* and *FICA Taxes Payable—HI* for the amounts withheld.

Federal Income Taxes

Employers are required to withhold a percentage of their employees' wages for income tax purposes. We explained in Unit 4 the methods of ascertaining the amounts to be withheld from wages for income tax purposes.

EMPLOYEE'S EARNINGS RECORD

WEEK	19-- WEEK ENDING	TOTAL WORKED DAYS	TOTAL WORKED HRS.	REG. EARN. HRS.	REG. EARN. RATE	REG. EARN. AMOUNT	O.T. EARN. HRS.	O.T. EARN. RATE	O.T. EARN. AMOUNT	FICA OASDI	FICA HI	FEDERAL INCOME TAX	STATE INCOME TAX	GROUP INSURANCE	NET PAID CK. NO.	NET PAID AMOUNT	CUMULATIVE EARNINGS	TIME LOST
1	1/3	5	44	40	5 20	208 00	4	7 80	31 20	14 83	3 47	4 00	4 78	9 00	510	203 12	2239 20	
2	1/10	5	42	40	5 20	208 00	2	7 80	15 60	13 86	3 24	2 00	4 47	9 00	706	191 03	2462 80	
3	1/17	6	44	40	5 20	208 00	4	7 80	31 20	14 83	3 47	4 00	4 78	9 00	898	203 12	2702 00	
4																		
5																		
6																		
7																		
8																		
9																		
10																		
11																		
12																		
13																		
QUARTER TOTAL																		
1																		
2																		
13																		
QUARTER TOTAL																		
SEMIANNUAL TOTAL																		

SEX F	SEX M	DEPARTMENT	OCCUPATION	WORKS IN (STATE)	S.S. ACCOUNT NO.	NAME—LAST	FIRST	MIDDLE	NO. W/H ALLOW.	MARITAL STATUS
	X	A-10	Clerk-Typist	XXX	204-43-1186	Amand	Jorge	Luis	2	M

Illustration 6-2   Employee's Earnings Record (page 1)

As with FICA taxes withheld, the employer also owes to the IRS the federal income taxes withheld from the employees' pay. You should keep a separate account in the general ledger for recording the employer's *liability* for the amount of federal income taxes withheld. A suitable title for this account is *Employees Federal Income Taxes Payable*, which may be abbreviated to read *Employees FIT Payable*. The account is credited for the total amount of federal income taxes withheld each payday and is subsequently debited for the amounts paid to a depositary or to the IRS.

State and City Income Taxes

Employers may be required to withhold state and city income taxes in addition to the federal income taxes that are withheld. You should keep a separate account in the general ledger for recording the employer's *liability* for the amount of each kind of income tax withheld. Account titles that may be used are: *Employees State Income Taxes (SIT) Payable* and *Employees City Income Taxes (CIT) Payable*.

Employees' Contributions to State Funds

A few states require employees to contribute to state unemployment compensation or disability funds. In states where employee contributions are required, the employer deducts the amount of the contributions from the employees' wages at the time the wages are paid. The *liability* for employees' contributions may be recorded in the same account as the employer's contributions; namely, *SUTA Taxes Payable*. Or, a separate ledger account, such as *SUTA Taxes Payable—State A* and *SUTA Taxes Payable—State B*, may be opened for each state. If the contributions of employees are to a disability benefit fund, this amount is usually reported separately to the state and should be recorded in a separate liability account such as *Employees Disability Contributions Payable*.

Net Pay

The total of the net amount paid to the employees each payday is credited to either the *Cash* account or the *Salaries Payable* account.

RECORDING PAYROLL TAXES

In this section we shall analyze the journal entries that are made to record the *employer's* payroll taxes, each of which has been discussed in preceding units:

1. *FICA*—taxes imposed under the Federal Insurance Contributions Act for old-age, survivors, and disability insurance (OASDI) and hospital insurance (HI) benefits.

2. *FUTA*—taxes imposed under the Federal Unemployment Tax Act.

3. *SUTA*—contributions to the unemployment compensation funds of one or more states.

The following accounts will be needed in the general ledger if the employer is subject to FICA taxes, FUTA taxes, and SUTA taxes:

1. *Payroll Taxes*—an expense account in which are recorded the FICA, FUTA, and SUTA taxes on the employer.

2. *FICA Taxes Payable—OASDI*—a liability account in which is recorded the liability of the employer for the tax withheld from employees' wages plus the employer's portion of the tax.

3. *FICA Taxes Payable—HI*—a liability account in which is recorded the liability of the employer for the tax withheld from employees' wages plus the employer's portion of the tax.

4. *FUTA Taxes Payable*—a liability account showing the accumulation of the employer's federal unemployment taxes payable to the federal government.

5. *SUTA Taxes Payable*—a liability account showing the amount payable to state unemployment compensation fund(s).

The following journal entry to record the payroll taxes includes a debit to the tax expense account for the total of the employer's payroll taxes and credits to the various tax liability accounts:

	Debit	Credit
Payroll Taxes	XXX	
Liabilities (Various Taxes) . . .		XXX
To record the payroll taxes and liabilities of the employer.		

FICA Taxes—Employer

The law states specifically that deductions made from the wages of employees under FICA should be recorded immediately as liabilities on the books of the company. The law does not require that employers record their part of the FICA taxes at the time the *wages* are paid. However, in order to place the tax expense in the accounting period in which it was incurred, the common practice is to record the employer's FICA tax liabilities each payday.

The taxes withheld from the employees' wages represent liabilities of the employer. They do not constitute expenses of the employer since the employer simply withholds the amount of the taxes. However, the taxes on the employer represent both business expenses and liabilities of the employer. Because the employer's FICA contributions are a *business expense*, they are deductible by the *employer* for federal income tax purposes (as are the costs of all other payroll taxes).

SUTA Taxes

Under the state unemployment compensation laws, employers are required to pay contributions into one or more state unemployment compensation funds. When an employer is required to make contributions to the state unemployment compensation funds of more than one state, it may be advisable to keep a separate liability account for the contributions payable to each state.

FUTA Tax

An employer subject to the gross FUTA tax of 6.2% may be able to claim credit in paying the federal tax because of contributions made to state unemployment compensation funds. As discussed in Unit 5, the maximum credit that may be claimed is 5.4%, even though the amount of state contributions is more than or less than 5.4%. Thus, the net FUTA tax (6.2% - 5.4%) is .8%. Although you do not actually claim the credit against the FUTA tax until Form 940 or Form 940-EZ is filed with the Internal Revenue Service, it is acceptable accounting practice to record the FUTA tax at the net amount (.8%) at the time you make the entry to record the employer's payroll taxes.

EXAMPLE:

The employees of the Absicon Company earn wages during the year amounting to $26,400, all of which is subject to the gross FUTA tax of 6.2%. The company is also required to make contributions to the unemployment compensation fund of the state in which the business is located at the rate of 2.8% of the wages paid each employee. The federal and state unemployment taxes are computed as follows:

SUTA tax, 2.8% of $26,400 =		$739.20	
Gross FUTA tax, 6.2% of $26,400 = ...	$1,636.80		
Less credit for SUTA tax, 5.4% of $26,400 = ..	-1,425.60	211.20	(net FUTA tax)
Total unemployment taxes ..		$950.40	

More simply, the net FUTA tax may be calculated by multiplying the taxable wages, $26,400, by the net FUTA tax rate, .8%, yielding $211.20.

The recording of the employer's FUTA tax for each pay period at .8% also applies to employers who, due to their state's liability for Title XII advances, have a net FUTA tax in excess of .8%. Since the exact rate is not known until November and the payment of the penalty is not made until the last deposit of the year, the FUTA tax expense for each payroll during the year is calculated at .8%. The extra FUTA tax, due to the penalty charge, can be recorded as a single adjusting entry at the end of the year:

	Debit	Credit
Payroll Taxes	XXX	
FUTA Taxes Payable		XXX
To record the employer's penalty for the year for the state's nonpayment of Title XII advances.		

The FUTA tax, like the FICA taxes and the contributions to the state for unemployment compensation purposes, is a social security tax. Thus, the FUTA tax can be charged to the same expense account as the other payroll taxes on the employer, the Payroll Taxes account. However, since employers may be required to pay the net FUTA tax quarterly, and to pay the FICA taxes more frequently, it is advisable to keep separate liability accounts for recording these two taxes of the employer.

Entries to Record Wages and Payroll Taxes

In the following illustrations of recording (or journalizing) wages and the payroll taxes imposed under both the federal and state laws, the employer is responsible for the following taxes:

1. FICA tax—OASDI on employees: 6.2%.
2. FICA tax—HI on employees: 1.45%.
3. FIT withheld from employees.
4. FICA tax—OASDI on employers: 6.2%.
5. FICA tax—HI on employers: 1.45%.
6. Net FUTA tax: .8%.
7. SUTA tax: 2.4%.

The weekly payroll amounts to $3,200, and the entire amount is subject to all social security and unemployment taxes. You may record this information in two separate journal entries. In the first entry, you might record the wages expense of the employer and the liabilities for the FICA taxes and FIT withheld in a two-column general journal as follows:

	Debit	Credit
Wages Expense	3,200.00	
FICA Taxes Payable—OASDI		198.40
FICA Taxes Payable—HI		46.40
Employees FIT Payable		230.00
Cash		2,725.20
To record the payment of wages and the liability for the employees' FICA taxes and FIT withheld.		

We can analyze this entry in T-accounts as shown below:

WAGES EXPENSE

3,200.00	

This debit represents the employees' gross earnings for the pay period. This results in an increase in the operating expenses of the employer.

FICA TAXES PAYABLE—OASDI

	198.40

This credit results in an increase in a liability of the employer.

The amount credited to FICA Taxes Payable—OASDI is computed as follows:

6.2% of $3,200 = $198.40, amount deducted from employees' wages

FICA TAXES PAYABLE—HI

	46.40

This credit results in an increase in a liability of the employer.

The amount credited to FICA Taxes Payable—HI is computed as follows:

1.45% of $3,200 = $46.40, amount deducted from employees' wages

EMPLOYEES FIT PAYABLE

	230.00

This credit results in an increase in a liability of the employer.

The amount credited to Employees FIT Payable is obtained by using one of the withholding methods explained in Unit 4.

CASH

	2,725.20

This credit results in a decrease in an asset.

The amount credited to Cash is computed as follows:

$3,200.00, gross wages earned
-474.80, employees' taxes withheld
$2,725.20, net amount paid employees

In the second entry, you can record the employer's payroll taxes as follows:

	Debit	Credit
Payroll Taxes	347.20	
FICA Taxes Payable—OASDI		198.40
FICA Taxes Payable—HI		46.40
FUTA Taxes Payable		25.60
SUTA Taxes Payable		76.80

To record the payroll taxes and the employer's liability for the taxes.

Let's analyze this entry by means of T-accounts as shown below:

PAYROLL TAXES

347.20	

This debit results in an increase in the operating expenses.

The amount debited to Payroll Taxes is computed as follows:

6.2% of $3,200 =	$198.40,	employer's OASDI tax
1.45% of $3,200 =	46.40,	employer's HI tax
.8% of $3,200 =	25.60,	employer's net FUTA tax
2.4% of $3,200 =	76.80,	employer's SUTA tax
Total payroll taxes	$347.20	

FICA TAXES PAYABLE—OASDI

	198.40
	198.40

The second credit amount, representing the employer's OASDI tax, also increases the employer's liability. The amount is determined as shown in the computation of the payroll taxes.

FICA TAXES PAYABLE—HI

	46.40
	46.40

The second credit amount, representing the employer's HI tax, also increases the employer's liability. The amount is determined as shown in the computation of the payroll taxes.

FUTA TAXES PAYABLE

	25.60
	This credit results in an increase in a liability of the employer. The amount is determined as shown in the computation of the payroll taxes.

SUTA TAXES PAYABLE

	76.80
	This credit results in an increase in a liability of the employer. The amount is determined as shown in the computation of the payroll taxes.

In the preceding illustration no contributions were required of employees for state unemployment compensation purposes. Assume that the employees had been required to make contributions of 1% to state unemployment compensation funds. The payroll entry would then appear as follows:

	Debit	Credit
Wages Expense	3,200.00	
FICA Taxes Payable—OASDI		198.40
FICA Taxes Payable—HI . . .		46.40
Employees FIT Payable		230.00
SUTA Taxes Payable		32.00
Cash		2,693.20

To record the payment of wages and the liability for the employees' FICA, FIT, and SUTA taxes withheld.

In a small company with few employees, you can calculate the hours worked, determine net pay, and prepare the paychecks or pay envelopes in a relatively short period of time. For such companies, a journal entry wherein you directly credit the cash account for the total net pay is a logical, efficient procedure.

In larger companies, however, the calculation of hours worked, the determination of net pay, and the preparation of paychecks may extend over the greater part of a workday, or even longer. In such companies because of the workload involved in meeting each payroll, especially when the paychecks must be mailed to far-flung branch offices, the paychecks may be prepared several days in advance of their actual distribution to the workers. Further, the preparation of the workers' paychecks may occur in one accounting period, although the actual payment is made in the following accounting period. Thus, to show an accurate picture of the firm's liability for the payroll, at the time of recording the payroll the net pay is accrued and credited to a liability account such as Salaries Payable or Accrued Salaries Payable, instead of to the cash account. Later, when the paychecks are given to the workers, an entry is made to record the payment of the payroll. In this entry the liability account Salaries Payable is debited and the cash account is credited.

RECORDING WORKERS' COMPENSATION INSURANCE EXPENSE

As we indicated in Unit 1, most states have passed laws that require employers to provide workers' compensation insurance to protect their employees against losses due to injury or death incurred during employment. The expense account, *Workers' Compensation Insurance Expense,* can be used to record the premiums paid by the company to provide this coverage.

Usually the employer estimates and pays the premium in advance. The insurance premium, often based upon the total gross payroll of the business, may be stated in terms of an amount for each $100 of weekly wages paid to employees. At the end of the year, all the payrolls are audited and the company pays an additional premium or receives credit for an overpayment. Since the premium rate varies with the hazard involved in the work performed, your personnel and payroll records should provide for a careful classification of employees by kind or grade of work and a summary of labor costs according to the insurance premium classifications.

EXAMPLE:

In the McMahon Company there are only two different grades of work—office clerical and machine shop. The premium rates for 1994 are $.18 per $100 of payroll for the office clerical workers, and $2.90 per $100 of payroll for the machine-shop workers. Based upon past experience and budgetary projections for 1994, the company estimates its annual premium to be $8,900 and sends a check for that amount to the insurance carrier at the beginning of the year. The entry to record this transaction is:

Workers' Compensation Insurance Expense	8,900.00	
Cash		8,900.00

The effect of this entry, when posted to the ledger accounts, is an increase in the operating expenses of the company and a decrease in the assets.

At the end of 1994 the payrolls for the year are audited and analyzed and the current rates are applied to determine the actual premium as follows:

Work Grade	Total Payroll	Rate per $100	Premium
Office clerical ...	$ 81,000	$ .18	$ 145.80
Machine shop ...	312,000	2.90	9,048.00
Total	$393,000		$9,193.80
Less estimated premium paid in January ..			8,900.00
Balance due...........................			$ 293.80

A check is written for the balance due the insurance company, and the following entry is made in the journal:

Workers' Compensation		
Insurance Expense	293.80	
Cash...................		293.80

Professional Tip

An effective way to reduce workers' compensation costs is for employers to assist their disabled workers in finding jobs which they are capable of performing despite a work-related injury. As long as the job offer is made in good faith (and not just to avoid payment of benefits), the employee must accept the job offer.

RECORDING THE DEPOSIT OR PAYMENT OF PAYROLL TAXES

The journal entries required to record the deposit or payment of FICA taxes and income taxes withheld and the payment of FUTA and SUTA taxes are explained below.

Depositing FICA Taxes and Federal Income Taxes Withheld

As was explained to you in Unit 3, the requirements for depositing FICA taxes and federal income taxes withheld from employees' wages vary in relation to the total volume of such taxes.

EXAMPLE:

On April 15, the ledger accounts FICA Taxes Payable—OASDI, FICA Taxes Payable—HI, and Employees FIT Payable of the Nannan Company appear as follows:

FICA TAXES PAYABLE—OASDI

	4/15	697.07
	4/15	697.07
		1,394.14

FICA TAXES PAYABLE—HI

	4/15	163.02
	4/15	163.02
		326.04

EMPLOYEES FIT PAYABLE

	4/15	1,601.19

The company is required to complete Form 8109 and to deposit the FICA and the federal income taxes. The following journal entry is made to record this deposit:

FICA Taxes Payable—OASDI .	1,394.14	
FICA Taxes Payable—HI	326.04	
Employees FIT Payable	1,601.19	
Cash		3,321.37

When this entry is posted, the debits of $1,394.14 and $326.04 to FICA Taxes Payable—OASDI and FICA Taxes Payable—HI remove the liabilities for the employer's share, as well as the employees' share, of the FICA taxes imposed. The debit of $1,601.19 to Employees FIT Payable removes the liability for the total amount of federal income taxes withheld from the employees' wages during the period. The credit of $3,321.37 to the cash account reduces the assets of the company.

Paying State or City Income Taxes

When the employer turns over to the state or to the city the amount of income taxes withheld from employees' wages, the appropriate journal entry would be recorded as follows:

	Debit	Credit
Employees SIT Payable	XXX	
or		
Employees CIT Payable	XXX	
Cash		XXX

Paying FUTA and SUTA Taxes

At the time of completing Form 8109 and depositing the FUTA taxes that have accumulated during the preceding calendar quarter, an entry is made as follows:

	Debit	Credit
FUTA Taxes Payable	XXX	
Cash		XXX

Employers subject to the net FUTA tax plus a penalty for Title XII advances (see Unit 5, pages 180-181) must make an adjusting entry prior to the last payment of the FUTA tax for the year. Since the amount of the penalty is not known until the fourth quarter, the penalty has not yet been recorded as a payroll tax expense. Therefore, an adjusting entry is made on

December 31 to record the expense and the liability. This liability will be paid in January, in addition to the payment for the fourth quarter net FUTA tax.

The quarterly payment of state unemployment contributions is recorded as follows:

	Debit	Credit
SUTA Taxes Payable	XXX	
Cash		XXX

RECORDING END-OF-PERIOD ADJUSTMENTS

In most cases, the end of the fiscal (accounting) period does not coincide with the end of the payroll period. Therefore, adjustments are commonly made to record the end-of-period wages and accrued vacation pay.

Wages

To record the adjustment for end-of-period wages, the wages for this last payroll period must be split between the fiscal period just ending (accrued wages) and the fiscal period just beginning. For instance, if the fiscal period ends on Wednesday and the employees are paid every Friday, the wages earned by the employees on Monday, Tuesday, and Wednesday are an expense of the fiscal period just ended. However, the wages earned on Thursday and Friday (payday) are an expense of the new fiscal period.

In order to record the wage expense properly for the fiscal period ended, an adjusting entry must be made on the last day of the fiscal period. However, since there is no actual wage payment, there is no need to credit any withholding accounts. The credit part of the entry is made to a single liability account for the total wage expense. In the case above, the wage expenses of Monday, Tuesday, and Wednesday would be recorded in the following adjusting entry:

	Debit	Credit
Wages Expense	XXX	
Wages Payable		XXX
To record wages incurred but unpaid as of the end of the fiscal period.		

In a situation where the employer holds back one week's pay (earnings for the current week are not paid until the following Friday), the adjusting entry for the example shown above would be for eight days (one full week plus Monday, Tuesday, and Wednesday).

Vacation Pay

Another adjustment required at the end of the accounting period concerns vacation pay. If a company has a vacation policy, the employees earn the right for paid future absences during the current period. Therefore, a liability should be accrued at the end of the current period. Whether the adjustment is made each payday, each month, or each year, the expense must be recorded when the liability is created, not necessarily in the period in which it is paid.

EXAMPLE:

The employees of the Dansly Company are entitled to one day's vacation for each month worked. The average daily pay for each of the 50 employees is $130. The adjusting entry to record the vacation expense of $6,500 ($130 x 50) at the end of each month is:

Vacation Benefits Expense . . .	6,500.00	
Vacation Benefits Payable .		6,500.00

When employees eventually use their vacation time, the payment is recorded by debiting Vacation Benefits Payable, not Wages Expense. This expense was previously recorded in the adjusting entry, as shown above.

Adjusting entries of this type are also required for postretirement benefits such as health care and pension. These benefits must be reported as expenses during the employees' working years when the entitlements are earned.

RECORDING TRANSACTIONS PERTAINING TO OTHER PAYROLL DEDUCTIONS

Up to this point in our discussion of deductions that are made from wages and salaries, we have been limited to FICA taxes, state unemployment contributions, and income taxes. However, most companies have other deductions that must be taken into consideration when the payroll is prepared. Regardless of the number of deductions or the types of deductions that are made from employees' wages, we must provide a systematic means of keeping a record of the total wages for each employee, the deductions for each purpose, and the net amount paid. It is impossible to say that a certain type of record is satisfactory for every organization or even for each company doing a certain kind of business. Each business organization has its own problems and peculiarities that will affect the type of record needed. It is important, therefore, that we keep all the records required by law, as well as those needed for other purposes.

Although it is usually advisable to have a separate column in the payroll register for each deduction, the payroll register may become too cumbersome if there are too many columns for deductions. In many businesses, therefore, it is common practice to use a payroll register with a separate column for each of the major deductions, and to lump all other deductions together in one column headed "Other Deductions." Some companies use only one column for deductions and place the entire total in that column. If this practice is followed, it is usually necessary to have a supplementary record of deductions showing a detailed breakdown of the total for each employee. This supplementary record is then used as the basis for obtaining the figure for total deductions shown in the payroll register.

The deductions for FICA taxes, income taxes, disability benefits, and state unemployment benefits are required by law. Most other payroll deductions are the result of company policies, collective bargaining agreements, or court orders. Some of the purposes for which deductions may be made are:

1. Group insurance.
2. Health insurance.
3. Purchase of government bonds.
4. Union dues.
5. Garnishment of wages.
6. Pension and retirement benefits.

Group Insurance

Many companies have a group insurance program for employees. Such programs usually permit employees to obtain life insurance at a much lower rate than would be possible if the employee purchased the insurance as an individual. Under some group insurance plans, the employer and the employee share the cost of the insurance premium. The employees' share may be deducted from their wages every payday, every month, or every quarter.

When recording a payroll in which deductions are made from employees' wages for group insurance, the amount withheld from their wages is applied toward the payment of their share of the premium. The total amount withheld is recorded as a credit to a *liability* account with a title such as *Group Insurance Premiums Collected* or *Group Insurance Payments Withheld*. This general ledger account serves the same purpose as the accounts used to record payroll taxes withheld from employees' wages.

Health Insurance

Many companies have developed their own health insurance plans for employees, or are members of private insurance groups that provide coverage for employees of companies that are members of the group. If employees bear the cost or a portion of the cost of such insurance, the portion paid by the employees is usually deducted every payday, monthly, or quarterly from the wages of the employees. (This voluntary form of insurance protection should in no way be confused with the health insurance program for the aged. The latter program, Medicare, is discussed in Appendix A.)

The amounts withheld from the employees' wages for health insurance are credited to a *liability* account such as *Health Insurance Premiums Collected*. Employers often pay the premium for health insurance in advance to the insurance carrier. At the time of paying the premium, a prepaid expense account such as *Prepaid Health Insurance* is debited for the amount paid the carrier. Periodically this account is adjusted through the health insurance or fringe benefit expense account.

Purchase of Government Savings Bonds

Employees are encouraged to invest a certain amount of their wages in government savings bonds. Such plans or similar savings plans encourage employees to save a certain amount of each salary payment. The theory behind such deductions is that most employees will not miss a small amount that is set aside each payday, and over a period of time the deductions accumulate into a sizable amount.

Employees authorize their employer to make payroll deductions for the purchase of savings bonds by completing authorization forms that indicate how much is to be withheld and how frequently. The amounts that are withheld from the paychecks are set aside by the employer, acting in a trustee position, until a sufficient amount is available for the purchase of savings bonds for the employees. The minimum denomination for Series EE savings bonds for new participants in a payroll savings plan is $100. A $100 bond can be purchased as soon as the participant has accumulated the $50 purchase price in his or her withholding account.

EXAMPLE:

Wayne Richards has authorized his employer to withhold $10 from his pay every two weeks toward the purchase of a Series EE U.S. savings bond, which has a maturity value of $100. At the time of preparing each biweekly payroll, the employer credits the *liability* account *U.S. Savings Bonds Deductions Payable* for $10. After the employer has recorded five similar entries, the balance of the liability account will be $50, the amount required for the purchase of one $100 Series EE U.S. savings bond. At this time the employer purchases the bond, which is later delivered to the employee. The journal entry to record this transaction includes a debit of $50 to the liability account *U.S. Savings Bonds Deductions Payable* and a corresponding credit to the cash account.

Union Dues

In companies in which employees are members of unions that require employees to pay dues to the union, many employees pay their dues, assessments, and initiation fees through deductions from wages. This withholding of union dues from employees' wages by the employer is known as a *check-off system*.

Amounts withheld from union members' wages are credited to a *liability* account such as *Union Dues Payable*. Monthly, or as agreed upon by the union and the employer, the amounts withheld are turned over to the treasurer of the union. At this time a journal entry is made in which the payment of union dues is recorded by debiting the liability account and crediting the cash account.

Garnishment of Wages

Garnishment refers to the legal or equitable procedure by means of which a portion of the wages of any person is required to be withheld for payment of a debt. Through the garnishment process, a creditor, with the aid of the courts, may require the employer to hold back a portion of the debtor's wages and pay that amount to the court or to the creditor. In some companies the amounts to be held back are deducted each payday from the employee's wages.

NEWS ALERT NEWS ALERT NEWS ALERT

Under the Family Support Act, by 1994 all states must permit child-support garnishment from the beginning of the support payments. In the past, some states garnished wages for child support only after the parent had fallen behind in payments.

Under the Consumer Credit Protection Act, the amount of wages subject to garnishment is in general limited to 25% of a worker's disposable earnings. *Disposable earnings* are the earnings remaining after withholding for income taxes and for other amounts required by law. (In cases of support orders, the limits on the amounts that can be taken from an employee's pay range from 50% to 65% of weekly disposable wages, depending on the employee's number of dependents.)

The provisions of the Consumer Credit Protection Act also prohibit an employer from discharging an employee simply because the employee's wages are subject to garnishment for one indebtedness. If another garnishment for a second indebtedness should arise, the worker could be discharged, provided a considerable amount of time had *not* elapsed between the two occasions of indebtedness. It is possible that the lapse of time could make the first garnishment immaterial. The payroll manager should also be aware that state garnishment laws that are more favorable to employees have priority over the federal law.

Pension and Retirement Benefits

Since in many instances social security benefits are inadequate for retired employees and their dependents, many firms provide pension and retirement plans that will supplement the government benefits. Although the benefit formulas and eligibility rules vary, the coverage is about the same for production workers, office employees, and managers. Many pension plans are financed solely by employer contributions, but other plans involve employee contributions. Once these contributions are deducted from the employees' pay, they become a liability for the employer and are recorded as such in the payroll entry.

Some employers also provide their employees with the opportunity to set up their own Individual Retirement Accounts (IRA) through a payroll deduction plan (see page 8). These voluntary contributions are deducted from the paychecks of the employees who desire to set up their own retirement accounts. These deductions are recorded as a liability in the payroll entry. This liability account will be cleared as the employer pays the contributions to the financial institution that is in charge of each employee's retirement account.

SUMMARY OF ACCOUNTS USED IN RECORDING PAYROLL TRANSACTIONS

The following listing summarizes some of the general ledger accounts that may be used to record payroll transactions:

1. *Wages and Salaries*—an operating expense account in which the gross payroll is recorded.

2. *Payroll Taxes*—an operating expense account in which are recorded all payroll taxes on the employer under FICA, FUTA, and the various state unemployment compensation laws.

3. *Workers' Compensation Insurance Expense*—an operating expense account in which are recorded the premiums paid by the company to provide coverage for employees against employment-related injury or death.

4. *Vacation Benefits Expense*—an operating expense account in which are recorded the costs of the vacation time that has been earned by employees.

5. *FICA Taxes Payable—OASDI*—a current liability account in which are recorded deductions made from employees' wages for OASDI taxes. When the liability for the employer's portion of the OASDI tax is recorded, the amount may also be credited to this account.

6. *FICA Taxes Payable—HI*—a current liability account in which are recorded deductions made from employees' wages for HI taxes. When the liability for the employer's portion of the HI tax is recorded, the amount may also be credited to this account.

7. *FUTA Taxes Payable*—a current liability account in which is recorded the employer's federal unemployment taxes.

8. *SUTA Taxes Payable*—a current liability account in which are recorded the amounts due the states for the employer's unemployment compensation contributions. This account may also be credited for amounts deducted from employees' wages, if employees are required to contribute to state unemployment compensation funds.

9. *Employees FIT Payable*—a current liability account in which are recorded deductions made from employees' wages for federal income taxes.

10. *Employees SIT Payable*—a current liability account in which are recorded deductions made from employees' wages for state income taxes.

11. *Health Insurance Premiums Collected*—a current liability account in which are recorded deductions made from employees' wages for their share of the premiums paid for health insurance coverage.

12. *Union Dues Payable*—a current liability account in which are recorded the deductions made from union members' wages for their union dues, assessments, or initiation fees.

13. *Wages Payable*—a current liability account in which are recorded the wages that have been earned by employees but not yet paid to them.

14. *Vacation Benefits Payable*—a current liability account in which are recorded the costs of vacation time that has been earned by employees but not yet used.

ILLUSTRATIVE CASE

The following illustrative case shows the accounting procedures used by the Brookins Company in recording payroll transactions during the third quarter of its fiscal year. The fiscal year of the company ends on June 30, 1994. Employees are paid semimonthly on the 15th and the last day of the month. When the 15th or the last day of the month falls on Saturday or Sunday, employees are paid on the preceding Friday.

On January 1, 1994, the balances of the accounts used in recording payroll transactions are as shown below. These account balances are shown in the general ledger on pages 235 and 236.

Acct. No.	Account Title	Account Balance
11	Cash	$85,000.00
20	FICA Taxes Payable—OASDI	734.29
21	FICA Taxes Payable—HI	171.73
22	FUTA Taxes Payable	122.00
23	SUTA Taxes Payable	40.50
25	Employees FIT Payable	1,472.00
26	Employees SIT Payable	474.42
28	Union Dues Payable	80.00
51	Wages and Salaries	46,500.00
55	Payroll Taxes	4,254.50

The first $59,700 in wages and salaries paid is subject to the OASDI tax on both the employer (6.2%) and the employees (6.2%). The total wages and salaries paid are subject to the HI tax on both the employer (1.45%) and the employees (1.45%). The employer is also subject to a net FUTA tax of .8%, based on the first $7,000 in earnings paid each employee during a calendar year; and a SUTA tax of 2.3%, based on the first $7,000 in earnings paid during a calendar year. The state does not require contributions of employees for unemployment compensation or disability insurance.

The wage-bracket method is used to determine the amount of federal income taxes to be withheld from the employees' earnings. The state income tax law requires that a graduated percentage of the gross earnings of each employee be withheld each payday. Under the check-off system, union dues are withheld each payday from the union workers, who are employed in the plant. On or before the fourth of each month the dues collected during the preceding month are turned over to the treasurer of the union.

In the following narrative of transactions, the January 14 payroll transaction is explained in detail at the bottom of page 231. All other transactions are stated briefly. Adjacent to the narrative are the journal entries to record the transactions. The ledger accounts showing the transactions posted are on pages 235 and 236.

NARRATIVE OF TRANSACTIONS	JOURNAL	P.R.	Debit	Credit
	1994			
Jan. 4. Paid the treasurer of the union $80, representing the union dues withheld from the workers' earnings during the month of December.	Jan. 4 Union Dues Payable	28	80.00	
	Cash	11		80.00
	To record the payment of the union dues withheld during December, 1993.			
Jan. 14. Paid total wages and salaries of all employees, $3,890. All the earnings are taxable under FICA. In addition to the social security taxes, the company withheld $455 from the employees' earnings for federal income taxes, $85.58 for state income taxes, and $45 for union dues. (See the explanation of the January 14 payroll transaction given at the bottom of this page.)	14 Wages and Salaries	51	3,890.00	
	FICA Taxes Payable—OASDI	20		241.18
	FICA Taxes Payable—HI	21		56.41
	Employees FIT Payable	25		455.00
	Employees SIT Payable	26		85.58
	Union Dues Payable	28		45.00
	Cash	11		3,006.83
	To record the payment of wages and the liabilities for the employees' taxes withheld.			
Jan. 14. Recorded the employer's payroll taxes for the first pay in January. All the earnings are taxable under FICA, FUTA, and SUTA.	14 Payroll Taxes	55	418.18	
	FICA Taxes Payable—OASDI	20		241.18
	FICA Taxes Payable—HI	21		56.41
	FUTA Taxes Payable	22		31.12
	SUTA Taxes Payable	23		89.47
	To record the payroll taxes and liabilities of the employer.			
Jan. 18. Completed Form 8109 and deposited with a Federal Reserve bank the FICA taxes and employees' federal income taxes withheld on the two December, 1993, payrolls. At the end of December the total liability for FICA taxes and federal income taxes withheld was $2,378.02. (January 17 is Martin Luther King, Jr.'s birthday, which is a bank holiday.)	18 FICA Taxes Payable—OASDI	20	734.29	
	FICA Taxes Payable—HI	21	171.73	
	Employees FIT Payable	25	1,472.00	
	Cash	11		2,378.02
	To record the deposit of FICA taxes and federal income taxes withheld for the December 15 and 31, 1993, payrolls.			

The analysis of the January 14 payroll transaction follows:

1. Wages and Salaries is debited for $3,890, the total of the employees' gross earnings.
2. FICA Taxes Payable—OASDI is credited for $241.18, the amount withheld from the employees' earnings for OASDI taxes.
3. FICA Taxes Payable—HI is credited for $56.41, the amount withheld from the employees' earnings for HI taxes.
4. Employees FIT Payable is credited for $455, the amount withheld from employees' earnings for federal income tax purposes.
5. Employees SIT Payable is credited for $85.58, the amount withheld from employees' earnings for state income taxes.
6. Union Dues Payable is credited for $45, the amount withheld from union members' earnings.
7. Cash is credited for $3,006.83, the net amount paid the employees ($3,890 gross earnings − $241.18 OASDI − $56.41 HI − $455 FIT − $85.58 SIT − $45 union dues).

8. Payroll Taxes is debited for $418.18, the amount of taxes imposed on the employer under FICA, FUTA, and SUTA. The computation of the total payroll taxes is:

FICA—OASDI:	6.2% of $3,890 =	$241.18
FICA—HI:	1.45% of $3,890 =	56.41
FUTA:	.8% of $3,890 =	31.12
SUTA:	2.3% of $3,890 =	89.47
Total payroll taxes		$418.18

9. FICA Taxes Payable—OASDI is credited for the amount of tax on the employer, which is 6.2% of $3,890, or $241.18.
10. FICA Taxes Payable—HI is credited for the amount of tax on the employer, which is 1.45% of $3,890, or $56.41.
11. FUTA Taxes Payable is credited for $31.12, the liability incurred because of the taxes imposed on the employer under FUTA.
12. SUTA Taxes Payable is credited for $89.47, the amount of the contributions payable to the state.

NARRATIVE OF TRANSACTIONS

JOURNAL

PAGE *15*

			P.R.	Debit	Credit

1994

Jan. 18. Paid the treasurer of the state $474.42, representing the amount of state income taxes withheld from the workers' earnings during the last quarter of 1993.

			P.R.	Debit	Credit
Jan.	18	Employees SIT Payable	26	474.42	
		Cash	11		474.42
		To record the payment of the state income taxes withheld during the fourth quarter of 1993.			

Jan. 31. Paid total wages and salaries, $4,100. All of this amount constitutes taxable earnings under FICA. Withheld $483 for federal income taxes, $90.20 for state income taxes, and $45 for union dues

			P.R.	Debit	Credit
	31	Wages and Salaries	51	4,100.00	
		FICA Taxes Payable—OASDI	20		254.20
		FICA Taxes Payable—HI	21		59.45
		Employees FIT Payable	25		483.00
		Employees SIT Payable	26		90.20
		Union Dues Payable	28		45.00
		Cash	11		3,168.15
		To record the payment of wages and the liabilities for the employees' taxes withheld.			

Jan. 31. Recorded the employer's payroll taxes for this payroll. All the earnings are taxable under FICA, FUTA, and SUTA.

			P.R.	Debit	Credit
	31	Payroll Taxes	55	440.75	
		FICA Taxes Payable—OASDI	20		254.20
		FICA Taxes Payable—HI	21		59.45
		FUTA Taxes Payable	22		32.80
		SUTA Taxes Payable	23		94.30
		To record the payroll taxes and liabilities of the employer.			

Jan. 31. Completed Form 8109 and deposited $122 with a Federal Reserve bank to remove the liability for FUTA taxes for the fourth quarter, 1993.

			P.R.	Debit	Credit
	31	FUTA Taxes Payable	22	122.00	
		Cash	11		122.00
		To record the deposit of FUTA taxes for the fourth quarter of 1993.			

Jan. 31. Filed the state unemployment contributions return for the quarter ending December 31, 1993, and paid $40.50 to the state unemployment compensation fund.

			P.R.	Debit	Credit
	31	SUTA Taxes Payable	23	40.50	
		Cash	11		40.50
		To record payment of contributions to state unemployment compensation fund for the fourth quarter of 1993.			

Jan. 31. Filed the Employer's Annual Federal Unemployment (FUTA) Tax Return, Form 940-EZ, for the preceding calendar year. No journal entry is required since the 1993 liability for FUTA taxes was removed by the timely deposit on January 31, 1994. No taxes were paid at the time of filing the annual return.

Jan. 31. Filed the quarterly return (Form 941) with the IRS Center for the period ended December 31, 1993. No journal entry is required since the 1993 liability for FICA taxes and employees' federal income taxes withheld was removed by the timely deposit on January 18, 1994. No taxes were paid or deposited at the time of filing Form 941.

Feb. 4. Paid the treasurer of the union $90, representing the union dues withheld from the workers' earnings during the month of January.

			P.R.	Debit	Credit
Feb.	4	Union Dues Payable	28	90.00	
		Cash	11		90.00
		To record the payment of the union dues withheld during January, 1994.			

NARRATIVE OF TRANSACTIONS	JOURNAL		PAGE 16	
		P.R.	Debit	Credit

NARRATIVE OF TRANSACTIONS	JOURNAL	P.R.	Debit	Credit
	1994			
Feb. 15. Paid total wages and salaries, $4,000. All of this amount is taxable under FICA. Withheld $470 for federal income taxes, $88 or state income taxes, and $45 for union dues.	Feb.　15　Wages and Salaries	51	4,000.00	
	FICA Taxes Payable—OASDI	20		248.00
	FICA Taxes Payable—HI	21		58.00
	Employees FIT Payable	25		470.00
	Employees SIT Payable	26		88.00
	Union Dues Payable	28		45.00
	Cash	11		3,091.00
	To record the payment of wages and the liabilities for the employees' taxes withheld.			
Feb. 15. Recorded the employer's payroll taxes. All the earnings are taxable under FICA, FUTA, and SUTA.	15　Payroll Taxes	55	430.00	
	FICA Taxes Payable—OASDI	20		248.00
	FICA Taxes Payable—HI	21		58.00
	FUTA Taxes Payable	22		32.00
	SUTA Taxes Payable	23		92.00
	To record the payroll taxes and liabilities of the employer.			
Feb. 15. Completed Form 8109 and deposited $2,160.48 with a Federal Reserve bank to remove the liability for the FICA taxes and the employees' federal income taxes withheld on the January 14 and January 31 payrolls.	15　FICA Taxes Payable—OASDI	20	990.76	
	FICA Taxes Payable—HI	21	231.72	
	Employees FIT Payable	25	938.00	
	Cash	11		2,160.48
	To record the deposit of FICA taxes and federal income taxes withheld for the January 14 and January 31, 1994, payrolls.			
Feb. 28. Paid total wages and salaries, $4,250. All of this amount is taxable under FICA. Withheld $502 for federal income taxes, $93.50 for state income taxes, and $50 for union dues.	28　Wages and Salaries	51	4,250.00	
	FICA Taxes Payable—OASDI	20		263.50
	FICA Taxes Payable—HI	21		61.63
	Employees FIT Payable	25		502.00
	Employees SIT Payable	26		93.50
	Union Dues Payable	28		50.00
	Cash	11		3,279.37
	To record the payment of wages and the liabilities for the employees' taxes withheld.			
Feb. 28. Recorded the employer's payroll taxes. All the earnings are taxable under FICA, FUTA, and SUTA.	28　Payroll Taxes	55	456.88	
	FICA Taxes Payable—OASDI	20		263.50
	FICA Taxes Payable—HI	21		61.63
	FUTA Taxes Payable	22		34.00
	SUTA Taxes Payable	23		97.75
	To record the payroll taxes and liabilities of the employer.			
Mar. 4. Paid the treasurer of the union $95, representing the union dues withheld from the workers' earnings during the month of February.	Mar.　4　Union Dues Payable	28	95.00	
	Cash	11		95.00
	To record the payment of the union dues withheld during February, 1994.			
Mar. 15. Paid total wages and salaries, $4,300. All of this amount is taxable under FICA. Withheld $554 for federal income taxes, $94.60 for state income taxes, and $50 for union dues.	15　Wages and Salaries	51	4,300	
	FICA Taxes Payable—OASDI	20		266.60
	FICA Taxes Payable—HI	21		62.35
	Employees FIT Payable	25		554.00
	Employees SIT Payable	26		94.60
	Union Dues Payable	28		50.00
	Cash	11		3,272.45
	To record the payment of wages and the liabilities for the employees' taxes withheld.			

GENERAL LEDGER

UNION DUES PAYABLE   28

Date	Item	P.R.	Dr.	Cr.	Balance Dr.	Balance Cr.
1994						
Jan. 1	Bal.	√				80.00
4		J15	80.00			-------------
14		J15		45.00		45.00
31		J15		45.00		90.00
Feb. 4		J15	90.00			-------------
15		J16		45.00		45.00
28		J16		50.00		95.00
Mar. 4		J16	95.00			-------------
15		J16		50.00		50.00
31		J17		50.00		100.00

WAGES AND SALARIES   51

Date	Item	P.R.	Dr.	Cr.	Balance Dr.	Balance Cr.
1994						
Jan. 1	Bal.	√			46,500.00	
14		J15	3,890.00		50,390.00	
31		J15	4,100.00		54,490.00	
Feb. 15		J16	4,000.00		58,490.00	
28		J16	4,250.00		62,740.00	
Mar. 15		J16	4,300.00		67,040.00	
31		J17	4,320.00		71,360.00	

PAYROLL TAXES   55

Date	Item	P.R.	Dr.	Cr.	Balance Dr.	Balance Cr.
1994						
Jan. 1	Bal.	√			4,254.50	
14		J15	418.18		4,672.68	
31		J15	440.75		5,113.43	
Feb. 15		J16	430.00		5,543.43	
28		J16	456.88		6,000.31	
Mar. 15		J17	462.25		6,462.56	
31		J17	464.40		6,926.96	

GLOSSARY

Business expense—cost of operating a business that is deductible by the employer for federal income tax purposes.

Check-off system—withholding of union dues from employees' wages by the employer.

Disposable earnings—the earnings remaining after withholding for income taxes and for other amounts required by law.

Garnishment—legal or equitable procedure by means of which a portion of the wages of any person is required to be withheld for payment of a debt.

Group insurance—life insurance program for employees at a low cost.

Journal entry—a transaction recorded in the accounting system of a business.

Payroll journal—book of original entry used for recording each payroll transaction and as the source for posting to appropriate general ledger accounts.

QUESTIONS FOR REVIEW

1. What are the main kinds of information contained in a payroll register?
2. For what reason are "distribution" columns sometimes provided in the payroll register?
3. Explain how to prove the accuracy of the totals of the payroll register.
4. What are the primary uses of the information contained in the payroll register?
5. Which payroll record is used by the employer in completing Forms W-2?
6. Explain the use of the "Cumulative" column in the employee's earnings record.
7. In Philadelphia, Pennsylvania, most workers are subject to three income taxes upon their earnings—federal, state, and city. Should an employer in Philadelphia record the liability for the withholding of all three income taxes in one liability account such as Income Taxes Payable?
8. What effect does the recording of the employer's portion of the FICA taxes have on the accounts in the general ledger?
9. When is it necessary to provide the account, Employees Disability Contributions Payable?
10. What special accounts must usually be opened in the general ledger to record payroll tax entries?
11. Does the recording of the social security taxes imposed on employers represent an increase or a decrease in owner's equity?
12. May the employer's FICA, FUTA, and SUTA taxes be deducted from gross income when the employer's federal income tax return is prepared?
13. Is it necessary for an employer who is subject to FICA and FUTA taxes to keep a separate expense account for the taxes under each act?
14. What is the effect of each of the following postings upon the assets, liabilities, and owner's equity of a company?
    a. A debit to Wages.
    b. A credit to FICA Taxes Payable—HI.
    c. A debit to SUTA Taxes Payable.
    d. A credit to Cash.
15. Why is it necessary to classify employees by kind of work performed when calculating the cost of workers' compensation insurance?
16. What accounts are debited and credited when an employer records the deposit of FICA taxes and federal income taxes that have been withheld?
17. Does the payment of the social security taxes withheld from employees' wages represent an increase or a decrease in owner's equity?
18. When are expenses of benefits such as vacation pay and retirement pay recorded? Explain.
19. Along with five payroll deductions required by law (FICA—OASDI and HI, Employees FIT, Employees SIT, and Employees CIT), five other deductions are typically made from the employees' earnings in the Cranston Company. What methods are available to the company in recording these ten deductions in the payroll register?
20. What journal entry is made at the time an employer turns over to the union treasurer the union dues that have been withheld under a check-off system?
21. What is meant by the *garnishment* of wages?

QUESTIONS FOR DISCUSSION

1. In what respect does an employee's earnings record resemble a ledger?
2. The Golic Corporation has undertaken a cost study of its operations. One area of concern to the company is the total cost of labor, particularly the cost of employee benefits. Prepare a list of the different kinds of costs that a company might incur as part of its "total package" salary cost.
3. A company subject to FICA taxes prepares a balance sheet at the end of each month. Which of the 12 monthly balance sheets will show liabilities for FICA taxes?
4. a. On which financial statement will a debit balance in the payroll taxes account appear?
   b. How should this account balance be classified on this financial statement?
5. Assume that an account is kept for Employees FIT Payable.
   a. On which financial statement will the account balance appear?
   b. How should the account balance be classified on this financial statement?

Date _____   Name _____

PRACTICAL PROBLEMS

Omit the writing of explanations for the journal entries.

6-1. a. An employer, Gail Winters, is subject to FICA taxes but exempt from FUTA and SUTA taxes. During the last quarter of the year, her employees earned monthly wages of $8,500, all of which is taxable. The amount of federal income taxes withheld each month is $1,040. Journalize the payment of wages and record the payroll tax on November 30.

JOURNAL

	DATE		DESCRIPTION	POST. REF.	DEBIT	CREDIT	
1							1
2							2
3							3
4							4
5							5
6							6
7							7
8							8
9							9
10							10

b. Prior to posting the November 30 payroll transaction, there were zero balances in the FICA Taxes Payable—OASDI, the FICA Taxes Payable—HI, and the Employees FIT Payable accounts. Winters is required to deposit with a Federal Reserve bank the FICA taxes and income taxes withheld on the November 30 payroll. Journalize the deposit of the payroll taxes on December 15.

JOURNAL

	DATE		DESCRIPTION	POST. REF.	DEBIT	CREDIT	
1							1
2							2
3							3
4							4
5							5
6							6

6-2. The employees of the Morton Music Company earn total wages of $4,690 during January. The total amount is taxable under FICA, FUTA, and SUTA. The state contribution rate for the company is 3.6%. The amount withheld for federal income taxes is $685. Journalize the payment of the monthly wages and record the payroll taxes.

JOURNAL

	DATE	DESCRIPTION	POST. REF.	DEBIT	CREDIT	
1						1
2						2
3						3
4						4
5						5
6						6
7						7
8						8
9						9
10						10
11						11

6-3. Tex, Inc., has a semimonthly payroll of $38,000 on May 15. The total payroll is taxable under FICA Taxes—HI, $32,850 is taxable under FICA Taxes—OASDI, and $29,300 is taxable under FUTA and SUTA. The state contribution rate for the company is 3.1%. The amount withheld for federal income taxes is $5,780. The amount withheld for state income taxes is $809. Journalize the payment of the wages and record the payroll taxes on May 15.

JOURNAL

	DATE	DESCRIPTION	POST. REF.	DEBIT	CREDIT	
1						1
2						2
3						3
4						4
5						5
6						6
7						7
8						8
9						9
10						10
11						11
12						12

6-4. Refer to Problem 6-3. Assume that the employees of Tex, Inc., are also required to pay state contributions (disability insurance) of 1% on the taxable payroll of $29,300, and that the employees' contributions are to be deducted by the employer. Journalize the May 15 payment of wages and record the payroll taxes, assuming that the state contributions of the employer and the employees are kept in separate accounts.

JOURNAL

	DATE		DESCRIPTION	POST. REF.	DEBIT	CREDIT	
1							1
2							2
3							3
4							4
5							5
6							6
7							7
8							8
9							9
10							10
11							11
12							12
13							13
14							14
15							15

6-5. The employees of the Pelter Company earn wages of $12,000 for the two weeks ending April 20. The entire amount of wages is subject to the FICA taxes, but only $9,800 is taxable under the federal and state unemployment compensation laws. The state contribution rate of the employer is 2.9%. Journalize the payment of the wages and record the payroll taxes on April 20. (Ignore employee income tax in this problem.)

JOURNAL

	DATE	DESCRIPTION	POST. REF.	DEBIT	CREDIT	
1						1
2						2
3						3
4						4
5						5
6						6
7						7
8						8
9						9
10						10
11						11

6-6. Refer to Problem 6-5. Assume that all employees are subject to state unemployment contributions of .5% on the taxable wages of $9,800, and that the employees' contributions are to be deducted by the employer. Journalize the payment of the wages and record the payroll taxes, assuming that the contributions of the employer and the employees are recorded in one account, SUTA Taxes Payable.

JOURNAL

	DATE	DESCRIPTION	POST. REF.	DEBIT	CREDIT	
1						1
2						2
3						3
4						4
5						5
6						6
7						7
8						8
9						9
10						10
11						11
12						12

6-7. The following information pertains to the payroll of the Furphy Textile Company on June 1:

a.   The total wages earned by employees are $2,180.
b.   The state unemployment insurance contribution rate is 2.5%.
c.   The entire amount of wages is taxable under FICA, FUTA, and SUTA.
d.   The amount withheld from the employees' wages for federal income taxes is $309; for state income taxes, $43.10; and for group insurance, $16.80.

Journalize the payment of wages and record the payroll taxes on June 1.

JOURNAL

	DATE	DESCRIPTION	POST. REF.	DEBIT	CREDIT	
1						1
2						2
3						3
4						4
5						5
6						6
7						7
8						8
9						9
10						10
11						11
12						12
13						13
14						14
15						15

6-8. On December 30, 1994, the Reuter Company has a balance of $98.75 in the FUTA Taxes Payable account. This represents the employer's liability for the fourth quarter taxes. Journalize the entry the Reuter Company should make in January, 1995, to record the last deposit of FUTA taxes for 1994.

JOURNAL

	DATE		DESCRIPTION	POST. REF.	DEBIT	CREDIT	
1							1
2							2
3							3
4							4
5							5
6							6

6-9. On December 30, 1994, the Mayes Company has a balance of $134.95 in the FUTA Taxes Payable account, which represents their liability for the fourth quarter taxes. However, the Mayes Company is an employer in a state where employers are liable for a penalty of .6% for Title XII advances. The company has not recorded any of the penalty during the year.

Journalize the adjusting entry to be made on December 31 (the total taxable payroll for FUTA for the year was $212,500), and also the entry to deposit the FUTA taxes on January 31, 1995.

JOURNAL

	DATE		DESCRIPTION	POST. REF.	DEBIT	CREDIT	
1							1
2							2
3							3
4							4
5							5
6							6

6-10. In Oregon, employers who are covered by the state Workers' Compensation Law must withhold employee contributions from the wages of covered employees at the rate of 14¢ for each day or part of a day that the worker is employed. Every covered employer is assessed 14¢ per day for each worker employed for each day or part of a day. The employer-employee contributions for workers' compensation are collected monthly, quarterly, or annually by the employer's insurance carrier, according to a schedule agreed upon by the employer and the carrier. The insurance carrier remits the contributions to the state's Workers' Compensation Department.

The Brunansky Company, a covered employer in Oregon, turns over the employer-employee workers' compensation contributions to its insurance carrier by the 15th of each month for the preceding month. During the month of July the number of full employee-days worked by the company's employees was 3,110; the number of part-time employee-days was 364.

a. The amount the company should have withheld from its full-time and part-time employees during the month of July for workers' compensation insurance is ... $_____

b. The title you would give to the general ledger account to which the amount withheld from the employees' earnings would be credited is:

c. Journalize the entry on July 31 to record the employer's liability for workers' compensation insurance for the month.

JOURNAL

	DATE	DESCRIPTION	POST. REF.	DEBIT	CREDIT	
1						1
2						2
3						3
4						4
5						5

d. Journalize the entry on August 15 to record payment to the insurance carrier of the amount withheld from the employees' earnings for workers' compensation insurance and the amount of the employer's liability.

JOURNAL

	DATE	DESCRIPTION	POST. REF.	DEBIT	CREDIT	
1						1
2						2
3						3
4						4
5						5

6-11. On the form on page 247 are the amounts that appear in the Earnings to Date column of the employees' earnings records for 10 workers in the Unger Company. These amounts represent the cumulative taxable earnings for each worker as of October 18, the company's last payday. The gross amount of earnings to be paid each worker on the next payday, October 25, is also given on the form.

In the state where the Unger Company is located, the tax rates and bases are as follows:

Tax on Employees:

FICA—OASDI	6.2% on first $59,700
FICA—HI	1.45% on *total earnings*
SUTA	.5% on first $8,000

Tax on Employer:

FICA—OASDI	6.2% on first $59,700
FICA—HI	1.45% on *total earnings*
FUTA	.8% on first $7,000
SUTA	1.8% on first $8,000

In the appropriate columns of the form on page 247, do the following:

1. Calculate the amount to be withheld from each employee's earnings on October 25 for (a) FICA—OASDI, (b) FICA—HI, and (c) SUTA, and determine the total employee taxes.
2. Record the portion of each employee's earnings that is taxable under FICA, FUTA, and SUTA and calculate the total employer's payroll taxes on the October 25 payroll.

Practical Problem 6-11

THE UNGER COMPANY

Employee	Earnings to Date	Gross Earnings Oct. 25	Taxes to Be Withheld from Employees' Earnings Under FICA OASDI	HI	SUTA	Employer Taxes Portion of Employees' Earnings Taxable Under FICA OASDI	HI	FUTA	SUTA
1. Weiser, Robert A.	$58,990	$790							
2. Stankard, Laurie C.	14,950	295							
3. Grow, Joan L.	4,060	240							
4. Rowe, Paul C.	8,190	235							
5. Mc Namara, Joyce M.	7,460	195							
6. O'Connor, Roger T.	59,410	810							
7. Carson, Ronald B.	8,905	280							
8. Kenny, Ginni C.	4,325	175							
9. Devery, Virginia S.	57,010	590							
10. Wilson, Joe W.	3,615	205							
Total Employee Taxes			$ 1.(a)	$ 1.(b)	$ 1.(c)				
Total Taxable Earnings						$	$	$	$
X Applicable Tax Rate									
Totals						$	$	$	$
Total Payroll Taxes							$ _____		2.

247

6-12. In the Illustrative Case in this unit, payroll transactions for the Brookins Company were analyzed, journalized, and posted for the third quarter of the fiscal year. In this problem you are to record the payroll transactions for the last quarter of the firm's fiscal year. The last quarter begins on April 1, 1994.

Refer to the Illustrative Case on pages 230 to 236 and proceed as follows:

a. Analyze and journalize the transactions described in the following narrative. Use the two-column journal paper provided on pages 251 to 254. Omit the writing of explanations in the journal entries.

b. Post the journal entries to the general ledger accounts on pages 255 to 260.

Narrative of Transactions:

April 1. Paid the treasurer of the union the amount of union dues withheld from workers' earnings during March.

15. Payroll: $6,105. All wages and salaries taxable. Withheld $565 for federal income taxes, $107.32 for state income taxes, and $50 for union dues.

15. Paid the treasurer of the state the amount of state income taxes withheld from workers' earnings during the first quarter of 1994.

15. Completed Form 8109 and deposited funds in a Federal Reserve bank to remove the liability for FICA taxes and employees' federal income taxes withheld on the March payrolls.

29. Payroll: $5,850. All wages and salaries taxable. Withheld $509 for federal income taxes, $128.90 for state income taxes, and $55 for union dues.

29. Filed the Employer's Quarterly Federal Tax Return (Form 941) for the period ended March 31. No journal entry is required since the FICA taxes and federal income taxes withheld have been timely deposited in a Federal Reserve bank.

29. Completed the quarterly deposit (Form 8109) for the period ended March 31 and deposited the FUTA taxes in a Federal Reserve bank.

29. Filed the state contribution return for the quarter ended March 31 and paid the amount to the state unemployment compensation fund.

May 2. Paid the treasurer of the union the amount of union dues withheld from workers' earnings during April.

13. Payroll: $5,810. All wages and salaries taxable. Withheld $507 for federal income taxes, $125.05 for state income taxes, and $55 for union dues.

16. Completed Form 8109 and deposited funds with a Federal Reserve bank to remove the liability for FICA taxes and federal income taxes withheld on the April payrolls.

31. Payroll: $6,060. All wages and salaries taxable. Withheld $533 for federal income taxes, $119.00 for state income taxes, and $50 for union dues.

June 3. Paid the treasurer of the union the amount of union dues withheld from workers' earnings during May.

15. Payroll: $6,380. All wages and salaries taxable, except only $5,000 is taxable under FUTA and SUTA. Withheld $549 for federal income taxes, $128.70 for state income taxes, and $50 for union dues.

15. Completed Form 8109 and deposited funds with a Federal Reserve bank to remove the liability for FICA taxes and federal income taxes withheld on the May payrolls.

30. Payroll: $6,250. All wages and salaries taxable, except only $4,770 is taxable under FUTA and SUTA. Withheld $538 for federal income taxes, $127.60 for state income taxes, and $50 for union dues.

c. Answer the following questions:

(1) The total amount of the liability for FICA taxes and federal income taxes withheld as of June 30 is . . . . $_____

(2) The total amount of the liability for state income taxes withheld as of June 30 is . . . . $_____

(3) The amount of FUTA taxes that must be paid to the federal government on or before August 1, 1994 is . . . . $_____

(4) The amount of contributions that must be paid into the state unemployment compensation fund on or before August 1, 1994 is . . . . $_____

(5) The total amount due the treasurer of the union is . . . . $_____

(6) The total amount of wages and salaries expense since the beginning of the fiscal year is . . . . $_____

(7) The total amount of payroll taxes expense since the beginning of the fiscal year is . . . . $_____

(8) Using the partial journal below, journalize the entry to record the vacation accrual at the end of the company's fiscal year. The amount of the Brookins Company's vacation accrual for the fiscal year is $15,000.

JOURNAL

	DATE	DESCRIPTION	POST. REF.	DEBIT	CREDIT	
1						1
2						2
3						3
4						4
5						5
6						6

Date _____   Name _____

Practical Problem 6-12

	DATE		DESCRIPTION	POST. REF.	DEBIT	CREDIT	
1							1
2							2
3							3
4							4
5							5
6							6
7							7
8							8
9							9
10							10
11							11
12							12
13							13
14							14
15							15
16							16
17							17
18							18
19							19
20							20
21							21
22							22
23							23
24							24
25							25
26							26
27							27
28							28
29							29
30							30
31							31
32							32
33							33
34							34

JOURNAL

	DATE		DESCRIPTION	POST. REF.	DEBIT	CREDIT	
1							1
2							2
3							3
4							4
5							5
6							6
7							7
8							8
9							9
10							10
11							11
12							12
13							13
14							14
15							15
16							16
17							17
18							18
19							19
20							20
21							21
22							22
23							23
24							24
25							25
26							26
27							27
28							28
29							29
30							30
31							31
32							32
33							33
34							34

Practical Problem 6-12

JOURNAL

	DATE		DESCRIPTION	POST. REF.	DEBIT	CREDIT	
1							1
2							2
3							3
4							4
5							5
6							6
7							7
8							8
9							9
10							10
11							11
12							12
13							13
14							14
15							15
16							16
17							17
18							18
19							19
20							20
21							21
22							22
23							23
24							24
25							25
26							26
27							27
28							28
29							29
30							30
31							31
32							32
33							33
34							34

JOURNAL

	DATE		DESCRIPTION	POST. REF.	DEBIT	CREDIT	
1							1
2							2
3							3
4							4
5							5
6							6
7							7
8							8
9							9
10							10
11							11
12							12
13							13
14							14
15							15
16							16
17							17
18							18
19							19
20							20
21							21
22							22
23							23
24							24
25							25
26							26
27							27
28							28
29							29
30							30
31							31
32							32
33							33
34							34

Date _____   Name _____

Practical Problem 6-12

CASH

DATE		ITEM	POST. REF.	DEBIT	CREDIT	BALANCE	
						DEBIT	CREDIT
1994 Apr.	1	Balance	√			5 8 2 3 3 04	

Practical Problem 6-12

FICA TAXES PAYABLE—OASDI ACCOUNT NO. 20

DATE	ITEM	POST. REF.	DEBIT	CREDIT	BALANCE	
					DEBIT	CREDIT
1994 Apr. 1	Balance	√				1 0 6 8 88

Practical Problem 6-12

| ACCOUNT | FICA TAXES PAYABLE—HI | | ACCOUNT NO. 21 |

DATE		ITEM	POST. REF.	DEBIT	CREDIT	BALANCE DEBIT	BALANCE CREDIT
1994 Apr.	1	Balance	√				2 4 9 98

Practical Problem 6-12

ACCOUNT   **FUTA TAXES PAYABLE**   ACCOUNT NO. 22

DATE		ITEM	POST. REF.	DEBIT	CREDIT	BALANCE	
						DEBIT	CREDIT
1994 Apr.	1	Balance	√				1 9 8 88

ACCOUNT   **SUTA TAXES PAYABLE**   ACCOUNT NO. 23

DATE		ITEM	POST. REF.	DEBIT	CREDIT	BALANCE	
						DEBIT	CREDIT
1994 Apr.	1	Balance	√				5 7 1 78

Practical Problem 6-12

ACCOUNT **EMPLOYEES FIT PAYABLE** ACCOUNT NO. 25

DATE	ITEM	POST. REF.	DEBIT	CREDIT	BALANCE DEBIT	BALANCE CREDIT
1994 Apr. 1	Balance	√				1 1 2 4 00

ACCOUNT **EMPLOYEES SIT PAYABLE** ACCOUNT NO. 26

DATE	ITEM	POST. REF.	DEBIT	CREDIT	BALANCE DEBIT	BALANCE CREDIT
1994 Apr. 1	Balance	√				5 4 6 92

Practical Problem 6-12

ACCOUNT   **UNION DUES PAYABLE**   ACCOUNT NO. 28

DATE		ITEM	POST. REF.	DEBIT	CREDIT	BALANCE	
						DEBIT	CREDIT
1994 Apr.	1	Balance	√				1 0 0 00

ACCOUNT   **WAGES AND SALARIES**   ACCOUNT NO. 51

DATE		ITEM	POST. REF.	DEBIT	CREDIT	BALANCE	
						DEBIT	CREDIT
1994 Apr.	1	Balance	√			7 1 3 6 0 00	

ACCOUNT   **PAYROLL TAXES**   ACCOUNT NO. 55

DATE		ITEM	POST. REF.	DEBIT	CREDIT	BALANCE	
						DEBIT	CREDIT
1994 Apr.	1	Balance	√			6 9 2 6 96	

✳ CONTINUING PAYROLL PROBLEM

In this last phase of your work on the Continuing Payroll Problem, you will record the amounts withheld for group insurance and health insurance and calculate the net pay for each employee. Refer to the partially completed payroll register upon which you were working at the end of Unit 5 and proceed as follows:

(1) In the appropriate column of the payroll register, record the amount to be withheld for group life insurance. Each employee contributes 85¢ each week toward the cost of group insurance coverage, with the exception of McGarry and Porth, who are not yet eligible for coverage under the company plan.

(2) Record the amount to be withheld for health insurance. Each employee contributes $1.65 each week toward the cost of health insurance.

(3) Record the net pay for each employee. The net pay for each employee is obtained by subtracting the total amount of all deductions from the total earnings.

(4) Each worker is to be paid by check. Assign check numbers commencing with No. 313.

(5) Foot all money columns of the payroll register and prove the accuracy of the column totals.

(6) On a separate sheet of paper:
(a) Prepare the journal entries as of January 12 to record the payroll and the payroll taxes for the week ending January 7. Credit Salaries Payable for the total net pay.

Use the following tax rates and bases: employer's FICA—OASDI, 6.2% on the first $59,700; employer's FICA—HI, 1.45% on total earnings; FUTA, .8% on the first $7,000; and SUTA, 3.5% on the first $8,000.
(b) Prepare the journal entry to record the payment of the payroll on January 14, when the paychecks are distributed to all workers.

Your work on the Continuing Payroll Problem is now completed and you may be asked to submit your payroll register to your instructor. The experience you have gained in working on each of the succeeding phases of the Continuing Payroll Problem will aid you in undertaking the payroll work involved in Unit 7. In Unit 7, the Comprehensive Payroll Project, you will be responsible for all aspects of payroll operations for a company for an entire calendar quarter.

CASE PROBLEMS

Case 6-1   How to Meet the Need for Temporary Help

The Zettek Electronics Company is a small manufacturer that has been in operation for several years. During its existence, the company has maintained a core of approximately 60 assembly-line personnel. This work force has been able to complete all contracts without the need for additional employees. Periodically, when a rush order or a large-volume contract is received, the company is able to have the staff work overtime without employing additional personnel.

Recently, the company has secured a lucrative contract that will last approximately three months. Management feels that the present employees can complete the job, but to do so will require the use of extensive overtime. Mark Cramer, the Controller, has become concerned about the high cost of overtime for these types of contracts. He is presently evaluating other solutions to the company's short-term labor needs.

One alternative approach would be to hire about 20 temporary employees. These employees would work for the duration of the contract (three months) and then be terminated. When future contracts are obtained, the individuals could be rehired.

Cramer is also considering the use of Expert Help, Inc., a company that supplies temporary help. The people supplied are the employees of Expert Help, Inc., who pays their wages and all the taxes on the wages. The Zettek Company will be charged a set fee for each hour worked by each person supplied. The cost per hour is approximately 30% more than the comparable cost of hiring temporary help as employees of the Zettek Company.

The present method of working the staff overtime to meet the company's needs has not been ruled out. The four shop supervisors have met with Cramer and recommended that this method be continued.

As Controller of the Zettek Electronics Company, evaluate the three alternatives, analyzing the advantages and disadvantages of each.

Case 6-2 Budgeting for Fringe Benefits

Frank Flynn is the payroll manager for the Powlus Supply Company. During the budgeting process, Sam Kinder, the Director of Finance, has asked Flynn to arrive at a set percentage that could be applied to each budgeted salary figure to cover the fringe benefits cost that will be incurred by the Powlus Company for each employee.

After some discussion, it was determined that the best way to calculate this percentage would be to base the fringe benefits cost on the average salary paid by the company.

Kinder wants this fringe benefits percentage to cover payroll taxes (FICA, FUTA, and SUTA) and other benefits costs covered by the company (workers' compensation expense, health insurance costs, and vacation pay).

Flynn gathers the following information in order to complete the analysis:

Average annual salary	$24,000
FICA rates	6.2% and 1.45%
FUTA	0.8% on 1st $7,000
SUTA	3.3% on 1st $10,400
Workers' compensation costs	$.97 per $100 of payroll
Health insurance costs	$75.15 per month
Vacation pay earned	2 weeks' pay earned each year to be used in following year.

Calculate the percentage that can be used in the budget.

PAYROLL PROJECT

GOALS OF THIS UNIT

Unit 7 consists of a simulation, or practice set, for payroll accounting. After completing this unit, you will have applied the knowledge acquired in this course to practical payroll situations. This unit is a culmination of the information presented in the textbook.

After completing the simulation, you will have experienced the following:

1. Preparing payroll registers.
2. Maintaining employees' earnings records.
3. Journalizing and posting payroll and payroll tax entries.
4. Completing federal, state, and city tax deposit forms and journalizing the transactions.
5. Preparing various quarter-end and year-end payroll tax forms.
6. Making the accrual entry for the payroll at the end of a year.

The Payroll Project is designed to provide you with extended practice in keeping payroll records and accounting for payroll transactions. Your completion of this project involves an application of the information learned in the preceding units. The work provided is similar to that prevailing in the office of every employer in the United States who is subject to the provisions of the federal wage and hour law, income tax withholding laws, the social security laws, and the unemployment compensation laws.

In many large businesses with hundreds or thousands of employees, payroll records are often kept as subsidiary records of the general ledger accounts. Under such a system, the totals in the payroll ledger are transferred to the general ledger control account when the books are closed at the end of the fiscal period. The purpose of this course is to acquaint you with the effect of payroll transactions upon the general accounting records, as well as to present the details of recording payroll transactions. Therefore, general ledger accounts, rather than subsidiary pay-roll ledger accounts, will be used for all payroll transactions.

In this project you are employed by the Glo-Brite Paint Company. As the payroll clerk in the accounting department, you have been in charge of the payroll records since the company first began operations on January 5 of the current year. The company employs about 800 individuals; but for the purpose of this project, payroll records will be kept for only a dozen or so employees. This will avoid duplication and detailed work from which no additional learning experience would be gained. By understanding the principles of payroll accounting for a few employees, you should be able to keep similar records for several hundred employees since the principles involved are the same.

For purposes of this project, you will assume that the payroll records, tax reports, and deposits have been completed and filed for the first three quarters of this year. Your work will involve the processing of the payrolls for the last quarter of the year and the completion of the last quarterly and annual tax reports and forms.

BOOKS OF ACCOUNT AND PAYROLL RECORDS

The books of account and payroll records that you will use in this project are described below.

Journal

You will use a two-column general journal to record all transactions affecting the accounts in the general ledger. This book of original entry serves as a posting medium for transactions affecting the payroll accounts.

General Ledger

A general ledger is used in keeping the payroll accounts. The ledger is ruled with balance-column ruling, which makes it possible to keep a continuous record of each account balance. Some of the ledger accounts will have beginning balances that were carried over from the first three quarters of the year.

The following chart of accounts has been used in opening the general ledger accounts on pages 289 to 296. The Glo-Brite Paint Company has other accounts in its general ledger, but those listed in the partial chart of accounts are the only accounts required in completing this project.

PARTIAL CHART OF ACCOUNTS

ACCOUNT TITLE	ACCOUNT NO.
Cash	11
Payroll Cash	12
FICA Taxes Payable—OASDI	20.1
FICA Taxes Payable—HI	20.2
FUTA Taxes Payable	21
SUTA Taxes Payable	22
Employees SUTA Payable	23
Employees FIT Payable	24
Employees SIT Payable	25
Employees CIT Payable	26
Group Insurance Premiums Collected	27
Union Dues Payable	28
Administrative Salaries	51
Office Salaries	52
Sales Salaries	53
Plant Wages	54
Payroll Taxes	56

Payroll Register

The payroll register provides the information that is needed for journalizing each payroll and for posting to the employees' earnings records.

Employee's Earnings Record

The employee's earnings record provides a summary of each employee's earnings, deductions, and taxable wages. The information to be recorded in this record is posted from the payroll register.

From the personnel data given at the top of the next page, an employee's earnings record has been maintained for each employee on pages 298 to 304. On the first line of each of these records, the employee's cumulative figures for the first three quarters of the year are shown. Note that only one-half page has been used for each employee's earnings record. In actual practice, however, both sides of a complete sheet would be used for the same employee.

GENERAL INFORMATION

The home office and the manufacturing plant of the Glo-Brite Paint Company are located at 2215 Salvador Street, Philadelphia, PA 19175-0682. The company's federal identification number is 31-0450660; the state identifying number is 46-3-3300; the city identifying number is 501-6791855.

Regular Hours of Work

The workweek for all employees is 40 hours. The office is open from 8:00 a.m. to 5:00 p.m. each day, except weekends. One hour is allowed for lunch, 12:00 p.m. to 1:00 p.m.

The plant operates on a five-day workweek of eight hours per day. The normal working hours in the plant are from 7:00 a.m. to 11:00 a.m. and 12:00 p.m. to 4:00 p.m.

Overtime

All employees except the president, the sales manager, sales representatives, and supervisors are paid *time and a half* for any overtime exceeding 40 hours a week.

Workers in the plant are paid *time and a half* for any hours worked over eight each workday. The overtime rate for any work scheduled on Saturdays, Sundays, or holidays is *twice* the regular hourly rate of pay.

Timekeeping

All office and plant employees, except the president, the sales manager, sales representatives, and supervisors, are required to ring in and out daily on a time clock. Those employees who ring in and out are required to notify the time clerk of the reason for lost time. (This information is required under the unemployment compensation laws of some states.) The time clerk prepares a weekly report of the hours worked by each employee.

PERSONNEL DATA—October 1, 19—

BONNO, Anthony Victor, 694 Bristol Avenue, Philadelphia, PA 19135-0617. Married, claiming 4 withholding allowances. Telephone, 555-9827. Social Security No. 537-10-3481. Position, mixer operator in Plant. Wages, $7.65 per hour. Group insurance, $24,000.

FERGUSON, James Claude, 808 Sixth Street, Philadelphia, PA 19106-0995. Married, claiming 5 withholding allowances. Telephone, 555-8065. Social Security No. 486-03-8645. Position, sales manager. Salary, $32,500 per year. Group insurance, $49,000. Department: Sales.

FORD, Catherine Louise, 18 Dundee Avenue, Philadelphia, PA 19151-1919. Divorced, claiming 2 withholding allowances. Telephone, 555-0235. Social Security No. 213-09-4567. Position, executive secretary. Salary, $975 per month. Group insurance, $18,000. Department: Office.

MANN, Dewey Wilson, 3007 Bisque Drive, Philadelphia, PA 19199-0718. Married, claiming 4 withholding allowances. Telephone, 555-0774. Social Security No. 282-37-9352. Position, sales representative. Salary, $1,950 per month. Group insurance, $35,000. Department: Sales.

O'NEILL, Joseph Tyler, 2100 Broad Street, Philadelphia, PA 19121-7189. Married, claiming 3 withholding allowances. Telephone, 555-2332. Social Security No. 897-04-1534. Position, president. Salary, $60,000 per year. Group insurance, $90,000. Department: Administrative.

RUSSELL, Virginia Aloise, 8004 Dowling Road, Philadelphia, PA 19135-9001. Single, claiming 1 withholding allowance. Telephone, 555-3681. Social Security No. 314-21-6337. Position, time clerk. Salary, $845 per month. Group insurance, $15,000. Department: Office.

RYAN, Norman Allen, 7300 Harrison Street, Philadelphia, PA 19124-6699. Married, claiming 4 withholding allowances. Telephone, 555-6660. Social Security No. 526-23-1223. Position, electrician in Plant. Wages, $9.80 per hour. Group insurance, $31,000.

SOKOWSKI, Thomas James, 133 Cornwells Street, Philadelphia, PA 19171-5718. Married, claiming 2 withholding allowances. Telephone, 555-5136. Social Security No. 662-04-8832. Position, supervisor in Plant. Salary, $450 per week. Group insurance, $35,000.

STUDENT, 7018 Erdrick Street, Philadelphia, PA 19135-8517. Single, claiming 1 withholding allowance. Position, accounting trainee. Salary, $650 per month. Group insurance, $12,000. Department: Office.

WILLIAMS, Ruth Virginia, 9433 State Street, Philadelphia, PA 19149-0819. Single, claiming 0 withholding allowances. Telephone, 555-5845. Social Security No. 518-30-6741. Position, programmer. Salary, $1,235 per month. Group insurance, $22,000. Department: Office.

Payday

Employees are paid biweekly on Friday. The first payday in the fourth quarter is Friday, October 9.

Since the weekly time clerk's report is not finished until the Monday following the end of each week, the first pay (October 9) will be for the two weeks, September 20—26 and September 27—October 3. The company, in effect, holds back one week's pay. This policy applies to all employees. The next payday (October 23) will cover the days worked in the weeks ending October 10 and October 17.

Payroll Taxes—Contributions and Withholdings

Payroll taxes are levied upon the Glo-Brite Paint Company and its employees as shown at the top of page 266.

Depositing Taxes

The company is required to deposit federal, state, and city taxes during this quarter. The deposit rules that affect the company are shown at the top of page 267.

Group Insurance

The company carries group life insurance on all its employees in an amount equal to one and one-half times the annual salary or wages paid each employee. Employees are fully covered under the group insurance program when they are employed full-time. A notation has been made on each employee's earnings record to show that each month 30¢ for each $1,000 of insurance coverage is deducted from the employee's earnings to pay a portion of the premium cost. This deduction is only made on the *last payday of each month*. The amount withheld is credited to a liability account entitled Group Insurance Premiums Collected.

The employer pays whatever additional premium is charged, which varies each year depending upon the average age of the employees and other factors. The employer is required to pay an estimated premium in advance at the beginning of the year. This amount is recorded as a debit to Prepaid Group Insurance in the general ledger. Prepaid Group Insurance is an asset account that will be adjusted at the end of the year by crediting it for the employees' share of the premium that was collected by withholding from their earnings during the year. The account is also credited

PAYROLL TAXES LEVIED UPON THE GLO-BRITE PAINT COMPANY AND ITS EMPLOYEES

Federal Income Taxes (FIT)	Withheld from each employee's gross earnings in accordance with information given on Form W-4 and employee's earnings record. Wage-bracket method is used to determine FIT withholding.*
Pennsylvania State Income Taxes (SIT)	2.8% withheld from each employee's gross earnings during the fourth quarter.
Philadelphia City Income Taxes (CIT)	4.96% withheld from gross earnings of each employee.*
Pennsylvania State Unemployment Taxes (SUTA)	*Employer:* 3.5% on first $8,000 gross earnings paid each employee during the calendar year.
	Employee: 0.15% on all wages paid.*
Federal Un-employment Taxes (FUTA)	Net tax rate of .8% on first $7,000 gross earnings paid each worker in the calendar year.
Federal Insurance Contributions Act (FICA)	*OASDI—* *Employer* *and* *Employee:* 6.2% on first $59,700 gross earnings paid each worker in the calendar year.
	HI— *Employer* *and* *Employee:* 1.45% on total gross earnings paid each worker in the calendar year.

*Tax withholdings for FIT, CIT, and SUTA are based on rates used in 1993. Rates for 1994 were not available at the time of publishing.

for the company's share of the premium. At the same time, this amount will be charged to an appropriate expense account, after which the prepaid group insurance account will balance provided the insurance year is the same as the company's fiscal year. Otherwise, the balance of the account at the end of the fiscal year will represent a prepaid expense (asset).

Union Dues

All workers in the plant, except the supervisors, are union members. Under the check-off system, $8 is deducted *each payday* from the plant workers' earnings for union dues, assessments, and initiation fees. A notation to this effect has been made on each plant worker's earnings record. On or before the tenth of each month, the amounts withheld during the preceding month are turned over to the treasurer of the union.

Distribution of Labor Costs

The salaries and wages are to be charged to the labor cost accounts as follows:

PERSONNEL	ACCOUNT TO BE CHARGED
President	Administrative Salaries
Executive Secretary Programmer Time Clerk . . . . Student (Accounting Trainee)	Office Salaries
Sales Manager . . . . Sales Representatives	Sales Salaries
Workers . . . . Supervisors	Plant Wages

NARRATIVE OF PAYROLL TRANSACTIONS

October 9, 19—

No. **1.** The first payroll in October was for the two workweeks that ended on September 26 and October 3. This payroll transaction has been entered for you in the payroll register, the employees' earnings records, the general journal, and the general ledger. By reviewing the calculations of the wages and deductions in the payroll register and the posting of the information to the employees' earnings records, you can see the procedure to be followed each payday.

Wages and salaries are paid by issuing special payroll checks. When such checks are received at the bank on which they are drawn, they will be charged against the payroll cash account.

The following rules are observed in computing earnings each pay period:

1. Do not make any deduction from an employee's earnings if the employee loses less than 15 minutes of time in any day. Time lost that exceeds 15 minutes is rounded to the nearest quarter-hour and deducted. If the time lost by an employee is not to be deducted, the time clerk will make a notation to that effect on the Time Clerk's Report.

DEPOSIT RULES FOR THE GLO-BRITE PAINT COMPANY	
Federal	The FICA taxes and FIT taxes must be deposited on or before the 15th of the month following the month in which the taxes were withheld. Since Glo-Brite is a new employer and has no tax liabilities during the lookback period, the company is subject to the monthly deposit rule.
Pennsylvania	The withheld state income taxes must be remitted within three banking days after the semimonthly periods ending on the 15th and the last day of the month. Since the state taxes withheld total $1,000 or more each quarter, the company must remit the withheld taxes semimonthly.
Philadelphia	The withheld city wage tax must be remitted within three banking days after the pay date. Since the city taxes total $250 or more each month, the company is subject to the three-day rule.

2. In completing the time record columns of the payroll register for all workers, you should place an 8 in the day column for each full day worked. If less than a full day is worked, show the actual hours for which the employee is being paid.

3. In the case of an employee who begins work during a pay period, compute the earnings by multiplying one full week worked, if any, by the weekly rate. For any partial week, compute the earnings for that week by multiplying the hours worked by the hourly rate of pay.

4. If time lost by a salaried employee is to be deducted from his or her pay, determine the employee's pay by multiplying the actual hours worked for that week by the hourly rate. The following schedule shows the weekly and hourly wage rates of the salaried employees:

EMPLOYEE	WEEKLY RATE	HOURLY RATE
Ferguson, James C. . .	$ 625.00	$15.63
Ford, Catherine L. . .	225.00	5.63
Mann, Dewey W. . . .	450.00	11.25
O'Neill, Joseph T. . . .	1,153.85	28.85
Russell, Virginia A. . .	195.00	4.88
Sokowski, Thomas J.	450.00	11.25
Student	150.00	3.75
Williams, Ruth V. . . .	285.00	7.13

5. In the case of plant workers, other than supervisors, employment is on an hourly basis. Compute the wages by multiplying the number of hours worked during the pay period by the employee's hourly rate.

The information needed and the sequence of steps that are completed for the payroll are presented in the following discussion.

The time clerk prepared Time Clerk's Reports Nos. 38 and 39, as shown on page 268, from the time cards used by the employees for these workweeks. Inasmuch as the president, sales manager, the sales representatives, and the supervisors do not ring in and out on the time clock, their records are not included in the time clerk's report; but their salaries must be included in the payroll.

① The following schedule shows the hourly wage rates of the two hourly employees that were used in preparing the payroll register for the payday on October 9.

EMPLOYEE	HOURLY RATE
Bonno, Anthony V.	$7.65
Ryan, Norman A.	9.80

② The entry required for each employee is recorded in the payroll register (see page 306). The names of all employees are listed in alphabetical order, including yours as "Student." The fold-out payroll register forms that are needed to complete this project are bound at the back of the book on pages 306 to 308.

No deduction has been made for the time lost by Williams. Thus, the total number of hours (80) for which payment was made is recorded in the Regular Earnings Hours column of the payroll register. However, a notation of the time lost (D) was made in the Time Record column. When posting to Williams' earnings record, 80 hours is recorded in the Regular Earnings Hours column, since there was no deduction for the time lost.

In computing the federal income taxes to be withheld, the wage-bracket tables in Tax Table B at the back of the book were used. Each payroll in the project requires the use of the tax tables for a *biweekly payroll period*.

Each payday $8 was deducted from the earnings of the plant workers, except the supervisor, for union dues.

Payroll check numbers were assigned beginning with check No. 672.

In the Labor Cost Distribution columns at the extreme right of the payroll register, each employee's gross earnings were recorded in that column which identifies the department in which the employee regularly works. The totals of the Labor Cost Distribution columns provide the amounts to be charged to the appropriate salary and wage expense accounts and aid department managers and supervisors in comparing the actual labor costs with the budgeted amounts.

Once the net pay of each employee was determined, all the amount columns in the payroll register were footed, proved, and ruled.

③ An entry was made in the journal on page 280 transferring from the regular cash account to the payroll cash account the amount of the check issued to Payroll to cover the net amount of the payroll; next, the entry was posted.

④ Information from the payroll register was posted to the employees' earnings records (see pages 298-304).

Note that when posting the deductions for each employee, a column has been provided in the earnings record for recording each deduction for FICA (OASDI and HI), SUTA, FIT, SIT, and CIT. All other deductions for each employee are to be totaled and recorded as one amount in the Other Deductions column. Subsidiary ledgers are maintained for Group Insurance Premiums Collected and Union Dues Withheld. Thus, any question about the amounts withheld from an employee's earnings may be answered by referring to the appropriate subsidiary ledger. In this project your work will not involve any recording in or reference to the subsidiary ledgers.

⑤ The proper journal entry was made to record salaries, wages, taxes, and the net amount of cash paid. The journal entry to record the payroll for the first pay in the fourth quarter is shown below and in the general journal on page 280.

Administrative Salaries	2,307.69	
Office Salaries	1,710.00	
Sales Salaries	2,150.00	
Plant Wages	2,296.00	
FICA Taxes Payable—OASDI		524.75
FICA Taxes Payable—HI		122.74
Employees SUTA Payable . .		12.72
Employees FIT Payable		714.00
Employees SIT Payable		236.99
Employees CIT Payable		419.80
Union Dues Payable		16.00
Payroll Cash		6,416.69

The amounts charged the salary and wage expense accounts were obtained from the totals of the Labor Cost Distribution columns in the payroll register. As shown in the listing of the distribution of labor costs on page 266, the salaries and wages were charged as follows:

TIME CLERK'S REPORT NO. 38
For the Week Ending September 26, 19--

EMPLOYEE	TIME RECORD						TIME WORKED	TIME LOST
	S	M	T	W	T	F	S		
Bonno, A. V. ..		8	8	8	8	8		40 hrs.	. . .
Ford, C. L.		8	8	8	8	8		40 hrs.	. . .
Russell, V. A. .		8	8	8	8	8		40 hrs.	. . .
Ryan, N. A.		8	8	8	8	8		40 hrs.	. . .
Student		8	8	8	8	8		40 hrs.	. . .
Williams, R. V.		8	8	D	8	8		32 hrs.	8 hrs.*

*Time lost because of personal business; charged to personal leave; no deduction for this time lost.

D = lost full day

TIME CLERK'S REPORT NO. 39
For the Week Ending October 3, 19--

EMPLOYEE	TIME RECORD						TIME WORKED	TIME LOST
	S	M	T	W	T	F	S		
Bonno, A. V. ..		8	8	8	8	8		40 hrs.	. . .
Ford, C. L.		8	8	8	8	8		40 hrs.	. . .
Russell, V. A. .		8	8	8	8	8		40 hrs.	. . .
Ryan, N. A.		8	8	8	8	8		40 hrs.	. . .
Student		8	8	8	8	8		40 hrs.	. . .
Williams, R. V.		8	8	8	8	8		40 hrs.	. . .

ADMINISTRATIVE SALARIES

Joseph T. O'Neill (President)

OFFICE SALARIES

Catherine L. Ford (Executive Secretary)
Virginia A. Russell (Time Clerk)
Student (Accounting Trainee)
Ruth V. Williams (Programmer)

SALES SALARIES

James C. Ferguson (Sales Manager)
Dewey W. Mann (Sales Representative)

PLANT WAGES

Anthony V. Bonno (Mixer Operator)
Norman A. Ryan (Electrician)
Thomas J. Sokowski (Supervisor)

FICA Taxes Payable—OASDI and FICA Taxes Payable—HI were credited for $524.75 and $122.74 respectively, the amounts deducted from employees' wages.

Employees SUTA Payable, Employees FIT Payable, Employees SIT Payable, Employees CIT Payable, and Union Dues Payable were credited for the total amount withheld for each kind of deduction from employees' wages. In subsequent payroll transactions, Group Insurance Premiums Collected will be credited for the amounts withheld from employees' wages for this type of deduction. Finally, Payroll Cash was credited for the sum of the net amounts paid all employees.

⑥ The payroll taxes for this pay were then recorded in the general journal on page 280 as follows:

Payroll Taxes	735.19	
FICA Taxes Payable—OASDI		524.75
FICA Taxes Payable—HI . . .		122.72
FUTA Taxes Payable		16.32
SUTA Taxes Payable		71.40

Payroll Taxes was debited for the sum of the employer's FICA, FUTA, and SUTA taxes. The taxable earnings used in calculating each of these payroll taxes was obtained from the appropriate column totals of the payroll register. The computation of the debit to Payroll Taxes was:

FICA—OASDI:	6.2% of $8,463.69 =	$524.75
FICA—HI:	1.45% of $8,463.69 =	122.72
FUTA:	.8% of $2,040.00 =	16.32
SUTA:	3.5% of $2,040.00 =	71.40
Total Payroll Taxes		$735.19

FICA Taxes Payable—OASDI was credited for $524.75, the amount of the liability for the employer's portion of the tax. FICA Taxes Payable—HI was credited for $122.72, the amount of the liability for the employer's share of this tax. FUTA Taxes Payable was credited for the amount of the tax on the employer for federal unemployment purposes ($16.32). SUTA Taxes Payable was credited for the amount of the contribution required of the employer under the state unemployment compensation law. This is the same amount, $71.40, that was charged as part of the debit to Payroll Taxes.

⑦ The journal entries were posted to the proper ledger accounts on pages 289-296.

October 14

No. 2. Since the Glo-Brite Paint Company withholds the City of Philadelphia income tax, you are required to deposit the taxes with the Department of Revenue. The deposit rule that affects the Glo-Brite Paint Company states that if the withheld tax is $250 or more in any month, you must deposit the tax within three banking days subsequent to each pay date. The withheld tax for the October 9 payday was $419.80.

① Prepare the journal entry to record the deposit of the taxes and post to the appropriate ledger accounts.

② Complete one of the Philadelphia income tax depository forms (Form W-7) which appear on pages 312-314.

October 15

This is the day on which the deposit of FICA and FIT taxes for the September payrolls is due at the bank. However, in order to concentrate on fourth quarter payrolls, we will assume that the deposit was made and the appropriate entry was completed.

October 20

No. 3. On this date the Glo-Brite Paint Company is required to deposit the Pennsylvania state income taxes withheld from the October 9 payroll.

The deposit rule states that if the employer expects the aggregate amount withheld each quarter to be $1,000 or more, the employer must pay the withheld tax semimonthly. The tax, along with the deposit statement (Form PA 501R), must be remitted within three banking days after the close of the semimonthly periods ending on the 15th and the last day of the month.

① Prepare the journal entry to record the deposit of the taxes and post to the appropriate ledger accounts.

② Complete one of the Pennsylvania deposit statements (Form PA-501R) which appear on pages 310-312. The company's telephone number is (215) 555-9559.

October 23

No. 4. Prepare the payroll for the last pay period of October from Time Clerk's Reports Nos. 40 and 41 below.

The proper procedure in recording the payroll is as follows:

① Complete the payroll register.

Inasmuch as only a portion of the payroll register sheet was used in recording the October 9 payroll, the October 23 payroll should be recorded on the same sheet to save space. On the first blank ruled line after the October 9 payroll, insert "Payday October 23—For Period Ending October 17, 19—." On the following lines record the payroll information for the last pay date of October. When recording succeeding payrolls, continue to conserve space by recording two payrolls on each separate payroll register sheet. In recording the payroll in actual practice, the payroll clerk might begin at the top of a new sheet.

The workers in the plant (Bonno and Ryan) are paid *time and a half* for any hours worked over eight each workday, and *twice* the regular hourly rate for work on Saturdays, Sundays, or holidays.

With this pay period, the *cumulative earnings* of several employees exceed the taxable income base set up by FUTA. This factor must be considered in preparing the payroll register and calculating the employer's payroll taxes. Refer to each employee's earnings record to see the amount of cumulative earnings.

Also, be sure to deduct 30¢ premium for each $1,000 of group insurance carried by each employee.

② Make the entry transferring from Cash to Payroll Cash the net amount of the total payroll, and post.

③ Post the required information from the payroll register to each employee's earnings record.

④ Record in the journal the salaries, wages, taxes withheld, group insurance premiums collected, union dues withheld, and net amount paid, and post to the proper ledger accounts.

The entry required to record the October 23 payroll is the same as that to record the October 9 payroll, except it is necessary to record the liability for the amount withheld from the employees' wages to pay their part of the group

TIME CLERK'S REPORT NO. 40								
For the Week Ending October 10, 19--								
EMPLOYEE	TIME RECORD						TIME WORKED	TIME LOST
	S	M	T	W	T	F	S		
Bonno, A. V. ..		8	8	8	8	8	4	44 hrs.	. . .
Ford, C. L.		4	8	8	8	8		36 hrs.	4 hrs.*
Russell, V. A. ..		8	8	8	8	8		40 hrs.	. . .
Ryan, N. A. ...		8	8	8	8	8		40 hrs.	. . .
Student		8	8	8	8	8		40 hrs.	. . .
Williams, R. V.		8	8	8	8	8		40 hrs.	. . .

*Time lost on account of death of relative; charged against annual personal leave; no deduction for time lost.

TIME CLERK'S REPORT NO. 41								
For the Week Ending October 17, 19--								
EMPLOYEE	TIME RECORD						TIME WORKED	TIME LOST
	S	M	T	W	T	F	S		
Bonno, A. V. ..		8	8	8	8	8		40 hrs.	. . .
Ford, C. L.		8	8	8	8	8		40 hrs.	. . .
Russell, V. A. .		8	8	8	8	8		40 hrs.	. . .
Ryan, N. A.		8	8	8	8	8	8	48 hrs.	. . .
Student		8	8	8	8	8		40 hrs.	. . .
Williams, R. V.		8	8	8	8	8		40 hrs.	. . .

insurance premium. The amount withheld should be recorded as a credit to Group Insurance Premiums Collected.

⑤ Record in the journal the employer's payroll taxes and the liabilities created, and post to the appropriate ledger accounts.

October 28

No. **5.** Deposit with the City of Philadelphia the amount of city income taxes withheld from the October 23 payroll.

November 4

No. **6.** Deposit with the State of Pennsylvania the amount of state income taxes withheld from the October 23 payroll.

No. **7.** Virginia Russell completed a new Form W-4, changing the number of withholding allowances to 2. Change Russell's earnings record (her marital status has not changed) and reflect this change in the November 6 pay.

No. **8.** Thomas J. Sokowski completed a new Form W-4, showing that his marital status is now single and that the number of withholding allowances remains at 2. Change Sokowski's earnings record accordingly and reflect this change in the November 6 pay.

November 6

No. **9.** Pay the treasurer of the union the amount of union dues withheld during the month of October.

No. **10.** Prepare the payroll for the first pay in November from Time Clerk's Reports Nos. 42 and 43 and record the paychecks issued to all employees. Record this payroll at the top of the second payroll register sheet.

Note: Virginia Russell worked only 38 hours in the week ending October 24. Therefore, calculate her pay for that week by multiplying 38 by $4.88 (her hourly rate). Ruth Williams worked only 39 hours in the week ending October 24. Therefore, calculate her pay for that week by multiplying 39 by $7.13 (her hourly rate).

Also, record the employer's payroll taxes.

November 11

No. **11.** Deposit with the City of Philadelphia the amount of city income taxes withheld from the November 6 payroll.

November 13

No. **12.** Because of her excessive tardiness and absenteeism, the company discharged Ruth V. Williams today. For the week ending November 7, she was late a total of six hours; and for this week, she missed one full day and was late two hours on another day. In lieu of two weeks' notice, Williams was given two full weeks' pay ($570.00).

Along with her dismissal pay ($570.00), she was paid for the week ending November 7 (34 hours, or $242.42) and the days worked this current week (30

TIME CLERK'S REPORT NO. 42								
For the Week Ending October 24, 19--								
EMPLOYEE	**TIME RECORD**						**TIME WORKED**	**TIME LOST**
	S	M	T	W	T	F	S	
Bonno, A. V. ..		8	8	8	8	8		40 hrs.	. . .
Ford, C. L.		8	8	8	8	8		40 hrs.	. . .
Russell, V. A. ..		8	8	8	8	6		38 hrs.	2 hrs.*
Ryan, N. A.		8	8	8	8	8	1	41 hrs.	. . .
Student		8	8	8	8	8		40 hrs.	. . .
Williams, R. V.		8	8	8	7	8		39 hrs.	1 hr.**

*Time lost on account of auto accident; deduct 2 hours' pay.
**Time lost because of tardiness; deduct 1 hour's pay.

TIME CLERK'S REPORT NO. 43								
For the Week Ending October 31, 19--								
EMPLOYEE	**TIME RECORD**						**TIME WORKED**	**TIME LOST**
	S	M	T	W	T	F	S	
Bonno, A. V. ..		8	8	8	8	8		40 hrs.	. . .
Ford, C. L.		8	8	8	8	8		40 hrs.	. . .
Russell, V. A. ..		8	8	8	8	8		40 hrs.	. . .
Ryan, N. A.		8	8	8	8	8		40 hrs.	. . .
Student		8	8	8	8	8		40 hrs.	. . .
Williams, R. V.		8	8	8	8	8		40 hrs.	. . .

hours, or $213.90). The total pay for the two partial weeks is $456.32.

① Record a separate entry in the payroll register to show Williams' total earnings, deductions, and net pay. The two weeks' dismissal pay is subject to all payroll taxes. Use the tax table for the biweekly payroll period for the total gross pay ($1,026.32) of Williams.

The deduction for group insurance premiums is $6.60. In the Time Record column make a note of Williams' discharge as of this date. Indicate the payroll check number used to prepare the final check for Williams. When posting to the earnings record, make a notation of Williams' discharge on this date.

② Prepare the journal entries to transfer the net cash and to record Williams' final pay and the employer's payroll taxes. Post to the ledger accounts.

③ Prepare a Wage and Tax Statement, Form W-2, which will be given to Williams with her final paycheck. Use the blank Form W-2 on page 319. Box "a" should be left blank since the Glo-Brite Paint Company does not use a control number to identify individual Forms W-2.

November 16

No. 13. Deposit with the City Bank the amount of FICA taxes and federal income taxes for the October payrolls. Since the company is subject to the monthly deposit rule, the deposit is due on the fifteenth of the following month. See the deposit

requirements that are explained on pages 83-85. November 15 is a Sunday; therefore, the deposit is to be made on the next business day.

① Prepare the journal entry to record the deposit of the taxes and post to the appropriate ledger accounts.

② Complete the Federal Tax Deposit Coupon, Form 8109, to accompany the remittance, using one of the preinscribed forms on page 309. The company's telephone number is (215) 555-9559.

November 17

No. 14. Prepare an employee's earnings record for Beth Anne Woods, a new employee who began work today, Tuesday. Woods is single and claims one withholding allowance. She is employed as a programmer at a monthly salary of $1,300. Address, 8102 Franklin Court, Philadelphia, PA 19105-0915. Telephone, 555-1128. Social Security No. 724-03-1587. She is eligible for group insurance coverage of $23,000 immediately, although her first deduction for group insurance will not be made until December 18.

Department: Office.
Weekly rate: $300.00.
Hourly rate: $7.50.

November 18

No. 15. Deposit with the State of Pennsylvania the amount of state income taxes withheld from the November 6 and 13 (Ruth V. Williams) payrolls.

TIME CLERK'S REPORT NO. 44									
For the Week Ending November 7, 19--									
EMPLOYEE	**TIME RECORD**							**TIME WORKED**	**TIME LOST**
	S	M	T	W	T	F	S		
Bonno, A. V. ..		8	8	8	8	8		40 hrs.	. . .
Ford, C. L.		8	8	8	8	8		40 hrs.	. . .
Russell, V. A. ..		8	8	8	8	8		40 hrs.	. . .
Ryan, N. A.		8	8	8	8	8		40 hrs.	. . .
Student		8	8	8	8	8		40 hrs.	. . .
Williams, R. V.		6	8	7	7	6		34 hrs.	6 hrs.*

*Time lost because of tardiness; deduct 6 hours' pay.

TIME CLERK'S REPORT NO. 45									
For the Week Ending November 14, 19--									
EMPLOYEE	**TIME RECORD**							**TIME WORKED**	**TIME LOST**
	S	M	T	W	T	F	S		
Bonno, A. V. ..	...	...	8	8	8			24 hrs.	. . .
Ford, C. L.	8	8	8	8	8			40 hrs.	. . .
Russell, V. A. .	8	8	8	8	8			40 hrs.	. . .
Ryan, N. A.	8	8	8	8	8	2		42 hrs.	. . .
Student	8	8	8	8	8			40 hrs.	. . .
Williams, R. V.	D	8	8	6	8			30 hrs.	10 hrs.*

*Time lost because of tardiness: deduct 2 hours' pay; and unexcused absence: deduct 8 hours' pay.

November 20

No. 16. Prepare the payroll for the last pay of November from Time Clerk's Reports Nos. 44 and 45, on page 272, and record the paychecks issued all employees. *Remember to deduct the premiums on the group insurance for each employee.*

Also, record the employer's payroll taxes.

November 25

No. 17. Deposit with the City of Philadelphia the amount of city income taxes withheld from the November 13 and 20 payrolls.

No. 18. Salary increases of $26 per month, effective for the two weeks covered in the December 4 payroll, are given to Catherine L. Ford and Virginia A. Russell. The group insurance coverage for Ford will remain at $18,000; for Russell, it will be increased to $16,000. Update the employees' earnings records accordingly. The new wage rates, effective for the December 4 payroll, are:

EMPLOYEE	WEEKLY RATE	HOURLY RATE
Ford, Catherine L. . .	$231.00	$5.78
Russell, Virginia A. . .	201.00	5.03

November 30

No. 19. Prepare an employee's earnings record for Paul Winston Young, the president's nephew, who began work today. Young is single and claims one withholding allowance. He is training as a field sales representative in the city where the home office is located. His beginning salary is $1,000 per month. Address, 7936 Holmes Drive, Philadelphia, PA 19107-6107. Telephone, 555-2096. Social Security No. 432-07-6057. Young is eligible for group insurance coverage of $18,000.

Department: Sales.
Weekly rate: $230.77.
Hourly rate: $5.77.

December 3

No. 20. Deposit with the State of Pennsylvania the amount of state income taxes withheld from the November 20 payroll.

December 4

No. 21. Prepare the payroll for the first pay of December from Time Clerk's Reports Nos. 46 and 47 and record the paychecks issued all employees. Record this payroll at the top of the third payroll register sheet.

Note: Thursday, November 26, is a paid holiday for all workers.

Also, record the employer's payroll taxes.

No. 22. Anthony V. Bonno reports the birth of a son and completes an amended Form W-4, showing his total withholding allowances to be five. Change his earnings record accordingly, and implement the change in allowance status in the December 18 payroll.

	TIME CLERK'S REPORT NO. 46						
	For the Week Ending November 21, 19--						
EMPLOYEE	S	M	T	W	T	F	S	TIME WORKED	TIME LOST

TIME CLERK'S REPORT NO. 46 — For the Week Ending November 21, 19--

EMPLOYEE	S	M	T	W	T	F	S	TIME WORKED	TIME LOST
Bonno, A. V. ..		8	8	8	8	8		40 hrs.	...
Ford, C. L.		8	8	8	8	8		40 hrs.	...
Russell, V. A. ..		8	8	8	8	8		40 hrs.	...
Ryan, N. A. ...		8	8	8	4	8		36 hrs.	4 hrs.*
Student		8	8	8	8	8		40 hrs.	...
Woods, B. A. ..		...	8	8	8	8		32 hrs.	...

*Time lost on account of personal business; deduct 4 hours' pay.

TIME CLERK'S REPORT NO. 47 — For the Week Ending November 28, 19--

EMPLOYEE	S	M	T	W	T	F	S	TIME WORKED	TIME LOST
Bonno, A. V. ..		8	8	8	PAID HOLIDAY	8	8	48 hrs.	...
Ford, C. L.		8	8	8	PAID HOLIDAY	8		40 hrs.	...
Russell, V. A. .		8	8	8	PAID HOLIDAY	8		40 hrs.	...
Ryan, N. A. ...		9	10	8	PAID HOLIDAY	8		43 hrs.	...
Student		8	8	8	PAID HOLIDAY	8		40 hrs.	...
Woods, B. A. ..		8	8	8	PAID HOLIDAY	8		40 hrs.	...

No. 23. Both Anthony Bonno and Norman Ryan have been notified that their union dues will increase to $9 per pay starting with the last pay of the year. Reflect these increases in the December 18 pay, and show the changes on their earnings records.

December 9

No. 24. Pay the treasurer of the union the amount of union dues withheld during the month of November.

No. 25. Deposit with the City of Philadelphia the amount of city income taxes withheld from the December 4 payroll.

December 11

No. 26. The payroll department was informed that Virginia A. Russell was killed in an automobile accident on her way home from work Thursday, December 10.

December 14

No. 27. ① Make a separate entry in the payroll register to record the issuance of a check payable to the estate of Virginia A. Russell. This check covers Russell's work for the weeks ending December 5 and 12 ($361.96) plus her accrued vacation pay ($402.00).

Russell's final biweekly pay for time worked ($361.96) and the vacation pay ($402.00) are subject to FICA, FUTA, and SUTA taxes. Since Russell's cumulative earnings have surpassed the taxable earnings figures established by FUTA and SUTA, there will not be any unemployment tax on the employer; however, the earnings are subject to the employee's share of the SUTA tax. This final pay is not subject to withholding for FIT, SIT, or CIT purposes. The deduction for group insurance premiums is $4.80.

② Make a notation of Russell's death in the payroll register and on her earnings record.

③ Prepare journal entries to transfer the net pay and to record Russell's final pay and the employer's payroll taxes. Post to the ledger accounts.

④ Prepare a Wage and Tax Statement, Form W-2, which will be given to the executor of the estate along with the final paycheck. Report the final gross pay ($763.96) in Boxes 3 and 5, but not in Boxes 1, 17, and 20. Use the blank Form W-2 on page 319.

In addition, the unpaid wages and vacation pay must be reported on Form 1099-MISC. A Form 1096 must also be completed. These forms will be completed in February before their due date. (See Transaction Nos. 42 and 43.)

December 15

No. 28. Deposit with the City Bank the amount of FICA taxes and federal income taxes for the November payrolls.

December 18

No. 29. Deposit with the State of Pennsylvania the amount of state income taxes withheld from the December 4 payroll.

No. 30. Glo-Brite has been notified by the insurance company that there will be no premium charge for the month of December on the policy for Virginia Russell. Write a check on the regular cash account, payable to the estate of Virginia A. Russell, for the amount that was withheld for insurance from her December 14 pay.

No. 31. Prepare an employee's earnings record for Richard Lloyd Zimmerman, who was employed today as time clerk to take the place left vacant by the death of Virginia A. Russell last week. His beginning salary is $780 per month. Address, 900 South Clark Street, Philadelphia, PA 19195-6247. Telephone, 555-2104. Social Security No. 897-12-1502. Zimmerman is married and claims one withholding allowance. Zimmerman is eligible for group insurance coverage of $14,000, although no deduction for group insurance premiums will be made until the last payday in January.

Department: Office.
Weekly rate: $180.00.
Hourly rate: $4.50.

No. 32. In this pay, the president of the company, Joseph O'Neill, is paid his annual bonus. This year his bonus is $4,000. For withholding purposes, the bonus is considered a supplemental payment and is added to his gross pay, and the aggregate amount is taxed. To determine the federal income tax, use the *Table of Allowance Values* along with *Tax Table A*.

Effective with this pay, O'Neill completed a new Form W-4 changing his total withholding allowances to four. Previously, he had claimed fewer allowances than he had been using on his tax return. Change his earnings record accordingly.

Prepare the payroll for the latter pay of December from Time Clerk's Reports Nos. 48 and 49 and record the paychecks issued all employees. Also, record the employer's payroll taxes.

Note: After posting the information for this last pay to the employees' earnings records, calculate and enter the quarterly and yearly totals on each earnings record.

December 23

No. 33. Deposit with the City of Philadelphia the amount of city income taxes withheld from the December 18 payroll.

> **NOTE: This completes the project insofar as recording the payroll transactions for the last quarter is concerned. The following additional transactions are given to illustrate different types of transactions arising in connection with the accounting for payrolls and payroll taxes. Record these transactions in the journal, but *do not* post to the ledger.**

January 6

No. 34. Deposit with the State of Pennsylvania the amount of state income taxes withheld from the December 18 payroll.

January 8

No. 35. Pay the treasurer of the union the amount of union dues withheld during the month of December.

January 15

No. 36. Deposit with the City Bank the amount of FICA taxes and federal income taxes for the December payrolls.

Complete the Federal Tax Deposit Coupon, Form 8109, using one of the preinscribed forms on page 309.

February 1

No. 37. Prepare Form 941, Employer's Quarterly Federal Tax Return, with respect to wages paid during the last calendar quarter. A blank Form 941 is reproduced on page 316. The information needed in preparing the return should be obtained from the ledger accounts, the payroll registers, the employees' earnings records, and the Federal Tax Deposit forms.

Form 941 and all forms that follow are to be signed by the president of the company, Joseph T. O'Neill.

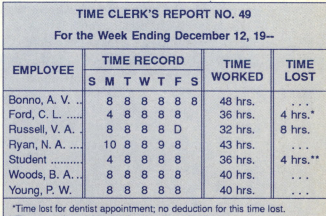

TIME CLERK'S REPORT NO. 48									
For the Week Ending December 5, 19--									
EMPLOYEE	**TIME RECORD**							**TIME WORKED**	**TIME LOST**
	S	**M**	**T**	**W**	**T**	**F**	**S**		
Bonno, A. V. ..		8	8	8	8	8	4	44 hrs.	. . .
Ford, C. L.		8	8	8	8	8		40 hrs.	. . .
Russell, V. A. ..		8	8	8	8	8		40 hrs.	. . .
Ryan, N. A.		8	9	9	9	9		44 hrs.	. . .
Student		8	8	7	8	8		39 hrs.	1 hr.*
Woods, B. A....		8	8	8	8	8		40 hrs.	. . .
Young, P. W.		8	8	8	8	8		40 hrs.	. . .

*Time lost because of tardiness; deduct 1 hour's pay.

TIME CLERK'S REPORT NO. 49									
For the Week Ending December 12, 19--									
EMPLOYEE	**TIME RECORD**							**TIME WORKED**	**TIME LOST**
	S	**M**	**T**	**W**	**T**	**F**	**S**		
Bonno, A. V. ..		8	8	8	8	8		48 hrs.	. . .
Ford, C. L.		4	8	8	8	8		36 hrs.	4 hrs.*
Russell, V. A. .		8	8	8	8	D		32 hrs.	8 hrs.
Ryan, N. A.		10	8	8	9	8		43 hrs.	. . .
Student		4	8	8	8	8		36 hrs.	4 hrs.**
Woods, B. A....		8	8	8	8	8		40 hrs.	. . .
Young, P. W.		8	8	8	8	8		40 hrs.	. . .

*Time lost for dentist appointment; no deduction for this time lost.
**Time spent in training session; no deduction in pay.

No. 38. ① Complete Form 940-EZ, Employer's Annual Federal Unemployment (FUTA) Tax Return, using the blank form reproduced on page 317, and also Form 8109, Federal Tax Deposit Coupon, using the blank form reproduced on page 310. The information needed in preparing these forms can be obtained from the ledger accounts, the payroll registers, the employees' earnings records, and the following:

(a) Contributions paid to the Pennsylvania unemployment fund for the year amount to $3,131.55. (This amount includes the employer's and the employees' contributions for the fourth quarter which will be determined and paid in Transaction No. 39.)

(b) FUTA taxable wages for the first three quarters: $65,490.00

(c) FUTA tax liability by quarter:
1st quarter—$272.71
2d quarter—$140.33
3d quarter—$110.88

(d) All deposits for the first three quarters were made on the dates they were due.

Journalize the entry to record the deposit included with Form 8109.

No. 39. ① Prepare Form UC-2, Employer's Report for Unemployment Compensation—Fourth Quarter, using the blank form reproduced on page 318. In Pennsylvania, a credit week is any calendar week during the quarter in which the employee earned at least $50 (without regard to when paid). The telephone number of the company is (215) 555-9559. All other information needed in preparing the form can be obtained from the ledger accounts, the payroll registers, and the employees' earnings records.

② Journalize the entry to record the payment of the taxes for the fourth quarter.

No. 40. Complete Form W-2, Wage and Tax Statement, for each employee, using the blank statements reproduced on pages 320-324. Use each employee's earnings record to obtain the information needed to complete the forms.

No. 41. Complete Form W-3, Transmittal of Wage and Tax Statements, using the blank form reproduced on page 325. Use the information on Forms W-2 to complete this form.

No. 42. Complete Form 1099-MISC, Miscellaneous Income, for the unpaid wages and vacation pay of Virginia A. Russell. The full amount of the December 14 payment must be reported in Box 3. The blank form is reproduced on page 326.

Note: Wages paid after an employee dies were previously reported as nonemployee compensation in Box 7 on Form 1099-MISC. These wages are now to be reported as prizes and awards in Box 3, so that the IRS will not seek self-employment tax on such amounts.

No. 43. Complete Form 1096, Annual Summary and Transmittal of U.S. Information Returns, using the blank form reproduced on page 326. Use the information on Form 1099-MISC to complete this form.

No. 44. Prepare Form PA-W3R, Employer Quarterly Reconciliation Return of Income Tax Withheld, using the blank form reproduced on page 314. The telephone number of the company is (215) 555-9559.

No. 45. Prepare the Annual Reconciliation of Wage Tax for Philadelphia, using the blank form reproduced on page 315.

QUESTIONS ON THE PAYROLL PROJECT

1. The total payroll tax expense incurred by the employer on salaries and wages paid during the quarter ended December 31 was .... $ _____

2. The total payroll tax expense incurred by the employer on the salary of Joseph T. O'Neill during the fourth quarter was .... $ _____

3. The amount of the group insurance premiums collected from employees during the quarter ended December 31 was .... $ _____

4. O'Neill has decided to give all current employees (excluding himself) a bonus payment during January equal to 5% of their total gross pay for last year. Determine the total of this bonus payment. .... $ _____

5. On the financial statements prepared at the end of its first year of operations, the company must show an accurate picture of all expenses and all liabilities incurred. The last payday of the year was December 18. However, the payment to the employees on that day did not include the weeks ending December 19 and 26 and the four days (December 28-31) in the following week. These earnings will be reflected in the January payrolls. Two-column journal paper is provided below for use in journalizing the following entry.

   Prepare the adjusting entry as of December 31 to record the salaries and wages that have accrued but remain unpaid as of the end of the year. When calculating the amount of the accrual for each hourly worker, assume each employee worked eight hours on each day during the period with no overtime. For each salaried worker, the accrual will amount to 14/10 of the worker's biweekly earnings, except for Zimmerman who worked only ten days.

   Each of the labor cost accounts should be debited for the appropriate amount of the accrual, and Salaries and Wages Payable should be credited for the total amount of the accrual. There is no liability for payroll taxes on the accrued salaries and wages until the workers are actually paid. Therefore, the company follows the practice of not accruing payroll taxes.

6. Also prepare the adjusting entry as of December 31 to record the accrued vacation pay as of the end of the year. Record the expense in a Vacation Benefits Expense account, and credit the appropriate liability account. Use the journal paper provided below.

   As of December 31, the vacation time earned but not used by each employee is listed below.

Bonno	two weeks	Sokowski	two weeks
Ferguson	three weeks	Student	two weeks
Ford	two weeks	Woods	none
Mann	one week	Young	none
O'Neill	four weeks	Zimmerman	none
Ryan	two weeks		

JOURNAL

Page

	DATE	DESCRIPTION	POST. REF.	DEBIT	CREDIT	
1						1
2						2
3						3
4						4
5						5
6						6
7						7
8						8
9						9
10						10
11						11

ACCOUNTING RECORDS AND REPORTS

Contents

Item	To Be Used with	Page
Journal	Payroll Project	280
General Ledger	Payroll Project	289
Employees' Earnings Records	Payroll Project	298
Payroll Register—Steimer Company	Continuing Payroll Problem	305
Payroll Register—Glo-Brite Paint Company	Payroll Project	306
Federal Tax Deposit Coupons (Form 8109)	Payroll Project	309
Employer Deposit Statement— Pennsylvania (Form PA-501R)	Payroll Project	310
Employer's Depository Return— City of Philadelphia (Form W-7)	Payroll Project	312
Employer Quarterly Reconciliation of Pennsylvania Income Tax Withheld (Form PA-W3R)	Payroll Project	314
Annual Reconciliation of Wage Tax—Philadelphia	Payroll Project	315
Employer's Quarterly Federal Tax Return (Form 941)	Payroll Project	316
Employer's Annual Federal Unemployment (FUTA) Tax Return (Form 940-EZ)	Payroll Project	317
Employer's Report for Unemployment Compensation— Pennsylvania (Form UC-2)	Payroll Project	318
Wage and Tax Statements (Form W-2)	Payroll Project	319
Transmittal of Wage and Tax Statements (Form W-3)	Payroll Project	325
Miscellaneous Income (Form 1099-MISC)	Payroll Project	326
Annual Summary and Transmittal of U.S. Information Returns (Form 1096)	Payroll Project	326

	DATE		DESCRIPTION	POST. REF.	DEBIT					CREDIT					
1	19-- Oct.	9	Payroll Cash	12	6	4	1	6	69						1
2			Cash	11						6	4	1	6	69	2
3															3
4		9	Administrative Salaries	51	2	3	0	7	69						4
5			Office Salaries	52	1	7	1	0	00						5
6			Sales Salaries	53	2	1	5	0	00						6
7			Plant Wages	54	2	2	9	6	00						7
8			FICA Taxes Payable—OASDI	20.1							5	2	4	75	8
9			FICA Taxes Payable—HI	20.2							1	2	2	74	9
10			Employees SUTA Payable	23								1	2	72	10
11			Employees FIT Payable	24							7	1	4	00	11
12			Employees SIT Payable	25							2	3	6	99	12
13			Employees CIT Payable	26							4	1	9	80	13
14			Union Dues Payable	28								1	6	00	14
15			Payroll Cash	12						6	4	1	6	69	15
16															16
17		9	Payroll Taxes	56		7	3	5	19						17
18			FICA Taxes Payable—OASDI	20.1							5	2	4	75	18
19			FICA Taxes Payable—HI	20.2							1	2	2	72	19
20			FUTA Taxes Payable	21								1	6	32	20
21			SUTA Taxes Payable	22								7	1	40	21
22															22
23															23
24															24
25															25
26															26
27															27
28															28
29															29
30															30
31															31
32															32
33															33
34															34

JOURNAL

Page ___

	DATE	DESCRIPTION	POST. REF.	DEBIT	CREDIT	
1						1
2						2
3						3
4						4
5						5
6						6
7						7
8						8
9						9
10						10
11						11
12						12
13						13
14						14
15						15
16						16
17						17
18						18
19						19
20						20
21						21
22						22
23						23
24						24
25						25
26						26
27						27
28						28
29						29
30						30
31						31
32						32
33						33
34						34

JOURNAL

Page

	DATE		DESCRIPTION	POST. REF.	DEBIT	CREDIT	
1							1
2							2
3							3
4							4
5							5
6							6
7							7
8							8
9							9
10							10
11							11
12							12
13							13
14							14
15							15
16							16
17							17
18							18
19							19
20							20
21							21
22							22
23							23
24							24
25							25
26							26
27							27
28							28
29							29
30							30
31							31
32							32
33							33
34							34

282

JOURNAL

Page

	DATE		DESCRIPTION	POST. REF.	DEBIT	CREDIT	
1							1
2							2
3							3
4							4
5							5
6							6
7							7
8							8
9							9
10							10
11							11
12							12
13							13
14							14
15							15
16							16
17							17
18							18
19							19
20							20
21							21
22							22
23							23
24							24
25							25
26							26
27							27
28							28
29							29
30							30
31							31
32							32
33							33
34							34

	DATE		DESCRIPTION	POST. REF.	DEBIT	CREDIT	
1							1
2							2
3							3
4							4
5							5
6							6
7							7
8							8
9							9
10							10
11							11
12							12
13							13
14							14
15							15
16							16
17							17
18							18
19							19
20							20
21							21
22							22
23							23
24							24
25							25
26							26
27							27
28							28
29							29
30							30
31							31
32							32
33							33
34							34

	DATE		DESCRIPTION	POST. REF.	DEBIT	CREDIT	
1							1
2							2
3							3
4							4
5							5
6							6
7							7
8							8
9							9
10							10
11							11
12							12
13							13
14							14
15							15
16							16
17							17
18							18
19							19
20							20
21							21
22							22
23							23
24							24
25							25
26							26
27							27
28							28
29							29
30							30
31							31
32							32
33							33
34							34

	DATE		DESCRIPTION	POST. REF.	DEBIT	CREDIT	
1							1
2							2
3							3
4							4
5							5
6							6
7							7
8							8
9							9
10							10
11							11
12							12
13							13
14							14
15							15
16							16
17							17
18							18
19							19
20							20
21							21
22							22
23							23
24							24
25							25
26							26
27							27
28							28
29							29
30							30
31							31
32							32
33							33
34							34

	DATE		DESCRIPTION	POST. REF.	DEBIT	CREDIT	
1							1
2							2
3							3
4							4
5							5
6							6
7							7
8							8
9							9
10							10
11							11
12							12
13							13
14							14
15							15
16							16
17							17
18							18
19							19
20							20
21							21
22							22
23							23
24							24
25							25
26							26
27							27
28							28
29							29
30							30
31							31
32							32
33							33
34							34

	DATE		DESCRIPTION	POST. REF.	DEBIT	CREDIT	
1							1
2							2
3							3
4							4
5							5
6							6
7							7
8							8
9							9
10							10
11							11
12							12
13							13
14							14
15							15
16							16
17							17
18							18
19							19
20							20
21							21
22							22
23							23
24							24
25							25
26							26
27							27
28							28
29							29
30							30
31							31
32							32
33							33
34							34

GENERAL LEDGER

ACCOUNT **CASH**   ACCOUNT NO. **11**

DATE		ITEM	POST. REF.	DEBIT	CREDIT	BALANCE DEBIT	BALANCE CREDIT
19-- Oct.	1	*Balance*	√			8 9 8 4 6 33	
	9		J41		6 4 1 6 69	8 3 4 2 9 64	

DATE		ITEM	POST. REF.	DEBIT	CREDIT	BALANCE	
						DEBIT	CREDIT
19-- Oct.	9		J41	6 4 1 6 69		6 4 1 6 69	
	9		J41		6 4 1 6 69	– – – –	– – – –

DATE		ITEM	POST. REF.	DEBIT	CREDIT	BALANCE	
						DEBIT	CREDIT
19-- Oct.	9		J41		5 2 4 75		5 2 4 75
	9		J41		5 2 4 75		1 0 4 9 50

ACCOUNT **FICA TAXES PAYABLE—HI**   ACCOUNT NO. 20.2

DATE		ITEM	POST. REF.	DEBIT	CREDIT	BALANCE DEBIT	BALANCE CREDIT
19-- Oct.	9		J41		1 2 2 74		1 2 2 74
	9		J41		1 2 2 72		2 4 5 46

ACCOUNT **FUTA TAXES PAYABLE**   ACCOUNT NO. 21

DATE		ITEM	POST. REF.	DEBIT	CREDIT	BALANCE DEBIT	BALANCE CREDIT
19-- Oct.	9		J41		1 6 32		1 6 32

ACCOUNT **SUTA TAXES PAYABLE**   ACCOUNT NO. 22

DATE		ITEM	POST. REF.	DEBIT	CREDIT	BALANCE DEBIT	BALANCE CREDIT
19-- Oct.	9		J41		7 1 40		7 1 40

ACCOUNT **EMPLOYEES SUTA PAYABLE**   ACCOUNT NO. 23

DATE		ITEM	POST. REF.	DEBIT	CREDIT	BALANCE	
						DEBIT	CREDIT
19-- Oct.	9		J41		1 2 72		1 2 72

ACCOUNT **EMPLOYEES FIT PAYABLE**   ACCOUNT NO. 24

DATE		ITEM	POST. REF.	DEBIT	CREDIT	BALANCE	
						DEBIT	CREDIT
19-- Oct.	9		J41		7 1 4 00		7 1 4 00

ACCOUNT **EMPLOYEES SIT PAYABLE**   ACCOUNT NO. 25

DATE		ITEM	POST. REF.	DEBIT	CREDIT	BALANCE	
						DEBIT	CREDIT
19-- Oct.	9		J41		2 3 6 99		2 3 6 99

ACCOUNT **EMPLOYEES CIT PAYABLE**   ACCOUNT NO. 26

DATE		ITEM	POST. REF.	DEBIT	CREDIT	BALANCE	
						DEBIT	CREDIT
19-- Oct.	9		J41		4 1 9 80		4 1 9 80

ACCOUNT **GROUP INSURANCE PREMIUMS COLLECTED**   ACCOUNT NO. 27

DATE	ITEM	POST. REF.	DEBIT	CREDIT	BALANCE	
					DEBIT	CREDIT

ACCOUNT **UNION DUES PAYABLE**   ACCOUNT NO. 28

DATE		ITEM	POST. REF.	DEBIT	CREDIT	BALANCE	
						DEBIT	CREDIT
19-- Oct.	9		J41		1 6 00		1 6 00

ACCOUNT **ADMINISTRATIVE SALARIES** ACCOUNT NO. 51

DATE		ITEM	POST. REF.	DEBIT	CREDIT	BALANCE	
						DEBIT	CREDIT
19-- Oct.	1	*Balance*	√			4 2 6 9 2 27	
	9		J41	2 3 0 7 69		4 4 9 9 9 96	

ACCOUNT **OFFICE SALARIES** ACCOUNT NO. 52

DATE		ITEM	POST. REF.	DEBIT	CREDIT	BALANCE	
						DEBIT	CREDIT
19-- Oct.	1	*Balance*	√			2 8 3 5 0 00	
	9		J41	1 7 1 0 00		3 0 0 6 0 00	

ACCOUNT **SALES SALARIES** ACCOUNT NO. 53

DATE		ITEM	POST. REF.	DEBIT	CREDIT	BALANCE	
						DEBIT	CREDIT
19-- Oct.	1	*Balance*	√			2 8 5 2 5 00	
	9		J41	2 1 5 0 00		3 0 6 7 5 00	

ACCOUNT **PLANT WAGES**   ACCOUNT NO. 54

DATE		ITEM	POST. REF.	DEBIT	CREDIT	BALANCE DEBIT	BALANCE CREDIT
19-- Oct.	1	Balance	√			4 2 6 5 7 30	
	9		J41	2 2 9 6 00		4 4 9 5 3 30	

ACCOUNT **PAYROLL TAXES**   ACCOUNT NO. 56

DATE		ITEM	POST. REF.	DEBIT	CREDIT	BALANCE DEBIT	BALANCE CREDIT
19-- Oct.	1	Balance	√			1 3 9 0 6 21	
	9		J41	7 3 5 19		1 4 6 4 1 40	

EMPLOYEES' EARNINGS RECORDS

Employee Payroll Record — BONNO, Anthony Victor

DEPARTMENT	OCCUPATION	WORKS IN (STATE)	SEX	S.S. ACCOUNT NO.	NAME—LAST	FIRST	MIDDLE	MARITAL STATUS	W/H ALLOW.
Plant	Mixer Operator	PA	M X	537-10-3481	BONNO	Anthony	Victor	M	4

SALARY: $
WEEKLY RATE: $
HOURLY RATE: $ 7.65
OVERTIME RATE: $ 11.48

GROUP INSURANCE: $24,000--30¢/M
OTHER DEDUCTIONS INFORMATION — UNION DUES: $8 each pay

19__ PAYDAY	REGULAR EARNINGS HRS.	RATE	AMOUNT	OVERTIME EARNINGS HRS.	RATE	AMOUNT	CUMULATIVE EARNINGS	FICA OASDI	HI	SUTA	FIT	SIT	CIT	OTHER DEDUCTIONS	CK. NO.	NET PAID AMOUNT
YEAR-TO-DATE TOTAL			10 2 9 3 40			10 2 8 60	113 2 2 00	7 0 1 96	1 6 4 17	1 6 98	3 1 0 00	3 1 7 02	5 6 1 66	2 1 6 80		90 3 3 41
1 10/9	80	7 65	6 1 2 00				119 3 4 00	3 7 94	8 87	92	2 00	1 7 14	3 0 36	8 00	672	5 0 6 77
2																
3																
4																
5																
6																
QUARTER TOTAL																
YEARLY TOTAL																

Employee Payroll Record — FERGUSON, James Claude

DEPARTMENT	OCCUPATION	WORKS IN (STATE)	SEX	S.S. ACCOUNT NO.	NAME—LAST	FIRST	MIDDLE	MARITAL STATUS	W/H ALLOW.
Sales	Sales Manager	PA	M X	486-03-8645	FERGUSON	James	Claude	M	5

SALARY: $ 32,500/yr.
WEEKLY RATE: $ 625.00
HOURLY RATE: $ 15.63
OVERTIME RATE: $

GROUP INSURANCE: $49,000--30¢/M
OTHER DEDUCTIONS INFORMATION — UNION DUES:

19__ PAYDAY	REGULAR EARNINGS HRS.	RATE	AMOUNT	OVERTIME EARNINGS HRS.	RATE	AMOUNT	CUMULATIVE EARNINGS	FICA OASDI	HI	SUTA	FIT	SIT	CIT	OTHER DEDUCTIONS	CK. NO.	NET PAID AMOUNT
YEAR-TO-DATE TOTAL			231 2 5 00				231 2 5 00	14 3 3 75	3 3 5 31	3 4 69	17 9 1 00	6 4 7 50	11 4 7 00	1 3 2 30		176 0 3 45
1 10/9	80		12 5 0 00				243 7 5 00	7 7 50	1 8 13	1 88	8 4 00	3 5 00	6 2 00		673	9 7 1 49
2																
3																
4																
5																
6																
QUARTER TOTAL																
YEARLY TOTAL																

Employee 1

Field	Value
DEPARTMENT	Office
OCCUPATION	Executive Secretary
WORKS IN (STATE)	PA
S.S. ACCOUNT NO.	213-09-4567
NAME—LAST	FORD
FIRST	Catherine
MIDDLE	Louise
SEX	F X
MARITAL STATUS	S
W/H ALLOW.	2
GROUP INSURANCE	$18,000--30¢/M

SALARY	$ 975/mo.
WEEKLY RATE	$ 225.00
HOURLY RATE	$ 5.63
OVERTIME RATE	$ 8.45

19__ PAYDAY	REGULAR EARNINGS HRS.	RATE	AMOUNT	OVERTIME EARNINGS HRS.	RATE	AMOUNT	CUMULATIVE EARNINGS	FICA OASDI	HI	SUTA	FIT	SIT	CIT	UNION DUES	OTHER DEDUCTIONS OTHER	CK. NO.	NET PAID AMOUNT
YEAR-TO-DATE TOTAL			6300 00				6300 00	390 60	91 35	9 45	439 00	176 40	312 48		37 80		4842 92
1 10/9	80		450 00				6750 00	27 90	6 53	68	27 00	12 60	22 32			674	352 97
2																	
3																	
4																	
5																	
6																	
QUARTER TOTAL																	
YEARLY TOTAL																	

Employee 2

Field	Value
DEPARTMENT	Sales
OCCUPATION	Sales Representative
WORKS IN (STATE)	PA
S.S. ACCOUNT NO.	282-37-9352
NAME—LAST	MANN
FIRST	Dewey
MIDDLE	Wilson
SEX	F X
MARITAL STATUS	M
W/H ALLOW.	4
GROUP INSURANCE	$35,000--30¢/M

SALARY	$ 1,950/mo.
WEEKLY RATE	$ 450.00
HOURLY RATE	$ 11.25
OVERTIME RATE	$

19__ PAYDAY	REGULAR EARNINGS HRS.	RATE	AMOUNT	OVERTIME EARNINGS HRS.	RATE	AMOUNT	CUMULATIVE EARNINGS	FICA OASDI	HI	SUTA	FIT	SIT	CIT	UNION DUES	OTHER DEDUCTIONS OTHER	CK. NO.	NET PAID AMOUNT
YEAR-TO-DATE TOTAL			5400 00				5400 00	334 80	78 30	8 10	332 00	151 20	267 84		31 50		4196 26
1 10/9	80		900 00				6300 00	55 80	13 05	1 35	47 00	25 20	44 64			675	712 96
2																	
3																	
4																	
5																	
6																	
QUARTER TOTAL																	
YEARLY TOTAL																	

Employee Payroll Record — O'NEILL, Joseph Tyler

Field	Value	Field	Value
DEPARTMENT	Admin.	OCCUPATION	President
WORKS IN (STATE)	PA	SEX	M (X)
S.S. ACCOUNT NO.	897-04-1534	NAME—LAST	O'NEILL
FIRST	Joseph	MIDDLE	Tyler
W/H ALLOW.	3	MARITAL STATUS	M
SALARY	$60,000/yr.	WEEKLY RATE	$1,153.85
HOURLY RATE	$28.85	OVERTIME RATE	$
GROUP INSURANCE	$90,000--30¢/M		

	REGULAR EARNINGS			OVERTIME EARNINGS				CUMULATIVE EARNINGS	DEDUCTIONS								CK. NO.	NET PAID AMOUNT
19__ PAYDAY	HRS.	RATE	AMOUNT	HRS.	RATE	AMOUNT			FICA OASDI	FICA HI	SUTA	FIT	SIT	CIT	OTHER DEDUCTIONS		
YEAR-TO-DATE TOTAL			426 9 2 27					426 9 2 27	26 4 6 92	6 1 9 04	6 4 04	61 1 6 00	11 9 38	21 1 7 54	2 0 2 50		297 3 0 85
1 10/9	80		23 0 7 69					449 9 9 96	1 4 3 08	3 3 46	3 46	3 3 1 00	6 4 62	1 1 4 46		676	16 1 7 61
2																	
3																	
4																	
5																	
6																	
QUARTER TOTAL																	
YEARLY TOTAL																	

Employee Payroll Record — RUSSELL, Virginia Aloise

Field	Value	Field	Value
DEPARTMENT	Office	OCCUPATION	Time Clerk
WORKS IN (STATE)	PA	SEX	F (X)
S.S. ACCOUNT NO.	314-21-6337	NAME—LAST	RUSSELL
FIRST	Virginia	MIDDLE	Aloise
W/H ALLOW.	1	MARITAL STATUS	S
SALARY	$845/mo.	WEEKLY RATE	$195.00
HOURLY RATE	$4.88	OVERTIME RATE	$7.32
GROUP INSURANCE	$15,000--30¢/M		

	REGULAR EARNINGS			OVERTIME EARNINGS				CUMULATIVE EARNINGS	DEDUCTIONS								CK. NO.	NET PAID AMOUNT
19__ PAYDAY	HRS.	RATE	AMOUNT	HRS.	RATE	AMOUNT			FICA OASDI	FICA HI	SUTA	FIT	SIT	CIT	OTHER DEDUCTIONS		
YEAR-TO-DATE TOTAL			62 4 0 00					62 4 0 00	3 8 6 88	9 0 48	9 36	4 4 2 00	1 7 4 72	3 0 9 44	3 1 50		47 9 5 62
1 10/9	80		3 9 0 00					66 3 0 00	2 4 18	5 66	59	3 1 00	1 0 92	1 9 34		677	2 9 8 31
2																	
3																	
4																	
5																	
6																	
QUARTER TOTAL																	
YEARLY TOTAL																	

Payroll Ledger Card — Left

Field	Value
DEPARTMENT	Plant
OCCUPATION	Electrician
WORKS IN (STATE)	PA
NAME—LAST	RYAN
FIRST	Norman
MIDDLE	Allen
S.S. ACCOUNT NO.	526-23-1223
SEX	M
MARITAL STATUS	M
W/H ALLOW.	4
GROUP INSURANCE	$31,000--30¢/M
OTHER DEDUCTIONS INFORMATION — UNION DUES	$8 each pay
SALARY	$
WEEKLY RATE	$
HOURLY RATE	$ 9.80
OVERTIME RATE	$ 14.70

	REGULAR EARNINGS HRS.	RATE	AMOUNT	OVERTIME EARNINGS HRS.	RATE	AMOUNT	CUMULATIVE EARNINGS	FICA OASDI	HI	SUTA	FIT	SIT	CIT	OTHER DEDUCTIONS	CK. NO.	NET PAID AMOUNT
YEAR-TO-DATE TOTAL			132 87 50			13 97 80	146 85 30	9 10 49	2 12 94	2 2 03	8 70 00	4 11 19	7 28 34	2 35 70		112 94 61
1 10/9	80	9 80	7 84 00	.			154 69 30	4 8 61	1 1 37	1 18	2 9 00	2 1 95	3 8 89	8 00	678	6 25 00
2																
3																
4																
5																
6																
QUARTER TOTAL																
YEARLY TOTAL																

Payroll Ledger Card — Right

Field	Value
DEPARTMENT	Plant
OCCUPATION	Supervisor
WORKS IN (STATE)	PA
NAME—LAST	SOKOWSKI
FIRST	Thomas
MIDDLE	James
S.S. ACCOUNT NO.	662-04-8832
SEX	X
MARITAL STATUS	M
W/H ALLOW.	2
GROUP INSURANCE	$35,000--30¢/M
SALARY	$ 450.00
WEEKLY RATE	$
HOURLY RATE	$ 11.25
OVERTIME RATE	$

	REGULAR EARNINGS HRS.	RATE	AMOUNT	OVERTIME EARNINGS HRS.	RATE	AMOUNT	CUMULATIVE EARNINGS	FICA OASDI	HI	SUTA	FIT	SIT	CIT	OTHER DEDUCTIONS	CK. NO.	NET PAID AMOUNT
YEAR-TO-DATE TOTAL			166 50 00				166 50 00	10 32 30	2 41 43	2 4 98	16 02 00	4 66 20	8 25 84	9 4 50		123 62 75
1 10/9	80		9 00 00				175 50 00	5 5 80	1 3 05	1 35	7 4 00	2 5 20	4 4 64		679	6 85 96
2																
3																
4																
5																
6																
QUARTER TOTAL																
YEARLY TOTAL																

301

Employee Record — Left

Field	Value
DEPARTMENT	Office
OCCUPATION	Accounting Trainee
WORKS IN (STATE)	PA
NAME—LAST	
S.S. ACCOUNT NO.	
SEX	M / F
FIRST	
MIDDLE	
MARITAL STATUS	S
W/H ALLOW.	1
GROUP INSURANCE	$12,000--30¢/M
SALARY	$ 650/mo.
WEEKLY RATE	$ 150.00
HOURLY RATE	$ 3.75
OVERTIME RATE	$ 5.63

19__ PAYDAY	REGULAR EARNINGS HRS.	RATE	AMOUNT	OVERTIME EARNINGS HRS.	RATE	AMOUNT	CUMULATIVE EARNINGS	FICA OASDI	FICA HI	SUTA	FIT	SIT	CIT	OTHER DEDUCTIONS	CK. NO.	NET PAID AMOUNT
YEAR-TO-DATE TOTAL			5550 00				5550 00	344 10	80 48	8 33	409 00	155 40	275 28	32 40		4245 01
1 10/9	80		300 00				5850 00	18 60	4 35	45	18 00	8 40	14 88		680	235 32
2																
3																
4																
5																
6																
QUARTER TOTAL																
YEARLY TOTAL																

Employee Record — Right

Field	Value
DEPARTMENT	Office
OCCUPATION	Programmer
WORKS IN (STATE)	PA
NAME—LAST	WILLIAMS
S.S. ACCOUNT NO.	518-30-6741
SEX	M / F (X)
FIRST	Ruth
MIDDLE	Virginia
MARITAL STATUS	S
W/H ALLOW.	0
GROUP INSURANCE	$22,000--30¢/M
SALARY	$ 1,235/mo.
WEEKLY RATE	$ 285.00
HOURLY RATE	$ 7.13
OVERTIME RATE	$ 10.70

19__ PAYDAY	REGULAR EARNINGS HRS.	RATE	AMOUNT	OVERTIME EARNINGS HRS.	RATE	AMOUNT	CUMULATIVE EARNINGS	FICA OASDI	FICA HI	SUTA	FIT	SIT	CIT	OTHER DEDUCTIONS	CK. NO.	NET PAID AMOUNT
YEAR-TO-DATE TOTAL			10260 00				10260 00	636 12	148 77	15 39	1306 00	287 28	508 86	59 40		7298 18
1 10/9	80		570 00				10830 00	35 34	8 27	86	71 00	15 96	28 27		681	410 30
2																
3																
4																
5																
6																
QUARTER TOTAL																
YEARLY TOTAL																

DEPARTMENT	OCCUPATION	WORKS IN (STATE)	SEX		S.S. ACCOUNT NO.	NAME—LAST	FIRST	MIDDLE
			M	F				

OTHER DEDUCTIONS INFORMATION						
GROUP INSURANCE	UNION DUES	OTHER	SALARY	$	W/H ALLOW.	MARITAL STATUS
			WEEKLY RATE	$		
			HOURLY RATE	$		
			OVERTIME RATE	$		

	19___ PAYDAY	REGULAR EARNINGS			OVERTIME EARNINGS			CUMULATIVE EARNINGS	DEDUCTIONS							NET PAID	
		HRS.	RATE	AMOUNT	HRS.	RATE	AMOUNT		FICA OASDI	FICA HI	SUTA	FIT	SIT	CIT	OTHER DEDUCTIONS	CK. NO.	AMOUNT
YEAR-TO-DATE TOTAL																	
1																	
2																	
3																	
4																	
5																	
6																	
QUARTER TOTAL																	
YEARLY TOTAL																	

DEPARTMENT	OCCUPATION	WORKS IN (STATE)	SEX		S.S. ACCOUNT NO.	NAME—LAST	FIRST	MIDDLE
			M	F				

OTHER DEDUCTIONS INFORMATION						
GROUP INSURANCE	UNION DUES	OTHER	SALARY	$	W/H ALLOW.	MARITAL STATUS
			WEEKLY RATE	$		
			HOURLY RATE	$		
			OVERTIME RATE	$		

	19___ PAYDAY	REGULAR EARNINGS			OVERTIME EARNINGS			CUMULATIVE EARNINGS	DEDUCTIONS							NET PAID	
		HRS.	RATE	AMOUNT	HRS.	RATE	AMOUNT		FICA OASDI	FICA HI	SUTA	FIT	SIT	CIT	OTHER DEDUCTIONS	CK. NO.	AMOUNT
YEAR-TO-DATE TOTAL																	
1																	
2																	
3																	
4																	
5																	
6																	
QUARTER TOTAL																	
YEARLY TOTAL																	

DEPARTMENT

OCCUPATION

WORKS IN (STATE)

S.S. ACCOUNT NO.

NAME—LAST FIRST MIDDLE

SEX M F

MARITAL STATUS

W/H ALLOW.

GROUP INSURANCE

OTHER DEDUCTIONS INFORMATION

UNION DUES OTHER

SALARY $
WEEKLY RATE $
HOURLY RATE $
OVERTIME RATE $

NET PAID

DEDUCTIONS

| REGULAR EARNINGS | | | OVERTIME EARNINGS | | | CUMULATIVE EARNINGS | FICA | | FIT | SIT | CIT | SUTA | OTHER DEDUCTIONS | CK. NO. | AMOUNT |
| HRS. | RATE | AMOUNT | HRS. | RATE | AMOUNT | | OASDI | HI | | | | | | | |

19 ___ PAYDAY

YEAR-TO-DATE TOTAL
1
2
3
4
5
6
QUARTER TOTAL
YEARLY TOTAL

DEPARTMENT

OCCUPATION

WORKS IN (STATE)

S.S. ACCOUNT NO.

NAME—LAST FIRST MIDDLE

SEX M F

MARITAL STATUS

W/H ALLOW.

GROUP INSURANCE

OTHER DEDUCTIONS INFORMATION

UNION DUES OTHER

SALARY $
WEEKLY RATE $
HOURLY RATE $
OVERTIME RATE $

NET PAID

DEDUCTIONS

REGULAR EARNINGS — HRS., RATE, AMOUNT
OVERTIME EARNINGS — HRS., RATE, AMOUNT
CUMULATIVE EARNINGS
FICA — OASDI, HI, FIT, SIT, CIT, SUTA, OTHER DEDUCTIONS, CK. NO., AMOUNT

19 ___ PAYDAY

YEAR-TO-DATE TOTAL
1
2
3
4
5
6
QUARTER TOTAL
YEARLY TOTAL

	TIME CARD NO.	NAME	MARITAL STATUS	NO. W/H ALLOW.	REGULAR EARNINGS			OVERTIME EARNINGS		
					HOURS WORKED	RATE PER HOUR	AMOUNT	HOURS WORKED	RATE PER HOUR	AMOUNT
1										
2										
3										
4										
5										
6										
7										
8										
9										
10										
11										
12										
13										
14										
15										
16										
17										
18										
19										
20										
21										
22										
23										
24										
25										
26										
27										
28										
29										
30										
31										
32										
33										
34										
35										

STEIMER COMPANY, INC.
PAYROLL REGISTER

TOTAL EARNINGS	DEDUCTIONS								CHECK NO.
	OASDI TAX	HI TAX	FIT	SIT	CIT	SUTA	GROUP INS.	HEALTH INS.	

	NAME	MARITAL STATUS	No. W/H ALLOW.	TIME RECORD															REGULAR EARNINGS			OVERTIME EA	
				S	M	T	W	T	F	S	S	M	T	W	T	F	S	HOURS	RATE	AMOUNT	HOURS	RATE
1																						
2																						
3																						
4																						
5																						
6																						
7																						
8																						
9																						
10																						
11																						
12																						
13																						
14																						
15																						
16																						
17																						
18																						
19																						
20																						
21																						
22																						
23																						
24																						
25																						
26																						
27																						
28																						
29																						
30																						
31																						
32																						
33																						
34																						
35																						
36																						

GLO-BRITE PAINT COMPANY

RNINGS	TOTAL EARNINGS	DEDUCTIONS								NET PAID		TAX	
MOUNT		OASDI	HI	SUTA	FIT	SIT	CIT	GROUP INS.	UNION DUES	CHECK NO.	AMOUNT	OASDI	HI

Transaction No. 13

AMOUNT OF DEPOSIT (Do NOT type; please print.)

Mark the "X" in this box only if there is a change to Employer Identification Number (EIN) or Name.

See Instructions on page 1.

DOLLARS | CENTS

BANK NAME/ DATE STAMP

EIN 31-0450660

GLO-BRITE PAINT COMPANY
2215 SALVADOR STREET
PHILADELPHIA, PA 19175-0682

IRS USE ONLY

Darken only one TYPE OF TAX		a n d	Darken only one TAX PERIOD
941	Sch. A		1st Quarter
990C	1120		2nd Quarter
943	990T		3rd Quarter
720	990PF		4th Quarter
CT-1	1042		
940			62

Telephone number (   )

FOR BANK USE IN MICR ENCODING

Federal Tax Deposit Coupon
Form 8109

Transaction No. 28

AMOUNT OF DEPOSIT (Do NOT type; please print.)

Mark the "X" in this box only if there is a change to Employer Identification Number (EIN) or Name.

See Instructions on page 1.

DOLLARS | CENTS

BANK NAME/ DATE STAMP

EIN 31-0450660

GLO-BRITE PAINT COMPANY
2215 SALVADOR STREET
PHILADELPHIA, PA 19175-0682

IRS USE ONLY

Darken only one TYPE OF TAX		a n d	Darken only one TAX PERIOD
941	Sch. A		1st Quarter
990C	1120		2nd Quarter
943	990T		3rd Quarter
720	990PF		4th Quarter
CT-1	1042		
940			62

Telephone number (   )

FOR BANK USE IN MICR ENCODING

Federal Tax Deposit Coupon
Form 8109

Transaction No. 36

AMOUNT OF DEPOSIT (Do NOT type; please print.)

Mark the "X" in this box only if there is a change to Employer Identification Number (EIN) or Name.

See Instructions on page 1.

DOLLARS | CENTS

BANK NAME/ DATE STAMP

EIN 31-0450660

GLO-BRITE PAINT COMPANY
2215 SALVADOR STREET
PHILADELPHIA, PA 19175-0682

IRS USE ONLY

Darken only one TYPE OF TAX		a n d	Darken only one TAX PERIOD
941	Sch. A		1st Quarter
990C	1120		2nd Quarter
943	990T		3rd Quarter
720	990PF		4th Quarter
CT-1	1042		
940			62

Telephone number (   )

FOR BANK USE IN MICR ENCODING

Federal Tax Deposit Coupon
Form 8109

Transaction No. 38

AMOUNT OF DEPOSIT (Do NOT type; please print.)

DOLLARS	CENTS

Mark the "X" in this box only if there is a change to Employer Identification Number (EIN) or Name.

See Instructions on page 1.

EIN 31-0450660

BANK NAME/ DATE STAMP

GLO-BRITE PAINT COMPANY
2215 SALVADOR STREET
PHILADELPHIA, PA 19175-0682

IRS USE ONLY

Darken only one TYPE OF TAX		a n d	Darken only one TAX PERIOD
941	Sch. A		1st Quarter
990C	1120		2nd Quarter
943	990T		3rd Quarter
720	990PF		4th Quarter
CT-1	1042		
940			

62

Telephone number ( )

FOR BANK USE IN MICR ENCODING

Federal Tax Deposit Coupon
Form 8109

Transaction No. 3

EMPLOYER DEPOSIT STATEMENT OF INCOME TAX WITHHELD
Use Only When Employers Do Not Have Preprinted Coupons
ALL EMPLOYERS MUST FILE A PA-W3 RETURN FOR EACH QUARTER

PA-501R
PA DEPARTMENT OF REVENUE

19--

EIN	QUARTER	QUARTER ENDING	DUE DATE	TYPE FILER	EXPECTED 3-MONTH WITHHOLDING WILL BE:
31-0450660	9-04	10/15/--	10/20/--	MONTHLY ☐	$300 OR MORE BUT LESS THAN $1,000 TAX
				SEMI-MONTHLY ☐	$1,000 OR MORE TAX

DATE WAGES WERE FIRST PAID

BUSINESS NAME AND ADDRESS

Glo-Brite Paint Company
2215 Salvador Street
Philadelphia, PA 19175-0682

1.	GROSS COMPENSATION	
2.	PA INCOME TAX WITHHELD	
3.	LESS CREDITS	
4.	PLUS INTEREST	
5.	PAYMENT	

DATE	TELEPHONE NUMBER ( )	SIGNATURE	TITLE

Transaction No. 6

EMPLOYER DEPOSIT STATEMENT OF INCOME TAX WITHHELD
Use Only When Employers Do Not Have Preprinted Coupons
ALL EMPLOYERS MUST FILE A PA-W3 RETURN FOR EACH QUARTER

PA-501R
PA DEPARTMENT OF REVENUE

19--

EIN	QUARTER	QUARTER ENDING	DUE DATE	TYPE FILER	EXPECTED 3-MONTH WITHHOLDING WILL BE:
31-0450660	9-04	10/31/--	11/4/--	MONTHLY ☐	$300 OR MORE BUT LESS THAN $1,000 TAX
				SEMI-MONTHLY ☐	$1,000 OR MORE TAX

DATE WAGES WERE FIRST PAID

BUSINESS NAME AND ADDRESS

Glo-Brite Paint Company
2215 Salvador Street
Philadelphia, PA 19175-0682

1.	GROSS COMPENSATION	
2.	PA INCOME TAX WITHHELD	
3.	LESS CREDITS	
4.	PLUS INTEREST	
5.	PAYMENT	

DATE	TELEPHONE NUMBER ( )	SIGNATURE	TITLE

Transaction No. 15

PA-501R
PA DEPARTMENT OF REVENUE

19--

EIN	QUARTER	QUARTER ENDING	DUE DATE	TYPE FILER	EXPECTED 3-MONTH WITHHOLDING WILL BE:
31-0450660	9-04	11/15/--	11/18/--	**M**ONTHLY ☐	$300 OR MORE BUT LESS THAN $1,000 TAX
				SEMI-MONTHLY ☐	$1,000 OR MORE TAX

DATE WAGES WERE FIRST PAID

BUSINESS NAME AND ADDRESS

Glo-Brite Paint Company
2215 Salvador Street
Philadelphia, PA 19175-0682

1.	GROSS COMPENSATION	
2.	PA INCOME TAX WITHHELD	
3.	LESS CREDITS	
4.	PLUS INTEREST	
5.	PAYMENT	

DATE	TELEPHONE NUMBER ( )	SIGNATURE	TITLE

Transaction No. 20

PA-501R
PA DEPARTMENT OF REVENUE

19--

EIN	QUARTER	QUARTER ENDING	DUE DATE	TYPE FILER	EXPECTED 3-MONTH WITHHOLDING WILL BE:
31-0450660	9-04	11/30/--	12/3/--	**M**ONTHLY ☐	$300 OR MORE BUT LESS THAN $1,000 TAX
				SEMI-MONTHLY ☐	$1,000 OR MORE TAX

DATE WAGES WERE FIRST PAID

BUSINESS NAME AND ADDRESS

Glo-Brite Paint Company
2215 Salvador Street
Philadelphia, PA 19175-0682

1.	GROSS COMPENSATION	
2.	PA INCOME TAX WITHHELD	
3.	LESS CREDITS	
4.	PLUS INTEREST	
5.	PAYMENT	

DATE	TELEPHONE NUMBER ( )	SIGNATURE	TITLE

Transaction No. 29

PA-501R
PA DEPARTMENT OF REVENUE

19--

EIN	QUARTER	QUARTER ENDING	DUE DATE	TYPE FILER	EXPECTED 3-MONTH WITHHOLDING WILL BE:
31-0450660	9-04	12/15/--	12/18/--	**M**ONTHLY ☐	$300 OR MORE BUT LESS THAN $1,000 TAX
				SEMI-MONTHLY ☐	$1,000 OR MORE TAX

DATE WAGES WERE FIRST PAID

BUSINESS NAME AND ADDRESS

Glo-Brite Paint Company
2215 Salvador Street
Philadelphia, PA 19175-0682

1.	GROSS COMPENSATION	
2.	PA INCOME TAX WITHHELD	
3.	LESS CREDITS	
4.	PLUS INTEREST	
5.	PAYMENT	

DATE	TELEPHONE NUMBER ( )	SIGNATURE	TITLE

Transaction No. 34

PA-501R
PA DEPARTMENT OF REVENUE

19__

EIN	QUARTER	QUARTER ENDING	DUE DATE	TYPE FILER	EXPECTED 3-MONTH WITHHOLDING WILL BE:
31-0450660	9-04	12/31/--	1/6/--	MONTHLY ☐	$300 OR MORE BUT LESS THAN $1,000 TAX
				SEMI-MONTHLY ☐	$1,000 OR MORE TAX

DATE WAGES WERE FIRST PAID

BUSINESS NAME AND ADDRESS

Glo-Brite Paint Company
2215 Salvador Street
Philadelphia, PA 19175-0682

1.	GROSS COMPENSATION	
2.	PA INCOME TAX WITHHELD	
3.	LESS CREDITS	
4.	PLUS INTEREST	
5.	PAYMENT	

DATE	TELEPHONE NUMBER ( )	SIGNATURE	TITLE

Transaction No. 2

THE CITY OF PHILADELPHIA
EMPLOYER'S DEPOSITORY RETURN
OF TAX WITHHELD (W7)

Glo-Brite Paint Company
2215 Salvador Street
Philadelphia, PA 19175-0682

T.D.	TOT. P.
T.P.	T.B.
I.&P.	I.&P. BAL.

FILE RETURN AND
PAY TAX FOR

Week No.	41
FROM	10/4/--
TO	10/10/--

W - 7

PERIOD	TYPE	S.I.C.	ACCOUNT NO.
4	1	501	6791855

1. TOTAL COMPENSATION (INCLUDE VALUE OF PERSONAL USE OF EMPLOYER OWNED VEHICLE)		
2. DEDUCT COMPENSATION PAID NON-RESIDENTS FOR SERVICES OUTSIDE PHILADELPHIA		
3. TAXABLE COMPENSATION (LINE 1 MINUS LINE 2)		
4A NUMBER OF RESIDENTS	PORTION OF LINE 3 PAID TO RESIDENTS	
4B NUMBER OF NON-RESIDENTS	PORTION OF LINE 3 PAID TO NON-RESIDENTS NOTE: (4A + 4B MUST EQUAL LINE 3)	

83-T-474

5. LINE 4A-TAX Withheld at 4.96%	6. LINE 4B-TAX Withheld at 4.3125%	7. TOTAL Block 5 Plus Block 6	8. Penalty + Interest (See Reverse)	9. TOTAL-Block 7 plus Block 8

PLEASE ANSWER FULLY
Have you ceased being an employer? ....
Have you discontinued or sold business? ....
If yes, give date ....
If sold, give name of new owner(s) ....

Transaction No. 5

THE CITY OF PHILADELPHIA
EMPLOYER'S DEPOSITORY RETURN
OF TAX WITHHELD (W7)

Glo-Brite Paint Company
2215 Salvador Street
Philadelphia, PA 19175-0682

T.D.	TOT. P.
T.P.	T.B.
I.&P.	I.&P. BAL.

FILE RETURN AND
PAY TAX FOR

Week No.	43
FROM	10/18/--
TO	10/24/--

W - 7

PERIOD	TYPE	S.I.C.	ACCOUNT NO.
4	1	501	6791855

1. TOTAL COMPENSATION (INCLUDE VALUE OF PERSONAL USE OF EMPLOYER OWNED VEHICLE)		
2. DEDUCT COMPENSATION PAID NON-RESIDENTS FOR SERVICES OUTSIDE PHILADELPHIA		
3. TAXABLE COMPENSATION (LINE 1 MINUS LINE 2)		
4A NUMBER OF RESIDENTS	PORTION OF LINE 3 PAID TO RESIDENTS	
4B NUMBER OF NON-RESIDENTS	PORTION OF LINE 3 PAID TO NON-RESIDENTS NOTE: (4A + 4B MUST EQUAL LINE 3)	

83-T-474

5. LINE 4A-TAX Withheld at 4.96%	6. LINE 4B-TAX Withheld at 4.3125%	7. TOTAL Block 5 Plus Block 6	8. Penalty + Interest (See Reverse)	9. TOTAL-Block 7 plus Block 8

PLEASE ANSWER FULLY
Have you ceased being an employer? ....
Have you discontinued or sold business? ....
If yes, give date ....
If sold, give name of new owner(s) ....

Transaction No. 11

Glo-Brite Paint Company
2215 Salvador Street
Philadelphia, PA 19175-0682

FILE RETURN AND PAY TAX FOR	
Week No.	45
FROM	11/1/--
TO	11/7/--

W - 7

T.D.		TOT. P.	
T. P.		T.B.	
I.&P.		I.&P. BAL.	

PERIOD	TYPE	S.I.C.	ACCOUNT NO.
4	1	501	6791855

1. TOTAL COMPENSATION (INCLUDE VALUE OF PERSONAL USE OF EMPLOYER OWNED VEHICLE)
2. DEDUCT COMPENSATION PAID NON-RESIDENTS FOR SERVICES OUTSIDE PHILADELPHIA
3. TAXABLE COMPENSATION (LINE 1 MINUS LINE 2)
4A. NUMBER OF RESIDENTS / PORTION OF LINE 3 PAID TO RESIDENTS
4B. NUMBER OF NON-RESIDENTS / PORTION OF LINE 3 PAID TO NON-RESIDENTS NOTE: (4A + 4B MUST EQUAL LINE 3)

83-T-474

5. LINE 4A-TAX Withheld at 4.96%	6. LINE 4B-TAX Withheld at 4.3125%	7. TOTAL Block 5 Plus Block 6	8. Penalty + Interest (See Reverse)	9. TOTAL-Block 7 plus Block 8

PLEASE ANSWER FULLY
Have you ceased being an employer? ....
Have you discontinued or sold business? ....
If yes, give date ....
If sold, give name of new owner(s) ....

Transaction No. 17

Glo-Brite Paint Company
2215 Salvador Street
Philadelphia, PA 19175-0682

FILE RETURN AND PAY TAX FOR	
Week No.	47
FROM	11/15/--
TO	11/21/--

W - 7

T.D.		TOT. P.	
T. P.		T.B.	
I.&P.		I.&P. BAL.	

PERIOD	TYPE	S.I.C.	ACCOUNT NO.
4	1	501	6791855

1. TOTAL COMPENSATION (INCLUDE VALUE OF PERSONAL USE OF EMPLOYER OWNED VEHICLE)
2. DEDUCT COMPENSATION PAID NON-RESIDENTS FOR SERVICES OUTSIDE PHILADELPHIA
3. TAXABLE COMPENSATION (LINE 1 MINUS LINE 2)
4A. NUMBER OF RESIDENTS / PORTION OF LINE 3 PAID TO RESIDENTS
4B. NUMBER OF NON-RESIDENTS / PORTION OF LINE 3 PAID TO NON-RESIDENTS NOTE: (4A + 4B MUST EQUAL LINE 3)

83-T-474

5. LINE 4A-TAX Withheld at 4.96%	6. LINE 4B-TAX Withheld at 4.3125%	7. TOTAL Block 5 Plus Block 6	8. Penalty + Interest (See Reverse)	9. TOTAL-Block 7 plus Block 8

PLEASE ANSWER FULLY
Have you ceased being an employer? ....
Have you discontinued or sold business? ....
If yes, give date ....
If sold, give name of new owner(s) ....

Transaction No. 25

Glo-Brite Paint Company
2215 Salvador Street
Philadelphia, PA 19175-0682

FILE RETURN AND PAY TAX FOR	
Week No.	49
FROM	11/29/--
TO	12/5/--

W - 7

T.D.		TOT. P.	
T. P.		T.B.	
I.&P.		I.&P. BAL.	

PERIOD	TYPE	S.I.C.	ACCOUNT NO.
4	1	501	6791855

1. TOTAL COMPENSATION (INCLUDE VALUE OF PERSONAL USE OF EMPLOYER OWNED VEHICLE)
2. DEDUCT COMPENSATION PAID NON-RESIDENTS FOR SERVICES OUTSIDE PHILADELPHIA
3. TAXABLE COMPENSATION (LINE 1 MINUS LINE 2)
4A. NUMBER OF RESIDENTS / PORTION OF LINE 3 PAID TO RESIDENTS
4B. NUMBER OF NON-RESIDENTS / PORTION OF LINE 3 PAID TO NON-RESIDENTS NOTE: (4A + 4B MUST EQUAL LINE 3)

83-T-474

5. LINE 4A-TAX Withheld at 4.96%	6. LINE 4B-TAX Withheld at 4.3125%	7. TOTAL Block 5 Plus Block 6	8. Penalty + Interest (See Reverse)	9. TOTAL-Block 7 plus Block 8

PLEASE ANSWER FULLY
Have you ceased being an employer? ....
Have you discontinued or sold business? ....
If yes, give date ....
If sold, give name of new owner(s) ....

THE CITY OF PHILADELPHIA
EMPLOYER'S DEPOSITORY RETURN
OF TAX WITHHELD (W7)

Glo-Brite Paint Company
2215 Salvador Street
Philadelphia, PA 19175-0682

FILE RETURN AND PAY TAX FOR	
Week No.	51
FROM	12/13/--
TO	12/19/--

W - 7

T.D.		TOT. P.	
T. P.		T.B.	
L&P.		L&P. BAL.	

PERIOD	TYPE	S.I.C.	ACCOUNT NO.
4	1	501	6791855

	1. TOTAL COMPENSATION (INCLUDE VALUE OF PERSONAL USE OF EMPLOYER OWNED VEHICLE)	
	2. DEDUCT COMPENSATION PAID NON-RESIDENTS FOR SERVICES OUTSIDE PHILADELPHIA	
	3. TAXABLE COMPENSATION (LINE 1 MINUS LINE 2)	
4A	NUMBER OF RESIDENTS / PORTION OF LINE 3 PAID TO RESIDENTS	
4B	NUMBER OF NON-RESIDENTS / PORTION OF LINE 3 PAID TO NON-RESIDENTS NOTE: (4A + 4B MUST EQUAL LINE 3)	

83-T-474

5. LINE 4A-TAX Withheld at 4.96%	6. LINE 4B-TAX Withheld at 4.3125%	7. TOTAL Block 5 Plus Block 6	8. Penalty + Interest (See Reverse)	9. TOTAL-Block 7 plus Block 8

PLEASE ANSWER FULLY
Have you ceased being an employer? ....
Have you discontinued or sold business? ....
If yes, give date ....
If sold, give name of new owner(s) ....

PA-W3R
COMMONWEALTH OF PENNSYLVANIA
DEPARTMENT OF REVENUE

EMPLOYER QUARTERLY RECONCILIATION RETURN OF INCOME TAX WITHHELD
For Use ONLY When Employers Do Not Have
Preprinted Coupons

19--

EIN	QUARTER	QUARTER ENDING	DUE DATE	BUSINESS NAME AND ADDRESS
31-0450660	9-04	12/31/--	2/1/--	Glo-Brite Paint Company 2215 Salvador Street Philadelphia, PA 19175-0682

RECORD OF PA WITHHOLDING TAX BY PERIOD			
Period	Semi-monthly Filer	Monthly Filer	Quarterly Filer
1			
2			
3			
4			
5			
6			
Total			

7. TOTAL COMPENSATION SUBJECT TO PA TAX	
8. TOTAL PA WITHHOLDING TAX (FROM LEFT)	
9. TOTAL DEPOSITS FOR QUARTER (INCLUDING PRIOR OVERPAYMENTS)	
10. TAX DUE (IF LINE 9 IS LESS THAN LINE 8)	
11. OVERPAYMENT (IF LINE 9 IS GREATER THAN LINE 8)	
12. PAYMENT	

Under penalties of perjury, I declare that I have examined this return and to the best of my knowledge and belief, it is true, correct and complete.

Date	Telephone Number ( )	Signature	Title

ANNUAL RECONCILIATION OF WAGE TAX

Due Date:
2/28/--

19--

Print your numbers like this:

| 1 | 2 | 3 | 4 | 5 | 6 | 7 | 8 | 9 | 0 |

Glo-Brite Paint Company
2215 Salvador Street
Philadelphia, PA 19175-0682

Type
Tax   W

SEE INSTRUCTIONS ON BACK

DATE WAGES TERMINATED: _____   ACCOUNT NO.   6 7 9 1 8 5 5
(IF APPLICABLE)

DATE BUSINESS TERMINATED: _____
(IF APPLICABLE)

PREPARER'S DAYTIME PHONE : _____

Note: "A" and "B" Denote Employees, Not Gross Wages

A. Number of Taxable Philadelphia Residents

B. Number of Taxable Non-Residents

1. Taxable Residents Compensation   0 0

2. Line 1 times .0496 (4.96%)

3. Taxable Non-Residents Compensation

4. Line 3 times .043125 (4.3125%)

5. Total Tax Due (Line 2 plus Line 4)

6. Tax Previously Paid For 19--

---DO NOT DETACH---

NAME: ACCOUNT NO.
                                               TYPE TAX: PERIOD: YEAR:

If Line 5 is Greater Than Line 6, Use Line 7

7. Tax Due (Line 5 Minus Line 6)
Make Check Payable To: City of Philadelphia

If line 5 is less than line 6, use line 8

8. Tax Overpaid (Line 6 Less Line 5)
     (SEE INSTRUCTIONS)

Signature: _____   Date _____

I certify that all amounts indicated as due the City of Philadelphia on this return were actually withheld from the gross compensation paid
by this taxpayer to its employees during the period(s) covered by this filing, and that I am authorized to so state.

Form **941**

4141

Department of the Treasury
Internal Revenue Service

Employer's Quarterly Federal Tax Return

▶ See separate instructions for information on completing this return.
Please type or print.

Enter state code for state in which deposits made ▶ [:] (see page 2 of instructions).

Name (as distinguished from trade name)

Date quarter ended
DEC 31, 19--

OMB No. 1545-0029

Trade name, if any
GLO-BRITE PAINT COMPANY

Employer identification number
31-0450660

Address (number and street)
2215 SALVADOR ST.

City, state, and ZIP code
PHILADELPHIA, PA
19175-0682

T	
FF	
FD	
FP	
I	
T	

If address is different from prior return, check here ▶ [ ]

IRS Use

1 1 1 1 1 1 1 1 1 1	2	3 3 3 3 3 3	4 4 4

| 5 5 5 | 6 | 7 | 8 8 8 8 8 8 | 9 9 9 | 10 10 10 10 10 10 10 10 10 |

If you do not have to file returns in the future, check here ▶ [ ] and enter date final wages paid ▶

If you are a seasonal employer, see **Seasonal employers** on page 2 and check here (see instructions) ▶ [ ]

1	Number of employees (except household) employed in the pay period that includes March 12th ▶		
2	Total wages and tips subject to withholding, plus other compensation	**2**	
3	Total income tax withheld from wages, tips, and sick pay	**3**	
4	Adjustment of withheld income tax for preceding quarters of calendar year .	**4**	
5	Adjusted total of income tax withheld (line 3 as adjusted by line 4—see instructions) . .	**5**	
6a	Taxable social security wages . . . . $_____ × 12.4% (.124) =	**6a**	
b	Taxable social security tips . . . . . . $_____ × 12.4% (.124) =	**6b**	
7	Taxable Medicare wages and tips . . . $_____ × 2.9% (.029) =	**7**	
8	Total social security and Medicare taxes (add lines 6a, 6b, and 7). Check here if wages are not subject to social security and/or Medicare tax . . . . ▶ [ ]	**8**	
9	Adjustment of social security and Medicare taxes (see instructions for required explanation) Sick Pay $_____ ± Fractions of Cents $_____ ± Other $_____ =	**9**	
10	Adjusted total of social security and Medicare taxes (line 8 as adjusted by line 9—see instructions)	**10**	
11	**Total taxes** (add lines 5 and 10)	**11**	
12	Advance earned income credit (EIC) payments made to employees, if any . . .	**12**	
13	Net taxes (subtract line 12 from line 11). This should equal line 17, column (d) below (or line D of Schedule B (Form 941))	**13**	
14	Total deposits for quarter, including overpayment applied from a prior quarter	**14**	
15	**Balance due** (subtract line 14 from line 13). Pay to Internal Revenue Service	**15**	
16	Overpayment, if line 14 is more than line 13, enter excess here ▶ $_____ and check if to be: [ ] Applied to next return OR [ ] Refunded.		

17	Monthly Summary of Federal Tax Liability.

• Monthly depositors: Complete line 17, columns (a) through (d) and check here . . . . ▶ [ ]

• Semiweekly depositors: Complete Schedule B and check here . . . . ▶ [ ]

• All filers: If line 13 is less than $500, you need not complete line 17 or Schedule B.

(a) First month liability	(b) Second month liability	(c) Third month liability	(d) Total liability for quarter

Sign Here

Under penalties of perjury, I declare that I have examined this return, including accompanying schedules and statements, and to the best of my knowledge and belief, it is true, correct, and complete.

Signature ▶

Print Your Name and Title ▶

Date ▶

Form **941**

Form **940-EZ**

Department of the Treasury
Internal Revenue Service

**Employer's Annual Federal
Unemployment (FUTA) Tax Return**

OMB No. 1545-1110

19--

T	
FF	
FD	
FP	
I	
T	

If incorrect,
make any
necessary
changes. ▶

Name (as distinguished from trade name)

Trade name, if any
GLO-BRITE PAINT COMPANY

Address and ZIP code
**2215 SALVADOR ST. PHILADELPHIA,
PA 19175-0682**

Calendar year
19--

Employer identification number
31 - 0450660

*Follow the chart under **Who May Use Form 940-EZ** on page 2. If you cannot use Form 940-EZ, you must use Form 940 instead.*

A   Enter the amount of contributions paid to your state unemployment fund. (See instructions for line A on page 4.)▶ $ ....

B   (1) Enter the name of the state where you have to pay contributions . . . . ▶ ....
       (2) Enter your state reporting number as shown on state unemployment tax return. ▶ ....

If you will not have to file returns in the future, check here (see *Who Must File,* on page 2) **complete, and sign the return** . . . . . ▶ ☐

If this is an Amended Return check here . . . . ▶ ☐

Part I   Taxable Wages and FUTA Tax

1	Total payments (including payments shown on lines 2 and 3) during the calendar year for services of employees	**1**		
2	Exempt payments. (Explain all exempt payments, attaching additional sheets if necessary.) ▶	**2**		
3	Payments for services of more than $7,000. Enter only amounts over the first $7,000 paid to each employee. Do not include any exempt payments from line 2. Do not use state wage limitation. The $7,000 amount is the Federal wage base. Your state wage base may be different	**3**		
4	Total exempt payments (add lines 2 and 3)	**4**	
5	**Total taxable wages** (subtract line 4 from line 1) . . . . ▶	**5**	
6	**FUTA tax.** Multiply the wages on line 5 by .008 and enter here. (If the result is over $100, also complete Part II.)	**6**	
7	Total FUTA tax deposited for the year, including any overpayment applied from a prior year (from your records)	**7**	
8	**Amount you owe** (subtract line 7 from line 6). This should be $100 or less. Pay to "Internal Revenue Service". ▶	**8**	
9	Overpayment (subtract line 6 from line 7). Check if it is to be: ☐ **Applied to next return,** or ☐ **Refunded** ▶	**9**	

Part II   Record of Quarterly Federal Unemployment Tax Liability (Do not include state liability.) Complete only if line 6 is over $100.

Quarter	First (Jan. 1 – Mar. 31)	Second (Apr. 1 – June 30)	Third (July 1 – Sept. 30)	Fourth (Oct. 1 – Dec. 31)	Total for year
Liability for quarter	272.71	140.33	110.88		

Under penalties of perjury, I declare that I have examined this return, including accompanying schedules and statements, and, to the best of my knowledge and belief, it is true, correct, and complete, and that no part of any payment made to a state unemployment fund claimed as a credit was, or is to be, deducted from the payments to employees.

Signature ▶   Title (Owner, etc.) ▶   Date ▶

Form **940-EZ**

EMPLOYER'S REPORT FOR UNEMPLOYMENT COMPENSATION
READ INSTRUCTIONS ON REVERSE SIDE OF EMPLOYER'S COPY
ANSWER EACH ITEM. TYPE OR PRINT IN INK

UC-2A'S

PA FORM	QTR.	YEAR
UC-2	4TH 19--	

| INV. OR R.D. CLEARANCE | EMPL. ALPHA INDEX | CASHIER'S TRANSMITTAL NUMBER | 1. TOTAL NUMBER OF COVERED EMPLOYES IN PAY PERIOD INCL. 12TH OF MONTH INCLUDE EMPLOYES WHOSE WAGES EXCEED TAXABLE LIMIT. IF NONE ENTER "0". | FIRST MONTH | SECOND MONTH | THIRD MONTH |

I CERTIFY THAT THE INFORMATION ON FORMS UC-2/2A/2B IS TRUE AND CORRECT TO THE BEST OF MY KNOWLEDGE AND BELIEF. NO PART OF THE AMOUNT OF EMPLOYER CONTRIBUTIONS REPORTED ON TAXABLE WAGES WAS DEDUCTED OR IS TO BE DEDUCTED FROM THE EMPLOYE'S WAGES.

SIGN HERE
DO NOT PRINT _____
SIGNATURE OF OWNER, PARTNER, RESPONSIBLE OFFICER OR AUTHORIZED AGENT

TITLE _____ DATE _____

GIVE EXACT TITLE

EMPLOYER'S CONTRIBUTION RATE ▶ .035

EMPLOYER'S ACCT. NO. 46-3-3300

GLO-BRITE PAINT COMPANY
2215 SALVADOR STREET
PHILADELPHIA, PA 19175-0682

2. GROSS WAGES	$
2A. EMPLOYE CONTRIBUTIONS WITHHELD. WITHHOLDING RATE IS:	$
3. TAXABLE WAGES FOR EMPLOYER CONTRIBUTIONS	$
4. EMPLOYER CONTRIBUTIONS DUE (RATE X ITEM 3)	$
4A. TOTAL CONTRIBUTIONS DUE (ITEM 2A + 4)	$
5. INTEREST DUE SEE INSTRUCTIONS	$
6. PENALTY DUE SEE INSTRUCTIONS	$
7. TOTAL REMITTANCE (ITEM 4A + 5 + 6)	$

FOR DEPT. USE

DO NOT WRITE IN THIS SPACE

MAKE CHECKS PAYABLE TO:
PA UC FUND

SUBJECTIVITY DATE

DATE PAYMENT RECEIVED

REPORT TIMELY

REPORT DELINQUENT DATE

POST CASH CREDIT

WE $
C $
I $
P $

EXAMINED BY

IF ADDRESS HAS CHANGED, PLEASE CORRECT
UC-2B PORTION OF THIS FORM

EMPLOYER'S QUARTERLY REPORT OF
WAGES PAID TO EACH EMPLOYE

PA FORM	
UC-2A	
QTR.	YEAR
4TH 19--	

7A. TEL. NO. OF PREPARER _____

8. TOTAL NUMBER OF PAGES IN THIS REPORT ▷

9. GROSS WAGES (MUST AGREE WITH ITEM 2 ABOVE AND TOTALS OF ITEM 14) ▷ $

10. TOTAL NUMBER OF EMPLOYEES LISTED IN ITEM 13 ON ALL PAGES ▷

11. PLANT NUMBER ▷

FOR DEPT. USE

12. EMPLOYE'S SOC. SEC. ACCT. NO.	13. NAME OF EMPLOYE (TYPE OR PRINT IN INK)			14. GR. WAGES PD. THIS QTR.	15. CREDIT WEEKS
	FIRST NAME	INITIAL	LAST NAME		

LIST ANY ADDITIONAL EMPLOYES ON FORM UC-2A SUPPLEMENT OR ON CONTINUATION SHEETS APPROVED BY THE DEPARTMENT.

TOTAL FOR THIS PAGE _____

Transaction No. 12

a Control number	22222	Void ☐	For Official Use Only ▶		

b Employer's identification number		1 Wages, tips, other compensation	2 Federal income tax withheld

c Employer's name, address, and ZIP code	3 Social security wages	4 Social security tax withheld
	5 Medicare wages and tips	6 Medicare tax withheld
	7 Social security tips	8 Allocated tips

d Employee's social security number	9 Advance EIC payment	10 Dependent care benefits

e Employee's name (first, middle initial, last)	11 Nonqualified plans	12 Benefits included in Box 1
	13 See Instrs. for Box 13	14 Other

15 Statutory employee ☐	Deceased ☐	Pension plan ☐	Legal rep. ☐	942 emp. ☐	Subtotal ☐	Deferred compensation ☐

f Employee's address and ZIP code

16 State	Employer's state I.D. No.	17 State wages, tips, etc.	18 State income tax	19 Locality name	20 Local wages, tips, etc.	21 Local income tax

Department of the Treasury—Internal Revenue Service

Form **W-2** Wage and Tax Statement **19--**

Copy A For Social Security Administration

Transaction No. 27

a Control number	22222	Void ☐	For Official Use Only ▶		

b Employer's identification number		1 Wages, tips, other compensation	2 Federal income tax withheld

c Employer's name, address, and ZIP code	3 Social security wages	4 Social security tax withheld
	5 Medicare wages and tips	6 Medicare tax withheld
	7 Social security tips	8 Allocated tips

d Employee's social security number	9 Advance EIC payment	10 Dependent care benefits

e Employee's name (first, middle initial, last)	11 Nonqualified plans	12 Benefits included in Box 1
	13 See Instrs. for Box 13	14 Other

15 Statutory employee ☐	Deceased ☐	Pension plan ☐	Legal rep. ☐	942 emp. ☐	Subtotal ☐	Deferred compensation ☐

f Employee's address and ZIP code

16 State	Employer's state I.D. No.	17 State wages, tips, etc.	18 State income tax	19 Locality name	20 Local wages, tips, etc.	21 Local income tax

Department of the Treasury—Internal Revenue Service

Form **W-2** Wage and Tax Statement **19--**

Copy A For Social Security Administration

a Control number	22222	Void ☐	For Official Use Only ▶		
b Employer's identification number			**1** Wages, tips, other compensation	**2** Federal Income tax withheld
c Employer's name, address, and ZIP code			**3** Social security wages	**4** Social security tax withheld
			5 Medicare wages and tips	**6** Medicare tax withheld
			7 Social security tips	**8** Allocated tips
d Employee's social security number			**9** Advance EIC payment	**10** Dependent care benefits
e Employee's name (first, middle initial, last)			**11** Nonqualified plans	**12** Benefits included in Box 1
			13 See Instrs. for Box 13	**14** Other

15 Statutory employee ☐	Deceased ☐	Pension plan ☐	Legal rep. ☐	942 emp. ☐	Subtotal ☐	Deferred compensation ☐

f Employee's address and ZIP code

16 State	Employer's state I.D. No.	17 State wages, tips, etc.	18 State income tax	19 Locality name	20 Local wages, tips, etc.	21 Local income tax

Department of the Treasury—Internal Revenue Service

Form **W-2** Wage and Tax Statement **19--**

Copy A For Social Security Administration

---

a Control number	22222	Void ☐	For Official Use Only ▶		
b Employer's identification number			**1** Wages, tips, other compensation	**2** Federal Income tax withheld
c Employer's name, address, and ZIP code			**3** Social security wages	**4** Social security tax withheld
			5 Medicare wages and tips	**6** Medicare tax withheld
			7 Social security tips	**8** Allocated tips
d Employee's social security number			**9** Advance EIC payment	**10** Dependent care benefits
e Employee's name (first, middle initial, last)			**11** Nonqualified plans	**12** Benefits included in Box 1
			13 See Instrs. for Box 13	**14** Other

15 Statutory employee ☐	Deceased ☐	Pension plan ☐	Legal rep. ☐	942 emp. ☐	Subtotal ☐	Deferred compensation ☐

f Employee's address and ZIP code

16 State	Employer's state I.D. No.	17 State wages, tips, etc.	18 State income tax	19 Locality name	20 Local wages, tips, etc.	21 Local income tax

Department of the Treasury—Internal Revenue Service

Form **W-2** Wage and Tax Statement **19--**

Copy A For Social Security Administration

a Control number	22222	Void ☐	For Official Use Only ▶		
b Employer's identification number			**1** Wages, tips, other compensation		**2** Federal income tax withheld
c Employer's name, address, and ZIP code			**3** Social security wages		**4** Social security tax withheld
			5 Medicare wages and tips		**6** Medicare tax withheld
			7 Social security tips		**8** Allocated tips
d Employee's social security number			**9** Advance EIC payment		**10** Dependent care benefits
e Employee's name (first, middle initial, last)			**11** Nonqualified plans		**12** Benefits included in Box 1
			13 See Instrs. for Box 13		**14** Other

15 Statutory employee ☐	Deceased ☐	Pension plan ☐	Legal rep. ☐	942 emp. ☐	Subtotal ☐	Deferred compensation ☐

f Employee's address and ZIP code

16 State	Employer's state I.D. No.	**17** State wages, tips, etc.	**18** State income tax	**19** Locality name	**20** Local wages, tips, etc.	**21** Local income tax

Department of the Treasury—Internal Revenue Service

Form **W-2** Wage and Tax Statement **19--**

Copy A For Social Security Administration

---

a Control number	22222	Void ☐	For Official Use Only ▶		
b Employer's identification number			**1** Wages, tips, other compensation		**2** Federal income tax withheld
c Employer's name, address, and ZIP code			**3** Social security wages		**4** Social security tax withheld
			5 Medicare wages and tips		**6** Medicare tax withheld
			7 Social security tips		**8** Allocated tips
d Employee's social security number			**9** Advance EIC payment		**10** Dependent care benefits
e Employee's name (first, middle initial, last)			**11** Nonqualified plans		**12** Benefits included in Box 1
			13 See Instrs. for Box 13		**14** Other

15 Statutory employee ☐	Deceased ☐	Pension plan ☐	Legal rep. ☐	942 emp. ☐	Subtotal ☐	Deferred compensation ☐

f Employee's address and ZIP code

16 State	Employer's state I.D. No.	**17** State wages, tips, etc.	**18** State income tax	**19** Locality name	**20** Local wages, tips, etc.	**21** Local income tax

Department of the Treasury—Internal Revenue Service

Form **W-2** Wage and Tax Statement **19--**

Copy A For Social Security Administration

a Control number	22222	Void ☐	For Official Use Only ▶		
b Employer's identification number			1 Wages, tips, other compensation	2 Federal income tax withheld
c Employer's name, address, and ZIP code			3 Social security wages	4 Social security tax withheld
			5 Medicare wages and tips	6 Medicare tax withheld
			7 Social security tips	8 Allocated tips
d Employee's social security number			9 Advance EIC payment	10 Dependent care benefits
e Employee's name (first, middle initial, last)			11 Nonqualified plans	12 Benefits included in Box 1
			13 See Instrs. for Box 13	14 Other

15 Statutory employee ☐	Deceased ☐	Pension plan ☐	Legal rep. ☐	942 emp. ☐	Subtotal ☐	Deferred compensation ☐

f Employee's address and ZIP code

16 State	Employer's state I.D. No.	17 State wages, tips, etc.	18 State income tax	19 Locality name	20 Local wages, tips, etc.	21 Local income tax

Department of the Treasury—Internal Revenue Service

Form **W-2** Wage and Tax Statement **19--**

Copy A For Social Security Administration

---

a Control number	22222	Void ☐	For Official Use Only ▶		
b Employer's identification number			1 Wages, tips, other compensation	2 Federal income tax withheld
c Employer's name, address, and ZIP code			3 Social security wages	4 Social security tax withheld
			5 Medicare wages and tips	6 Medicare tax withheld
			7 Social security tips	8 Allocated tips
d Employee's social security number			9 Advance EIC payment	10 Dependent care benefits
e Employee's name (first, middle initial, last)			11 Nonqualified plans	12 Benefits included in Box 1
			13 See Instrs. for Box 13	14 Other

15 Statutory employee ☐	Deceased ☐	Pension plan ☐	Legal rep. ☐	942 emp. ☐	Subtotal ☐	Deferred compensation ☐

f Employee's address and ZIP code

16 State	Employer's state I.D. No.	17 State wages, tips, etc.	18 State income tax	19 Locality name	20 Local wages, tips, etc.	21 Local income tax

Department of the Treasury—Internal Revenue Service

Form **W-2** Wage and Tax Statement **19--**

Copy A For Social Security Administration

Transaction No. 40

a Control number	22222	Void ☐	For Official Use Only ▶		

b Employer's identification number		**1** Wages, tips, other compensation	**2** Federal income tax withheld
c Employer's name, address, and ZIP code		**3** Social security wages	**4** Social security tax withheld
		5 Medicare wages and tips	**6** Medicare tax withheld
		7 Social security tips	**8** Allocated tips
d Employee's social security number		**9** Advance EIC payment	**10** Dependent care benefits
e Employee's name (first, middle initial, last)		**11** Nonqualified plans	**12** Benefits included in Box 1
		13 See Instrs. for Box 13	**14** Other

15 Statutory employee ☐	Deceased ☐	Pension plan ☐	Legal rep. ☐	942 emp. ☐	Subtotal ☐	Deferred compensation ☐

f Employee's address and ZIP code

16 State	Employer's state I.D. No.	**17** State wages, tips, etc.	**18** State income tax	**19** Locality name	**20** Local wages, tips, etc.	**21** Local income tax

Department of the Treasury—Internal Revenue Service

Form **W-2** Wage and Tax Statement **19--**

Copy A For Social Security Administration

---

a Control number	22222	Void ☐	For Official Use Only ▶		

b Employer's identification number		**1** Wages, tips, other compensation	**2** Federal income tax withheld
c Employer's name, address, and ZIP code		**3** Social security wages	**4** Social security tax withheld
		5 Medicare wages and tips	**6** Medicare tax withheld
		7 Social security tips	**8** Allocated tips
d Employee's social security number		**9** Advance EIC payment	**10** Dependent care benefits
e Employee's name (first, middle initial, last)		**11** Nonqualified plans	**12** Benefits included in Box 1
		13 See Instrs. for Box 13	**14** Other

15 Statutory employee ☐	Deceased ☐	Pension plan ☐	Legal rep. ☐	942 emp. ☐	Subtotal ☐	Deferred compensation ☐

f Employee's address and ZIP code

16 State	Employer's state I.D. No.	**17** State wages, tips, etc.	**18** State income tax	**19** Locality name	**20** Local wages, tips, etc.	**21** Local income tax

Department of the Treasury—Internal Revenue Service

Form **W-2** Wage and Tax Statement **19--**

Copy A For Social Security Administration

Transaction No. 40

a Control number	22222	Void ☐	For Official Use Only ▶

b Employer's identification number	1 Wages, tips, other compensation	2 Federal Income tax withheld

c Employer's name, address, and ZIP code	3 Social security wages	4 Social security tax withheld
	5 Medicare wages and tips	6 Medicare tax withheld
	7 Social security tips	8 Allocated tips

d Employee's social security number	9 Advance EIC payment	10 Dependent care benefits

e Employee's name (first, middle initial, last)	11 Nonqualified plans	12 Benefits included in Box 1
	13 See Instrs. for Box 13	14 Other

15 Statutory employee ☐	Deceased ☐	Pension plan ☐	Legal rep. ☐	942 emp. ☐	Subtotal ☐	Deferred compensation ☐

f Employee's address and ZIP code

16 State	Employer's state I.D. No.	17 State wages, tips, etc.	18 State income tax	19 Locality name	20 Local wages, tips, etc.	21 Local income tax

Department of the Treasury—Internal Revenue Service

Form **W-2** Wage and Tax Statement **19--**

Copy A For Social Security Administration

---

a Control number	22222	Void ☐	For Official Use Only ▶

b Employer's identification number	1 Wages, tips, other compensation	2 Federal Income tax withheld

c Employer's name, address, and ZIP code	3 Social security wages	4 Social security tax withheld
	5 Medicare wages and tips	6 Medicare tax withheld
	7 Social security tips	8 Allocated tips

d Employee's social security number	9 Advance EIC payment	10 Dependent care benefits

e Employee's name (first, middle initial, last)	11 Nonqualified plans	12 Benefits included in Box 1
	13 See Instrs. for Box 13	14 Other

15 Statutory employee ☐	Deceased ☐	Pension plan ☐	Legal rep. ☐	942 emp. ☐	Subtotal ☐	Deferred compensation ☐

f Employee's address and ZIP code

16 State	Employer's state I.D. No.	17 State wages, tips, etc.	18 State income tax	19 Locality name	20 Local wages, tips, etc.	21 Local income tax

Department of the Treasury—Internal Revenue Service

Form **W-2** Wage and Tax Statement **19--**

Copy A For Social Security Administration

a	Control number		For Official Use Only ▶ OMB No. 1545-0008			

b	**Kind of Payer** ▶	941/941E ☐	Military ☐	943 ☐	1 Wages, tips, other compensation	2 Federal income tax withheld
		CT-1 ☐	942 ☐	Medicare govt. emp. ☐	3 Social security wages	4 Social security tax withheld

c Total number of statements	d Establishment number	5 Medicare wages and tips	6 Medicare tax withheld
	e Employer's identification number	7 Social security tips	8 Allocated tips

f Employer's name	9 Advance EIC payments	10 Dependent care benefits
	11 Nonqualified plans	12 Deferred compensation
	13 Adjusted total social security wages and tips	
	14 Adjusted total Medicare wages and tips	
g Employer's address and ZIP code		
h Other EIN used this year	15 Income tax withheld by third-party payer	

i Employer's state I.D. No.					

Under penalties of perjury, I declare that I have examined this return and accompanying documents, and, to the best of my knowledge and belief, they are true, correct, and complete.

Signature ▶ _____   Title ▶ _____   Date ▶ _____

Telephone number (_____) _____

Form **W-3 Transmittal of Wage and Tax Statements 19--**

Department of the Treasury
Internal Revenue Service

Transaction No. 42

9595 ☐ VOID ☐ CORRECTED

PAYER'S name, street address, city, state, and ZIP code		1 Rents $	OMB No. 1545-0115	
		2 Royalties $	19--	Miscellaneous Income
		3 Prizes, awards, etc. $		
PAYER'S Federal identification number	RECIPIENT'S identification number	4 Federal income tax withheld $	5 Fishing boat proceeds $	Copy A
RECIPIENT'S name		6 Medical and health care payments $	7 Nonemployee compensation	For Internal Revenue Service Center
Street address (including apt. no.)		8 Substitute payments in lieu of dividends or interest $	9 Payer made direct sales of $5,000 or more of consumer products to a buyer (recipient) for resale ▶ ☐	File with Form 1096. For Paperwork Reduction Act Notice and instructions for
City, state, and ZIP code		10 Crop insurance proceeds $	11 State income tax withheld $	completing this form, see Instructions for
Account number (optional)	2nd TIN Not. ☐	12 State/Payer's state number		Forms 1099, 1098, 5498, and W-2G.

Form **1099-MISC**

Department of the Treasury - Internal Revenue Service

Transaction No. 43

Form **1096** Department of the Treasury Internal Revenue Service	**Annual Summary and Transmittal of U.S. Information Returns**	OMB No. 1545-0108 19--

ATTACH IRS LABEL HERE

FILER'S name

Street address (including room or suite number)

City, state, and ZIP code

| If you are not using a preprinted label, enter in box 1 or 2 below the identification number you used as the filer on the information returns being transmitted. Do not fill in both boxes 1 and 2. | Name of person to contact if the IRS needs more information

Telephone number ( ) | **For Official Use Only** ☐☐☐☐☐☐☐ ☐☐ |
|---|---|---|

1 Employer identification number	2 Social security number	3 Total number of forms	4 Federal income tax withheld $	5 Total amount reported with this Form 1096 $

Check only one box below to indicate the type of form being transmitted.	If this is your FINAL return, check here . . . ▶ ☐

W-2G 32	1098 81	1099-A 80	1099-B 79	1099-DIV 91	1099-G 86	1099-INT 92	1099-MISC 95	1099-OID 96	1099-PATR 97	1099-R 98	1099-S 75	5498 28
☐	☐	☐	☐	☐	☐	☐	☐	☐	☐	☐	☐	☐

Please return this entire page to the Internal Revenue Service. Photocopies are NOT acceptable.

Under penalties of perjury, I declare that I have examined this return and accompanying documents, and, to the best of my knowledge and belief, they are true, correct, and complete.

Signature ▶ .... Title ▶ .... Date ▶ ....

SOCIAL SECURITY BENEFITS

Usually when we refer to *social security benefits*, we are speaking about old-age, survivors, or disability insurance benefits—those which are discussed in this appendix. Since these benefits are provided for under Title II of the Social Security Act, sometimes they are known as *Title II benefits*. Social security benefits, also called *OASDI benefits*, are paid to workers, their spouses, children, and parents, and to widows, widowers, and some divorced persons.

As the employees of a firm near retirement age, they may approach the payroll manager to find out what retirement benefits and hospital and medical benefits they are entitled to under their social security coverage. Then, too, if workers become disabled or die, their families may turn to the payroll manager for advice as to their rights to disability benefits or survivors benefits. Thus, this appendix discusses the benefits related to the two programs of old-age, survivors, and disability insurance and health insurance for the aged and disabled.

OLD-AGE, SURVIVORS, AND DISABILITY BENEFITS

Benefits payable under the old-age, survivors, and disability program may be classified as:

1. Old-age or disability benefits paid to the worker.
2. Benefits for dependents of a retired or disabled worker.
3. Benefits for surviving family members of a deceased worker.
4. Lump-sum death payments.

For individuals and their families to be eligible for most benefits, the person must be "fully insured." Lump-sum benefits and certain survivor benefits are payable, however, if the individual is only "currently insured." A knowledge of the meaning of such terms as quarter of coverage, fully insured, currently insured, and average monthly wage is needed to understand the method of computing the various benefits to which individuals, their dependents, or their survivors may be entitled.

Quarter of Coverage

A calendar quarter is a period of three consecutive calendar months ending on March 31, June 30, September 30, or December 31. A *quarter of coverage* refers to the minimum amount of wages or self-employment income with which individuals must be credited in a calendar quarter if they are to receive credit toward being insured for that period. Quarters of coverage are used in determining whether workers, as classified below, are fully insured, currently insured, or insured for disability benefits.

Wage-Earners. In 1993 a worker received one quarter of coverage, up to a maximum of four, for each $590 of earnings in the calendar year.

Self-Employed Persons. The individual's net earnings from self-employment must amount to at least $400 for the taxable year before any quarters in that year can be credited with self-employment income. For 1993 a self-employed person was credited with one quarter of coverage for each calendar quarter in which $590 or more in self-employment income was allocated.

Farm Workers. The quarters of coverage earned by farm workers are based on wages received during the calendar year, not during the calendar quarter. A farm worker may earn a maximum of four quarters of coverage each year. For 1993 a farm worker was credited with one quarter of coverage, up to a total of four, for each $590 earned during the year.

Fully Insured Individual

To be eligible for most retirement and disability benefits, a worker must be fully insured. To be *fully insured*, a worker normally needs between six and 40 quarters of coverage. The number of quarters needed depends on when the person reaches a specified age or dies. When 40 quarters of coverage (10 years), have been obtained, the worker is fully insured for life and need not be concerned about counting the number of quarters of coverage.

Currently Insured Individual

Although individuals must be fully insured before they or their families can obtain retirement benefits, lump-sum benefits and certain survivor benefits are payable if the individuals are only currently insured.

To be *currently insured*, individuals must have at least six quarters of coverage during the 13-quarter period ending with (1) the quarter in which they died, or (2) the quarter in which they became entitled to old-age insurance benefits or most recently became entitled to disability benefits. The quarters of coverage need not have been consecutive within such 13-quarter period.

Primary Insurance Amount

The *primary insurance amount (PIA)* is a person's monthly retirement or disability benefit and the base upon which monthly benefits of the worker's family

and survivors are calculated. Social security benefits are calculated according to one of several methods, depending, generally, on the year in which the worker reached age 62, died, or became disabled.

Under the 1977 amendments to the Social Security Act, a formula is used to determine the PIA of workers who reach age 62, become disabled, or die. By means of the formula, benefits are kept up-to-date with increases in prices after a worker becomes eligible for benefits. In the formula, the PIA is derived from the worker's *averaged indexed monthly earnings*. By means of *indexing*, the worker's average monthly earnings are updated, or adjusted, to reflect changes in wage levels up to the time of entitlement to benefits.

Cost-of-Living Increases in Benefits

Generally automatic increases in social security benefits are tied to increases in the cost of living as measured by the Consumer Price Index. For example, starting with the benefit checks received in January, 1993, there was a 3% cost-of-living increase in the social security benefits. For those receiving benefit checks commencing in January, 1994, the cost-of-living adjustment (COLA) in benefits is 2.6%.

Wage Credits for Veterans and Service Personnel

Prior to 1957 service personnel were given wage credits of $160 for each month of active service, although at that time they paid no social security tax. Beginning in 1957 service personnel are covered like other employees and pay FICA tax on their basic pay; but they receive additional wage credits up to $1,200 each year.

Reduced Benefits

The Social Security Amendments of 1983 provided that the age at which a person can retire with no reduction in benefits will eventually be raised to 67. However, this change, which will be phased in gradually, does not affect workers born in 1937 or earlier. Early retirement with reduced benefits will still be permitted at age 62, but workers who retire exactly at age 62 in the year 2022 or later will get only 70% of their full benefits.

In the meantime, for persons currently reaching retirement age, 65 is still the age at which full benefits may be received. If a worker chooses to claim old-age benefits before age 65, the amount of the monthly benefits will be permanently reduced. If employees commence to receive benefits at age 62, the earliest age at which they can qualify, the amount of reduction is about 20%. For each month after age 62 that the worker waits before applying for benefits, the reduction will be less.

Eligible widows or widowers may receive reduced benefits as early as age 60. If the worker at any time received a reduced benefit, the widow or widower may not receive more than the greater of (a) a benefit equal to the amount the worker would be getting if alive, or (b) 82.5% of the worker's PIA. For a widow or widower whose worker spouse was receiving an unreduced benefit, the age-60 benefit will be 71.5% of the worker's PIA. If the benefit is taken at age 62, it will be 82.9% of the worker's PIA.

Severely disabled widows and widowers and surviving divorced spouses may receive reduced benefits at age 50. The benefits for such a person age 50-59 equal 71.5% of the worker's unreduced benefit.

The spouse or divorced spouse of a worker who is getting benefits may also become entitled to reduced benefits on reaching age 62. The benefit payable to one whose benefits start at age 62 is reduced by about 25%.

Persons, such as a widowed mother, may be receiving benefits only because they are caring for a child of the deceased worker. In such cases, those persons are not subject to the reduction provisions, even though they may receive benefits at an early age.

The benefit payable to a husband, wife, mother, father, widow, or widower may be reduced by the amount of a government pension to which the person is entitled on the basis of his or her own work in government service not covered by social security. Thus, government workers are prevented from getting both a full public (government) pension and a social security benefit of a spouse, mother, or father.

KINDS OF SOCIAL SECURITY BENEFITS

Several different kinds of benefits are provided under the social security system, each depending upon the relationship of the beneficiary to the retired, deceased, or disabled worker. As mentioned before, the worker, upon whose earnings record the benefits are based, must have attained a certain insured status and acquired quarters of coverage. In addition, an application for such benefits must be filed.

Illustration A-1 shows in summary form the kinds of benefits available and the qualifications needed by the insured worker or his or her beneficiary in order to receive these benefits.

Disability Benefits

Title II of the Social Security Act provides the following types of protection for the disabled worker:

1. Monthly cash benefits for disabled workers and their families.
2. Protection of the workers' wage records while they are disabled so that any low earnings obtained during the period of disability will have minimal effect upon the workers' wage records.
3. Monthly cash benefits for severely disabled widows and widowers and surviving divorced spouses who are age 50 and over.
4. Monthly cash benefits for a disabled child beneficiary age 18 or older.
5. Vocational rehabilitation services for social security disability beneficiaries who are capable of being restored to productive activity.

Workers who have become so severely disabled that they are unable to work can protect their rights to future benefits for themselves and their families by applying to have their social security records "frozen." Thus, after a five-month waiting period, monthly disability benefits are payable to workers and their families while the workers are disabled. Although the worker does not have to be completely helpless to be considered disabled, the disability must be so severe that it prevents the worker from doing any substantial gainful work. Further, the disability must last, or be expected to last, for at least 12 full months or result in death.

As we indicated earlier in this appendix, generally disabled workers must have enough quarters of coverage so that if the workers are already at retirement age, they would be fully insured and have 20 quarters of coverage in the 40-quarter period ending with the one in which the workers become disabled. There are exceptions, however. For example, blind persons need only be fully insured, and workers who are disabled at age 24-30 can qualify if they worked half of the time between age 21 and the onset of disability.

Family Benefits

The monthly payments to members of a retired or a disabled worker's family and the payments to the survivors of an insured worker are equal to a certain percentage of the worker's benefit. Family benefits are generally calculated in relation to the worker's PIA, even though benefits were obtained before age 65. However, there is a limit on the amount that one family may obtain in total benefits, and some of these benefits may be reduced if taken early.

The benefits payable to members of the worker's family, before any reductions are applied because of age or limitations upon total family benefits, are as follows:

Relationship of Family Member to Worker	Percentage of Worker's Benefit to Be Received
Wife, husband, divorced wife, or divorced husband	50% while worker is alive
Child	50% while worker is alive and 75% if worker is dead
Widow, widower, or surviving divorced spouse	100% if of full retirement age; 75% if he or she is caring for worker's child
Dependent grandchild	50% if worker is alive; 75% if worker is dead; child's parents must be dead or disabled
Dependent parent who outlives the worker	82½%; if both parents qualify, a total of 150% is received

Benefits for Divorced Persons

A divorced woman may receive a wife's or a widow's benefit if she was married to her former husband (the insured worker) for at least 10 years. Similar benefits are payable to divorced men.

Divorced spouses who have been divorced for at least 2 years may draw benefits at age 62 if the former spouse is eligible for retirement benefits. It is of no consequence whether the former spouse's benefits have been claimed or if they have been suspended because of substantial employment.

Students' Benefits

Generally benefits for a child end when the child reaches age 18 unless the child is a full-time student or has a disability. Benefits end for elementary or high school students when they reach age 19.

Benefits for Aliens and Prisoners

The Social Security Amendments of 1983 placed limitations on the benefits received by some aliens and prisoners. If an alien is receiving benefits as a dependent or a survivor of an insured worker and has been outside the United States for 6 consecutive months, the benefits will be suspended. Exceptions are made for young children and beneficiaries who lived in the United States for at least 5 years and had a relationship with the worker which established eligibility for benefits. Benefits may also be continued where international social security agreements are in force.

If a person is confined in jail for a felony, benefits may not be paid that person, except in limited circumstances where the felon is participating in an approved rehabilitation program. The benefits payable to a felon's spouse or child are not affected.

Benefits for the Self-Employed

Old-age, survivors, and disability benefits and hospital insurance benefits are payable to self-employed persons and their dependents or survivors under the same conditions as to wage earners and their dependents or survivors.

Benefits for Employees of Carriers

Companies engaged as carriers and employees of carriers are exempted under FICA, as indicated in Unit 3. To provide old-age and disability benefits for workers in these occupations, special legislation has been enacted governing railroads and other carriers, as well as the employees of carriers.

The Railroad Retirement Tax Act sets up the provisions under which employees of carriers subject to the Interstate Commerce Act may retire and become eligible for annuities. The term "annuity" is substituted for the term "benefit" used under the Social Security Act, but both terms have a similar meaning and are commonly referred to as old-age insurance. Details about benefits and taxes can be obtained from the Railroad Retirement Tax Act and the Carriers' Taxing Act.

Special Minimum Benefit

Special provision is made for persons who have worked in jobs covered by social security for many years but at rather low earnings levels. Such workers can qualify for a special benefit that is somewhat higher than that available to them under the regular benefit computation provisions of the law. Thus, workers can receive a benefit equal to $11.50 times the number of years over 10 (up to 30) that they have been covered by the law and have met certain minimum earnings requirements set forth in the law. The special benefits payable under these provisions will be automatically adjusted for cost-of-living increases in the future.

Working After Benefits Start—the Retirement Test

Under the social security system, it is expected that workers will retire, at least partially, when they reach retirement age. If they do not retire, at least partially, they ordinarily are unable to collect their benefits. The *retirement test* or *annual earnings test*, which is provided by law, determines to what extent workers

KINDS OF SOCIAL SECURITY BENEFITS

(1) Old-Age or Disability Benefits

Person to Receive Benefits	Eligibility Requirements — The insured individual must be:
Retired worker, age 62 or older	Fully insured
Disabled worker (except one who is blind), any age under 65	Both fully insured and insured for disability benefits

(2) Benefits for Dependents of Retired or Disabled Workers

Spouse, or divorced spouse, age 62 or older . . . .
Spouse, any age, if caring for child (except student age 18 or over) entitled to benefits . . . .
Unmarried child, grandchild, or great-grandchild if —
(a) under age 18, or
(b) under age 19 and a full-time elementary or secondary school student, or
(c) age 18 or older with a disability that began before age 22.

> Fully insured for old-age benefits or insured for disability benefits, whichever is applicable.

(3) Survivor Benefits

Widow, widower, or divorced person, age 60 or older or age 50–59 and able to meet a special definition of disability   Fully insured

Widow, widower, or divorced parent of deceased worker's child, any age, caring for a young child entitled to benefits . . . .
Unmarried child, grandchild, or great-grandchild if child is —
(a) under age 18, or
(b) under age 19 and a full-time elementary or secondary school student, or
(c) age 18 or older with a disability that began before age 22.

> Either fully insured or currently insured

Dependent parents, 62 or older . . . .   Fully insured

(4) Lump-Sum Death Payment ($255)

Paid only, in order of priority, to (1) worker's widow or widower living with worker at time of death, (2) worker's widow or widower not living with worker but eligible on worker's earnings record, or (3) eligible surviving child . . . .   Either fully insured or currently insured

Illustration A-1. Kinds of Social Security Benefits

and self-employed persons may continue to have earnings and still collect their full social security benefits. The retirement test applies to a worker's earnings whether or not the work is covered by the Social Security Act. As explained below, different annual amounts of earnings are applied in the retirement test, depending on whether the retired worker is over or under age 65.

Retired Workers, Age 65 to 70. In 1994, it is anticipated that workers age 65 through 69 will be able to earn $10,920 without losing any benefits. For each $3 in excess of the stipulated earnings limit, $1 is deducted from the benefits paid the worker and any family members who may be receiving benefits. How-

ever, *during the first year of eligibility only,* a monthly earnings test is also applied to determine the amount of benefits to be received. Thus, in 1994, workers who reach age 65 and retire will be paid a full benefit for any month in which they neither earn more than $910 nor are substantially self-employed, regardless of their total earnings. After the initial year of retirement, however, the monthly measure in the retirement test is eliminated.

When retired persons commence to work after receiving benefits, their wages are subject to social security and Medicare taxes, regardless of their age. Some who delay their retirement and work beyond age 65 receive extra benefit credits, as explained in a later section.

Retired Workers, Age 62 to 64.
Workers retiring in 1994 at ages 62 to 64 can expect to earn $7,920 without losing any benefits. *In the first year of eligibility only*, a monthly test applies whereby workers are paid full benefits for those months in which they neither earn more than $660 nor are substantially self-employed. In the second and succeeding years of eligibility, annual earnings tests are applied to determine any excess earnings. The retired worker loses $1 for each $2 in excess of the stipulated earnings limit.

Retired Workers, Age 70 and Over.
At age 70 benefits are paid retired workers, no matter how much they earn.

Increased Benefits for Workers Who Delay Retirement

A person may earn increased social security benefits by working beyond the full retirement age (currently age 65). The amount of the increase is based on the credit the worker receives for each month of delayed retirement. In turn, the amount of credit allowed depends on the worker's birth date, as shown in the following listing:

Birth Date	Amount of Credit Received
1916 or earlier	1/12% per month (1% per year)
1917 through 1924	1/4% per month (3% per year)
1925 or later	3 1/2% to 8% per year, depending on birth date

By deferring their claims for benefits, wage earners will generally be able to qualify for a higher primary insurance amount in the years ahead. Thus, the deferral of increased benefits will appeal to those workers who, beyond age 65, continue to enjoy not only good health but also good earnings.

MEDICAL CARE FOR AGED AND NEEDY

The 1965 amendments to the Social Security Act established a three-part program of medical care for the aged and the needy: (1) hospital insurance benefits for the aged and disabled, (2) supplementary medical insurance benefits for the aged and disabled, and (3) medical assistance to the needy.

The first of these programs, hospital insurance benefits for the aged and disabled, is sometimes called Basic Medicare, Part A Medicare, or hospital insurance. The *hospital insurance (HI) plan* provides protection against the costs of certain hospital and related services. The plan is financed by a separate hospital insurance tax paid by employees, employers, and the self-employed. The tax provisions are discussed on pages 76 and 79.

The second program, the *supplementary medical insurance benefits* for the aged and disabled, is often referred to as supplementary, voluntary, voluntary supplementary Medicare, the medical insurance program, or Part B Medicare. This voluntary supplementary program for the aged and disabled is designed to cover the costs of doctors' services and a number of other items and services not covered under the basic program. The program is largely financed by monthly premiums from those who enroll and by matching contributions from the federal government. Under this plan the federal government usually pays 80% of the reasonable costs or charges for covered services after the individual pays a deductible each year. The individual also pays the additional 20% that Medicare does not pay.

The third program is popularly called *Medicaid*. Under this program medical assistance is provided to aged and needy persons by means of a joint federal-state program.

APPLYING FOR SOCIAL SECURITY BENEFITS

Generally social security benefits are paid only if applied for by the person who is entitled to receive them. The application for benefits must be completed by the applicant if he or she is at least 18 years of age, mentally competent, and physically capable of filling out the form. In all other situations the application may be filed on behalf of the eligible person by a legal guardian, other legal representative, or by the person who is caring for the applicant.

Special application forms are available for applying for benefits under the old-age, survivors, and disability insurance program. The proper forms may be obtained from the nearest district office of the Social Security Administration, which will also give applicants any help they may need in preparing the application, including notary services, free of charge.

After the claimant has filed an application with the district office of the Social Security Administration, the application is forwarded to the appropriate payment center for final approval. If the claim is found correct, it is approved by the Social Security Administration, and the United States Treasury is notified that payment should be made. Benefits commence with the month in which the person meets the eligibility requirements, and the benefit checks are usually mailed so that they will be received on the third day of the month following the month for which payment is due. The entitlement to benefits ends with the month preceding the month in which an event occurs that causes the cessation of entitlement. Thus, if a beneficiary should die in April, the benefit entitlement would end with the preceding March.

It is important that claims for benefits be filed promptly. Generally, benefits are payable retroactively; however, some benefit payments may be limited or lost if application is made too late.

Proof of Age

Applicants for benefits may be required to give evidence of their right to receive benefits or the amount of such benefits. If age is a condition to entitlement, the applicant may be required to file a proof of age showing the date of birth. Evidence based on such records as those listed below may be acceptable:

1. Public records of birth (birth certificate)
2. Church records of birth or baptism established or recorded before the age of five
3. Census Bureau notification of registration of birth
4. Hospital birth record or certificate
5. Foreign records of birth
6. Physician's or midwife's birth record
7. Certification, on approved form, of Bible or other family record
8. Naturalization records
9. Immigration papers
10. Military records
11. Passports
12. School records
13. Vaccination records
14. Insurance policy
15. Labor union or fraternal organization records
16. Marriage records
17. Other evidence of probative value, such as employment records and voting records

Statement of Employer

The individual's wage record kept by the Social Security Administration may be several months in arrears since the posting of wages earned to the wage records of individuals is a tremendous task.[1] Therefore, the Administration may request the employer to complete a Statement of Employer, Form SSA-7011-F4, in order to bring an individual's wage record up-to-date. Thus, the computation of the individual's benefits will include the most recent earnings.

Electronic Transfer of Social Security Benefits

Beneficiaries of social security benefits may elect to have their monthly benefits electronically transferred to their bank, savings and loan association, credit union, or other qualified financial organization. The beneficiary is aided by the electronic transfer of benefits in that the possibility of loss is reduced and the process of depositing is eliminated. The beneficiary is further assured that the deposit will be made while the beneficiary is absent from his or her home or is away during any temporary period of relocation.

Taxability and Assignability of Benefits

A portion of a worker's social security benefits is included in taxable income for federal income tax purposes. The amount of benefits taxable is determined by a complicated formula that relates the worker's adjusted gross income and as much as 85% of the social security benefits to a base amount set by the government.

Social security benefits cannot be assigned and generally the benefits are not subject to levy, garnishment, or attachment. However, the benefits may be attached in order to collect delinquent federal taxes or to enforce an obligation to make child-support or alimony payments.

---

[1]As indicated in Unit 3, workers should check on the status of their social security accounts from time to time to make sure that their earnings have been properly credited. Form SSA-7004-SM, used to request a statement of earnings, is described on page 82. This form may be obtained by calling the toll-free number 1-800-772-1213.

At the end of the quarter, the quarterly report is displayed. At the end of the year, the W-2 statements of earnings and withholdings are displayed from the yearly earnings and withholdings fields that have accumulated during the year.

SOFTWARE PROGRAM OVERVIEW

The software you will be using makes use of a standard user interface that utilizes pull-down menus, movable overlapping windows, mouse support, list windows, and help windows. This standard interface is similar to the interface used in many other software applications. Most of the techniques you will learn can be applied to many other software packages.

Using a Mouse

The Computerized Payroll Accounting software works with a mouse. If you have a mouse on your computer, the pointer will be displayed on your screen as a small rectangle (▮) or arrow (↗). The pointer moves on the screen as you move the mouse. The following functions can be performed with a mouse:

Point	Move the pointer to a specific location on the screen.
Click	Quickly press and release the left mouse button.
Drag	Press and hold down the left mouse button and move the mouse.
Point and Click	Pointing to an object on the screen and clicking the mouse button is "clicking on the object." For example, if you are directed to "click on" the Ok button, you should point to the Ok button and click the left mouse button.

Pull-Down Menus

One of the ways you can communicate with the computer is with a menu. A **Menu** is a list of commands. Figure B-1 shows the parts of the Computerized Payroll Accounting menu system.

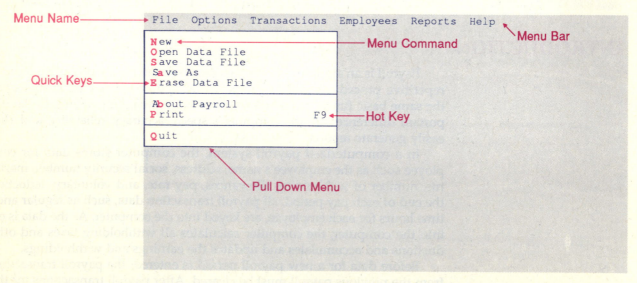

Figure B-1. Pull Down Menus

- **Menu Bar.** The **Menu Bar** is the top line of the screen showing the menus available.
- **Menu Name.** Each of the words on the Menu Bar is the name of one of the pull down menus. If a menu name is "dimmed," it is not available.

- **Pull Down Menu.** A Pull Down Menu is a list of commands that appears immediately below the selected menu.
- **Menu Command.** The menu commands are the menu items such as New and Open Data File shown in the File menu in Figure B-1. They are referred to as commands because they command the computer to perform a particular action.
- **Quick Keys.** Each menu name and each menu command has a quick key associated with it. The quick keys appear on the screen either as a bright or underlined letter (within the menu or command name). The quick keys allow for easy menu or menu command selection.
- **Hot Keys.** Some menu options can be selected without pulling down a menu by simply pressing a key. Frequently used menu commands (such as Print) can be quickly selected with Hot Keys. If a menu command has a Hot Key it will be shown on the pull down menu.

Table B-1 below describes keyboard keys that you will find useful when working with the pull-down menus.

Key	Function
Alt	Use this key to transfer control to the Menu Bar to select a pull-down menu.
Esc	Use this key to release control from the Menu Bar or to remove any pull-down menu.
Down Arrow	Use this key to pull down a menu. Each time this key is pressed while a menu is pulled down, the highlight bar will move down to the next menu command. If the highlight bar is on the last command, it will wrap around to the first command.
Up Arrow	Use this key to move the highlight bar up to the previous command within a pull-down menu.
Right Arrow	This key selects the next menu.
Left Arrow	This key selects the previous menu.
Enter	Use this key to choose the currently highlighted menu or menu command.

Table B-1.   Keys Used with Pull-Down Menus

Selecting and Choosing Menus and Menu Commands

With the Computerized Payroll Accounting software, the terms **select** and **choose** have different meanings. When menus on the menu bar or menu commands are selected they are highlighted. When a highlighted (or selected) menu or command is chosen, the software will take the appropriate action. Dimmed commands are not available at the current time (you may need to select another command before using a dimmed command).

Using the Keyboard to Pull Down a Menu and Choose a Menu Command

1 Press the Alt key.

When the Alt key is pressed, the first menu on the menu bar (File) is selected.

2   Press the Left or Right Arrow key to select a menu.

As you move through the menus with the left and right arrow keys, any menus that are inactive (dimmed) are skipped.

3   Press Enter to choose the selected menu.

The chosen menu will appear with the first menu command highlighted. If the File menu were chosen, the screen would appear as shown in Figure B-1.

Hint: If the name in the menu bar has a highlighted or underlined letter, you can press Alt to select the menu bar, and then type the letter that is highlighted or underlined. For example, to pull down the Help menu, press Alt+H (while holding down the Alt key, press H).

4   Use the Up and Down Arrow keys to select the menu command, then press Enter to choose the command.

Hint: If the menu command has a highlighted or underlined letter, you can choose a menu command by typing the letter that is highlighted or underlined. For example, to choose Open Data File, you would type **O**. These highlighted letters are called **Quick Keys** because they allow you to quickly select menu commands with the keyboard.

Using a Mouse to Pull Down a Menu and Choose a Menu Command

1   Pull down the menu by pointing to the name of the menu on the menu bar and clicking the left mouse button.

2   Point to the menu command and click the left mouse button.

Hint: To move directly to a menu item, you can point to the menu name and drag the highlight bar down the menu until the menu command is highlighted, and then release the mouse button.

WINDOWS

You interact with the computer to perform payroll processing procedures through windows. A **window** is a rectangular area of the screen in which the software is communicating with the user. Often the screen contains only one window. At times, two or more overlapping windows appear on the screen. However, only one window is active at a time. The Computerized Payroll Accounting software uses four different types of windows: data entry, list, dialog, and report windows.

Data Entry Windows

Data is keyed into the computer from the computer's keyboard and displayed in data entry windows as it is keyed. This process is called **data entry**. Figure B-2 shows the parts of a data entry window.

- **Window Title.** The title of the data entry window.
- **Close Button.** The equal sign (=) in the upper left hand corner of the screen is the close button. Clicking on the close button with the mouse tells the computer to close the window. The window can be closed from the keyboard by pressing the Esc key.
- **Title Bar.** Any data entry window with a wide title bar, like the one shown, can be moved with the mouse. To move a window, point to the title bar with the mouse, then click-and-drag the window where desired. As the window is dragged, an outlined image of the window follows your movements. When the mouse button is released, the window moves to where the outlined image was. The window will remain in its new location during your computer session and until the software is restarted. The contents of a window underneath

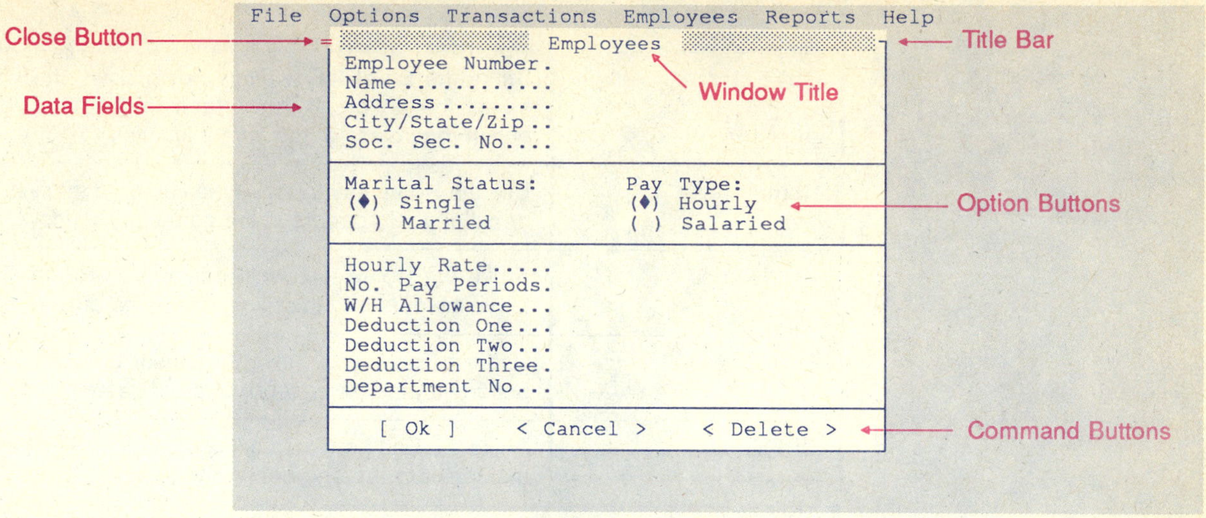

Figure B-2. Data Entry Window

a movable window may be viewed by clicking-and-holding the mouse button down while the mouse is pointing to the title bar.

- **Data Fields.** Data fields are used to enter data or change (edit) previously entered data.
- **Option Buttons.** You can select only one option at a time. The selected option contains a diamond shaped character in parentheses (♦).
- **Command Buttons.** A command button initiates an immediate action. Choosing a command button is referred to as "pushing" the button. Command buttons are located along the bottom of the windows. A command button is pushed by clicking on it with the mouse or by tabbing to it with the Tab key and pressing Enter. The default command button is always highlighted (selected). The default command button can be pushed from anywhere in the window by pressing Ctrl-Enter.

Data fields and buttons should be keyed or selected in the normal tab sequence. The **tab sequence** is the logical sequence that the computer is expecting each data field and/or button to be entered. It is usually left-to-right and top-to-bottom. The Tab key moves the cursor to the next data field or button in the tab sequence. The Shift-Tab keystroke combination moves the cursor to the previous data field or button in the tab sequence. Table B-2 below describes keys that you will find useful when working with data entry windows.

Key	Function
Tab	Use this key to move the cursor to the next data field or button in the tab sequence.
Shift-Tab	Strike the Tab key while holding down the Shift key to move the cursor backward to the previous data field or button in the tab sequence.
Enter	If the cursor is positioned on a command button, the command button will be executed. If the cursor is positioned on an option button, that option will be selected and the cursor will move to the next data field or button in the tab sequence. If the cursor is in a data field, the data will be accepted and the cursor will move to the next data field or button in the tab sequence.

Key	Function
Ctrl-Enter	Strike the Enter key while holding down the Ctrl key to select the action of the default (highlighted) command button regardless of the cursor location.
Home	Use the Home key to move the cursor to the first data field or button that appears in the data entry window.
Ctrl-Home	Strike the Home key while holding down the Ctrl key to move the cursor to the beginning of the **current data field**.
End	Use the End key to move the cursor to the last command button on the bottom (end) of the data entry window.
Ctrl-End	Strike the End key while holding down the Ctrl key to move the cursor to the end of the **current data field**.
Down Arrow	Use this key (↓) to move down to the next data field or button. If the cursor is positioned on one of the command buttons at the bottom of the window it will wrap around to the first data field/button.
Up Arrow	Use this key (↑) to move up to the previous data field or button. If the cursor is located in the first data field/button, it will wrap around to the last button.
Right Arrow	Use this key (→) to move one position to the right within the current data field.
Left Arrow	Use this key (←) to move one position to the left within the current data field.
Insert	Use this key to toggle between insert and overstrike mode. When a data field is selected, it always defaults to the insert mode. When in insert mode, the cursor is displayed as a blinking underscore (_). When in overstrike mode, the cursor appears as a blinking square (■).
Backspace	Within a data field, use this key to erase the character immediately to the left of the cursor.
Delete	Within a data field, use this key to erase the character at the current cursor position.
Space Bar	Use this key to select the button the cursor is currently positioned on.
Esc	Use this key to close and remove the current window from the display screen.

Table B-2. Keys Used with Data Entry Windows

List Windows

A List window allows you to search and select items from lists. List windows are typically displayed on top of data entry windows. An example of an employee list window displayed on top of the Employees data entry window is shown in Figure B-3.

When a list window is opened, no other menu commands can be chosen until the list window has been dismissed.

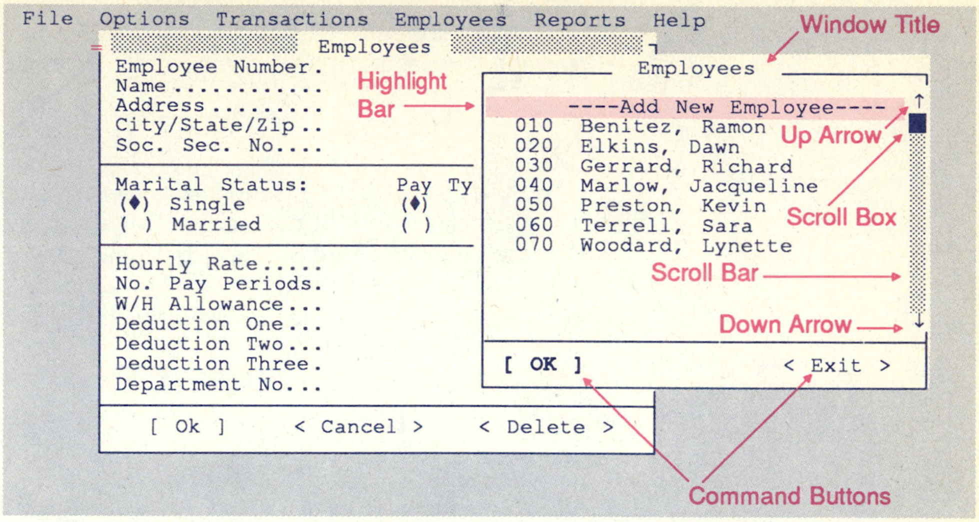

Figure B-3. List Window

The **highlight bar** identifies the selected item in a list window. When a list window appears, the first item in the list is selected. The **scroll bar** is a bar on the right side of the list window that represents the range of items in the list window and is used in conjunction with the scroll box to view items that exist beyond the borders of the window. The **scroll box** indicates the relative position of the selected item within the range of items in the list.

Using the Keyboard to Select and Choose Employees from the List Window

1 Use the Up Arrow, Down Arrow, Page Up, Page Down, Home, and End keys to select the desired item from the list.

2 Press Enter to choose the selected item or press Esc to cancel the list window.

   When an employee is chosen, the list window is closed and the employee's data is inserted into the data entry window.

Using A Mouse to Select and Choose Employees from the List Window

1 Use the mouse operations shown in Table B-3 to select the desired employee.

Action	Mouse Operations
Scroll Up One Line	Click on the up arrow (↑) located at the top of the scroll bar to scroll upward (you may also click on the line immediately above the first item in the list window).
Scroll Down One Line	Click on the down arrow (↓) located at the bottom of the scroll bar to scroll downward (you may also click on the line immediately below the last item in the list window).
Scroll to Top	Click on the top of the scroll bar just below the up arrow.
Scroll to Bottom	Click on the bottom of the scroll bar just above the down arrow.
Scroll Anywhere	Click on the scroll bar at the relative position. For example, to scroll to the middle of the list, click on the middle of the scroll bar.

Table B-3.   Mouse Operations

2 Choose the selected Employee by clicking on the Ok command button (click on the Cancel command button to exit without choosing an employee).

Dialog Windows

The purpose of dialog windows is to provide informational and error messages. A decision from the user may be required. When a dialog window appears, one of the command buttons must be chosen before other menu commands can be selected. Figure B-4 shows the dialog window that will appear if the payroll system is ended before data has been saved.

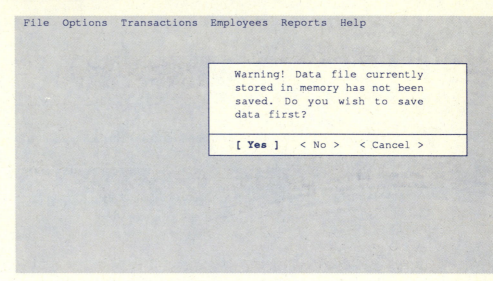

File   Options   Transactions   Employees   Reports   Help

```
Warning! Data file currently
stored in memory has not been
saved. Do you wish to save
data first?

[ Yes ]    < No >    < Cancel >
```

Figure B-4. Dialog Window

Using the Keyboard to Select and Choose Command Buttons from a Dialog Window

1 Use the Right and Left Arrow keys or the Tab and Shift-Tab keys to select the desired command button.

2 Press Enter to choose the selected (highlighted) command button.

If you have a mouse, click on the desired command button.

Report Windows

When a command is chosen from the Report menu or one of the Help commands is chosen, the corresponding information is displayed in a report window so that it can be viewed and/or printed on an attached printer.

Some reports have a **Selection Options** dialog window. You can restrict the data that appears on the report. For example, if the range of employees is 010 to 050, only employees with employee numbers from 010 through 050 will be printed.

After pushing the Ok command button, the selected report will appear in the scrollable Report Window as illustrated in Figure B-5. The report can be printed on an attached printer by either pulling down the File menu and choosing the Print command or by pressing the F9 key (the Hot Key for the Print command).

Using the Keyboard to Scroll Data in a Report Window

1 Use the Up Arrow, Down Arrow, Page Up, Page Down, Home, and End keys to view the data in the report window.

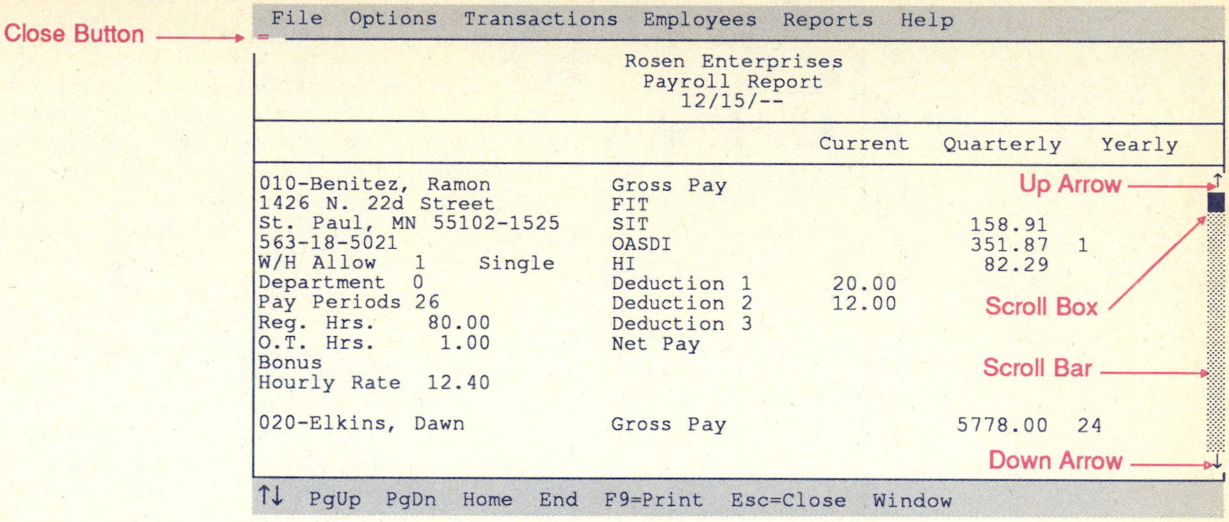

Close Button ──────→

```
 File  Options  Transactions  Employees  Reports  Help
                        Rosen Enterprises
                        Payroll Report
                           12/15/--

                                   Current   Quarterly   Yearly

010-Benitez, Ramon         Gross Pay                              Up Arrow ──→ ↑
1426 N. 22d Street         FIT                                              ▓
St. Paul, MN 55102-1525    SIT                       158.91
563-18-5021                OASDI                     351.87   1
W/H Allow   1    Single    HI                         82.29
Department  0              Deduction 1    20.00                  Scroll Box
Pay Periods 26             Deduction 2    12.00
Reg. Hrs.    80.00         Deduction 3
O.T. Hrs.     1.00         Net Pay                               Scroll Bar ──→
Bonus
Hourly Rate 12.40

020-Elkins, Dawn           Gross Pay                 5778.00  24
                                                                Down Arrow ──→ ↓

↑↓  PgUp  PgDn  Home  End  F9=Print  Esc=Close  Window
```

Figure B-5.   Report Window

2   Press Esc to close the window.

Using a Mouse to Scroll Data in a Report Window

1   Use the mouse operations described in Table B-3 to view the report.

2   Close the window by clicking on the equal sign (=) in the upper left corner of the window.

Printing the Contents of a Report Window

At any time while a report is displayed in a report window, the contents of the report window can be printed by pulling down the File menu and selecting the Print command. As a short cut, you can simply press the F9 function key. When the Print menu command is chosen, the Print Options data entry window shown in Figure B-6 will appear.

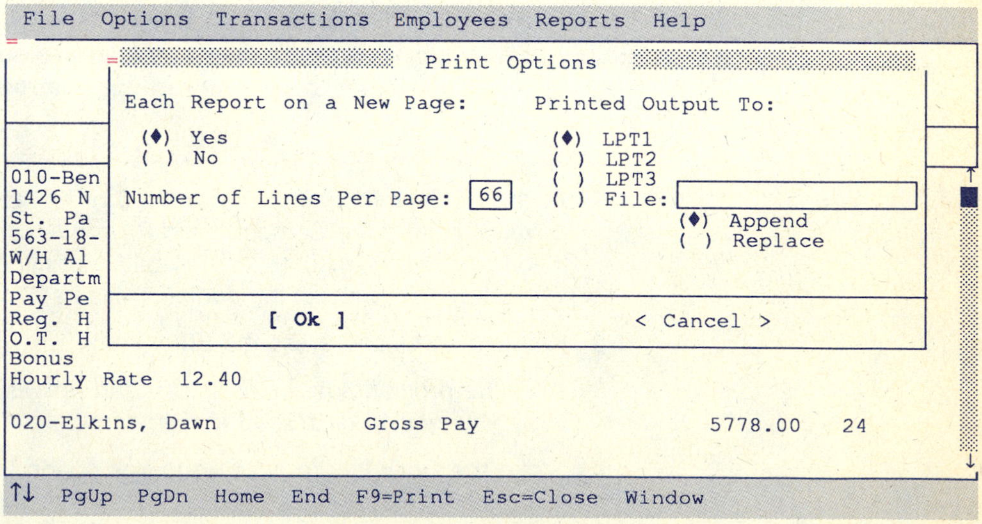

```
 File  Options  Transactions  Employees  Reports  Help
 =
  =░░░░░░░░░░░░░░░░░░░  Print Options  ░░░░░░░░░░░░░░░░░

       Each Report on a New Page:     Printed Output To:

        (♦) Yes                        (♦) LPT1
        ( ) No                         ( ) LPT2
                                       ( ) LPT3
010-Ben  Number of Lines Per Page: [66]  ( ) File: [          ]
1426 N
St. Pa                                      (♦) Append
563-18-                                     ( ) Replace
W/H Al
Departm
Pay Pe
Reg. H            [ Ok ]                   < Cancel >
O.T. H
Bonus
Hourly Rate  12.40

020-Elkins, Dawn          Gross Pay              5778.00   24

↑↓  PgUp  PgDn  Home  End  F9=Print  Esc=Close  Window
```

Figure B-6.   Print Options

Each of the buttons and data fields on the Print Options data entry window are described in Table B-4.

Button/Data Field	Explanation
Each Report on a New Page	If this option button is set to Yes, each report will be printed on a new page. If this button is set to No, the computer will space down several lines between reports, thus conserving paper.
Number of Lines Per Page	This number represents the number of print lines that will fit on each page of paper. This option is necessary for a printer that feeds individual sheets of paper.
Printed Output To	If your computer has several printers attached, this option allows you to direct the output to a specific printer. To direct the report to a file, you must: (1) key the file name of the disk file that is to receive the output and (2) set the option buttons to indicate whether the output is to be added to the end of an existing file (Append) or a new file created (Replace). There are many uses for a file containing a printed report (for example, it could be printed later with the DOS Print command or it could be merged into a word processing document).
Ok	The Ok command button directs the computer to print the report. Once the report begins printing it may be stopped by pressing the Esc key.
Cancel	The Cancel command button directs the computer to dismiss the Print Options data entry window and return to the Report Window.

Table B-4. Data Fields and Buttons for Print Options Data Entry Window

START-UP PROCEDURES

To bring up the Computerized Payroll Accounting software, you must load a program called **PAYROLL**. The start-up procedure varies considerably depending on the type of computer system you are using. The procedure is different for (1) a floppy disk system, (2) a hard disk system, (3) a workstation on a network, or (4) a hard disk system with a graphics user interface, such as Microsoft Windows[1] or IBM's OS/2.[2] Whatever the environment, the start-up is quite simple.

Floppy Disk Based System Start-Up

1   At the DOS prompt (DOS version 2.0 or higher), set the default drive to the drive containing the Computerized Payroll Accounting software. For example, if you have the Computerized Payroll Accounting program disk in Drive A, you would key "A:" (without the quotation marks). A> will appear on your screen.

2   Key PAYROLL and press the Enter key.

3   After the program loads, the Initial Start-up Display window will appear, asking if you would like to read about payroll.

4   Strike the Enter key to accept the Yes option (if using a mouse, click on the Yes button). To select the No option, strike the Tab key to activate the No

---

[1] Microsoft and Windows are registered trademarks of Microsoft Corporation. Any reference to Microsoft or Windows refers to this footnote.

[2] IBM and OS/2 are registered trademarks of IBM Corporation. Any reference to IBM or OS/2 refers to this footnote.

button, then strike Enter. (If using a mouse, click on the No button.) Choosing the No option will bypass the window displays explained in Steps 5 and 6. Next, the Select Display Type window will appear. (Proceed directly to Step 7.)

5   If the computer you are using has a color graphics board, strike the Enter key to accept the Color option. (If using a mouse, click on the Color button.) If the computer you are using has a color graphics adapter board with a monochrome monitor, strike the Tab key to activate the MonoChrome button, then strike Enter. (If using a mouse, click on the MonoChrome button.) After either option has been chosen, the first copyright display window will appear.

Note: If the software detects that you are using a computer configured with a non-graphics adapter board, or you have previously set the display type to monochrome, the Select Display Type window will be bypassed and will not appear during start-up.

6   If you are using the keyboard, strike the PgDn key two times to view the next two copyright information screens, then strike the Esc key to exit. If you are using a mouse, use the scroll bar to scroll down through the next two copyright information screens, then click on the Close Box to exit.

7   When the Menu Bar appears on an empty display screen, the Computerized Payroll Accounting software is ready to use.

Hard Disk Based System Start-Up

1   From the C prompt (assuming your hard disk is Drive C), set the default drive and directory to the drive and directory containing the Computerized Payroll Accounting software.

Hint: For example, if the software is stored on drive C in a directory called PAYACCT, you would:
(a) Key "C:" (without quotes) to set the default drive to Drive C.
(b) At the C> prompt, key "CD \PAYACCT" (without quotes) to set the default directory to PAYACCT.

2   Key PAYROLL and press the Enter key.

3   When the Initial Start-up Display window appears, follow the procedure described above, beginning with step number 4.

Network or Graphic User Interface

1   Because of the large number of networks available and because of the flexible program selection methods of the graphic user interfaces, it is not possible to provide step-by-step procedures for start-up. Your instructor will provide you with the necessary start-up procedures.

2   After start-up is completed, the Initial Start-up Display window will appear. Follow the procedure described above, beginning with step number 4.

OPERATING PROCEDURES

The payroll operating procedures consist of loading a payroll data file, preparing a new payroll, keying employee maintenance (additions, changes, and deletions), keying payroll transactions, and generating payroll reports. At the end of the quarter, the quarterly report is printed and the quarterly accumulators are cleared. At the end of the year, the W-2 statements are printed and the yearly accumulators cleared.

File Menu

The pull-down File menu, shown in Figure B-7, consists of commands that handle all the Computerized Payroll Accounting input and output operations. Each of these commands are described below.

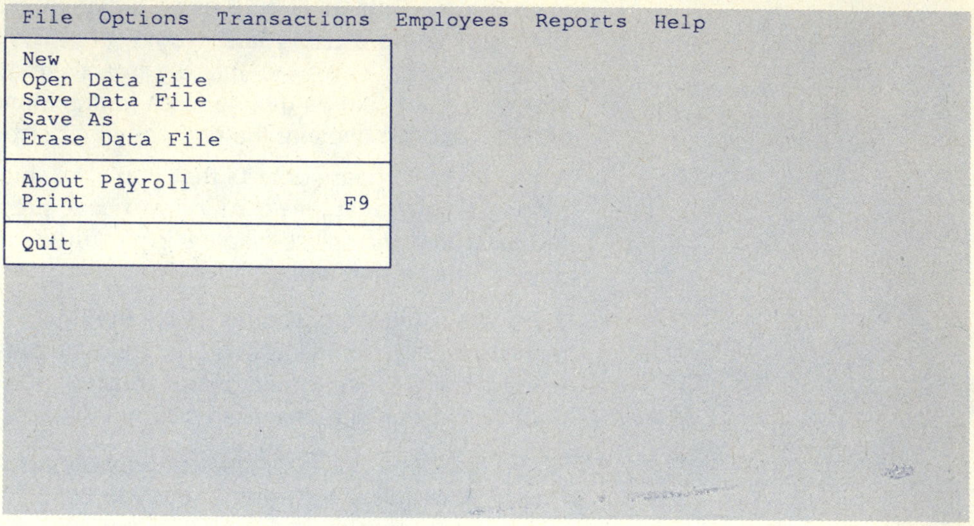

```
File  Options  Transactions  Employees  Reports  Help
┌─────────────────────────┐
│ New                     │
│ Open Data File          │
│ Save Data File          │
│ Save As                 │
│ Erase Data File         │
├─────────────────────────┤
│ About Payroll           │
│ Print              F9   │
├─────────────────────────┤
│ Quit                    │
└─────────────────────────┘
```

Figure B-7.   File Menu

New. This menu command erases any existing data in the computer's memory and establishes empty payroll system files. The New menu command does **not** remove any data from disk.

Open Data File. Before stored data can be processed, it must be loaded from disk into the computer's memory with the Open Data File menu command.

1   Choose the Open Data File menu command from the File menu.

The Open Data File data entry window will appear. If you have previously entered a Path and File name during this session, they will appear in the Path and File data fields. If not, the Path field will default to the current path and the File field will be blank.

2   Key the path name to the drive and directory that contains the data file you wish to load.

If you are loading a template file (a file provided with the software), key the path to the drive and directory containing the template files (usually the same drive and directory containing the payroll software). If you are loading a previously saved data file, key the path to the drive and directory containing your data files.

The path used depends on the configuration of your computer system and the location of the template files and data files.

3   Key the file name you wish to load.

To view a list of files currently stored in the designated path, push the Directory button by clicking on it with the mouse or pressing the END key to move the cursor to the Directory button and press Enter.

4   To load the file, push the Ok command button by clicking on it with the mouse or pressing Ctrl-Enter.

Save Data File. The Save Data File command saves your data to disk so that you can continue a problem in a later session. The data will be saved to a file on disk with the path and filename currently displayed near the upper right corner of the screen.

1 Choose the Save Data File command from the File menu.

Hint: Before you use the Save Data File command, check the current file name in the upper right corner of the screen to make certain you want to save with this path and name. If you wish to save your data with a path or filename different from the current path and file, use the Save As command.

Save As. The Save As command is the same as the Save Data File command except you save your data with a path and/or filename different from the path and filename shown in the upper right corner of the screen. This menu command is useful for making a **backup**, or copy of a data file. For example, you may want a backup of your data file before preparing for a new payroll period, or before clearing quarterly and yearly accumulators. To make a backup copy, load the data file you wish to backup and use the Save As command to save it with a different name.

1 Choose the Save As menu command.

2 Key the path and file name under which you would like the data file saved.

3 Push the Ok button.

Erase Data File. This command erases a data file stored on disk. You might want to delete a file that is no longer needed (perhaps to free up disk space). This command erases data from disk but not from memory. To erase data from memory use the New menu command.

About Payroll. When the About Payroll command is chosen, a report window will appear. The contents of the report window consist of copyright text information regarding the current version of the Computerized Payroll Accounting software. After viewing the contents of the report window, click on the Close Box or strike the Esc key to dismiss the window.

Print. The purpose of the Print menu command is to print the report displayed in the Report Window. This process was described earlier under the Report Window section.

Quit. The Quit menu command is used to exit the accounting software. When the Quit command is chosen, the computer checks to see if the current data in its memory has been saved. If not, a dialog window will appear asking if you wish to save your data to disk.

Options Menu

The Options pull-down menu, shown in Figure B-8 on page 348, contains commands that enable the user to specify general information about the company and computer problem to be solved. When the Options pull-down menu is selected from the Menu bar, the commands described in the following material will become available for execution.

General Information Data Entry Window. The purpose of the General Information data entry window is to provide information to the payroll software for reference during execution. You are required to supply the Run Date (usually the last day of the pay period), your name, company name, and problem name. This information will be listed on each of your computer generated reports.

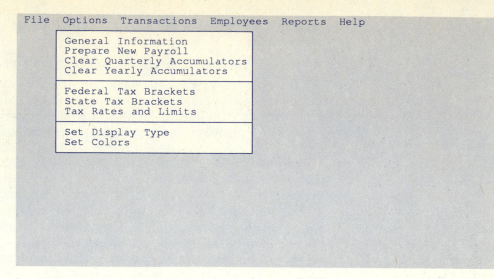

Figure B-8. Options Menu

Prepare New Payroll. The purpose of the Prepare New Payroll command is to erase the previous pay period transactions data prior to keying the current pay period data. You can correct the payroll transactions and reprint the payroll reports at any time **until** the Prepare New Payroll command is chosen to begin the next payroll period. If you do not select the Prepare New Payroll command before entering transactions for a new period, the computer assumes that you are correcting the transactions from the previous pay period rather than entering transactions for a new period. You must select Prepare New Payroll option before entering the current period's transactions.

1 Choose Prepare New Payroll from the Options menu.

2 When the dialog window appears, push the Ok button.

Clear Quarterly Accumulators. After printing and verifying the quarterly report and before processing the first payroll of the new quarter, you must instruct the computer to reset the quarterly accumulators to zero so that the next quarter's totals can be accumulated. When the Clear Quarterly Accumulators command is chosen, the current payroll data is also cleared.

1 Choose Clear Quarterly Accumulators from the Options menu.

2 When the dialog window appears, push the Ok button.

Clear Yearly Accumulators. After the W-2 statements are run and before the first payroll of the new year is run, the yearly accumulators must be reset to zero so that the totals for the next year can be accumulated. The Clear Yearly Accumulators options also clears the quarterly accumulators and the current payroll data.

1 Choose Clear Yearly Accumulators from the Options menu.

2 When the dialog window appears, push the Ok button.

Federal Tax Brackets, State Tax Brackets, Tax Rates and Limits. The Federal Tax Brackets command may be used to update the federal withholdings by referring to IRS Circular E (Employer's Tax Guide, Table 7, Annual Payroll). The State Tax Brackets command may be used to change the state taxable rate percentage (and limit if necessary). The Tax Rates and Limits command may be used to update various tax rates, upper limits, and allowance amounts required by the software to calculate employee and employer payroll taxes.

You will not be required to use these commands to complete the payroll processing tasks in the student project. It is recommended that you not change these rates when working the payroll problems. If the rates or percentages are changed, the calculated withholding amounts will no longer match the solutions provided to your instructor.

Set Display Type. The software checks the video card in your computer to determine whether you are using a monochrome or color monitor. In some cases monochrome monitors with graphics capability are mistakenly identified by the software as color monitors. The result is a "fuzzy" display that is difficult to read. If this occurs, you can choose the Set Display Type menu command and force the correct display type. When this command is selected, the Select Display type window will appear. Choose the display type desired by pushing either the "Color" or "MonoChrome" command button.

If the software recognizes that you are using a computer with a monochrome monitor, or the Set Display Type has been set to monochrome, the Set Colors command will be dimmed and unavailable.

Set Colors. If you are using a color monitor, you may modify the colors that appear on the screen with the Set Colors Dialog window. Once set, color settings will remain in effect during your computer session and will be saved to disk along with your data.

1   Push the Change button to change the colors.

A new, sample color combination will be displayed in the window boxes.

2   Continue pushing the Change button until the color combination that you prefer appears.

3   Push the Ok button to record your selection.

Transactions Menu

The pull-down Transactions menu, shown in Figure B-9, provides an Opening Balances command that may be used to enter the opening balance data when establishing a computerized payroll system, and a Payroll Transactions command that is used to enter payroll transaction data. When the Transactions menu is selected from the menu bar, the Opening Balances and Payroll Transactions commands described in this section will become available for execution.

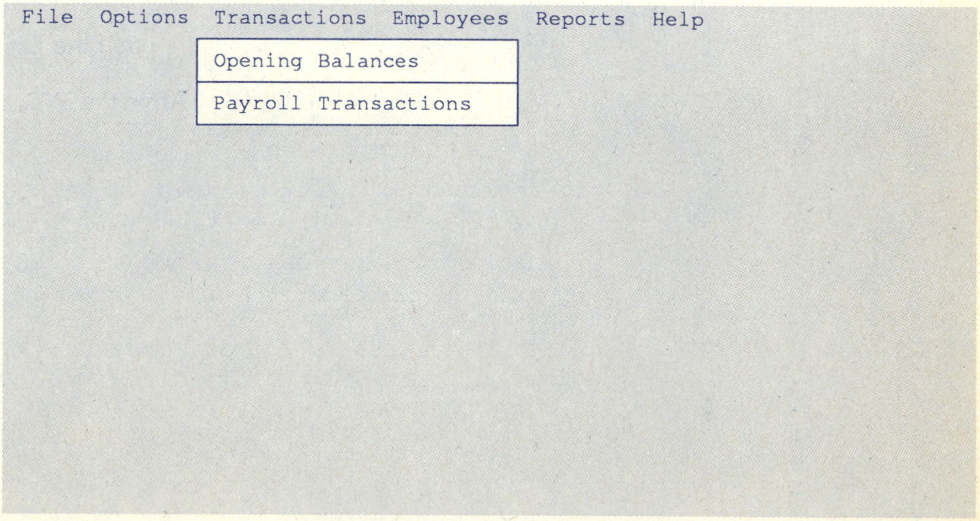

```
File   Options   Transactions   Employees   Reports   Help
                 ┌─────────────────────────┐
                 │  Opening Balances        │
                 │  Payroll Transactions    │
                 └─────────────────────────┘
```

Figure B-9.   Transactions Menu

Opening Balances. The Opening Balances command enables the user to enter, correct, and delete historical payroll data (quarter-to-date and year-to-date earnings and withholdings) that may be keyed into the computer in order to set up a new computerized payroll system. You will not be required to use this command to complete the problems in this text.

Payroll Transactions. The purpose of the Payroll Transactions data entry window is to identify the employees to be paid for the current pay period, to key the hours worked for hourly employees, and to enter any extra pay. After a transaction is entered, the computer performs the payroll calculations and updates the employee's record. The transaction remains in memory until the computer is directed to prepare a new payroll.

1   Choose the Payroll Transactions command from the Transactions menu.

   When the Payroll Transactions command is chosen from the Transactions menu, the data entry window with an employee list window will appear, as shown in Figure B-10.

```
 File  Options  Transactions  Employees  Reports  Help

░░░░░░░░░░░░░░░░░ Payroll Transaction            Employees
                                          ┌──────────────────────────┐
Employee No ....                          │ 010  Benitez, Ramon      │↑
Name............                          │ 020  Elkins, Dawn        │■
Type of Pay ....                          │ 030  Gerrard, Richard    │
           Current Pay Informa            │ 040  Marlow, Jacqueline  │
Regular Hours ..                          │ 050  Preston, Kevin      │
Overtime Hours .                          │ 060  Terrell, Sara       │
Bonus..........                           │ 070  Woodard, Lynette    │
(♦) Calculate Taxes                       │                          │
( ) Key Taxes                             │                          │
           Withholding Informa            │                          │
FIT.............                          │                          │↓
SIT.............                          │                          │
OASDI...........                          │ [ OK ]          < Exit > │
HI..............                          └──────────────────────────┘

      [ Pay ]              < Don't Pay >
```

Figure B-10.   Payroll Transactions Data Entry Window

After you have chosen the employee to pay, you may add a new employee to the payroll while keying payroll transactions by pressing the F2 hot key (or by pulling down the Employees menu and choosing the Maintain Employees command). The procedure to add a new employee is discussed in the next section under the Employees menu.

2   Choose the employee to be paid from the employee list window.

   The list window will be dismissed and the Employee No., Name, and Type of Pay will be displayed as shown in Figure B-11.

   To erase transaction data already entered and remove an employee from the pay status, select the employee, then push the Don't Pay button.

3   Key the Current Pay Information. If the employee is paid Hourly, key the Regular and Overtime hours. If the employee is to be paid additional pay, key the Extra Pay.

   Leave the option button set to Calculate Taxes unless you wish to key the withholding tax information rather than have the computer calculate taxes.

4   Push the Pay button.

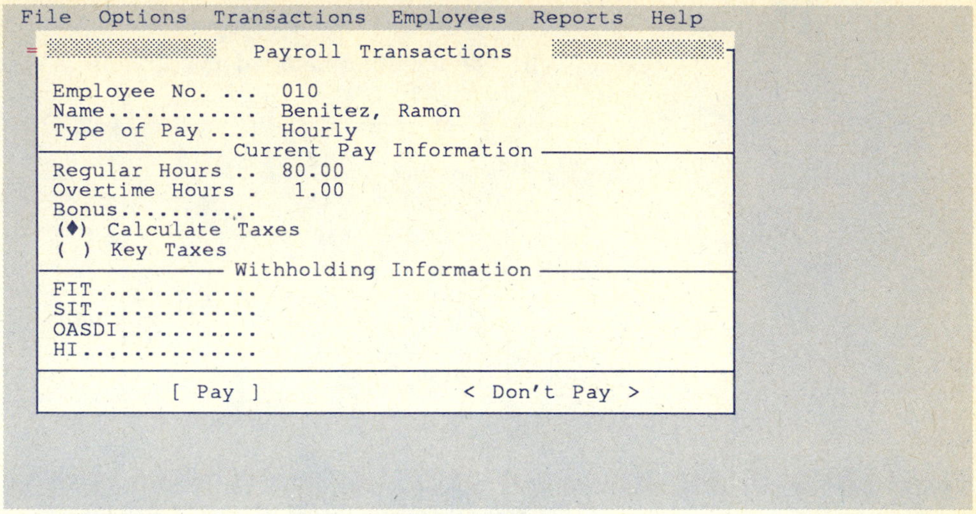

```
 File  Options  Transactions  Employees  Reports  Help
 =▒▒▒▒▒▒▒▒▒▒▒▒▒         Payroll Transactions        ▒▒▒▒▒▒▒▒▒▒▒▒▒┐

   Employee No. ...  010
   Name............  Benitez, Ramon
   Type of Pay ....  Hourly
   ─────────────────  Current Pay Information ──────────
   Regular Hours ..  80.00
   Overtime Hours .   1.00
   Bonus...........
   (♦) Calculate Taxes
   ( ) Key Taxes
   ──────────────── Withholding Information ──────────
   FIT.............
   SIT.............
   OASDI...........
   HI..............

            [ Pay ]                    < Don't Pay >
```

Figure B-11. Payroll Transactions

Note: Employees will appear in the list box with the >> symbol immediately to the left of their employee numbers when they have had transaction data entered for the current pay period and are to be paid.

If you must change employee data that affects payroll calculations (marital status, pay type, pay rate, pay periods per year, withholding allowances, or voluntary deductions), use this procedure: (1) select the employee from the list window, (2) eliminate the employee from being paid by pushing the Don't Pay button, (3) correct the employee's data using the Maintain Employees option, then (4) reenter the employee's payroll transaction data so the computer can recalculate the payroll information.

Employees Menu

Whenever necessary, new employees must be added, data must be changed, and employees no longer employed must be deleted. The Employees menu, shown in Figure B-12, provides a command that lists all employees that currently exist in the computer, and a command that enables the user to add, change, and delete employee records. When the Employees menu is selected from the Payroll menu bar, the two commands described in this section become available for execution.

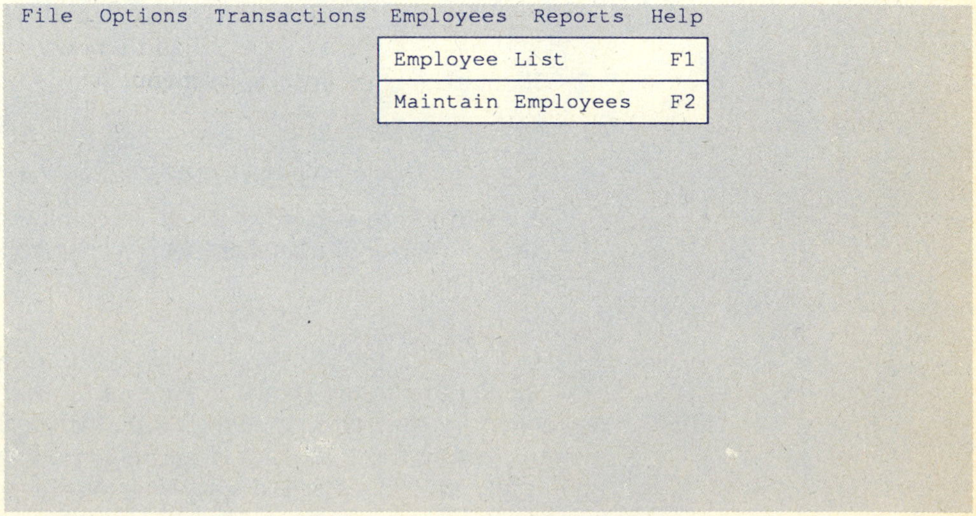

```
 File  Options  Transactions  Employees  Reports  Help
                              ┌─────────────────────────┐
                              │ Employee List        F1 │
                              ├─────────────────────────┤
                              │ Maintain Employees   F2 │
                              └─────────────────────────┘
```

Figure B-12. Employees Menu

1 Choose the Maintain Employees command from the Employees menu.

The Maintain Employees data entry window is illustrated in Figure B-13.

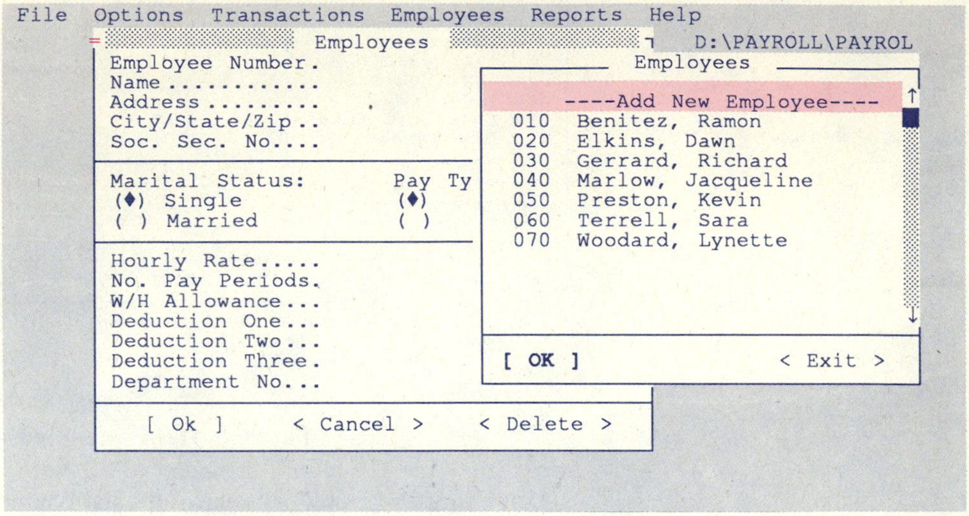

```
File   Options   Transactions   Employees   Reports   Help
  =                    Employees                  ┐    D:\PAYROLL\PAYROL
  Employee Number .                            Employees
  Name . . . . . . . . . . . .
  Address . . . . . . . . .                 ----Add New Employee----    ↑
  City/State/Zip ..               010   Benitez,  Ramon                 ■
  Soc. Sec. No.. . .              020   Elkins,   Dawn
                                  030   Gerrard,  Richard
  Marital Status:        Pay Ty   040   Marlow,   Jacqueline
  (♦) Single             (♦)      050   Preston,  Kevin
  ( ) Married            ( )      060   Terrell,  Sara
                                  070   Woodard,  Lynette
  Hourly Rate . . . . .
  No. Pay Periods .
  W/H Allowance . . .
  Deduction One . . .
  Deduction Two . . .                                                   ↓
  Deduction Three .               [ OK ]                    < Exit >
  Department No . . .

       [ Ok ]        < Cancel >       < Delete >
```

Figure B-13. Maintain Employees Data Entry Window

Adding a New Employee

2 Choose ----Add New Employee---- from the list window.

3 Key the employee data and set the Marital Status and Pay Type option buttons.

4 Push the Ok button.

Changing Employee Data

2 Choose the employee you wish to change from the list window.

The list window will be dismissed and the data for the chosen employee will be displayed.

3 Use the Tab key to position the cursor to the field you wish to change and rekey the correct data.

4 Push the Ok button.

Deleting an Employee

2 Choose the employee you wish to delete.

3 Push the delete button.

When the Delete Employee dialog window appears, push the Ok button.

You will not be allowed to delete an employee with cumulative earnings for the current year until after the Clear Yearly Accumulators command has been selected.

Reports Menu

The Reports menu, shown in Figure B-14, provides access to reports that are generated by the payroll system. Recall, the procedure to display and print the payroll reports was discussed in the Software Program Overview section earlier in this text. Once a report is displayed, it may be printed to an attached printer by choosing the Print command (in the File menu) or by pressing the F9 hot key. Each payroll report is described in the following section.

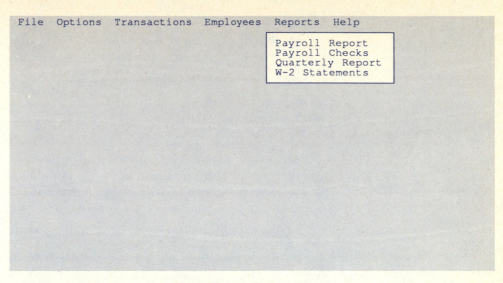

```
File  Options  Transactions  Employees  Reports  Help
                                       ┌─────────────────┐
                                       │ Payroll Report  │
                                       │ Payroll Checks  │
                                       │ Quarterly Report│
                                       │ W-2 Statements  │
                                       └─────────────────┘
```

Figure B-14.   Reports Menu

Payroll Report. The payroll report, which must be generated each pay period, actually contains two reports. The first report lists employee data, with current, quarterly, and yearly earnings and withholdings. A payroll summary is listed at the end of the report. The second report provides the journal entries resulting from the current payroll.

1 Choose the Payroll Report command from the Reports menu.

The Selection Options dialog window will appear allowing you to select the employees that you wish to appear on the report.

Hint: Use the F1 hot key to obtain a list window containing the numbers and names of all employees.

2 Key the range of employees.

3 Push the Ok button.

Payroll Checks. The payroll checks have two parts: (1) the check stub, which contains all current, quarterly, and year-to-date earnings and withholding information; and (2) the check itself.

1 Choose the Payroll Checks command from the Reports menu.

The Selection Options dialog window will appear allowing you to select the employees for which checks are to be prepared and the beginning check number.

2 Key the range of employees for which the checks are to be printed and the beginning check number.

3 Push the Ok button.

Quarterly Report. At the end of each quarter, the quarterly report must be run. The company uses it to report OASDI (social security) and HI (Medicare) taxable wages to the Internal Revenue Service.

1 Choose the Quarterly Report command from the Reports menu.

W-2 Statements. At the end of the year, the company must provide a W-2 statement to each employee paid during the past year. The W-2 statement is used for individual tax reporting purposes.

1   Choose the W-2 Statements option from the Reports menu.

The Selection Options dialog window will appear allowing you to select the employees that you wish to appear on the report.

2   Key the range of employees.

3   Push the Ok button.

Help Menu

Help windows have been provided as quick references when using the computerized payroll software to aid in the operation of the computer and software.

The Help pull-down menu may be accessed at any time during program execution. Operational information is provided in scrollable window displays.

1   Choose the desired Help command from the Help pull-down menu.

2   Use the keyboard (or mouse if available) to scroll through the help information.

3   Press the Esc key (or click on the Close Box (=) located in the upper left corner of the help window) to dismiss the help window display.

When a help window is dismissed, the computer returns to the point of interruption so processing may continue.

TUTORIAL PROBLEM

This tutorial problem illustrates the principles and procedures required to process payroll transactions using the Computerized Payroll Accounting software. You will perform the operating procedures necessary to add a new employee and make changes to employee data. In addition you will process the last payroll for the month of December for Rosen Enterprises. Since this is the last payroll of the year it will include the end-of-quarter and end-of-year reports. The information required to complete the December 31 payroll is listed below.

Instructions

Each of the step-by-step instructions below lists a task to be completed at the computer. If you need additional explanation for the task, a page reference is provided from the Operating Procedures section of this appendix.

Step 1: Remove the Tutorial Problem Audit Test found on page 361. Answer the questions for the December 31 payroll as you complete processing for the pay period.

Step 2: Bring up the Computerized Payroll Accounting software. (Page 344)

At the DOS prompt, key PAYROLL (or follow the instructions provided by your instructor).

Step 3: Load the opening balances template file, PAYROLL1. (Page 346)

Pull down the File menu and choose the Open Data File menu command. Key into the Path field the drive and directory containing the template files. Key a file name of PAYROLL1 and push the Ok button.

Step 4: When the General Information data entry window appears, set the run date to December 31 of the current year and enter your name. (Page 347)

Key December 31 of the current year (in the mm/dd/yy format) in the Run Date field, key your name in the Student Name field, then push the Ok button. Verify that the Company Name field contains Rosen Enterprises, and that the Problem Name field contains Tutorial Problem. If not, you may have loaded the wrong template file.

Step 5: Use the Save As command to save data to disk with a file name of XXX-1 (where XXX are your initials). (Page 347)

Pull down the File menu and choose the Save As menu command. Key the path to the drive and directory that contains your data files. Key a file name of XXX-1 where XXX are your initials. Push the Ok button.

Step 6: Enter employee maintenance data. (Page 352)

Pull down the Employees menu and choose the Maintain Employees command. Key the following employee maintenance data:

Addition of New Employee:

Yoshino, Sachi
6728 Linden Creek Dr.
St. Paul, MN 55104-2060

Assign employee number 080 (to place the new employee in alphabetical sequence); social security number, 484-72-3565; married; salaried,

$1,050.00; pay periods per year, 12; withholding allowances, 2; deduction one, $30.00; deduction two, $11.00; department number not used.

Changes to Current Employees:

- Benitez, Ramon: Change the marital status to married and the number of withholding allowances to 2.

- Marlow, Jacqueline: Change the number of withholding allowances to 5.

- Woodard, Lynette: Change Deduction 2 to $14.95.

Step 7: Prepare a new payroll. (Page 348)

Pull down the Options menu, choose the Prepare New Payroll menu command. When the Prepare New Payroll dialog window appears, push the Ok button to erase the previous pay period transaction data.

Step 8: Key the payroll transactions. (Page 350)

Pull down the Transactions menu and choose the Payroll Transactions menu command. Key the following payroll transaction data (use the Calculate Taxes option):

Employees to be Paid this Pay Period:

Employee Number	Employee Name	Regular Hours	Overtime Hours	Extra Pay
010	Benitez, Ramon	80		
020	Elkins, Dawn	80	5.50	
030	Gerrard, Richard	75		
040	Marlow, Jacqueline	(salaried)		$150.00
050	Preston, Kevin	(salaried)		$ 75.00
060	Terrell, Sara	(salaried)		
070	Woodard, Lynette	80	3.50	
080	Yoshino, Sachi	(salaried)		

Step 9: Display the Payroll Report and Journal Entries Report. (Page 353)

Pull down the Reports menu and choose the Payroll Report menu command. When the Selection Options dialog window appears, key a range of employees from 010 to 080 (if not already specified). The payroll report for Employee 010, Ramon Benitez, is shown in Figure B-15 followed by the payroll summary. The journal entries report is shown in Figure B-16 (your display will include a payroll report for all employees).

```
                        Rosen Enterprises
                        Payroll Report
                           12/31/--
--------------------------------------------------------------------

                                  Current    Quarterly    Yearly
--------------------------------------------------------------------
010-Benitez, Ramon       Gross Pay   992.00    6667.25   24633.00
1426 N. 22d Street       FIT          85.92     819.08    3139.12
St. Paul, MN 55102-1525  SIT          27.78     186.69     689.73
563-18-5021              OASDI        61.50     413.37    1527.24
W/H Allow   2   Married  HI           14.38      96.67     357.17
Department  0            Deduction 1  20.00
```

Pay Periods	26	Deduction 2	12.00
Reg. Hrs.	80.00	Deduction 3	
O.T. Hrs.		Net Pay	770.42
Bonus			
Hourly Rate	12.40		

Payroll summary:	Gross Pay	8814.85	52529.53	100977.39
	FIT	842.10	6098.95	12298.11
	SIT	246.81	1470.83	2827.37
	OASDI	546.53	3256.22	6260.60
	HI	127.80	761.65	1464.15
	Deduction 1	177.50		
	Deduction 2	109.95		
	Deduction 3			
	Net Pay	6764.16		

Figure B-15.   Payroll Report

Rosen Enterprises
Journal Entries
12/31/--

Account Title	Debit	Credit
Payroll Cash	6764.16	
Cash		6764.16
Salary Expense	8814.85	
Employees' FIT Payable		842.10
Employees' SIT Payable		246.81
FICA Tax Payable—OASDI		546.53
FICA TAX Payable—HI		127.80
Deduction 1 Payable		177.50
Deduction 2 Payable		109.95
Payroll Cash		6764.16
Payroll Taxes Expense	792.12	
FICA Taxes Payable—OASDI		546.53
FICA Taxes Payable—HI		127.80
FUTA Taxes Payable		15.63
SUTA Taxes Payable		102.16

Figure B-16.   Journal Entries Report

Step 10:   Display payroll checks. (Page 353)

Pull down the Reports menu and choose the Payroll Checks menu command. When the Selection Options window appears, key an employee range of 010 to 080 (if not already specified) and a beginning check number of 3501, then push the Ok button to display the checks for all employees. The first check is illustrated in Figure B-17 (your display will include checks for all employees).

Check No. 3501

Date 12/31/--

		Current	Quarterly	Yearly
010-Benitez, Ramon	Gross Pay	992.00	6667.25	24633.00
1426 N. 22d Street	FIT	85.92	819.08	3139.12
St. Paul, MN 55102-1525	SIT	27.78	186.69	689.73
563-18-5021	OASDI	61.50	413.37	1527.24
W/H Allow 2 Married	HI	14.38	96.67	357.17
Department 0	Deduction 1	20.00		
Pay Periods 26	Deduction 2	12.00		
Reg. Hrs. 80.00	Deduction 3			
O.T. Hrs.	Net Pay	770.42		
Bonus				
Hourly Rate 12.40				

National State Bank
DownTown Office
Anycity, State 12345-1234

Rosen Enterprises

Check No. 3501

PAY
TO THE
ORDER   Benitez, Ramon
OF

Date	Amount
12/31/--	770.42

Figure B-17.   Payroll Check

Step 11:   Display the quarterly report. (Page 353)

Pull down the Reports menu, choose the Quarterly Report menu command, and display the quarterly report as of the end of the fourth quarter (December 31, 19--). The report is shown in Figure B-18.

Rosen Enterprises
Quarterly Report
12/31/--

Social Security #	Employee Name	Taxable OASDI	Taxable HI
563-18-5021	Benitez, Ramon	6667.25	6667.25
543-62-6539	Elkins, Dawn	6889.95	6889.95
581-30-3968	Gerrard, Richard	6941.13	6941.13
443-56-8642	Marlow, Jacqueline	7419.03	7419.03
440-51-4565	Preston, Kevin	8842.55	8842.55
734-74-6830	Terrell, Sara	8777.55	8777.55
485-15-6327	Woodard, Lynette	5942.07	5942.07
484-72-3565	Yoshino, Sachi	1050.00	1050.00
	Totals	52529.53	52529.53
	Total Employees 8		

Figure B-18.   Quarterly Report

Step 12: Display the W-2 statements. (Page 353)

Pull down the Reports menu, choose the W-2 Statements menu command, and display the W-2 statements as of the end of the year. When the Selections Options dialog window appears, select an employee range of 010 to 080 (all employees). The first statement is shown in Figure B-19 (your display will show statements for all employees).

19-- Wage and Tax Statement

	Wages	OASDI Tax	HI Tax
Rosen Enterprises	24633.00	1527.24	357.17

Social Security No.	Federal Tax	OASDI Wages	HI Wages
563-18-5021	3139.12	24633.00	24633.00

	State Tax
	689.73

Benitez, Ramon
1426 N. 22d Street
St. Paul, MN 55102-1525

Figure B-19. W-2 Statement

Step 13: Save your data to disk with a file name of XXX-1. (Page 346)

Pull down the File menu and choose the Save Data File command (to save your data to the current drive/directory with the current filename).

Step 14: End the session. (Page 347)

From the File menu, choose the Quit command.

Note: After verifying the accuracy of the quarterly report and the W-2 statements, the Clear Yearly Accumulators command must be run prior to processing the first payroll of the new calendar year.

TUTORIAL PROBLEM AUDIT TEST

Use the payroll file you saved under file name XXX-1 to answer the following questions for the December 31 payroll.

Payroll Report

1. What is the total net pay for Dawn Elkins? .... _____

2. What is the current gross pay for Kevin Preston? .... _____

3. What is the amount of HI withheld for the quarter for Sara Terrell? ... _____

4. What is the total current net pay for all employees? .... _____

5. What is the total yearly gross pay for all employees? .... _____

Journal Entries Report

6. What is the amount of the credit to Employees' Federal Income Tax Payable? .... _____

7. What is the amount of the credit to FICA Tax Payable—HI? .... _____

8. What is the amount of the debit to Salary Expense? .... _____

Payroll Checks

9. What is the current gross pay shown on the check stub for the check written to Richard Gerrard? .... _____

10. What is the net amount of the check to Sachi Yoshino? .... _____

Quarterly Report

11. What is the Taxable OASDI amount for Lynette Woodard? .... _____

12. What is the total Taxable HI (Medicare) amount for all employees for the quarter? .... _____

W-2 Statements

13. What is the amount of State Tax shown for Ramon Benitez? .... _____

14. What is the amount of HI Tax shown for Jacqueline Marlow? .... _____

STUDENT PROJECT

The employee data for Surgical Supply, Inc. are stored on the disk (as of September 24 of the current year) under the file name PAYROLL2. The biweekly payroll from September 24 through December 31 of the current year will be run for Surgical Supply, Inc. You will perform the operating procedures necessary to maintain employee data and process the payroll each pay period. Since December 31 is both the end of a quarter and the end of the year, the December 31 payroll will include the end-of-quarter report and W-2 statements.

OCTOBER 8 PAYROLL

The step-by-step instructions for completing the October 8 payroll (for the weeks ending September 30 and October 8) are listed below.

Step 1: Remove the Student Project Audit Test found on page 369. Answer the questions for the October 8 payroll as you complete processing for the pay period.

Step 2: Bring up the Computerized Payroll Accounting software.

Step 3: Load the opening balances template file, PAYROLL2.

Step 4: When the General Information data entry window appears, set the run date to October 8 of the current year and enter your name in the Student name field.

Step 5: Prepare a new payroll.

Step 6: Enter the following payroll transactions:

Employees to be Paid this Pay Period:

Employee Number	Employee Name	Regular Hours	Overtime Hours	Extra Pay
210	Alder, Jeanne	80		
220	Dittrich, Michael	72		
230	Harding, Stephen	(salaried)		
240	Olmstead, Christine	80		
250	Sheng, Tien	(salaried)		
260	Thatcher, Scott	80	2.5	

Step 7: Print or display a payroll report for all employees.

Step 8: Print or display payroll checks for all employees. Begin check numbering with Check No. 835.

Step 9: Use the Save As command to save the October 8 payroll to disk with a file name of XXX-1008 (where XXX are your initials and 1008 represents month 10, day 08).

Step 10: Proceed to the October 22 payroll. If necessary, end your payroll session.

OCTOBER 22 PAYROLL

The step-by-step instructions for completing the October 22 payroll (for the weeks ending October 15 and October 22) follow.

Step 1: Answer the questions for the October 22 payroll on the Audit Test as you complete processing for the pay period.

Step 2: If you quit the software after processing the previous pay period, perform the following steps:
(a) Bring up the Computerized Payroll Accounting software.
(b) Load your file containing the last pay period data (XXX-1008).

Step 3: Set the run date to October 22 of the current year in the General Information data entry window.

Step 4: Enter the following employee maintenance data.
- Dittrich, Michael: Change the marital status to married and the number of withholding allowances to 2.
- Sheng, Tien: Change the amount of Deduction 1 (group insurance) to $21.95.

Step 5: Prepare a new payroll.

Step 6: Enter the following payroll transactions:

Employees to be Paid this Pay Period:

Employee Number	Employee Name	Regular Hours	Overtime Hours	Extra Pay
210	Alder, Jeanne	80	1.75	
220	Dittrich, Michael	80		
230	Harding, Stephen	(salaried)		
240	Olmstead, Christine	80	3.0	
250	Sheng, Tien	(salaried)		
260	Thatcher, Scott	68		

Step 7: Print or display a payroll report for all employees.

Step 8: Print or display payroll checks for all employees. Continue the previous check numbering by entering a beginning Check No. 841.

Step 9: Use the Save As command to save the October 22 payroll to disk with a file name of XXX-1022 (where XXX are your initials and 1022 represents month 10, day 22).

Step 10: Proceed to the November 5 payroll. If necessary, end your payroll session.

NOVEMBER 5 PAYROLL

The step-by-step instructions for completing the November 5 payroll (for the weeks ending October 29 and November 5) are listed below.

Step 1: Answer the questions for the November 5 payroll on the Audit Test as you complete processing for the pay period.

Step 2: If you quit the software after processing the previous pay period, perform the following steps:
(a) Bring up the Computerized Payroll Accounting software.
(b) Load your file containing the last pay period data (XXX-1022).

Step 3: Set the run date to November 5 of the current year in the General Information data entry window.

Step 4: Prepare a new payroll.

Step 5: Enter the following payroll transactions:

Employees to be Paid this Pay Period:

Employee Number	Employee Name	Regular Hours	Overtime Hours	Extra Pay
210	Alder, Jeanne	80		
220	Dittrich, Michael			$840.00
				(two weeks vacation pay)
230	Harding, Stephen	(salaried)		
240	Olmstead, Christine	80		
250	Sheng, Tien	(salaried)		
260	Thatcher, Scott	80		

Step 6: Print or display a payroll report for all employees.

Step 7: Print or display payroll checks for all employees. Continue the previous check numbering by entering a beginning Check No. 847.

Step 8: Use the Save As command to save the November 5 payroll to disk with a file name of XXX-1105 (where XXX are your initials and 1105 represents month 11, day 05).

Step 9: Proceed to the November 19 payroll. If necessary, end your payroll session.

NOVEMBER 19 PAYROLL

The step-by-step instructions for completing the November 19 payroll (for the weeks ending November 12 and November 19) are listed below.

Step 1: Answer the questions for the November 19 payroll on the Audit Test as you complete processing for the pay period.

Step 2: If you quit the software after processing the previous pay period, perform the following steps:

(a) Bring up the Computerized Payroll Accounting software.
(b) Load your file containing the last pay period data (XXX-1105).

Step 3: Set the run date to November 19 of the current year in the General Information data entry window.

Step 4: Add the following employee.

Lawson, Helen
19566 Ashby Lane
Boise, ID 83705-9210

Assign employee number 235 (to place the new employee in alphabetical sequence); social security number, 448-62-7364; married; hourly rate, $9.95; pay periods per year, 26; withholding allowances, 2; deduction one (group insurance), $20.00; deduction two (union dues), $4.00; department number not used.

Step 5: Prepare a new payroll.

Step 6: Enter the following payroll transactions:

Employees to be Paid this Pay Period:

Employee Number	Employee Name	Regular Hours	Overtime Hours	Extra Pay
210	Alder, Jeanne	80	6.5	
220	Dittrich, Michael	80		
230	Harding, Stephen	(salaried)		
235	Lawson, Helen	40		
240	Olmstead, Christine	40		$446.00
		(one week vacation pay)		
250	Sheng, Tien	(salaried)		
260	Thatcher, Scott	80	5.0	

Step 7: Print or display a payroll report for all employees.

Step 8: Print or display payroll checks for all employees. Continue the previous check numbering by entering a beginning Check No. 853.

Step 9: Use the Save As command to save the November 19 payroll to disk with a file name of XXX-1119.

Step 10: Proceed to the December 3 payroll. If necessary, end your payroll session.

DECEMBER 3 PAYROLL

The step-by-step instructions for completing the December 3 payroll (for the weeks ending November 26 and December 3) are listed below.

Step 1: Answer the questions for the December 3 payroll on the Audit Test as you complete processing for the pay period.

Step 2: If you quit the software after processing the previous pay period, perform the following steps:
(a) Bring up the Computerized Payroll Accounting software.
(b) Load your file containing the last pay period data (XXX-1119).

Step 3: Set the run date to December 3 of the current year in the General Information data entry window.

Step 4: Prepare a new payroll.

Step 5: Enter the following payroll transactions:

Employees to be Paid this Pay Period:

Employee Number	Employee Name	Regular Hours	Overtime Hours	Extra Pay
210	Alder, Jeanne	80		
220	Dittrich, Michael	64		
230	Harding, Stephen	(salaried)		
235	Lawson, Helen	80		
240	Olmstead, Christine	80	3.75	
250	Sheng, Tien	(salaried)		
260	Thatcher, Scott	80		

Step 6: Print or display a payroll report for all employees.

Step 7: Print or display payroll checks for all employees. Continue the previous check numbering by entering a beginning Check No. 860.

Step 8: Use the Save As command to save the December 3 payroll to disk with a file name of XXX-1203.

Step 9: Proceed to the December 17 payroll. If necessary, end your payroll session.

DECEMBER 17 PAYROLL

The step-by-step instructions for completing the December 17 payroll (for the weeks ending December 10 and December 17) are listed below.

Step 1: Answer the questions for the December 17 payroll on the Audit Test as you complete processing for the pay period.

Step 2: If you quit the software after processing the previous pay period, perform the following steps:
(a) Bring up the Computerized Payroll Accounting software.
(b) Load your file containing the last pay period data (XXX-1203).

Step 3: Set the run date to December 17 of the current year in the General Information data entry window.

Step 4: Prepare a new payroll.

Step 5: Enter the following payroll transactions:

Employees to be Paid this Pay Period:

Employee Number	Employee Name	Regular Hours	Overtime Hours	Extra Pay
210	Alder, Jeanne	80		
220	Dittrich, Michael	80	7.0	
230	Harding, Stephen	(salaried)		
235	Lawson, Helen	80		
240	Olmstead, Christine	80		
250	Sheng, Tien	(salaried)		
260	Thatcher, Scott	80		

Step 6: Print or display a payroll report for all employees.

Step 7: Print or display payroll checks for all employees. Continue the previous check numbering by entering a beginning Check No. 867.

Step 8: Use the Save As command to save the December 17 payroll to disk with a file name of XXX-1217.

Step 9: Proceed to the December 31 payroll. If necessary, end your payroll session.

DECEMBER 31 PAYROLL

The step-by-step instructions for completing the December 31 payroll (for the weeks ending December 24 and December 31), and for generating the quarterly report and W-2 statements are listed below.

Step 1: Answer the questions for the December 31 payroll on the Audit Test as you complete processing for the pay period, end-of-quarter, and end-of-year.

Step 2: If you quit the software after processing the previous pay period, perform the following steps:

(a) Bring up the Computerized Payroll Accounting software.

(b) Load your file containing the last pay period data (XXX-1217).

Step 3: Set the run date to December 31 of the current year in the General Information data entry window.

Step 4: Prepare a new payroll.

Step 5: Enter the following payroll transactions:

Employees to be Paid this Pay Period:

Employee Number	Employee Name	Regular Hours	Overtime Hours	Extra Pay
210	Alder, Jeanne	80	5.25	
220	Dittrich, Michael	80		
230	Harding, Stephen	(salaried)		$225.00 (bonus)
235	Lawson, Helen	80	6.0	
240	Olmstead, Christine	80		
250	Sheng, Tien	(salaried)		$225.00 (bonus)
260	Thatcher, Scott	80	4.5	

Step 6: Print or display a payroll report for all employees.

Step 7: Print or display payroll checks for all employees. Continue the previous check numbering by entering a beginning Check No. 874.

Step 8: Print or display a quarterly report.

Step 9: Print or display the W-2 statements for all employees.

Step 10: Use the Save As command to save the December 31 payroll to disk with a file name of XXX-1231.

Step 11: End the computerized payroll session.

STUDENT PROJECT AUDIT TEST

OCTOBER 8 PAYROLL: (Use the payroll file you saved under file name XXX-1008 to answer the following questions for the October 8 payroll.)

Payroll Report

1. What are the number of withholding allowances for Michael Dittrich? . _____
2. What is the current gross pay for Christine Olmstead? . . . . _____
3. What is the amount of HI withheld for the quarter for Scott Thatcher? . _____
4. What is the total current net pay for all employees? . . . . _____
5. What is the total yearly gross pay for all employees? . . . . _____

Journal Entries Report

6. What is the amount of the debit to Salary Expense? . . . . _____
7. What is the amount of the debit to Payroll Taxes Expense? . . . . _____
8. What is the amount of the credit to Cash? . . . . _____

Payroll Checks

9. What is the check number for the check written to Stephen Harding? . _____
10. What is the amount of the check to Tien Sheng? . . . . _____

- -

STUDENT PROJECT AUDIT TEST

OCTOBER 22 PAYROLL: (Use the payroll file you saved under file name XXX-1022 to answer the following questions for the October 22 payroll.)

Payroll Report

1. What is the current gross pay for Jeanne Alder? . . . . _____
2. What is the current amount of OASDI withheld for Jeanne Alder? . . . . _____
3. What is the total current net pay for all employees? . . . . _____
4. What is the total yearly gross pay for all employees? . . . . _____

Journal Entries Report

5. What is the amount of the debit to Salary Expense? . . . . _____
6. What is the amount of the debit to Payroll Taxes Expense? . . . . _____
7. What is the amount of the credit to Cash? . . . . _____

Payroll Checks

8. What is the check number for the check written to Christine Olmstead? _____
9. What is the amount of the check to Christine Olmstead? . . . . _____

STUDENT PROJECT AUDIT TEST

NOVEMBER 5 PAYROLL: (Use the payroll file you saved under file name XXX-1105 to answer the following questions for the November 5 payroll.)

Payroll Report

1. What is the current amount of FIT withheld for Michael Dittrich? . . . . . _____

2. What is the total current gross pay for all employees? . . . . _____

3. What is the total group insurance (Deduction 1) for all employees? . . . _____

4. What is the total union dues (Deduction 2) for all employees? . . . . _____

Journal Entries Report

5. What is the amount of the credit to FICA Taxes Payable—OASDI? . . . _____

6. What is the amount of the credit to FICA Taxes Payable—HI? . . . . _____

7. What is the amount of the debit to Payroll Taxes Expense? . . . . _____

Payroll Checks

8. What is the check number for the check written to Scott Thatcher? . . . _____

9. What is the amount of the check to Michael Dittrich? . . . . _____

STUDENT PROJECT AUDIT TEST

NOVEMBER 19 PAYROLL: (Use the payroll file you saved under file name XXX-1119 to answer the following questions for the November 19 payroll.)

Payroll Report

1. What is the amount of FIT withheld for the year for Christine Olmstead? . . . . _____

2. What is the total current net pay for all employees? . . . . _____

3. What is the total yearly gross pay for all employees? . . . . _____

Journal Entries Report

4. What is the amount of the Credit to Cash? . . . . _____

5. What is the amount of the debit to Payroll Taxes Expense? . . . . _____

6. What is the amount of the debit to Salary Expense? . . . . _____

Payroll Checks

7. What is the check number for the check written to Helen Lawson? . . . _____

8. What is the amount of the check to Helen Lawson? . . . . _____

STUDENT PROJECT AUDIT TEST

DECEMBER 3 PAYROLL: (Use the payroll file you saved under file name XXX-1203 to answer the following questions for the December 3 payroll.)

Payroll Report

1. What is the current gross pay for Christine Olmstead? . . . . _____
2. What is the current amount of OASDI withheld for Stephen Harding? . _____
3. What is the total current net pay for all employees? . . . . _____
4. What is the total yearly gross pay for all employees? . . . . _____

Journal Entries Report

5. What is the amount of the debit to Salary Expense? . . . . _____
6. What is the amount of the credit to Employees' SIT Payable? . . . . _____
7. What is the amount of the debit to Payroll Taxes Expense? . . . . _____

Payroll Checks

8. What is the check number for the check written to Tien Sheng? . . . . . _____
9. What is the amount of the check to Tien Sheng? . . . . _____

- -

STUDENT PROJECT AUDIT TEST

DECEMBER 17 PAYROLL: (Use the payroll file you saved under file name XXX-1217 to answer the following questions for the December 17 payroll.)

Payroll Report

1. What is the social security number of Stephen Harding? . . . . _____
2. What is Scott Thatcher's zip code? . . . . _____
3. What is the current amount of SIT withheld for Jeanne Alder? . . . . _____
4. What is the total current net pay for all employees? . . . . _____
5. What is the total yearly gross pay for all employees? . . . . _____

Journal Entries Report

6. What is the amount of the debit to Salary Expense? . . . . _____
7. What is the amount of the debit to Payroll Taxes Expense? . . . . _____

Payroll Checks

8. What is the check number for the check written to Helen Lawson? . . . _____
9. What is the amount of the check to Michael Dittrich? . . . . _____

STUDENT PROJECT AUDIT TEST

DECEMBER 31 PAYROLL: (Use the payroll file you saved under file name XXX-1231 to answer the following questions for the December 31 payroll.)

Payroll Report

1. What are the number of withholding allowances for Scott Thatcher? . . _____

2. What is Jeanne Alder's street address? . . . . _____

3. What is the amount of SIT withheld for the year for Stephen Harding? _____

4. What is the total current net pay for all employees? . . . . _____

5. What is the total yearly gross pay for all employees? . . . . _____

Journal Entries Report

6. What is the amount of the debit to Salary Expense? . . . . _____

7. What is the amount of the debit to Payroll Taxes Expense? . . . . _____

Payroll Checks

8. What is the check number for the check written to Scott Thatcher? . . . _____

9. What is the amount of the check to Scott Thatcher? . . . . _____

Quarterly Report

10. What is the taxable OASDI (social security) amount for Jeanne Alder? _____

11. What is the total taxable HI (Medicare) amount for all employees for
    the quarter? . . . . _____

W-2 Statements

12. What is the amount of total wages earned for Stephen Harding? . . . . _____

13. What is the total taxable HI Wages for Tien Sheng? . . . . _____

14. What is the total HI tax for Tien Sheng? . . . . _____

15. What is the total State tax for Scott Thatcher? . . . . _____

MASTERY PROJECT

In this project you will be required to perform the operating procedures necessary to add a new employee, make changes to employee data, and enter payroll transactions for the pay period that ended December 31 for Kenton Corporation with a minimum of instruction. Since this is the last payroll of the year it will include the end-of-quarter and end-of-year reports. The information required to complete the December 31 payroll is listed below.

DECEMBER 31 PAYROLL

The payroll data for the December 31 payroll are listed below.

Addition of New Employee:

Preston, Gerald
6382 Winding Way Dr.
St. Paul, MN 55107-5739

Assign employee number 055; social security number, 572-68-2679; single; hourly rate, $10.60; pay periods per year, 26; withholding allowances, one; deduction one, $17.50; deduction two, $14.25; department number not used.

Changes to Current Employees:

- Cantey, Paul: Change Deduction 2 to $14.25.
- Nettles, Todd: Change number of withholding allowances to five.
- Skelly, Michelle: Change salary to $1,325.00 per pay period.

Employees to be Paid this Pay Period:

Employee Number	Employee Name	Regular Hours	Overtime Hours	Extra Pay
010	Cantey, Paul	80		$150.00
020	Flanagan, Connie	80	3.5	$150.00
030	Hayashi, Sumio	80		$150.00
040	Kinsey, Rebecca	(salaried)		$250.00
050	Nettles, Todd	(salaried)		$250.00
055	Preston, Gerald	56		
060	Skelly, Michelle	(salaried)		$250.00
070	Wurst, Tracy	80	7.0	$150.00

Instructions:

To solve the mastery project, complete the tasks listed below.

- Load the opening balances template file, PAYROLL3.
- Set the run date to December 31 of the current year.
- Save the data to your data disk or directory with a name of XXX-3.
- Process the December 31 payroll.
- Display the December 31 payroll report, payroll checks (starting check number, 1077), quarterly report, and W-2 statements.
- Save your data with a file name of XXX-3.
- End the session.

MASTERY PROJECT AUDIT TEST

Use the payroll file you saved under file name XXX-3 to answer the following questions for the December 31 payroll.

Payroll Report

1. What is the total net pay for Paul Cantey? .... _____

2. What is the current gross pay for Connie Flanagan? .... _____

3. What is the amount of HI withheld for the quarter for Rebecca Kinsey? _____

4. What is the total current net pay for all employees? .... _____

5. What is the total yearly gross pay for all employees? .... _____

Journal Entries Report

6. What is the amount of the credit to Employees' Federal Income Tax Payable? .... _____

7. What is the amount of the credit to FICA Tax Payable—HI? .... _____

8. What is the amount of the debit to Salary Expense? .... _____

Payroll Checks

9. What is the gross pay shown on the check stub for the check written to Michelle Skelly? .... _____

10. What is the net amount of the check to Tracy Wurst? .... _____

Quarterly Report

11. What is the Taxable OASDI amount for Connie Flanagan? .... _____

12. What is the total Taxable HI (Medicare) amount for all employees for the quarter? .... _____

W-2 Statements

13. What is the amount of State Tax shown for Rebecca Kinsey? .... _____

14. What is the amount of HI (Medicare) Tax shown for Todd Nettles? ... _____

TAX TABLE
A

TABLE OF ALLOWANCE VALUES

Payroll period	Amount of one withholding allowance:
Weekly	$ 45.19
Biweekly	90.38
Semimonthly	97.92
Monthly	195.83
Quarterly	587.50
Semiannual	1,175.00
Annual	2,350.00
Daily or miscellaneous (per day of such period)	9.04

TABLES FOR PERCENTAGE METHOD OF WITHHOLDING
(Effective January 1, 1993)

TABLE 1—WEEKLY Payroll Period

(a) SINGLE person (including head of household)—

If the amount of wages (after subtracting withholding allowances) is:

The amount of income tax to withhold is:

Not over $49. . . . . $0

Over—	But not over—		of excess over—
$49	—$451 . . .	15%	—$49
$451	—$942 . . .	$60.30 plus 28%	—$451
$942	. . . .	$197.78 plus 31%	—$942

(b) MARRIED person—

If the amount of wages (after subtracting withholding allowances) is:

The amount of income tax to withhold is:

Not over $119 . . . . . $0

Over—	But not over—		of excess over—
$119	—$784 . . .	15%	—$119
$784	—$1,563 . . .	$99.75 plus 28%	—$784
$1,563	. . . .	$317.87 plus 31%	—$1,563

TABLE 2—BIWEEKLY Payroll Period

(a) SINGLE person (including head of household)—

If the amount of wages (after subtracting withholding allowances) is:

The amount of income tax to withhold is:

Not over $97. . . . . $0

Over—	But not over—		of excess over—
$97	—$902 . . .	15%	—$97
$902	—$1,884 . .	$120.75 plus 28%	—$902
$1,884	. . . .	$395.71 plus 31%	—$1,884

(b) MARRIED person—

If the amount of wages (after subtracting withholding allowances) is:

The amount of income tax to withhold is:

Not over $238 . . . . . $0

Over—	But not over—		of excess over—
$238	—$1,567 . . .	15%	—$238
$1,567	—$3,125 . . .	$199.35 plus 28%	—$1,567
$3,125	. . . .	$635.59 plus 31%	—$3,125

TABLE 3—SEMIMONTHLY Payroll Period

(a) SINGLE person (including head of household)—

If the amount of wages (after subtracting withholding allowances) is:

The amount of income tax to withhold is:

Not over $105 . . . . $0

Over—	But not over—		of excess over—
$105	—$977 . . .	15%	—$105
$977	—$2,041 . .	$130.80 plus 28%	—$977
$2,041	. . . . . .	$428.72 plus 31%	—$2,041

(b) MARRIED person—

If the amount of wages (after subtracting withholding allowances) is:

The amount of income tax to withhold is:

Not over $258 . . . . $0

Over—	But not over—		of excess over—
$258	—$1,698 . . .	15%	—$258
$1,698	—$3,385 . . .	$216.00 plus 28%	—$1,698
$3,385	. . . .	$688.36 plus 31%	—$3,385

TABLE 4—MONTHLY Payroll Period

(a) SINGLE person (including head of household)—

If the amount of wages (after subtracting withholding allowances) is:

The amount of income tax to withhold is:

Not over $210 . . . . $0

Over—	But not over—		of excess over—
$210	—$1,954 . .	15%	—$210
$1,954	—$4,081 . .	$261.60 plus 28%	—$1,954
$4,081	. . . . . .	$857.16 plus 31%	—$4,081

(b) MARRIED person—

If the amount of wages (after subtracting withholding allowances) is:

The amount of income tax to withhold is:

Not over $517 . . . . $0

Over—	But not over—		of excess over—
$517	—$3,396 . . .	15%	—$517
$3,396	—$6,771 . . .	$431.85 plus 28%	—$3,396
$6,771	. . . .	$1,376.85 plus 31%	—$6,771

TABLES FOR PERCENTAGE METHOD OF WITHHOLDING
(Effective January 1, 1993)

TABLE 5—QUARTERLY Payroll Period

(a) SINGLE person (including head of household)—

If the amount of wages (after subtracting withholding allowances) is:
The amount of income tax to withhold is:

Not over $631 . . . . $0

Over—	But not over—		of excess over—
$631	—$5,863 . .	15%	—$631
$5,863	—$12,244 . .	$784.80 plus 28%	—$5,863
$12,244	. . . . . .	$2,571.48 plus 31%	—$12,244

(b) MARRIED person—

If the amount of wages (after subtracting withholding allowances) is:
The amount of income tax to withhold is:

Not over $1,550 . . . . $0

Over—	But not over—		of excess over—
$1,550	—$10,188 . .	15%	—$1,550
$10,188	—$20,313 . .	$1,295.70 plus 28%	—$10,188
$20,313	. . . . . .	$4,130.70 plus 31%	—$20,313

TABLE 6—SEMIANNUAL Payroll Period

(a) SINGLE person (including head of household)—

If the amount of wages (after subtracting withholding allowances) is:
The amount of income tax to withhold is:

Not over $1,263 . . . $0

Over—	But not over—		of excess over—
$1,263	—$11,725 . .	15%	—$1,263
$11,725	—$24,488 . .	$1,569.30 plus 28%	—$11,725
$24,488	. . . . . .	$5,142.94 plus 31%	—$24,488

(b) MARRIED person—

If the amount of wages (after subtracting withholding allowances) is:
The amount of income tax to withhold is:

Not over $3,100 . . . . $0

Over—	But not over—		of excess over—
$3,100	—$20,375 . .	15%	—$3,100
$20,375	—$40,625 . .	$2,591.25 plus 28%	—$20,375
$40,625	. . . . . .	$8,261.25 plus 31%	—$40,625

TABLE 7—ANNUAL Payroll Period

(a) SINGLE person (including head of household)—

If the amount of wages (after subtracting withholding allowances) is:
The amount of income tax to withhold is:

Not over $2,525 . . . $0

Over—	But not over—		of excess over—
$2,525	—$23,450 . .	15%	—$2,525
$23,450	—$48,975 . .	$3,138.75 plus 28%	—$23,450
$48,975	. . . . . .	$10,285.75 plus 31%	—$48,975

(b) MARRIED person—

If the amount of wages (after subtracting withholding allowances) is:
The amount of income tax to withhold is:

Not over $6,200 . . . . $0

Over—	But not over—		of excess over—
$6,200	—$40,750 . .	15%	—$6,200
$40,750	—$81,250 . .	$5,182.50 plus 28%	—$40,750
$81,250	. . . . . .	$16,522.50 plus 31%	—$81,250

TABLE 8—DAILY or MISCELLANEOUS Payroll Period

(a) SINGLE person (including head of household)—

If the amount of wages (after subtracting withholding allowances) divided by the number of days in the payroll period is:
The amount of income tax to withhold per day is:

Not over $9.70 . . . . $0

Over—	But not over—		of excess over—
$9.70	—$90.20 . .	15%	—$9.70
$90.20	—$188.40 . .	$12.08 plus 28%	—$90.20
$188.40	. . . . . .	$39.58 plus 31%	—$188.40

(b) MARRIED person—

If the amount of wages (after subtracting withholding allowances) divided by the number of days in the payroll period is:
The amount of income tax to withhold per day is:

Not over $23.80 . . . . $0

Over—	But not over—		of excess over—
$23.80	—$156.70 . .	15%	—$23.80
$156.70	—$312.50 . .	$19.94 plus 28%	—$156.70
$312.50	. . . . . .	$63.56 plus 31%	—$312.50

TAX TABLE
B

WAGE-BRACKET WITHHOLDING TABLES

WEEKLY Payroll Period — Employee NOT MARRIED — Effective January 1, 1993

And the wages are— / And the number of withholding allowances claimed is— / The amount of income tax to be withheld shall be—

At least	But less than	0	1	2	3	4	5	6	7	8	9	10
$0	$50	$0	$0	$0	$0	$0	$0	$0	$0	$0	$0	$0
50	55	1	0	0	0	0	0	0	0	0	0	0
55	60	1	0	0	0	0	0	0	0	0	0	0
60	65	2	0	0	0	0	0	0	0	0	0	0
65	70	3	0	0	0	0	0	0	0	0	0	0
70	75	4	0	0	0	0	0	0	0	0	0	0
75	80	4	0	0	0	0	0	0	0	0	0	0
80	85	5	0	0	0	0	0	0	0	0	0	0
85	90	6	0	0	0	0	0	0	0	0	0	0
90	95	7	0	0	0	0	0	0	0	0	0	0
95	100	7	1	0	0	0	0	0	0	0	0	0
100	105	8	1	0	0	0	0	0	0	0	0	0
105	110	9	2	0	0	0	0	0	0	0	0	0
110	115	9	3	0	0	0	0	0	0	0	0	0
115	120	10	4	0	0	0	0	0	0	0	0	0
120	125	11	4	0	0	0	0	0	0	0	0	0
125	130	12	5	0	0	0	0	0	0	0	0	0
130	135	12	6	0	0	0	0	0	0	0	0	0
135	140	13	7	0	0	0	0	0	0	0	0	0
140	145	14	7	1	0	0	0	0	0	0	0	0
145	150	15	8	1	0	0	0	0	0	0	0	0
150	155	15	9	2	0	0	0	0	0	0	0	0
155	160	16	10	3	0	0	0	0	0	0	0	0
160	165	17	10	4	0	0	0	0	0	0	0	0
165	170	18	11	4	0	0	0	0	0	0	0	0
170	175	19	12	5	0	0	0	0	0	0	0	0
175	180	19	13	6	0	0	0	0	0	0	0	0
180	185	20	14	7	0	0	0	0	0	0	0	0
185	190	21	15	7	1	0	0	0	0	0	0	0
190	195	22	15	8	1	0	0	0	0	0	0	0
195	200	22	16	9	2	0	0	0	0	0	0	0
200	210	23	17	10	3	0	0	0	0	0	0	0
210	220	25	19	12	5	0	0	0	0	0	0	0
220	230	26	20	13	6	0	0	0	0	0	0	0
230	240	28	21	14	8	1	0	0	0	0	0	0
240	250	29	23	16	9	2	0	0	0	0	0	0
250	260	31	24	17	11	4	0	0	0	0	0	0
260	270	32	26	19	12	5	0	0	0	0	0	0
270	280	34	27	20	14	7	0	0	0	0	0	0
280	290	35	29	22	15	8	2	0	0	0	0	0
290	300	37	30	23	17	10	3	0	0	0	0	0
300	310	38	32	25	18	11	5	0	0	0	0	0
310	320	40	33	26	20	13	6	0	0	0	0	0
320	330	41	35	28	21	14	8	1	0	0	0	0
330	340	43	36	29	23	16	9	2	0	0	0	0
340	350	44	38	31	24	17	11	4	0	0	0	0
350	360	46	39	32	26	19	12	5	0	0	0	0
360	370	47	41	34	27	20	14	7	0	0	0	0
370	380	49	42	35	29	22	15	8	2	0	0	0
380	390	50	44	37	30	23	17	10	3	0	0	0
390	400	52	45	38	32	25	18	11	5	0	0	0
400	410	53	47	40	33	26	20	13	6	0	0	0
410	420	55	48	41	35	28	21	14	8	1	0	0
420	430	56	50	43	36	29	23	16	9	2	0	0
430	440	58	51	44	38	31	24	17	11	4	0	0
440	450	59	53	46	39	32	26	19	12	5	0	0
450	460	61	54	47	41	34	27	20	14	7	0	0
460	470	64	56	49	42	35	29	22	15	8	2	0
470	480	67	57	50	44	37	30	23	17	10	3	0
480	490	70	59	51	45	38	32	25	18	11	5	0
490	500	73	60	53	47	40	33	26	20	13	6	0
500	510	75	63	54	48	41	35	28	21	14	8	1
510	520	78	66	56	50	43	36	29	23	16	9	2
520	530	81	68	57	51	44	38	31	24	17	11	4
530	540	84	71	59	53	46	39	32	26	19	12	5
540	550	87	74	61	54	47	41	34	27	20	14	7
550	560	89	77	64	55	49	42	35	29	22	15	8
560	570	92	80	67	58	50	44	37	30	23	17	10
570	580	95	82	70	61	52	45	38	32	25	18	11
580	590	98	85	73	64	53	47	40	33	26	19	13

WEEKLY Payroll Period — Employee NOT MARRIED — Effective January 1, 1993

And the wages are— / And the number of withholding allowances claimed is— / The amount of income tax to be withheld shall be—

At least	But less than	0	1	2	3	4	5	6	7	8	9	10
$590	$600	$101	$88	$75	$63	$55	$48	$41	$35	$28	$21	$14
600	610	103	91	78	66	56	50	43	36	29	22	16
610	620	106	94	81	68	58	51	44	38	31	24	17
620	630	109	96	84	71	59	53	46	39	32	25	19
630	640	112	99	87	74	61	54	47	41	34	27	20
640	650	115	102	89	77	64	56	49	42	35	28	22
650	660	117	105	92	80	67	57	50	44	37	30	23
660	670	120	108	95	82	70	59	53	45	38	31	25
670	680	123	110	98	85	72	60	55	47	40	33	26
680	690	126	113	101	88	75	63	55	48	41	34	28
690	700	129	116	103	91	78	65	56	50	43	36	29
700	710	131	119	106	94	81	68	58	51	44	37	31
710	720	134	122	109	96	84	71	59	53	46	39	32
720	730	137	124	112	99	86	74	61	54	47	41	34
730	740	140	127	115	102	89	77	64	56	49	42	35
740	750	143	130	117	105	92	79	67	57	50	44	37
750	760	145	133	120	108	95	82	70	59	52	45	38
760	770	148	136	123	110	98	85	72	60	53	47	40
770	780	151	138	126	113	100	88	75	63	55	48	41
780	790	154	141	129	116	103	91	78	65	56	50	43
790	800	157	144	131	119	106	93	81	68	58	51	44
800	810	159	147	134	122	109	96	84	71	59	52	46
810	820	162	150	137	124	112	99	86	74	61	54	47
820	830	165	152	140	127	114	102	89	76	64	55	49
830	840	168	155	143	130	117	105	92	79	67	57	50
840	850	171	158	145	133	120	107	95	82	69	58	52
850	860	173	161	148	135	123	110	98	85	72	60	53
860	870	176	164	151	138	126	113	100	88	75	62	55
870	880	179	166	154	141	128	116	103	91	78	65	56
880	890	182	169	157	144	131	119	106	93	81	68	58
890	900	185	172	159	147	134	121	109	96	83	71	59
900	910	187	175	162	149	137	124	111	99	86	74	61
910	920	190	178	165	152	140	127	114	102	89	76	64
920	930	193	180	168	155	142	130	117	105	91	79	67
930	940	196	183	171	158	145	133	120	107	94	82	69
940	950	199	186	173	161	148	135	123	110	97	85	72
950	960	202	189	176	164	151	138	126	113	100	88	75
960	970	205	192	179	166	154	141	128	116	103	90	78
970	980	208	194	182	169	156	144	131	119	106	93	81
980	990	211	197	185	172	159	147	134	121	109	96	83
990	1,000	214	200	187	175	162	149	137	124	111	99	86
1,000	1,010	217	203	190	178	165	152	140	127	114	102	89
1,010	1,020	220	206	193	180	168	155	142	130	117	105	92
1,020	1,030	224	209	196	183	170	158	145	133	119	107	95
1,030	1,040	227	213	199	186	173	161	148	135	123	110	97
1,040	1,050	230	216	202	189	176	163	151	138	125	113	100
1,050	1,060	233	219	205	192	179	166	154	141	128	115	103
1,060	1,070	236	222	208	196	182	169	156	144	131	118	106
1,070	1,080	239	225	211	199	184	172	159	147	134	121	109
1,080	1,090	242	228	214	202	187	175	162	149	137	124	111
1,090	1,100	245	231	217	203	190	177	165	152	139	127	114
1,100	1,110	248	234	220	206	193	180	168	155	142	130	117
1,110	1,120	251	237	223	209	196	183	170	158	145	132	120
1,120	1,130	255	241	227	213	199	186	173	161	148	135	123
1,130	1,140	258	244	230	216	202	189	176	163	151	138	125
1,140	1,150	261	247	233	219	205	191	179	166	153	141	128
1,150	1,160	264	250	236	222	208	194	182	168	156	144	131
1,160	1,170	267	253	239	225	211	197	184	172	159	146	134
1,170	1,180	270	256	242	228	214	200	187	175	162	149	137
1,180	1,190	273	259	245	231	217	203	190	177	165	152	139
1,190	1,200	276	262	248	234	220	206	193	179	167	155	142
1,200	1,210	279	265	251	237	223	209	196	182	170	158	145
1,210	1,220	282	268	254	240	226	212	198	184	172	160	148
1,220	1,230	286	272	258	244	230	216	202	187	176	163	151
1,230	1,240	289	275	261	247	233	219	205	191	179	166	153
1,240	1,250	292	278	264	250	236	222	208	194	181	169	156

$1,250 and over — Use Table 1(a) for a SINGLE person

WAGE-BRACKET WITHHOLDING TABLES

WEEKLY Payroll Period — Employee MARRIED — Effective January 1, 1993

And the wages are— / And the number of withholding allowances claimed is—

The amount of income tax to be withheld shall be—

At least	But less than	0	1	2	3	4	5	6	7	8	9	10
$0	$125	0	0	0	0	0	0	0	0	0	0	0
125	135	1	0	0	0	0	0	0	0	0	0	0
135	140	2	0	0	0	0	0	0	0	0	0	0
140	145	3	0	0	0	0	0	0	0	0	0	0
145	150	4	0	0	0	0	0	0	0	0	0	0
150	155	5	0	0	0	0	0	0	0	0	0	0
155	160	6	0	0	0	0	0	0	0	0	0	0
160	165	6	0	0	0	0	0	0	0	0	0	0
165	170	7	0	0	0	0	0	0	0	0	0	0
170	175	8	1	0	0	0	0	0	0	0	0	0
175	180	9	2	0	0	0	0	0	0	0	0	0
180	185	9	3	0	0	0	0	0	0	0	0	0
185	190	10	3	0	0	0	0	0	0	0	0	0
190	195	11	4	0	0	0	0	0	0	0	0	0
195	200	12	5	0	0	0	0	0	0	0	0	0
200	210	13	6	0	0	0	0	0	0	0	0	0
210	220	14	8	1	0	0	0	0	0	0	0	0
220	230	16	9	2	0	0	0	0	0	0	0	0
230	240	17	11	4	0	0	0	0	0	0	0	0
240	250	19	12	5	0	0	0	0	0	0	0	0
250	260	20	14	7	0	0	0	0	0	0	0	0
260	270	22	15	8	1	0	0	0	0	0	0	0
270	280	23	17	10	3	0	0	0	0	0	0	0
280	290	25	18	11	5	0	0	0	0	0	0	0
290	300	26	20	13	6	0	0	0	0	0	0	0
300	310	28	21	14	8	1	0	0	0	0	0	0
310	320	29	23	16	9	2	0	0	0	0	0	0
320	330	31	24	17	11	4	0	0	0	0	0	0
330	340	32	26	19	12	5	0	0	0	0	0	0
340	350	34	27	20	14	7	0	0	0	0	0	0
350	360	35	29	22	15	8	1	0	0	0	0	0
360	370	37	30	23	17	10	3	0	0	0	0	0
370	380	38	32	25	18	11	4	0	0	0	0	0
380	390	40	33	26	20	13	6	0	0	0	0	0

At least	But less than	0	1	2	3	4	5	6	7	8	9	10
390	400	41	35	28	21	14	7	1	0	0	0	0
400	410	43	36	29	23	16	9	2	0	0	0	0
410	420	44	38	31	24	17	10	4	0	0	0	0
420	430	46	39	32	26	19	12	5	0	0	0	0
430	440	47	41	34	27	20	13	7	0	0	0	0
440	450	49	42	35	29	22	15	8	1	0	0	0
450	460	50	44	37	30	23	16	10	3	0	0	0
460	470	52	45	38	32	25	18	11	4	0	0	0
470	480	53	47	40	33	26	19	13	6	0	0	0
480	490	55	48	41	35	28	21	14	7	0	0	0
490	500	56	50	43	36	29	22	16	9	2	0	0
500	510	58	51	44	38	31	24	18	11	4	0	0
510	520	59	53	46	39	32	25	19	12	5	0	0
520	530	61	54	47	41	34	27	21	14	7	0	0
530	540	62	56	49	42	35	28	22	15	8	1	0
540	550	64	57	50	44	37	30	24	17	10	3	0
550	560	65	59	52	45	38	31	25	18	11	4	0
560	570	67	60	53	47	40	33	27	20	13	6	0
570	580	68	62	55	48	41	34	28	21	14	7	0
580	590	70	63	56	50	43	36	30	23	16	9	2
590	600	71	65	58	51	44	37	31	24	17	10	3
600	610	73	66	59	53	46	39	33	26	19	12	5
610	620	74	68	61	54	47	40	34	27	20	13	6
620	630	76	69	62	56	49	42	36	29	22	15	8
630	640	77	71	64	57	50	43	37	30	23	16	9
640	650	79	72	65	59	52	45	39	32	25	18	11
650	660	80	74	67	60	53	46	41	34	27	20	13
660	670	82	75	68	62	55	48	42	35	28	21	14
670	680	83	77	70	63	56	49	44	37	30	23	16
680	690	85	78	71	65	58	51	45	38	31	24	17
690	700	86	80	73	66	59	52	46	39	32	25	19
700	710	88	81	74	68	61	54	47	40	34	27	20
710	720	89	83	76	69	62	55	49	42	35	28	22
720	730	91	84	77	71	64	57	50	43	37	30	23
730	740	92	86	79	72	65	58	52	45	38	31	25

WEEKLY Payroll Period — Employee MARRIED — Effective January 1, 1993

And the wages are— / And the number of withholding allowances claimed is—

The amount of income tax to be withheld shall be—

At least	But less than	0	1	2	3	4	5	6	7	8	9	10
$740	$750	94	87	80	74	67	60	53	46	40	33	26
750	760	95	89	82	75	68	61	55	48	41	34	28
760	770	97	90	83	77	70	63	56	49	43	36	29
770	780	98	92	85	78	71	64	58	51	44	37	31
780	790	100	93	86	80	73	66	59	52	46	39	32
790	800	103	95	88	81	74	67	61	54	47	40	34
800	810	106	96	89	83	76	69	62	55	49	42	35
810	820	108	98	91	84	77	70	64	57	50	43	37
820	830	111	99	92	86	79	72	65	58	52	45	38
830	840	114	101	94	87	80	73	67	60	53	46	40
840	850	117	104	95	89	82	75	68	61	55	48	41
850	860	120	107	98	90	83	76	70	63	56	49	43
860	870	122	110	100	92	85	78	71	64	58	51	44
870	880	125	113	103	93	86	79	73	66	59	52	46
880	890	128	115	105	95	88	81	74	67	61	54	47
890	900	131	118	106	96	89	82	76	69	62	55	49
900	910	134	121	108	98	91	84	77	70	64	57	50
910	920	136	124	111	99	92	85	79	72	65	58	52
920	930	139	127	114	101	94	87	80	73	67	60	53
930	940	142	129	117	104	95	88	82	75	68	61	55
940	950	145	132	120	107	98	90	83	76	70	63	56
950	960	148	135	122	110	100	91	84	77	71	64	58
960	970	150	138	125	112	103	93	86	79	73	66	59
970	980	153	141	128	115	105	94	88	80	74	67	61
980	990	156	143	131	118	108	96	89	82	76	69	62
990	1,000	159	146	134	121	108	97	90	83	77	70	64
1,000	1,010	162	149	136	124	111	98	92	85	78	71	65
1,010	1,020	164	152	139	126	114	101	94	87	80	73	67
1,020	1,030	167	155	142	129	116	104	95	88	82	75	68
1,030	1,040	170	157	145	132	119	107	96	90	83	76	70
1,040	1,050	173	160	148	135	122	110	98	91	85	78	71
1,050	1,060	176	163	150	138	125	112	100	93	86	79	73
1,060	1,070	178	166	153	140	128	115	103	94	88	81	74
1,070	1,080	181	169	156	143	131	118	105	96	89	82	76
1,080	1,090	184	171	159	146	133	121	108	97	91	84	77

At least	But less than	0	1	2	3	4	5	6	7	8	9	10
1,090	1,100	187	174	162	149	136	124	111	99	92	85	79
1,100	1,110	190	177	164	152	139	126	114	101	94	87	80
1,110	1,120	192	180	167	154	142	129	117	104	95	88	82
1,120	1,130	195	183	170	157	145	132	119	107	97	90	83
1,130	1,140	198	185	173	160	147	135	122	109	98	91	85
1,140	1,150	201	188	176	163	150	138	125	112	100	93	86
1,150	1,160	204	191	178	166	153	140	128	115	102	94	88
1,160	1,170	206	194	181	168	156	143	131	118	105	96	89
1,170	1,180	209	197	184	171	159	146	133	121	108	97	91
1,180	1,190	212	199	187	174	161	149	136	123	111	99	92
1,190	1,200	215	202	190	177	164	152	139	126	114	101	94
1,200	1,210	218	205	192	180	167	154	142	129	116	104	95
1,210	1,220	220	208	195	182	170	157	145	132	119	107	97
1,220	1,230	223	211	198	185	173	160	147	135	122	109	98
1,230	1,240	226	213	201	188	175	163	150	137	125	112	100
1,240	1,250	229	216	204	191	178	166	153	140	128	115	102
1,250	1,260	232	219	206	194	181	168	156	143	130	118	105
1,260	1,270	234	222	209	196	184	171	159	146	133	121	108
1,270	1,280	237	225	212	199	187	174	161	149	136	123	111
1,280	1,290	240	227	215	202	189	177	164	151	139	126	114
1,290	1,300	243	230	218	205	192	180	167	154	142	129	116
1,300	1,310	246	233	220	208	195	182	170	157	144	132	119
1,310	1,320	248	236	223	210	198	185	173	160	147	135	122
1,320	1,330	251	239	226	213	201	188	175	163	150	137	125
1,330	1,340	254	241	229	216	203	191	178	165	153	140	128
1,340	1,350	257	244	232	219	206	194	181	168	156	143	130
1,350	1,360	260	247	234	222	209	196	184	171	158	146	133
1,360	1,370	262	250	237	224	212	199	187	174	161	149	136
1,370	1,380	265	253	240	227	215	202	189	177	164	151	139
1,380	1,390	268	255	243	230	217	205	192	179	167	154	142
1,390	1,400	271	258	246	233	220	208	195	182	170	157	144
$1,400 and over		Use Table 1(b) for a MARRIED person										

WAGE-BRACKET WITHHOLDING TABLES

BIWEEKLY Payroll Period — Employee NOT MARRIED — Effective January 1, 1993

And the wages are— / And the number of withholding allowances claimed is— / The amount of income tax to be withheld shall be—

At least	But less than	0	1	2	3	4	5	6	7	8	9	10
$0	$100	$0	$0	$0	$0	$0	$0	$0	$0	$0	$0	$0
100	105	1	0	0	0	0	0	0	0	0	0	0
105	110	2	0	0	0	0	0	0	0	0	0	0
110	115	2	0	0	0	0	0	0	0	0	0	0
115	120	3	0	0	0	0	0	0	0	0	0	0
120	125	4	0	0	0	0	0	0	0	0	0	0
125	130	5	0	0	0	0	0	0	0	0	0	0
130	135	5	0	0	0	0	0	0	0	0	0	0
135	140	6	0	0	0	0	0	0	0	0	0	0
140	145	7	0	0	0	0	0	0	0	0	0	0
145	150	8	0	0	0	0	0	0	0	0	0	0
150	155	8	0	0	0	0	0	0	0	0	0	0
155	160	9	0	0	0	0	0	0	0	0	0	0
160	165	10	0	0	0	0	0	0	0	0	0	0
165	170	11	0	0	0	0	0	0	0	0	0	0
170	175	11	0	0	0	0	0	0	0	0	0	0
175	180	12	0	0	0	0	0	0	0	0	0	0
180	185	13	0	0	0	0	0	0	0	0	0	0
185	190	14	0	0	0	0	0	0	0	0	0	0
190	195	14	0	0	0	0	0	0	0	0	0	0
195	200	15	2	0	0	0	0	0	0	0	0	0
200	205	16	2	0	0	0	0	0	0	0	0	0
205	210	17	3	0	0	0	0	0	0	0	0	0
210	215	17	4	0	0	0	0	0	0	0	0	0
215	220	18	5	0	0	0	0	0	0	0	0	0
220	225	19	5	0	0	0	0	0	0	0	0	0
225	230	20	6	0	0	0	0	0	0	0	0	0
230	235	20	7	0	0	0	0	0	0	0	0	0
235	240	21	8	0	0	0	0	0	0	0	0	0
240	245	22	8	0	0	0	0	0	0	0	0	0
245	250	23	9	0	0	0	0	0	0	0	0	0
250	260	24	10	0	0	0	0	0	0	0	0	0
260	270	25	11	0	0	0	0	0	0	0	0	0
270	280	27	12	0	0	0	0	0	0	0	0	0
280	290	28	13	1	0	0	0	0	0	0	0	0
290	300	30	16	3	0	0	0	0	0	0	0	0
300	310	31	17	4	0	0	0	0	0	0	0	0
310	320	33	18	6	0	0	0	0	0	0	0	0
320	330	34	19	7	0	0	0	0	0	0	0	0
330	340	36	21	9	0	0	0	0	0	0	0	0
340	350	37	24	10	0	0	0	0	0	0	0	0
350	360	39	25	12	0	0	0	0	0	0	0	0
360	370	40	27	13	0	0	0	0	0	0	0	0
370	380	42	28	15	1	0	0	0	0	0	0	0
380	390	43	30	16	3	0	0	0	0	0	0	0
390	400	45	31	18	4	0	0	0	0	0	0	0
400	410	46	33	19	6	0	0	0	0	0	0	0
410	420	48	34	21	7	0	0	0	0	0	0	0
420	430	49	36	22	9	0	0	0	0	0	0	0
430	440	51	37	24	10	0	0	0	0	0	0	0
440	450	52	39	25	12	0	0	0	0	0	0	0
450	460	54	40	27	13	0	0	0	0	0	0	0
460	470	55	42	28	15	1	0	0	0	0	0	0
470	480	57	43	30	16	3	0	0	0	0	0	0
480	490	58	45	31	18	4	0	0	0	0	0	0
490	500	60	46	33	19	5	0	0	0	0	0	0
500	520	62	48	35	21	8	0	0	0	0	0	0
520	540	65	51	38	24	11	0	0	0	0	0	0
540	560	68	54	41	27	14	0	0	0	0	0	0
560	580	71	57	44	30	17	3	0	0	0	0	0
580	600	74	60	47	33	20	6	0	0	0	0	0
600	620	77	63	50	36	23	9	0	0	0	0	0
620	640	80	66	53	39	26	12	0	0	0	0	0
640	660	83	69	56	42	29	15	2	0	0	0	0
660	680	86	72	59	45	32	18	5	0	0	0	0
680	700	89	75	62	48	35	21	8	0	0	0	0
700	720	92	78	65	51	38	24	11	0	0	0	0
720	740	95	81	68	54	41	27	14	1	0	0	0
740	760	98	84	71	57	44	30	17	3	0	0	0
760	780	101	87	74	60	47	33	20	6	0	0	0

BIWEEKLY Payroll Period — Employee NOT MARRIED — Effective January 1, 1993

And the wages are— / And the number of withholding allowances claimed is— / The amount of income tax to be withheld shall be—

At least	But less than	0	1	2	3	4	5	6	7	8	9	10
$780	$800	$104	$90	$77	$63	$50	$36	$23	$9	$0	$0	$0
800	820	107	93	80	66	53	39	26	12	1	0	0
820	840	110	96	83	69	56	42	29	15	4	0	0
840	860	113	99	86	72	59	45	32	18	7	0	0
860	880	116	102	89	75	62	48	35	21	10	0	0
880	900	119	105	92	78	65	51	38	24	13	0	0
900	920	123	108	95	81	68	54	41	27	16	3	0
920	940	129	111	98	84	71	57	44	30	19	6	0
940	960	134	114	101	87	74	60	47	33	22	9	0
960	980	140	117	104	90	77	63	50	36	25	12	0
980	1,000	145	120	107	93	80	66	53	39	28	15	0
1,000	1,020	151	126	110	96	83	69	56	42	31	18	3
1,020	1,040	157	131	113	99	86	72	59	45	34	21	6
1,040	1,060	162	137	116	102	89	75	62	48	37	24	9
1,060	1,080	168	142	119	105	92	78	65	51	40	27	12
1,080	1,100	173	148	123	108	95	81	68	54	43	30	15
1,100	1,120	179	154	128	111	98	84	71	57	46	33	18
1,120	1,140	185	159	134	114	101	87	74	60	49	36	21
1,140	1,160	190	165	140	117	104	90	77	63	52	39	24
1,160	1,180	196	170	145	120	107	93	80	66	55	42	27
1,180	1,200	201	176	151	125	110	96	83	69	58	45	30
1,200	1,220	207	182	156	131	113	99	86	72	61	48	33
1,220	1,240	213	187	162	137	116	102	89	75	64	51	36
1,240	1,260	218	193	168	142	119	105	92	78	67	54	39
1,260	1,280	224	198	173	148	123	108	95	81	70	57	42
1,280	1,300	229	204	179	153	128	111	98	84	73	60	45
1,300	1,320	235	210	184	159	134	114	101	87	76	63	48
1,320	1,340	241	215	190	165	139	117	104	90	79	66	51
1,340	1,360	246	221	196	170	145	120	107	93	82	69	54
1,360	1,380	252	226	201	176	151	125	110	96	85	72	57
1,380	1,400	257	232	207	181	156	131	113	99	88	75	60
1,400	1,420	263	238	212	187	162	136	116	102	91	78	63
1,420	1,440	269	243	218	193	167	142	119	105	94	81	66
1,440	1,460	274	249	224	198	173	148	122	108	97	84	69
1,460	1,480	280	254	229	204	179	153	128	111	100	87	72
1,480	1,500	285	260	235	209	184	159	134	114	103	90	75
1,500	1,520	291	266	240	215	190	164	139	117	106	93	78
1,520	1,540	297	271	246	221	195	170	145	120	109	96	81
1,540	1,560	302	277	252	226	201	176	150	125	112	99	84
1,560	1,580	308	282	257	232	207	181	156	131	115	102	87
1,580	1,600	313	288	263	237	212	187	162	136	118	105	90
1,600	1,620	319	294	268	243	218	192	167	142	122	108	93
1,620	1,640	325	299	274	249	223	198	173	147	128	111	96
1,640	1,660	330	305	279	254	229	204	178	153	133	114	99
1,660	1,680	336	310	285	260	235	209	184	159	139	117	102
1,680	1,700	341	316	291	265	240	215	190	164	145	120	105
1,700	1,720	347	322	296	271	246	220	195	170	150	125	108
1,720	1,740	353	327	302	277	251	226	201	175	156	130	111
1,740	1,760	358	333	308	282	257	232	206	181	161	136	114
1,760	1,780	364	338	313	288	263	237	212	187	167	142	118
1,780	1,800	369	344	319	293	268	243	218	192	173	147	122
1,800	1,820	375	350	324	299	274	248	223	198	178	153	128
1,820	1,840	381	355	330	305	279	254	229	203	184	158	133
1,840	1,860	386	361	336	310	285	260	234	209	189	164	139
1,860	1,880	392	366	341	316	291	265	240	215	195	170	144
1,880	1,900	398	372	347	321	296	271	246	220	201	175	150
1,900	1,920	404	378	352	327	302	276	251	226	206	181	156
1,920	1,940	410	383	358	333	307	282	257	231	212	186	161
1,940	1,960	416	389	364	338	313	288	262	237	217	192	167
1,960	1,980	422	394	369	344	319	293	268	243	223	198	172
1,980	2,000	429	401	375	349	324	299	274	248	229	203	178
2,000	2,020	435	407	380	355	330	304	279	254	234	209	184
2,020	2,040	441	413	386	361	335	310	285	259	240	214	189
2,040	2,060	447	419	392	366	341	316	290	265	245	220	195
2,060	2,080	453	425	397	372	347	321	296	271	251	226	201

$2,080 and over		Use Table 2(a) for a SINGLE person

WAGE-BRACKET WITHHOLDING TABLES

BIWEEKLY Payroll Period — Employee MARRIED — Effective January 1, 1993

And the wages are—		And the number of withholding allowances claimed is—										
At least	But less than	0	1	2	3	4	5	6	7	8	9	10
		The amount of income tax to be withheld shall be—										
$1,340	$1,360	$167	$153	$140	$126	$113	$99	$85	$72	$58	$45	$31
1,360	1,380	170	156	143	129	116	102	88	75	61	48	34
1,380	1,400	173	159	146	132	119	105	91	78	64	51	37
1,400	1,420	176	162	149	135	122	108	94	81	67	54	40
1,420	1,440	179	165	152	138	125	111	97	84	70	57	43
1,440	1,460	182	168	155	141	128	114	100	87	73	60	46
1,460	1,480	185	171	158	144	131	117	103	90	76	63	49
1,480	1,500	188	174	161	147	134	120	106	93	79	66	52
1,500	1,520	191	177	164	150	137	123	109	96	82	69	55
1,520	1,540	194	180	167	153	140	126	112	99	85	72	58
1,540	1,560	197	183	170	156	143	129	115	102	88	75	61
1,560	1,580	200	186	173	159	146	132	118	105	91	78	64
1,580	1,600	206	189	176	162	149	135	121	108	94	81	67
1,600	1,620	211	192	179	165	152	138	124	111	97	84	70
1,620	1,640	217	195	182	168	155	141	127	114	100	87	73
1,640	1,660	222	198	185	171	158	144	130	117	103	90	76
1,660	1,680	228	203	188	174	161	147	133	120	106	93	79
1,680	1,700	234	208	191	177	164	150	136	123	109	96	82
1,700	1,720	239	214	194	180	167	153	139	126	112	99	85
1,720	1,740	245	220	197	183	170	156	142	129	115	102	88
1,740	1,760	250	225	200	186	173	159	145	132	118	105	91
1,760	1,780	256	231	205	189	176	162	148	135	121	108	94
1,780	1,800	262	236	211	192	179	165	151	138	124	111	97
1,800	1,820	267	242	217	195	182	168	154	141	127	114	100
1,820	1,840	273	248	222	198	185	171	157	144	130	117	103
1,840	1,860	278	253	228	203	188	174	160	147	133	120	106
1,860	1,880	284	259	233	208	191	177	163	150	136	123	109
1,880	1,900	290	264	239	214	194	180	166	153	139	126	112
1,900	1,920	295	270	245	219	197	183	169	156	142	129	115
1,920	1,940	301	276	250	225	200	186	172	159	145	132	118
1,940	1,960	306	281	256	231	205	189	175	162	148	135	121
1,960	1,980	312	287	261	236	211	192	178	165	151	138	124
1,980	2,000	318	292	267	242	216	195	181	168	154	141	127
2,000	2,020	323	298	273	247	222	198	184	171	157	144	130
2,020	2,040	329	304	278	253	228	202	187	174	160	147	133
2,040	2,060	334	309	284	259	233	208	190	177	163	150	136
2,060	2,080	340	315	290	264	239	214	193	180	166	153	139
2,080	2,100	346	320	295	270	244	219	196	183	169	156	142
2,100	2,120	351	326	301	275	250	225	199	186	172	159	145
2,120	2,140	357	332	306	281	256	230	205	189	175	162	148
2,140	2,160	362	337	312	287	261	236	211	192	178	165	151
2,160	2,180	368	343	317	292	267	242	216	195	181	168	154
2,180	2,200	374	348	323	298	272	247	222	198	184	171	157
2,200	2,220	379	354	329	303	278	253	227	202	187	174	160
2,220	2,240	385	360	334	309	284	258	233	208	190	177	163
2,240	2,260	390	365	340	315	289	264	239	213	193	180	166
2,260	2,280	396	371	345	320	295	270	244	219	196	183	169
2,280	2,300	402	377	351	326	300	275	250	224	205	186	172
2,300	2,320	407	382	357	331	306	281	255	230	210	189	175
2,320	2,340	413	388	362	337	312	286	261	236	216	192	178
2,340	2,360	418	393	368	343	317	292	267	241	216	195	181
2,360	2,380	424	399	373	348	323	298	272	247	222	198	184
2,380	2,400	430	404	379	354	328	303	278	253	227	202	187
2,400	2,420	435	410	385	359	334	309	283	258	233	208	190
2,420	2,440	441	416	390	365	340	314	289	264	238	213	193
2,440	2,460	446	421	396	371	345	320	295	269	244	219	196
2,460	2,480	452	427	401	376	351	326	300	275	250	224	199
2,480	2,500	458	432	407	382	356	331	306	281	255	230	205
2,500	2,520	463	438	413	387	362	337	311	286	261	236	210
2,520	2,540	469	444	418	393	368	342	317	292	266	241	216
2,540	2,560	474	449	424	399	373	348	323	297	272	247	221
2,560	2,580	480	455	429	404	379	354	328	303	278	252	227
2,580	2,600	486	460	435	410	384	359	334	309	283	258	233
2,600	2,620	491	466	441	415	390	365	339	314	289	264	238
2,620	2,640	497	472	446	421	396	370	345	320	294	269	244
$2,640 and over		Use Table 2(b) for a MARRIED person										

BIWEEKLY Payroll Period — Employee MARRIED — Effective January 1, 1993

And the wages are—		And the number of withholding allowances claimed is—										
At least	But less than	0	1	2	3	4	5	6	7	8	9	10
		The amount of income tax to be withheld shall be—										
$0	$245	$0	$0	$0	$0	$0	$0	$0	$0	$0	$0	$0
245	250	1	0	0	0	0	0	0	0	0	0	0
250	260	2	0	0	0	0	0	0	0	0	0	0
260	270	4	0	0	0	0	0	0	0	0	0	0
270	280	5	0	0	0	0	0	0	0	0	0	0
280	290	7	0	0	0	0	0	0	0	0	0	0
290	300	8	0	0	0	0	0	0	0	0	0	0
300	310	10	0	0	0	0	0	0	0	0	0	0
310	320	11	0	0	0	0	0	0	0	0	0	0
320	330	13	0	0	0	0	0	0	0	0	0	0
330	340	14	1	0	0	0	0	0	0	0	0	0
340	350	16	2	0	0	0	0	0	0	0	0	0
350	360	17	4	0	0	0	0	0	0	0	0	0
360	370	19	5	0	0	0	0	0	0	0	0	0
370	380	20	7	0	0	0	0	0	0	0	0	0
380	390	22	8	0	0	0	0	0	0	0	0	0
390	400	23	10	0	0	0	0	0	0	0	0	0
400	410	25	11	0	0	0	0	0	0	0	0	0
410	420	26	13	1	0	0	0	0	0	0	0	0
420	430	28	14	2	0	0	0	0	0	0	0	0
430	440	29	16	4	0	0	0	0	0	0	0	0
440	450	31	17	5	0	0	0	0	0	0	0	0
450	460	32	19	7	0	0	0	0	0	0	0	0
460	470	34	20	8	0	0	0	0	0	0	0	0
470	480	35	22	10	0	0	0	0	0	0	0	0
480	490	37	23	11	0	0	0	0	0	0	0	0
490	500	38	25	13	0	0	0	0	0	0	0	0
500	520	41	27	14	0	0	0	0	0	0	0	0
520	540	44	30	17	3	0	0	0	0	0	0	0
540	560	47	33	20	6	0	0	0	0	0	0	0
560	580	50	36	23	9	0	0	0	0	0	0	0
580	600	53	39	26	12	0	0	0	0	0	0	0
600	620	56	42	29	15	2	0	0	0	0	0	0
620	640	59	45	32	18	5	0	0	0	0	0	0
640	660	62	48	35	21	8	0	0	0	0	0	0
660	680	65	51	38	24	11	0	0	0	0	0	0
680	700	68	54	41	27	14	0	0	0	0	0	0
700	720	71	57	44	30	17	3	0	0	0	0	0
720	740	74	60	47	33	20	6	0	0	0	0	0
740	760	77	63	50	36	23	9	0	0	0	0	0
760	780	80	66	53	39	26	12	0	0	0	0	0
780	800	83	69	56	42	29	15	1	0	0	0	0
800	820	86	72	59	45	32	18	4	0	0	0	0
820	840	89	75	62	48	35	21	7	0	0	0	0
840	860	92	78	65	51	38	24	10	0	0	0	0
860	880	95	81	68	54	41	27	13	0	0	0	0
880	900	98	84	71	57	44	30	16	3	0	0	0
900	920	101	87	74	60	47	33	19	6	0	0	0
920	940	104	90	77	63	50	36	22	9	0	0	0
940	960	107	93	80	66	53	39	25	12	0	0	0
960	980	110	96	83	69	56	42	28	15	1	0	0
980	1,000	113	99	86	72	59	45	31	18	4	0	0
1,000	1,020	116	102	89	75	62	48	34	21	7	0	0
1,020	1,040	119	105	92	78	65	51	37	24	10	0	0
1,040	1,060	122	108	95	81	68	54	40	27	13	0	0
1,060	1,080	125	111	98	84	71	57	43	30	16	3	0
1,080	1,100	128	114	101	87	74	60	46	33	19	6	0
1,100	1,120	131	117	104	90	77	63	49	36	22	9	0
1,120	1,140	134	120	107	93	80	66	52	39	25	12	0
1,140	1,160	137	123	110	96	83	69	55	42	28	15	1
1,160	1,180	140	126	113	99	86	72	58	45	31	18	4
1,180	1,200	143	129	116	102	89	75	61	48	34	21	7
1,200	1,220	146	132	119	105	92	78	64	51	37	24	10
1,220	1,240	149	135	122	108	95	81	67	54	40	27	13
1,240	1,260	152	138	125	111	98	84	70	57	43	30	16
1,260	1,280	155	141	128	114	101	87	73	60	46	33	19
1,280	1,300	158	144	131	117	104	90	76	63	49	36	22
1,300	1,320	161	147	134	120	107	93	79	66	52	39	25
1,320	1,340	164	150	137	123	110	96	82	69	55	42	28

WAGE-BRACKET WITHHOLDING TABLES

SEMIMONTHLY Payroll Period—Employee NOT MARRIED—Effective January 1, 1993

And the number of withholding allowances claimed is—
The amount of income tax to be withheld shall be—

At least	But less than	0	1	2	3	4	5	6	7	8	9	10
$0	$110	$0	$0	$0	$0	$0	$0	$0	$0	$0	$0	$0
110	115	1	0	0	0	0	0	0	0	0	0	0
115	120	2	0	0	0	0	0	0	0	0	0	0
120	125	2	0	0	0	0	0	0	0	0	0	0
125	130	3	0	0	0	0	0	0	0	0	0	0
130	135	4	0	0	0	0	0	0	0	0	0	0
135	140	4	0	0	0	0	0	0	0	0	0	0
140	145	5	0	0	0	0	0	0	0	0	0	0
145	150	6	0	0	0	0	0	0	0	0	0	0
150	155	7	0	0	0	0	0	0	0	0	0	0
155	160	8	0	0	0	0	0	0	0	0	0	0
160	165	9	0	0	0	0	0	0	0	0	0	0
165	170	9	0	0	0	0	0	0	0	0	0	0
170	175	10	0	0	0	0	0	0	0	0	0	0
175	180	11	0	0	0	0	0	0	0	0	0	0
180	185	12	0	0	0	0	0	0	0	0	0	0
185	190	12	0	0	0	0	0	0	0	0	0	0
190	195	13	0	0	0	0	0	0	0	0	0	0
195	200	14	0	0	0	0	0	0	0	0	0	0
200	205	15	0	0	0	0	0	0	0	0	0	0
205	210	15	0	0	0	0	0	0	0	0	0	0
210	215	16	1	0	0	0	0	0	0	0	0	0
215	220	17	2	0	0	0	0	0	0	0	0	0
220	225	18	3	0	0	0	0	0	0	0	0	0
225	230	18	3	1	0	0	0	0	0	0	0	0
230	235	19	4	2	0	0	0	0	0	0	0	0
235	240	20	5	4	0	0	0	0	0	0	0	0
240	245	21	6	5	0	0	0	0	0	0	0	0
245	250	21	6	7	0	0	0	0	0	0	0	0
250	260	22	7	8	0	0	0	0	0	0	0	0
260	270	24	9	10	0	0	0	0	0	0	0	0
270	280	25	11	11	0	0	0	0	0	0	0	0
280	290	27	12	13	0	0	0	0	0	0	0	0
290	300	28	14	14	0	0	0	0	0	0	0	0
300	310	30	15	16	1	0	0	0	0	0	0	0
310	320	31	17	2	0	0	0	0	0	0	0	0
320	330	33	18	4	0	0	0	0	0	0	0	0
330	340	34	20	5	0	0	0	0	0	0	0	0
340	350	36	21	7	0	0	0	0	0	0	0	0
350	360	37	23	8	0	0	0	0	0	0	0	0
360	370	39	24	10	0	0	0	0	0	0	0	0
370	380	40	26	11	0	0	0	0	0	0	0	0
380	390	42	27	13	0	0	0	0	0	0	0	0
390	400	43	29	14	0	0	0	0	0	0	0	0
400	410	45	30	16	1	0	0	0	0	0	0	0
410	420	46	32	17	2	0	0	0	0	0	0	0
420	430	48	33	19	4	0	0	0	0	0	0	0
430	440	49	35	20	5	0	0	0	0	0	0	0
440	450	51	36	22	7	0	0	0	0	0	0	0
450	460	52	38	23	8	0	0	0	0	0	0	0
460	470	54	39	25	10	0	0	0	0	0	0	0
470	480	55	41	26	11	0	0	0	0	0	0	0
480	490	57	42	28	13	0	0	0	0	0	0	0
490	500	58	44	29	14	0	0	0	0	0	0	0
500	520	61	46	31	17	2	0	0	0	0	0	0
520	540	64	49	34	20	5	0	0	0	0	0	0
540	560	67	52	37	23	8	0	0	0	0	0	0
560	580	70	55	40	26	11	0	0	0	0	0	0
580	600	73	58	43	29	14	0	0	0	0	0	0
600	620	76	61	46	32	17	2	0	0	0	0	0
620	640	79	64	49	35	20	5	0	0	0	0	0
640	660	82	67	52	38	23	8	0	0	0	0	0
660	680	85	70	55	41	26	11	0	0	0	0	0
680	700	88	73	58	44	29	14	0	0	0	0	0
700	720	91	76	61	47	32	17	3	0	0	0	0
720	740	94	79	64	50	35	20	6	0	0	0	0
740	760	97	82	67	53	38	23	9	0	0	0	0
760	780	100	85	70	56	41	26	12	0	0	0	0
780	800	103	88	73	59	44	29	15	0	0	0	0
800	820	106	91	76	62	47	32	18	3	0	0	0

SEMIMONTHLY Payroll Period—Employee NOT MARRIED—Effective January 1, 1993

And the number of withholding allowances claimed is—
The amount of income tax to be withheld shall be—

At least	But less than	0	1	2	3	4	5	6	7	8	9	10
$820	$840	$109	$94	$79	$65	$50	$35	$21	$6	$0	$0	$0
840	860	112	97	82	68	53	38	24	9	0	0	0
860	880	115	100	85	71	56	41	27	12	0	0	0
880	900	118	103	88	74	59	44	30	15	3	0	0
900	920	121	106	91	77	62	47	33	18	3	0	0
920	940	124	109	94	80	65	50	36	21	6	0	0
940	960	127	112	97	83	68	53	39	24	9	0	0
960	980	130	115	100	86	71	56	42	27	12	0	0
980	1,000	134	118	103	89	74	59	45	30	15	1	0
1,000	1,020	140	121	106	92	77	62	48	33	18	4	0
1,020	1,040	146	124	109	95	80	65	51	36	21	7	0
1,040	1,060	151	127	112	98	83	68	54	39	24	10	0
1,060	1,080	157	130	115	101	86	71	57	42	27	13	0
1,080	1,100	162	135	118	104	89	74	60	45	30	16	1
1,100	1,120	168	141	121	107	92	77	63	48	33	19	4
1,120	1,140	174	146	124	110	95	80	66	51	36	22	7
1,140	1,160	179	152	127	113	98	83	69	54	39	25	10
1,160	1,180	185	157	130	116	101	86	72	57	42	28	13
1,180	1,200	190	163	136	119	104	89	75	60	45	31	16
1,200	1,220	196	169	141	122	107	92	78	63	48	34	19
1,220	1,240	202	174	147	125	110	95	81	66	51	37	22
1,240	1,260	207	180	152	128	113	98	84	69	54	40	25
1,260	1,280	213	185	158	131	116	101	87	72	57	43	28
1,280	1,300	218	191	164	136	119	104	90	75	60	46	31
1,300	1,320	224	197	169	142	122	107	93	78	63	49	34
1,320	1,340	230	202	175	147	125	110	96	81	66	52	37
1,340	1,360	235	208	180	153	128	113	99	84	69	55	40
1,360	1,380	241	213	186	159	131	116	102	87	72	58	43
1,380	1,400	246	219	192	164	137	119	105	90	75	61	46
1,400	1,420	252	225	197	170	142	122	108	93	78	64	49
1,420	1,440	258	230	203	175	148	125	111	96	81	67	52
1,440	1,460	263	236	208	181	154	128	114	99	84	70	55
1,460	1,480	269	241	214	187	159	132	117	102	87	73	58
1,480	1,500	274	247	220	192	165	137	120	105	90	76	61
1,500	1,520	280	253	225	198	170	143	123	108	93	79	64
1,520	1,540	286	258	231	203	176	149	126	111	96	82	67
1,540	1,560	291	264	236	209	182	154	129	114	99	85	70
1,560	1,580	297	269	242	215	187	160	132	117	102	88	73
1,580	1,600	302	275	248	220	193	165	138	120	105	91	76
1,600	1,620	308	281	253	226	198	171	143	123	108	94	79
1,620	1,640	314	286	259	231	204	177	149	126	111	97	82
1,640	1,660	319	292	264	237	210	182	155	129	114	100	85
1,660	1,680	325	297	270	243	215	188	160	133	117	103	88
1,680	1,700	330	303	276	248	221	193	166	138	120	106	91
1,700	1,720	336	309	281	254	226	199	171	144	123	109	94
1,720	1,740	342	314	287	259	232	205	177	150	126	112	97
1,740	1,760	347	320	292	265	238	210	183	155	129	115	100
1,760	1,780	353	325	298	271	243	216	188	161	133	118	103
1,780	1,800	358	331	304	276	249	221	194	166	139	121	106
1,800	1,820	364	337	309	282	254	227	199	172	145	124	109
1,820	1,840	370	342	315	287	260	233	205	178	150	127	112
1,840	1,860	375	348	320	293	266	238	211	183	156	130	115
1,860	1,880	381	353	326	299	271	244	216	189	161	135	118
1,880	1,900	386	359	332	304	277	249	222	194	167	140	121
1,900	1,920	392	365	337	309	282	255	227	200	173	145	124
1,920	1,940	398	370	343	315	288	261	233	206	178	151	127
1,940	1,960	403	376	348	321	294	266	239	211	184	156	130
1,960	1,980	409	381	354	327	299	272	244	217	189	162	135
1,980	2,000	414	387	360	332	305	277	250	222	195	168	140
2,000	2,020	420	393	365	338	310	283	255	228	201	173	146
2,020	2,040	426	398	371	343	316	289	261	234	206	179	151
2,040	2,060	431	404	376	349	322	294	267	239	212	184	157
2,060	2,080	438	409	382	355	327	300	272	245	217	190	163
2,080	2,100	444	414	388	360	333	305	278	250	223	196	168
2,100	2,120	450	421	393	366	338	311	283	256	229	201	174

$2,120 and over — Use Table 3(a) for a SINGLE person

WAGE-BRACKET WITHHOLDING TABLES

SEMIMONTHLY Payroll Period — Employee MARRIED — Effective January 1, 1993

And the wages are— / And the number of withholding allowances claimed is— / The amount of income tax to be withheld shall be—

At least	But less than	0	1	2	3	4	5	6	7	8	9	10
$0	$260	$0	$0	$0	$0	$0	$0	$0	$0	$0	$0	$0
260	270	1	0	0	0	0	0	0	0	0	0	0
270	280	3	0	0	0	0	0	0	0	0	0	0
280	290	4	0	0	0	0	0	0	0	0	0	0
290	300	6	0	0	0	0	0	0	0	0	0	0
300	310	7	0	0	0	0	0	0	0	0	0	0
310	320	9	0	0	0	0	0	0	0	0	0	0
320	330	10	0	0	0	0	0	0	0	0	0	0
330	340	12	0	0	0	0	0	0	0	0	0	0
340	350	13	0	0	0	0	0	0	0	0	0	0
350	360	15	0	0	0	0	0	0	0	0	0	0
360	370	16	1	0	0	0	0	0	0	0	0	0
370	380	18	3	0	0	0	0	0	0	0	0	0
380	390	19	4	0	0	0	0	0	0	0	0	0
390	400	21	6	0	0	0	0	0	0	0	0	0
400	410	22	7	0	0	0	0	0	0	0	0	0
410	420	24	9	0	0	0	0	0	0	0	0	0
420	430	25	10	0	0	0	0	0	0	0	0	0
430	440	27	12	0	0	0	0	0	0	0	0	0
440	450	28	13	0	0	0	0	0	0	0	0	0
450	460	30	15	0	0	0	0	0	0	0	0	0
460	470	31	16	1	0	0	0	0	0	0	0	0
470	480	33	18	3	0	0	0	0	0	0	0	0
480	490	34	19	4	0	0	0	0	0	0	0	0
490	500	36	21	6	0	0	0	0	0	0	0	0
500	520	38	23	8	0	0	0	0	0	0	0	0
520	540	41	26	11	0	0	0	0	0	0	0	0
540	560	44	29	14	0	0	0	0	0	0	0	0
560	580	47	32	17	3	0	0	0	0	0	0	0
580	600	50	35	20	6	0	0	0	0	0	0	0
600	620	53	38	23	9	0	0	0	0	0	0	0
620	640	56	41	26	12	0	0	0	0	0	0	0
640	660	59	44	29	15	0	0	0	0	0	0	0
660	680	62	47	32	18	3	0	0	0	0	0	0
680	700	65	50	35	21	6	0	0	0	0	0	0
700	720	68	53	38	24	9	0	0	0	0	0	0
720	740	71	56	41	27	12	0	0	0	0	0	0
740	760	74	59	44	30	15	0	0	0	0	0	0
760	780	77	62	47	33	18	3	0	0	0	0	0
780	800	80	65	50	36	21	6	0	0	0	0	0
800	820	83	68	53	39	24	9	0	0	0	0	0
820	840	86	71	56	42	27	12	0	0	0	0	0
840	860	89	74	59	45	30	15	1	0	0	0	0
860	880	92	77	62	48	33	18	4	0	0	0	0
880	900	95	80	65	51	36	21	7	0	0	0	0
900	920	98	83	68	54	39	24	10	0	0	0	0
920	940	101	86	71	57	42	27	13	0	0	0	0
940	960	104	89	74	60	45	30	16	1	0	0	0
960	980	107	92	77	63	48	33	19	4	0	0	0
980	1,000	110	95	80	66	51	36	22	7	0	0	0
1,000	1,020	113	98	83	69	54	39	25	10	0	0	0
1,020	1,040	116	101	86	72	57	42	28	13	0	0	0
1,040	1,060	119	104	89	75	60	45	31	16	1	0	0
1,060	1,080	122	107	92	78	63	48	34	19	4	0	0
1,080	1,100	125	110	95	81	66	51	37	22	7	0	0
1,100	1,120	128	113	98	84	69	54	40	25	10	0	0
1,120	1,140	131	116	101	87	72	57	43	28	13	0	0
1,140	1,160	134	119	104	90	75	60	46	31	16	2	0
1,160	1,180	137	122	107	93	78	63	49	34	19	5	0
1,180	1,200	140	125	110	96	81	66	52	37	22	8	0
1,200	1,220	143	128	113	99	84	69	55	40	25	11	0
1,220	1,240	146	131	116	102	87	72	58	43	28	14	0
1,240	1,260	149	134	119	105	90	75	61	46	31	17	2
1,260	1,280	152	137	122	108	93	78	64	49	34	20	5
1,280	1,300	155	140	125	111	96	81	67	52	37	23	8
1,300	1,320	158	143	128	114	99	84	70	55	40	26	11
1,320	1,340	161	146	131	117	102	87	73	58	43	29	14
1,340	1,360	164	149	134	120	105	90	76	61	46	32	17
1,360	1,380	167	152	137	123	108	93	79	64	49	35	20
1,380	1,400	170	155	140	126	111	96	82	67	52	38	23

SEMIMONTHLY Payroll Period — Employee MARRIED — Effective January 1, 1993

And the wages are— / And the number of withholding allowances claimed is— / The amount of income tax to be withheld shall be—

At least	But less than	0	1	2	3	4	5	6	7	8	9	10
$1,400	$1,420	$173	$158	$143	$129	$114	$99	$85	$70	$55	$41	$26
1,420	1,440	176	161	146	132	117	102	88	73	58	44	29
1,440	1,460	179	164	149	135	120	105	91	76	61	47	32
1,460	1,480	182	167	152	138	123	108	94	79	64	50	35
1,480	1,500	185	170	155	141	126	111	97	82	67	53	38
1,500	1,520	188	173	158	144	129	114	100	85	70	56	41
1,520	1,540	191	176	161	147	132	117	103	88	73	59	44
1,540	1,560	194	179	164	150	135	120	106	91	76	62	47
1,560	1,580	197	182	167	153	138	123	109	94	79	65	50
1,580	1,600	200	185	170	156	141	126	112	97	82	68	53
1,600	1,620	203	188	173	159	144	129	115	100	85	71	56
1,620	1,640	206	191	176	162	147	132	118	103	88	74	59
1,640	1,660	209	194	179	165	150	135	121	106	91	77	62
1,660	1,680	212	197	182	168	153	138	124	109	94	80	65
1,680	1,700	215	200	185	171	156	141	127	112	97	83	68
1,700	1,720	219	203	188	174	159	144	130	115	100	86	71
1,720	1,740	225	206	191	177	162	147	133	118	103	89	74
1,740	1,760	231	209	194	180	165	150	136	121	106	92	77
1,760	1,780	236	212	197	183	168	153	139	124	109	95	80
1,780	1,800	242	215	200	186	171	156	142	127	112	98	83
1,800	1,820	247	220	203	189	174	159	145	130	115	101	86
1,820	1,840	253	226	206	192	177	162	148	133	118	104	89
1,840	1,860	259	231	209	195	180	165	151	136	121	107	92
1,860	1,880	264	237	212	198	183	168	154	139	124	110	95
1,880	1,900	270	242	215	201	186	171	157	142	127	113	98
1,900	1,920	275	248	220	204	189	174	160	145	130	116	101
1,920	1,940	281	254	226	207	192	177	163	148	133	119	104
1,940	1,960	287	259	232	210	195	180	166	151	136	122	107
1,960	1,980	292	265	237	213	198	183	169	154	139	125	110
1,980	2,000	298	270	243	216	201	186	172	157	142	128	113
2,000	2,020	303	276	248	221	204	189	175	160	145	131	116
2,020	2,040	309	282	254	227	207	192	178	163	148	134	119
2,040	2,060	315	287	260	232	210	195	181	166	151	137	122
2,060	2,080	320	293	265	238	213	198	184	169	154	140	125
2,080	2,100	326	298	271	243	216	201	187	172	157	143	128
2,100	2,120	331	304	276	249	222	204	190	175	160	146	131
2,120	2,140	337	310	282	255	227	207	193	178	163	149	134
2,140	2,160	343	315	288	260	233	210	196	181	166	152	137
2,160	2,180	348	321	293	266	238	213	199	184	169	155	140
2,180	2,200	354	326	299	271	244	217	202	187	172	158	143
2,200	2,220	359	332	304	277	250	222	205	190	175	161	146
2,220	2,240	365	338	310	283	255	228	208	193	178	164	149
2,240	2,260	371	343	316	288	261	233	211	196	181	167	152
2,260	2,280	376	349	321	294	266	239	214	199	184	170	155
2,280	2,300	382	354	327	299	272	245	217	202	187	173	158
2,300	2,320	387	360	332	305	277	250	223	205	190	176	161
2,320	2,340	393	366	338	311	283	256	228	208	193	179	164
2,340	2,360	399	371	344	316	289	261	234	211	196	182	167
2,360	2,380	404	377	349	322	294	267	239	214	199	185	170
2,380	2,400	410	382	355	327	300	273	245	218	202	188	173
2,400	2,420	415	388	360	333	306	278	251	223	205	191	176
2,420	2,440	421	394	366	339	311	284	256	229	208	194	179
2,440	2,460	427	399	372	344	317	289	262	235	211	197	182
2,460	2,480	432	405	377	350	322	295	268	240	214	200	185
2,480	2,500	438	410	383	355	328	301	273	246	218	203	188
2,500	2,520	443	416	388	361	334	306	279	251	224	206	191
2,520	2,540	449	422	394	367	339	312	284	257	230	209	194
2,540	2,560	455	427	400	372	345	317	290	263	235	212	197
2,560	2,580	460	433	405	378	350	323	295	268	241	215	200
2,580	2,600	466	438	411	383	356	329	301	274	246	219	203
2,600	2,620	471	444	416	389	362	334	307	279	252	225	206
2,620	2,640	477	450	422	395	367	340	312	285	258	230	209
2,640	2,660	483	455	428	400	373	345	318	291	263	236	212
2,660	2,680	488	461	433	406	378	351	324	296	269	241	215
2,680	2,700	494	466	439	411	383	357	329	302	274	247	220
$2,700 and over		Use Table 3(b) for a MARRIED person										

WAGE-BRACKET WITHHOLDING TABLES

MONTHLY Payroll Period — Employee NOT MARRIED — Effective January 1, 1993

And the wages are—		And the number of withholding allowances claimed is—										
At least	But less than	0	1	2	3	4	5	6	7	8	9	10
		The amount of income tax to be withheld shall be—										
$0	$210	$0	$0	$0	$0	$0	$0	$0	$0	$0	$0	$0
210	220	1	0	0	0	0	0	0	0	0	0	0
220	230	2	0	0	0	0	0	0	0	0	0	0
230	240	4	0	0	0	0	0	0	0	0	0	0
240	250	5	0	0	0	0	0	0	0	0	0	0
250	260	7	0	0	0	0	0	0	0	0	0	0
260	270	8	0	0	0	0	0	0	0	0	0	0
270	280	10	0	0	0	0	0	0	0	0	0	0
280	290	11	0	0	0	0	0	0	0	0	0	0
290	300	13	0	0	0	0	0	0	0	0	0	0
300	320	15	0	0	0	0	0	0	0	0	0	0
320	340	18	0	0	0	0	0	0	0	0	0	0
340	360	21	0	0	0	0	0	0	0	0	0	0
360	380	24	0	0	0	0	0	0	0	0	0	0
380	400	27	0	0	0	0	0	0	0	0	0	0
400	420	30	1	0	0	0	0	0	0	0	0	0
420	440	33	4	0	0	0	0	0	0	0	0	0
440	460	36	7	0	0	0	0	0	0	0	0	0
460	480	39	10	0	0	0	0	0	0	0	0	0
480	500	42	13	0	0	0	0	0	0	0	0	0
500	520	45	16	0	0	0	0	0	0	0	0	0
520	540	48	19	0	0	0	0	0	0	0	0	0
540	560	51	22	0	0	0	0	0	0	0	0	0
560	580	54	25	0	0	0	0	0	0	0	0	0
580	600	57	28	0	0	0	0	0	0	0	0	0
600	640	61	32	3	0	0	0	0	0	0	0	0
640	680	67	38	9	0	0	0	0	0	0	0	0
680	720	73	44	15	0	0	0	0	0	0	0	0
720	760	79	50	21	0	0	0	0	0	0	0	0
760	800	85	56	27	0	0	0	0	0	0	0	0
800	840	91	62	33	3	0	0	0	0	0	0	0
840	880	97	68	39	9	0	0	0	0	0	0	0
880	920	103	74	45	15	0	0	0	0	0	0	0
920	960	109	80	51	21	0	0	0	0	0	0	0
960	1,000	115	86	57	27	0	0	0	0	0	0	0
1,000	1,040	121	92	63	33	4	0	0	0	0	0	0
1,040	1,080	127	98	69	39	10	0	0	0	0	0	0
1,080	1,120	133	104	75	45	16	0	0	0	0	0	0
1,120	1,160	139	110	81	51	22	0	0	0	0	0	0
1,160	1,200	145	116	87	57	28	0	0	0	0	0	0
1,200	1,240	151	122	93	63	34	5	0	0	0	0	0
1,240	1,280	157	128	99	69	40	11	0	0	0	0	0
1,280	1,320	163	134	105	75	46	17	0	0	0	0	0
1,320	1,360	169	140	111	81	52	23	0	0	0	0	0
1,360	1,400	175	146	117	87	58	29	0	0	0	0	0
1,400	1,440	181	152	123	93	64	35	5	0	0	0	0
1,440	1,480	187	158	129	99	70	41	11	0	0	0	0
1,480	1,520	193	164	135	105	76	47	17	0	0	0	0
1,520	1,560	199	170	141	111	82	53	23	0	0	0	0
1,560	1,600	205	176	147	117	88	59	29	0	0	0	0
1,600	1,640	211	182	153	123	94	65	35	6	0	0	0
1,640	1,680	217	188	159	129	100	71	41	12	0	0	0
1,680	1,720	223	194	165	135	106	77	47	18	0	0	0
1,720	1,760	229	200	171	141	112	83	53	24	0	0	0
1,760	1,800	235	206	177	147	118	89	59	30	0	0	0
1,800	1,840	241	212	183	153	124	95	65	36	6	0	0
1,840	1,880	247	218	189	159	130	101	71	42	12	0	0
1,880	1,920	253	224	195	165	136	107	77	48	18	0	0
1,920	1,960	259	230	201	171	142	113	83	54	24	0	0
1,960	2,000	265	236	207	177	148	119	89	60	30	1	0
2,000	2,040	280	242	213	183	154	125	95	66	36	7	0
2,040	2,080	291	248	219	189	160	131	101	72	42	13	0
2,080	2,120	302	254	225	195	166	137	107	78	48	19	0
2,120	2,160	314	260	231	201	172	143	113	84	54	25	2
2,160	2,200	325	270	237	207	178	149	119	90	60	31	8
2,200	2,240	336	281	243	213	184	155	125	96	66	37	14
2,240	2,280	347	292	249	219	190	161	131	102	72	43	20
2,280	2,320	358	304	255	225	196	167	137	108	78	49	26
2,320	2,360	370	315	261	231	202	173	143	114	84	55	32
2,360	2,400	381	326	271	237	208	179	149	120	90	61	—

MONTHLY Payroll Period — Employee NOT MARRIED — Effective January 1, 1993

And the wages are—		And the number of withholding allowances claimed is—										
At least	But less than	0	1	2	3	4	5	6	7	8	9	10
		The amount of income tax to be withheld shall be—										
$2,400	$2,440	$392	$337	$282	$243	$214	$185	$155	$126	$96	$67	$38
2,440	2,480	403	348	294	249	226	191	161	132	102	73	44
2,480	2,520	414	360	305	255	232	197	167	138	108	79	50
2,520	2,560	426	371	316	261	232	203	173	144	114	85	56
2,560	2,600	437	382	327	272	238	209	179	150	120	91	62
2,600	2,640	448	393	338	283	244	215	185	156	126	97	68
2,640	2,680	459	404	350	295	250	221	191	162	132	103	74
2,680	2,720	470	416	361	306	256	227	197	168	138	109	80
2,720	2,760	482	427	372	317	262	233	203	174	144	115	86
2,760	2,800	493	438	383	328	273	239	209	180	150	121	92
2,800	2,840	504	449	394	339	285	245	215	186	156	127	98
2,840	2,880	515	460	406	351	296	251	221	192	162	133	104
2,880	2,920	526	472	417	362	307	257	227	198	168	139	110
2,920	2,960	538	483	428	373	318	263	233	204	174	145	116
2,960	3,000	549	494	439	384	329	275	239	210	180	151	122
3,000	3,040	560	505	450	395	341	286	245	216	186	157	128
3,040	3,080	571	516	462	407	352	297	251	222	192	163	134
3,080	3,120	582	528	473	418	363	308	257	228	198	169	140
3,120	3,160	594	539	484	429	374	319	265	234	204	175	146
3,160	3,200	605	550	495	440	385	331	276	240	210	181	152
3,200	3,240	616	561	506	451	397	342	287	246	216	187	158
3,240	3,280	627	572	518	463	408	353	298	252	222	193	164
3,280	3,320	638	584	529	474	419	364	309	258	228	199	170
3,320	3,360	650	595	540	485	430	375	321	266	234	205	176
3,360	3,400	661	606	551	496	441	387	332	277	240	211	182
3,400	3,440	672	617	562	507	453	398	343	288	246	217	188
3,440	3,480	683	628	574	519	464	409	354	299	252	223	194
3,480	3,520	694	640	585	530	475	420	365	311	258	229	200
3,520	3,560	706	651	596	541	486	431	377	322	267	235	206
3,560	3,600	717	662	607	552	497	443	388	333	278	241	212
3,600	3,640	728	673	618	563	509	454	399	344	289	247	218
3,640	3,680	739	684	630	575	520	465	410	355	301	253	224
3,680	3,720	750	696	641	586	531	476	421	367	312	259	230
3,720	3,760	762	707	652	597	542	487	433	378	323	268	236
3,760	3,800	773	718	663	608	553	499	444	389	334	279	242
3,800	3,840	784	729	674	619	565	510	455	400	345	290	248
3,840	3,880	795	740	686	631	576	521	466	411	357	302	254
3,880	3,920	806	752	697	642	587	532	477	423	368	313	260
3,920	3,960	818	763	708	653	598	543	489	434	379	324	269
3,960	4,000	829	774	719	664	609	555	500	445	390	335	280
4,000	4,040	840	785	730	675	621	566	511	456	401	346	292
4,040	4,080	851	796	742	687	632	577	522	467	413	358	303
4,080	4,120	863	808	753	698	643	588	533	479	424	369	314
4,120	4,160	875	819	764	709	654	599	545	490	435	380	325
4,160	4,200	888	830	775	720	665	611	556	501	446	391	336
4,200	4,240	900	841	786	731	677	622	567	512	457	402	348
4,240	4,280	913	852	798	743	688	633	578	523	469	414	359
4,280	4,320	925	864	809	754	699	644	589	535	480	425	370
4,320	4,360	937	877	820	765	710	655	601	546	491	436	381
4,360	4,400	950	889	831	776	721	667	612	557	502	447	392
4,400	4,440	962	901	842	787	733	678	623	568	513	458	404
4,440	4,480	975	914	854	799	744	689	634	579	525	470	415
4,480	4,520	987	926	866	810	755	700	645	591	536	481	426
4,520	4,560	999	939	878	822	767	711	657	602	547	492	437
4,560	4,600	1,012	951	890	833	777	723	668	613	558	503	448
4,600	4,640	1,024	963	903	843	789	734	679	624	569	514	460
4,640	4,680	1,037	976	915	855	800	745	690	635	581	526	471
4,680	4,720	1,049	988	928	867	811	756	701	647	592	537	482
4,720	4,760	1,061	1,001	940	879	822	767	713	658	603	548	493
4,760	4,800	1,074	1,013	952	892	833	779	724	669	614	559	504
4,800	4,840	1,086	1,025	965	904	845	790	735	680	625	570	516
4,840	4,880	1,099	1,038	977	916	856	801	746	691	637	582	527
4,880	4,920	1,111	1,050	990	929	868	812	757	703	648	593	538
4,920	4,960	1,123	1,063	1,002	941	881	823	769	714	659	604	549
4,960	5,000	1,136	1,075	1,014	954	893	835	780	725	670	615	560
$5,000 and over		Use Table 4(a) for a SINGLE person										

WAGE-BRACKET WITHHOLDING TABLES

MONTHLY Payroll Period — Employee MARRIED — Effective January 1, 1993

And the wages are— / And the number of withholding allowances claimed is— / The amount of income tax to be withheld shall be—

At least	But less than	0	1	2	3	4	5	6	7	8	9	10
$0	520	$0	$0	$0	$0	$0	$0	$0	$0	$0	$0	$0
520	540	2	0	0	0	0	0	0	0	0	0	0
540	560	5	0	0	0	0	0	0	0	0	0	0
560	580	8	0	0	0	0	0	0	0	0	0	0
580	600	11	0	0	0	0	0	0	0	0	0	0
600	640	16	0	0	0	0	0	0	0	0	0	0
640	680	22	0	0	0	0	0	0	0	0	0	0
680	720	28	0	0	0	0	0	0	0	0	0	0
720	760	34	4	0	0	0	0	0	0	0	0	0
760	800	40	10	0	0	0	0	0	0	0	0	0
800	840	46	16	0	0	0	0	0	0	0	0	0
840	880	52	22	0	0	0	0	0	0	0	0	0
880	920	58	28	0	0	0	0	0	0	0	0	0
920	960	64	34	5	0	0	0	0	0	0	0	0
960	1,000	70	40	11	0	0	0	0	0	0	0	0
1,000	1,040	76	46	17	0	0	0	0	0	0	0	0
1,040	1,080	82	52	23	0	0	0	0	0	0	0	0
1,080	1,120	88	58	29	0	0	0	0	0	0	0	0
1,120	1,160	94	64	35	5	0	0	0	0	0	0	0
1,160	1,200	100	70	41	11	0	0	0	0	0	0	0
1,200	1,240	106	76	47	17	0	0	0	0	0	0	0
1,240	1,280	112	82	53	23	0	0	0	0	0	0	0
1,280	1,320	118	88	59	29	0	0	0	0	0	0	0
1,320	1,360	124	94	65	35	6	0	0	0	0	0	0
1,360	1,400	130	100	71	41	12	0	0	0	0	0	0
1,400	1,440	136	106	77	47	18	0	0	0	0	0	0
1,440	1,480	142	112	83	53	24	0	0	0	0	0	0
1,480	1,520	148	118	89	59	30	1	0	0	0	0	0
1,520	1,560	154	124	95	65	36	7	0	0	0	0	0
1,560	1,600	160	130	101	71	42	13	0	0	0	0	0
1,600	1,640	166	136	107	77	48	19	0	0	0	0	0
1,640	1,680	172	142	113	83	54	25	0	0	0	0	0
1,680	1,720	178	148	119	89	60	31	0	0	0	0	0
1,720	1,760	184	154	125	95	66	37	7	0	0	0	0
1,760	1,800	190	160	131	101	72	43	13	0	0	0	0
1,800	1,840	196	166	137	107	78	49	19	0	0	0	0
1,840	1,880	202	172	143	113	84	55	25	0	0	0	0
1,880	1,920	208	178	149	119	90	61	31	2	0	0	0
1,920	1,960	214	184	155	125	96	67	37	8	0	0	0
1,960	2,000	220	190	161	131	102	73	43	14	0	0	0
2,000	2,040	226	196	167	137	108	79	49	20	0	0	0
2,040	2,080	232	202	173	143	114	85	55	26	0	0	0
2,080	2,120	238	208	179	149	120	91	61	32	0	0	0
2,120	2,160	244	214	185	155	126	97	67	38	9	0	0
2,160	2,200	250	220	191	161	132	103	73	44	15	0	0
2,200	2,240	256	226	197	167	138	109	79	50	21	0	0
2,240	2,280	262	232	203	173	144	115	85	56	27	0	0
2,280	2,320	268	238	209	179	150	121	91	62	33	3	0
2,320	2,360	274	244	215	185	156	127	97	68	39	9	0
2,360	2,400	280	250	221	191	162	133	103	74	45	15	0
2,400	2,440	286	256	227	197	168	139	109	80	51	21	0
2,440	2,480	292	262	233	203	174	145	115	86	57	27	0
2,480	2,520	298	268	239	209	180	151	121	92	63	33	4
2,520	2,560	304	274	245	215	186	157	127	98	69	39	10
2,560	2,600	310	280	251	221	192	163	133	104	75	45	16
2,600	2,640	316	286	257	227	198	169	139	110	81	51	22
2,640	2,680	322	292	263	233	204	175	145	116	87	57	28
2,680	2,720	328	298	269	239	210	181	151	122	93	63	34
2,720	2,760	334	304	275	245	216	187	157	128	99	69	40
2,760	2,800	340	310	281	251	222	193	163	134	105	75	46
2,800	2,840	346	316	287	257	228	199	169	140	111	81	52
2,840	2,880	352	322	293	263	234	205	175	146	117	87	58
2,880	2,920	358	328	299	269	240	211	181	152	123	93	64
2,920	2,960	364	334	305	275	246	217	187	158	129	99	70
2,960	3,000	370	340	311	281	252	223	193	164	135	105	76
3,000	3,040	376	346	317	287	258	229	199	170	141	111	82
3,040	3,080	382	352	323	293	264	235	205	176	147	117	88
3,080	3,120	388	358	329	299	270	241	211	182	153	123	94
3,120	3,160	394	364	335	305	276	247	217	188	159	129	100
3,160	3,200	400	370	341	311	282	253	223	194	165	135	106

MONTHLY Payroll Period — Employee MARRIED — Effective January 1, 1993

And the wages are— / And the number of withholding allowances claimed is— / The amount of income tax to be withheld shall be—

At least	But less than	0	1	2	3	4	5	6	7	8	9	10
$3,200	3,240	$406	$376	$347	$317	$288	$259	$229	$200	$171	$141	$112
3,240	3,280	412	382	353	323	294	265	235	206	177	147	118
3,280	3,320	418	388	359	329	300	271	241	212	183	153	124
3,320	3,360	424	394	365	335	306	277	247	218	189	159	130
3,360	3,400	430	400	371	341	312	283	253	224	195	165	136
3,400	3,440	439	406	377	347	318	289	259	230	201	171	142
3,440	3,480	450	412	383	353	324	295	265	236	207	177	148
3,480	3,520	461	418	389	359	330	301	271	242	213	183	154
3,520	3,560	472	424	395	365	336	307	277	248	219	189	160
3,560	3,600	483	430	401	371	342	313	283	254	225	195	166
3,600	3,640	495	440	407	377	348	319	289	260	231	201	172
3,640	3,680	506	451	413	383	354	325	295	266	237	207	178
3,680	3,720	517	462	419	389	360	331	301	272	243	213	184
3,720	3,760	528	473	425	395	366	337	307	278	249	219	190
3,760	3,800	539	485	431	401	372	343	313	284	255	225	196
3,800	3,840	551	496	441	407	378	349	319	290	261	231	202
3,840	3,880	562	507	452	413	384	355	325	296	267	237	208
3,880	3,920	573	518	463	419	390	361	331	302	273	243	214
3,920	3,960	584	529	475	425	396	367	337	308	279	249	220
3,960	4,000	595	541	486	431	402	373	343	314	285	255	226
4,000	4,040	607	552	497	442	408	379	349	320	291	261	232
4,040	4,080	618	563	508	453	414	385	355	326	297	267	238
4,080	4,120	629	574	519	465	420	391	361	332	303	273	244
4,120	4,160	640	585	531	476	426	397	367	338	309	279	250
4,160	4,200	651	597	542	487	432	403	373	344	315	285	256
4,200	4,240	663	608	553	498	443	409	379	350	321	291	262
4,240	4,280	674	619	564	509	455	415	385	356	327	297	268
4,280	4,320	685	630	575	521	466	421	391	362	333	303	274
4,320	4,360	696	641	587	532	477	427	397	368	339	309	280
4,360	4,400	707	653	598	543	488	433	403	374	345	315	286
4,400	4,440	719	664	609	554	499	444	409	380	351	321	292
4,440	4,480	730	675	620	565	511	456	415	386	357	327	298
4,480	4,520	741	686	631	577	522	467	421	392	363	333	304
4,520	4,560	752	697	643	588	533	478	427	398	369	339	310
4,560	4,600	763	709	654	599	544	489	434	404	375	345	316
4,600	4,640	775	720	665	610	555	500	446	410	381	351	322
4,640	4,680	786	731	676	621	567	512	457	416	387	357	328
4,680	4,720	797	742	687	633	578	523	468	422	393	363	334
4,720	4,760	808	753	699	644	589	534	479	428	399	369	340
4,760	4,800	819	765	710	655	600	545	490	436	405	375	346
4,800	4,840	831	776	721	666	611	556	502	447	411	381	352
4,840	4,880	842	787	732	677	623	568	513	458	417	387	358
4,880	4,920	853	798	743	689	634	579	524	469	423	393	364
4,920	4,960	864	809	755	700	645	590	535	480	429	399	370
4,960	5,000	875	821	766	711	656	601	546	492	437	405	376
5,000	5,040	887	832	777	722	667	612	558	503	448	411	382
5,040	5,080	898	843	788	733	679	624	569	514	459	417	388
5,080	5,120	909	854	799	745	690	635	580	525	470	423	394
5,120	5,160	920	865	811	756	701	646	591	536	482	429	400
5,160	5,200	931	877	822	767	712	657	602	548	493	438	406
5,200	5,240	943	888	833	778	723	668	614	559	504	449	412
5,240	5,280	954	899	844	789	735	680	625	570	515	460	418
5,280	5,320	965	910	855	801	746	691	636	581	526	472	424
5,320	5,360	976	921	867	812	757	702	647	592	538	483	430
5,360	5,400	987	933	878	823	768	713	658	604	549	494	439
5,400	5,440	999	944	889	834	779	724	670	615	560	505	450
5,440	5,480	1,010	955	900	845	791	736	681	626	571	516	462
5,480	5,520	1,021	966	911	857	802	747	692	637	582	528	473
5,520	5,560	1,032	977	923	868	813	758	703	648	594	539	484
5,560	5,600	1,043	989	934	879	824	769	714	660	605	550	495
5,600	5,640	1,055	1,000	945	890	835	780	726	671	616	561	506
5,640	5,680	1,066	1,011	956	901	847	792	737	682	627	572	518
5,680	5,720	1,077	1,022	967	913	858	803	748	693	638	584	529
5,720	5,760	1,088	1,033	979	924	869	814	759	704	650	595	540
5,760	5,800	1,099	1,045	990	935	880	825	770	716	661	606	551
$5,800 and over		Use Table 4(b) for a MARRIED person										

WAGE-BRACKET WITHHOLDING TABLES

DAILY or MISC Payroll Period—Employee NOT MARRIED — Effective January 1, 1993

At least	But less than	0	1	2	3	4	5	6	7	8	9	10
		The amount of income tax to be withheld shall be—										
$0	$12	$0	$0	$0	$0	$0	$0	$0	$0	$0	$0	$0
12	15	0	0	0	0	0	0	0	0	0	0	0
15	18	1	0	0	0	0	0	0	0	0	0	0
18	21	1	1	0	0	0	0	0	0	0	0	0
21	24	2	1	0	0	0	0	0	0	0	0	0
24	27	2	0	0	0	0	0	0	0	0	0	0
27	30	3	1	0	0	0	0	0	0	0	0	0
30	33	3	1	1	0	0	0	0	0	0	0	0
33	36	4	2	1	0	0	0	0	0	0	0	0
36	39	4	3	1	0	0	0	0	0	0	0	0
39	42	5	3	2	1	0	0	0	0	0	0	0
42	45	5	4	2	1	0	0	0	0	0	0	0
45	48	6	4	3	1	0	0	0	0	0	0	0
48	51	6	5	3	2	1	0	0	0	0	0	0
51	54	6	5	4	2	1	0	0	0	0	0	0
54	57	7	6	4	3	2	0	0	0	0	0	0
57	60	7	6	5	3	2	1	0	0	0	0	0
60	63	8	7	5	4	3	1	0	0	0	0	0
63	66	8	7	6	4	3	1	1	0	0	0	0
66	69	9	7	6	5	4	2	1	0	0	0	0
69	72	9	8	6	5	4	2	1	0	0	0	0
72	75	10	8	7	6	5	3	2	1	0	0	0
75	78	10	9	7	6	5	3	2	1	0	0	0
78	81	11	9	8	7	6	4	3	1	1	0	0
81	84	11	10	8	7	6	4	3	2	1	0	0
84	87	11	10	9	7	6	5	4	2	1	1	0
87	90	12	11	9	8	7	5	4	3	2	1	0
90	93	13	11	10	8	7	5	4	3	2	1	0
93	96	13	12	10	9	8	6	5	3	2	1	1
96	99	14	12	11	9	8	6	5	4	3	2	1
99	102	15	13	11	10	9	7	6	5	4	3	1
102	105	16	14	12	11	10	8	7	5	4	3	2
105	108	16	14	13	11	10	8	7	6	5	4	2
108	111	17	15	14	12	11	9	8	6	5	4	3
111	114	18	16	15	13	12	9	8	7	6	5	3
114	117	19	17	14	12	10	9	8	6	5	4	2
117	120	20	17	15	13	11	10	8	7	5	4	3
120	123	21	18	16	14	12	10	9	7	6	4	3
123	126	22	19	17	15	12	11	9	8	6	5	4
126	129	23	20	17	15	13	11	10	8	7	5	4
129	132	23	21	18	16	14	11	10	9	7	6	5
132	135	24	22	19	17	15	12	11	9	8	6	5
135	138	25	23	20	18	16	13	11	10	8	7	6
138	141	26	23	21	19	17	14	12	10	9	7	6
141	144	27	24	22	20	17	15	13	11	10	8	7
144	147	28	25	22	20	18	16	13	12	10	8	7
147	150	28	26	23	21	19	17	14	13	11	9	8
150	153	29	27	24	22	20	17	15	13	11	9	8
153	156	30	27	25	23	21	18	16	15	12	10	9
156	159	31	28	26	23	22	19	17	16	13	11	9
159	162	32	29	27	24	22	19	17	17	14	12	10
162	165	33	30	28	26	23	20	18	18	15	13	11
165	168	34	31	29	27	24	21	19	19	16	14	12
168	171	35	32	30	28	25	22	20	20	17	15	13
171	174	35	33	31	29	27	22	22	20	17	15	13
174	177	36	33	31	28	26	23	21	18	16	13	11
177	180	37	34	32	29	27	24	22	19	17	15	12
180	183	38	35	32	30	28	25	22	20	18	16	13
183	186	38	36	33	31	29	26	23	21	19	17	14
186	189	39	37	34	32	30	26	24	22	20	17	15
189	192	40	38	35	33	30	28	25	22	20	17	15
192	195	41	38	36	34	31	28	26	23	21	18	16
195	198	42	40	37	35	32	29	27	24	22	19	17
198	201	43	41	38	36	33	30	28	25	23	20	18
201	204	44	42	40	37	34	31	28	25	23	21	18
204	207	45	42	40	38	34	32	29	27	24	22	19
207	210	46	43	41	39	35	33	30	28	25	23	20
210	213	47	44	42	40	36	34	31	29	26	24	21
213	216	48	45	43	41	37	35	32	29	27	25	22
216	219	49	46	44	43	38	36	33	30	27	25	22

DAILY or MISC Payroll Period—Employee NOT MARRIED — Effective January 1, 1993

At least	But less than	0	1	2	3	4	5	6	7	8	9	10
		The amount of income tax to be withheld shall be—										
$219	$222	$50	$47	$44	$41	$38	$36	$33	$31	$28	$26	$23
222	225	50	48	45	42	39	37	34	32	29	27	24
225	228	51	49	46	43	40	38	35	33	30	27	25
228	231	52	50	47	44	41	38	36	33	31	28	26
231	234	53	50	48	45	42	39	37	34	32	29	27
234	237	54	51	49	46	43	40	38	35	33	30	27
237	240	55	52	49	47	44	41	39	36	33	31	28
240	243	56	53	50	47	45	42	39	37	34	32	29
243	246	57	54	51	49	46	43	40	38	35	33	30
246	249	58	55	52	49	47	44	41	38	36	33	31
249	252	59	56	53	50	48	45	42	39	37	34	32
252	255	60	57	54	51	49	46	43	40	38	35	33
255	258	61	58	55	52	49	47	44	41	38	36	33
258	261	62	59	56	53	50	48	45	42	39	37	34
261	264	63	60	57	54	51	49	46	43	40	38	35
264	267	63	61	58	55	52	49	47	44	41	38	36
267	270	64	62	59	56	53	50	48	45	42	39	37
270	273	65	63	60	57	54	51	49	46	43	40	38
273	276	66	63	61	58	55	52	49	47	44	41	38
276	279	67	64	62	59	56	53	50	48	45	42	39
279	282	68	65	63	60	57	54	51	49	46	43	40
282	285	69	66	63	61	58	55	52	49	47	44	41
285	288	70	67	64	62	59	56	53	50	48	45	42
288	291	71	68	65	63	60	57	54	51	48	46	43
291	294	72	69	66	63	61	58	55	52	49	47	44
294	297	73	70	67	64	62	59	56	53	50	48	45
297	300	74	70	68	65	62	60	57	54	51	48	46
300	303	75	71	69	66	63	61	58	55	52	49	47
303	306	76	72	70	67	64	62	59	56	53	50	48
306	309	76	73	71	68	65	62	60	57	54	51	48
309	312	77	74	71	69	66	63	61	58	55	52	49
312	315	78	75	72	70	67	64	62	59	56	53	50
315	318	79	76	73	71	68	65	62	60	57	54	51
318	321	80	77	74	72	69	66	63	61	58	55	52
321	324	81	78	75	73	70	67	64	62	59	56	53
324	327	82	79	76	74	71	68	65	62	60	57	54
327	330	83	80	77	75	72	69	66	63	61	58	55
330	333	84	81	78	76	73	70	67	64	62	59	56
333	336	85	82	79	76	74	71	68	65	62	60	57
336	339	86	83	80	77	75	72	69	66	63	61	58
339	341	87	84	81	78	75	73	70	67	64	61	59
341	343	88	84	82	79	76	73	71	68	65	62	59
343	345	88	85	83	80	77	74	71	68	66	63	60
345	347	89	86	83	80	78	74	72	69	67	63	60
347	349	89	86	84	81	78	75	72	69	67	64	61
349	351	90	87	84	81	79	76	73	70	67	64	62
351	353	90	87	85	82	79	76	73	71	68	65	62
353	355	91	88	85	83	80	77	74	71	69	66	63
355	357	92	89	86	83	81	78	75	72	69	66	63
357	359	92	89	87	84	81	78	75	73	70	67	64
359	361	93	90	87	84	82	79	76	73	70	68	65
361	363	93	91	88	85	82	79	77	74	71	68	65
363	365	94	91	88	86	83	80	77	74	72	69	66
365	367	95	92	89	86	83	81	78	75	72	69	67
367	369	95	92	90	87	84	81	78	76	73	70	67
369	371	96	93	90	87	85	82	79	76	73	71	68
371	373	96	93	91	88	85	82	80	77	74	71	68
373	375	97	94	91	89	86	83	80	77	75	72	69
375	377	98	95	92	89	86	84	81	78	75	72	70
377	379	98	95	92	90	87	84	81	79	76	73	70
379	381	99	96	93	91	88	85	82	79	77	74	71
381	383	99	97	94	91	88	85	83	80	77	74	72
383	385	100	97	95	92	89	86	83	80	78	75	72
385	387	100	98	95	92	90	87	84	81	78	76	73
387	389	101	98	96	93	90	87	84	82	79	76	73
389	391	102	99	96	94	91	88	85	82	80	77	74
$391 and over		Use Table 8(a) for a SINGLE person										

WAGE-BRACKET WITHHOLDING TABLES

DAILY or MISC Payroll Period — Employee MARRIED — Effective January 1, 1993

And the wages are—		And the number of withholding allowances claimed is—										
At least	But less than	0	1	2	3	4	5	6	7	8	9	10
		The amount of income tax to be withheld shall be—										
$0	$27	$0	$0	$0	$0	$0	$0	$0	$0	$0	$0	$0
27	30	1	0	0	0	0	0	0	0	0	0	0
30	33	1	0	0	0	0	0	0	0	0	0	0
33	36	2	1	0	0	0	0	0	0	0	0	0
36	39	2	1	0	0	0	0	0	0	0	0	0
39	42	3	1	0	0	0	0	0	0	0	0	0
42	45	3	2	0	0	0	0	0	0	0	0	0
45	48	3	2	1	0	0	0	0	0	0	0	0
48	51	4	2	1	0	0	0	0	0	0	0	0
51	54	4	3	2	0	0	0	0	0	0	0	0
54	57	5	3	2	1	0	0	0	0	0	0	0
57	60	5	4	2	1	0	0	0	0	0	0	0
60	63	6	4	3	1	0	0	0	0	0	0	0
63	66	6	5	3	2	0	0	0	0	0	0	0
66	69	7	5	4	2	1	0	0	0	0	0	0
69	72	7	6	4	3	1	0	0	0	0	0	0
72	75	8	6	5	3	2	0	0	0	0	0	0
75	78	8	7	5	4	2	1	0	0	0	0	0
78	81	9	7	6	4	3	1	0	0	0	0	0
81	84	9	7	6	5	3	2	1	0	0	0	0
84	87	9	8	7	5	4	2	1	0	0	0	0
87	90	10	8	7	6	4	3	1	0	0	0	0
90	93	10	9	7	6	5	3	2	0	0	0	0
93	96	11	9	8	7	5	4	2	1	0	0	0
96	99	11	10	8	7	6	4	3	1	0	0	0
99	102	11	10	9	7	6	5	3	2	1	0	0
102	105	12	11	9	8	7	5	4	2	1	0	0
105	108	12	11	10	8	7	6	4	3	2	0	0
108	111	13	11	10	9	7	6	5	3	2	1	0
111	114	13	12	11	9	8	7	5	4	2	1	0
114	117	14	12	11	10	8	7	6	4	3	1	0
117	120	14	13	11	10	9	7	6	5	3	2	1
120	123	15	13	12	11	9	8	7	5	4	2	1
123	126	15	14	12	11	10	8	7	6	4	3	1
126	129	16	14	13	11	10	9	7	6	5	3	2
129	132	16	15	13	12	11	9	8	7	5	4	2
132	135	16	15	14	12	11	10	8	7	6	4	3
135	138	17	15	14	13	11	10	9	7	6	5	3
138	141	17	16	14	13	12	10	9	8	6	5	4
141	144	18	16	15	14	12	11	10	8	7	6	4
144	147	18	17	15	14	13	11	10	9	7	6	5
147	150	19	17	16	15	13	12	10	9	8	6	5
150	153	19	18	16	15	14	12	11	10	8	7	6
153	156	20	18	17	15	14	13	11	10	9	7	6
156	159	20	19	17	16	15	13	12	11	9	8	6
159	162	21	19	18	16	15	14	12	11	10	8	7
162	165	22	20	18	17	16	14	13	11	10	9	7
165	168	22	20	19	17	16	15	13	12	11	9	8
168	171	23	21	19	18	16	15	14	12	11	10	8
171	174	24	22	20	18	17	16	14	13	11	10	9
174	177	25	23	20	19	17	16	15	13	12	11	9
177	180	26	24	21	19	18	16	15	14	12	11	10
180	183	27	25	22	20	18	17	15	14	13	11	10
183	186	28	25	23	20	19	17	16	15	13	12	11
186	189	29	26	24	21	19	18	16	15	14	12	11
189	192	29	27	24	22	20	18	17	16	14	13	11
192	195	30	28	25	23	20	19	17	16	15	13	12
195	198	31	29	26	24	21	19	18	16	15	14	12
198	201	32	30	27	24	22	20	18	17	16	14	13
201	204	33	30	28	25	23	20	19	17	16	15	13
204	207	34	31	29	26	24	21	19	18	17	15	14
207	210	35	32	30	27	25	22	20	18	17	16	14
210	213	36	33	31	28	26	23	21	19	18	16	15
213	216	37	34	32	29	27	24	22	19	18	17	15
216	219	37	35	32	30	27	25	22	20	19	17	16
219	222	38	35	33	30	28	25	23	21	19	18	16
222	225	39	36	34	31	29	26	24	21	19	18	17
225	228	40	37	35	32	30	27	25	22	20	19	17
228	231	40	38	36	33	31	28	26	23	21	19	18
231	234	41	39	36	34	31	29	26	24	21	19	18

DAILY or MISC Payroll Period — Employee MARRIED — Effective January 1, 1993

And the wages are—		And the number of withholding allowances claimed is—										
At least	But less than	0	1	2	3	4	5	6	7	8	9	10
		The amount of income tax to be withheld shall be—										
$234	$237	$42	$39	$37	$34	$32	$29	$27	$24	$22	$20	$18
237	240	43	40	38	35	33	30	28	25	23	20	19
240	243	44	41	39	36	34	31	28	26	24	21	19
243	246	45	42	39	37	34	32	29	27	24	22	20
246	249	45	43	40	38	35	33	30	28	25	23	20
249	252	46	44	41	39	36	34	31	28	26	23	21
252	255	47	44	42	39	37	34	32	29	27	24	22
255	258	48	45	43	40	38	35	33	30	28	25	23
258	261	49	46	44	41	39	36	34	31	28	26	23
261	264	50	47	44	42	39	37	34	32	29	27	24
264	267	50	48	45	43	40	38	35	33	30	28	25
267	270	51	49	46	44	41	39	36	34	31	28	26
270	273	52	50	47	44	42	39	37	34	32	29	27
273	276	53	50	48	45	43	40	38	35	33	30	28
276	279	54	51	49	46	44	41	39	36	34	31	28
279	282	55	52	50	47	44	42	39	37	34	32	29
282	285	55	53	50	48	45	43	40	38	35	33	30
285	288	56	54	51	49	46	44	41	39	36	34	31
288	291	57	55	52	50	47	44	42	39	37	34	32
291	294	58	55	53	50	48	45	43	40	38	35	33
294	297	59	56	54	51	49	46	44	41	39	36	33
297	300	59	57	55	52	50	47	44	42	39	37	34
300	303	60	58	55	53	50	48	45	43	40	38	35
303	306	61	59	56	54	51	49	46	44	41	39	36
306	309	62	60	57	55	52	49	47	44	42	39	37
309	312	63	60	58	55	53	50	48	45	43	40	38
312	315	64	61	59	56	54	51	49	46	44	41	39
315	318	65	62	60	57	55	52	49	47	44	42	40
318	321	66	63	61	58	55	53	50	48	45	43	40
321	324	67	64	61	59	56	54	51	49	46	44	41
324	327	68	65	62	60	57	55	52	49	47	44	42
327	330	68	66	63	61	58	55	53	50	48	45	43
330	333	69	67	64	61	59	56	54	51	49	46	44
333	336	70	68	65	62	60	57	55	52	49	47	44
336	339	71	68	66	63	60	58	55	53	50	48	45
339	341	72	69	66	64	61	59	56	54	51	48	46
341	343	73	70	67	64	62	59	57	54	52	49	47
343	345	73	71	68	65	62	60	57	55	52	50	47
345	347	74	71	68	66	63	60	58	55	53	50	48
347	349	75	72	69	66	63	61	58	56	53	51	48
349	351	75	72	70	67	64	62	59	56	54	51	49
351	353	76	73	70	67	65	62	60	57	54	52	49
353	355	77	74	71	68	65	63	60	57	55	52	50
355	357	77	74	72	69	66	63	61	58	55	53	50
357	359	78	75	72	69	66	64	61	58	56	53	51
359	361	78	75	73	70	67	64	62	59	57	54	52
361	363	79	76	73	71	68	65	62	60	57	55	52
363	365	80	77	74	71	68	66	63	60	58	55	53
365	367	80	77	75	72	69	66	64	61	58	56	53
367	369	81	78	75	72	70	67	64	61	59	56	54
369	371	81	79	76	73	70	67	65	62	60	57	54
371	373	82	79	76	74	71	68	65	63	60	57	55
373	375	83	80	77	74	71	69	66	63	61	58	55
375	377	83	80	78	75	72	69	67	64	61	59	56
377	379	84	81	78	75	73	70	67	64	62	59	57
379	381	84	82	79	76	73	70	68	65	62	60	57
381	383	85	82	79	77	74	71	68	66	63	60	58
383	385	86	83	80	77	74	72	69	66	63	61	58
385	387	86	84	81	78	75	72	70	67	64	61	59
387	389	87	84	81	78	75	73	70	67	65	62	59
389	391	88	85	82	79	76	74	71	68	65	62	60
391	393	88	86	83	80	77	74	72	69	66	63	61
393	395	89	86	84	80	78	75	72	70	67	64	61
395	397	89	87	84	81	78	75	73	70	67	64	62
397	399	90	87	84	82	79	76	73	71	68	65	62

$399 and over — Use Table 8(b) for a MARRIED person

INDEX

A

Absences, under FLSA, 35
Accounting system, payroll: 10, 17; manual, 17
Accounts, summary of, used in recording payroll transactions, 229
Adjusting entry: to record vacation pay at end of period, 227; to record wages at end-of-period , 227
Advances: under federal income tax withholding law, 120; under FICA, 73
Affirmative action: 5; plan, 5
Age Discrimination in Employment Act (ADEA), 5, 13
Agricultural workers: tax deposit requirements for employers of, 86; under federal income tax withholding law, 120; under FUTA, 175
Allocation of tips, large food and beverage establishments, 74, 120
Allowance: for dependents, 122; personal, 122; special withholding, 122; table of allowance values for percentage method of income tax withholding, 126; withholding, 122
American Payroll Association (APA): 2; Certified Payroll Professional certificate, 2; code of ethics, 2
Americans with Disabilities Act (ADA), 5
Annual earnings test, 330
Annual Return of Withheld Federal Income Tax (Form 945), 140, 141, *illus.*, 142
Annual Summary and Transmittal of U.S. Information Returns (Form 1096), 144
Annuities, under federal income tax withholding law, 125
Application: for employer identification number (Form SS-4), 79; for employment, 12, *illus.*, 14-15; for social security benefits, 332; for social security card (Form SS-5), 79
Application for Filing Information Returns Magnetically/Electronically (Form 4419), 144
Autogen, 86
Automatic payroll depositing, 48
Average indexed monthly earnings, 328

B

Backup withholding: 141; reported on Form 945, 88, 141
Benefits, under social security: 327; aliens and prisoners, 330; annual earnings test, 330; applying for, 332; cost-of-living increases in, 328; disability, 329; divorced persons, 330; electronic transfer of, 333; employees of carriers, 330; family, 329; hospital insurance, 332; kinds of, 329, 331; lump-sum death payment, 331; old-age, survivors, and disability, 327; proof of age, 333; reduced, 328; retirement test, 330; self-employed individuals, 330; special minimum benefit, 330; students', 330; taxability and assignability, 333; workers who delay retirement, 332; working after benefits start, 330
Benefits, under state unemployment compensation laws: as a result of major disaster, 194; disability, 10, 194; disqualification of, 193; eligibility for, 193; employee, 193; ex-service personnel, 194; federal employees, 194; federal emergency, 195; state disability benefit laws, 10; summary of sources and duration of, 195; supplemental unemployment (SUB), 194
Biweekly, payment of salary, 28
Bonuses, under FICA, 73

C

Cash: paying wages and salaries in, 46; payment of FICA taxes, 91
Certain Government Payments (Form 1099-G), 143
Certified Payroll Professional certificate, 2
Change of status form, *illus.*, 17
Check: immediate credit item, 86; paying wages and salaries by, 18, 47
Check-off system, 229
Check stub, showing payroll deductions, *illus.*, 20, 48
Child labor restrictions under FLSA: 32; agricultural occupations, 33; certificate of age, 33; nonfarm occupations, 32

Child support, withholding for, 126
Circular E, Employer's Tax Guide, 140
City income taxes: entry to record liability, 222; entry to record payment, 226
Civil Rights Act of 1964: 2, 13; Executive Order 11246, 5
Close button, 338
Clothes-changing time, as working time, 34
Coffee breaks, under FLSA, 35
Command buttons, 339
Commission: 45; on sales or insurance premiums, under FICA, 73
Common-law relationship, 70
Common-law test, 70
Compressed workweek, 26
Constructively paid wages, 179
Contribution report, SUTA, 190
Core time, 26
Cumulative withholding, for federal income tax withholding, 129
Currently insured individual, for social security benefits, 328
Current Tax Payment Act of 1943, 6, 117

D

Data entry window, 338
Data fields, 339
Davis-Bacon Act of 1931, 8, 9
Daylight-saving time, under FLSA, 36
Death payment, lump-sum, 331
Deceased person's wages, under federal income tax withholding law, 121
Delinquent taxes, withholding to collect, 126
Dependency allowances, under state unemployment compensation, 193
Dependents, allowances for, under federal income tax withholding law, 122
Deposit requirements, FICA: for employers of agricultural workers, 86; for employers of household employees, 86; for employers of nonagricultural workers, 83, for state and local government employers, 86; summary of, 85
Deposits of FICA and income taxes withheld: depositaries, 83; employers of agricultural workers, 86; employers of household employees, 86; end of calen-

dar quarter, 85; immediate credit item, 86; lookback period, 84; monthly, 84; $100,000 one-day rule, 84; procedures for making, 86; safe harbor rule, 85; semiweekly, 84; state and local government employers, 86; summary of rules for nonagricultural employers, 85; timeliness of, 86

Disability benefits: 10; under social security, 327, 331; under SUTA, 194

Disability funds, recording employees' contributions to state, 222

Disaster Relief Act, 194

Dismissal payments: under federal income tax withholding law, 119; under FICA, 73

Distributions from Pensions, Annuities, Retirement or Profit-Sharing Plans, IRAs, Insurance Contracts, etc. (Form 1099-R), 143

Dividends and Distributions (Form 1099-DIV), 143

Divorced persons, social security benefits for, 330

Domestic service: under federal income tax withholding law, 121; under FICA, 72; under FUTA, 175

E

Earned income credit (EIC): 132; advance payment of, 132; advance payments shown on Form 941, 90; computing the advance payment of, 133; employer's returns and records, 134; paying the advance to employees, 133

Earned Income Credit Advance Payment Certificate (Form W-5), 132, *illus.*, 133

Earnings: annual test, 330; disposable, 229; statement, *illus.*, 48

Earnings record, employee's 17, 219, *illus.*, 19, 221

Educational assistance: under federal income tax withholding law, 120; under FICA, 75

Electronic funds transfer system (EFTS), 48

Electronic reporting of information returns, 144

Electronic transfer: of social security benefits, 333; paying wages and salaries by, 47

Emergency Unemployment Compensation Act, 195

Employee: defined under federal income tax withholding law, 118; defined under FICA, 69; defined under FUTA, 174; defined under SUTA, 176; history record, 16; SUTA contributions, 181; tipped, 29

Employee Retirement Income Security Act of 1974, *see* ERISA

Employee's earnings record, 17, 219, *illus.*, 19, 221

Employee's Withholding Allowance Certificate (Form W-4): 123, *illus.*, 123; magnetic media/electronic reporting, 145; submitting to IRS, 125

Employer: application for identification number (Form SS-4), 79; contributions to state unemployment compensation funds, 7, 181; defined under federal income tax withholding law, 118; defined under FICA, 71; defined under FUTA, 174; defined under SUTA, 174; FICA Taxes, 77; FLSA requirements, 3, 36; negative-balance and positive-balance,

for SUTA, 184; of household employees, 86; records for income taxes withheld, 145; state and local government 86

Employer Deposit Statement of Income Tax Withheld (Form PA-501R, Pennsylvania), 146, *illus.*, 146

Employer Quarterly Reconciliation Return of Income Tax Withheld (Form PA-W3R, Pennsylvania), 146, *illus.*, 147

Employer's Annual Federal Unemployment (FUTA) Tax Return (Form 940), 186, *illus.*, 187-188

Employer's Annual Federal Unemployment (FUTA) Tax Return (Form 940-EZ), 187, *illus.*, 190

Employer's Annual Information Return of Tip Income and Allocated Tips (Form 8027), 74, 120, 143

Employer's Annual Tax Return for Agricultural Employees (Form 943), 83, 86, 141

Employer's Depository Return of Tax Withheld, City of Philadelphia (Form W-7), 147, *illus.*, 148

Employer's Monthly Federal Tax Return (Form 941-M), 83, 141

Employer's Quarterly Federal Tax Return (Form 941): 83, 88, 141; completing, 88; filing, 88; *illus*, 89; signing, 88; sources of information for completing, 90

Employer's Quarterly Tax Return for Household Employees (Form 942), 83, 86, 141

Employer's Report for Unemployment Compensation (Form UC-2, Pennsylvania), *illus.*, 192

Employer's returns: Form 941, 83, 88, 141; Form 941-M, 83, 141; Form 942, 83, 86, 141; Form 943, 83, 86, 141; magnetic media/electronic reporting, 144; summary of major returns, 83, 141; under federal income tax withholding law, 140

Employer's Tax Guide (Circular E), 140

Employment: application for, 12, *illus.*, 14-15; defined under FICA, 72; laws for fair, 4; permanent part-time, 27; transfers of, under SUTA, 177

End-of-period adjustments, recording, 227

Enterprise coverage, under FLSA, 26

Equal Employment Opportunity Commission (EEOC), 4, 13

Equal Pay Law, 30

ERISA: 7; disclosure requirements, 9; individual retirement account (IRA), 8; simplified employee pension plan (SEP), 8; The Pension Benefit Guaranty Corporation, 7; vesting, 7

Executive orders: 5; affirmative action, 5; Executive Order 11246, 5

Exempt employees: under FICA, 71; under FLSA, 31; under FUTA, 175

Exemption: from FLSA, 31; no-tax-liability, 124; personal, under federal income tax withholding law, 122; status of workers under FLSA, 31

Experience rating: reserve-ratio formula, 184; under FUTA, 180; under SUTA, 181

F

Fair Credit Reporting Act of 1968, 16

Fair employment laws: 4; Age Discrimination in Employment Act of 1967, 5; Americans with Disabilities Act (ADA), 5; Civil Rights Act of 1964, 4; executive orders, 5; records retention, 5

Fair Labor Standards Act, *see* FLSA

Family and Medical Leave Act of 1993 (FMLA), 9, 30

Family benefits, determining maximum, under social security, 329

Federal Disability Insurance Trust Fund, 6

Federal emergency benefits for unemployment, 195

Federal government employees: FICA coverage, 71; unemployment benefits under SUTA, 194

Federal income tax: entry to record deposit, 226; entry to record liability, 220

Federal income tax withholding law: annualizing wages, 129; cumulative withholding, 129; main methods of withholding, 126; part-year employment, 130; percentage method, 126; quarterly averaging of wages, 128; standard deduction, 126; substantially similar methods, 130; supplemental wages, 130; vacation pay, 130; voluntary agreement to withhold additional tax, 124; wage-bracket method, 127; withholding less tax than required, 124

Federal Insurance Contributions Act, *see* FICA

Federal Old-Age and Survivors' Trust Fund, 6

Federal payroll laws, summary of information required by major, 3

Federal Tax Deposit Coupon (Form 8109): 83, 86, 188; for depositing agricultural withheld income and FICA taxes, 83, 86; for depositing FUTA taxes, 83, 188; for depositing withheld income and FICA taxes, 83, 86; *illus.*, 87, 191

Federal Unemployment Tax Act, *see* FUTA

Federal Wage and Hour Law, *see* FLSA

FICA: 6; common-law relationship, 70; common-law test, 70; coverage, 69; depositaries, 83; deposit requirements for employers of agricultural workers, 86; deposit requirements for employers of nonagricultural workers, 83; educational assistance, 75; employee defined, 69; employees of a corporation, 70; employees of not-for-profit organizations, 71; employer defined, 71; employers of household employees, 86; employment defined, 72; end of quarter deposit of taxes, 85; exempt employees, 71; federal government employees, 71; filing Form 941, 91; government payments and employer payments, 71; HI tax, 6, 69; independent contractors, 70; lookback period for deposit of taxes, 84; meals and lodging, 75; Medicare, 6, 332; monthly deposit of taxes, 84; OASDI tax, 6, 69; $100,000 one-day deposit rule, 84; partnerships, 91; paying taxes, 91; penalties, 92, 93-94; privately printed forms, 91; procedures for making deposits, 86; quarterly returns, 82; recording employee taxes, 220; reporting information on magnetic media, 92; returns, 82; safe harbor rule for depositing taxes, 85; self-employed persons, 78; semiweekly deposit of taxes, 84; sick pay, 75; simplified employee pension plan (SEP), 75; state and local government employees, 71, 86; taxable wage bases, 76; taxable wages, 72; tax rates, 76; tips, 74; voluntary coverage, 72

FICA taxes: entry to record deposit of, 226; entry to record liability, 223; recording employee, 220; recording employer, 222
Flexible time, 26
Flexible work schedule, 26
Flextime, 26
FLSA: 2, 17, 25; agricultural occupations, 33; areas not covered, 34; certificate of age, 33; child-labor restrictions, 32; coverage, 25; enterprise coverage, 26; equal pay law, 30; exempt employees, 31; exemption for executive, administrative, and professional employees, 31; exemption for highly skilled computer professionals, 32; exemption status of workers under, 31; Federal Wage and Hour Law, 2; individual employee coverage, 28; minimum wages, 28; nonfarm occupations, 32; overtime hours, 29; overtime pay, 29; penalties, 33; records requirements, 36; short test of exemption, 32; summary of information required by, 3; tips, 29, 119; wages defined, 28; workweek defined, 29
Food and beverage establishments, reporting rules, 119
Forms: I-9 (Employment Eligibility Verification), 9; PA-W3R (Employer Quarterly Reconciliation Return of Income Tax Withheld), 146, illus., 147; PA-501R (Employer Deposit Statement of Income Tax Withheld), 146, illus., 146; SS-4 (Application for Employer Identification Number), 79, illus., 80; SS-5 (Application for a Social Security Card), 79, illus., 81; SSA-7004-SM (Request for Earnings and Benefit Estimate Statement), 82; SSA-7011-F4 (Statement of Employer), 333; UC-2 (Employer's Report for Unemployment Compensation), illus., 192; W-2 (Wage and Tax Statement), 18, 120, 135, illus., 135; W-2c (Statement of Corrected Income and Tax Amounts), 138, illus., 138; W-3 (Transmittal of Wage and Tax Statements), 139, illus., 139; W-3c (Transmittal of Corrected Income and Tax Statements), 140; W-4 (Employee's Withholding Allowance Certificate), 123, illus., 123; W-4P (Withholding Certificate for Pension or Annuity Payments), 125; W-4S (Request for Federal Income Tax Withholding from Sick Pay), 125; W-5 (Earned Income Credit Advance Payment Certificate), 132, illus., 133; W-7 (The City of Philadelphia Employer's Depository Return of Tax Withheld), 147, illus., 148; 940 (Employer's Annual Federal Unemployment [FUTA] Tax Return), 186, illus., 187-188; 940-EZ (Employer's Annual Federal Unemployment [FUTA] Tax Return), 187, illus., 190; 941 (Employer's Quarterly Federal Tax Return), 83, 88, 141, illus., 89; 941c (Supporting Statement to Correct Information), 83; 941-M (Employer's Monthly Federal Tax Return), 83, 141; 941PR (Employer's Quarterly Federal Tax Return), 83; 941SS (Employer's Quarterly Federal Tax Return), 83; 941-V (Form 941 Payment Voucher), 83; 942 (Employer's Quarterly Tax Return for Household Employees), 83, 86, 141; 943 (Employer's Annual Tax Return for Agricultural Employees), 83, 86, 141; 945 (Annual Return of Withheld Federal Income Tax), 88, 140, 141, illus., 142; 945-A (Annual Record of Federal Tax Liability), 141; 1096 (Annual Summary and Transmittal of U.S. Information Returns), 144; 1099-DIV (Dividends and Distributions), 143; 1099-G (Certain Government Payments), 143; 1099-INT (Interest Income), 143; 1099-MISC (Miscellaneous Income), 143, illus., 144; 1099-PATR (Taxable Distributions Received from Cooperatives), 143; 1099-R (Distributions From Pensions, Annuities, Retirement or Profit-Sharing Plans, IRAs, Insurance Contracts, etc.), 143; 2159 (Payroll Deduction Agreement), 126; 4070 (Employee's Report of Tips to Employer), 74, 119, illus., 74; 4070-A (Employee's Daily Record of Tips), 119; 4137 (Social Security and Medicare Tax on Unreported Tip Income), 74; 4419 (Application for Filing Information Returns Magnetically/Electronically), 144; 4782 (Employee Moving Expense Information), 121; 5498 (Individual Retirement Arrangement Information), 143; 6466 (Transmittal of Magnetic Media of Form W-4, Employee's Withholding Allowance Certificate), 145; 8027 (Employer's Annual Information Return of Tip Income and Allocated Tips), 74, 120, 143; 8109 (Federal Tax Deposit Coupon), 83, 86, 188, illus., 191; 8109-B (Federal Tax Deposit Coupon), illus., 87; 8508 (Request for Waiver from Filing Information Returns on Magnetic Media), 145; 8655 (Reporting Agent Authorization), 92
Form W-2, magnetic media/electronic reporting, 144
Form W-3, where to file, 140
Form W-4: magnetic media/electronic reporting, 145; submitting to IRS, 125
Form 940: filing, 186; payment of balance of taxes due, 186; signing, 186; sources of information for completing, 189
Form 941: 83, 88; completing, 88; filing, 91; privately printed, 91; signing, 88; sources of information for completing, 90; where to file, 91
Fractional cents: computing FICA taxes, 77; computing hourly and overtime rates, 43
Fringe benefits, noncash: under federal income tax withholding law, 119; under FICA, 73
Fully insured individual, for social security benefits, 328
FUTA: 6, 173; annual return (Form 940), 186, illus., 187-188; annual return (Form 940-EZ), 187, illus., 190; coverage under, 174; credits against tax, 179; employee, 174; employers, 174; entry to record liability for tax, 224; entry to record payment of tax, 226; exempt employment, 175; experience rating, 180; funds, 195; penalties, 189; quarterly deposit form, 188; recording taxes, 223; records requirements, 3, 7; tax rate, 179; Title XII advances, 180; wages, 178

G

Garnishment of wages, 229
Gifts, Christmas, under FICA, 73

Government contractors, antidiscrimination regulation for, 5
Governments, as employers: under federal income tax law, 118; under FUTA, 176
Gross earnings, 42
Gross wages, rounding off, for federal income tax withholding, 126, 127
Group insurance, recording payroll deduction for, 228
Guaranteed annual wage payments, under FICA, 73

H

Health insurance, recording deduction for, 228
Hiring notice, 16, illus., 16
Holidays, legal, 10
Hospital employees: overtime pay for, 30; under FUTA, 176
Hospital insurance (HI) plan: 6, 332; taxable wage base, 76; tax rate, 76
Hot keys, 337
Household employees, tax deposit requirements for employers of, 86
Human resources records: application for employment, 12, illus., 14-15; change of status form, illus., 17; employee history record, 16; hiring notice, 16, illus., 16; reference inquiry, 13; requisition for personnel, 12
Human resources system, 10, 11; procedures, illus., 11

I

Identification number: employer's, 79
Idle time or standby payments, under FICA, 73
Immediate credit item, 86
Immigration Reform and Control Act of 1986 (IRCA): 9; Form I-9 (Employment Eligibility Verification), 9
Incentive plans, 44
Income, self-employment, 78
Income tax withholding, state and local, 6, 145
Income tax withholding law, federal: 6; advances, 120; backup withholding, 88; coverage under, 118; deposits, 83, 86; educational assistance, 120; employees, 118; employers, 118; exempt payments, 120; noncash fringe benefits, 119; records requirements, 145; summary of information required by law, 3
Independent contractor, test for, 71
Indexing, to determine social security benefits, 328
Individual account plan, for supplemental unemployment benefits, 195
Individual employee coverage, under FLSA, 28
Individual retirement account (IRA): 8, 134; deductible contributions, 134; nondeductible contributions, 134
Individual Retirement Arrangement Information (Form 5498), 143
Information reports, under SUTA, 189
Information returns: for income tax, 143; Form 1096, 144; Form 1099-DIV, 143; Form 1099-G, 143; Form 1099-INT, 143; Form 1099-MISC, 143; Form 1099-PATR, 143; Form 1099-R, 143; Form 5498, 143; Form 8027, 143; magnetic

media/electronic reporting of, 144; major, 143

Insurance: group, 228; health, 228; workers' compensation, 9

Interest Income (Form 1099-INT), 143

Interest rate for tax underpayments and overpayments, 93

Internal Revenue Service Centers, 91

Interstate employees, under SUTA, 176

Investigative consumer report, 16

IRA, see Individual retirement account

J

Job cost card, 37, illus., 39

Job sharing, 27

Journal, payroll, 219

Jury duty pay, under FICA, 73

L

Legal holidays, 10

List windows, 340

Local income taxes: withholding laws, 6

Lodging, under FICA, 75

Lookback period, 84

Lump-sum death payment, 331

M

Magnetic media reporting: FICA information, 92; Form W-2, 144; Form W-4, 125, 145; information returns, 144

McNamara-O'Hara Service Contract Act of 1965, 8

Meal periods, as working time, 35

Meals and lodging: under federal income tax withholding law, 119; under FICA, 75

Medicaid, 332

Medical care for aged and needy, 332

Medicare, 6, 332

Menu, 336; bar, 336; command, 337; employees, 351; file, 346; help, 354; hot keys, 337; name, 336; options, 347; pulldown, 337; quick keys, 337; reports, 352; transactions, 349

Merit rating, under FUTA, 180

Minimum wages: and maximum hours laws, state, 4; laborers for government contractors, 8; paying workers less than, 28; under FLSA, 2, 28

Miscellaneous Income (Form 1099-MISC), 143

Mom and pop stores, 26

Moving expense reimbursement: under federal income tax withholding law, 121; under FICA, 73

N

Negative-balance employers, SUTA, 184

Net pay, entry to record, 222

Nonprofit organizations, as employers, under federal income tax withholding law, 118

Nontaxable wages, under FUTA, 178

No-tax-liability exemption, under federal income tax withholding law, 124

O

OASDI benefits, 327

Occupational Safety and Health Act (OSHA) of 1970, 8

Old-age, survivors, and disability insurance program (OASDI): 69, 327; taxable wage base, 76; tax rate, 76

Operating procedures for Computerized Payroll Accounting, 345

Overtime earnings for pieceworkers, 44

Overtime hours, 29

Overtime pay, 29

P

Partial unemployment: 191; notices, under SUTA, 191

Part-time employment, permanent, 27

Part-year employment, federal income tax withholding method, 130

Pay-as-you-go basis, of income tax withholding, 117

Paycheck, 18, illus., 20

Payroll, entry to record, 220

Payroll account at bank, 47

Payroll accounting system: 10, 17; manual, 17; procedures, illus., 18

Payroll deductions: garnishment of wages, 229; group insurance, 228; health insurance, 228; pension and retirement benefits, 229; purchase of government savings bonds, 228; union dues, 229

Payroll journal, 219

Payroll laws, summary of information required by major federal, 3

Payroll rate, change in, 16

Payroll records: employee's earnings record, 17, 219, illus., 19, 221; federal laws affecting the need for, 7; payroll register, 17, 217, illus., 19, 218-219; state laws affecting the need for, 9

Payroll register: 17, 217, illus., 19, 218-219; proving totals of, 218; using information in, 219

Payroll sheet, supplementary, 46, illus., 46

Payroll slip, illus., 48

Payroll taxes: entries to record, 222; entry to record deposit of FICA taxes and federal income taxes withheld, 226; entry to record employer FICA taxes, 222; entry to record FUTA, 223; entry to record payment of FUTA and SUTA taxes, 226; entry to record payment of state or city income taxes, 226; entry to record SUTA, 223; entry to record withholdings, 220

Penalties: bad checks in payment of employment taxes, 94; failure to file employment tax returns, 93; failure to file or furnish information returns, 94; failure to furnish wage and tax statements, 94; failure to make timely deposits, 94; failure to pay over employment taxes, 93; failure to supply identification number, 94; the 100% penalty, 93; under FICA, FUTA, and federal income tax withholding law, 92, 93-94; under FLSA, 33; under FUTA, 189; under SUTA, 191

Pension and retirement benefits, recording payroll deductions for, 229

Pension plans: income tax withholding, 125; simplified employee (SEP), under FICA, 75; under ERISA, 7

Percentage method of income tax withholding: 126; tables, 382-384

Permanent part-time employment, 27

Personal allowances, under federal income tax withholding law, 122

Personnel records: federal laws affecting the need for, 7; state laws affecting need for, 9

Piece rate: computing wages and salaries, 44; system, 44

Pieceworkers, overtime earnings for, 44

Pooled-fund laws, SUTA, 181

Pooled-fund plan, for supplemental unemployment benefits, 194

Positive-balance employers, SUTA, 184

Prehire inquiries, 13

Preliminary and postliminary activities, as working time, 35

Primary insurance amount (PIA): 328; calculating, 328

Principal activities, working time, 34

Privately printed forms, Form 941, 91

Profit-sharing plans, 45

Q

Quarterly averaging of wages, for federal income tax withholding, 128

Quarterly deposits: for FICA and income taxes withheld, 85; under FUTA, 188

Quarter of coverage under FICA: 327; for farm workers, 328; for self-employed persons, 328; for wage earners, 328

Quick keys, 337

R

Railroad Retirement Tax Act, 72

Railroad Unemployment Insurance Act, 176

Railroad workers, exclusion from FICA, 72

Reciprocal agreements, state income tax withholding, 146

Reciprocal arrangements, SUTA, 177

Records, employers: advance EIC payments, 134; for income taxes withheld, 145; human resources, see Human resources records; payroll, see Payroll records

Reference inquiry form, 13

Remuneration, total, defined under FLSA, 2, 28

Report windows, 342

Request for Earnings and Benefit Estimate Statement (Form SSA-7004-SM), 82

Request for Federal Income Tax Withholding from Sick Pay (Form W-4S), 125

Requisition for personnel, 12, illus., 12

Reserve-ratio formula, SUTA, 184

Rest periods, 35

Retirement benefits, recording payroll deductions for, 229

Retirement test, 330

Returns, summary of major, filed by employers, 83, 141

S

Safe harbor rule, 85

Salaries and wages: commissions, 45; converting monthly salary rates to hourly rate, 43; converting weekly wage rates to hourly rates, 42; fractional cents, 43; incentive plans, 44; methods of computing, 42; methods of paying, 46; paying by check, 47; paying by electronic transfer, 47; paying in cash, 46; piece rate, 44; profit-sharing plans, 45; time rate, 42

Salary, 28

Self-employed persons, social security coverage, 78, 328

Self-Employment Contributions Act (SECA), 6, 69, 78

Self-employment income: 78; reporting, 78; social security benefits, 328; taxable year, 78; taxes, 79

Semimonthly payment of salary, 28

Separation reports, SUTA, 191

Sick pay: under federal income tax withholding law, 121, 125; under FICA, 73, 75

Simplified employee pension plan (SEP), 8; employee contributions under FICA, 75

Social Security Act: 6, 63, 173; summary of information required by, 3; Title II of, 327

Social Security Administration offices, 140

Social security benefits, see Benefits, under social security

Social security card: illus., 82; application for (Form SS-5), 79, illus., 81

Social security taxes, entry to record, 223, 224

Special withholding allowance, under federal income tax withholding law, 122

Staggered work schedule, 26

Standard deduction, 126

Start-up procedures for Computerized Payroll Accounting, 344

State and local government employees: compensatory time off, 30; FICA coverage, 71

State and local government employers: tax deposit requirements, 86; voluntary coverage under FICA, 72

State disability benefit laws, 10

State income tax: reciprocal agreements, 146; recording liability, 222; recording payment, 226; types of returns or reports, 146; withholding, 145; withholding laws, 6

Statement of Corrected Income and Tax Amounts (Form W-2c), 138

Statement of Employer (Form SSA-7011-F4), 333

State minimum wage and maximum hours laws, 4

State time-off-to-vote laws, 10

State unemployment compensation funds: calculating the contribution rate, 184; employee and employer contributions, 181; experience rating, 181; recording employees' contributions, 222; summary of sources and duration of benefits, 195; voluntary contributions, 185

State unemployment compensation laws: benefits for ex-service personnel, 194; benefits for federal employees, 194; benefits for unemployed as a result of major disaster, 194; benefits under, 193; contribution reports, 190; coverage under, 174; dependency allowances, 193; disability benefits, 194; disqualification of benefits, 193; eligibility for benefits, 193; federal emergency benefits, 195; interstate employees, 176; partial unemployment notices, 191; pooled-fund laws, 181; reciprocal arrangements, 177; separation reports, 191; status reports, 190; summary of, 182-183; supplemental unemployment benefits, 194; transfer of employment, 177; wage information reports, 191, illus., 192

State Unemployment Tax Acts, see SUTA

Status reports, unemployment compensation, 190

Stock payments, under FICA, 73

Students' benefits, under social security, 330

Supplemental unemployment benefits (SUB): 194; individual-account plan, 195; pooled-fund plan, 194

Supplemental wage payments: federal income tax withholding, 119, 130; paid along with regular wages, 130; paid separately from regular wages, 131; vacation pay, 130

Supplementary Medical Insurance plan, 6, 332

Supplementary payroll Sheet, illus., 46

Supporting Statement to Correct Information (Form 941c), 83

Survivors benefits, 327, 331

SUTA: 7, 173; calculating contribution rate, 184; coverage of interstate employees, 176-177; coverage under, 174; employee and employer contributions, 181; employee benefits, 193; entry to record payment of tax, 226; entry to record liability, 223, 224; experience rating, 180, 181; information reports, 189; penalties, 191; pooled-fund laws, 181; reciprocal arrangements, 177; recording employees' contributions, 225; tax rates, 181; transfers of employment, 177; voluntary contributions, 185; wages, 179

System, human resources, 10, 11

System, payroll accounting, 17

T

Tables: allowance values for percentage method of federal income tax withholding, 126; computing employee's excess of wages over allowances claimed, 128; percentage method of withholding, 382-384; wage-bracket method of withholding, 387-396

Taxable Distributions Received from Cooperatives (Form 1099-PATR), 143

Taxable wage base: under FICA, 76; under FUTA, 178

Tax deposits, see Deposits of FICA and income taxes withheld

Taxlink, 88

Tax overpayments and underpayments, interest rate on, 93

Taxpayer Identification Numbers (TINS), 141

Tax rate: under FICA, 76; under FUTA, 179; under SUTA, 181

Telecommuting, 27

Time card: 36, illus., 38; continental system, 36, illus., 38; job cost card, illus., 39; Timekeeper, 40, illus., 40

Time clock: computerized, 40; mechanical, 37

Timekeeping: 36; computerized time and attendance recording systems, 40, Illus., 41; fractional parts of an hour, 41; mechanical time-clock system, 37; time cards, 36; time sheets, 36

Time-off-to-vote laws, state, 10

Time rate, computing, 42

Time sheet, 36, illus., 37

Tipped employee: defined under FICA, 74; defined under FLSA, 29

Tips: 29; allocation of, by large food and beverage establishments, 74, 120; Employee's Report of Tips to Employer (Form 4070), illus., 74; federal income tax withholding, 119; taxable under FICA, 74

Title bar, 338

Title XII advances, under FUTA, 180

Total remuneration, defined under FLSA, 2

Training sessions, as working time, 35

Transfer of employment, under SUTA, 177

Transmittal of Corrected Income and Tax Statements (Form W-3c), 140

Transmittal of Wage and Tax Statements (Form W-3), 139, illus., 139; where to file, 140

Travel time, as working time, 34

U

Unclaimed wages, 48

Unemployment compensation: benefits, 193; reports required of employer, 186; state programs, 7; summary of sources and duration of benefits, 195; summary of state laws, 182-183; taxes and credits, 179

Unemployment insurance, taxes, 6, 173

Unemployment tax law, summary of information required by, 3

Union dues, recording payroll deductions for, 229

U.S. citizens residing abroad, under federal income tax withholding law, 121

U.S. savings bonds, recording deduction for purchase of, 228

V

Vacation pay: recording end-of-period adjustment, 227; under federal income tax law, 119, 130; under FICA, 73

Vesting, 7

Veterans and service personnel, wage credits under social security, 328

Vietnam Era Veterans' Readjustment Act of 1974, 8

Vocational Rehabilitation Act of 1973, 8

Voluntary contributions to state unemployment funds, 185

Voluntary coverage, under FICA, 72

W

Wage and Hour Division of U.S. Department of Labor, 4, 25

Wage and Hour Law, see FLSA

Wage and Tax Statement: Form W-2, 18, 120, 135, illus., 135; instructions for completing, 136-137; magnetic media/electronic reporting, 144; privately printed forms, 140

Wage base, taxable: under FICA, 76; under FUTA, 178

Wage-bracket method of withholding federal income tax: 127; tables, 387-396

Wage credits, for veterans and service personnel, 328

Wage information reports, SUTA, 191, illus., 192

Wage rates: converting monthly salary rates to hourly rates, 43; converting weekly wage rates to hourly rates, 42; incentive plans, 44; piece rate, 44; table of decimal equivalents used for conversion into weekly, hourly, and hourly overtime, 43; table of weekly, converted to hourly rates, 42; time rate, 42

Wages: annualizing, for federal income tax withholding, 129; constructively paid, 179; defined under EIC, 132; defined under federal income tax withholding law, 119; defined under FICA, 72; defined under FLSA, 28; defined under FUTA, 178; defined under SUTA, 179; entries to record, 223; exempt from income tax withholding, 120; garnishment of, 229; guaranteed annual payments, 73; nontaxable, under FUTA, 178; payments to dependents after employee's death, 73; quarterly averaging of, for federal income tax withholding, 128; recording end-of-period adjustments, 227; retroactive increases, 73; taxable under

FICA, 72; taxable under FUTA, 178; unclaimed, 48

Wages and salaries: commissions, 45; converting monthly salary rates to hourly rates, 43; converting weekly wage rates to hourly rates, 42; fractional cents, 43; incentive plans, 44; methods of computing, 42; methods of paying, 46; paying by check, 47; paying by electronic transfer, 47; paying in cash, 46; piece rate, 44; profit-sharing plans, 45; time rate, 42

Walsh-Healey Public Contracts Act of 1936, 8

Wash-up time, as working time, 34

Weekly time report, *illus.*, 37

Welfare plan, under ERISA, 7

Windows: data-entry, 338; dialog, 342; list, 340; report, 342

Window title, 338

Withholding: backup, 141; for child support, 126; income tax laws, 6; tips, *see* Tips

Withholding allowances: 122; for dependents, 122; personal, 122; special, 122

Withholding Certificate for Pension or Annuity Payments (Form W-4P), 125

Withholding certificates, 122; invalid, 124

Workers' compensation: laws, 9; recording insurance expense, 225

Working time: absences, 35; clothes-changing time and wash-up, 34; daylight-saving time, 36; determining employee's, 34; fractional parts of an hour, 41; meal periods, 35; preliminary and postliminary activities, 35; principal activities, 34; rest periods and coffee breaks, 35; tardiness, 35; training sessions, 35; travel time, 34

Work schedules: compressed workweek, 26; flexible, 26; job sharing, 27; permanent part-time employment, 27; staggered, 26; telecommuting, 27; types of, 26-27

Work-sharing, 27

Workweek: compressed, 26; defined under FLSA, 29; 4/40, 26